Nation Maker

A lean, mean, political machine, with a sardonic smile.

SIR JOHN A. MACDONALD:

His Life, Our Times

VOLUME TWO: 1867–1891

RICHARD GWYN

RANDOM HOUSE CANADA

PUBLISHED BY RANDOM HOUSE CANADA

Published in 2011 by Random House Canada, a division of Random House of Canada Limited, Toronto. Distributed in Canada by Random House of Canada Limited.
www.randomhouse.ca

LIBRARY AND ARCHIVES CANADA CATALOGUING IN PUBLICATION

Gwyn, Richard, 1934-
John A. : the man who made us : the life and times of John A. Macdonald / Richard Gwyn.

Vol. 2. has title: Nation maker : Sir John A. Macdonald : his life, our times.
Includes bibliographical references and indexes.
Contents: v. 1. 1815–1867 — v. 2. 1867–1891.

ISBN 978-0-679-31475-2 (v. 1).—ISBN 978-0-307-35644-4 (v. 2)

1. Macdonald, John A. (John Alexander), 1815–1891. 2. Canada—History—19th century. 3. Canada—Politics and government—19th century. 4. Prime ministers—Canada—Biography. I. Title. II. Title: Nation maker.

FC521.M29G89 2007 971.05'1092 C2007-903422-5

Text and cover design by CS Richardson

Cover image: Library and Archives Canada, C-005327

Printed and bound in the United States of America

2 4 6 8 9 7 5 3 1

To my father,
Philip Eustace Congreve Jermy Gwyn,
1899–1976;
a good man

Contents

Prologue

[Confederation will be] an event which will make us historical—not with my will would another person take my place.
John A. Macdonald to Governor General Lord Monck, June 26, 1866

In the year 1867, three countries underwent transformational change. In Japan, a new emperor initiated the Meiji Restoration to turn a feudal society into a modern industrial power. In Germany, twenty-two northern states led by Prussia formed themselves into a North German Federation, which its chancellor, Otto von Bismarck, would soon unify with southern German states to form a new German Empire. And on July 1, a handful of British colonies in the northeast corner of North America reorganized themselves into a confederation.

The objective of these colonies—Ontario and Quebec emerging from the preceding United Province of Canada, with Nova Scotia and New Brunswick joining them—was by far the least ambitious of the three. Confederation's prime purpose was to enable the people above the border with the United States to continue being what they already were—British North Americans—rather than becoming Americans. As a secondary goal, far less widely accepted, the exercise aimed to develop a "new nationality" for those living in the Dominion of Canada.

While modest, Canada's ambitions may well have been the most difficult to fulfill. The new dominion had little of the stuff of which nation-states are customarily made. Canada lay next door to an overwhelming neighbour, and it was difficult to distinguish its inhabitants, French Canadians excepted, from those to the south. Its own people knew almost nothing about each other: Maritimers had always looked eastwards back to Britain or southwards to the rich New England market; and the populations of Ontario and Quebec were separated by profound differences in language, ethnicity and religion. The harsh winters and the vast distances between settlements isolated Canadians even further from each other. The country itself was more a stretched out subcontinent than a country; the American journalist Horace Greeley got it right when he called it "an eel-skin of settled country"—one composed of widely scattered towns and pioneer farms in clearings hacked out of primeval forests, with almost all these fragments of civilization huddled against a border that was arbitrary and invisible.

In no respect was the Canada created by Confederation a nation-state. It was still a British colony, with no say whatever in its foreign affairs. It possessed less autonomy than little-developed states such as Haiti or Liberia. Rather than a nation, it was a patchwork quilt of three nations, English, French and Aboriginal. Nor did it fulfill the customary purpose of a nation—to enable a distinctive ethnic group to take its place on the international stage. Robert MacNeil, the long-time public affairs host of PBS television, once observed that his native Canada was not an "inevitable nation"—unlike Denmark, for instance, which provides a homeland for Danish people, or Japan for the Japanese. Inevitably, the attempt to create a new Canadian nationality would have to be quietly abandoned.

Canada's very existence constituted a denial of geography, demography and commerce. Compared to the United States—Canadians engaged in such comparisons incessantly—the country was poor, provincial, underdeveloped and almost entirely lacking life's pleasantries (except in some quarters in Montreal and in the care and pride with which the people built their churches). The British parliamentarian Charles Dilke, who visited in 1869, wrote that "a fog of unenterprise hung over the land: roads were wanting, houses rude, swamps undrained, plains untilled." Many of its best and brightest inhabitants moved to the United States, while the immigrants it needed so desperately either went to America directly or came to Canada, saw what was on offer and left.

Soon after Confederation, the *Times* of London took a look at Canada and winced. The newspaper doubted that Canada could survive, because it lacked "the body, the vital organs, the circulation and the muscular force that are to give adequate power to these wide-spread limbs." The analysis of the *New York Times* was similar but for its triumphant tone: "When the experiment of the 'Dominion' shall have failed, as fail it must, a process of peaceful absorption will give Canada her proper place in the Great North American republic."

In both Britain and the United States, the prevailing judgment among the small number of those reasonably well informed on the matter was that the new confederation would quickly vanish—by joining its neighbour. That merger would greatly improve the standard of living of most Canadians, and it could be done easily, in two short steps: first independence, then annexation. As for the first, many in the Mother Country wished Canada would leave the nest, to end the risk of a British-American conflict initiated by some border incident. Lord Monck, who as governor general had played a critical part in achieving Confederation, thought this way, and on his return home to England told the House of Lords that it was "in the interests of the Mother Country that [Canada] should be taught to look forward to independence." Once that was achieved, all Canada needed to do was knock on the right door in Washington, where many of the most powerful men—including President Andrew Johnson, Secretary of State William Seward and Charles Sumner, chairman of the Senate Committee on Foreign Relations—were annexationists.

In both countries, informed opinion agreed. In Britain, a few months before Confederation, the Oxford history professor and influential commentator Goldwin Smith forecast that the "British North American colonies will in time, and probably at no very distant time, unite themselves politically with [the United States] of which they are already by race, position, commercial ties and the characteristics of their institutions a part." On Confederation's eve, the prominent U.S. historian George Bancroft advised Seward that Canada would soon "break into parts & follow the strong attraction of the immensely massive weight of the United States."

Instead, Canada followed its own version of manifest destiny. This choice, illogical though it may have seemed, was the product of two causes. The first was that the great majority of Canadians, for reasons often opaque, but ranging from loyalty, to a conviction of cultural superiority, to pleasure in belonging to the world's greatest empire, were determined not to become Americans. The other was that the man who led them at this time happened to be Sir John A. Macdonald. Among all the ablest nineteenth-century democratic leaders, including Lincoln, Disraeli and Gladstone, he was one of the most skilled and most experienced, and probably the most wily. He was also exceptionally determined, whether in pursuit of his country's interests or of his own. What follows is Sir John A.'s story to its end, and Canada's at its beginning.

ONE

Present at the Creation

In thirty days, for weal or for woe, the Confederate Government will be inaugurated. By the exercise of common sense and a limited amount of the patriotism which goes by the name of self-interest, I have no doubt the Union will be good for the Country's weal.
Macdonald to Newfoundland politician Ambrose Shea, June 3, 1867

Confederation Day, on July 1, 1867, passed tolerably well. All across Ontario, large crowds turned out to watch the parades and fireworks, listen to concerts by military bands, eat free steaks carved from oxen roasting on spits, sit through speeches by politicians, and cheer on games of cricket or croquet, with sack races for the children. The excitement was equally high in the English sections of Montreal. In Nova Scotia, though, several newspapers bordered their front page in black, and the government forbade distribution of the governor general's proclamation. In Quebec, the crowds were sparse, Montreal's powerful Bishop Ignace Bourget delayed expressing even grudging approval for Confederation until the day had passed, and George-Étienne Cartier's own newspaper, *La Minerve*, informed readers that Confederation provided a direct route to "l'indépendence politique."

All that really mattered was that Confederation had happened. For the first time ever, colonials had written their own constitution.

They had done so despite having only two federal models as guides, in Switzerland and the United States. In Britain, the only role model that mattered, sovereignty was singular, residing in its entirety in the king in Parliament. The constitution itself, the British North America Act, if breaking no new ground politically or legally, was nevertheless in some respects remarkably ambitious. To join the Maritimes to the old Canada in fact as well as in law, the new dominion pledged to build a railway across the five hundred miles of wilderness between Quebec City and Halifax. It also declared itself ready to extend all the way to the Pacific—which, if the western colonies agreed, would make the country the second largest in the world after Russia.

John A. Macdonald was the man behind this extravagant commitment. Cartier, his Quebec ally, had originally opposed it, concerned that it would add too many anglophones to the new nation; George Brown, his long-time opponent but an irreplaceable partner in the Confederation project, preferred a mini-federation that excluded even the Maritimes. Macdonald himself had been skeptical at first, fearing that the West would attract immigrants away from the still under-populated Ontario. But then he had changed his mind: "The Americans must not get behind us," he wrote to a friend. With the purchase of Alaska from Russia early in 1867, the United States had already turned its gaze northwards; other attempts to expand beyond the forty-ninth parallel were certain to follow.* The first came in December of that same year, when Minnesota senator Alexander Ramsey placed a resolution before the Senate Committee on Foreign Relations proposing that Canada, in return for a favourable trade pact, "cede to the United States the districts of North America west of longitude 90 degrees." The

* For a time, Secretary of State Seward also considered buying Greenland from Denmark, in a kind of giant pincer movement.

resolution failed, but the larger contest between Canada and the United States over dividing North America had begun. One country had to lose.

The contest was hopelessly unequal. The United States was much larger, incomparably richer, far more developed and, with the Civil War won, confident and energetic. Above all, after a near century as a nation-state, it knew what it was, while the new dominion did not. A great many Canadians didn't even want to be Canadian, whether Canadiens in Quebec or, as would soon become apparent, Nova Scotians too. The uneven mix of support, indifference and resistance within the country to even the idea of a larger Canada, along with the U.S. interest in annexing its northern neighbour, measured the task ahead for Macdonald.

Despite a few glitches, Confederation Day passed better than tolerably well for Macdonald personally. It invested him with a quality he had long been lacking—gravitas. He now had the title of Prime Minister, the Right Honourable Sir John A. Macdonald, rather than, as earlier, Premier, the Honourable John A. Macdonald*. As further augmented his persona, after a decade as a rackety widower, he again had a wife, and so a portion of that prized Victorian virtue of respectability. She was Susan Agnes Bernard, twenty-one years his junior, whom he had married the previous February in London.

He was now, at fifty-two, in full middle age. He had changed little. He had no grey hairs. His torso was still angular, his indifference to food offsetting his excessive intake of liquor. He never exercised

* In fact, Macdonald most times referred to himself as "Premier," no doubt because this had been his title for so many of his pre-Confederation years.

A "New Nation", a first-ever Prime Minister, and more work than ever.

beyond walking the short distance to work, but his energy remained exceptional. He put in long hours and was still capable of ferocious bursts of effort. Even on holiday at the cottage he later bought in Rivière-du-Loup, he diligently went through the official papers from Ottawa and replied to incoming letters until the early afternoon.

Liberal MP Charles Langelier, who sat across from him in the House of Commons in the 1880s, left the best description of Macdonald from these years: "His eyes lively and his look pleasant. A charming smile, an enormous mass of curly hair, a slim build, his walk an elegant nonchalance, and a nose that made up his whole glory." Nature had indeed given Macdonald the priceless political asset of being distinctive. Wherever he went—out on the hustings, attending some grand public event or talking to urchins on the street—he was recognized and attracted a crowd. In political cartoons too, especially those by the brilliant J.W. Bengough in the weekly satirical magazine *Grip*, he jumped right off the page into the consciousness of readers. Bengough could be savage about Macdonald's political and administrative misdeeds but not about him personally, casting him in the engaging roles of a naughty schoolboy, a street-smart scamp, an artful dodger.

A large part of Macdonald's distinctiveness was of his own deliberate invention. In an era when shrub-sized beards were the style, he was always clean-shaven; he wore attention-getting clothes, such as bright red cravats and trousers with large checks. As time went by—the influence of a chatelaine, no doubt—he more often wore grey trousers and a matching Prince Albert jacket, although still with a red cravat. But that mass of hair and glorious nose ensured that almost everyone knew him at once. During his one trip out west, by train late in life, an old-timer, unaware who he was, described him as a "seedy beggar." Macdonald, overhearing the comment, shot back, "Yes, a rum 'un to look at, but a rare 'un to go."

Langelier was also correct in his description of the new prime minister's "elegant nonchalance." Macdonald's habitual response to the flaws and follies of humankind was an amused insouciance. In the House of Commons, he typically reacted to some assault on his policies or his morals with a quip, the best of which made his outraged opponent laugh at himself. Wit, spontaneous and unrehearsed, was his hallmark: accosted by a suffragette demanding to know why he but not she had the vote, he pondered and then replied, "Madame, I cannot conceive." Although all politicians are actors, or ought to be, few have been so utterly at ease in their skin as Macdonald was. He accepted himself for the bad as well as the good, never apologizing for his drinking or for his procrastination in making decisions. As Sir Joseph Pope, his last and ablest secretary, put it, "He knew every chord of the human heart; he understood every passion that swayed man's nature." This acceptance made him a good politician, but it was also innate. He understood women well and enjoyed their company, even though, lacking the vote, they were of no consequence politically. They, in return, "worshipped him," in the judgment of editor John Willison of the Liberal Toronto *Globe*.

Macdonald's knowledge of people earned him a collateral political gift—he knew how to manipulate them. By Confederation, he had won over to his side a former Liberal leader and premier, John Sandfield Macdonald, and a former Liberal cabinet minister with a strong following, Thomas D'Arcy McGee. His first cabinet included three Liberal front-benchers, lured there to sustain the illusion he was leading a Liberal-Conservative coalition.* Several Liberal members of Parliament deliberately avoided talking to him for fear he would seduce them into crossing the floor. One Liberal MP, talking to him in some corner of the Parliament Buildings, was overheard to say, "Oh Sir John, I do so love you. If only I could trust you."

The bond between him and his own MPs and supporters was even closer, of course, almost intimate. Scarcely any of them ever turned away from him, mesmerized by his charm and the hours he spent in the Commons listening to the incoherent addresses of backbenchers and then praising them lavishly. He distributed patronage plums, either directly to his supporters or to others they wished to please. In fact, though, many got nothing—yet, as Willison noted, they still "went through fire and water for him," because they loved him.

As for ordinary Canadians, they, according to the journalist M.O. Hammond, "flocked to his railway coach, they hung about his carriage, and they invaded his hotel rooms." Macdonald's own analysis was even better: "They prefer John A. drunk to George Brown sober." He made them laugh, never talked down to them, and paid them the compliment of always speaking spontaneously, never from a text, and usually without notes. To make his points, he ambled along in a conversational style, waiting until a heckler intervened to give him the chance to be rude about Brown or to "hive the Grits." Macdonald treated all people as his equal, whether a coach driver or a British duke. He once walked out on George Monro Grant, the principal of Queen's University and one of the country's most eminent men, so he could talk to a barber. Grant had persuaded Macdonald's sister Margaret to invite him

* The Opposition's title was still predominantly "Reform" at this time, but for simplicity's sake its eventual title of "Liberal" is used throughout this volume.

to her Kingston house so he could have a private after-dinner conversation with the visiting prime minister, no doubt about university funding. Through the meal they chattered amicably, but before any business could be done, Macdonald slipped away. When Margaret remonstrated with Macdonald later, he explained that he had gone to a pub to converse with a barber "who controls thirty votes"—in contrast to Grant, who, like all high-minded intellectuals, "prefers to make up his own mind." The ever-political Macdonald made sure this story leaked out.

After Confederation, he gained another asset. The event turned him into Canada's first celebrity—the only one until Toronto's Ned Hanlan won the world rowing championship in England in 1879. People wrote to him not just to ask for patronage or to complain about some policy, but also to tell him their personal concerns. Among Macdonald's responses to these letters is one to Francis Jones of Kemptville: "I have your letter of the 25th informing me that there are suspicious strangers about Smiths Falls. Many thanks for the information. I shall cause immediate inquiries to be made." Another, to an E. Stone Wiggins, reads: "I am not a sufficient mathematician to be able fully to appreciate your long sought-for solution to the bisection of an Angle by purely mathematical means." In a country where the people across its expanse had so little in common, Macdonald belonged to everyone. He was both their leader and their friend.

All these attributes diverted attention from the most considerable of Macdonald's qualities: he was exceptionally intelligent, with a subtle and capacious mind. Usually, Macdonald sheathed his intelligence, so as not to block voters' sight of him. He only brandished it offstage, as when he held his own in private discussions with Britain's ablest public figures, including a late-night, brandy-fuelled review of politics and literature with Benjamin Disraeli, his "twin" in wit, theatrical looks and Machiavellian guile. His schooling had ended at sixteen, but he never stopped learning. Pope described him as an "omnivorous" reader; he read not just politics, law and biography, but novels and poetry. He dropped lines from Shakespeare, Milton, Sheridan, Trollope and Dickens into his speeches, not to impress but to illuminate an idea or advance an argument. When he reached the town of Victoria on his western tour, he remarked that there "the day is always in the afternoon"— an apt allusion to Tennyson's "The Lotos-Eaters."* Once, while praising the "good memory and a vicious fluency of speech" of a leading Conservative member, he dismissed the MP's career prospects because he was "altogether devoid of reading."

He most certainly had his defects. He drank far too much, regularly going on prolonged benders. "John A. carried out of the lunchroom hopelessly drunk," the senior official Edmund Meredith recorded in his diary after one early cabinet meeting. (Besides cold beef and mutton, sherry, port and whisky were all available in the cabinet room, and at reduced prices.) Macdonald also had a quick temper. On one occasion he suffered a defeat in the Commons after he ruined a make-up meeting with a key, wavering MP by showering him with abuse over past wrongs. He could be cynical too, as when he exclaimed, "There is no gratitude to be expected from the public; I learned that long ago." And he could be crass. In 1872, in advance of an imminent election, Macdonald enacted legislation to protect the legal status of unions, but wrote soon after to the editor of the Conservative *Mail* newspaper, reminding him that it was one thing to attack capitalists but "when the present excitement is over, you must look to them & not to the employed for support." Over time,

---

* Tennyson's lines read: "In the afternoon they came unto a land / In which it seemed always afternoon. / All round the coast the languid air did swoon, / Breathing like one that hath a weary dream."

he became careless about administration, describing his early attempts to advance efficiency, long since abandoned, as those of "a devil of a reformer."*

Action for the sake of action was never part of his "long game." He loved to quote the dictum attributed to William Pitt the Younger—"The first, second and third requisites of a Prime Minister are patience." Macdonald also maintained a huge patronage machine. He extracted from businessmen with whom the government was dealing—railway companies in particular, but also suppliers and contractors—considerable amounts of cash that he applied to the Conservative Party, though never to himself.

But there was no smallness in the man. Bengough caught this quality memorably in the central line of *Grip*'s epitaph after his death: "He was no harsh, self-righteous Pharisee." Few public figures had a bleaker private life: during just his first marriage he endured the Job-like blows of having a wife who quickly became an invalid and opium addict, a deeply loved son who died as an infant, and a second son who was mostly alienated from him, yet he never lost his innate optimism or his zest for life. He never despaired, and he never complained.

Although Macdonald could be unremittingly harsh towards opponents, such as George Brown, there was no meanness in him. The religious and ethnic animosities that so disfigured nineteenth-century Canadian public life would have worn down the spirits of any national leader, but he never succumbed to the temptation to side with the majority against the minority. His early policy towards the French, "treat them as a nation and they will respond as a free people usually do—generously," would not

* Macdonald was always scrupulous about protocol, insisting that "forms are things." When Edgar Dewdney, a senior Indian Affairs official and personal friend, sent his reports directly to him as his departmental minister, Macdonald instructed him always to send them first to his deputy minister.

be equalled by any English-Canadian public figure for a century. The same was true for his dealings with Aboriginals: Macdonald understood Indians better than any prime minister would for the next century, let alone any predecessor. In his dealings with them he made mistakes, but they were the product of political and administrative miscalculations, never of prejudice.

In *Heaven's Command*, his chronicle of the British Empire, James Morris wrote that Disraeli was "the one Prime Minister who could be described as a loveable human being." Macdonald is the nearest Canadian equivalent—his failings making him all the more human. Canadians understood this appeal instinctively, and that is why they voted for him time and time again. They trusted him because they knew he cared about their country and about them.

Among the post-Confederation challenges that soon faced Macdonald, one of the most considerable resided in the Quadrilateral—the house he was renting on Daly Street in Ottawa. Its drains stank to high heaven. "We can't make room for you just now," Macdonald advised his sister Louisa after she inquired about coming up from Kingston. "The fact is our drain is stopped up and my study, where I do all my work, had so offensive a smell that it began to affect my health." He explained that his mother-in-law, Mrs. Theodora Bernard, had given up her bedroom so he could use it as a temporary office and taken possession of her son's room, and that her son, Colonel Bernard, was "now sleeping in the garret." Three months later, Macdonald was still having to turn Louisa away: "I am now living in lodgings . . . the lower part of the house is almost useless." For lack of any trunk sewers (until 1874), the local drains, made of wood or common clay with no cemented joints, were not only smelly but a serious health hazard.

Leaky sewers and the absence of any municipal supply of running water were everyday realities in Ottawa, while the fact that wire screens had yet to be invented meant that flies poured into the houses to "hold Parliament on the kitchen tablecloths," in the wonderful phrase of Lady Macdonald in the diary she started a few days after Confederation. In *The Private Capital*, Sandra Fraser Gwyn opened the rearward lens still wider: "Even at the most elegant parties, the air was dank with the smell of stale perspiration. Teeth, even in rosebud mouths, were frequently snaggled and discoloured. The roads were full of mud and manure; the wooden side-walks covered with clots of spittle, tobacco juice, and worse." And at the city's centre, where the Bank of Canada stands today, pigs rooted among the refuse.

Today, the Bank of Canada looks down at this downtown intersection in Ottawa; back then, pigs feasted at it.

Macdonald fitted perfectly into this new country, where it was just about impossible for people to put on airs or take themselves too seriously. He focused intently on his task, to keep Canada free of American entanglements or close embrace and to gain the time for this odd political entity to grow from adolescence to maturity, to, as he put it, "turn gristle into bone." And he did it all while muffling his resolve with jaunty quips and elegant nonchalance.

TWO

Agnes of God

I do so like to identify myself with all my husband's pursuits and occupations. . . . I would soon fall out of his life if I went my own ways.

Lady Macdonald, in her diary, July 7, 1867

Of all Canada's leaders, Macdonald was the most gregarious. His friends ranged from British lords who welcomed him into their country houses to an Ottawa hansom-cab driver who insisted on transporting him to and from the Parliament Buildings free of charge during his years out of power. He was also the most solitary leader. His first wife, Isabella, succumbed to illness and became bed-ridden and an opium dependent for most of the fourteen years of their marriage. He lived very much on his own when at home with Isabella, often eating by himself in their darkened, silent house. After her death in 1857, he lived alone for another decade, frequently in boarding houses in one of the three cities where the rotating capital was located.

During this time, his family circle narrowed: his father was the first to die, and then his mother, the person he was closest to his whole life. He moved away from Kingston, and so from his two sisters, Louisa and Margaret. His surviving son, Hugh John, lived with Margaret and steadily grew away from him. Macdonald had many friends, and many colleagues and cronies, but he had no partner. He had no one to care for him who loved him unreservedly.

Suddenly, in London, on February 16, 1867, towards the end of the final negotiations on the new constitution, he married Susan Agnes Bernard. The marriage was almost entirely a union of convenience. He, as prime minister, needed a hostess and housekeeper. She, at thirty-one, and neither a beauty nor the possessor of a substantial dowry, ignored warnings by her brother, Hewitt, about Macdonald's drinking and accepted his offer, which promised to save her from a life without husband, home and children.

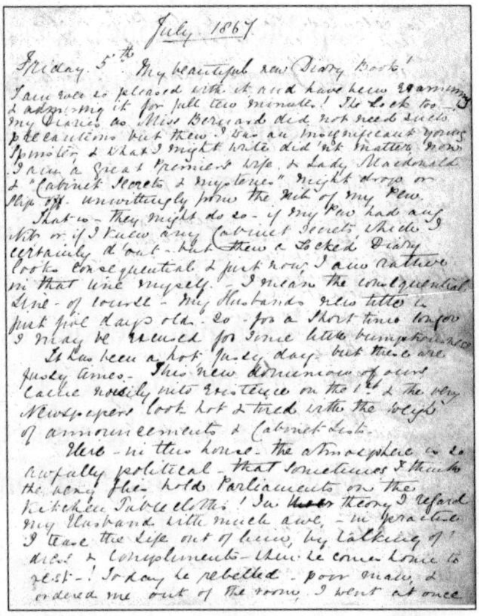
July 1867

Friday 5th My beautiful new Diary Book! I am sure so pleased with it and have been examining & admiring it for full two minutes! The Lock too—My Diaries as Miss Bernard did not need such precautions but then I was an insignificant young Spinster, & what I might write did'nt matter, now I am a Great Premier's wife, & Lady Macdonald & "Cabinet Secrets & mysteries" might drop or slip off unwittingly from the nib of my Pen.

That is—they might do so—if my Pen had any Nib or if I knew any Cabinet Secrets which I certainly do'nt—but then a Locked Diary looks consequential & just now, I am rather in that line myself.—I mean the consequential line—of course—my Husband's new title is just five days old. So—for a short time longer I may be excused for some little bumptiousness.

It has been a hot, fussy day—but these are fussy times. This new Dominion of ours came noisily into existence on the 1st & the very Newspapers look hot & tired with the weight of announcements & Cabinet Lists.

Here—in this house—the atmosphere is so awfully political—that sometimes I think the very Flies hold Parliaments on the Kitchen Tablecloths! In theory I regard my Husband with much awe,—in practice I tease the life out of him, by talking of dress & compliments—then he comes home to rest—! Today he rebelled—poor man, & ordered me out of the room, I went at once

The first entry, on July 5, 1867, in Lady Macdonald's diary—the only one known to have been kept by a prime ministerial spouse.

Rather to her surprise, Agnes fell totally and delightedly in love with John A. "I often look in astonishment at him," she wrote early on in her diary.* "He is so wise." Effortlessly, Macdonald became the focus of her life. "He comes in with a very moody brow," she wrote, "tired and oppressed, his voice weak, his step slow, and ten minutes after he is making clever jokes and laughing like a schoolboy with his hands in his pockets and his head thrown back." Another day she added, "I think he likes me to be near him; he is so equable and good-natured that being near him is always refreshing."

Agnes's role in Macdonald's life was far greater than she ever gave herself credit for. E.B. Biggar, the prime minister's first

---

* Lady Macdonald's diary covers the years 1867–69 quite extensively, but later entries are scarce.

capable biographer, speculated that the heavy-drinking Macdonald would not have lived ten years beyond Confederation but for her. By tempering his habit and by caring for him, Agnes enabled him to live for a quarter-century after July 1, 1867. She thus won for him the crucial extra time he needed to complete the Canadian Pacific Railway, which turned Canada into a nation reaching from sea to sea and so ended the risk that the West might, in one way or another, become part of the United States. In her own way, Lady Macdonald can be ranked beside George Brown's wife, Anne, as a Mother of Confederation.

All the early biographers portrayed Agnes Macdonald as a paragon of Victorian virtue—the Angel of the House. Later commentators have been less kind. One governor general's wife described her as ruling Ottawa society with "a rod of iron," while John Thompson, a senior cabinet minister and Canada's fifth prime minister, called her "a mole-catcher of a wife" and described Macdonald's home life as "tormenting." Over the years, the prevailing image of Agnes hardened into that of a battle-axe with a passion for making moralistic judgments. This assessment seems to be justified: when a cabinet minister committed the outrageous offence of marrying a divorced woman, Macdonald's relaxed response was to quote the maxim "Beneath the belt, there is no wisdom,"* but Agnes exiled the couple from Ottawa society. Louise Reynolds's excellent biography, *Agnes*, was far more sympathetic, but she still noted Agnes's "bleak piety."

There were, in fact, two Agneses—as historians Donald Creighton and Sandra Fraser Gwyn have noted. To distinguish

---

* The maxim's source was a seventeenth-century English writer, Sir Matthew Hale. In the original version it was "below the girdle," then the term for a man's belt.

Lady Macdonald, just after Confederation: young, slim and delighted she had "found something worth living for—living in—my husband's heart and love."

them, it's useful to call one "Agnes" and the other "Lady Macdonald." They had commonalities, of course: neither was considered pretty, whether the slim, statuesque figure of 1867 or the more matronly form of later years. Both were deeply religious, and neither had a sense of humour. Still, Agnes possessed a genuine sense of fun, delighting in physical abandon—as when she rode the train's cow-catcher through the Rockies. Lady Macdonald fretted about social proprieties and stood on her dignity. Agnes felt free to sit on the stone steps leading up the Centre Block, reading a book until her husband left for the day. She was awed that, after so many years as "an insignificant spinster," she had "found something worth living for—living in—my husband's heart and love."* Lady Macdonald was no less pleased, but even

* Lady Macdonald's diary.

early on was unafraid to "tease the life out of him by talking of dress and compliments when he comes home."

Agnes was plucky, gregarious and at times a perceptive observer. When she first saw Macdonald, in 1858 in the old legislature, she was struck by his "forcible yet changeable face, with such a mixture of strength and vivacity," and went on to describe his "bushy, dark peculiar hair as he leaned on his elbows and looked down." In many respects, Agnes operated shrewdly, improving her French by taking lessons from the Grey Nuns and helping Macdonald by talking to francophone MPs in their own tongue. (In her diary, though, she noted crossly, "The French seem always wanting everything, and they get everything.") She studied politics by noting what he did, watching intently "the results of his marvellous skill in the diplomatic line—all of this helped to weary & yet excite me, a Novice in this kind of life." She understood that doing nothing was sometimes the best thing: "As long as I can help him by being cheery & smiling, I am quite satisfied," she wrote. She took note of the crowd of supplicants waiting for hours outside the prime minister's office: "I try to be patient with them, for does it not concern their daily bread?" She and he learned sign language so that, as she sat in the Common's gallery and he at his desk below, they could exchange secret messages. "I do so like to identify myself with all my husband's pursuits and occupations," she noted astutely. "He is so busy and so much older than I that I would soon fall out of his life if I went my own ways."

Agnes, though, was cursed by a lack of social self-confidence, gaining it only after she had fully assumed her "Lady Macdonald" character. Her day job was to be Macdonald's hostess and chatelaine, but she lacked any of the light touches that give social occasions spirit and vitality. She possessed none of the silky assurance of Charlotte Rose, the wife of Macdonald's finance minister and close friend, John Rose. "She is so clever but her stories savour of such worldliness that I fear she is dangerous," Agnes observed sourly.* When the Roses moved to London in 1869, she wrote in relief, "I think I feared her cosy yet cutting smile." More intimidating still was the beautiful, flirtatious, impeccably gowned Lucianne Desbarats, the wife of the Queen's printer, who in her diary dismissed one of Lady Macdonald's social events as "boring. No dancing."

Even when there was no competition to unnerve her, Agnes remained conscious of her own clumsiness. "I pour tea very untidily," she wrote sadly of her "kettle-drums" or small tea parties. "Tea and games for supper, but it was very stupid. I could do nothing to promote gaiety." No one intimidated her more on such occasions than Macdonald himself: "He was charming, and we could never have done without him." On another occasion, her party had just begun when he was called away on some cabinet crisis. She wrote afterwards, "I never enjoy myself much when he does not assist, and his pleasant easy manner makes all go well." It's not easy being married to a Pied Piper when tuneless oneself.

Predictably, it came to be assumed that Agnes's personal inclinations on public matters could influence her husband. His first biographer, J.E. Collins, wrote that Macdonald, "it is whispered, is in the habit of consulting her when he is about to take some important step." In fact, on decisions about matters of state, Macdonald did exactly as he wished. There's a tone of almost girlish delight in Agnes's diary entry about her inability to advance the cause of a petitioner for a post: she did all she could, she noted, but, "as is usual for him on these occasions, [he] looked very benign, very gracious, very pleasant—but answered not one word! He never does."

---

* In referring to stories that "savour of such worldliness," she may have had in mind Charlotte Rose's predilection for literary works such as *Cometh Up As a Flower*, in which a married woman admits to an admirer that she loves him.

Agnes's second personality, as Lady Macdonald, would not appear in its full imperious aspect for a decade; after 1878, she did indeed rule Ottawa society with "a rod of iron." The contrasting characters of Agnes and Lady Macdonald were never entirely alone on the stage; her readiness to moralize was evident from the beginning, while traces of the gayer Agnes were still visible during Lady Macdonald's long years as a widow.

Whichever aspect of her was dominant, Agnes's solace was religion. She was an Anglican who followed an unusually puritanical and censorious version of that doctrine, which she inherited from her mother, Theodora. She adored her mother and was in utter thrall to her. Agnes took "a right stand against Balls . . . and theatricals," even boycotting them, and she disliked "all games of cards but Patience [solitaire]," granting this exception because Macdonald used the game to slow down his racing mind after a hard day in the office.*

St. Alban's, in the Sandy Hill area of Ottawa, became her church. She persuaded Macdonald to attend Sunday services regularly, although sometimes he insisted on going to Presbyterian and Methodist services to mix with voters of other denominations. She found it far more difficult to introduce family prayers into the household: "How to arrange it I do not know," she wrote in her diary. "Sir John rises late—it is his only quiet time of rest. Then Hewitt says he has not time—he goes out early." No doubt Macdonald and Hewitt were in cahoots in their explanations for resisting reform.

Nevertheless, Agnes was able to make Sunday a true day of

* Agnes recorded in her diary, "We read that Albert the Good [Victoria's consort] was fond of" patience—knowledge that provided further reinforcement for its acceptability.

rest. Macdonald had got into a bachelor's habit of filling up the emptiness of Sundays by treating them as another working day. "I made it for months a subject of very earnest prayer that my husband might prevent Sunday visitors . . . on anything but very pressing matters," Agnes recorded in her diary. God answered her plea. On November 17, 1867, she wrote euphorically to herself, "This has been a very quiet, happy day. . . . He—my own dear, kind husband—has been mercifully taught to see the right in this thing, and now we have so much happy rest after our morning service."

~

Prayer was not enough to overcome one devil in Agnes's life. No passages in her diary are more poignant than those where she discusses Macdonald's drinking and her efforts to get him to slow down, as he had promised before their marriage. She could never bring herself to describe the devil she was trying to exorcise; the words "liquor" and "drinking" never appear in her diary, let alone "drunk." The descriptions are all indirect: "Some things have happened to make this a rather trying week," or "his headaches, which gave me pain." At times, she was optimistic, but always tentatively: "The shadow that has for so long dimmed [life's] brightness has passed away. I trust its memory may never fade—but keep as ever, watchful and humble." She gave up wine, "for example's sake," and blamed herself when this sacrifice proved insufficient: "I was overconfident, vain, presumptuous in my sense of power." She managed to limit his intake by accompanying him on election campaigns and by waiting for him for hours at the Parliament Buildings until he emerged from some interminable debate.

Soon after Confederation, Macdonald did cut back. By the spring of 1868, Agnes could write, in triumph and in gratitude, "My darling so cheery and in good health. . . . Who am I to have been made the Instrument of so much improvement. God in his great mercy has so ordered it." And, after an evening at a concert, "I never had a happier evening. John was in such boyish spirits." But then would come the inevitable relapses, which she always blamed on herself, never on him: "I know that I troubled my darling; my over-anxiety was the cause of it." Sometimes she almost flagellated herself: "I fancied I could do much, and I failed signally. I am more humble now." After each failure she would become more deeply, almost more desperately, religious. His lapses continued, and gradually she retreated from the fight. But Agnes never gave up. She looked after him with assiduous care and unstinting affection.

Agnes also did her best to build a family around Macdonald. In January 1868, Hugh John, by now eighteen, distant from his father and with their relationship no warmer than formal, came for a visit during a break from his studies at the University of Toronto. Agnes noted that Hugh John "has been brought up necessarily much away from his father," while Macdonald "never remains long at his, that is Hugh's, home with his Aunts." The tell-tale phrase in her account was her designation "Hugh's home."

Then, astonishingly, Agnes herself expanded the family by becoming pregnant at the advanced age, for the time, of thirty-three. As was the custom then, her first reference to her condition, late in June 1869, was indirect: "My strength feels failing somehow and I am not feeling well." A few weeks later, she joyously threw aside all inhibitions: "Can it be that someday I shall have the sweet happiness of being a Mother? It seems too wonderful and yet so beautiful—I can hardly express what a new life it has given me. What a new life."

None of this caused Agnes to slacken in the most vital contribution she was making to her husband: to bring order into Macdonald's personal life. For the first time since he had left his parents' home, his fires were lit on time, his meals were served properly and promptly, his house was kept clean, his servants were supervised, the flow of visitors at all hours was controlled, and large weekly dinners were organized so he could invite all his MPs in rotation. One consequence was that Macdonald's own habits became more orderly. His days became much more regular, often broken by a restful nap in the afternoon. He rose early, read the newspapers and the official papers, stopped at 9:30 for a light breakfast, and then, assisted by a single secretary, personally answered all his incoming letters by hand.

Agnes knew she was doing the right thing, because Macdonald let her know it. Whenever Macdonald praised her, she blossomed: "We had a large dinner party last night—12—and everything was nice indeed," she wrote on one occasion. "John seemed in such good spirits, & so satisfied that I was ever so happy." Sometimes she got everything right: "My house is warm and cosy with the blazing fire and the bright gaslights as we trundled in after our cold drive, and John said, 'How comfortable this is.'" One wonderful moment she recorded in her diary: "As I write, the clock is striking ten; the house is very quiet. John lies reading near me on the sofa. Do you think it was very wicked of me to rest my head on his shoulder while he read me [Tennyson's] 'Locksley Hall'?"

While Agnes clearly loved him absolutely, it's impossible to know Macdonald's own thoughts about their relationship, because not a single letter from him to her survives. Almost certainly, Agnes destroyed the correspondence during her widowhood, perhaps out of melancholy or possibly out of pride that only she knew their full story. Macdonald's attitude to his second wife was always one of respect, affection, loyalty and fidelity, but his feelings towards her, to the extent it's possible to guess at them, were never stronger than these. No doubt their age difference was a factor, and their temperaments—his jaunty, hers judgmental—put them apart. Perhaps Macdonald had endured too much pain to ever again open himself up fully to another person, as he once had briefly to Isabella. And then, of course, he always maintained a mistress—politics.

Essentially, Agnes gave him a sanctuary. Within it, Macdonald experienced a force virtually unknown to him since he left his family home: female tenderness. "My darling held me in his arms until just now when I feared to disturb his precious sleep and I got up softly, turning out the gas, and left him." In this way Agnes won for him that extra decade and a half it took to give the country a spine.

THREE

Modest Country; Ambitious Leader

There must always be working men, men to work with their hands, to be poor, to be industrious, to be unfortunate, to suffer; it is the will of God, and the destiny of the race.

Halifax *Evening Express*

The country Macdonald presided over in 1867 can be quickly described. It stretched from Cape Breton Island to just beyond the Great Lakes. Its population was 3.5 million, one in three of them French and some 105,000 Aboriginal. The dominion's only real city was Montreal, with 115,000 inhabitants; Toronto and Quebec City each had about 60,000. The principal exports were lumber and grain. Manufacturing was starting up, but only a few companies had more than a dozen employees; one exception was the agricultural implements manufacturer Massey, which won two awards at the great Paris Exposition of 1867. The new nation's principal asset was abundant space, except that little arable land now remained to attract new settlers.

Canada's dominant characteristic was its Britishness: cricket was more popular than baseball, and no social success matched getting an invitation from the titled incumbent at Rideau Hall. Every bit as important, Canada was outgrowing its pioneer phase, often rowdy, raunchy and uninhibitedly bibulous, and becoming a Victorian society—a condition it would retain far longer than its Britishness, right through to the early 1960s.

Four in five Canadians were farmers, many having only a few acres of stony or swampy land. Their working hours were long, their work was brutally hard and their small houses (often just shacks) were dark and chilly. Because they owned their land, though, they were independent and self-sufficient, an achievement impossible had they remained on the other side of the Atlantic. Although workers in the towns earned more money in good times, they had it much harder. They had to rent accommodation and had no woodlots to supply fuel for the long winters. Not that the towns, Montreal excepted, were very different from the countryside. In Toronto, local newspapers carried notices such as "Lost, a roan cow, horns inclined inward, last seen on Queen Street east."

Everywhere, entertainment was limited to hellfire speeches by itinerant preachers, concerts by military bands, and an occasional show put on by touring actors, usually over-age and drunken. The people themselves staged their own barn-raisings, ploughing competitions and fall fairs. Food often went bad, and water, especially in towns, was frequently befouled. Death, from diseases such as smallpox, typhoid and diphtheria, let alone from the ministrations of doctors who wielded unsterilized instruments with unwashed hands, came early and was a commonplace among young children. Visits to dentists were sorties into horror.* Despite the best efforts of educational reformers such as Egerton Ryerson, who took as his creed, "Education is a public good; ignorance is a public evil," it was not until 1874 that Ontario made primary education compulsory.

* Doctors at least made house calls and were in abundant supply, although few had ever been to university. One notable exception was Macdonald's senior minister Charles Tupper, a medical graduate from the University of Edinburgh.

Even then, up to half the children often stayed away to do essential farm work. In Quebec, almost half the population over twenty years of age could not read or write. And as the towns expanded, Canadians faced challenges mostly unknown in the villages they had emigrated from—overcrowded slums, pollution and prostitution. Only if they read Charles Dickens had they even heard of such things.

The principal antidote to all this hardship was drink. Each year, every man, woman and child in the country consumed an average of four gallons of alcohol. Macdonald wasn't in the least unusual in his habit, although, as society grew ever more Victorian, he became an odd man out in public life, particularly because he never hid his drinking or apologized for it. Canada's defining attitudes were those of practicality, realism and stoicism; matters theoretical or aesthetical seldom provoked the least interest. As historian Donald Creighton described Canadians of this era, "For them the favorite myths of the Enlightenment did not possess an even quaintly antiquarian interest. . . . God, not government, these British Americans believed, could alone effect the regeneration of mankind." Significantly, in 1867, there were just two public libraries in the entire country.

If there was little that was fancy in the country, a great deal was solid. Loyalty—to marriage, family, church, employer, political party, clan or tribe, and to Queen and country—was the supreme national virtue. Belief in the cardinal importance of the rule of law was near universal. No one, least of all Macdonald, would have doubted the Charlottetown *Examiner*'s assertion that "the prosperity and civilization of the nation are dependent upon the enforcement of discipline and the preservation of order." Rural areas had neither police nor scarcely any crime,* and Canada's soon-to-be-acquired

* In 1880, the notorious massacre of the Black Donnellys occurred in Ontario's Biddulph Township, but it resulted from a feud the Donnellys and others had brought with them from Ireland.

"Far West" would develop radically differently from the same flatlands below the border because of the presence of Macdonald's North-West Mounted Police. Still, Canada was a rough place, and brawls broke out frequently between Green and Orange Irish as well as between French and Irish during labour strikes. But there was none of the general acceptance of violence so widespread in the United States, the lynch mobs and vigilante squads, the gangs of New York and the deliberately provoked Indian wars. While the now-iconic phrase "Peace, Order and Good Government" was never used at this time to describe the state's founding purpose, Canada from its beginning was an unusually peaceable kingdom.*

Religion mattered greatly—more so than to Americans, with their strict constitutional separation of church and state. Canadians attended church regularly and rarely divorced. In the two decades after 1867, there were around 300,000 divorces in the United States, compared with 116 in Canada. As Principal Grant of Queen's University summed it up: "Church-going habits are universal. Family worship is generally observed. Family life is pure." And while much about nineteenth-century Canada shocks today's sensibilities—such as public executions to which crowds flocked, bringing their children—those earlier Canadians would have been as shocked that, a century later, old people are warehoused in institutions rather than living with their children and grandchildren.

There was no democracy in Canada, the vote being limited to those men who owned sufficient property. Canadians regarded the U.S.-style universal male franchise as "mob rule." As the Ottawa *Times* put it in 1869, "The besetting sin of democracy is its inevitable tendency to level down . . . to debase everything to its own level, to pull down, never to elevate." There was, though, a rough

* For a history of what insiders call POGG, see *John A: The Man Who Made Us*, vol. 1, pp. 402–3.

and ready egalitarianism and a complete absence of any class system, whether based on birth, as in Britain, or on extremes of wealth and poverty, as in the United States. Macdonald understood the distinction. Although he opposed the universal franchise to the end of his days, on the grounds that it amounted to rule by those with no financial stake in the system, he also proclaimed proudly, "Classes and systems have not had time to grow here naturally. We have no aristocracy but of virtue and talent."

The highest social virtues were those of respectability and propriety. A pin-neat house attracted more praise than a large one. As the Toronto *Mail* warned its readers, "One impropriety is often the parent of a long succession of crimes." These attitudes were quintessentially Victorian. Queen Victoria had been on the throne for thirty years, but it had taken time for her attitudes and values to take hold in Britain, and a lot longer for them to cross the Atlantic. From the 1860s on, however, Victorianism flooded into Canada like an unstoppable tide.

The Victorians have generally had a bad press, being identified most commonly with sexual repression and overstuffed furniture. But a good case can be made that they were the most interesting generation ever. They were hypocritical for sure, but their seriousness, moral steadfastness and sheer sturdiness are beyond question. They needed these heroic qualities, because they had to cope with two revolutions of a magnitude never equalled before.

The initial challenge was the second wave of the Industrial Revolution. The first, in the eighteenth century, consisted of brilliant inventions in mechanized devices and steam engines concocted by solitary geniuses. The second used advances in financing, corporate organization and the systemization of research to spew out endless new marvels—railways, steamships, steam tractors, electricity, streetcars, the telegraph, telephones, typewriters and sewing machines, to name but a few. The consequences of these inventions went far beyond efficiency and convenience: streetcars created suburbs by making it possible for people to live at a distance from their work; railways created national markets, with the print media as the first beneficiary; and typewriters generated jobs for women in previously male-only offices. They also created an entire new class—a proletariat of industrial workers who formed unions that could bargain with their employers over wages and working conditions.

The intellectual revolution that burst forth was even more radical in its implications. Charles Darwin's *The Origin of Species* (1859) and *The Descent of Man* (1871), by questioning man's divine creation, compelled Victorians to reconsider their unquestioning faith in God and the Bible. Canadians, even if they occupied the rim of the known world, were well aware of this existential challenge. Principal William Dawson of McGill University warned that the new doctrines "threaten to overthrow the whole fabric of society as at present constituted." With considerable insight, he identified as especially pernicious "the ideas of struggle for existence and survival of the fittest." This creed, now known as social Darwinism, gave credibility to racism, and in Canada it fed the notion that Aboriginals were savages.

Victorians reacted to the intellectual and moral threat in one of three ways: by becoming even firmer in their faith (Torontonians, for example, gained the title of "Good" for their city by banning streetcars on Sundays); by exploring alternatives such as spirituality; or by concluding that religion had to refashion itself by helping to make earth more heavenly. This last response became a prime source of the Victorians' faith in the possibility of endless progress, pursued in Britain by Christian Socialism and in Canada, soon after the century's turn, by the Social Gospel movement. Moral earnestness became an integral part of Canadian identity. Soon after Confederation, the first Humane Society for animals was established, followed by the Children's Aid Society. As a direct consequence of the new public morality, the Woman's Christian Temperance Union was established in 1874, representing the initial entry by women into public debate. Canada's first strong labour movement, the Knights of Labor, imported from the United States, had both a moral and an economic mission. In *Grip* magazine, J.W. Bengough, himself the product of evangelical Presbyterianism, espoused causes like women's suffrage and temperance at the same time as he lashed out at the rich: "The explicit curse of heaven has been against those who grind the faces of the poor."

Things did get better, gradually, in early Canada. Universities, such as Toronto, Queen's, McGill and Dalhousie, were growing. Sports were organized, with inter-city leagues for lacrosse, baseball, cricket and hockey. Despite limited schooling for many, each household subscribed on average to at least one newspaper or journal. Cities began to acquire some urban niceties: in Toronto in 1869, the first version of Eaton's department store opened. There and in Montreal, some homeowners planted trees, and the *Canadian Monthly* called for "proper parks and grounds for health, stillness, exercise and innocent recreation." Henry George, the American radical, attracted huge audiences, particularly in Hamilton, by asking the fundamental, unanswerable question of the age: Why was there "advancing poverty amid advancing wealth"? All the changes did leave people unsettled. Professor Goldwin Smith, after he moved to Toronto in the 1870s, wrote of the horror of "unsexed female students who go about with their hair cut short and smoking in the streets."

Macdonald didn't believe in progress—in this sense he wasn't a Victorian. As John Willison of the Toronto *Globe* wrote in his *Reminiscences*, "For the evangelical school of reconstructionists who would remake the world in their own image and redeem mankind by legislation, he had only a complacent tolerance." And as Macdonald himself put it in the Commons, "I am satisfied to confine myself to practical things. . . . I am satisfied not to have a reputation for indulging in imaginary schemes and harbouring visionary ideas."

Overwhelmingly, Canadians agreed with him. Everyone hated taxes; few supported government spending (except on their own town). Governments, especially Macdonald's, were prepared to spend money (that is, to borrow it) for nation- and economy-building projects like canals, railways and land surveys, but that was it. There was no Poor Law, as in Britain; charity was the responsibility of the churches, not the government. Even public funding of education was criticized: "There is no reason or justice in making one man pay for the education of another man's children," complained the *Bystander*. Those without jobs were not "the unemployed" but the "idle poor" or the "undeserving poor."* The one way nineteenth-century governments were more interventionist than those of today was in their ample exercise of patronage: it was employed mainly for partisan political purposes, but sometimes as a welfare program for old guys whose legs had given out, or as a kind of affirmative action program to apportion public posts among all the regional, religious and racial groups.

Even if the government had wanted to do more, it would have been hard pressed. The entire federal civil service comprised just 2,660 people; the Department of Justice, for which Macdonald

---

* The word "unemployed" cannot be found in the *Oxford English Dictionary* before 1888.

was responsible after Confederation, had all of eight employees—the deputy minister, five lawyers and two messengers (sorely needed in those pre-telephone days). Whether Conservative or Liberal, no government enacted any social legislation in Ottawa until a half-century later, in 1927.*

Macdonald believed that human nature did not change; by logical extension, there was therefore no point in trying to make the world a better place. This attitude didn't make him politically inert. Specific public ills seized his attention. In 1871, he fired off a letter to his close namesake, Ontario premier John Sandfield Macdonald: "The sight of the immense masses of timber constantly passing my windows every morning constantly suggests to my mind . . . [that] we are destroying the timber of Canada and there is scarcely any possibility of replacing it." He urged Ontario and Quebec to jointly study Norwegian and German cutting practices, but because the jurisdiction was provincial he could take no action himself and nothing was done. Within the federal ambit, he was free to act, and every now and then he did: the Bank Act of 1871 was one of the most important and successful items of legislation enacted in Canadian history; one of its key consequences has been a near absence of bank failures in Canada in contrast to their regularly falling like leaves south of the border. He implemented legal protection for women from "seduction" (provided they were "of previously chaste character") ahead of any other country in the British Empire, and in 1869 he abolished public executions, although after Britain had done so.

About power itself, and his interest in it, Macdonald was not the least coy. "I don't care for office for the sake of money, but for

---

* This initiative was a modest old-age pension scheme, and it became politically acceptable only because earlier initiatives had been taken to help returned veterans of the First World War.

the sake of power and for the sake of carrying out my own views of what is best for the country," he said. Power was a means to an end—though he enjoyed having it immensely, not least because he was so good at exercising it. He had a clear idea of why he wanted power: to make certain Canada did not become American, either by conquest or by handing itself over to its overpowering neighbour. He also had a clear idea of how this goal must be achieved: by stretching Canada into a continental nation that would be a mirror image of its rival, and by winning enough time for the new dominion to mature into a true nation.

The new prime minister approached this objective warily, recognizing that progress wouldn't come easily and that there would be setbacks. In 1868, he commented to the new governor general, Lord Lisgar, "At present we are all mere politicians, but by and by it may be to the good luck for some of us to rise to the level of national statesmen."* He was just as cautious in public. At the new Parliament's first session, he avoided giving the government leader's usual inspirational opening speech by giving no speech at all. He did so because he was not yet a real prime minister, one elected by the people with a mandate, but only a prime minister whom the governor general had picked to get the show going. So, before the summer of 1867 was over, Macdonald called his first election.

As in all elections, Macdonald left nothing to chance. Two days after Confederation Day, he wrote to Toronto bishop John Lynch to jog his memory: "I have a claim upon the confidence and support of the Catholics of Upper Canada . . . [because] if they have

* The newcomer's title at this time was actually Sir John Young, but he was soon ennobled as Lord Lisgar, and this title is used throughout the text.

secured a Separate School Bill, if they have received any money grants for their Educational Institutions, or if they have received any appointments to Office above the rank of a Landing Waiter, it is due to myself." In case this wasn't enough, Macdonald reminded His Grace that Liberal leader George Brown's *Globe* had long been "zealously employed in reviling the Catholic Hierarchy from the Pope downwards." Earlier, he had persuaded John Sandfield Macdonald, a former Liberal (Reform) leader, to turn Conservative and become the first premier of Ontario, although, oddly, for a time he also sat in the House of Commons as a Liberal.

The results trickled in through September and October, with individual constituencies still holding elections on different days.* Macdonald won comfortably, although not overwhelmingly. Overall, he won 101 seats to the 80 of the various opposition parties. Especially pleasing to him, he won in Ontario, where George Brown went down to personal defeat. Although Brown remained a major force in the Liberal Party, he would never again return to Parliament. The election results were disappointing only in Nova Scotia where an anti-Confederate tide swept all but one seat. Macdonald dismissed this outcome as "a small cloud of opposition no bigger than a man's hand." In fact, the cloud was sizeable and dark.

The 1867 election result was decisive in one enduring way. The Conservative Party emerged from it as Canada's first genuine national party. The Quebec *bleu* MPs were now Conservatives, intermingled in the Commons with their anglophone colleagues.

---

* By sheer oversight, the British North America Act left the provinces responsible for the local rules for federal elections. These rules differed widely: Nova Scotia required all constituency elections to be held on the same day, and New Brunswick implemented the secret ballot. Macdonald pledged to achieve uniformity by making the entire system a federal responsibility, but he didn't get round to it until 1885.

By contrast, the Opposition was made up of an alliance between the Liberals and the Quebec *rouges*, and even lacked an agreed leader when Brown was not replaced. The Conservatives were also an organized party, thanks to their control of patronage and their system—Macdonald's—for distributing the plums. On the government side at least, the era of the "loose fish"—of MPs making up their own minds how to vote—was coming to an end. Macdonald had recognized the need for a strong party organization and set out to build one. As he wrote to his Montreal *Gazette* friend Brown Chamberlin in 1868, "The difficulty is that there is no great party interested in fighting the battle of the Dominion." It would take the Liberals another two decades to copy his example.

Macdonald was now prime minister by the free choice of the people, or at least of a majority of the 15 per cent of them entitled to vote. He set November 7 for the opening of the first Parliament of the new Confederation of Canada.

But for that architectural gem the Library of Parliament, which would not be completed until 1876, everything was ready in Ottawa for Canada's first MPs and senators. The three imposing buildings on Parliament Hill—the East Block, the West Block and the Parliament Building—were all complete. Macdonald left no recorded comment about the place where he would spend much of his life, but Edward Blake, a leading Liberal, summed up the general opinion by describing it as "one of the greatest examples of magnitude without convenience on the face of the earth." In summer the building was too hot, because the windows couldn't be opened, and in winter too cold, because only wood was used in the central heating plants (supposedly so the buildings wouldn't be blackened by soot from coal fires, but probably to justify

No one liked Ottawa, but the Parliament Buildings, completed just in time, gave the nation a centre and, as important, a rare example of national daring.

patronage contracts). The ventilation system worked erratically, and the gas lighting sucked oxygen from the air.

There were 181 MPs, compared to the 130 members of the old United Province of Canada legislature, for whom the buildings had originally been designed. They had only to endure these discomforts for about three months each year—the length of the annual sessions, from which members gained the nickname "sessionals." Their pay, at six hundred dollars per annum, was adequate, but in no way ample.* And they had few material aides—no offices or

* The pay rate was increased to a thousand dollars in 1873.

secretaries, nothing but a box of stationery and, later, a travelling trunk. There were some perks. Parliament's facilities included a hairdressing salon where members could have their scalps massaged by a steam-driven hairbrush. And in the basement of the Parliament Building there was a saloon and restaurant that was exempt from all licensing laws. Wilfrid Laurier later estimated that, by midnight, "at least fifty per cent of the members [were] more or less under the influence of liquor." Debating tactics included throwing books, papers and, at least once, firecrackers, singing songs, and, as heckling, mimicking cats, roosters and bagpipes. The Speaker sat not at one end of the chamber, as today, but in the middle of one long side. Until 1875, there was no Hansard.*

Ottawa itself, a former lumber town of about twenty thousand inhabitants, attracted nothing but rude comments. Macdonald's son, Hugh John, described it as "almost like a city of the Dead." That label was not really fair. Unlike Quebec City, one of the previous three "rotating" capitals, it at least boasted the occasional "theatrical"—for example, *Sketches in India*, presented by Mr. Vining Brown and Miss Florence Grosvenor. On Sparks Street, passersby could halt at Bates's store to watch miniature steam engines driving coffee- and spice-grinding machines. The town did have one good hotel, the Russell House, where the cost of a champagne lunch for two (the principal meal of the day) was three dollars, with no tips expected. The salaries of public servants were scant, though; even the judges of the Supreme Court sometimes arranged bank loans to draw on their salaries up to nine months in advance. After 1867, Ottawa made efforts to look more like a national capital. A municipal police force was created,

* The principal beneficiaries of this failure to record debates were parliamentary reporters, who got commissions from MPs to report their speeches in full in the newspapers and earned money on the side by writing up the proceedings of parliamentary committees.

though initially its principal activity was chasing skaters off the canal on winter Sundays, and civic authorities began to enforce a bylaw requiring the removal of night-soil from backyard privies.

Rideau Hall, the governor general's residence, functioned like a mini-court for which there was no equivalent in dourly republican Washington. Occasions there could be quite grand, though sometimes raucous, as when the chief justice of the Supreme Court of Canada became blind drunk at a reception. But these functions were also egalitarian: no fewer than one in ten Ottawans were considered eligible for invitations—doctors, lawyers and civil servants as well as "shop-keepers, butchers, bakers and tradesmen of every quality." The other grace note was the august Rideau Club, of which Macdonald and George-Étienne Cartier were founding members, though it excluded anyone in trade from membership.

Macdonald attempted to make things better. He proposed that the government buy and redevelop the entire downtown block between Wellington and Sparks streets and that a new Rideau Hall be built on Nepean Point, looking out on the Ottawa River. The cabinet turned him down on the grounds of cost. Not until after the Second World War would another attempt be made to give Ottawa the appearance of a national capital. Macdonald's ambitions for the Library of Parliament were also well ahead of their time. In 1868, he told the Commons that the library should take the same position "as that of the British Museum . . . and must be open to all students or readers desiring reference to scarce and valuable stores of information." Nothing happened. All in all, the platform on which Macdonald had to build a nation was a rickety one

~

Confederation's first Throne Speech was read out to the new Parliament on November 7, 1867, by the soon-to-depart Governor General Lord Monck. It was a workmanlike declaration. MPs were told they would be invited to consider measures for "the adoption of a uniform postal system; for the proper management and maintenance of public works and the properties of the Dominion; for the adoption of a well-considered scheme of militia organization and defence; for the proper administration of Indian affairs; for the introduction of uniform laws respecting patents of invention and discovery." Its one visionary note was a reference to "the important subject of western, territorial expansion."

Before the opening, Macdonald had to unsnarl one small in-house snag and another that could have been very large indeed. The minor fracas derived from the fact that Alexander Tilloch Galt, the minister of finance, suddenly resigned because the cabinet had refused to accept a particular policy he favoured. Macdonald replaced him with John Rose, a close friend and a successful corporate lawyer, who, as a Montrealer, could take over from Galt the responsibility for representing Quebec's English Protestants.

Here, Macdonald was genuinely innovative. From the very beginning, he constructed his cabinets so that they represented regions as well as religious and ethnic groups. No precedent for a consciously constructed national cabinet existed in either Britain or the United States. The balance Macdonald settled on throughout his first term, until 1872, was five cabinet ministers from Ontario, four from Quebec (three of them francophones), and two each from Nova Scotia and New Brunswick. As he explained in the Commons on April 3, 1868, although "the theory of the constitution made no such requirement," he believed "the confidence of every section of the Confederation should be invited and secured by the recognition of its right to Cabinet representation." Before his second election, in 1872, he took care to let it be known that his second cabinet would include both a Catholic Irish minister and a representative of the Orange Order. Later, he added cabinet representatives from the new provinces as they joined—Manitoba, British Columbia, Prince Edward Island. The intent was to give the regions a voice at the centre, as a substitute for the U.S. system of a powerful Senate with equal representation for all states. In fact, most ministers functioned principally the other way around—as voices speaking to their regions on behalf of the federal government.

Macdonald was aware of the problem but could conceive of no solution. He advised one supporter that "it will not conduce to the good of the Country" to accept the "right of any nationalities, as such, to a share in the Government": the consequence could be "endless disputes between the different people who have sought a home in Canada." After the 1872 election, Macdonald expressed pleasure that two senior ministers, Cartier and Finance Minister Francis Hincks, after being defeated in their home ridings, had chosen to contest and win seats in the new provinces of Manitoba and British Columbia. Unrealistically, he rejoiced that this dispersal of cabinet talent had given "the coup de grace to sectionalism forever."

The second snag Macdonald had to deal with had the potential to split apart his entire government, except that it never went beyond threats and hurt feelings. In the fall of 1867, D'Arcy McGee, by this time outside the cabinet, reported to Macdonald that he had picked up rumours about rebellious talks going on between Cartier and Galt. He warned Macdonald that "Cartier is only waiting a change of opportunities to separate from and break up your administration." Apparently, both Cartier and Galt (whom Macdonald dismissed as "unstable as water") were miffed that, at Confederation, Macdonald had been ennobled as a Knight Commander of the Bath while they and others had received only

Companionships of the Bath. McGee added that Cartier was also talking to Macdonald's old opponent, George Brown.

Something was indeed going on. Brown reported in a letter to his wife, Anne, that "Cartier . . . sent me a letter suggesting a political alliance and my return to Parliament." Brown responded fulsomely, praising Cartier for having "run the risk of political death" by committing himself during the preliminary negotiations for Confederation, in contrast to Macdonald, who "ran no risk whatever." Cartier suggested that Brown meet him for confidential talks. However, when Brown consulted Alexander Mackenzie, the Liberals' parliamentary leader, Mackenzie expressed grave alarm at the potential damage to party morale if news of these backstage negotiations ever leaked out.

The plot ended in 1868, when Macdonald reached into his patronage bag to placate his disaffected colleagues. Cartier got a baronetcy, a title higher than Macdonald's because it made his knighthood hereditary (though only a gesture, because he had no son). Galt got his knighthood the following year.

There was so much housekeeping to be done in the new dominion that in 1868 Macdonald called two sessions of Parliament. A total of seventy-two acts were passed, dealing with everything from disentangling the activities of the federal and provincial governments to enacting new regulations so the federal government could carry out a host of new responsibilities—from trade and commerce to banking, navigation and shipping, and bankruptcy and criminal law.

During this period, what has since become Canada's principal political activity—wrangling between Ottawa and the provinces over money and jurisdiction—scarcely existed. The common judgment that Macdonald set out from the start to undermine the new provincial governments is plain wrong. Macdonald was certainly a centralist, and he had little respect for the provincial governments. He told Brown Chamberlin that "the General Gov't or Parliament should pay no more regard to the status or position of the Local Governments than they would to the prospects of the ruling party in the Corporation of Quebec or Montreal." And he confided to Edmund Meredith, one of the deputy ministers, that he intended to "hand over all the loose and doubtful fish to the local governments where they could be clearly watched and killed off like nits."

But Macdonald moved with great caution. In 1868, he circulated to the premiers a memorandum he had drafted as justice minister on how Ottawa would exercise its constitutional power to disallow provincial legislation it judged was either *ultra vires* (outside their jurisdiction) or damaging to national interests. He pledged to implement this intrusive power "very seldom" and only when the provinces had clearly exceeded their authority. The unanimous response from provincial capitals was highly favourable.

No federal-provincial clash occurred until 1871, when the government of New Brunswick passed legislation to replace the existing system of separate schools with a secular public school system. Although Ottawa had a residual power to protect separate schools that had "existed in law" at the time of Confederation, Macdonald, supported by Cartier, refused to intervene despite pressure from Quebec MPs. His reasoning was that the federal power to override provincial legislation dealing with education did not apply, because New Brunswick's system existed only in fact, not in law. He referred the matter to the Judicial Committee of the Privy Council in London, which sustained his judgment. In defence of his decision, Macdonald said, "The constitution would not be worth the paper it is written on unless the rights of the

Provincial Legislatures were supported." Rather, New Brunswick Catholics had to do the work themselves, by "us[ing] their influence in favour of those candidates who will promise to do them justice."

At this time, the most important characteristic of provincial governments was that they scarcely existed at all. In 1869, Quebec employed just ninety-two civil servants. All provincial governments were small, inexperienced and amateurish. In contrast, the federal government was staffed by the civil servants who had previously run the United Province of Canada, and all the best politicians were there—the veteran Conservatives and Liberals as well as newcomers such as Leonard Tilley from New Brunswick and Charles Tupper from Nova Scotia. Moreover, because dual seats were allowed, many of the best men—Alexander Mackenzie, Edward Blake and Cartier and the premiers of both Ontario and Quebec—sat in both the federal and the provincial legislatures, reducing the latter to the political equivalent of railway sidings.

In these early years, Macdonald often acted like a kindly godfather to the provincial governments. "In going over the Acts of your Legislature," he wrote to Sandfield Macdonald, "I observe a misprint in Ca. 3, Sec. 3—the word 'person' in it, should be 'purpose.'" He did the same with Quebec's Pierre-Joseph-Olivier Chauveau, also a Conservative, but more diplomatically, routing his comments through his Quebec ministers. When he was shown a draft of some of the province's legislation, he told a Quebec colleague he would "draft a Bill which I think will hold water and do all that is necessary."

In only one area did Macdonald expand federal jurisdiction. Immigration was a joint responsibility, but the provinces lacked the money and imagination to act. "Are you not going to do anything on the subject of a new Emigration Establishment?" Macdonald pleaded with Sandfield Macdonald. It would be "a great pity," he continued, if the provinces could not agree on a national system. "They would jar and clash with each other & create uncertainty in Europe," he cautioned. Eventually, as he told Chamberlin, "I had to take them [immigration matters] into my own hands. The Local Governments would do nothing, and the French were not very anxious on the subject."

Macdonald's commitment to centralism was real, but its character has repeatedly been misperceived. He had no interest in gaining more power in order to enact worthy reform legislation or to improve the material lives of people. He was a centralist because he was a nationalist. He wanted power in order to nurture a fragile, fragmented collection of quasi-colonies into a nation that could survive alongside the most dynamic nation-state in the world.

But before he could fulfill any of these plans, he had first to shore up the existing building so that it remained in one piece.

FOUR

A Triumph; A Tragedy

We must qualify ourselves to fulfill the spirit of tolerance and forbearance. It is our only means to make a great nation of a small people.

Thomas D'Arcy McGee

Just four months after Canadians came together to create a new nation, a sizeable number—the majority of Nova Scotians—did their best to leave. To magnify the nation-building challenge that now confronted Macdonald, this secessionist threat came at the same time he was trying to double the new nation's size in the West.

The British North America Act provided for Canada to acquire Rupert's Land, that vast tract of land given to the Hudson's Bay Company in 1670. It encompassed most of the present-day prairie provinces and extended westwards to the height of the Rockies and eastwards, across northern Ontario and Quebec, all the way to Labrador.* In the first session of the first post-Confederation Parliament, the government introduced a resolution to allow it to

* The territory was named after the dashing Royalist cavalry general Prince Rupert of the Rhine, who secured the charter for his Company of Adventurers from Charles II, his cousin.

buy the territory. The minister sponsoring the resolution, William McDougall, who as editor of the *North American* newspaper had advocated western expansion as early as the 1850s, argued persuasively, "either we must expand or contract." The resolution passed easily, and Macdonald dispatched McDougall and Cartier to London to negotiate the financial terms of the takeover with the Colonial Office and the Hudson's Bay Company.

In the eastern provinces, Macdonald was on the defensive. Nova Scotians had entered Confederation reluctantly and angrily. Not only had Macdonald and his ally Charles Tupper, the provincial premier, orchestrated events so that the people of this once separate colony had had no say in the matter, but, yet more deviously, they had arranged things so that the provincial legislature, which had achieved Responsible Government, or self-government, even earlier than Canada, never debated the Confederation terms. Further, soon after Confederation, Nova Scotians realized that they were obliged to pay the higher tariffs of the old United Province of Canada, which were now the national standard, and, worse, that all customs duties that were due would now actually be collected. They worried further that Ottawa's plans for expansion to the West meant that less money would be dispatched down east. A backlash was inevitable.

Retribution came in the fall of 1867, when the first elections for the federal Parliament were held as well as those for each of the four provincial legislatures. Of the fifty-five federal and provincial constituencies in Nova Scotia, anti-Confederates won fifty-two: all but one of the nineteen federal seats, and all but two of the thirty-six provincial seats. The single Confederate survivor of substance was Charles Tupper, fearless and indefatigable but prone to crashing misjudgments and verbal excess in both content and volume. Although a devout Baptist, Tupper was famously known as the "Ram of Cumberland" for his flirtatious attentions to the ladies. The "antis" now not only commanded the provincial government but, because most Nova Scotian merchants feared impending competition from Canada, possessed a fatter electoral war chest. Above all, in Joseph Howe, they had the province's one politician of genuinely high repute.

To Macdonald, Howe was "the tallest head," the one who, unless won over to the Canadian side, might actually lead Nova Scotians out of Confederation. Newly elected as one of the "Noble Eighteen" anti-Confederates in the Dominion Parliament, he went to Ottawa and promptly made impassioned speeches against Confederation. He also planned to cross the Atlantic to Britain to plead his cause with the government there. Here, Howe had a weak spot: the son of a United Empire Loyalist, he described himself as a "dear lover of old England" and admitted publicly that, to save her, he would "blow up Nova Scotia into the air, or scuttle her." Separation, he confessed to Macdonald, might lead to Nova Scotia eventually joining the United States.

Knowing Howe's doubts, Macdonald, as he often did at the beginning of some crisis, became over-optimistic. He treated the election setbacks philosophically, observing that, whenever "there was a junction between a large and a small Country, the smaller was always more opposed to it." He confided to supporters that, no matter how much Nova Scotia complained, it was powerless to do any serious harm.

Serious harm was indeed possible. Of the two newcomers to Confederation, Nova Scotia mattered far more than New Brunswick. It possessed a far larger population (some 350,000) and a more developed economy (extensive fisheries, shipbuilding yards and, in Cape Breton, the new country's only coal mines). Halifax was also the site of a major Royal Navy base. If Nova Scotia left, Canada would, effectively, no longer stretch out to the Atlantic, and so could never become a truly continental-sized nation. Furthermore, New Brunswick might well follow it out of Confederation. Such an unravelling might persuade Britain to abandon the whole project of building a new nation, allowing Washington to pick up the pieces. Indeed, Governor General Monck warned the colonial secretary that the break-up of the union so soon after its creation would make "the maintenance of British power or the existence of British institutions in America . . . impossible."

To heighten this risk, a disturbing political change had just taken place in London. Benjamin Disraeli's Conservative government had been defeated. In the new Liberal government, many of its ministers, including the foreign secretary and the colonial secretary, and even Prime Minister William Gladstone himself, were suspected to be "separatists" who doubted the value of maintaining colonies. American annexationists took notice: General Benjamin Butler, a Massachusetts congressman, made a flying visit to Prince Edward Island, reporting back—inaccurately but damagingly—that everyone there was talking about joining the United States.

All was not lost, by any means. It was one thing for Nova Scotians to want to leave, but quite another for them to find somewhere to go. The once-mooted alternative of a Maritime Union was a chimera: the anti-Confederates sent emissaries to their neighbours but got only evasive replies. Britain had indicated clearly in the lead-up to Confederation that it wanted to withdraw from its commitments in North America, so was most unlikely to accept Nova Scotia as a reborn, separate colony. Heady talk in the province of annexation forced Canadians to pay attention, but most Nova Scotians were scared of it themselves, and the United States was highly unlikely to offend Britain for so minor a territorial gain.

One real threat did exist, which Macdonald spotted immediately. While the chances that Howe's mission to London would succeed were slight, Macdonald realized, as he told Jonathan McCully, a leading local supporter, that the separatists in the British government might be "weak enough" to tell Howe "to give the new system a fair trial for a year or two." Such temporizing would encourage the anti-Confederates to redouble their efforts.

Macdonald's strategy was the exact opposite of the one he had deployed to haul Nova Scotia into Confederation. He put no pressure on Nova Scotians either directly, by threatening a cutback in funds, or indirectly, by trying to incite London once again to apply "the imperial screw." And he avoided any confrontation with the "antis." His objective became not to herd the Nova Scotians back into Confederation but to get them to walk themselves back in. As he explained to Ambrose Shea, a Newfoundland ally, it was important "to the Dominion that this state of perpetual 'sulk' in which the Nova Scotians indulge" should come to an end. He wanted them in, but contentedly so—more or less.

He had in mind the bigger picture. Pacifying Nova Scotia and acquiring Rupert's Land weren't the only items on his nation-building agenda. Macdonald was also eyeing Newfoundland and Prince Edward Island, and he was even looking all the way west to the Pacific, to the Crown colony of British Columbia. If he could haul in all of these, the new nation would gain the coherence of a state bounded on three sides by salt water and, even more important, would become a continental-sized state like the United States.

Macdonald's agenda could scarcely have been more ambitious. By wretched ill-timing, he had also to deal with a personal problem that distracted his thoughts and wore down his energies.

Before his marriage to Agnes, Macdonald had drawn up a prenuptial agreement that transferred to her a sizeable share of his assets. This arrangement had probably been suggested by Agnes's brother, Hewitt Bernard, who, as Macdonald's deputy minister, knew him well and worried that his drinking might leave her a pauper. As a side benefit, these assets, once transferred to her, could not be seized if he ever tumbled into debt.

Right after Confederation, Macdonald's finances improved considerably. His prime ministerial salary was $5,000. He could also count on some $2,000 a year in profits from his law practice, which he still maintained in Kingston; as well, Agnes kept a far closer eye on their spending than he ever had.

In 1864, Macdonald's law partner, Archibald Macdonnell, had died suddenly. Absorbed as he was in grand political affairs, Macdonald took some years to realize that Macdonnell, acting on his own, had used the firm's cash to engage in some highly risky investments—in some instances, very possibly, criminal ones. By May 1867, Macdonald came to the shocked realization that he and the Macdonnell estate owed jointly some $64,000 (around $1 million today).* His principal creditor was Kingston's Commercial Bank of Canada, which charged a steep interest rate of 7 per cent. When this bank failed the following year, it was taken over by the Merchants' Bank of Canada, owned by Hugh Allan, the country's wealthiest man. A February 1868 letter from Macdonald reveals some of the frantic attempts he was making to stay afloat. He had tried to sell some of the land he owned but had been offered only $300 instead

---

* Financial figures in this section are taken from the detailed account provided by J.K. Johnson in his and Peter Waite's joint profile of Macdonald in *The Dictionary of Canadian Biography.*

of the $500 he thought the lots were worth. He was considering selling off his best asset, "the Guelph property, at a good price." By early 1869, Macdonald's debt had risen to $80,000 (worth close to $1.5 million today). Another bank, the Bank of Upper Canada, began an action against him to recover debts. In a September 1869 letter to his principal creditor, Allan, Macdonald pointed out that if this bank took him to court, "I shall be unable legally to carry out the proposition I have made to you." This carefully judged pressure prompted Allan's bank to reach a settlement with him for his outstanding debts. In one remedial action, Macdonald took out a $12,000 joint mortgage with Agnes against property he owned in Kingston.

Macdonald struggled on in this way for another year. Then, in 1870, a wealthy Toronto friend, D.L. Macpherson, realizing how close to penury the prime minister had become, organized a private subscription among businessmen which raised $67,000 and placed the money in a trust fund from which Macdonald could draw sums to cover his living expenses, but with the principal reserved for the use of his wife and family. "He relinquished the profits of his profession," Macpherson explained, "and in the service of his country became not a richer but a poorer man." The stress and humiliation of this financial crisis, coinciding with his vast exercises in nation-building, caused Macdonald to relapse again into heavy drinking late in 1868, despite Agnes's prayers and ministrations.

No other Canadian prime minister has ever had to cope with such personal financial pressure; Sir Joseph Pope wrote in his *Memoirs* that "in the autumn of 1869, I do not think [Macdonald] was worth one shilling." Yet Macdonald never showed the least sign of depression, self-pity or loss of confidence. His lifelong attitude, as expressed in his wonderful advice to the financially strapped Toronto *Mail* editor T.C. Patteson, was, "Why, man, do you expect to go through this world without trials or worries? . . . As for present debts, treat them as Fakhreddin in Tancred treated his—He played with his debts, caressed them, toyed with them—What would I do without those darling debts, said he." Later, Macdonald supplemented this advice: "As to debts and troubles, these come to us 'as Sparks fly upward' . . . but they disappear like summer flies and new ones come. Take things pleasantly and, when fortune empties her chamber pot on your head—Smile and say, 'We are going to have a summer shower.'"

In the late 1860s, fortune had not yet finished emptying her chamber pot on Macdonald's head: he was about to lose a close friend and an invaluable ally.

Macdonald's lost ally, and Confederation's lost bard, was Thomas D'Arcy McGee. By the time of Confederation, McGee was no longer the spirited charmer he had once been. Heavy drinking and declining health had reduced him, at the age of forty-three, to a shadow of the vital elf he had once been.* He had become politically reckless, lashing out at Fenian sympathies among Catholic Irish communities in Ontario and Montreal, and ignoring warnings, including from Macdonald, that he was risking violent retaliation. McGee was not among the cabinet ministers announced on Confederation Day, principally because of the new rules of regional balance, but also because he no longer carried his old political weight. That fall, he received no party funds to help him in his election campaign, and he won his seat in Montreal very narrowly. His future now depended on patronage. Macdonald promised him the position of commissioner of patents, a job with

* Sometime in 1867, McGee did take the pledge, and from then to the end drank not a drop.

light duties and a salary of three thousand dollars. Though repelled by the thought of taking such a "subordinate office," McGee was drawn to it, because he would no longer have to "devote myself to those infernal gods, the publishers."

McGee could still sing. One of his late writings included the uncanny perception that "In a sense we are all foreigners to America: European civilization is foreign to us; the Christian religion is foreign to us." One of the verses he composed during this period ascends towards poetry:

Give me again, my harp of yew,
In consecrated soil 'twas grown—
Shut out the day star from my view,
And leave me with the night alone.

Ugly enough to be compared to a monkey but with a gorgeous voice, D'Arcy McGee gave the nation what it most needed—poetry and a sense of soul.

His real song remained Canada. In the spring of 1867, returning from London once the British North America Act was passed, McGee was met at the station in Montreal by a welcoming crowd. He told them, "Other politics that have been preached in British North America will grow old and lose their lustre, but the conciliation of class and class . . . the policy of linking together all our people . . . of linking order to order, of smoothing down the sharp and wounding edge of hostile prejudice—this policy will never grow old." At the Ottawa railway station, where an even larger crowd had gathered to greet him, he gave his recipe for Canadian greatness: "We must qualify ourselves to fulfill the spirit of tolerance and forbearance. It is our only means to make a great nation of a small people."

Here McGee was articulating what his friend and political leader Macdonald was trying to do—to weave together all the disparate elements within the new nation into a kind of peaceable kingdom. Their perspectives were not the same—McGee always looked directly at Canada, while Macdonald kept a close eye on Britain and America—but their objectives were identical.

On St. Patrick's Day, March 17, 1868, a dinner was held at Ottawa's Russell House hotel to honour McGee, where Macdonald and Cartier praised him fulsomely. A short time later, on April 7, he lingered late in the Commons, gossiping and chatting with Macdonald about political matters. When the debate finally ended after midnight, McGee and another MP, Robert MacFarlane, put on their coats, lit up cigars and walked out into the clear, sharp night, the ground covered by a light fall of new snow. At the corner of Sparks and Metcalfe streets they exchanged goodnights, McGee continuing alone on Sparks Street to Mrs. Trotter's boarding house. At the door, he took out his key just as Mrs. Trotter opened it from the inside. At that moment there was a loud explosion.

All day, Agnes Macdonald had experienced a sense of foreboding. Macdonald didn't get home until after two in the morning. Waiting up for him, she wrote later, "a sort of dread came upon me, as I looked out into the cold, still bright moonlight, that something might happen to him at that hour coming home alone." But then she "heard the carriage wheels & flew down to open the door for my Husband."

Shortly afterwards, Agnes heard a frantic knocking on the door. "Springing up I threw on a wrapper & ran into my dressing-room, just in time to see John throw up the window & to hear him call out, 'Is there anything the matter?'" "McGee is murdered, lying in the street. Shot thro' the head," the messenger shouted back. Macdonald, accompanied by Hewitt Bernard, immediately raced into town by carriage, where they found McGee still lying where he had fallen outside the boarding house. Macdonald cradled McGee's head in his arms and held him until a doctor arrived to confirm that he was dead. Only then did Macdonald and the others carry his body to a couch inside. Back home, his overcoat sodden with blood, Macdonald collapsed. As Agnes wrote, "He was much agitated, for him whose self command is so wonderful . . . his face a ghostly white."

That night, Macdonald slept for just two hours, then went to the office to fire off telegrams demanding that those involved—Fenians, as was assumed universally—be arrested and brought to justice. In the Commons, Macdonald began his tribute: "His hand was open to everyone. His heart was made for friends. And his enmities were written in water." He faltered, stopped and had to begin again: "He was too good, too generous to be rich. Yet he has left us a sacred legacy." He went on to declare that McGee's widow and two young daughters now "belong to the state" and would receive a government annuity.*

In a letter written to Bishop Connolly of Halifax, Macdonald wrote that McGee "was just in the beginning of his usefulness." Out of politics and into a sinecure, he could have "devote[d] himself to literary pursuits." In fact, McGee's true gift was as a speaker, and it's likely his words would not have translated well onto a blank page without the magic he invested in them through his wonderful voice. What is certain is that post-Confederation Canada missed him. So did Macdonald, as he continued on without

---

* Macdonald, in a later letter to Joseph Howe, said the amount was intended to be $2,000 a year, but the Opposition demurred and it was reduced to $1,200, with additional money being raised by public subscription. In addition, McGee's two daughters received a lump sum of £1,000 each.

The assassinated McGee was given a full state funeral, and people crowded the streets to mourn him. In his eulogy delivered in the Commons, Macdonald said, "His heart was made for friends. And his enmities were written in water," faltered, then added, "He has left us a sacred legacy."

the bard beside him to challenge and tease him—and perhaps to stretch him further than he might otherwise have gone.

The trial of McGee's alleged killer, Patrick Whelan, a twenty-eight-year-old tailor, was close to a shambles. Whelan confessed to being involved in the affair but denied firing any shots, and he named no accomplices. Proof of a Fenian connection to the murder has never been uncovered. At the trial, Macdonald displayed rage at the death of his friend and a capacity for revenge as he sat beside the presiding judge. In the spectators' gallery, Agnes watched with a sharp eye as Whelan "munched apples . . . and watched the flies creep on the ceiling and laughed when the Constable's foot slipped." Then, with a softness amid the sharpness, she wrote about Whelan's solitary wait for the jury's verdict: "They tell me he cannot feel. . . . But how can a living healthy man, young and active, in whose veins the blood bounds quick and strong, [how] can he know he shall be sentenced to hang by the neck until his body be dead, and not feel!" Whelan was found guilty. Although he possessed a revolver of the same kind that fired the lethal bullet, he never admitted guilt. He was hanged on February 11, 1869, after speaking his final words: "God save Ireland and God save my soul."

By this time, Nova Scotians had started to walk themselves back into Confederation. The turnaround began in London, when Gladstone, the new prime minister, and Lord Granville, his colonial secretary, made it clear to Joseph Howe that Nova Scotia's request to be released from Confederation was unthinkable.

Howe was now living on what he called "old savings of one kind or another"—loans from supporters that they, and he, knew he could never repay. On his return from his disappointing mission to England, he was finally ready to hear what Macdonald had to propose.

In fact, Macdonald had almost botched his first attempt to reach out to Howe. As he explained to Tupper, he had thought of "writing him a letter to greet him on his arrival" in Ottawa in 1867, offering such plums as "a seat in the Cabinet, a Railway Commissionership, a vacant Senatorship," but he did not follow through because he was concerned that his "letter might be misunderstood and looked on as an attempt to offer him personal advancement." He decided, instead, to deal with some of Nova Scotia's specific grievances. To placate public discontent over the new dominion tariffs, he made imports of corn, corn meal and flour duty free and lowered the rate on sugar.

All along, Macdonald was well aware that federal patronage was the best way to connect him to Howe. It had to be offered, though, in a decorous way. In September 1868, he confided to Howe his concern that there was no Nova Scotian on the Railway Commission, which had been set up to oversee the Intercolonial

Railway, the Quebec City–Halifax line pledged in the constitution. He hoped "you will speedily see your way to the nomination of a Nova Scotian of standing."* A few weeks later, he advised Howe that, with great regret, he had had to fill three penitentiary director vacancies after having "held these appointments open as long as possible."

By delaying making patronage appointments, Macdonald was angering his own supporters. Tupper protested, saying that local supporters were "completely paralyzed" by the scarcity of appointments and contracts, but Macdonald reminded him that he was playing a game "that was settled between you and myself." At this game, Macdonald was the master. The favours he distributed to his supporters reminded wavering anti-Confederates of what they were missing. And the occasional plums he granted to the "enemy" signalled to them that he was serious about making a deal. Soon, hardline "antis" began to suspect that Howe was at least thinking of getting into bed with the enemy, if not yet sleeping with him. Macdonald was beginning to isolate Howe from his own supporters.

In parallel, the Colonial Office, clearly with Macdonald's knowledge if not at his instigation, advised Howe it had "confidence" the dominion might be ready to "relax or modify any arrangements . . . which may prejudice the peculiar interests of Nova Scotia." This gentle turn of the Imperial screw informed Howe that he might be able to get what were known as "better terms" for his province—in other words, more money than had been provided for in the BNA Act. When Howe boarded a ship to return to Canada, he found that Tupper and Leonard Tilley were

* The commission's sole purpose was to distribute patronage and limit construction costs. Sandford Fleming, the railway's chief engineer, fought manfully to keep patronage down and construction standards up, but he had only intermittent success.

also aboard. Tilley, the former New Brunswick premier, now one of Macdonald's ministers, joined him at breakfast one morning; as Tilley later reported to Macdonald, Howe let on during the meal that he was ready to "abandon our opposition to Confederation if some concessions are made."

Immediately, Macdonald moved from the wings to centre stage. In August 1868 he accepted an invitation from Howe to go to Halifax. The anti-Confederates, led by Premier William Annand, refused to talk to him. But after he met Howe privately in a church, Macdonald knew that the repeal cause was lost. Howe agreed to arrange a meeting between him and some moderate anti-Confederates, and the encounter went comparatively well.

By November, Macdonald had escalated his attentions to Howe to the level of unashamed flattery. Howe was "the sole means, but the certain means" of resolving the crisis, Macdonald wrote. "You are the Nova Scotia Mirabeau," he said, comparing Howe to Honoré Mirabeau, the moderate French revolutionary who conducted secret negotiations with Louis XVI which might have saved the king's life and saved France from the Terror. Later, he emphasized to Howe how important it was that he "gain the prestige of extracting from the Dominion Government some important concessions for Nova Scotia." The way to do this would be for Finance Minister John Rose to go to Halifax to negotiate with Howe. But Rose would then have to talk to Annand's provincial government and cede it a share of the credit. Macdonald's solution was for Howe and the Canadian representatives to meet on neutral territory, outside the province. Once Howe agreed to this plan, Macdonald wrote triumphantly to Rose: "Nova Scotia is about to take the shilling and enlist in the Union, though I'm afraid it will consider itself for a time as a conscript rather than as a volunteer."

On January 15, 1869, Howe and Rose met secretly in Portland, Maine. They readily reached a two-part agreement: Canada would assume all of Nova Scotia's provincial debt of close to $2 million and increase its annual subsidy to the province by $85,000 a year. The federal cabinet quickly ratified the agreement. On January 30, 1869, Howe joined Macdonald's cabinet.

Before he could do so, Howe, as the rules still required, had to resign his seat and win a by-election as a Conservative candidate. The campaign was bitter, nasty and exceedingly expensive: all told, Howe and his anti-Confederate opponent spent an incredible $50,000.* Howe won by just 313 votes, down from his margin of 2,141 in 1867.

As a cabinet minister, Howe made the news headlines only once, as a result of a speech he delivered to the Young Men's Christian Association in Ottawa on February 27, 1872. There, he unloaded all his hurt feelings towards Britain, claiming that the Mother Country no longer cared about the colonies and describing its recent dealings with Canada in trilateral negotiations in Washington as an attempt "to buy her own peace at the sacrifice of our interests." Macdonald hastily reassured the governor general that Howe's outburst had been "inexcusable . . . and disloyal." More realistically, he told a supporter that Howe's indiscretion proved that "the veteran should not lag superfluous on the stage." In 1873, Macdonald appointed Howe lieutenant-governor of Nova Scotia, but he died a few weeks later. As a rebel against Confederation, Howe's great weakness was to be too loyal to Britain.

It took Nova Scotians some time to see themselves as anything more than Confederation conscripts. In August 1869, when Governor General Lisgar made his first visit to Halifax, not a single provincial

---

* The two sides also taught Canadians lessons in the black arts of electoral fraud. The safe way to bribe voters was to overpay for staple supplies such as flour, pigs and transportation. No system was ever perfect, though; one voter, pressured by a creditor to mark his ballot against Confederation, refused to do so and ended up in a debtors' jail.

cabinet minister attended the official welcoming reception. And in advance of a provincial election in 1871, the anti-Confederate provincial government barred federal civil servants from voting. The real source of this rancour was economic hard times. Once conditions improved, particularly in the form of the record fish catches from 1869 on, so did relations between Nova Scotia and Canada. Most of the MPs who had come to Ottawa as anti-Confederates eventually joined the Conservative Party.

The story did not end there. In a Commons debate on the "better terms" Macdonald had promised to Nova Scotia, the Opposition and even some Conservatives from other provinces argued strongly that Ottawa should never have been so generous. So began the federal-provincial haggling about money and jurisdiction that has dominated Canadian political debate ever since.

FIVE

Who Speaks for Canada?

Subtle and powerful logic of his mind / Chilly as the fin of a dead fish
Two descriptions of Edward Blake

The better terms Macdonald had convinced Joseph Howe to accept were in fact quite modest. They merely brought Nova Scotia up to the level Leonard Tilley had secured for New Brunswick in the pre-Confederation negotiations. Edward Blake, the most prominent member of the Liberal Opposition in Ottawa and, simultaneously, a leading member of the Ontario legislature, considered the terms dangerous—not for the additional money Ottawa had to send to Halifax every year, but because of the constitutional precedent the new terms set. The money had to come from revenues raised by the federal government in the other provinces, even though they had not been given any opportunity to discuss and approve this change. To Blake, this affair raised a cardinal issue of Canadian politics: namely, "Who speaks for Canada?" in the phrase that so dominated late twentieth-century federal-provincial debates. Did the federal government alone have this role, or, instead, did Ottawa and the provinces conjointly, in some manner not mentioned in the constitution?

Until the twenty-first century, Edward Blake was the only Liberal leader who never became prime minister. He is also the only Canadian political leader of any party who was born in a log cabin. His father, William Hume Blake, of Anglo-Irish stock, emigrated, switched from the Anglican ministry to law, quickly built a successful practice, became a Reform politician and ended his career as head of the Ontario Court of Chancery. Edward himself was a standout at school and won the silver medal in classics at the University of Toronto. His law practice was an instant success, and by the time he entered politics in 1867, his wealth topped $100,000, an astounding amount for a man of thirty-three.

Blake was six feet tall and broad-shouldered, with a great wave of chestnut hair falling across a massive forehead. His speeches were masterpieces of organization, erudition and penetration, but they were also interminable, often stretching to five hours. Intellectually, he was exceptional: the historian Peter Waite has marvelled at "his powers of application, his range of knowledge, [and] the subtle and powerful logic of his mind," while also describing him as "wound up like a spring." Blake resembled some huge rare bird, beautiful but as clumsy as a dodo, repeatedly treading on the feet of those clustered around to admire him, as well as on his own. He was known to walk right by old friends without acknowledging them. Nothing he said ever touched anyone's emotions, yet whenever he was criticized, he broke into tears. "Shut up in that great brain," Waite continued, "he was unable in his groping, clumsy shyness to reach the people around him. He was outrageously sensitive to slights, real and imagined. He would also sleep or read a newspaper through the speeches of his political friends." His handshake was described as "chilly as the fin of a dead fish." As a cabinet minister and as party leader, he was forever resigning.

Blake inherited these psychological problems—"neurasthenia," in the term of the time, manifesting itself in bouts of headaches, insomnia, exhaustion and nervousness—from his formidable father and his deeply pious mother, Catherine, who was determined that her son should be not just great, but also very good. Blake doubted his ability to share his mother's Anglican faith, and once confessed to her that he could not achieve any emotional commitment to Christianity.* Unlike Macdonald, he was never a happy political warrior. He did, however, hold to the highest moral standards, once urging Macdonald to "understand the importance of legislating on general principles." He died in 1912; his last request was that a single-word inscription should be carved onto his headstone: "Misunderstood."

Liberal leader Edward Blake possessed the finest legal mind in Canada in the nineteenth century but his poor social skills presented him from reaching his full potential.

The relationship between Blake and Macdonald was prickly—though, on Macdonald's side, respectful.† In October 1868, he sounded Blake out on whether he might accept the same position his father had held on the Court of Chancery. Macdonald told

---

* When Blake's beloved daughter—"the *flower* of my life"—died in 1863, his mother told him, "The Lord I think in taking her meant to arouse yr attention to the madness & folly of living only for this world." Such a comment would have unhinged any sane person.

† Blake's attitude to Macdonald was predominantly scornful, but he could never quite escape the man. Once, he called at the Colonial Office in London to be greeted by a senior official who infuriated him by opening the conversation with "Well, I hope our friend Sir John Macdonald is getting along all right."

the incumbent, Philip VanKoughnet, a staunch Conservative who wanted to retire, "I said I had no right to ask him . . . without offering it to him—but under the circumstances would ask him to give me some idea whether he could take it." Blake begged for time to consider the proposal. His father warned him, "Be on your guard," but Catherine Blake told her son, "We have always found J.A.M. kind and considerate." His father relented, saying the post "would afford leisure and opportunity for communion with God." The plan came to a halt when the other judges declined to change their posts. Blake then wrote to Macdonald that this outcome "coincides with my own wishes." It's a toss-up whether Macdonald was trying to remove a formidable opponent from the political scene or to fill a key post with the best available person, as he did often in his judicial appointments. Beyond doubt, the Liberals wanted Blake to remain active in politics, and when VanKoughnet's death a year later reopened the post they successfully pressured him to stay active in politics.

As the best legal mind in the country, Blake made his most significant contribution to Canada as a constitutional critic. At the hearings of the Judicial Committee of the Privy Council, Britain's arbiter of the legal and constitutional doings of its colonies, Blake's arguments on behalf of Ontario in several legal cases played a key part in shifting Canada's constitutional character away from the centralized federation Macdonald had envisaged to a far more decentralized, province-oriented, federal system. Blake's first step along this path took place in 1869, after Macdonald had introduced legislation in the House of Commons to authorize payment of the better terms he had promised to Howe and to Nova Scotia.

Blake spoke twice on this subject, first in the Commons in June 1869, and then in the Ontario legislature in November. In Ottawa, he argued that, because the British North America Act was British legislation, it could only be altered by the Parliament of Westminster, provided that all those who had been involved in drafting the constitution, including the four provinces, agreed. Clearly thinking of Quebec as the next supplicant for "better terms," he posed the awkward question, "When will the floodgates now opened be closed again?" At Queen's Park in Toronto, he went further, breaking radically new ground. "Our province [Ontario] agreed to part with a certain part of its jurisdiction upon certain conditions," he said, and these conditions were embodied into an Imperial act that gave us security, "a charter of our rights." He concluded precisely, "This compact under which we have surrendered so much of our rights is not alterable except by the power that made it."

In both legislatures, Blake's speeches were usually received in uncomprehending silence. On this occasion, a couple of Liberal MPs supported his arguments, and one Conservative broke ranks to point out that each Ontarian paid twenty-seven cents into the federal coffers and in return received only six, while in comparison Nova Scotians were about to get eighteen cents each, while paying in only five and a half.

The press dismissed Blake's arguments as "political quackery." Macdonald, well aware that legalisms seldom influence people's minds, said nothing at all. The resolution for better terms for Nova Scotia passed easily. Yet Blake was the first to advance the concept of Confederation as a "compact" between the provinces, which had got together to create a federal government to fulfill certain common functions. The federal government thus was not, as people commonly assumed, the embodiment of the nation, with the provinces as junior governments.* At the time, all these arguments amounted to no more than clever legalisms. In practical terms, Ontario and Quebec had not even existed before Confederation, so they had lacked any government to speak for them; moreover, as colonies, they and the two newcomers, Nova Scotia and New Brunswick, had possessed no right to negotiate, let alone sign a treaty. In recent years, however, Blake's interpretation of Confederation—that a multiplicity speaks for Canada—has become far closer to the country's political and legal character than Macdonald's vision for it. Despite all his political shortcomings, Blake always had a better sense of the future than did the political master, Macdonald. In his speeches, Blake used the word "destinies" rather than "destiny" to describe how Canada was likely to develop, and he declared that the "separate interests" of each province had to be "directed by separate governments."

Macdonald's contrasting vision of Canada was not unitary, as often has been assumed. Thus, among other reasons, he wanted the federal government to be powerful so it could "protect the rights of minorities." At the same time, it was no coincidence that the constitution of which he had been the principal author used throughout the term "union" rather than "federation." Macdonald wanted to build a nation out of an entity that lacked any distinct identity or internal commonality other than that borrowed from Britain. To this end he had, as he said during the Confederation Debates of 1865, "given the General Legislature all the great subjects of legislation . . . all the powers which are incidental to sovereignty."

About legal specifics, Macdonald was always far more reticent. Unlike Blake, with his quest for constitutional purity, his manner

* The "compact theory" of Confederation has always been credited to Quebec lawyer T.J.J. Loranger, who, in 1883 and 1884, published his two-volume *Lettres sur l'interprétation de la constitution fédérale*. Loranger was indeed the first to describe the concept at length, but its originator was Blake.

of progressing was pragmatic—he muddled through. "The whole of our present system is an experiment," he explained to the Reverend John Cook on February 3, 1868. Cook had written to Macdonald denouncing the new Quebec legislature as "unmitigated humbug." Macdonald replied that "the question is not whether your Local Parliament is of much use, as it is whether it will not serve as a safety valve and relieve us from the conflict of the races." This letter, long overlooked, goes to the heart of Macdonald's constitutional thinking. He sought harmony among all the races, religions and regions so that he could get on with the real task of building a continental nation.

To Macdonald, harmony between the federal government and the provinces was an essential component of this package. He spelled this goal out in a December 11, 1868, letter to Brown Chamberlin, editor of the Montreal *Gazette*: "The questions of conflict of jurisdiction have pretty nearly all developed themselves, and must ere long be settled," he wrote. To settle them satisfactorily, "they should be approached in a statesmanlike spirit, and not in a vain attempt on the part either of the Local or Dominion Statesmen, to gain a victory." He expressed satisfaction that "while you, an ardent Dominion man, say I yield too much, for the sake of peace, to the Provincial magnates," those same provincial heavyweights claimed that he was invading their "Local rights and powers." In his own mind, he was achieving a golden mean. Moreover, Macdonald was much closer to the Canadian character than was Blake, who, for all his advocacy of provincial rights, was really interested only in Ontario, quarrelling about the "better terms" offered to any new province and dismissing British Columbia as a barren "sea of mountains."

With Nova Scotia now fully back in, Macdonald set out to increase his Atlantic catch. "What a glorious programme it would be to go down to Parliament next Session," he wrote to Tupper at the start of 1869, "with Nova Scotia pacified, Newfoundland voluntarily joining & the acquisition of Hudson's Bay." Instead, Newfoundlanders wriggled off his hook.

Two delegates from the island, Frederick Carter and Ambrose Shea, had attended the 1864 Quebec City Conference and returned home Confederates. Although Carter went on to become premier, Newfoundland stood aside from joining the new nation, primarily because local merchants opposed it. Then a series of disastrous fishery failures put a third of the population on relief, and opinion shifted. The legislature approved draft terms of union, and had an election been held in 1868, as Macdonald devoutly hoped it would be, Newfoundlanders would almost certainly have endorsed union.

Carter, though, had promised to give voters a clear choice, and he delayed the election to 1869, allowing Newfoundlanders to decide their future democratically. By the time the election was held, an exceptional harvest of seals and cod had reversed public opinion yet again. The anti-Confederates had the merchants and the Catholic Church on side, as well as an exceptional orator, Charles Fox Bennett, who initiated a tradition of electoral hyperbole in Newfoundland by warning that Confederation would "send your sons to die on the desert sands of Canada."* Of the thirty seats at stake, the Confederates won just nine.

Macdonald's response was restrained. In a report to Governor General Lisgar, he dismissed a recommendation by Newfoundland's governor, Sir Stephen Hill, that the election result be ignored and

*The most hyperbolic rhetoric was in the dispatch sent to the Colonial Office by Governor Stephen Hill. The defeat, he reported, was due to the "ignorant, lawless, prejudiced body [of] . . . unfit subjects for educated and intellectual men to reason with."

the island press-ganged into Confederation by Imperial decree. That would never do, Macdonald wrote, since "we have had an infinity of trouble with Nova Scotia . . . because the question was not submitted to the electors." In a rare conversion to democracy, Macdonald concluded, "we should accept their decision."

Macdonald never again raised his hopes about Newfoundland, wryly comparing the political effect of a single good fish catch to "the Bulls that we read of in Holy Writ, they 'waxed fat and kicked.'" He remained as competitive as ever, though, never forgiving the defeat. In 1872, when Allan, the country's leading ship owner, told Macdonald he planned to initiate a new shipping line between Montreal and Liverpool, with stops at Halifax and St. John's, Macdonald responded: "As a matter of policy we had better let the Island feel all the inconvenience of isolation," because "once the Canadian Government agreed that your Steamers should touch the Island, [it] could not well withdraw the assent." The ever-confident Allan went ahead anyway, judging a lucrative mail contract for the island worth Macdonald's wrath. Three-quarters of a century would pass before Newfoundlanders changed their minds about their relationship with Canada. The choice they made then would again be a democratic one.

SIX

Good Times and Hard Times

The worst that could happen to Canada would be annexation to a free and prosperous country.

Sir John Michel, the British officer commanding Canada's forces

The two years from mid-1867 to mid-1869 were probably the most satisfying Macdonald ever experienced, in both his personal and his political life. Being a Celt and knowing that tragedy is an integral part of life, he would have appreciated his good run even while assuming it couldn't last for long. When it arrived, however, the end of this exceptional period for Macdonald would come with brutal suddenness and be grossly unfair. Nevertheless, as a measure of his contentment, Macdonald drank not a drop for about nine months.

Macdonald's reasons for feeling so ebullient were obvious. He had exchanged the drudgery of small-time politics for the exhilarating challenge of nation-building; he was successfully avoiding the humiliation of personal bankruptcy; and for the first time he had a partner who adored him and worked tirelessly on his behalf—enabling him, for instance, to invite Conservative MPs to dinner, to bond with them and keep up with caucus gossip. The wider universe was unfolding as agreeably. Macdonald's parliamentary majority would soon be enlarged by Nova Scotian MPs. Construction had begun on the five-hundred-mile-long Intercolonial Railway to link Halifax to the nation's heartland and would be completed in 1876. There were even signs that the economy was coming out of the doldrums.

Most encouragingly, the items listed in the North-West Territory file kept being ticked off. In London, a deal was done—its terms dictated by the colonial secretary and assented to by the Canadian envoys, George-Étienne Cartier and William McDougall. The Hudson's Bay Company (HBC) agreed that its territory, Rupert's Land, could be expropriated for the handsome sum of £300,000 (Britain advancing an equivalent loan to Canada for the purchase), as well as 45,000 acres of land around its 120 trading posts and the right to claim one-twentieth of the cultivatable prairie land.* In June 1869, Parliament approved an act to set up a temporary administration to run the territory until a permanent government could be established. McDougall was chosen to be the first lieutenant-governor, his term to start on December 1, 1869, when he would take over from the company's governor, William Mactavish.

The interests of all three parties involved—Britain, Canada and the HBC—neatly dovetailed. Macdonald exulted that the vast territory was on the brink of becoming truly Canadian as "the land of hope for the hardy youth of the provinces as they seek new homes . . . when Canada becomes the highway of immigration from Europe to those fertile valleys." Just one detail was missing. None of the people living in the territory—mostly Indians, but also some nine thousand Métis (both French and English) centred in the Red River Colony and around a thousand whites (some newcomers but

---

* Actually, the Hudson's Bay Company was now owned by a mysterious group of investors called the International Finance Corporation, which had quietly bought up its shares and was about to make a plump profit.

mostly retired HBC officials)—had been told anything about these arrangements, let alone asked what they thought of them.

This purchase of Rupert's Land would stretch Canada to the foothills of the Rockies. The next step would be to add the Crown colony of British Columbia to the nation. There, Canada's own version of manifest destiny was unfolding as it should. In May 1868, a public meeting in Victoria resulted in the creation of a fledgling Confederation League led by a politician who had changed his name from the prosaic William Smith to Amor de Cosmos, or Lover of the Universe. Macdonald had already begun communicating with BC politicians. In some letters he referred to "the Great Pacific Railway," although cautioning, "It is perhaps premature to speculate much on this just now." But the impossible dream was beginning to seem a probability. In August 1869, the colonial secretary, Lord Granville, sent a note to the new British Columbia lieutenant-governor advising him that "the establishment of a British line of communication between the Atlantic and Pacific Oceans," by way of a railway across Canada, would accomplish the crucial goal of connecting Liverpool to the ports of Japan and China; Britain's commercial self-interests and Macdonald's dream were now as one.

There was also a personal reason for Macdonald's exuberance. Agnes's pregnancy had reached its natural conclusion. It hadn't been easy. Often she'd felt "headachy" or languid. She'd given up most activities, spending her days at the Quadrilateral with her mother, Theodora, and taking walks with her "darling." But she'd kept up with her duties as a hostess. On January 1, 1869, the Macdonalds had held their traditional New Year's Day at-home. Large numbers came, enjoyed themselves and behaved properly, making it, in Agnes's words, "the happiest New Year's Day I can remember since I was a child." As her confinement approached, Macdonald was "a tender, loving care-taker and nurse." Her labour, which began at 4 a.m. on February 7, was exceedingly difficult and lasted a full day and a half. Chloroform, the soporific of the time, was used to ease her suffering, and the doctor had to resort to the use of forceps. Finally, at 3:15 p.m. on February 8, a girl was born to an exhausted Agnes and a delighted John A. They named her Mary.

With a wife who loved him and now a daughter, Macdonald was, for the first time in his life, on the cusp of a normal family life.

It's impossible to know when the parents began to suspect that their joy was premature. Agnes's early comments about Mary are proud and tender: "She is lying asleep in her blankets, my own darling baby—my little daughter, the sweet gift from Heaven, my Mary, dark-eyed, soft thing." And Macdonald nicknamed her his Baboo. But both would have struggled not to admit that Mary, as she lay motionless in her crib, unresponsive to their attentions and the world around her, with her head growing to an unusual size, was unlike other babies. Agnes's recovery from confinement had taken an exceptionally long nine weeks. She ended it by going to church, yet even there found herself in a "cold, dark frame." There is a melancholic ambivalence to her diary entry for late April: "My dear, dear little child. I have read nothing today—my heart is cold and dull—I seem to be waiting for something—perhaps it is for light."

Not until May 1, 1869, when Mary was three months old, did Agnes admit the truth to herself, as always expressing it obliquely in her diary: "The day has been stamped with the world's greatest seal—it is graven, I think, with the word 'disappointment.' Perhaps yesterday was one of the saddest times of my life—let it pass, let it die—only teach me, Heavenly Father, to see the lesson it was destined to teach, and while I learn it to do so cheerfully." Macdonald's unawareness lasted longer. As late as June 5, he ended a letter to a friend with the cheerful report, "I do not know whether I ever told you that a little Miss Macdonald made her appearance some three months ago, who flourishes greatly."

The doctors diagnosed Mary's condition as hydrocephalus, known popularly as water on the brain. She would never be able to stand, walk, feed herself or dress herself. Today, a shunt inserted into the skull could release the pressure of the accumulated brain fluid and incomparably improve chances for leading a near-normal life. But not then.

Once they realized their daughter would be forever grievously disadvantaged, the Macdonalds did not place her in an institution nor, so far as can be known, ever consider doing so. She was their daughter, and she would remain an important part of the family—supported and protected by her parents as she grew from baby to child to woman. They never hid her nor made any public reference to her condition. Word of her ailment sped through the Ottawa

At birth, Mary was to Lady Macdonald, "so wonderful and so beautiful,*" but within a few months she realized that her daughter was hydrocephalic, suffering a crippling handicap known as water on the brain.*

grapevine of course, but no guest at the Macdonalds' home was ever warned by his hosts to expect anything unusual. Visitors would watch in astonishment as the prime minister massaged Mary's thin, inert legs in the hope that forcing the blood to circulate would strengthen them, and listen entranced as he read fairy stories to her or, when she was older, told her about his political activities during the day just ended.

For Agnes, the tragedy meant that she would never fully realize the joys of wife and mother that she had anticipated with such delight. She surely went through a dark night of the soul, wondering how an all-powerful, beneficent God could allow such suffering to be inflicted on an innocent creature whom He had created. She must have wondered at some point why God had abandoned her, because the tragedy could only be explained as part of some divine plan that she lacked the intelligence and the piety to comprehend.

This crisis changed Agnes profoundly—or, more exactly, brought to the fore predispositions already inherent in her. From this point on, she was less Agnes in personality and more Lady Macdonald—censorious, severe, self-controlled and controlling. Among the entries in her diary, which she would soon abandon, the most revealing and honest was her early admonition to herself, "I also know that my love of Power is strong, so strong that I sometimes dread it; it influences me when I imagine I am influenced by a sense of right." She returned to that theme several times: "Often, I find what I thought at first to be a principle proves only an evidence of a selfish love of power." Clearly she was conscious of her failing and tried to resist it. But her deep religious sense strengthened the urge: whatever she was doing had to be right, because her motivation was right.

As for Macdonald, he responded in the same way he did to political or financial crises, accepting the facts as they were and doing the best he could. He never complained in any letter he wrote about the heavy expenses for nurses, caregivers and special treatments that Mary's condition required. But given that he and Agnes were so unalike in their characters, this tragedy served over time to push them further apart. Rather than coming together as a couple, they became two people who gave each other support, companionship and affection, but not more, although the flame John A. had lit in Agnes never died.

No evidence exists of any later relationship between Macdonald and any other woman (despite some hopeful claims by some families in Kingston and Ottawa); such a betrayal by a man who so prized loyalty is improbable. Nevertheless, he certainly enjoyed the company of attractive women. One such lady, a Mrs. Hooper, achieved the near impossible by persuading Macdonald to recommend that a plum patronage post, sheriff of Prince Edward County, be given to a Liberal—her brother Ham. In a letter to Ontario premier Sandfield Macdonald recommending young Ham for the post, Macdonald cited as justification that Mrs. Hooper was "very pretty," adding his praises for her "personal charms." Undoubtedly, it was all thoroughly innocent; just as undoubtedly, Macdonald greatly enjoyed her company.

However the Macdonalds' marriage evolved, the care and devotion with which Agnes looked after John never changed. And while Macdonald may never have experienced a normal family life, he did receive love both from Agnes and, in her own way, no less fully from Mary.

As a welcome distraction from personal stresses, political matters required Macdonald's attention. He needed to find a new finance minister after John Rose failed to win caucus approval for his proposed Bank Act, resigned and decided to move to London, England. The act would have granted special privileges to the Bank of Montreal, raising it to the status of a kind of privately owned Bank of Canada and reducing all the other banks to local institutions. The leading candidate for finance minister was Richard Cartwright, a highly regarded MP. Instead, Macdonald settled the prized portfolio on Francis Hincks, a former premier who was exceptionally intelligent but widely regarded as corrupt.

Sir Francis Hincks, the Father of Canada's Boring Banks.

This choice came at a cost to Macdonald: Cartwright crossed the floor soon after. Hincks went on to enact one of the most important pieces of financial legislation in Canadian history.* His 1871 Bank Act initiated a system of regulation—Scottish-style branch banks, unlike U.S.-style regional ones; and protection from foreign competition in exchange for respectably strict rules of financial probity—that close to a century and a half later would enable Canadians to brag that their "boring" banks were among the best in the world.

In politics, good times never last. For some time, Macdonald had been receiving warning signals that in London serious consideration

* The branch banking system—one of the principal reasons there were so few bank failures here in 2008–2009, unlike below the border—flourished from its beginning. Between 1868 and 1890, the number of branch banks almost quadrupled, from 123 to 426.

was being given to pulling back most of the British troops now stationed in the country's colonies.

There had been hints of this withdrawal even before Confederation, when ministers in the Conservative government in London had advanced the patently absurd proposition that the new union would make it possible for Canada to defend itself unaided. In the fall of 1867, General Sir John Michel, the British officer commanding all military forces in Canada, completed his term. Before leaving, he dispatched to Macdonald his analysis of the political and military state of the nation. Given that the United States was preoccupied with the demands of reconstruction following the Civil War, he wrote, it was "hardly to be conceived that she would think of endeavouring to annex Canada until these matters are satisfactorily adjusted." Therefore, "war between England and the United States will become more and more improbable." That was the good news.

The bad news, Michel continued, was that, should war with the United States somehow break out, Britain would suffer "pecuniary ruin and loss of prestige," but Canada would experience "annexation to a free and populous country." In his bluff, soldierly way, Michel was telling Macdonald that it was in Britain's interest to withdraw militarily from Canada to minimize the risk of an accidental war with the United States. He was also implicitly telling Macdonald that his obsession with keeping Canada apart from its neighbour accomplished nothing except to deny Canadians the abundant economic and other benefits available under a cross-border union. Michel has to have been reflecting a common opinion among members of the government in London.

Recent events had made Macdonald's task of keeping Britain close to Canada, and the reverse, considerably more difficult. Germany was fast emerging as a major power under Bismarck's leadership. In 1866 it had crushed Austria-Hungary in a war and would soon do the same to France. In these circumstances, it was important for most British troops to be at home. Moreover, a Liberal government headed by William Gladstone had now come to office. Gladstone had chosen Edward Cardwell as his minister of defence, the same man who, as colonial secretary, had successfully applied "the imperial screw" to Nova Scotia and New Brunswick to drive them into Confederation. Over time, Cardwell's views about relations with the colonies had changed considerably.*

On January 9, 1869, Cardwell submitted a memorandum to cabinet calling for the total forces in the colonies to be cut from 50,000 to 26,000. He soon disclosed that the British contingent in Canada would fall from 15,000 soldiers and sailors to just 6,000. When he was challenged that he was leaving the colonies defenceless, Cardwell responded, "The true defence of our colonies is that they live under the aegis of the name of England." Lord Monck, now retired, went further: "In time of peace [Canadians] must under no circumstances expect to see an Imperial soldier within their limits." The appalling prospect dawned in Ottawa that, soon, there might be no British troops at all in Canada.

Macdonald fought back as best he could. He pleaded with Lord Carnarvon, a former Conservative colonial secretary and good friend, to fight the cutbacks: "We greatly distrust the men at the helm in England," he wrote. "We are to be left the unaided victims of Irish discontent [the Fenians] and American hostility caused entirely by our being a portion of the Empire." He asked John Rose, now settled in London and with exceptional social and financial contacts, to spread the word about Canada's displeasure.

---

* It was the Duke of Wellington who had overloaded the number of troops in the colonies. After Waterloo, he had cannily shifted many soldiers to British posts abroad. There they were highly popular, making it extremely difficult to withdraw them. One British minister observed that local ladies were "frantic on the subject."

In return came a discreet twist of the Imperial screw. In June 1869, the new colonial secretary, Lord Granville, sent a dispatch to Governor General Lisgar which contained a broad hint that Britain was prepared to accept outright Canadian independence. He advised Lisgar that Britain had no desire to maintain Canada as a colony for even "a single year" if that condition became "injurious or distasteful" to Canadians. He asked Lisgar to inform him of any measures that might "gradually prepare both countries for a friendly relaxation" of the existing relationship.

Macdonald, the old fox, had been outfoxed. If he protested publicly, he would make his people aware that Britain was ready to let Canada go; his silence, though, could be interpreted as his consent. Then he got a lucky break. On July 15, 1869, Governor General Lisgar delivered a public speech in Quebec City in which, after defending the troop cutbacks, he said reassuringly that, if an actual war broke out, Britain was committed to "defend every part of the Empire with all the resources at its command." He concluded with a scaled-down version of Granville's dispatch to him. Canada, he said, was already "in reality independent," and it was time for Canadians to make up their minds whether to continue the connection to Britain or, "in due time of the maturity of the Dominion, to change it to some other form of alliance." The newspapers, even the *Globe*, severely criticized Lisgar for his indiscretion, and Macdonald let his displeasure be known in private. Thereafter, musings about Canada's future by members of the British government ceased.

Macdonald stepped back. When British critics of Gladstone's policy of pulling troops from the colonies attempted to organize a colonial conclave to bring pressure on the British government, he declared it was "not fitting" for Canada to send delegates. He wrote to Rose, "We are quite satisfied with our position," implying that he took at face value Britain's commitment to come to Canada's aid in time of need.

Meanwhile, Cardwell forged ahead. Late in 1869, he reduced the number of British troops due to remain in Canada from six thousand to just two thousand; in 1870, he decreed that all would be withdrawn but for a few to train the Canadian militia.

Except for the sailors who guarded the Royal Navy base at Halifax, Britain's military presence in Canada ended on November 11, 1871. The last to leave from the Citadel in Quebec City was a battalion of the 60th Rifles, a regiment that first came to Canada with the army led by General Wolfe, which climbed to the Plains of Abraham. These soldiers, in their distinctive green, marched through the narrow streets of the old capital to the strains of "Goodbye, Sweetheart, Goodbye" and "Auld Lang Syne." In the harbour, they boarded the steamer *Orontes* for the journey home.* Thereafter, Canada was defended by a symbolic border, by the will of its people and, for most of the next two decades, by the political skills of Sir John A. Macdonald.

* To offset all this, the U.S. Army had by now dwindled to 31,000, with fewer than 1,000 stationed along its northern border.

SEVEN

Manifest Destiny versus Manifest Destiny

The great ocean itself does not present more infinite variety than does this prairie-ocean. . . . This ocean has no past—time has been nought to it, and men have come and gone, leaving behind them no track, no vestige of their presence.

Captain W.F. Butler, *The Great Lone Land*, 1872

Across the vast expanse of the North-West Territories, extending from just west of the Great Lakes to the foothills of the Rockies, the single settlement (except for the Hudson's Bay Company forts that served the old fur trade) was the Red River Colony—a discontinuous narrow strip running from the village of Winnipeg for some fifty miles along the banks of the Red River. The settlers were mostly Métis, both French and English, but also some Canadians, Americans and HBC officials. Elsewhere, the footprint of the region's original hunter-gatherer inhabitants, the Cree and the Blackfoot Confederacy, and also some Sioux and Saulteaux, had been so light that they left scarcely a mark.

Below the forty-ninth parallel, where the landscape was the same, the scene was substantially different: settlement was taking place at an ever-quickening pace, with real towns growing up and railways and roads being built. While America's West was being tamed, Canada's North-West was as yet hardly touched. And

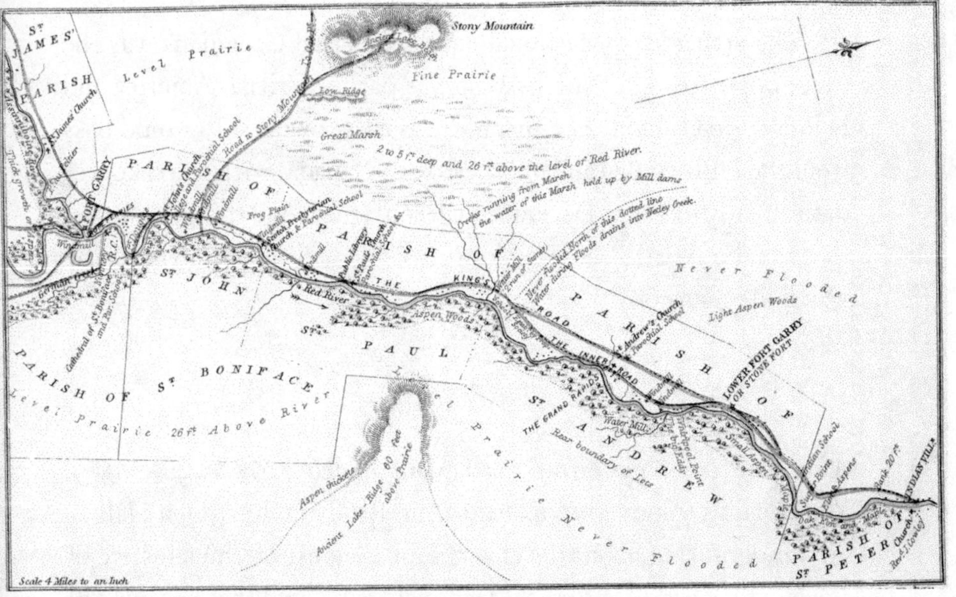

The Red River Settlement was small and had few graces, yet it bubbled with energy from the variety of its people—Métis, both French and English, Hudson's Bay officials, Indians of the Plains, newly arrived Canadians, and annexation-minded Americans.

with the purchase of Rupert's Land from the HBC not yet finalized, it still didn't even belong to Canada. Many Americans took for granted that the territory above the border would soon become their economic hinterland, and later part of America itself—especially a group of politicians and businessmen in Minnesota's capital of St. Paul and their allies in Washington, including some in the White House. Now that the Civil War was over, the nation's formidable energy was being applied to winning the West. It was, after all, their manifest destiny.*

---

* The term was coined by the journalist John O'Sullivan in 1845 in the *Democratic Review* magazine, where he wrote that "the right of our manifest destiny" was "to overspread and possess the whole of the continent which Providence has given us." Sullivan applied this concept specifically to the acquisition that same year of Oregon, to which the HBC also had a claim; it was later expanded to the continent.

The attitude of Macdonald and almost all Canadians was the exact opposite. The North-West was part of British America and belonged to Canada. Acquiring it was easy: ownership would pass from the HBC to Britain and then on to Canada, with the takeover date already fixed for December 1, 1869. It was one thing, however, to own the North-West; making it Canadian in more than title was quite another.

After the 1869 session of Parliament ended early in July 1869, Macdonald responded to a letter from R.G. Haliburton, a Halifax lawyer, inquiring about his chances for the post of chief justice of the North-West Territories. Macdonald explained that because the first administration would be provisional, he could not consider the request until a permanent government had been established. The real difficulty, Macdonald continued, was that "we are just now quite in the dark as to the wants and wishes of that Country, and we shall grope quietly along until we get a sufficient amount of information." In other letters of the time, he admitted, "We are in utter darkness as to the state of affairs there; what the wants and wishes of the people are—in fact, how the affairs are carried on at all," and "I am ignorant as possible of the future mode of administering the affairs of the country." Macdonald thus knew he knew little about the North-West Territories, and clearly he was uneasy about what might lie ahead.

He had good reasons to be wary. A small and comparatively poor colony of three and a half million people was about to undertake the largest real-estate deal in history, by acquiring a new territory half the size of Europe. When the takeover was first considered by the cabinet, only one minister besides William McDougall, the intended lieutenant-governor, supported it. Macdonald had overcome his own initial skepticism by taking the position that British America "must belong either to the American or British system of Government." Legal sovereignty and effective sovereignty were quite different, though. A key influence on Macdonald's thinking was a warning by one of his best ministers, Alexander Morris, that "if [the Americans] find no established institutions or organized government [in the West,] they will form an Association and commence a Government on their own." He was referring to the way American settlers in the 1840s had made northern Oregon American by creating facts on the ground. Canada's West thus had to be Canadianized, because the default alternative was for it to be Americanized, economically and demographically, and ultimately politically.

Macdonald's thinking about the North-West was, at one and the same time, simple and extravagantly ambitious. He took it for granted that, without the West, Canada could not become a great nation, and very likely would not survive at all. Canada had to be stretched out from sea to sea all the way to the Pacific, and the intervening prairies opened up to development by a transcontinental railway. It would bring in immigrants to work the land and build settlements, then transport their agricultural products via ship from Montreal to the British market. The horrendous costs of building this rail link for so small a market—just 25,000 Europeans in British Columbia, compared to well over a million in California—could bankrupt the nation. Macdonald's belief was not so much that if he built the railway, people and economic activity would come; rather, it was a conviction that the alternative was Canada's extinction.

The way Macdonald set out to realize this impossible dream marked the beginning of a new style of governance in North America. Below the border, the American West was being developed by the American people themselves: as individuals and families, they left their homes in the East (or in Europe), travelled westwards in covered wagons until they reached the last settlements, then continued on until they found unclaimed land. Canada's West, in contrast, would be developed by its government. The continental railway would be built by some form of public-private partnership. The entire territory would be surveyed by the government before any newcomers arrived. Justice would be administered and law and order enforced not by the settlers themselves but by a new institution—the first distinctively Canadian one—the North-West Mounted Police (later, the Royal Canadian Mounted Police). And government itself, in the form of Lieutenant-Governor McDougall and the planned provisional administration, would be there before the newcomers came in. It was all very different from the U.S. West, where governance was concocted by the settlers themselves.

If Macdonald felt able only to "grope along," he wasn't alone. To almost all Canadians, the North-West was *terra incognita*.* A key cross-border difference was that on the Canadian side of Lake Superior, the Precambrian Shield came right down to the lake, so that to get westwards Canadians had to cross hundreds of miles of bare granite, scrubby trees and interminable small lakes. South of the lake, though, the land was flat and open, so that Americans could easily roll westwards (and in their own wagons rather than en masse). Further, the lack of an intruding Precambrian Shield made it easy for western Americans wanting to look over the prairies above the border (often to sell liquor to the Indians) to ride northwards; Canadians coming in from Ontario had either

* The description of the prairies in one 1857 report was, "the climate is mild and cattle keep fat in winter as well as summer on its nutritious grasses."

to slog through the wilderness above Lake Superior or dip down into the United States to go west. This difference explains why HBC officials in Red River didn't communicate with their head office in London through Canada but by way of their outpost of York Factory on Hudson Bay and then on by ship. As a consequence, it took two weeks to get a letter from Red River to Ottawa, and the same for its reply. Once the trouble with the Red River settlers began, Macdonald came to realize that he was giving orders that arrived after the action he had requested had already been overtaken by new events. Telegrams moved far faster, but Macdonald suspected, almost certainly correctly, that their contents were being read by American telegraphers and passed to the annexationists.

Macdonald's limited knowledge of the West was compounded by sheer bad luck. In September 1869, he sent his Nova Scotia colleague Joseph Howe, now secretary of state for the provinces, on a fact-finding mission to Red River. Howe stayed only a week and talked to few people. When Howe met up with McDougall making his way towards his new post, a snowstorm was raging, and Howe hurried on rather than brief him about his discovery of potential local opposition to the Canadian takeover. He did not write his report until he was back in Ottawa. But Howe, who opposed western expansion, was the wrong person to be assessing what should be done there anyway. As he told a friend, "The country is not necessary to us . . . [and] will only be a drag upon our energies and resources."

Unfortunately, the one person who was best informed about Red River told the government almost nothing about what was going on there. The Edinburgh-born William Mactavish had worked himself up in the Hudson's Bay Company from clerk to the highest post in the territory—governor of Assiniboia. When he went to Ottawa in the summer of 1869, however, he was in the terminal stages of his battle with tuberculosis, so he saw few people and said little. In any case, Mactavish's judgment was as biased as Howe's. He wrote to a friend that Red River's "ultimate destiny" was to join the United States: "It is for the interests of settlers here that annexation should take place at once."

Macdonald's lack of knowledge might have been mitigated had the best contemporary description of the North-West and Red River been available to him—Captain Butler's *The Great Lone Land.* But Butler journeyed across the prairies a year later, in 1870. Somewhat like Lawrence of Arabia, William Butler, who went on to become a general, was one of those British Imperial soldiers with an aptitude for understanding unfamiliar people and places. His description of the Aboriginals of the plains as "the only perfect socialists or communists of the world, a people who held all things in common," whether "the land, the bison, the river and the moose," would have been appreciated instantly by someone of Macdonald's intelligence. He also noted regretfully that "possession of a horse is valued before that of a wife." He spotted a transformational challenge looming ahead for both the Métis and the Indians: "Year by year the prairies which once shook beneath the tread of countless bison are becoming denuded of animal life," he wrote. He foretold the hard future ahead of both these native people: "A vast country lying, as it were, silently awaiting the approach of the immense wave of human life which rolls unceasingly from Europe to America."

One of Butler's observations played an important part in Canadian history: "The region is without law, order or security," he wrote. Since the summer of 1869, Macdonald had been worrying about the same issue, with the American liquor trade in particular in mind, and Butler's comment encouraged him to establish the North-West Mounted Police. Unfortunately, the only Canadian sources of information available to Macdonald when he most needed them in 1869 were the reports of trips made there in the mid-1850s by Captain John Palliser and Henry Youle Hind, whose real focus was the agricultural potential of the North-West.

Only one person was really well informed about the people and politics of the North-West—James Wickes Taylor. He was an American and since the mid-1850s had been an ardent annexationist—in the best interests, he believed, of the people living there. Taylor had drafted Senator Ramsey's 1867 resolution calling on the United States to buy up the North-West, and he belonged to the syndicate that built a railway line from St. Paul towards the border, hoping to direct Red River's commerce southwards. Once the troubles broke out in Red River, Taylor was appointed by the State Department as a secret agent there. An individual of great charm, he went on to become an exceptionally well liked consul in Winnipeg, where he died in 1893. Unhappily, he was on the opposite side from Macdonald.

Besides knowing too little, Macdonald was handicapped in his campaign to secure the North-West for Canada by having to look too many ways at the same time. He had always to gaze intently westwards; but he also had to keep glancing back at Britain, to gauge how quickly the troops would be withdrawn from the country and how committed the Gladstone government really was to the colonies. Besides looking eastwards as well as westwards, he also had to look southwards, to assess how much support the Minnesota annexationists (or expansionists, as they termed themselves) could count on in Washington, in Congress and the White House.

In almost every way, the American annexationists held all the advantages. Canada possessed just two. One was the odd, obdurate insistence of the majority of Canadians on not becoming

American. The other was Macdonald himself, by now easily the most experienced and skilful, and beyond argument the wiliest, politician on the continent. He had no high cards, but he knew how to play almost any game.

The challenge from the South wasn't new. Americans had wanted to annex Canada even before the United States itself existed. The first Congress of the rebellious American colonies, in Philadelphia in 1775, had extended to Canada (although not to the other British North America colonies) an automatic right to enter the new union, a privilege extended to no other territory on the continent. When this offer was met by silence, the Americans undertook their first attempt at regime change by sending in armies, the key one led by General Benedict Arnold, who later changed sides. Later, they precipitated the War of 1812. It took the end of the Civil War, Lincoln's assassination and Reconstruction to turn Americans' interests inward, and even then they looked the other way while the various Fenian raids were launched across the border. As Macdonald never knew at the time, just before Canada's first elections in 1867, William Averill, the U.S. consul in the important posting of Montreal, sent a memorandum to Secretary of State William Seward proposing that action be taken to bring about Macdonald's defeat. Averill claimed that "some leaders of the Liberal Party . . . had represented to me they would be very glad to receive some assistance." He calculated that fifty thousand dollars, divided among Liberal candidates and supporting newspapers, would do the trick. Seward took no action. Nevertheless, Averill assumed it was proper for him to send to the secretary of state a proposal to intervene in Canadian politics, an act for which he suffered no penalty. Seward himself was an annexationist, as was President Andrew Johnson, who had replaced the slain Lincoln. In his last message to Congress as president, in December 1868, Johnson called for "the acquisition and incorporation of the several adjacent and insular countries"—Canada being the "adjacent" country, and Cuba and the Dominican Republic the "insular" ones. The clearest and loudest annexationist voice was that of Senator Charles Sumner, who mattered a great deal because, for the decade from 1861 to 1871, he was chairman of the Senate Committee on Foreign Relations.

Many Americans were annexationists. Having made war on each other for four years, the majority now wanted only to get on with their lives. The popular topics of debate were the Tammany Hall scandals, whether Mrs. Lincoln's widow's pension was too large, and, most contentiously, the new issue of women's rights. The *New York Times* viewed Canada's emergence with equanimity: "North America is certainly large enough for two families, even if they do not wish to board and lodge together," it stated. A few annexationists settled on a kinder, gentler version of manifest destiny, confident that Canada would, sooner or later, drop southwards like a "ripe fruit."

In the U.S. West, however, entirely new forces were in play. On May 10, 1868—by coincidence the same day MPs in Ottawa began debating the bill for the temporary government of the North-West Territories—a ceremony took place at Promontory Point, Utah. It marked the completion of the Central Pacific and Union Pacific railways—the first transcontinental railway—which connected Chicago with San Francisco.

Congress had already approved a charter for a second such railway, the Northern Pacific, to run from Boston to Puget Sound on the west coast. To Macdonald, its most relevant point was that its prairie section would be built unusually close to the forty-ninth parallel. The prospectus submitted to Congress by the Northern Pacific syndicate explained that this route would make it easy to push feeder lines into the Canadian prairies, which would then "become so Americanized in interest and feeling that they would be in effect severed from the new Dominion."

In 1868, the idea was picked up by the Minnesota legislature, which passed a resolution specifically linking construction of the Northern Pacific to acquisition of Canada's West. An early convert to the cause was Eugene Wheeler, the state's most prominent businessman and owner of the St. Paul *Press*. "If politically it [the North-West] belongs to Canada," the newspaper declared, "geographically and commercially, it belongs to Minnesota. . . . Canadian policy may propose, but American enterprise will dispose." Now that St. Paul was connected to the national railway network by a line to Duluth, other regions began to take an interest in exploiting the North-West as a commercial hinterland. Prompted by the Northern Pacific syndicate, politicians in Michigan and Illinois joined the cause. Michigan senator Zachariah Chandler ranted in the chamber: "This continent is our land and we may as well notify the world . . . that we will fight for it."

In Washington, once a new administration took office in March 1869, the annexationists gained the most powerful allies possible. Both the new president, General Ulysses S. Grant, and his secretary of state, Hamilton Fish, espoused the creed. Grant had come to office convinced that the absorption of Canada by the Union was not only inevitable but highly desirable for both parties.* At one of his first cabinet meetings, he made it clear that the acquisition of Canada was among his principal policy goals.

Fish thought likewise, though he operated much more cautiously. He laid down the rule that any actions taken had to be "short of war." He made his initial approach through Britain, when he met Sir Edward Thornton, the ambassador in Washington. How would Britain react to a takeover? he asked. Thornton replied

---

* This is the judgment of American historian Allan Nevins, the author of the authoritative *Hamilton Fish: The Inner History of the Grant Administration.*

that Britain had no desire to hold on to Canada, and if Canadians wanted to go, it would stand aside.

Macdonald soon heard of this exchange. In a letter to John Rose, his man in London, he angrily described Fish's meeting with Thornton as "a blackguard business," directing his irritation directly at Thornton for his indifference to Canada's interests. Word of Macdonald's annoyance got back to Thornton, who, in his next meeting with Fish, told him, "The Canadians find great fault with me for saying as openly as I do that we are ready to let them go whenever they wish." It was hardly the reaction Macdonald wanted.

Macdonald was fully aware that Fish's exploratory inquiries to the British ambassador were only the opening moves in a grand game in which Canada risked being treated like a pawn. Depending on how this game was played, Britain and America might emerge as fast friends or as bitter enemies. It was not a case of a mouse versus an elephant, in Pierre Trudeau's famous phrase, but of a mouse scurrying about among the legs of two elephants, doing its best to avoid extinction while the beasts made up their minds whether to make love or war.

The United States had come out of the Civil War with deep suspicions about, indeed outright anger at, British behaviour. By declaring neutrality, Britain had been able to treat the American South as the legal equal of the North and continue to do business with it. But Britain hadn't always acted like a neutral party. Turning a blind eye, it had allowed six Confederate raiders to be built in its shipyards, the first and most destructive vessel being the *Alabama*. Once launched, these warships sank fifty-eight Federal merchant ships before they were sunk themselves. Once the war ended, Washington demanded hundreds of millions in compensation, as well as an apology.

Britain, the Mother Country of the world's largest empire since Rome, would never accept the humiliation of issuing an apology. Neither could it afford the cost of reparations. Fish soon figured out that there was something Britain could afford to give to the United States to settle the dispute—that odd new entity, the Dominion of Canada.

In November 1869, the same month that McDougall began his mission in the West, President Grant told his ministers that, in exchange for Canada, he would be willing to settle the *Alabama* claims (as they came to be called) at once. In his diary, Fish wrote that such an agreement seemed agreeable to "every member of the Cabinet." At his next meeting with Thornton, he told the ambassador that "removal of the British flag" from North America would "render easy the settlement of all other questions between the two governments." He noted in his diary, "The Prest. evidently expects these [British] provinces to be annexed to the United States during his Administration." Although Fish himself believed "such is their destiny," he doubted it would happen "as soon as the President expects."

Macdonald, however, was determined to accomplish the opposite destiny for Canada, adding the North-West and then British Columbia to it as quickly as possible, so that the country would match the United States as a sea-to-sea nation. All the steps to achieve the first objective were in place—except for one. Until now, Macdonald had paid no attention to the attitudes and interests of the inhabitants of the territory's one settlement, the Red River Colony. Nor had he shown any awareness of the single most powerful group in the North-West—the Métis.

EIGHT

Champions of Two Nations

[Riel] is a clever fellow.
Macdonald to Lieutenant-Governor William McDougall

In the first comment he made about the events unfolding in Red River, Macdonald got it wrong. In a November 16, 1869, letter to John Rose in London, he recounted breezily that an American newspaper had reported that "the half-breeds at first attempted to oppose" Lieutenant-Governor William McDougall as he travelled to take up his duties in the Red River Colony, but that McDougall had proceeded on "in triumph."

Within a few days, after reading McDougall's first report, Macdonald realized that the trouble in the North-West was real. It transpired that first a group of Métis had forced a Canadian survey team to stop its work in the colony, and later a group of armed Métis had stopped McDougall at the border and prevented him from entering the territory he had been sent to govern.

Macdonald dispatched a carefully composed missive to McDougall. Accepting that Canada had no legal standing in the colony until the official takeover took place, on December 1, he assumed a cautious and conciliatory tone. "The point you must never forget," he instructed McDougall, "is that you are now approaching a Foreign Country, under the Government of the Hudson's Bay Company. . . . You cannot force your way in." In his report, McDougall had written that the local Catholic priests were supporting the Métis, perhaps even were inciting their resistance. Macdonald urged him not to quarrel with the priests, although, "once fairly in the saddle, if they attempt to obstruct your administration you can act summarily with them." Above all, cautioned Macdonald, "Your Government must not have an ill omen at the commencement, no blood must be shed."

Gradually, Macdonald came to comprehend the complexity of the small settlement of Red River. Its approximately eleven thousand citizens were divided between about ten thousand Métis (French predominantly, but many English) and a group of Canadians. Most of the Canadians were newcomers who accepted John Christian Schultz as their leader—an energetic, acquisitive businessman and a member of the expansionist Canada First movement. Macdonald soon learned that Schultz was "greatly disliked" by the Métis. There were also a few Americans, who were almost all annexationists and able to count on outside support—as shown by the sudden appointment of a consul to the territory. Finally, there were the HBC officials, who, as Macdonald came to realize, generally opposed the takeover because they worried about their positions and pensions.

Macdonald quickly learned that by appointing McDougall as the North-West's first Canadian governor, he had made one of the worst choices of his career. Some of McDougall's qualifications were certainly impressive. Early on, he had advocated expansion into the North-West and together with George-Étienne Cartier had negotiated its takeover in London. He was well educated, with advanced ideas on matters such as an elected Senate and the secret ballot; he was tall, heavily built, with luxuriant hair. But as a Liberal to begin, and now one of Macdonald's ministers, he had earned his nickname of "Wandering Willy"; although a Canada

First nationalist, he wasn't trusted by many of that persuasion, because he had once advocated annexation; French-Canadian colleagues kept their distance from him because he could not conceal his anti-Catholicism. As for the Métis, he described them as "semi-savages and serfs of yesterday." He was vain, erratic and irredeemably pigheaded. As Canada's intended first proconsul in the North-West, McDougall was utterly unfit for so demanding and delicate a task.

Sent out to be the first lieutenant-governor of the North-West Territory, William McDougall, overburdened with self-confidence while bereft of common sense, almost managed to lose it for Canada.

In his next letter to Rose, Macdonald admitted that he feared McDougall's "want of suavité will be a good deal in our way" and described Colonel John Stoughton Dennis, the head of the survey party the Métis had forced to stop work, as "cantankerous and ill-conditioned." Widening his concerns, he said that most of the Métis' priests came from France, so "their sympathies are not with us." As an antidote, Macdonald sent two representatives out to Red River to make contact with the Métis—Father Jean-Baptiste Thibault, a retired missionary, and Charles de Salaberry, a hero of the War of 1812. He hoped these men could build "a golden bridge" over which McDougall might make his way to his intended headquarters at Fort Garry.

Done much earlier, this effort to learn what was agitating the Métis might have made a substantial difference. By now, it was far too little too late. Along with McDougall's ineptitude, there was a cluster of reasons for the Métis discontent, principally that they would be overwhelmed by English Protestants; the influential

Bishop Alexandre Taché, Riel's patron, regarded immigration as "an actual fact" that would cause the Métis to "cease to be what we have hitherto been, an exceptional people." To heighten their unease, a plague of locusts had destroyed their 1868 harvest. But only one factor really mattered: among the Métis in Red River, there happened to be, at exactly the right time, exactly the right man. His name was Louis Riel.

Louis Riel is one of the most commanding and complex public personalities in Canadian history. More distinctive yet, he is the only truly romantic figure—fighting for a small, threatened people, and dying for them—that we have ever had. More has been written about him than about any other Canadian (far more than about Macdonald), and not only in books, articles and learned treatises, but also in poems, operas and plays for stage and television. Riel's own words, whether profound or trivial or incoherent, have been transcribed, annotated, translated and published, a tribute accorded to no other public figure. Once regarded as a traitor, he has since been sanctified by the state, with public statues erected in his honour. He now carries the title of Father of Manitoba. The long contest between Macdonald and Riel would end in his execution, to the great approval of most Canadians of the day (though by no means all), and not long afterwards he all but vanished from the public's memory (not in the West, though, nor among his own people). But in the court of public opinion today, Riel wins hands down in his contest with Macdonald.*

* A rare exception: in 2007, CBC Television staged a Greatest Canadian competition. Riel trailed in eleventh place, with Macdonald coming in eighth and so qualifying for the final round, if behind the hockey commentator Don Cherry.

A threatened people found the right man at the right time in Louis Riel.

At the time he began to make his mark, Riel cut an impressive figure: he was comparatively tall, broad-shouldered if a shade stout, and with a great mane of curly black hair. His character made a vivid impression: Oscar Malmros, the American consul in Red River, described him as "ambitious, quick of perception, though not profound, of indomitable energy, daring, excessively suspicious of others." There were incongruities, however. Once Riel became head of his provisional government, his daily dress became an English-style Victorian frock coat paired with moccasins. Yet he possessed a charisma that caused all who met him, foe or friend, to recognize they were in the presence of a natural leader. Macdonald spotted this trait even from a distance. Early on, he described Riel as "a clever fellow" and suggested to McDougall he should enlist him "in your future Police," if only as proof that "you are not going to leave the half-breeds out of the law."

Riel was actually only one-eighth Aboriginal, one grandmother being a Franco-Chipewyan Métisse. Most Métis were illiterate, but Riel was well educated—indeed better educated than Macdonald—if in a narrowly classical way. He knew the world outside, as few Métis did, having spent close to a decade in Montreal and some time in Chicago. He had never shot a buffalo and had few of the skills of a frontiersman. He almost never drank. Yet he was Métis to every nerve-end of his being, and the Métis embraced him as one of them. They would follow him without question, some to their deaths.

He was the eldest of eleven children in a close-knit and deeply religious family. His father, Jean-Louis Riel, whom he idolized, was one of the leading figures in Red River. At school, the young Riel attracted the attention of Bishop Taché, who arranged for him and two other Métis boys to go to the Petit Séminaire in Montreal in the hope they would become priests. He did well at his studies, but the sudden death of his father in 1866 sent him into a deep depression. In the summer of 1868, he abandoned his studies and returned home to help his struggling family.

The Red River he came back to was different from the one he had left. The English presence was becoming ever more pronounced: the village of Winnipeg, at the confluence of the Red and Assiniboine rivers, was expanding into a small town. With Confederation now a fact, it was plain that many more settlers from Ontario would soon arrive.

One of the great unknowables is whether Riel sensed early on that the era of the Métis might be over, and in a far more fundamental way than just disputes over who owned which plot of land. Having personal knowledge of the world outside, of its dynamism and energy, he may have guessed that his people were near the high point of their historical arc. Often in his contest with Macdonald, Riel performed almost as skilfully as the old pro. But he also made reckless mistakes, especially when challenged. In his later years, these outbursts could be attributed to his mental imbalance, his megalomania, his religious fanaticism, but his occasional self-destructiveness may have been the product of the unbearable stress of knowing how slight was his chance of rewriting history for his people.

On October 25, 1869, Riel appeared before the governing body of the Hudson's Bay Company at what would turn out to be its last meeting before being dissolved. He was asked to explain why he had turned back the Canadian survey party. His answer was far more a plea for his Métis than a paean of defiance: "They knew that they were in a sense poor and insignificant," he explained, but they "felt so much at being treated as if they were more insignificant than they really were."

~

The Métis of Red River, the offspring of unions between newcomers and natives, of colonizers and colonized, were a unique people—not just within the North-West, but anywhere in the world, despite the many similar liaisons elsewhere. They were part French and mostly part Cree, but also Blackfoot, Ojibwa, Saulteaux and Sioux. Even among the Métis as a whole, they were a distinct breed, the others being part English (actually, most often Scottish) rather than French. The French Métis were unforgettable—gregarious, impulsive, passionate, bold and vivacious, but also braggarts, credulous, superstitious and improvident. They wore long black coats, or capotes, and colourful Quebec-style sashes. They loved singing, bawling out, "En roulant ma boule," or "Youpe! Youpe! Sur la rivière," as they worked on riverboats. Above all, they loved dancing to the music of fiddles, combining Scottish reels and Indian dances into a form of square dance with their own calls, such as today's "Allemande left." They were deeply religious. Crime was virtually unknown, and doors were never locked. Their language, Michif, was unique, a combination of French and Cree. In comparison, their English counterparts were less distinctive, if more industrious and better farmers.

The Red River Colony was crucial to their development as a people. It was a semi-civilized dot in the middle of a kind of vast nature reserve, the HBC having done all it could to keep out settlers to protect its fur trade. The Métis dominated this community as no "half-breeds" did anywhere else, both in population and militarily. They had already demonstrated their prowess in victorious battles against the Selkirk Scottish settlers, at Seven Oaks in 1816, and over the Sioux, at Grand Coteau in 1851. Their basic military tactic was unknown elsewhere: they formed their Red River carts (made of wood, without a single nail) into a circle and dug shallow trenches to shield themselves from incoming fire. They dominated their community culturally as well, though as time passed the arrival of more white men, and particularly of more white women, altered local values and customs.

The buffalo were fundamental to the Métis way of life. Other groups hunted these animals too, Indians especially, along with some white professional hunters. But the Métis were the champions of the buffalo hunt. As horsemen, they were unmatched: Macdonald compared them to "centaurs." They were exceptional sharpshooters, able to fire at a buffalo at full gallop, hit it, reload by pouring in powder and spitting in an iron ball they carried in

A variant of those used by habitants along the St. Lawrence River, the Red River cart had not a single nail in it, nor any grease so its wheels would not seize up from the prairie dust.

their mouths, and fire again. More than just exceptional hunters, the Métis were also well organized. The whole community went out on hunts, women and children included, in a long line of Red River carts. Explorer Henry Youle Hind described a hunt in his 1858 report during his journey across the prairies:

> After the start from the settlement has been well made, a great council is held and a president elected. A number of captains are nominated by the president and people jointly. The captains then proceed to appoint their own policemen. . . . Their duty is to see that the laws of the hunt are strictly carried out. If a man ran a buffalo without permission before the general hunt began, his saddle and bridle were cut to pieces for the first offence; for the second offence of the same description his clothes were cut off his back. . . . At night the carts are placed in the form of a circle with the horses and cattle inside the ring, and it is the duty of the captains and their policemen to see that this is rightly done. . . . In sight of buffalo, the hunters are drawn up in a line, the president, captains and police being a few yards in advance, restraining the impatient hunters. Not yet, not yet is the subdued whisper of the president as the approach is cautiously made. Now! the president exclaims, and as the word leaves his lips the charge is made and the excited half-breeds are among the bewildered buffalo.

Back in Ottawa, almost no one appreciated the military capability of the Métis. Yet there were weaknesses among these people. The Métis culture was perfectly in tune with life on the western plains, at least as long as the buffalo flourished, but it had produced not a single lawyer, doctor or priest. As farmers, the Métis harvested only potatoes and barley, and in scant quantities. And the very success of their buffalo hunts meant that the Métis were, in effect, eating their own seed corn.

To an observer as intelligent as Riel, what was being done to the buffalo had to be as troubling as what Canada might do to the North-West. At their peak, there were probably more than fifty million buffalo across the western flatlands of North America. They moved north and south, from Texas to as far north as close to the treeline. Once a herd began to move, nothing could stop it. In Saskatchewan's Qu'Appelle Valley, travellers once watched for twenty-four hours as a continuous column of animals crossed a river at a rate of one hundred each minute. Standing as high as six feet and weighing up to two thousand pounds, the buffalo were the largest self-generating supply of food in the hemisphere. Far more than raw meat came from them: from their hides came moccasins, leggings and teepees; their long facial hairs were woven into ropes, their bladders became water bags, their bones were carved into knife handles and toboggan runners, and their dung fuelled fires. Pemmican, made from dried, shredded buffalo meat, was as long-lasting as salt cod.

The "tragedy of the commons"—the overexploitation of a resource that no one owns but to which everyone has access—would overtake the buffalo of the prairies, just as it would much later overtake the cod of the Northwest Atlantic. All the hunters contributed to this annihilation: the American professional hunters with their devastating repeater rifles, the Plains Indians with their wasteful "buffalo jumps" over cliffs and the Métis with their massive hunts. Hind described one Red River column as composed of "603 carts, 700 half-breeds, 200 Indians, 600 horses, 200 oxen, 400 dogs and one cat." They went out twice a year, in summer and fall. By the 1860s, they were sending some 2,500 cartloads of hides and pemmican to St. Paul each year. But profits weren't the only cause of the overkill. Thousands of carcasses were left untouched on the plains, many with only their tongues (the greatest delicacy) taken. One Métis historian reckoned that one in three slain buffalo was put to no use.

The decline in buffalo first became detectable in the 1860s; to maintain their highly profitable industry, the Red River Métis launched a third hunt during the winter. By the mid-1870s, the Red River hunt had virtually ended, with the animals being chased farther west. A decade later, all the buffalo were gone.* Many Métis left Red River at this time, desperately moving west in the hope some buffalo remained there. Others attempted to make the transition to the tedious, careworn life of a farmer.

In the way of this narrowing future for the Métis stood Riel. A failed seminarian with an education heavy on theology and Latin, and only twenty-five years old, he turned out to be an outstanding leader. Right after his first successes—stopping the survey party and halting McDougall at the border—Riel acted on an intuitive understanding that, now that he had once defied authority, caution and compromise meant defeat while boldness just might snatch victory.

Riel took a huge gamble. He sent his Métis followers to Upper Fort Garry, the HBC's headquarters. As came naturally to hunters, they slipped into the fort quietly, singly or in pairs, attracting no attention until they were ready to take command of the place—doing this bloodlessly. Riel was now controller of a real fort with six-pounder cannon and ample supplies of food and munitions. He was master of the Red River Colony.

Immediately, the American group in Red River came alive. Consul Malmros fired off a dispatch to the State Department,

* In the late 1870s, a Manitoba Métis, James McKay, purchased a bull buffalo and four heifers and nurtured them into a herd of twenty-three. From this stock and others in the United States, the buffalo numbers have been brought back to some half-million.

claiming (quite inaccurately in fact) that the "entire" French population and "over half" of the others favoured union with the United States. Senator Alexander Ramsey advised Washington that $100,000 would ensure "the success of the annexation movement," but he received only a noncommittal reply.

Success went to Riel's head. He had already given himself the title of President of Red River, and now he added another—*commandant en chef.* Thereafter, his tolerance for dissent dwindled markedly.

Macdonald had now to unravel two closely related yet separate problems. One was to get productive talks going with the Métis, "these refractory people," as he wrote to Rose on November 23. The other was to deter McDougall, the designated lieutenant-governor, from doing anything precipitate or aggressive. He wrote to Captain D.R. Cameron, a member of McDougall's party (and Charles Tupper's son-in-law), to emphasize that the Canadian group had "no power or authority to force [their] way into the Territory" and that they should "remain in the United States and watch events." He warned Cartier he was concerned that McDougall "seems inclined to act with a high hand" and, as soon as he was sworn in, to act authoritatively.

By now, Macdonald's sympathies had shifted towards the Métis. Their sense of grievance was understandable, he told Cartier; they had been told nothing and assumed they would be "handed over like a flock of sheep" and would "lose their lands and everything they value." Aware of the machinations of the Americans in Red River, and of others in Minnesota and Washington, he was now ready to concede a great deal to the Métis. Unfortunately, his representatives Thibault and de Salaberry had accomplished nothing (the latter had devoted himself to organizing a boy's band), and he had no way to communicate a message to them.

As an alternative, Macdonald set out to extract a sizeable concession from the most powerful player in the drama—Britain. Canada had agreed to take over Rupert's Land from the HBC in good faith, but the North-West was in no shape to be purchased. Canada's "true course," he told Cartier, "is to throw the responsibility on the Hudson's Bay [Company] and Her Majesty's Government." The date for the actual transfer was December 1. Macdonald telegraphed Rose in London: "Canada cannot accept North West until peaceable possession can be given." The takeover, therefore, had to be delayed. "Meanwhile, the money should remain on deposit and not be paid over. Answer."

It was a bold trick and a bare-faced one. Canada was refusing to pay the agreed amount to the HBC on the grounds that the property was not in an appropriate condition. In this exchange, Britain had already fired the first shot—one sure to prick Macdonald. Earlier, Lord Granville had sent Governor General Lisgar a dispatch in which he reported that the Queen was "gravely concerned" that the grievances of her subjects in Red River had not, apparently, been listened to.

Unflustered, Macdonald mustered up an argument that, in other circumstances, he would have admitted was bunkum. If McDougall plunged ahead and proclaimed himself lieutenant-governor, Macdonald told Rose, this action would end the authority of the Company. At that point, the people of Red River "might be forced, for the protection of their lives and property," to switch their loyalty to the only effective government remaining—to Riel and his Métis. This status would give Riel's insurgency "an apparent sanction in the eyes of the people of the United States." Macdonald was saying that Britain had to take back the territory or the United States would likely take it over.

That same day, Macdonald sent McDougall the single most important set of instructions he ever imparted to him. McDougall, he noted, was speaking of "crossing the line and being sworn in." But by "assuming the Government," he would immediately end the HBC's responsibility at a time when he himself lacked the force to ensure law and order in Red River. The result would be anarchy. Macdonald then unveiled an intriguing analysis of the situation: "In such a case, no matter how the anarchy is produced, it is quite open in the law of Nations for the inhabitants to form a Government *ex necessitate* [from necessity] for the protection of life and property." Once established, such a government would have "certain Sovereign rights by the *jus gentium* [laws common to all people], which might be very convenient for the United States, but exceedingly inconvenient for you." The outcome of hasty action by McDougall could be "an acknowledgement of such a Government by the United States."

McDougall did not get the letter, or at least not until it was too late. By some administrative bungle in Ottawa, the letter was given not to a special courier but to the post office. So McDougall went ahead and did what he thought was best—in reality, the worst possible course.

On December 1, 1869, even though no proclamation signed by the Queen had reached him, McDougall concocted a replacement. He sneaked across the border with a party of six assistants and two dogs, stopped at a deserted HBC post, and read out to an audience of snowbanks and the stars a supposed Royal Proclamation he had written and signed. He then scurried back to Pembina, Dakota. Meantime, he had given orders to his senior officer, Colonel John Stoughton Dennis, to go secretly to Red River to raise a contingent of loyalists to "attack, arrest, disarm or disperse" the insurgency. It was the exact opposite of what Macdonald wished.

International law was on Riel's side when, after preventing McDougall from entering the country, he created a Provisional Government of both the French and English Métis.

By a remarkable coincidence, Riel had arrived at the same conclusion as Macdonald, and at the same time. Almost certainly he was helped by the French priests and very likely one of the annexationists, perhaps Enos Stutsman—an amazing individual who, though born without legs, was a superb horseman—who got on very well with Riel. On November 22, a small group gathered around Riel to draft a constitution for a provisional government. A few days later they issued their justification: "A people when it has no Government is free to adopt one form of Government in preference to another."

Although Macdonald and Riel would never meet, they were as one at this moment. Both had concluded that the people of Red River had every legal right to form their own government in the absence of any British or Canadian one. They converged on yet another and even more vital matter: each was fighting for the survival of his nation, as he saw it.

Riel's immediate task was to persuade the English Métis that his provisional government was their government as much as for his own French Métis. He achieved this by a series of negotiating sessions to which each side sent twelve elected members. The French Métis argued for special protection for their language and religion; the English readily agreed. Although differences remained—the English Métis were wary of anything that suggested rebellion against the Crown—the give-and-take among the French and English Métis gained the provisional government considerable credibility. On January 8, 1870, Riel formally became its president.

For his part, Macdonald had still to get London to agree to a delay in the takeover. He did so by sheer persistence, as Granville, the colonial secretary, finally admitted to Gladstone: "We could not force the territory on Canada, if they put up their backs." Having gained the manoeuvring room he wanted, Macdonald now had to find the right person to initiate talks with the Métis, meaning Riel. On December 13, he sent McDougall—by now about to slink back to Canada, "very chop-fallen" in the prime minister's phase—one final letter. He brought McDougall up to date on a new development: "We have thought it well to send Mr. Smith up, as in his capacity as an official of the Hudson's Bay Coy, he will probably have no difficulty getting into the country." If McDougall was Macdonald's worst appointment during the crisis, Donald Smith would be his best.

Smith, Macdonald explained, would perform the role of a special commissioner to inquire into the causes of the discontent and to suggest solutions. Macdonald didn't reveal that the mandate he had given Smith included using special funds to buy Métis support for Canada's eventual takeover.

Donald Smith was one of the highest-achieving Canadians of the nineteenth century—in some respects one of the most admirable, and in others the most dislikeable. In either case, he was one of the richest Canadians of his time. Little remembered today, Smith is memorialized in Canada's most famous photograph—the tall, lean figure with a long grey beard and stovepipe hat, pounding at the Canadian Pacific Railway's last spike in the middle of the Rockies. By 1905, at eighty-five years old, he would hold simultaneously the posts of governor of the Hudson's Bay Company, president of the Bank of Montreal and Canadian high commissioner to London, and also the chancellorships of McGill University and the University of Aberdeen.

Macdonald's first successful countermove to Riel's resistance was to send Donald Smith, a rising star in the Hudson's Bay Company, to Red River as his representative. His mission was to get Riel to send delegates to Ottawa to negotiate a settlement. He succeeded.

Born in 1820 on Scotland's chill northeast coast, he emigrated to Canada as a teenager and was hired by the Hudson's Bay Company. In 1838, he was sent as a factor to harsh, frigid Labrador. He stayed there for three decades. Quarrels with his superiors did not help his cause, but during that time he built up an extremely profitable fur trade and, more remarkably, a substantial farm of cows, horses, sheep, hens, vegetables, fruits and hay. He worked inordinately hard, was unbelievably tough (he once walked the 550 miles to Montreal to receive treatment for an attack of snow-blindness), and was very shrewd, applying most of his salary to quietly buying up HBC shares. He slept little, ate little, and drank not at all. His one grace note was to send a letter or cable every day to his wife, Isabella, whenever they were apart. They were married "country style," which in Labrador bothered no one at all. Later, as he gained status, Smith remarried Isabella four times, the last just before he was ennobled as Lord Strathcona. Although he never retired, he mellowed into a philanthropist. His donations mounted to a staggering $7.5 million, including a college for women at McGill and an entire Canadian regiment, Lord Strathcona's Horse, which he dispatched to fight in the Boer War.

Macdonald met with Smith on the recommendation of George Stephen, a successful Montreal businessman and personal friend (also Smith's cousin). Macdonald summoned Smith to Ottawa and quizzed him about the standing of the HBC in Red River. He was greatly impressed by Smith's analysis that, unless Riel was pacified, "law and order and property will be at the mercy of the most lawless members of the community until the Americans step in and annex it."

On December 15, Smith left Ottawa for Red River, accompanied by Charles Tupper, who was going out to help his daughter, Captain Cameron's wife, pack up their belongings and return home. Also accompanying him were several thousand dollars to be used as bribes. The party arrived on December 27, 1869.

Back in Ottawa, Macdonald became cocky. He spent December 1, the original date for the transfer, reading a Trollope novel in front of a roaring fire.* "There never was much in the

---

* Most probably it was *Phineas Finn*, one of Trollope's Palliser series, published earlier that year and a brilliant political chronicle. Any biographer of John A. has to hope this was the book, because Trollope has one character in it make an observation that would have made Macdonald smile in agreement: "Life is so unlike theory."

insurrection," he told a Nova Scotia correspondent. Macdonald's optimism, as so often, was premature. It took Smith, no less devious than he, to arrange affairs in such a fashion that Macdonald would turn out to be right.

NINE

Building the Future; Ruining the Present

We must make Canada respect us.
Louis Riel

In the summer of 1869, when Macdonald was considering how best to administer the North-West Territories, he deliberately included Captain D.R. Cameron in Lieutenant-Governor William McDougall's original party. He told Cameron he was to be commissioner of police, or some such title, with responsibility for "seeing the Laws carried into effect—that peace is kept within the Territory—that all Frontier rowdyism is prevented, and the Indian tribes kept quiet." Here was the germ of an idea that would blossom into Canada's first distinctive national institution. That December, Macdonald wrote to Cameron, by then on his way to Red River, that "the best force would be Mounted Riflemen, trained to act as cavalry . . . this body should not be expressly Military but should be styled Police and have the bearing of the Irish Constabulary." He had John Rose send him a copy of "the Organization of the Irish Constabulary" from London.

During his entire political life, Macdonald would be a proud godfather of this force, initially called the North-West Mounted

Police, and in 1920 renamed the Royal Canadian Mounted Police. He dismissed critics' complaints that some police officers might actually have visited brothels out west or even have drunk too much. He beat back Opposition demands for the force to be scrapped on the grounds of cost. He concocted many schemes for improving the effectiveness of the force, including one that must be among the most significant missed opportunities in Canadian history. Early in 1870, Macdonald circulated within the government an order-in-council describing his plans for the force: it would consist of two hundred mounted men who would also be, as was most unusual, magistrates; all but fifty of them would be recruited in the West, and at least fifteen were to be French Canadians. Macdonald went even further: he called for the force to be "a mixed one of pure white and British and French half-breeds." Later, in the House of Commons, he described this composition as "a commingling of the races." Before this proposal could be implemented, Riel's uprising* and the sectarian hatreds it unleashed made his idea politically impossible. Had the races commingled successfully in this astoundingly successful police force, the succeeding blighted relationships between Europeans and Aboriginals in Canada might have unfolded differently.

Other concerns soon distracted Macdonald's attention from his Mounted Police (in fact, the force was not set up until 1873). On January 25, 1870, he received a deeply disturbing letter from Charles Brydges, a leading Canadian railway man. Brydges recounted a

* Until Canada gained ownership of the North-West, Riel was not engaged in a rebellion against it. Rather, in an attempt to secure better terms for the people of the North-West, he was merely resisting the actions of a potential future government.

conversation he had recently had with the president of the Northern Pacific Railway, who confirmed that his company planned to build its line close to the border, with spur lines running north, to make untenable "the construction on an independent line in British territory." Brydges further warned Macdonald that Washington intended to use the Northern Pacific's route "to prevent your getting control for Canada of the Hudson's Bay Territory." By return mail, Macdonald replied that it was clear the U.S. government was "resolved to do all they can short of war, to get possession of the western territory." It was imperative, therefore, "to show unmistakably our resolve to build the Pacific Railway."* Thus, even while dealing with the trouble in Red River, he had to figure out how so small a state could mount so mammoth a project as a transcontinental railway.

Within Red River, the Americans were now reaching a peak of influence and of confidence. Consul Malmros and Enos Stutsman often saw Riel privately; they gave him advice, offered bribes and described the manifold attractions of America. In January, Riel approved the transfer to American ownership of the local newspaper, the *Nor'Wester*, which promptly titled its next main story "Annexation Our Manifest Destiny." (The article's anonymous author was Malmros.) As well, Riel had by now befriended an ardent annexationist, William O'Donoghue. Born in Ireland, he had migrated to New York while still a boy, and while studying for the priesthood had moved to Red River to teach in St. Boniface. A supporter of the Fenians, if not a member himself, O'Donoghue quickly became close to Riel—who gave him the key post of secretary-treasurer in the provisional government. Winnipeg's leading hotel, Emmerling's, now flew the Stars and Stripes rather than the Union Jack. Across the border, the St. Paul *Press* boasted,

* Macdonald's proposed railway had as yet no fixed name; earlier in the year, he called it "the Great Pacific Railway."

"Every vestige of British power may be swept from the western half of the continent."

Riel clearly admired the United States and used it to lever concessions out of Ottawa. He knew, however, that the kind of collective rights the Métis were seeking were unknown there, and that the strict separation of church and state made state-funded Catholic schools impossible. It's highly unlikely, then, that he ever considered trying to join the North-West to its southern neighbour.

By now, Macdonald had begun to think that a dispatch of troops to Red River could not be avoided. Yet he was wary. "Looking at the matter from a Military point of view, the situation is rather uncomfortable," he wrote to Rose. "We cannot send troops through the United States. They would not give us permission . . . [and] all the men would desert if they did." He worried about the effect military preparations might have on Riel. To avoid any suggestion that force might be used, he rejected a request by the senior British officer in Canada, Colonel Garnet Wolseley, to accompany Donald Smith on his mission to Red River. "We are endeavouring to exert all peaceable means of bringing these poor people to reason," he told a Captain Healy. "If they fail, I suppose in the Spring some steps must be taken of a Military kind."

The first suggestions that force should be used had actually come from London. As early as November 25, 1869, Colonial Secretary Granville told Governor General Lisgar to be ready to "repress with the [Queen's] authority . . . any unlawful disturbance" and promised a one-year delay in the withdrawal of British troops. From early on, though, Macdonald considered force as an option. In late January 1870, he wrote to Rose, "The best plan will be to send a mixed expeditionary force of a small body of Regulars with some light artillery." These regulars would all be British troops in order to "convince the United States Government and people that Her Majesty's Government have no intention of abandoning this Continent." Such a contingent could disprove the "fixed idea at Washington that England wants to get rid of the Colonies."

London agreed to the plan, but on the condition that Canadian militia troops went as well. Macdonald's strategy now unfolded along two parallel lines. One was to end the annexation threat by dispatching an expeditionary force to Red River. The other was to do all he could to persuade Riel to negotiate, including suggesting that success in negotiations would remove the need for any military expedition. This plan lay behind Smith's mission at Red River. "Should you be able to prevail on the insurgents to send a deputation to Ottawa," Macdonald told Smith at their last meeting before he set off, "you can assure them that they will be received with all kindness." At the same time, though, Macdonald ordered work to begin on building boats to carry an expedition across the Great Lakes.

Macdonald wasn't the only one playing two hands simultaneously. At the same time as the Imperial government was telling Macdonald that British troops could be sent west to enable Canada to secure the North-West, Sir Edward Thornton, its ambassador in Washington, was telling Secretary of State Fish that, as the American recorded in his diary, Britain was "willing, even desirous" that Canada become independent. As Fish reported to a cabinet meeting, Thornton even suggested that the United States should maintain its restrictions on cross-border trade so that Canada's economic difficulties might trigger a popular demand for independence—this at a time when most observers, and Macdonald among them, took for granted that independence would lead inevitably to a political union in North America.

Smith made it to Red River on December 27, where he was met by Riel. This first encounter between these exceptional individuals—Smith incomparably more worldly than the Métis leader, but with the far younger Riel in full command of the territory—was amicable but accomplished little. Riel, unnerved by an emissary of Smith's calibre, ordered him to stay within Fort Garry, but agreed that anyone could call on him there. In return, Smith, while refusing to accept the legality of the provisional government, pledged not to challenge its authority. In his first report to Macdonald, Smith warned that "the power [is] entirely in the hands of Mr. Riel." He added, ominously, "The drift of the whole thing is evidently annexation."

Macdonald responded with minor concessions, such as a promise to delay extending Canada's high tariff rates to Red River. More creatively, he authorized Smith to invite a delegation from Red River to come to Ottawa to negotiate terms. More deviously, he assured Smith that "any pecuniary arrangements that you may make with individuals in the manner we spoke about, will be carried out here"—in other words, that all bribes would be paid. Smith, shrewdly guessing that direct talks between him and Riel, in his capacity as president of the provisional government, would go nowhere, convinced Riel to call a general meeting at which Smith could present his case to the Métis. He by now had distributed enough money to gain some supporters.

For two consecutive days in mid-January, amid temperatures of −20 °F (−29 °C), more than one thousand Red River citizens stood, twice, for five hours in the snow in Fort Garry's quadrangle, huddled in buffalo coats and otter hats around a few small fires. Smith read out a succession of lengthy documents and answered questions about them, every now and then crossing verbal swords with Riel. Of all the words Smith read out, the most effective by far was the Queen's declaration of her "sorrow and displeasure" that her Red River subjects should have been given cause to protest. Useful also was the colonial secretary's assurance that all their rights as British subjects would be respected. By the end of this saga, the crowd was ready to accept Smith's good faith. After an adjournment, Riel made a stirring speech calling on French and English Métis to elect delegates to draft a bill of rights setting out their claims. He concluded, trenchantly, "We claim no half rights . . . but all the rights we are entitled to . . . and, what is more, gentlemen, we will get them."

Persuading Riel to negotiate had been a considerable achievement for Smith. Riel's even larger achievement was, at the sessions on the bill of rights, to persuade hunters and farmers to come together despite differences in religion and race, and to put their trust in words that most could not read. A new bill of rights was drawn up, and, on February 10, Riel made public the names of the three delegates who would negotiate with Macdonald in Ottawa. Afterwards came fireworks and a night-long drunk in the pubs of Winnipeg. A few days later, the American flag was pulled down at the Emmerling Hotel, and the *Nor'Wester* soon returned to Canadian ownership.

Macdonald had won; so had Riel, and indeed so also had Donald Smith. Still to be determined was everyone's good faith.

As so often, Macdonald's response was to indulge in excessive optimism. He told Rose on March 11 that the propositions adopted at the Red River Conference were reasonable and could easily be settled in Ottawa with their delegates. Drawing on his political experience, he identified one risk: "The longer [Riel] remains in power, the more unwilling will he be to resign it." But Macdonald remained confident: "We will receive the delegation with all kindness, & I think beyond a doubt make an arrangement with them." If he failed, he had an alternative: the military expedition would be ready to leave by the end of April or early May.

Then Riel changed everything by making the single worst mistake of his life.

McDougall's order for his military commander to "arrest, disarm or disperse" the insurgents in Red River had been a miserable failure: no one had assembled to take on Riel. In the confusion, though, John Schultz, the leader of the Canadian faction, had gathered some forty supporters and convinced them to turn his Winnipeg house into a fort, his muddled motive being to keep stores of HBC pork out of the hands of insurgents. The Métis surrounded the building with men and two cannon dragged from nearby Fort Garry and forced its surrender. Riel found himself with some three dozen prisoners. Many escaped from Fort Garry after their wives smuggled in pen-knives hidden in cakes and pies, but most were soon recaptured. Schultz and a fellow Canada First nationalist, Charles Mair,

Riel was master of Red River when he gained Fort Gary, with its guns, thick walls and supplies.

got clean away, though. Confident in his string of successes, Riel announced that all the remaining prisoners would be released.

Instead, even more prisoners fell into his hands. Out on the flatlands at Portage la Prairie, a group of Canadian supporters decided to march on Fort Garry to free their kin, without realizing that Riel had already said he would release them. Along the way they spilt the first blood of the uprising when their ragged contingent arrested a solitary Métis on suspicion he was a spy. The man escaped, but then killed an innocent young Scottish settler he believed was about to rearrest him. The original group recaptured the Métis and beat him so severely that he died. Most of the Canadians now turned back towards their homes, but some, inexplicably, marched close to Fort Garry. As they neared the fort, they were surrounded by Métis horsemen and arrested. Riel's jails were now overflowing.

Badly shaken by this second uprising, Riel announced that the leader of this contingent, Charles Boulton, in fact a moderate, would be executed. Pleas by the mother of the slain Scottish boy, backed by Smith, convinced him to cancel the order. Peace returned to the settlement. Meanwhile, both Schultz and Mair came out of hiding and made an incredible mid-winter journey to the safety of the border, despite suffering snow-blindness and near starvation.

On March 2, Riel suddenly issued a new and terrifying announcement: one of the new prisoners would be put on trial for his life before a court headed by Ambroise Lépine, Riel's military commander in the provisional government. The prisoner was Thomas Scott, a surveyor from Ontario. On the very next day, after a bogus trial, he was executed.

Alexander Begg, a local historian and author of an excellent journal on the crisis, wrote that Riel was experiencing "brain fever" at this time. The general stress was getting to him, accentuated by his tendency to lose self-control when challenged. This time the arguments and pleas of Smith and the Protestant ministers could not convince Riel to reverse his decision. Perhaps fearing losing face, he refused to change his mind a second time.

The original caption on the photo describes the worst mistake Riel ever made: "Thomas Scott, Murdered by Riel on 4th March, 1870." Scott's bungled execution after a mock trial turned Riel into an object of hatred for Protestant Ontario.

Apologists for Riel have argued that Scott was a hard-drinking, brutal, racist Orangeman who shouted abuse at his guards until Riel had no choice but to silence him.* But character is not a crime. Scott's belligerence may have been caused by the fact he was suffering from diarrhoea and the toilet facilities were scanty. He may not even have deserved the demonizing of later Riel apologists. Historian J.M. Bumsted has challenged the conventional wisdom, finding "precious little evidence" that Scott was a bully, "no real evidence" that he drank heavily, "if at all," and, although an Orangeman, that he ever expressed anti-Catholic sentiments. Whatever Scott's character and behaviour, his trial was a travesty and his end an outrage. The trial was in French, a language he did not understand. No written accusation was made available to him, and he was not allowed to question hostile witnesses. The manner of his execution was worse. Smith reckoned that most members of the firing party were drunk. The wretched Scott may well have

* In one biography of Riel, Scott was described as an "unrelenting boozer," "violent and abusive," "hard-drinking, foul-mouthed," with a "violent temper" and prone to "fanatical and rather ridiculous ranting."

lingered for well over an hour after being shot, even moaning piteously while encased in his coffin. When Smith asked Riel why he had allowed this sentence, he answered: "We must make Canada respect us." In an interview with the Winnipeg *Sun* in June 1883, Riel provided perhaps the most convincing explanation: "I was really the leader, and whenever I believe myself to be right, no man has ever changed my opinion."

The news of Scott's execution reached Ottawa on April 4. Macdonald answered a question in the Commons, saying his information was limited, that he didn't yet know the victim's name, but there was no doubt that a man had been murdered. In a letter to his friend Lord Carnarvon a few days later, he began to sort out his thoughts: "The affair has been a good deal complicated by the barbarous murder of Scott," he wrote. "He was tried by a sham Court Martial under the orders of Riel, and condemned on the most frivolous pretexts." In Ontario, he continued, "the blood of the people is at fever heat," with widespread calls for retribution on Riel. Most worrying was that demands were now being made for the government to "refuse to receive any delegates commissioned by Riel."

Macdonald was determined to meet the delegates, and he remained confident that a deal could be done. His attitude to Riel, however, changed to one of contempt—an attitude that would reassert itself with disastrous consequences when, over a decade later, comparable tensions arose around Riel and the Métis much farther out in the North-West. For now, though, the resistance in Red River, previously a local affair, was attracting interest across the country.

TEN

Rage and Recovery

The Pacific Railway must be built by means of the land through which it has to pass.

Macdonald during "Manitoba" debate in Commons, May 1870

The execution of Thomas Scott changed the nature of the crisis from a possible civil war between the Métis and the Canadian government to a possible civil war among Canadians. From now on, French Canadians identified with Riel and the Métis, while English Canadians, above all the Orangemen of Ontario, identified with Scott. As for Macdonald, he not only had to look constantly at London, Washington and Red River, but now had also to keep a close eye on developments in his own backyard.

To this point, Quebecers had paid little attention to the West; it was a long way off and, to all but fur traders, was foreign. It had taken George-Étienne Cartier to grasp that the principal beneficiary of a transcontinental railway across the North-West would be Montreal, the country's natural transportation and financial centre, thereby dashing the aspirations the Toronto *Globe* had expressed in December 1869: "We hope to see a great new Upper Canada in the North-West." Ontario businessmen also counted on western grain getting to Britain by way of Toronto and the Erie Canal. Nationalists in Quebec still worried that the West, with its free land and rich soil, would attract habitants to move there to farm. That had always been the hope of the astute Bishop Alexandre Taché of St. Boniface, Riel's original patron. But Quebec's leaders wanted their people to stay home to ensure that the province remained overwhelmingly French; the newspaper *La Vérité* denounced emigration to the North-West as "a social calamity which all true patriots have a duty to fight with all legitimate means."

When the trouble began in Red River, few Quebecers took any notice. *Le Pays* described its own position as "considerable indifference," and *L'Événement* dismissed the Métis as "savage people . . . [whom] a few cases of beads would have satisfied." Quebec woke up to the crisis only after Ontario had begun to seethe. Then, because Quebec saw Ontario as anti-Quebec, it was anti-Ontario rather than pro-Riel.*

Anger in Ontario was predictable, because one of its own had been killed by French-speaking Roman Catholics. The anger quickly escalated into something far more threatening—not just rage, but well-organized rage. Its forcing agents were bigotry and sectarianism, but patriotism also played a part; Scott's murder catalyzed the first attempt to articulate a sense of Canada as itself, rather than as a collection of leftovers of British North America. The attempt failed, but it left behind footprints that others would follow later far more effectively.

* By far the best study of attitudes in Quebec to the West in the late nineteenth century is the chapter "Confederation and the North-West" in A.I. Silver's *The French-Canadian Idea of Confederation, 1864–1900*.

In April 1868, a year after Confederation, a group of aspirant poets and journalists who admired D'Arcy McGee got together in Ottawa to talk about their country—what it was and where it might go. They gave themselves the title "Canada Firsters." The best expression of these often naïve and confused ideas appeared in the *Globe* in a series titled "Our New Nationality," by a Toronto lawyer and journalist, W.A. Foster. He made the first attempt to describe a distinct Canadian identity: "We are a Northern people . . . more manly, more real, than the weak-marrowed bones and superstitions of an effeminate South." Others picked up this theme. Robert Haliburton, son of the author of the popular Sam Slick series, described Canada as "a Northern country, inhabited by the descendants of the north men."

Out of manliness and northernness, these men believed, had come a North American quite distinct from Americans in the United States. For some Canada Firsters, idealism was the spur: William Norman called on Canada to "fulfill her destiny, to be an asylum for the oppressed and downtrodden people of Europe." For others, it was bigotry: the popular historian George Robert Parkin observed that, unlike the "vagrant population of Italy and other countries of Southern Europe" that had come to the United States, Canada was composed of "the sturdy races of the North—Saxon and Celt, Scandinavian, Dane and Northern German." George Denison, the scion of a United Empire Loyalist family and a military authority, believed that what Canadians needed to make themselves distinct was "a rattling good war with the United States."*

The Canada Firsters would reach their peak in the mid-1870s, after the Oxford historian Goldwin Smith moved to Canada, joined the group and gave it credibility. Edward Blake was widely

* Denison wrote a book, *Cavalry Tactics*, which won first prize in an international competition organized by the czar of Russia.

expected to become its leader, but ultimately refused. Not long afterwards, the movement petered out. In the meantime, however, this first attempt at pan-Canadian nationalism escalated the protests against Scott's execution into a powerful popular cause.

John Christian Schultz and Charles Mair, the pair of counter-insurgents who escaped from Red River, were both Canada Firsters. They were intellectuals—Mair wrote two of Canada's first works of poetry, *Dreamland and Other Poems* and *Tecumseh*, and Schultz produced a number of learned articles that would earn him membership in the Royal Society of Canada. They were also romantics, attracted to the West because they believed that Canada's future lay there. Mair described it as "the garden of the world" in an article in the *Globe*. Later, both men championed the Indians: Mair called them "villainously wronged," and Schultz argued in the Senate that the treaties negotiated with them were grossly unfair.

Yet when they lived in Red River, both men were detested by the Métis. Mair received a horse-whipping from an enraged Métisse after he wrote in the *Globe* that Métis wives had a habit of "biting at the backs of their white sisters." Schultz, although bilingual and married to a Catholic, was deeply mistrusted by the Métis for his questionable business dealings as well as his leadership of the so-called Canada Party in Red River. Once they had made their harrowing escape across the border, the pair headed for Toronto, determined to arouse protests against Scott's execution.

By a fateful coincidence, strong emotions already existed in Quebec. There, the dominant creed at this time was a particular form of Catholicism known as ultramontanism, a right-wing doctrine that looked to Rome for guidance in all matters secular as well as religious. Its leader was Montreal bishop Ignace Bourget, who rejected any notion of separation between church and state. The "Catholic Program" he persuaded the Quebec bishops to adopt encouraged priests to direct their congregations on which way to vote during elections. These priests told their faithful to note that heaven was *bleu* and hell *rouge*, these happening to be the colours of the Liberal *rouges* and the conservative, pro-ultramontane *bleus*.

Connections existed between this movement and Red River. Bishop Taché was an ultramontane (as was Riel) and, at the time of the uprising, he was in Rome for the First Vatican Council, at which the church promulgated the doctrine of papal infallibility. Two powerful, directly contradictory movements were now headed for a collision—the ultramontanes and the Orange lodges. One was passionately pro-Rome, the other pro–British Empire; one hierarchical and authoritarian, the other democratic and populist. Both were arch-conservative and narrow.

The inevitable explosion ignited on April 6, 1870, the day Schultz and Mair made their first appearance in Toronto. Earlier, the feisty Denison had issued a challenge: "Is there an Ontario man who will not hold out a hand of welcome to these men? Any man who hesitates is no true Canadian." The Canada Firsters organized a rally at St. Lawrence Hall, and the mayor agreed to take part. When five thousand people tried to cram into the hall, the event was moved to the steps of City Hall, where more than ten thousand aroused citizens turned out. From then on, all the Orange lodges across Ontario were eager to assist Schultz and Mair. In succeeding rallies across the province, the rhetoric got ever wilder, with audiences shouting out, "Death to the murderers and tyrants of Fort Garry." To keep the rage at fever pitch, Schultz took to holding up a piece of rope, claiming it had been used "to bind the wrists of poor, murdered Scott."

From across the Ottawa River came the first angry response. The newspaper *L'union des Cantons de l'Est* remarked, "How much hatred there is in these Anglo-Saxon souls against everything which is French and Catholic." *L'Opinion publique* denounced the "fanatical Upper Canadian press."

These dragon seeds of a sectarian civil war had been sown at the very moment when the delegates from Red River were due to arrive in Ottawa. In the meetings to follow, Macdonald hoped to negotiate an agreement that would bring the North-West amicably into Canada.

Macdonald's immediate challenge was that many in Ontario—Denison most particularly—suspected that to appease Quebec he would never send a military expedition to Red River to restore order. Conversely, many in Quebec suspected he would dispatch the troops precisely to crush their Métis kin. In fact, he had by now made up his mind that the expedition "*must* go," while still telling Lord Carnarvon how important it was that the troops be "accepted, not as a hostile force, but as a friendly garrison." For that to happen, a satisfactory settlement with Riel's delegates was essential.

A separate issue was coming to the fore. Back in December, Governor General Lisgar had proclaimed an amnesty for all Métis involved in the uprising who had committed civil offences (such as breaking into Fort Garry and making use of HBC stores), provided they laid down their arms. Although the Métis had not put down their weapons, this technicality could be overlooked in normal times. But the times were abnormal. The Liberals, realizing how narrow was Macdonald's manoeuvring room, began to insist that he declare unequivocally that no amnesty would be granted to Riel or to anyone involved in Scott's death.

It was hard for Macdonald to hide his annoyance that so much damage had been done so unnecessarily. He told Adams Archibald, soon to replace McDougall as lieutenant-governor, that were it not for Scott's execution, all parties would "acquiesce in the propriety of letting by-gones be by-gones." For Macdonald, the only solution to the rift between the country's founding European races—with French Canadians calling now for a general amnesty, while Ontario's English Canadians insisted it exclude anyone involved in Scott's death—was "Time, the great healer of all evils." As for the amnesty issue itself, he would once again pass that responsibility back across the Atlantic to London on the grounds, true in law, if only just, that the North-West still belonged to Britain and not Canada.

When the delegates left Red River on March 24, they had no idea of the furore awaiting them until their train neared Toronto. There were three of them: a judge, John Black; a saloon-keeper, Alfred Scott (no relation to Thomas Scott); and a priest, Father Noël-Joseph Ritchot. A big man with a waist-length black beard, Ritchot had come to Red River from Quebec as a missionary in 1862. Though quiet and gentle, he was awed by no one. He was Riel's confidant and had acted as his adviser during the uprising.

As Riel's choice as a delegate to Ottawa, Father Noël-Joseph Ritchot won every round, from land for the Métis to making Manitoba a province, but for the last one—an amnesty for Riel.

Ritchot always denied this, but at his funeral in 1905, a fellow-priest from the time, Georges Dugas, described Ritchot as "the soul of the movement," adding, "It was he who launched it." In the negotiations, Ritchot would prove exceptionally skilful and persistent, even though handicapped by speaking little English.

Macdonald's first task was to make certain the delegates reached Ottawa safely. He sent word that they should not stop in Toronto but continue to Ogdensburg, New York, where a private coach would bring them to the capital. Once they had made it to Ottawa, however, some Canada Firsters arranged for two of the delegates to be arrested on a warrant for murder. A judge released them, almost certainly at Macdonald's direction. Thomas Scott's brother, Hugh, then had a second warrant taken out. Again they were arrested and again released.

Finally, on April 25, all three delegates got together with Macdonald and Cartier in Cartier's house in Ottawa. Ritchot insisted that the two politicians issue a declaration recognizing their visitors as representatives of the provisional government of the North-West. A version produced a day later referred to them only as "from the North-West." Ritchot protested but settled for their being granted "official status." He then declared that no negotiations of any kind could take place unless they made a clear statement that a general amnesty would be given for all offences committed during the insurgency. Macdonald responded that this decision would have to be made by the Imperial government, though he was certain it would be forthcoming. Ritchot accepted this response, even though Macdonald had actually committed himself to nothing. The subtleties of the language in translation no doubt escaped Ritchot and later led to prolonged charges and counter-charges between the two men.

When discussion turned to specifics in the bill of rights agreed on in Red River by the convention of elected delegates, Macdonald and Cartier found that Riel had unilaterally added last-minute demands, most notably that the region become a province rather than a territory—an idea the convention had specifically rejected because of the costs it would impose. But Macdonald and Cartier were ready to yield, and, in addition, quickly agreed to the demands for bilingualism and denominational schools. They also agreed to a special allotment of land for the Métis, an issue Ritchot would pursue with unflagging persistence. An initial offer of 100,000 acres grew to 1.4 million acres, including a special provision for the children of Métis families.

In gaining so much land for the Métis, Ritchot had done extraordinarily well—but not in one critical respect. Riel wanted a single huge block of land, which could serve as a kind of collective reserve for the Métis. What he was being offered were myriad small lots for individual Métis. At the public discussions back in Red River, Riel had made a most revealing statement: "We must seek to preserve the existence of our people. . . . Though in a sense British subjects, we must look on all coming from abroad [from Canada] as foreigners." What he meant was that the Métis, as "a new nation," had to live apart. Riel spelled this notion out in a letter he sent to Ritchot while he was in Ottawa: "Cette coutume des deux populations vivant separement soit maintenue pour la sauvegarde de nos droits." In effect, Riel was asking for an Indian reserve while, simultaneously, retaining all the rights of other Canadians; in other words, status as a distinct society (though the notion did not then exist). It was too much, and Ritchot may have recognized that or simply not fully understood what Riel sought. This misunderstanding would be repeated more than a decade later in Saskatchewan, with explosive consequences. On both occasions, though, Riel recognized clearly that what was needed to try to secure the future of his people was not transfers of plots of land to individual Métis but rather a collective land settlement.

At this point in the negotiations, Macdonald and Cartier at last showed their own hand. They agreed to the demand that the North-West Territories come into Confederation as a province. Only a very small part of it, the size of PEI, would be called Manitoba—in Cree, "God who speaks." Ottawa would retain ownership of the remainder of the territory and of the Crown lands within the mini-province. They would be used for national purposes—to develop a granary for the empire and as a building-block for a transnational railway. Otherwise, no deal was possible, because no Parliament would ever accept it. Having done so well on other matters, Ritchot agreed to these limitations. He did not know, however, that the British government had sent over an official, Sir Clinton Murdoch, to keep an eye on things, and that Murdoch had reported back his strong opposition to "an indemnity to Riel and his abettors for the execution of Scott." Ritchot, unlike Macdonald, most certainly did know how much he had failed to win.

By the end of April, when the work was all but finished, Ritchot noted in his daily journal that Macdonald had failed to show up because "indisposed." The accumulated strain had set him off on a prolonged binge. Cartier was left to settle the final details with Riel's delegation, though Macdonald did reappear just before they were completed. (Of the delegates, Ritchot remained in Ottawa to argue for a blanket amnesty, Black left the country to return to his native Scotland, and Scott, who had been receiving secret commissions to tell Americans how the negotiations were proceeding, just vanished from the scene, initially moving to New York.)

The Manitoba Bill was introduced into the Commons on May 1, 1870, and attracted almost no debate. The Métis would get a great deal of land; the country would get a fifth province (enlarged a bit at the last moment)—a second bilingual one that, before long, would receive critical attention from the Orange

Order. The federal government would get a huge reserve of Crown land. During the debate in the House of Commons, Macdonald explained the reason: "The land could not be handed over; it was of the greatest importance to the Dominion to have possession of it, for [financing] the Pacific Railway." Cartier said the same thing more directly: because a railway was soon to be built across the prairies and on to the Pacific, "the Dominion Parliament would soon require to control the wild [Crown] lands."

Manitoba came officially into existence on July 15, 1870. Its lieutenant-governor (also that of the now-reduced North-West Territories) was Adams Archibald, a Nova Scotian with no knowledge of the West, but intelligent, tactful and astute enough to take care that francophones held important posts in his administration. He was exactly the kind of proconsul Macdonald should have appointed a year earlier.

Later, Riel would claim for himself, and eventually would be granted, the title "Father of Manitoba." In fact, a good case can be made that Manitoba was the work of several fathers, including Macdonald and Cartier and, no less, a priest named Ritchot—all but one of the quartet being French.

When the Manitoba legislation came before the Commons, Sir Stafford Northcote, the governor of the Hudson's Bay Company, was watching from the galleries. In his diary, he commented on Macdonald's speech: "He seemed feeble, and looked ill, but spoke with great skill. He makes no pretension to oratory, but is clear and dextrous in statement and gave very ingenious turns to his difficult points." The most ingenious of the arguments Macdonald used to get the legislation approved was that the generous land grants for the Métis were the same as those offered to incoming

Loyalists decades earlier. Such a reference, Northcote noted, "was of course most acceptable to the Ontario men." The bill passed easily.

Northcote's concern about Macdonald's health was justified. Heavy drinking was only part of the problem.* For weeks now, Macdonald had felt intimations of some fundamental physical problem that periodically caused intense stabs of pain in his upper back and then vanished. On May 6, while he was in his office in the Parliament Buildings, a sudden pain burst through his entire body. He stood up to ease the pressure, lost his balance and fell full length on the carpet.

---

* Perceptively, Northcote spotted the particular way Macdonald performed when on a binge, recording that, although Macdonald continued to have official papers sent to him, "he is conscious of his inability to do any important business, and he does none."

ELEVEN

First the North-West; Then the West

True Loyalty's to Motherland
And not to Canada,
The love we bear is second-hand
To any step-mama.
British Colonist, Victoria, BC

Throughout the greater part of May 1870, the Ottawa *Times* kept a six-column obituary of Macdonald set in type so it could be used at any time. In his first report to Governor General Lisgar, Macdonald's doctor, James A. Grant, confided that he saw "little hope" the prime minister would survive. Parliament adjourned for the day and a huge crowd gathered at the entrance to the East Block, where Macdonald remained in his office. They were admonished to be very quiet.

Macdonald's condition was exceedingly serious. In Grant's diagnosis, he had passed a gallstone—a "biliary calculus"—of unusual size. The excruciating pain inflicted by the stone's descent caused him to pass out and fall to the floor.* The pain reoccurred

* E.B. Biggar included a detailed account in his *Anecdotal Life of Sir John Macdonald*: "The stone would not come away, and his nervous force was exhausted by the pain. His utter prostration left the muscles relaxed, and this relaxation let the stone pass away." In fact, it may not have been a gallstone but a kidney stone, larger and thus more painful.

several times, and he was treated with morphine. The passing of a gallstone, however, is not in itself lethal. From early on, Macdonald seemed to know he was going to survive: when Lady Macdonald, attempting to ease his discomfort, rubbed some whisky onto his chest, Macdonald quipped, "Oh, do it again, it seems to do me good." When his doctor limited his lunch to a half oyster on the grounds that the country's future depended on him, Macdonald retorted, "It seems strange that the hopes of Canada should depend on half an oyster."

Right across the country, the response to the medical crisis was massive and deeply personal. Macdonald had come to be seen as Canada's champion, and as its first celebrity. Dr. Grant issued bulletins every morning and evening. The biographer E.B. Biggar compared the extent of national anxiety and sympathy to that of Americans after Lincoln's assassination. It was during this period that Macdonald's friend David Macpherson learned how close to bankruptcy Macdonald was and set out to raise a "testimonial fund" to protect him and his family in future.

Lady Macdonald rose to the challenge of restoring him to full health by her exceptional powers of organization and decision. When he could not be moved initially from the East Block, his office there became a sickroom. All the clerks in the building were ordered out so there would be

SIR JOHN A. MACDONALD.

The following despatches from Ottawa convey a slightly improved account of Sir John A. Macdonald's condition, although, as our correspondent remarks, so long as there is a liability of a return of the spasmodic symptoms Sir John cannot be said to be out of danger:

(By Special Telegraph to the Globe).

OTTAWA, May 12, 1:30 p.m.

Dr. Campbell, of Montreal, arrived this morning to take medical charge of Sir John A. Macdonald, and will remain until to-morrow.

Sir John passed a pretty good night, and a more hopeful view is taken of his state to-day.

If he should have no fresh attacks the chances are considered in his favour. He is still in a dangerous state, however.

10 p.m.

Sir John A. Macdonald has improved to-day, and there is now some hope of his recovering.

So long as he is exposed to fresh attacks in his present state he cannot be considered out of danger.

He still occupies his rooms in the eastern Departmental buildings.

Globe *report of May 13, 1870, of the medical bulletin on Macdonald's condition after he passed a "biliary calculus." For a time it was feared he might die.*

no noise to disturb his rest. Agnes was at his side every day and through every night. Once Macdonald began to recover, she moved him to the more comfortable quarters of the Speaker's office, and on good days had him taken out to the clifftop behind the Library of Parliament to breathe in the fresh air and enjoy the splendid view out over the Ottawa River.

The long illness gave Agnes the opportunity to nurse Macdonald back to health—and to bring them close together again. It's possible she may have exaggerated the risks to Macdonald's life to give herself this role. Even before he collapsed, she had worried about his health. Earlier in the session, she realized he was working so hard on the Red River file that he often ate nothing between the breakfasts and suppers she provided for him at home. So she arranged for a light lunch to be brought to his office every day.

Once his recovery was well under way, Agnes arranged a holiday for Macdonald, something he needed desperately after years of intensive nation-building but had not been capable of arranging for himself. In mid-June the government steamer, *Druid*, took them down the Ottawa River to Montreal, then chugged on down the St. Lawrence towards the cooler breezes of the Gulf.* At Charlottetown, on July 8, Macdonald was carried ashore in an easy chair and taken by carriage to a house that had been prepared for their arrival. Within a week, he began taking short walks in the grounds. Agnes allowed few visitors to call, and almost no official papers to be sent to him. The holiday stretched out to seven weeks, until they returned to Ottawa by train on September 22.

---

* Macdonald had actually received an alternative offer—to recuperate on the other side of the continent. While he was recovering and absent from public duties, three delegates from British Columbia came to Ottawa to negotiate the Crown colony's entry into Confederation. Their mission accomplished, they suggested that Macdonald go back with them to Victoria. The long rail trip to San Francisco, though, was judged too demanding for him.

The next day, Macdonald wrote to his sister Margaret, promising, "I shall not do much work for some months but act in the Govt. as a Consulting Physician." In fact, within a few days he sent off a long letter to the governor general complaining about President Grant's decision to pardon the Fenian commander John O'Neill, who had led a cross-border raid back in 1866. Macdonald predicted that O'Neill, once free, would organize another raid—which indeed he did, a year later in Manitoba. Before long, Macdonald told a friend that the gallstone attack had given him "a new lease on easier terms." Rather than the government's consulting physician, he was already back to performing as its brain surgeon.

In fact, he was never fully the same again. He was close to sixty now, and his heavy drinking and neglect of himself while a widower had taken their toll. That October, he informed an inquirer, "I have now, thank God, quite recovered from my very severe attack." A year later, though, he admitted to his friend Judge James Robert Gowan, "Of course the severe attack I had last year has left its mark on me for life." He had lost some of his resilience, and his furious bursts of energy lasted for shorter periods. References to illnesses such as colds, influenza, a "touch of cholera," an attack of "catarrah of the stomach" and an unnamed "disease" that kept him confined to the house for eleven days began to occur much more frequently in his correspondence. He allowed himself breaks and ever-longer holidays. The lion wasn't yet in winter, but he was well into the fall.

In Macdonald's absence, Cartier successfully piloted the Manitoba Bill through Parliament. After its passage, Father Noël-Joseph Ritchot stayed on in Ottawa trying to secure from Cartier and

Signs of the strain on Macdonald can be seen in this photograph, taken a year later at William Notman's studio in Ottawa.

Lisgar a written commitment to a comprehensive amnesty, only to be told yet again that, while the matter looked exceedingly promising, the decision had to be made in London. Finally, to satisfy Ritchot, Cartier composed a long petition to the Queen that, under the priest's signature, urged her to "exercise Your Royal Prerogative of mercy by an act of amnesty."

By the end of June, Ritchot was back in Red River, where he presented a balanced report on the constitutional and land allocation agreements reached in Ottawa but expressed more confidence in the imminent arrival of a comprehensive amnesty than the facts warranted. Riel had a twenty-one-gun salute fired in the priest's honour, and the provisional government formally accepted the Manitoba Act. His duty done, Ritchot retired to his parish at St. Norbert, where he lived for the rest of his life. Bishop Alexandre Taché, however, was uneasy at the continued absence of a written commitment to a comprehensive amnesty. He went to Ottawa, met with Cartier, and asked him to arrange an audience with the governor general. Lisgar was dismissive and harsh, pointing out that Thomas Scott had been "murdered in cold blood," making the issuance of an amnesty at this time "injudicious, impolitic and dangerous." Offstage, Macdonald's stance was that no action should be taken on any amnesty "until the election is over."

~

By this time, the military expedition was making its slow and determined way towards Red River. Its commander was Colonel Garnet Wolseley, one of Britain's ablest officers, later leader of the expedition up the Nile to Khartoum in a failed attempt to rescue General Charles Gordon, where he used the skills of some three hundred Canadian voyageurs to get the troops over the

Nile cataracts. He ended his career as a field marshal and a viscount* but is remembered best as the model for Gilbert and Sullivan's "Very model of a modern major-general." For the expedition to Red River, Wolseley commanded twelve hundred men, four hundred of whom were British regulars and the rest Canadian militia from Ontario and Quebec, mostly anglo-Quebecers. Militarily, Wolseley's performance was exceptional: he took his mini-army, its cannon and supplies, across the tortuous, mosquito-infested portages and bare rock westward from the Lakehead without losing a man.†

Macdonald, still recuperating in Prince Edward Island, had a personal connection to the expeditionary force. His son, Hugh John, had long aspired to a military career and pleaded to be allowed to go. Macdonald refused, no doubt because of his lifelong skepticism about military life. Hugh John, by now twenty years old and in the militia, took his case to Cartier, arguing that, if he didn't go, he would be accused of being a coward. Cartier persuaded Macdonald to relent, and Ensign Macdonald joined the 16th Company of the First Ontario Rifles. Hugh John showed some aptitude for military life. He was indifferent to hardship and soon acquired an ability to "swear a little" and bawl out the ditty then popular among young men: "Mary, mother, we believe / That without sin you did conceive / Teach, we pray thee, us believing / How to sin without conceiving." The son's views about Riel were far harsher than his father's: he got into a "violent

---

* Late in his life, Wolseley made the uncannily accurate prediction that the eventual dominant powers in the world would be the U.S. and China, the latter only needing a "Peter the Great or Napoleon to make them so."

† The U.S. government at first allowed only one of Wolseley's ships to use its canal at Sault Ste. Marie, but ended its obstruction when word was passed to Washington that the Canadian government was thinking of retaliating by barring American ships from using the Welland Canal.

Hugh John Macdonald, aged 22, at this time alienated from his father and seeking a military career rather than the legal one his father insisted on.

debate" with Macdonald, "pitch[ing] into the whole policy of the government on the Red River matter."

Hugh John saw no action, but on his return still hoped for a military career. His father dashed his hopes. He told his sister Margaret that Hugh John "has had his 'Outing' & must now go to work." When the young man returned to Toronto, he discovered that his father had arranged for him to article with Robert Harrison, a prominent lawyer. He responded by having "a great battle about smoking downstairs" with his father at their Ottawa house, winning, so he boasted to a friend, by threatening to take his books upstairs and do all his reading in his bedroom.

Once on the prairie, the expeditionary force moved quickly. At last, in pouring rain, it neared the Red River settlement and made straight for the stone hulk of Fort Garry. It was deserted. As one British officer recorded, the soldiers were "enthusiastically greeted by a half-naked Indian, very drunk." Only at the last minute had Riel realized how precarious was his position. Accompanied by his annexationist friend William O'Donoghue, he fled just before the troops reached the fort, leaving behind the warm remains of his breakfast (which soldiers promptly ate). From the comparative safety of St. Boniface, Riel watched the contingent march through the settlement, remarking to O'Donoghue, "He who ruled in

Fort Garry yesterday is now a homeless wanderer with nothing to eat but two dried fishes." The two men set out on the long journey to the border, initially on horseback and, after losing their horses, on foot. Riel was safe, but he had lost his country.

The British troops left within a week. The Canadian militiamen in Red River, particularly the Orangemen, began a long reign of terror. Two Métis were killed in suspicious circumstances, and there were constant brawls. Blame rested with the local commanders, British and Canadian, and more so with the government, which, during Macdonald's convalescence, failed to issue clear directions for maintaining peace and order or to ensure that the incoming lieutenant-governor, Adams Archibald, made it to Red River and established civilian rule before the troops arrived.

In his seminal book *The Birth of Western Canada*, historian George Stanley wrote of Red River, "The serpent in this Eden was progress."* Progress—railways, the telegraph, mechanized farming, immigrants from Ontario and later Europe, and an organized government, police and legal system—was inevitable, and neither the Métis nor the Indians could continue to live in their traditional ways. The creation of the province of Manitoba, though only "postage-stamp sized," might benefit the Métis for a time, with its official bilingualism and separate schools provided for in the Manitoba Act, but within a few years the population balance in the province would tilt against the francophones as Ontario settlers poured in. Quickening this process was the decline of the buffalo and disputes over land claims. As early as 1874, the *Manitoba Free Press* was calling for an end to bilingualism and separate schools. Despairing of their future, many Métis took

* Published in Britain in 1936, Stanley's book sold only a few hundred copies in Canada. It took a second edition, published in the 1960s, for western Canadians, gaining confidence as their economy progressed, to appreciate the magnitude of this first survey of their history.

scrip (a title to land) and promptly sold it to speculators. Red River's Métis and francophone character eroded rapidly, and Riel's people moved farther west in the hope that, there, they could still be *gens libres*. The place many of them chose, on the banks of the South Saskatchewan River, was called Batoche.

Two issues now faced Macdonald. One was that Riel, still in the United States, wanted to come back—as he did secretly, several times. In response, the Orangemen bellowed that if Riel showed himself, they would arrest him, some threatening that a bullet would end the need for any trial. The simultaneous issue was that Riel and his supporters were demanding an amnesty to exonerate him—a demand echoed overwhelmingly by the press and the public in Quebec.

Whether Macdonald ever promised an amnesty to Bishop Taché or Father Ritchot or any Riel representative was a contentious question at that time, and has been so ever since. Beyond question, Macdonald and Cartier allowed both these emissaries to believe that a general amnesty from Britain would be forthcoming. But whether one was ever actually promised is quite another matter. The two governors general who studied the matter closely—Lisgar and Dufferin—concluded that no such promise had been made. Murdoch, the senior British official involved, who discussed the matter with Ritchot, thought likewise. The evidence is often confusing: although Ritchot recorded in his diary that Murdoch had told him the British government wanted to "pass the sponge" over the matter, Murdoch later told a parliamentary inquiry he had never made "any promise or expectation of an amnesty to Riel." Cartier and Ritchot also remember their conversations quite differently. Macdonald perhaps captured what was going on by explaining to Dufferin that, in their talks, these two negotiators had been "moving in different planes: Sir George referring to the amnesty exclusive of the persons charged with the death of Scott, and Father Ritchot always including them."

No all-knowing referee exists, but there is an acceptable alternative: the *Globe*, the newspaper owned by George Brown. In 1874, when the new Liberal government established a Special Commons Committee to investigate the Red River affair, the *Globe*, though severely critical of Macdonald for his handling of the crisis, reported that he had "evidently committed himself to nothing that could be laid hold of." Rather, Macdonald's and Cartier's talks with Taché and Ritchot had fallen "short of pledging the government to grant an amnesty." For Brown's paper to conclude that Macdonald was telling the truth in so vital a matter is persuasive. In Quebec, the pro-Liberal *Le National* also reached the same conclusion.*

Macdonald's solution was to bribe Riel to stay safely out of the country. Improperly using money from the secret-service fund (so it wouldn't appear in government records), augmented by six hundred dollars contributed by Donald Smith from the Hudson's Bay Company, he got Bishop Taché to pass the funds on to the fugitive. Riel was now out of reach, both of Canadian justice and of Orange retribution. One bit of evidence suggests strongly that an amnesty was part of this arrangement. A telegram exists, disappointingly undated, in which Macdonald tells Bishop Taché: "If you can succeed in keeping him out of the way, I will make his case mine, and I will carry the point." Riel's "case" has to have been an amnesty, although Riel then broke his side of the bargain

* The most intensive studies of the issue, Philippe Mailhot's doctoral dissertation, "Ritchot's Resistance," and Jane Graham's master's thesis, "The Riel Amnesty . . . 1869–75," reach contrary conclusions.

by sneaking back across the border. However inelegant, this solution worked—for a time.

The important matters were that the Red River resistance was over, that Manitoba was now a fact, and that it and the North-West were now Canadian. The way was open, perhaps, for Macdonald's major nation-building feat—a transnational railway.

During Macdonald's extended convalescence, Canada completed its expansion all the way to the west coast. This huge addition to the nation happened with unexpected ease. A serious problem did exist, as the lines at the opening of this chapter show: the loyalty of these people was to their British motherland, not to Canada. One leading citizen, Dr. John Sebastian Helmcken, expressed it vividly during a debate about Confederation in the BC legislature in the spring of 1870. "No union on account of love need be looked for," he warned. "Love for Canada has to be acquired by the prosperity of the country, and from our children." Indeed, British Columbians called Canadians "North American Chinamen," on the grounds that they too came, made money and left with all they had earned. Canada had one fragile asset to offer: it constituted the only way British Columbians could avoid becoming American Columbians, as very few wanted to do.

In the 1860s, British Columbia consisted of Victoria and of small groups of miners, prospectors, loggers, farmers and fishermen scattered through the rest of its vast territory. Of the total European population of around twenty thousand, four thousand lived in Victoria. It was a town of some substance: its streets were macadamized and illuminated by gaslight. It was a rather somnolent place: a visiting railway engineer noted that its shopkeepers "hated to be bothered with business, especially if there was a cricket match on, and they would all shut up shop in the event of a horse match." It was intensely British, with all the paraphernalia of a governor surrounded by a quasi-court.* Yet the only regular steamship service to the outside world was operated by Americans; outgoing letters carried American stamps; and for urban shopping, its citizens had to go to San Francisco.

On the eve of Confederation, the junior minister for the colonies had concluded that it seemed impossible "we should long hold B.C. from its natural annexation" to the U.S. Yet the next year, a Confederation League was formed in Victoria, with the self-styled Amor de Cosmos as its leader. An engaging eccentric who never entered an electric streetcar for fear he would be electrocuted, de Cosmos injected energy into the Confederate cause through his newspaper, *The British Colonist*, and his passionate speeches.† More decisive yet was Macdonald's success in 1869 in persuading the Colonial Office to appoint Anthony Musgrave as the colony's new governor. Earlier in Newfoundland, Musgrave had mobilized opinion for a time in favour of Confederation, and he set out to do the same on Canada's opposite side. As in Red River, there were local annexationists, and some 150 of them signed two petitions to President Grant asking him to accept the colony into the Union. Grant, however, took no action. Macdonald had also learned an important lesson in Red River. There, he had neglected to curry favour with HBC officials; in Victoria he made certain their equivalents could look forward to jobs or pensions. And so it happened that, during the spring session of 1870, the

* One visitor waxed so enthusiastic about the local scene that he wrote that the "keen intelligence and zeal in public affairs" of Victoria's citizens "suggests a parallel in the history of some of the minor states of ancient Greece and Italy."

† De Cosmos was noted for his fondness for using the first personal singular: a newspaper had to abridge one of his speeches when its compositor ran out of the letter "I."

BC legislature agreed to send three delegates to Ottawa to negotiate terms for Confederation.

Remarkably, the terms the delegates brought to Ottawa contained no mention of a railway to connect British Columbia to Canada, but only of a telegraph line and a wagon road across the Rockies. As the delegates travelled eastwards over the Union Pacific Railroad from San Francisco, however, they came to realize that the line Macdonald had been talking about could actually be built. When they finally arrived in Ottawa and began their talks with Cartier, he urged them to ask for a railway, the whole way. In his impulsive, confident way, Cartier pledged that the entire 2,700-mile line would be built in just ten years. (So extravagant an offer could only have been made with Macdonald's approval.)

Conservative MPs all but rebelled at the financial implications of the commitment Cartier had made. Macdonald, though, was by now back in Ottawa. He asked Joseph Trutch, the delegation's leader, to come to a meeting of the Conservative caucus to assure members that the explicit terms of the railway agreement would not be insisted on. As a reward, Trutch was promised lucrative railway construction contracts and the position of lieutenant-governor. By including Aboriginals and Chinese workers in the total, Macdonald also calculated British Columbia's population at a grossly exaggerated 120,000, thereby qualifying the province for six federal seats—far larger than its Representation by Population share—and for higher payments from Ottawa.

When the House of Commons came to debate the railway commitment, the criticism from the Opposition was intense. Liberal house leader Alexander Mackenzie described the promise as "insane." To get the legislation through, Cartier had to promise that no taxes would be raised to pay for the railway; this commitment reduced the government's subsidy options to those of generous land grants to the company and, as would come at a far higher cost politically, a commitment to the CPR that it would enjoy monopoly status in the West. Macdonald's contribution was to engage in some political deviousness. He persuaded Governor Musgrave to call the BC legislature to a special session at which he asked members to approve the terms of union immediately, without any discussion. Macdonald then claimed the BC legislature's decision amounted to "a treaty," so that "any alteration [of the terms] by Canada would be almost equivalent to a refusal to admit the Colony into the Union." Faced by a *fait accompli*, the opposition fell silent. On July 20, 1871, British Columbia formally entered Confederation as its sixth province. Macdonald had built a nation coast to coast. Only on a map, though, did it look impressive. Everything depended on a railway to give the attenuated entity a spine. As Macdonald explained later, "Until this great work is finished, our Dominion will be little more than a 'geographical expression.'" Until the railway was completed to the west coast, "We have as much interest in B. Columbia as in Australia"; only once the line was finished could Canada become "a great united country with a large inter-provincial trade and a common interest."

Before that could happen, however, Macdonald had to leave for Washington, and there fight for the nation he had created.

TWELVE

Bragging Rights

I do not know whether [Macdonald] is really an able man or not; that he is one of the duskiest horses that ever ran on any course is sure.

Lord de Grey to Lord Granville, 1871

For close to three months early in 1871, Macdonald engaged in what he called "the most difficult and disagreeable work that I have ever undertaken since I entered Public Life." The reason for this uncharacteristic hint of self-pity was that he found himself ensnared in a contest with an opponent he admired immensely—Great Britain itself.

Otherwise, Macdonald's circumstances could not have been more agreeable. He was in Washington, enjoying a mild winter. He was there as one of five members of a high-level British delegation at the most important conference between Britain and the United States since the Treaty of Ghent settled the War of 1812. He was lionized socially, invited to endless receptions and dinners by prominent hostesses. While protesting the burden of such engagements in letters home,* he no doubt found most

* The period of the Washington Conference, early March to early May 1871, is the most extensively recorded of all in Macdonald's life. He wrote many letters

pleasant the attentions of bare-shouldered Southern ladies.

At one reception, Macdonald met Ulysses S. Grant (his only encounter ever with a U.S. president). They discussed horses, or at least the excellent horses of someone they both knew—Nova Scotia's lieutenant-governor, Sir Charles Hastings Doyle. At another reception, he met General William Tecumseh Sherman, whom he described as a "singularly agreeable person." He enjoyed the Washington gossip, sending home amusing snippets, such as that senators and congressmen regularly had speeches printed in the congressional record which they had actually never given but had commissioned from "professional penny-a-liners." On one occasion, two congressmen engaged the same hack, and two identical speeches were preserved for posterity even though neither man had spoken a word of them.

The Washington Conference was called to settle all the outstanding continental issues between Britain and the United States. The negotiations really began with meetings in the fall of 1869 between U.S. Secretary of State Hamilton Fish and the British ambassador, Sir Edward Thornton, to discuss the huge compensation demanded by the United States to settle the *Alabama* claims for the Union ships sunk by Confederate raiders that Britain had allowed to be built in its shipyards during the Civil War. Fish suggested that these claims could be dealt with simply by Canada being added to the Union. The dominion, he said, was "ripe for independence and the only class opposed to it were those connected with the government, the bankers and the smugglers." In response, Thornton never disagreed that annexation might well be Canada's future, although insisting that the choice was for Canadians themselves to make.

---

to Cartier, Tupper, Rose, Lisgar and many others, simply because he was away from his home town.

Macdonald knew about these talks, and he was also aware that many British officials and politicians thought the same way. Lord Monck, the former governor general, had sent him a note as he prepared to go to Washington, expressing the hope that Macdonald's "experiment" in diplomacy would show him Canada was "nearly strong enough to walk alone." As he didn't know, Prime Minister Gladstone had already suggested to his cabinet that "we could sweeten the *Alabama* question for the United States by bringing in Canada."

Macdonald's position was all but impossible. He was but one member of the British delegation and had no official mandate to defend Canada's interests. He was caught in a tug of diplomatic war in which the two players were the current global superpower and its impending successor. The team he was on had no choice but to make a deal—if necessary, at Canada's expense. Yet he was bound, legally and morally, to make the best possible case for Britain's interests rather than Canada's. He could argue his cause only with his British colleagues, and only in private, so the Americans wouldn't know that the delegation across the table was divided. Lastly, the four co-commissioners he would have to argue with were Britain's best and brightest: a future chancellor of the Exchequer, a future viceroy of India, a future permanent head of the Foreign Office and a distinguished scholar of international law.* As well, keeping the minutes was Ambassador Thornton.

The Washington Conference was the most demanding exercise in *realpolitik* Macdonald ever undertook. He had no illusions about the magnitude of the task ahead of him; for close to three months, from February 26 to May 8, he never drank one drop too many. He and Lady Macdonald stayed at the Arlington Hotel, while the

* Montague Bernard, from Oxford University, was a distant relative of Agnes Macdonald.

Five of Britain's best and brightest, and one clever, guileful Canadian, gathered for the historic Washington Conference to settle all the outstanding quarrels between a declining superpower and a rising one. From the left: Lord Tenterden, Sir Stafford Northcote, Macdonald, Lord de Grey and Ripon and Sir Edward Thornton.

British team lived in a rented house, which, as Macdonald regretfully informed Charles Tupper, was bound to be "gay enough," because the leader of the delegation, Lord de Grey and Ripon, to give him his full title, was "known to be hospitable and has brought his cook with him."

Macdonald had one key advantage over his grander colleagues: his negotiating experience was unmatched, if in national rather than international affairs, as in fact makes precious little difference. At home, he had frequently had to deal with heated disputes between mutually hostile provinces and between extremist Orange Protestants and ultramontane Catholics. As additional support, he brought with him to Washington Lady Macdonald (the other delegates were alone), two officials (the others had none) and some priceless advice from Sir Francis Hincks, his finance minister. A savvy old pro, Hincks told Macdonald that "the coming negotiation is really a game of brag, and by bragging high, you must win." Victory, that is, would go to the one who claimed most convincingly to have been victorious. To this insight, Macdonald added a deft variation of his own: besides claiming a victory he might not really have achieved, he would also claim a defeat he had not really suffered—and secure compensation for it.*

In his annual message to Congress of December 5, 1870, President Grant set a record for being rude about his northern neighbour. He complained that Canada had been behaving like a "semi-independent but irresponsible agent" and accused the Canadian government of showing a lack of friendly feeling towards the United States. There was some truth to the latter complaint: the previous summer, a number of American vessels fishing in Canadian waters had been seized by Canadian patrol boats and their captains compelled to pay fines or have their nets and gear confiscated. The unfriendliness, however, had begun below the border. In 1866, the United States had decided not to renew its decade-long cross-border Reciprocity Treaty with Canada, chiefly as retribution for the widespread pro-Southern sympathy in the country during the Civil War. Canada took this decision hard. It was widely assumed that reciprocity was the reason for the country's lively economic growth, although in fact a larger cause had

* Despite the importance of the Washington Conference to Canada—the peaceful settlement of North America into its present form, and Canada's first appearance on the international stage—the only in-depth study by a Canadian historian is in the second volume of Donald Creighton's biography of Macdonald. In contrast, American historians have written two books and numerous articles on the subject, one of which describes Macdonald as "considered by some the ablest statesman of the era."

been the demand for war materials. Macdonald, a free-trader by nature, had attempted to persuade Washington to open talks on a new treaty, but was told that Congress would never approve.

Washington, however, had overlooked the fact that the Reciprocity Treaty had secured for Americans two valuable advantages: free entry into Canada's rich fishing grounds and free passage along the St. Lawrence River. As a result of Confederation, authority over these areas now resided with Canada, not Britain. Grant's complaint that American fishing boats were being "seized without notice or warning, in violation of the custom previously prevailing," was correct, but the action was completely legal.

Grant touched on another matter crucial to Canada in his speech. He declared ominously that the time was approaching when "the European political connection with this continent will cease," but he also extended an open hand across the Atlantic. The United States, he said, was ready for a "full and friendly adjustment" of all the financial claims against Britain arising out of the Civil War and had an "earnest desire for a conclusion consistent with the honour and dignity of both nations." These comments defined the agenda of the Washington Conference.

In the early 1870s, the world's geopolitical order underwent a transformation comparable to the end of the Cold War in the 1980s. In Europe the radical event was France's crushing defeat in the Franco-Prussian War of 1870–71 and the addition to the map of a united Germany. Simultaneously, Russia showed it had fully recovered from defeat in the Crimean War by declaring that it no longer accepted demilitarization of the Black Sea. Henceforth, Britain had to concentrate its diplomatic skills and military capability on Continental Europe. The last thing it needed was a conflict in North America precipitated by some friction along the Canada-U.S. border. As the august *Times* of London put it, crossly but perceptively, "the mother country has become the dependency of the colonies." In this new situation, Canada was in no way automatically expendable; honour and prestige mattered to Britain, as did the integrity of the Empire. But it did make Canada a useful pawn to be moved about the board—and even, if circumstances required, off it.

There was, however, one countervailing factor that Macdonald was not yet aware of: the British were in the process of reinventing their Empire. Created originally by naval power at the service of trade, the Empire was now turning into a source of glory and pride for its own sake. Britain had been divided between "Little Englanders," who saw no value in the colonies, and "Big Englanders," who hungered for fame and fortune. The latter group was winning now, one telling signal being the runaway success in 1869 of Charles Dilke's book *Greater Britain*, a paean to imperialism.* The real change lay just ahead, when Disraeli, in a famous speech at the Crystal Palace in 1872, embraced the newly enfranchised urban workers as allies, on the grounds that they, like him, believed in "maintaining the greatness of the kingdom and the empire" (as they did, if only for the sake of some colour in their hard lives). There were even signs that Gladstone's new Liberal government was beginning to distance itself from its anti-colony past. All these trends would give Macdonald some unanticipated leverage in Washington.

---

* Exceptionally talented, Dilke seemed headed for the prime ministership before he was brought down by an epic sex scandal involving a mistress and her maid—perhaps even all having been in the same bed at the same time.

The tap on Macdonald's shoulder came in February 1870, after Washington and London had agreed to set up a Joint High Commission to negotiate all outstanding issues between them and, by extension, those affecting Britain's dependency, Canada. Macdonald was London's second choice, after the well-connected John Rose—a friend of Prince Edward (later Edward VII) and Hamilton Fish as well as Macdonald. But Rose was married to an American and now lived permanently in England, and so could not represent Canada. Macdonald's first reaction to the invitation was to say no; Canada's influence would be slight and, as part of the British team, he would lose any right to criticize decisions reached by the two giants. However, as he told Governor General Lisgar, without any Canadian voice in the room the outcome might be "a sacrifice of the rights of the Dominion." So he accepted his role as a joint high commissioner, or, as they called each other, a "High Joint." He admitted to Rose: "I contemplate my visit to Washington with a good deal of anxiety. If things go well, my share in the Kudos will be but small, and if anything goes wrong, I will be made the scapegoat."

The trouble began at Macdonald's first meeting with the head of the delegation, Earl de Grey and Ripon, who came to see Macdonald at the Arlington Hotel to report on a conversation he had with "a leading [American] statesman"—Fish, undoubtedly—who told him, "The United States must have the inshore [Canadian] fisheries, but were ready to pay for them." Macdonald replied that Canada would accept only reciprocity or major tariff concessions for its fisheries, but not cash. Moreover, he warned that Britain "had no right to injure posterity by depriving Canada . . . of her fisheries." De Grey responded that his informant had made it clear that Congress would never accept reciprocity. Macdonald retorted that Canada's fisheries were far superior to those of the United States and that Canada might well surpass its neighbour as a maritime power. This first encounter confirmed for the duration of the conference de Grey's pre-meeting assessment of Macdonald—that he expected to have "a great deal of difficulty in bringing him to accept moderate terms."

In addition, an issue that interested only Canada—its fisheries—had emerged as a potential deal-breaker for the entire conference. To the surprise and then the dismay of both the British and the Americans, Macdonald wouldn't shut up about them. Day by day, it became apparent that a conference staged so that two of the world's most powerful nations could settle all their outstanding differences was being hijacked by a third-order interest of a second-rank power. As was almost surreal, Canadian concerns went on to occupy close to two-thirds of the time the delegates spent around the table. An American miscalculation contributed to this outcome: its delegation had insisted that the Canadian fisheries be the first item on the agenda, taking for granted that the matter would be disposed of easily.

In fact, Macdonald almost certainly knew full well he was exaggerating the importance to Canada of its fisheries; Hincks had told him they were "a mere expense." And since he knew that reciprocity was unattainable, he was bluffing when he insisted Canada could accept only reciprocity as payment for American access to its fishing grounds. Indeed, a year earlier he had told an American, George W. Brega, that cross-border free trade "could only be effected by the pressure of American interests upon Congress." Here, to an uncanny degree, Macdonald was anticipating the Washington lobbying strategy Canada would adopt more than a century later.* At the time, he simply refused to accept that

---

* That strategy, initiated by Ambassador Allan Gotlieb in the 1980s, involved lobbying Congress on issues that concerned Canada, such as reducing acid rain, by persuading Americans sympathetic to the cause to head up the lobbying effort. Macdonald even anticipated future Canadian tactics by hiring Brega to lobby for free trade with Canada, if unsuccessfully.

Canadian concerns merited any less attention than those of Britain and the United States. Most directly, Macdonald needed no instruction about the political importance of the fisheries, given the disproportionate number of ridings in the Maritimes.

During the conference, Macdonald's great handicap was that he was the lone Canadian voice. So he invented a second voice in support of his positions. He did so by writing regularly to his cabinet members back in Ottawa (where Cartier was acting prime minister) and asking their opinions about the issues of the day. The ministers understood that he wanted replies that could be shown to the other British delegates, in particular that they should instruct him to hold firm on key issues. Macdonald could then tell his British colleagues he had no choice but to follow the directions given him by his government. On one occasion, de Grey solicited support from his superior, Foreign Secretary Lord Granville, for his insistence that Macdonald's stand on Canada's fisheries not be allowed to bring the entire conference to a halt. Macdonald concocted a directive from his cabinet that instructed him to write to Colonial Secretary Lord Kimberley, asking whether Canada had the right to make decisions about its own fisheries. Kimberley, unaware he was being lured into a trap, answered forthrightly, "His Majesty's Government never had any intention of disposing of the fisheries of Canada without her consent."*

Macdonald called this response, which directly contradicted the parallel exchange between de Grey and Granville, a "floorer"; he then set out to use it to gain for himself what amounted to a veto over the entire conference. He was able to do so because

* The exclusively Canadian grounds extended only to the three-mile limit, and there was the usual haggling over whether these encompassed all the sea within bays whose headlands were far apart.

Britain and the United States had agreed to "bundle" all the outstanding issues together, so their alternatives were either to agree on everything or on nothing. The British team, recognizing that the saltwater fisheries belonged to Canada no differently from the way the inland, freshwater ones did, accepted defeat. On March 20, Granville instructed de Grey that any deal reached on the fishery "must be subject to ratification by the Canadian Parliament." A mere colony had won a veto over the outcome of a bilateral conference involving two of the world's most powerful nations. But this de facto veto was sharply double-edged. Should Macdonald actually shut down the conference for the sake of better terms for the fishery, he and Canada would pay a fearful price: unflagging hostility from both Britain and the United States. The pair would promptly have staged a second conference with no Canadian present.

From this point on, the Washington Conference became two conferences. The first involved the British-American negotiations; here, the parties reached important decisions with commendable speed, such as that international arbitrators should determine the scale of British reparations and, in return, that the United States would accept an expression of regret in place of an apology from Britain. The second conference pitched Macdonald against all the other delegates, though mostly it involved only Macdonald and de Grey.

Initially, Macdonald's opinion of de Grey was positive. He wrote to Lisgar, "He is quick in perception, cool in judgment, of imperturbable temper . . . [and] much liked as being frank and cordial." Indeed, de Grey was widely regarded as capable and decent. Although to the manor born, he had become a Christian Socialist. Later, as grand master of the Freemasons of England, he caused a sensation by converting to Roman Catholicism. After Washington, he won the ultimate Imperial prize as viceroy of India.* The difficulties between him and Macdonald were essentially that de Grey was seeking peace with the United States, while Macdonald was seeking victory over it.

Governor General Lord Lisgar, who broke all the rules of diplomatic and gentlemanly conduct by leaking to British delegates at the Washington Conference the contents of Macdonald's private letters to his cabinet in Ottawa.

Macdonald's obduracy led de Grey on one occasion to step out of character—he resorted to a bribe. During a conversation with Macdonald, as de Grey later recalled, "the words 'Privy Councillor' somehow escaped my lips." If Macdonald would stop ranting about the fishery, intimated de Grey, he could gain the honour of becoming the first colonial admitted to the Privy Council of Britain. The bribe worked—but only halfway. A year later, Macdonald made sure that the departing governor general, Lord Lisgar, passed on to his successor, Lord Dufferin, full information about the matter. At the conference, though, he continued on about the fishery.

On April 15, de Grey wrote to Lord Granville to let him know that, while Macdonald "professes to be unable to take a step without his colleagues in Ottawa, we learn from Ottawa that he has things in his own hands and has full discretion to act." Macdonald's ruse had been found out. The manner of the discovery was unfair and, more shocking yet, ungentlemanly. It turned out that Governor General Lisgar had been secretly sending to the British delegates copies of all Macdonald's letters to the

* While viceroy, de Grey won a war in Afghanistan.

cabinet and their replies—correspondence that had been sent to him because they concerned decisions being made by "his" ministers. Macdonald's co-commissioners now read what he really thought of them, such as that they were easily "squeezable" by the Americans and that "they seem to have only one thing on their minds, that is to go home to England with a Treaty in their pockets settling everything no matter at what cost to Canada." Lisgar, in his covering letter to de Grey, described Macdonald as "a huckster" who had "scarcely a shadow of consideration for imperial interests." Granville, more experienced in international affairs, appreciated that Macdonald was just doing what his job as prime minister required. He wrote to Gladstone that "Sir John A. Macdonald seems to have more to say for himself than his brother Commissioners admit." Even Gladstone agreed that Britain should not "be hustled about" by the United States on the fisheries.

Macdonald negotiated a compromise with de Grey: he agreed that the Americans could enter Canada's fishing grounds in return for a cash payment, but the term would last for only ten years. The amount of the payment would be decided through arbitration by an international panel. Here, Macdonald was overplaying his hand, and Fish, who at one time had suggested duty-free entry for coal, salt and lumber, withdrew the offer on the grounds that the Senate would never agree to it.

In fact, the fisheries were but a sideshow for Macdonald. The issue that really mattered to him was compensation from the United States for the Fenian raids. Although they had been defeated without great difficulty, these cross-border raids had inflicted a heavy cost in blood and property damage, and Canadians' feelings about them were similar to those of Americans about the *Alabama* claims. Compensation for the Fenian raids was the principal reason Macdonald had agreed to come to Washington.

But the issue of American compensation for these raids was

not even on the agenda. Either by incompetence or by calculation, the British had neglected to put the item on the list. They guessed, no doubt correctly, that the Grant administration would never accept losing face by admitting that its predecessors—Lincoln above all—had been at fault.

When de Grey finally told Macdonald there would be no American compensation for the Fenian damages, Macdonald realized that the country he loved had all along planned to use Canada as a sacrificial lamb, securing better terms on the *Alabama* claims by putting no pressure on the Americans to compensate Canada for the damages done by the Fenians. Still, continued de Grey, Canada could walk away with a reasonably full pocket. De Grey had done this by coming over to the Arlington hotel after church on Sunday, April 16, to tell Macdonald, as he later reported to Cartier in a confidential letter, "he was in a position to inform me, in strictest confidence . . . that Her Majesty's Government would, if all other matters were settled and it were not to be considered as a precedent, consent to pay Canada a sum of money [for Fenian damages] if the United States refused to do so." So the lamb was at least to be reasonably well fed.

De Grey's objective was comparatively straightforward: now that all the British-American issues had been resolved, he wanted to get a treaty signed and then ratified by the three legislatures—in Westminster, Washington and Ottawa. He needed Macdonald to pledge publicly to use his immense influence to ensure that the Parliament in Ottawa actually passed the treaty. Macdonald's aims were more complex: he still wanted a better deal for Canada's fisheries; even more, he wanted the British government to declare publicly that it would compensate Canada for the Fenian raids.

So began an elaborate and a prolonged diplomatic dance. Macdonald fired off a letter to de Grey declaring it was his strong conviction that the fisheries terms "will not be accepted by

Canada" and that he would find them difficult to justify or defend in the Canadian Parliament. The British delegates "all made speeches" at him in response, but he didn't back down. The heat increased during the first two weeks in April, until de Grey told Macdonald sternly that "a failure in the settlement of the Fishery question would involve a complete disruption of the negotiations." There were many in England, he warned, who would rejoice were Canada to confirm that "the Colonies were a danger and a burden." In return, Macdonald told de Grey that he was considering absenting himself from the conference, thereby letting the Americans know he doubted that the Canadian Parliament would sanction the treaty. De Grey retorted that he found such words "a grave statement to make." Two days later, Macdonald wrote to a Montreal friend that events over the next few days might be the "entering wedge" of a severance between Canada and Britain.

Having gone to the brink, Macdonald now took a step back. He downplayed his concerns about the fishery, asked that his reservations about the deal be "unmistakably and publicly affirmed" and agreed to present all the other aspects of the treaty to Parliament. Tempers began to cool—somewhat. As the conference neared its end, Macdonald wrote to de Grey emphasizing "the expediency of the Fenian matter being taken up without delay and settled by H.M. Government." In his last letter to Macdonald in Washington, however, de Grey cautioned, "You would incur a responsibility of the gravest kind if you were to withhold your signature."

De Grey had, in fact, made only a private verbal promise to Macdonald to compensate Canada for its Fenian losses. Late in July, two months after the conference ended, Macdonald felt sufficiently troubled by this to write to Lisgar: "I cannot for a moment suppose the British Government will hesitate to carry out the assurance given to me by Lord de Grey at Washington." He did not know that, at the end of the conference, de Grey had written to Lord Granville to say: "If he [Macdonald] gets the consent of the Canadian Parliament to the stipulations of the Treaty for which it is required, he will deserve reward, but if he does not, he ought to get nothing."

The Washington Conference ended on May 8, 1871. Both sides gave the other lavish dinners, and the Freemason lodges in Washington entertained the two British delegates who were members.

On the key issue of the *Alabama* claims, Britain and the United States agreed to set up a five-member international arbitration panel to determine the amount of the payments.* Britain made no apology for the *Alabama* affair, but did express regrets. The Canada-U.S. fishery dispute was settled when the Americans agreed to pay for entry for a ten-year term, with a three-member international panel to decide the amount of the payment. (The panel's decision, made public in 1877, gave Canada a totally unexpected award of $5.5 million. The United States was so annoyed by this settlement that it cancelled the deal when it expired in 1878.)

The conference's great achievement was to end the long history of hostilities between Britain and the United States in North America, to establish normal relations and, once time passed, to make it possible for a special relationship to develop between them. Canada gained the fisheries deal, the potential of British compensation for its Fenian losses and, because of the veto it possessed in the form of its Parliament's right to ratify the treaty, implicit U.S. acceptance of Canada's autonomous existence. The American

* Each side was to appoint one member of the arbitration panel, while the emperor of Brazil, the king of Italy and the president of Switzerland would each appoint their choices.

annexationist movement faded away, although the "ripe fruit" doctrine would linger for decades, and the power and allure of America would always affect the course of Canadian national development. But the decision on the existential choice in Canadian life—whether to continue as Canadians or to become Americans—would be made henceforth by Canadians, not by Americans.

Before leaving Washington, Macdonald stepped back to give himself a wider view. He understood the scale of the achievement: "It seems to me that if all the rest of the World were at War, Great Britain and the United States ought to be friends," he wrote in one letter home. As for Canada, "With a Treaty therefore once made, Canada has the game in her own hands. All fear of war will have been averted." In another letter, he added the cautionary note "I am no believer in eternal friendships between Nations."

After the delegates returned home, only two matters remained to be resolved: Britain's promise to pay Canada compensation for the damages caused by the Fenian raids, and Macdonald's promise to persuade the Canadian Parliament to ratify the treaty. The diplomatic dance between de Grey and Macdonald continued, and neither issue would be settled until early in 1872.

Macdonald had set the tone for the continuing dispute when he signed the treaty in Washington. He walked over to the table, picked up the pen and said to Fish, who was standing nearby, "Well, here go the fisheries."

This comment was a gross and deliberate exaggeration. In fact, the Halifax *Times*' judgment on the new fisheries arrangements was, "We have fished for twelve years alongside the United States, and were not ruined." The *Globe*, predictably, did fulminate that Macdonald had shown himself to be "but a poor parody of a statesman" who had "giv[en] away Canada's fisheries . . . asking nothing in return," and who, by failing to secure any compensation for the Fenian raids, of which no announcement had been made, had left Canadians "insulted, injured and outraged."

In fact, that was exactly the response Macdonald wanted. The *Globe*, and George Brown, knew nothing about de Grey's offer of compensation provided that Macdonald navigated the treaty through Parliament. The criticism of the fisheries deal, which Macdonald straight-facedly described to de Grey as a "universal storm," simply strengthened his hand in negotiating the Fenian payment. As for getting Parliament's approval, Macdonald calculated that the best way to do it was by doing nothing. He instructed Conservative newspapers to make no comment at all about the treaty, pro or con. He himself remained silent on the issue, initially to Brown's surprise, though the publisher gradually began to suspect that Macdonald was up to something.

No one was more unsettled by all of this than de Grey. He told his minister, Lord Granville, "I do not know whether he is really an able man or not; that he is one of the duskiest horses that ever ran on any course is sure, and that he has been playing his own game all along with unswerving steadiness, is plain enough."

While tacking back and forth, Macdonald knew exactly where he had to go. He wanted to get the promise of compensation for the Fenian raids made public and use it to secure Parliament's approval for the treaty, including the fisheries arrangements. He didn't know, though, that there was a large obstacle in his way. One of the letters he had written from Washington to his ministers in Ottawa, which Lisgar had passed on to the British delegation, contained the damning passage "Our true policy is to hold out to

England that we will not ratify the treaty . . . [so that] we can induce to a liberal offer."

This sentence soon provoked righteous fury in London. "Knavery is not too-harsh a word," said Colonial Secretary Kimberley. Gladstone was as angry: "I hope the 'liberal' offer which Sir John Macdonald intends to conjure from us will be *nil*." That is, no parliamentary approval, no payment.

At one time, Macdonald came close to a public breach. He warned Lisgar that, if Britain made the payment conditional on earlier parliamentary approval, "I should consider [this] a breach of the understanding and would at once abandon any attempt to reconcile my colleagues or the people of Canada" to the treaty.

Luck intervened. In the summer of 1871, British Columbia entered Confederation. To get it aboard, the government had to promise not just a transcontinental railway, but an immediate start to it and its completion in just ten years. Macdonald now had an inspired idea (or had it suggested to him): rather than a cash payment for the Fenian damages, London should agree to guarantee a loan—a commitment far easier to get through the Westminster Parliament. Kimberley wrote to Gladstone that the British government should not "make the assent of the Canadian Parliament to the Treaty a condition of our payment." The prime minister agreed, and so advised Queen Victoria. On January 22, 1872, Macdonald informed the governor general that the treaty would be placed before Parliament at its coming session and that assent was assured because Britain would announce in advance its intention to guarantee a £2.5 million loan to be spent by Canada on railways and canals.

Macdonald had played a trump card in his latest tournament of "the long game." Right afterwards, he had to pick up another weak hand. An election could not be delayed for long, the last one having been held in the fall of 1867, now close to the five-year statutory limit. The omens could not have been darker. The Conservatives had just lost Ontario—the country's richest and most populous province.

THIRTEEN

Railway First; Election Next

> The Government is obliged to stipulate that no foreigner is to appear as a shareholder. . . . The shares taken by you and our other American friends, will therefore have to stand in my name for some time.
>
> Hugh Allan to George Cass, summer 1872

From one perspective, 1872 was an excellent time for Macdonald to be asking Canadians what they thought of his government. Thanks to a worldwide boom, the economy was in excellent condition. All other aspects were decidedly unpromising. Many fishermen were upset that, as a consequence of the Washington Treaty, Americans would soon be back in their inshore waters. Macdonald's refusal to disallow New Brunswick legislation to end public funding of separate schools for Roman Catholics had stirred discontent in Quebec, no matter that Cartier warned publicly it could be used as a precedent to justify federal intervention in Quebec's own education system. Cartier himself seemed to be behaving strangely, as if suffering from some mysterious physical weakness. The most serious setback had happened in Macdonald's own province of Ontario, and with him partly responsible for it.

Since Confederation, Ontario had been run by Macdonald's Conservative ally and near-namesake, John Sandfield Macdonald, often known as "Little John" to distinguish him. A thoroughly decent man, he performed his duties as premier competently and with excellent intentions, but was too deferential to "Big John." Many Ontarians regarded him more as the representative of Ottawa than of themselves. Early in 1871, the Liberal leader, Edward Blake, capitalized on the furore Louis Riel had unleashed by his execution of Thomas Scott by moving a resolution declaring the act "cold-blooded murder" and demanding that "every effort should be made to bring to trial the perpetrators of this great crime." Badly rattled, Sandfield Macdonald called a snap election. He chose not to use a $1.5 million surplus generated by the good times to buy votes across the province—to the intense disgust of John A. "It is vexatious to see how Sandfield threw away his game," he told a friend, but he was unable to do anything to save his ally, because he was still at the conference in Washington. Sandfield Macdonald won the election, but narrowly, and one by one his "loose fish" wriggled away to the other side. In December 1871, he was forced to hand over the government to Blake.

Blake used his authority as premier to intensify his contest with Macdonald by again using Riel as a scapegoat. In February 1872, he moved a second motion deploring the fact that "no effectual steps have been taken to bring to justice the murderers of Thomas Scott," and followed up by issuing a five-thousand-dollar reward for Riel's capture.

At this point, the behaviour of Riel and William O'Donoghue, his one-time key supporter, seemed to give some substance to Blake's histrionics. Macdonald had got Riel out of the country by forwarding him funds through Bishop Taché. In mid-1871, Riel slipped back to his own home in the hamlet of St. Vital, living there while protected by his faithful Métis. Then O'Donoghue mustered up a cross-border raid by a sad group of forty Fenians—the last of the Fenian raids. These Irishmen were easily apprehended by

American soldiers. In the meantime, Riel had called upon Métis horsemen to guard the border. Lieutenant-Governor Adams Archibald went out to thank them for their loyalty, shaking the hand of each man—including Riel's. Archibald's well-intentioned but unwise gesture was reported in the Ontario press, along with the fact that Riel was back in Canada. In the minds of many Ontario voters, it became a fixed fact that Macdonald, to win votes in Quebec, was conniving to help Riel to escape justice for Scott's "murder."

Then something new and encouraging arrived on Macdonald's desk—a specific, and credible, proposal to build the transcontinental railway that he and Cartier had promised to British Columbia.

~

Suggestions for a coast-to-coast line were not new: Lord Durham had suggested it in his famous report of 1839, and in 1851 Joseph Howe had told a Halifax audience, "Many in the room will live to hear the whistle of a train in the passes of the Rocky Mountains." Not until 1862, however, was the first systematic study done. Its author was Sandford Fleming, then a thirty-five-year-old surveyor and engineer, who later became famous as the inventor of standard time. Entirely by himself, he calculated everything, even to the numbers of railway ties and telegraph poles, and estimated the total cost at a hundred million dollars— astoundingly close to the actual figure. By 1871, Fleming was still a lonely prophet, though the first such scheme, the Union Pacific line to California, had by now been completed. To turn Fleming's plan into reality, Macdonald needed someone who possessed either a great deal of money or partners able to raise it.

Railway financing in the nineteenth century was similar to the dot-com boom of the late twentieth century. Some entrepreneurs made fortunes; many more went bankrupt. The particular difficulty was that new lines could not make money until they were completed from end to end. In fact, profits were made principally out of insider trading and land speculation, rather than from operating the railway company. The critical step was to secure a monopoly licence from the government—most commonly through bribery. One American promoter, Jason "Jay" Gould, bested his rivals by distributing $500,000 in used bills from a huge portmanteau in a single day at the State House in Albany. In Canada, pre-Confederation premier Allan MacNab had famously said, "All my politics is railroads."

Remarkably, given that the topic would dominate his thinking for the greater part of his post-Confederation term in office, Macdonald at this time knew little about railways. He had never been a member of a syndicate, owned any railway shares or, unlike Cartier, worked as a solicitor for a major railway company. All he really knew about a transcontinental railway was that it had to be built—to give the overextended and underpopulated Canada a spine.

Initially, Macdonald groped along much as he had at the beginning of the Red River affair, and he made mistakes. The most effective way of minimizing Canada's daunting geographical problems—the barren Precambrian Shield and the high Rocky Mountains—was for the undertaking to be executed by a consortium of established companies, thereby spreading the costs and multiplying the potential traffic. Just such an array of companies already existed on both sides of the border. In Canada, there was the Grand Trunk Railway, its main line stretching from Quebec City to Sarnia. In the United States there was the Northern Pacific Railway, now completing its line from Duluth to St. Paul, and planning to go all the way to Puget Sound. The two lines could easily be merged into an international "road," with the Grand Trunk stretching out to Duluth, and the Northern Pacific running feeder-lines into the Canadian West from its line near the border.

This solution was so tempting that, when Macdonald received the first proposal, he reacted enthusiastically rather than analytically. The letter arrived early in February 1871. It came from Hugh Allan in Montreal, the owner of a vast and highly successful business empire. Macdonald quickly assured Allan that the government was "in no way connected with any Company or Companies" and would not make any decisions before Parliament approved the enabling legislation. "Meanwhile," he continued, "I see no objection to the Capitalists of Canada or of England (or of the United States for that matter) joining together & making proposals for the construction of the Road."

Macdonald's purpose was to encourage Allan to get involved in his project. By that casual inclusion of the United States in his sentence, he had given Allan a green light to go ahead and create the kind of railway company he already had in mind: an American-Canadian consortium in which control would reside south of the border, home to most of the money and to men who knew so much more about building and running railways. Inevitably, it would become the same as conjoining an elephant and a mouse. In his first step in pursuit of his national dream, Macdonald had stumbled badly.

There were three key players in Allan's scheme. The first was the robber baron, Hugh Allan himself. Scottish-born and a member of a shipping family, he would come to earn an annual income of half a million dollars (today, an incredible fifteen million dollars, and in fact more in real terms, since there was no income tax). His father emigrated to Montreal in 1816, when the young Allan was six; at thirteen, he left school to work in the family business. By the age of twenty-five, he was a partner in a large import company, and soon branched out himself into shipping, where he made early use of the new technologies of screw propellers and iron hulls. Once he became interested in a possible transcontinental line, he bought up several small railways radiating out from Montreal. Just about everything Allan touched turned to gold—telegraphs, railways, elevators, insurance companies, tobacco products, rolling mills, coal and iron mines; at his peak, he was president of sixteen companies. He was hard, self-contained and secretive, treating politicians and press and public with contempt and his employees like serfs, but also shrewd enough to learn fluent French. He built a gigantic house, Ravenscrag, high on Mount Royal, with a ballroom that accommodated several hundred guests.* Though a devout churchgoer, he gave almost nothing to charity. On one occasion when he was at Macdonald's home for dinner, Lady Macdonald asked him for a donation for her church, remarking, "You can't take it with you." From the far end of the table, Macdonald chimed in softly, "It would soon melt if he did."

Sir Hugh Allan, Canada's richest and most powerful businessman, who sold out to American railway promoters, sold out George-Étienne Cartier, sold out Macdonald. He then sold out his American partners. The result was the "Canadian Pacific Scandal."

Next, the tycoon, the banker Jay Cooke, described as a "red-white-and-blue huckster who could sell anything he put his mind

---

* Today, the Allan Memorial Institute, a psychiatric hospital and research centre.

to, with a dedication bordering on religious fervour."* Cooke was deeply religious, holding daily prayers for his family and staff in his enormous mansion in Philadelphia. Unlike Allan, he gave a tithe of his income to charity. In 1861, when Cooke was forty years old, he opened his own private banking house. He did spectacularly well during the Civil War, when he marketed war bonds, eventually selling $830 million worth. Afterwards, he caught the railway bug, became an agent for the Northern Pacific and boosted the idea of using Duluth as the base for a Canadian-American line to the Pacific. He was also an ardent annexationist and suggested that the best way to add the North-West to the United States was "the quiet emigration over the border of trustworthy men and their families." He was prepared to spend a great deal of money to assist manifest destiny.

Lastly, the Canadian-American George W. McMullen, who, born in Picton, Ontario, to well-off parents, moved to richer pastures below the border in his early twenties and ended up in Chicago as a successful businessman and owner of the *Chicago Evening Post*. He was inquisitive and inventive, as his later attempts to grow aphrodisiacs and build a long-distance cannon showed. In the spring of 1871, McMullen travelled to Ottawa in search of new business and heard talk of the transcontinental railway project. In subsequent meetings in Chicago and New York, he recruited prominent Americans, among them Jay Cooke.

In July 1871, just before British Columbia entered Confederation, McMullen brought several of his associates to Ottawa to meet Finance Minister Francis Hincks, who introduced them briefly to Macdonald. When the group returned, they

---

* The main sources for this chronicle are Alistair Sweeny's *George-Étienne Cartier*, Pierre Berton's *The National Dream*, W. Kaye Lamb's *History of the Canadian Pacific Railway*, and Leonard Irwin's *Pacific Railways and Nationalism in the Canadian-American Northwest, 1845–1873*.

assured Hincks they were ready to add prominent Canadians to their board of directors. Hincks was interested, particularly when they explained that free stock would be distributed to board members and that the syndicate was seeking "such persons as you think proper . . . from personal or political considerations." Hincks then travelled to Montreal to brief Allan on the opportunity.

In fact, Allan already knew about it; months earlier, Cooke's brother and business partner, Henry, had described it to him. Hincks let the group know that he favoured a scheme for a joint American-Canadian company, although the cabinet had not yet discussed it. Anyway, Allan had in his files Macdonald's telegram suggesting that American capitalists might join with their Canadian kin in the project. In September, Allan met with McMullen in Montreal and they agreed to form a company predominantly owned by the Northern Pacific, but nominally a joint venture. Allan would receive a large block of stock and forty thousand dollars (later upped to fifty thousand) for him to dispense, as McMullen put it, "among persons whose accession would be desirable."

Cooke was ecstatic at this breakthrough. He wrote to his brother, "The Canadian government is extremely friendly . . . and they will do all they can to connect with us at Manitoba and other points." He refined his plans somewhat, so the Northern Pacific would build eastwards from Duluth to Sault Ste. Marie, crossing into Canada there and reaching Montreal over Canadian lines (some of them Allan's). Westwards from Duluth, a "Saskatchewan Division" would run from Winnipeg to the Rockies, followed by a "Columbia Division" above the forty-ninth parallel. By the fall of 1871, Cooke was so sure of success he issued a new prospectus for bond sales, describing how the Northern Pacific was about to become "in all essentials an international enterprise" for "the vast and fertile portion of British America which extends from Winnipeg to the Rocky Mountains."

Macdonald's only formal meeting with Allan and his American backers was held in Ottawa in July 1871. They asked him about a charter for the Canadian portion of their international railway and were shocked when, in response, he said only that the government would consider all the proposals it received. Macdonald was now aware of the scale of the Americans' ambitions. As soon as they left his office, he wired John Rose in London and instructed him to spread word among the influential press that "the Dominion is about to construct Pacific Railway through British Territory." This telegram was the first clear statement that the Pacific Railway would be a Canadian line right across the West rather than just a feeder for the Northern Pacific. Still unclear was whether it had to be all-Canadian or whether some Canadian-American combination would be acceptable. In a letter to Rose, Macdonald noted that "[Allan] is connected with strong men in the United States," his only expression of concern being that the Americans might "ask a larger subsidy & more land than Parliament will be likely to grant them."

The crucial decision on the national composition of the company—whether joint or exclusively Canadian—had still to be addressed. Two days before Christmas, Macdonald wrote to a journalist friend and reassured him, "You may depend upon it we will see that Canadian interests are fully protected and that no American ring will be allowed to get control." He had at last stopped groping around and made the distinction between actual "control" of the project and some American financial involvement in it—this latter option being all but inevitable given that most financial houses in London were underwriters of the rival Grand Trunk, so the alternative of minority British funding was unlikely.

No documentary evidence exists to explain why and how Macdonald reached this decision. No doubt the approaching election was one consideration, because being seen as deferential to Americans could provoke a backlash. The main answer probably lies among Macdonald's own instincts. The specific purpose of the railway was to make certain that Canada would not become America. He knew, though, that any joint railway would inevitably become overwhelmingly American. Only if the company was predominantly Canadian could the railway line make Canada into a self-sustaining nation. Once Macdonald focused on the choices before him, there was no other conclusion he could come to. The best secondary evidence that his thinking followed this line is that he would soon insist that not only the company had to be all-Canadian but also the line itself. Despite the huge costs, it would have to follow a route across the wasteland of the Precambrian Shield above Lake Superior, rather than dipping down and reaching the West by way of the much gentler territory below the border.

The Americans had to be eased out of running the railway syndicate. For this to happen, though, Canadians would have to replace them. As Macdonald put it in one letter, "a feeling of fear arose in Ontario, especially in Toronto, that the Pacific Railway might get into American hands . . . and that in the construction of the Board, the interests of Ontario might be forgotten, or neglected."

Macdonald's choice was a man with shining political appeal. A leading Toronto financier, David Macpherson was a Conservative supporter and the personal friend who had raised the "testimonial trust" that protected Lady Macdonald and Mary. Macpherson agreed to assemble a syndicate to join with Allan, saying that Allan's original joint scheme "would place our great Transcontinental Railway forever under the absolute control of our rivals, our American neighbours."

By April 1872, Macdonald was able to inform Rose that Allan would be obliged to abandon his "Yankee confreres." As a consequence, he predicted, "we shall have a strong Company of Canadian capitalists who will undertake and finish the Railway." The solution was sensible, but it was already out of date. By now, Cooke and the other Americans had signed a secret agreement with Allan to set up a Canadian Pacific railway company in which the only important Canadian would be Allan himself. Of the $10 million issued to the founders, Allan would receive $1.5 million. His principal contribution would be to secure a charter for the company from Parliament. Other than in outward appearance, this company would be wholly American. As Cooke explained to one of his partners, American involvement was being kept secret because of "the political jealousies in the Dominion," and there was to be "no hint of the Northern Pacific connection."

As an additional complication, Macpherson could not overcome his mistrust of Allan. After a hostile meeting between them in Montreal, he returned to Toronto and convinced his associates to set up a rival company, the Inter-Oceanic Railway. It's quite possible, as Pierre Berton suggests in *The National Dream*, that Macpherson organized this company only as a dummy to be sold later to Allan's syndicate for a quick profit—a trick he had played once before. What is certain is that, once Allan actually won the huge railway contract, several members of Macpherson's syndicate pleaded to be taken on as directors; the Americans, themselves no slouches at such tactics, were shocked at such crassness.

Macdonald had failed to achieve the Montreal-Toronto railway alliance he had counted on. The project itself, though, kept on going. Allan reassured Macdonald that he had at last purged himself of his American partners. If Macdonald had seen two letters Allan sent out that summer, his confidence would have evaporated. One was to McMullen: "Yesterday, we entered into an agreement by which the Government bound itself to form a company of Canadians only. . . . Americans are to be carefully

To the very, very rich belong the spoils: Hugh Allan's Ravenscrag mansion in Montreal, with a ballroom designed for several hundred guests with ample room for servants to circulate.

excluded, in the fear that they will sell it to the Northern Pacific. But I fancy we can get over that some way or other." The other was to the Northern Pacific's incoming president, General George Cass: "The Government is obliged to stipulate that no foreigner is to appear as a shareholder, so as to avoid [a] cry of selling ourselves to the Northern Pacific. . . . The shares taken by you and our other American friends, will therefore have to stand in my name for some time."

By now, Allan was lying as barefacedly to his American partners as to the Canadian government. In addition to the impenetrable arrogance of a self-made multi-millionaire, he possessed the sublime self-confidence of someone who had never experienced failure. For all his talents, Allan knew nothing of politics or of public life; neither did he understand Macdonald. So he forged ahead obsessively, straight to disaster.

For Macdonald, the election was now all that mattered. He would not be able to announce any grand pan-Canadian railway consortium, but only enact legislation to create a Canadian Pacific Railway company to do the job—its board members and owners still unnamed. To win the election, he would need some luck. It turned up, taking form right in front of him, waiting for him to pick it up.

FOURTEEN

Gristle into Bone

The advent of the Grits to power just now would shake Confederation to its very centre.

Macdonald to Archbishop Thomas Connolly of Halifax

The election of 1872 worried Macdonald more than any he had waged since he'd first made it to the top as premier back in 1857. He showed his uneasiness by delaying the election to the very end of the five-year limit—and, even more sharply, by his manner of drinking. Instead of just binging, he was now quaffing it down consistently and heavily. Alexander Campbell, his former law partner and now a minister close to him, reported later that, during the actual election campaign, Macdonald "from the time he left Kingston after his own election . . . kept himself more or less under the influence of wine . . . and really has no clear recollection of what he did on many occasions."

Secondary factors would have heightened his sense of anxiety. The gallstone attack a year earlier had given Macdonald clear intimations of his mortality. He had survived the crisis, but also acquired a new fragility. In June 1872, in a letter to Rose, he admitted: "I only wish that I was physically a little stronger. However,

Mary Macdonald at the age of three. All hope of recovery was now gone: she could not feed herself, clothe herself, turn over in bed or stand. Visitors unaware of her condition would watch astonished as the prime minister massaged her shrunken limbs to try to cause the blood to circulate.

I think I will not break down in the Contest." His home life had changed profoundly. Each time he returned home from the office he went straight over to his daughter, Mary, now three, picked her up, wrapped himself around her, told her tales and made her laugh. But Mary's shrunken form and oversized head could not but signal that he had entered some kind of a hospital. As well, the early ease and intimacy between himself and Agnes had passed. One reason Macdonald spent such long hours in his office was that he could escape there from his sombre home into the rough and genial male company of the political arena; Parliament Hill served him as a sort of second home.

His actual political concerns were sizeable. As he wrote Archbishop Thomas Connolly of Halifax, "The advent of the Grits to power just now would shake Confederation to its very centre, and perhaps break it up." This analysis of the state of the nation was transparently self-serving. But from Macdonald's perspective, what was at risk was a critical and exceptionally difficult phase of nation-building, one that could make the nation or break it.

He had, in his first term, achieved the goal of stretching the nation from sea to sea so that, at least on maps, it now looked to be as substantial as the United States. Most of this impression was little more than a dream, and a good deal of bluff: in practical terms, British Columbia, the newest addition, was as distant from Canada "as Australia," as Macdonald himself had said; and the

North-West was peopled by Aboriginals and Métis, but scarcely any settlers. Canada was really no more than "a geographical expression." To become an actual country, it had to have a spine—a railway that could bind Canadians together and attract immigrants to start filling up the vast empty spaces. Yet, in Parliament's last session before the election, all that Macdonald had been able to do was pass legislation setting up the shell of a transnational railway company.

What Canada needed, Macdonald was convinced, was time. The Liberals had said nothing good about bringing British Columbia into Confederation or about his attempts to create a railway company to build a backbone of steel across the country. In no way did they wish to harm the nation, but their vision was modest. Blake viewed Confederation as a "compact" among the provinces rather than as a whole larger than its parts—that absurdly ambitious vision that Macdonald had in mind.

Time was the magic ingredient. The country needed it; Macdonald needed it; and the country needed him—his love of power justifying that last logical jump. Macdonald expressed this view most explicitly in another letter to Rose, on March 5, 1872: "I am, as you may fancy, exceedingly desirous of carrying the election again; not with any personal object, because I am weary of the whole thing, but Confederation is only yet in the gristle, and it will require five years more before it hardens into bone."

"Gristle into bone" became his war cry. In fact, gristle (cartilage) cannot harden into bone, the two being quite different substances. Macdonald knew that perfectly well, but it was an effective metaphor. Over time, he would alter the amount of time needed—a decade, a quarter-century, once as long as a century—before Canada could mature into a real nation rather than remaining "a prospective nation," as one Canada First nationalist put it. And over time, this would be exactly what happened. Macdonald's particular contribution was to win for Canadians the time for their country to mature into a second, distinctive North American nation.

First, however, he had to win the election.

No Canadian politician, either afterwards or before, has ever done better in elections than Macdonald. From Confederation on, he would compete in seven and win six. The core reason was simple: most people liked him a lot, both for himself and in comparison with anyone else available.

Ordinary people outright loved him, because he was funny, unstuffy, a natural showman, daring, treated all as equals and was adept at putting down hecklers in a way that never humiliated them. The irony here is that Macdonald always opposed widening the franchise, even though the poor and landless were his most ardent supporters, as were women, those others not welcomed at the ballot boxes. He never patronized his audiences; rather, he paid them the supreme compliment of never talking at them from a prepared text but rather talked with them, ad libbing his actual speech and coming out with his best lines whenever heckled or interrupted. Later, Wilfrid Laurier would be famous for the vote-winning attractiveness of his "sunny ways"; but Macdonald was the first of that seductive political breed in Canada.

Macdonald's other great asset was that he was ferociously competitive. Winning was everything to him. Whenever an election approached, he dropped everything and applied all his inventiveness and capacity for hard work to the challenge.

This time, one of his initiatives was to create a Conservative newspaper, the Toronto *Mail*, to rival the Liberals' Toronto *Globe*. He began a campaign to raise the needed funds, contributing ten thousand dollars himself, and persuaded an experienced journalist, T.C. Patteson, to become the editor, guaranteeing him a government sinecure if the venture failed. When he saw the first dummy edition, he worried its tone might be considered offensive: "You call G.B. [George Brown] a bully and a tyrant," he wrote to Patteson. "He is both, but is it wise to throw down the gauntlet so early and so offensively?" Soon his competitiveness took over: "The first number is a good one—*for a first number*," he wrote. "You must assume an appearance of dignity at the outset. The sooner, however, that you put on the war paint and commence to scalp the better."

One campaign idea he toyed with was for the Conservative Party to change its name to something more compelling, such as the Union Party, the Canadian Constitutional Party or the Constitutional Union Party. These titles, he argued, would signal that the party stood for "union with England against all Annexationists and Independents, and for British North America . . . against all anti-Confederates." The idea died, as did Macdonald's later suggestion that the party should be called an "Association of Union and Progress"—whatever that meant.

His electoral tricks were endless. He informed one candidate: "You will be surprised to receive an appointment as an Issuer of Marriage Licences." The candidate, who was an Ontario provincial member, was to accept the honour, "& then in a day or so you must write a letter of resignation." Macdonald had figured out that this individual could qualify himself to become a federal candidate simply by taking on a provincial post that, by law, required him to resign his legislature seat. He warned candidates against being too generous too early: "If you give a man five dollars before the nomination, he will have spent it and want another five dollars before polling."

As always, religion trumped everything else. Macdonald urged the bishop of Hamilton to "put the Episcopal screw" onto Kenny

Fitzpatrick, whom Macdonald wanted as a Catholic candidate but who kept protesting he was not sufficiently educated to be an MP; Macdonald explained that Canada's Parliament was fast becoming one where "only the leaders speak and the majority are satisfied with . . . giving silent votes with their party."

In one small way, the election of 1872 made Canadian political history. For the first time, a working-class candidate, H.B. Witton from Hamilton, was elected to Parliament—and as a Conservative. The person who made Witton's victory possible, and the source of Macdonald's great piece of electoral luck, was none other than George Brown.

George Brown, owner of The Globe, *moral and intellectual leader of the Liberals even though no longer in Parliament, was by far Macdonald's ablest opponent. Despite his abilities, Brown lost almost every contest.*

While Canada was still overwhelmingly rural, an urban proletariat was beginning to emerge in Montreal, Toronto and Hamilton, where industrial workers now made up close to one-fifth of the labour force. Canadian workers put in longer hours for less pay than their British and American equivalents, and their unions were weak or non-existent.

The idea of union activism was beginning to spread to Canada from Britain and the U.S., though. In 1871 the Toronto Trades Assembly was formed as a voice for the many union locals in the city. Its leaders seized on the idea of launching a Nine-Hour Movement, already victorious in

Britain.* On February 28, 1872, Typographical Union No. 19 informed printing firms in Toronto that its members wished to work nine hours a day instead of ten. The night compositors, the most skilled workers, met with Brown, the *Globe*'s proprietor, and he agreed to shorter hours and a pay raise. But when the less-skilled printers sought a similar agreement, Brown refused to meet with them. On March 25, every Typographical Union worker left his bench. Brown instantly formed an employers' consortium of various kinds of businesses that agreed to help the *Globe* resist "any attempt on the part of our Employees to dictate to us by what rules we shall govern our business."

The workers had their own countermeasures prepared. A newspaper called the *Ontario Workman* appeared on the streets to denounce oppression by the capitalists, and a succession of mass protest meetings organized by the Trades Assembly raised funds.† A pro-Conservative newspaper, *The Leader*, took the side of the strikers, giving them a public platform. Most adroitly, the strikers urged British workers to warn "mechanics" or skilled workers planning to emigrate that they would be coming to a land where the working man had no rights. The demonstrations escalated, and one rally brought out ten thousand men, women and children. Brown, though, had the law on his side. He had warrants issued against members of the Typographical Union's Vigilance Committee, and on April 16 thirteen were arrested on charges of conspiracy.

At this point, Macdonald rose in the House of Commons to announce that legislation would be introduced "to relieve Trade Unions from certain disabilities under which they labour." The

---

* American unions were more advanced: south of the border, the equivalent campaign was the Eight-Hour Movement.

† In one intriguing accomplishment, an early edition of the *Ontario Workman* ran a long extract from Karl Marx's recently published *Das Kapital*—even though it would not be published in English translation until 1882.

bill, he said, would place them on equal footing with unions in England. Brown's arrest warrants were valid because, under existing Canadian law, unions had no right to organize. In Britain, trade unions had this right under a law enacted by Gladstone's Liberal government. Canadian Liberals could hardly criticize British Liberals, so Macdonald's bill passed with scarcely a dissenting word. The case against the leaders of the Typographical Union was dropped abruptly. In the *Globe*, Brown declared that Macdonald's only motive had been to gain "a little cheap political capital."

That was precisely Macdonald's objective. Union leaders now appeared on platforms with Conservative candidates. The Toronto Trades Assembly staged a huge rally to express its gratitude, presenting a jewelled case to Lady Macdonald and providing Macdonald with an opportunity to charm the crowd by saying that, as a maker of cabinets, he was himself an industrial worker.

A bit more than electoral opportunism was involved. Macdonald was also worried that harsh labour laws in Canada would discourage

The Globe.

TORONTO, MONDAY, MARCH 25.

THE PRINTERS' STRIKE.

The Typographical Society held a general meeting on Saturday evening, and in their usual magnificent fashion "closed" the printing-offices of all the Master Printers who dared to resist their dictation and signed the declaration of independence published in another column. THE GLOBE OFFICE is consequently "*closed*." The effect of this is that all the members of the Society are forbidden to work in THE GLOBE office, under the penalty of being expelled from the Union and published in the Society's black-list, for the guidance of Union offices elsewhere.

We very much regret this, for the sake of a number of excellent men, who, strongly against their will and at the sacrifice of the interests of their families, are forced to leave comfortable situations at high rates of wages, which they have held for years.

So far as THE GLOBE office is concerned, we need hardly say, the "closing" is only metaphorical. A large number of hands have already gone, and others will no doubt follow to-day—but THE GLOBE will nevertheless appear with its accustomed regularity.

As we may be short-handed for a few days, it will be necessary that advertisements should be left at the office not later than 5 p.m. to secure insertion the following morning. Our advertising friends will oblige us by aiding us in this matter.

Brown's attempt to use the law to crush a strike by Globe *typographers prompted Macdonald to pass legislation to legalize trade unions. In one inadequate response, the* Globe *appealed: "Our advertising friends will oblige us by aiding us in this matter."*

immigration from Britain.* With his railway plans progressing, immigration had become a key nation-building policy. Earlier in the parliamentary session, he had enacted a Dominion Lands Act, which made a 160-acre lot, or quarter-section, available to settlers for a nominal ten-dollar fee. Two years earlier, he had initiated a comprehensive survey of the North-West to map these sections—one of the great administrative accomplishments of nineteenth-century Canada.

In due course, Witton was elected as a working-class, Macdonald Conservative, but thereafter he did precious little to advance labour's cause. "We had met him soon after the election when he dined in a rough suit," Lady Dufferin, the wife of the incoming governor general, recorded in her diary, "but he now wears evening clothes."†

Nevertheless, by scoring off Brown and by shaking the hands of industrial workers, Macdonald had gained momentum. He used it now to overcome other obstacles in his path.

The most troubling matter Macdonald had to settle before going to the polls was the demand for an amnesty for "misdeeds"—in Bishop Taché's delicate phrase—committed during the Red River Resistance. Early in 1872, Father Ritchot dispatched a petition to the governor general urging him to "proclaim the amnesty which was promised us when negotiating in Ottawa." Macdonald advised Governor General Lisgar that "no answer should be sent," and

* Much of the material in this section is drawn from Bernard Ostry's groundbreaking 1960 article "Conservatives, Liberals and Labour in the 1870s," in *Canadian Historical Review*.

† Witton lost his seat two years later, in the 1874 election. He made a "good transition" to the new Liberal government and was sent by them to a post in Vienna.

Lisgar in turn informed London that he had never made "an assurance or promise of an amnesty."

Taché made yet another attempt to secure an amnesty. He went to Ottawa and met with Macdonald, who told him forthrightly that "no government could stand that would endeavour to procure the amnesty." At this meeting, Macdonald came up with the idea of sending money to Riel, through Taché, to enable him to survive in the United States. That solution put the amnesty issue to rest—for a while. In the election campaign, whenever hecklers demanded to know when Riel would be brought to justice, Macdonald would reply solemnly, "Where is Riel? God knows. I wish I could lay my hands on him."

A $5,000 reward issued by the Ontario Liberal government for Riel's arrest made it risky for him to come back across the border. He did it repeatedly: once, after winning a seat in Manitoba, he slipped into the Parliament Building to sign the register as an elected MP.

The easiest of the outstanding issues requiring attention was the Washington Treaty. By delaying dealing with it for so long, Macdonald had allowed everyone's temper to cool. Not until May 3, 1872, did he bring it before Parliament. By then, he had received a copy of a message sent by the colonial secretary to Lisgar pledging that, once the treaty was passed, the British government would guarantee a £2.5 million loan for the railway.

Macdonald's speech was long—four hours—and one of his best. He recalled that he had been reluctant to become one of the commissioners, and had done so only to protect Canada's interests. Once in Washington, he had been forced to compromise so that Britain and the United States could make peace. Although he was unhappy about the fisheries settlement, it was at least now firmly established that Britain could not cede those fisheries without Canada's consent. He ended by asking MPs "to accept this treaty, to accept it with all its imperfections, to accept it for the sake of peace, and for the sake of the great Empire of which we form part." The debate was brief, and the treaty was ratified by a margin of two to one.

The last issue to be dealt with was the most important of all—the identity of the company that would build the railway. The enabling legislation had already been brought before the House and passed after a desultory debate. The government would review bids to build the line, and the winning company would receive thirty million dollars in cash and fifty million acres of prairie land in alternate blocks on either side of the line. Two important matters were left unsettled. One was how the government would respond to a new demand by British Columbia that the railway should extend to Vancouver Island by way of a succession of bridges across the island-dotted part of the Georgia Strait opposite Campbell River. (This would have required building no fewer than seven bridges spanning the deep, tide-ripped waters).

The other matter was a good deal more consequential: how the government would decide who should actually build and run the railway. As the *Commercial & Financial Chronicle* noted shrewdly, the bill allowed the government "to make almost any agreement it chose."

At this time, Macdonald was still trying to get David Macpherson to combine his Inter-Oceanic Railway with Hugh Allan's Canadian Pacific, but Macpherson was refusing to accept that Allan be named president of the company. He brushed aside Macdonald's compromise suggestion that, while Allan would have the top job, each could nominate the same number of members to the board.

Macpherson's suspicions were wholly justified. Despite Allan's promise to Macdonald, he was continuing his secret partnership with the Americans. He even convinced himself he was doing so for the country's sake, telling the Northern Pacific president, George Cass, he was "really doing a most patriotic act." While lying to Macdonald, Allan lied as amply to his American colleagues: he told them that, because Parliament could not approve legislation that put Americans in charge of a vital national project, all the stock of the Canadian Pacific would have to be held in the names of Canadians. American investors should place a certificate equal to one million dollars in gold in his own Merchants' Bank and, once the government awarded the contract, this money would be used by the Americans to buy shares from the Canadians who held them.*

All these intrigues were still a secret, though suspicions about Allan's dealings were beginning to leak out. As for Macdonald, he

---

* The Canadian shareholders of record included Donald Smith, William McDougall and J.J. Abbott, the company lawyer and, much later, briefly prime minister, as well as a number of MPs. Not all were privy to Allan's extraordinary scheme, but a number must have been.

was delighted with what had been accomplished during the parliamentary session. He told a friend that he and the Conservatives had "routed the Grits horse, foot and Artillery." He now called the election.

Macdonald set off immediately to campaign in western Ontario, hastily doubling back to Kingston when he heard that the contest in his own riding was close. He worked very hard in Ontario, spending two full months travelling, speaking, organizing local election campaigns and pushing back against the interventions of the new provincial Liberal government, which deployed all its patronage and influence to defeat the Conservatives. As he later told a supporter, "Had I not taken regularly to the stump, a thing that I have never done before, we should have been completely routed."

It was just enough. In his own riding, he won by only 130 votes. The *Canadian Parliamentary Guide* records the overall result as 104 seats for Macdonald and 96 for the opposition parties, leaving him with a bare majority of 8. In Nova Scotia, however, where the *Guide* gave Macdonald only 10 seats, most of the MPs, now that "better terms" had been gained, in fact consistently supported him. Macdonald's effective majority thus was nearer to 30. In the two new provinces, British Columbia and Manitoba, he won all of their 10 seats, a number far larger than their populations warranted.

He had, though, suffered one incalculable loss. Cartier, his partner for so many years, had been defeated in his own Montreal East riding. The person responsible was Hugh Allan.

For months now, both before and during the election, Allan had also been lying to Cartier, the man who had done much to guarantee him the presidency of the Canadian Pacific. Allan knew very little about politics, and he almost never bothered to vote. But he knew a great deal about power. He came to the conclusion that, to make certain his Canadian-American syndicate would gain the CPR contract, it was necessary for Cartier to be reduced to a powerless tool. Cartier at this time wielded immense influence, because he and Macdonald were close and, as the necessary foundation for their intimate alliance, because he controlled forty-five *bleu* MPs, who, as Allan noted, "voted in a solid phalanx for all his measures." If a significant number of these men ever wandered, their absence could "put the Government out of office." That would put the government at Allan's mercy.

Allan went after Cartier with chilling skill. He knew that Quebecers had long wanted a railway from Montreal to Ottawa through the country north of the Ottawa River, but that Cartier, as solicitor of the rival Grand Trunk, had consistently opposed this line. So Allan made "this *French* railroad scheme" into his own great cause. He subsidized newspapers that supported it and bought a controlling interest in the company's stock. He travelled along the intended route, visiting priests and influential people and speaking in fluent French at public meetings. Before long, he had twenty-seven of the forty-five *bleus* on side—demobilizing more than half of Cartier's army. At that point, Cartier buckled under and, to save his political career, promised the railway contract to Allan and his Canadian Pacific Railway.

Cartier had not only been reduced to a dependant but, with his declining health, was also in jeopardy in his own riding. To have any hope of holding his seat, he needed funds in large amounts. The only possible source was Allan.

The money did come in, and in staggering, unprecedented

amounts. But it was too late. Cartier's illness, finally diagnosed as Bright's disease, was rapidly eroding his inexhaustible energy and making his judgments erratic. His legs ballooned and he was able to give only two campaign speeches, both times speaking from a chair. Other factors came into play. The ultramontanes, led by Bishop Bourget, were determined to make Cartier pay for the Conservatives' treatment of Riel. Allan's claim that Cartier had opposed a "*French* railroad" stuck in the public's mind, and his opponent in the riding, an able young lawyer, was a strong candidate. On election night, Cartier was soundly defeated by a margin of three to one.

George-Étienne Cartier, "Brave as a lion," in Macdonald's phrase, lost his own riding to Allan's outpouring of money against him. To get Allan and his money back onto his side, Cartier ignored Macdonald's instructions and promised him the charter for the Pacific Railway. Illness took away first his judgment, then his life.

In one respect, Allan and Cartier were alike. Both were exceptionally self-confident, certain that they were right or that they could bring the situation back to the way it should be. In all else, they were strangers. Cartier lived life to the full, with lively parties, a mistress, a passion for bawling out songs and a well-stocked wine cellar. Allan kept life at a distance. Cartier was a passionate patriot; the Confederation pact between French and English was far more his than Macdonald's, and Montreal's long reign as Canada's principal industrial and financial city was his gift to his people. Allan's only interest was in himself. Cartier was a life force. Allan never had much to say: long after the Pacific Scandal, a federal civil servant who knew him asked whether he had made a mistake by getting involved in politics. After a long silence he replied, "Mebbe."* Cartier was a big man, Allan a very brainy small one. And it is Cartier who is remembered.

A replacement riding was quickly found for Cartier by Bishop Taché, who persuaded Riel to give up the nomination he had secured in the Manitoba riding of Provencher. But his political career was already over. A month after the election, Cartier boarded the steamship *Prussian* (owned, inevitably, by Allan) on his way to London to become a patient of the world's authority on Bright's disease. At this time, Macdonald advised Governor General Lisgar that Cartier's sickness was "incurable" and that he wasn't expected to last a year.

The election over, Macdonald now turned back to the Canadian Pacific issue. From this time on, he would have to deal with it alone.

---

* This anecdote is recounted in Pierre Berton's *National Dream*.

FIFTEEN

The Blunder

Is not bribery the corner-stone of Party Government?
Judge John D. Armour*

Towards the end of the 1872 election, Macdonald wrote to a candidate, James S. McQuaig of Picton, about the always delicate matter of election funds. "Our friends here have been liberal with contributions," he said, "and I can send you $1,000 without inconvenience." He wrote many other letters like that. On August 4, he urged Finance Minister Francis Hincks, "Spare no expense. There are many ways of covering it." Two days later, he instructed the manager of the Kingston branch of the Merchants' Bank to disburse seven thousand dollars to several candidates.

The matter of suspect electoral funding was of course not in the least new. The 1872 election was quite different, though, in both the size of the donations and the recklessness with which

* Mr. Justice Armour made this observation in an 1884 case, *The Queen v. Bunting*. His uncommon candour did not prevent him from going on to become chief justice of Ontario.

Macdonald chased after them. Alexander Campbell's brother, Charles, wrote to him in distress to say that Macdonald had persuaded him and a friend to sign jointly a note for $10,000 to be used as campaign funds. He then made the astonishing disclosure "the only security we have being Sir John's under-taking in writing as a *member of the Government to recoup us in the amount loaned him.*"* The prime minister thus had got himself on record as prepared to use government funds to repay an election contribution. The largest contribution by far came from Hugh Allan, the seeker of the contract to build the transcontinental railway. By the election's end, Allan's contributions to the Conservative Party topped an incredible $350,000. Out of this would come the Canadian Pacific Scandal— the worst political scandal by far in Canadian history.

Through much of the campaign, Macdonald acted as if desperate, almost unbalanced. Heavy drinking was a factor and, as made things worse, he repeatedly violated his practice of not making important decisions while on a binge. The underlying cause has to have been fear—the debilitating fear that he might well lose the election and his office as prime minister, and very likely afterwards the party leadership, leaving him like a beached whale. It could be said that, throughout the 1872 election, Macdonald was battling a double addiction—a dependency on both politics and liquor.

~

In many countries, political corruption was starting to be curbed. In Germany and in France, an understanding had developed that

---

* Charles Campbell included the emphasis in his letter. His brother, adept at backroom deals, was able to cover up this particular indiscretion.

the functioning of a modern nation-state required efficiency. Change was happening in Britain too, despite its age-old traditions of "rotten boroughs" or pocket constituencies where the local lord decided who won. In 1870, examinations were made standard for entry into the civil service, and the purchase of military commissions was abolished.*

But the idea of a meritocracy had not yet crossed the Atlantic. In the United States, General Ulysses S. Grant came to the presidency in 1869 wrapped in Civil War glory; by the time he left, eight years later, he and many of his closest colleagues had been enveloped in scandals, among them two vice-presidents, two secretaries of the treasury and one of war, and his personal private secretary. During the reign of "Boss" Tweed at New York's Tammany Hall from 1859 to 1871, something like a hundred million dollars was stolen from City Hall. Mark Twain dubbed the sale of corporate charters and rights to land, mines and lumber the "Great Barbeque."

If the United States, with its "spoils system," was a couple of decades behind leading European countries in the ethics of government, Canada lagged by about a half-century. All these practices were sanctified by history: the great pre-Confederation achievement of Responsible Government, or self-government, had been mostly about a transfer of patronage from the governor general to local politicians; Confederation itself had been accomplished by money being poured into New Brunswick to defeat an anti-Confederation government.

Patronage in Canada could be justified as necessary to accommodate the differing interests of the various regions, races and

---

* The best description of patronage came, predictably, from Benjamin Disraeli. It was, he said, "the outward and visible sign of an inward and spiritual grace, and that is Power."

religions. In the best study of patronage in Canada, *Spoils of Power*, political columnist Jeffrey Simpson concludes that "patronage, whatever its costs, has done its bit for national integration and stability."* This necessity was well understood. Goldwin Smith wrote that, although Macdonald's system was "undoubtedly one of corruption . . . the only excuse is the difficulty, if not to say the impossibility, of holding this heterogeneous and ill-cemented mass together in any other way." The journal *The Week* pointed out that Macdonald "did not come up through a trap door" but rather "he and his system are mainly the offspring of a necessity . . . among the members of Confederation[,] who can be held together only by such means."

Few nineteenth-century Canadians were greatly troubled by patronage.† At that time, jobs were not essential for self-esteem and status; rather, respectability was what mattered most, even if it still required a minimal income and a job. The politicians passed out the available jobs—the comfortable indoor ones especially—not to those best qualified to perform them, but to their supporters. No stigma was attached to gaining a cushy job by such means; seven relatives of Montreal's Archbishop Taschereau held government jobs, and it was no coincidence that Taschereau served Macdonald as a counterweight to the right-wing ultramontane Bishop Bourget. The most illuminating comment about the patronage system was made by Commons Speaker Timothy Anglin (actually a Liberal),

---

* Simpson's *Spoils of Power* is not only the best study but almost the only one. Other useful works are Gordon Stewart's *The Origins of Canadian Politics* and S.J.R. Noel's *Patrons, Clients, Brokers.*

† Elite opinion turned against patronage only when the economy had grown enough for the private sector to generate attractive jobs. Over time, however, the elite has become the principal beneficiary of patronage: few routine jobs—in the post office and customs houses, for example—are handed out any more, but, rather, judgeships, ambassadorships, senatorships and appointments to royal commissions and the boards of national institutions.

who, when forced to give up his post in 1877 because a company he owned had been given government contracts, said in his defence, "Everybody did it."* As a last justification for patronage, it was one of the few instances where Canadian politics was truly national; as the historian Gordon Stewart has written, "On patronage, English-Canadians and French-Canadians spoke the same language."

Macdonald neither invented Canadian-style patronage nor developed a unique system for it. It long pre-existed him and in an organized sense was first implemented in the 1840s by that pair of Canadian political heroes (for achieving Responsible Government) Robert Baldwin and Louis-Hippolyte LaFontaine. Wilfrid Laurier implemented a system almost identical to Macdonald's as soon as he came to power in 1896; Oliver Mowat, Ontario's first Liberal premier, did the same. Macdonald's patronage was, nevertheless, far more extensive than any earlier system and a good deal more intelligent. He used it not just to reward friends, but also to recruit converts. It was always his personal system, because of his unrivalled knowledge of people and politics. Over time, it became better organized, with MPs or constituency boards making recommendations to the appropriate ministers. But the final decisions were always his.

What was truly unique about Macdonald's patronage system was that, much as with his drinking, he never showed the least shame for what he did nor ever apologized for it. Indeed, Macdonald argued for patronage with some conviction: "Whenever an Office is vacant, it belongs to the party supporting the Government if within the party there is to be found a person competent to perform the duties," he told a Liberal MP. "Responsible Government cannot be carried out on any other principle." Moreover, he accepted that

---

* The "everybody did it" defence worked: within a year, Anglin had regained the Speakership.

when the other side gained power it would select its own friends for available posts, and that "no one could object to it." Any attempt to create a non-partisan civil service, he said, would be like "trying to put Canada back to the age of Adam and Eve."* Real change did not begin until the outbreak of the First World War, when the need to raise and maintain large armies showed that administrative efficiency mattered.

Macdonald used patronage for purposes other than partisanship. He made a respectable effort, if not always, to make merit a precondition for important judicial appointments. And he used patronage to look after what he called "wounded birds." He asked a senior official to give an appointment to a Mr. Geddes, an old schoolmate who had been "first boy" at his school and had "always beat" him, "but yet he has never got on." He instructed one minister to award the job of "sweeping and dusting about the [Parliament] buildings" to an old woman married to a "blackguard." In some respects, his patronage system resembled a charity, even an early version of affirmative action, since it enabled disadvantaged groups, like Irish Catholics, to catch up, a bit, with English Protestants. Macdonald also excluded himself and his family from the benefits of patronage, once infuriating Charles Tupper by refusing to allow government legal contracts to be given to the joint law partnership of their sons. Yet the charge of "corruptionist" has always stuck to Macdonald. In his day, a key reason was the brilliant, savage cartoons of him that J.W. Bengough published every week in *Grip*. That image became indelible largely because the Canadian Pacific Scandal was so huge and so far-reaching in its consequences.

---

* Royal commissions on improving the civil service were set up by both Liberal and Conservative governments in 1880–81, 1891–92, 1907–8 and 1911–12, but accomplished little.

By the end of the 1872 election, Macdonald found himself facing the most serious crisis of his entire career. The issue at stake was not whether he had accepted election funds from someone seeking government favours, or even from someone who had already been promised such favours. It was far worse. The question was whether he, the principal architect of Confederation and now Canada's nation-builder, had accepted funds from Americans who were seeking favours that would, effectively, hand over his national dream to them.

On July 12, 1872, while Macdonald was in Toronto in mid-campaign, he received a telegram from Hugh Allan. It was different in tone from their earlier communications, even threatening: "It is very important in the interest of Sir George [Cartier] and the government that the Pacific question be settled without delay. I send this from no personal interest but a storm is brewing."

Over the next few days, the nature of this supposed storm became clear. Macdonald's attempt to create a railway consortium combining Allan's Montreal-based Canadian Pacific and David Macpherson's Toronto-based Inter-Oceanic had failed, because Macpherson refused to believe that Allan was not a front for American interests. Allan moved quickly to gain complete control over the company that would build the transcontinental railway. By now, Allan had won more than half the *bleu* MPs to his side, making Cartier his dependant and so shrunken in stature that he asked Allan to speak on his behalf at a major public meeting. (The crowd pelted them both with rotten eggs.) What Cartier really wanted, to keep himself alive politically, was money.

Cartier was now reduced to the role of courier, carrying messages between Macdonald and Allan. In one, the Montreal robber baron assured Macdonald: "If the government will pledge itself to appoint directors favourable to me as president and to the allotment of stock, I will be satisfied." After failing in one more attempt to convince Macpherson to accept Allan as president of a joint syndicate, Macdonald telegraphed Cartier on July 26, authorizing him to assure Allan that the government would exercise its influence "to secure him the position of president." But all other matters—the allocation of stock and membership in the board of directors—would be set aside until after the election. He closed with the command "Answer."

No answer came for four days. Cartier had shown Macdonald's telegram to Allan, who asked him to write a memorandum pledging that, if no amalgamation with Macpherson could be achieved, the railway charter would be given to Allan's Canadian Pacific. If Cartier obliged, said Allan, this document would "satisfy our friends." In effect, Allan was requiring Cartier to guarantee him a charter that he could then interpret as he wished—rearranging it to accommodate his American partners. Cartier agreed, and Allan in exchange composed a memorandum that declared, "The friends of the [Canadian] Government will expect to be assisted with funds in the pending elections" and cited as "immediate requirements" a total of $110,000, including $35,000 for Macdonald. Cartier sent the two documents to Macdonald, who by this time was in Kingston.

Macdonald's reaction was one of disbelief. He had instructed Cartier to offer Allan the presidency; instead, Cartier had given him everything. Indeed, in his memorandum to Allan, Cartier went so far as to declare that there was "no doubt but that the Governor-in-Council will agree with the company for the construction and working out of the Canadian Pacific"— even though the legislation recently passed by Parliament had deliberately made no mention of who would build and operate the line.

In the middle of a fiercely fought election, with a close result likely even in his own riding of Kingston, Macdonald had to make a critical choice. Should he reject the entire plan, leaving the party without the election funds it needed so badly, or should he accept it, which would mean a secret commitment by the government to Allan's company? Facing these alternatives, Macdonald chose to say neither yes nor no; instead, he said, "No, but . . ."

Macdonald informed Cartier that the arrangement he had just made with Allan was unacceptable. Still acceptable, though, was his own July 26 telegram authorizing Cartier to offer Allan the presidency of a merged company. This offer must be "the basis of the agreement," he wired. When Cartier relayed this news, Allan, surprisingly, did not withdraw his offer of financial support. Instead, he promptly sent Macdonald ten thousand dollars. Thereafter, the money flowed in increasingly large amounts.

The election remained exceedingly tight, while at the same time Macdonald's drinking became ever more out of control. On August 26, Macdonald went down to the telegraph office in Kingston and dispatched to J.J. Abbott, Allan's lawyer, a cable that would become the best-known telegram in Canadian history. It read: "Immediate private. I must have another ten thousand. Will be the last time of calling. Do not fail me. Answer today." His signature, as always bold, followed at the bottom of the cable form that he scribbled out in the office. Abbott's reply came three days later: "Draw on me for ten thousand."

By sending this message and attaching his signature to it, Macdonald had not only cocked and fired a gun, but he had left it smoking profusely. For anyone in his position to have done so—above all, a skilled politician and practised lawyer—was an act of suicidal madness. A rough comparison might be the way that, in the early years of the Internet, many users did not realize that deleting embarrassing e-mails did not in fact eliminate them from their computers.

Despite this reckless lapse, Macdonald's other decisions made sense, based on what he knew at the time. Allan's abundant financial and transportation experience made him the best available choice to build a transcontinental railway; almost certainly, he was the only person in the country who could have pulled off so gigantic a project. As for the money, Allan, as a Conservative, would have been approached for election funding under any circumstances.

But two aspects of the agreement were patently indefensible. The scale of the funding—eventually $350,000—was without precedent. Such largesse made it inevitable that many Conservative candidates would breach the electoral laws, which technically were quite strict, as for instance that "treating," or small-scale bribing, was forbidden. As minister of justice, Macdonald was responsible for maintaining these laws. Moreover, although Macdonald had limited his commitment to making Allan president of the company, he had accepted a deluge of money from someone whose ambitions, as he knew full well from Cartier's communications, went far beyond possessing a corporate title. Macdonald did not confirm that Cartier, as he had instructed, had cancelled his broader commitment to Allan. He preferred not to know what Cartier was actually up to until the election was safely over. As a sin of omission rather than of commission, this lapse may not have broken the law, but it was unrestrainedly sleazy.

Most pointedly, Macdonald never asked Allan whether he was still in bed with his American partners. He simply assumed that Allan had cancelled the connection, as he had insisted. He had made it crystal clear that the Canadian Pacific was to be a Canadian project, accepting only minority involvement by British and American investors. A secret, majority holding by American railway financiers would violate this principle, particularly because so many of them sat on the board of the Northern Pacific, an enterprise that could succeed only by absorbing the Canadian

Pacific and turning Canada's transnational railway into an elongated branch line. Just one marginal defence exists for Macdonald's behaviour. Any American ownership of the Canadian Pacific was bound to become public eventually. The government would then fall, and a new government would cancel the deal. Macdonald persuaded himself that Allan, widely respected for his abilities, could not have been so self-deluded as to persevere with his American-backed syndicate.

As soon as the election was over, Macdonald resumed his efforts to pull off an amalgamated Ontario-Quebec company. Macpherson responded by calling Allan's scheme "an audacious, insolent, unpatriotic and gigantic swindle." Describing himself as "greatly chagrined," Macdonald argued back, pleading with Macpherson that his only objective was to ensure that the Canadian Pacific "should not be used against the party . . . [and] might serve an old friend like you—and through you, other friends."

In September 1872, Macpherson made his objections public. A statement by the Inter-Oceanic's executive committee formally rejected amalgamation and advanced a remarkably perceptive analysis: "It is perfectly futile to look to the United States for aid in this work as [the Canadian Pacific] is necessarily a rival to the several existing [American] Pacific railways." The Toronto company insisted that "Sir Hugh Allan's original scheme is unchanged" and that it would be "ill-advised and dangerous to the public interests."

In a long reply, Allan denied the charge. He argued that majority ownership by Canadian investors had always been understood as mandatory and that this was the case now. He admitted that there had been some earlier discussions with American investors, but claimed these negotiations had long since been closed. The government defended Allan's competence and patriotism, adding that the success of the railway project depended on its "complete identification with the public sentiment of the country."

Macdonald still had not asked Allan directly whether he had cut all his ties to his American partners. He was alarmed enough, nevertheless, to insist that Cartier clarify from his sickbed in London the agreement he had settled on with Allan: "Send the facts to me," he wrote to his old partner. "I fear the mention of the thing would break up the Council [cabinet] and the Government."

The analysis issued by the Inter-Oceanic Railway made its greatest impact not on Macdonald but on Allan. It snapped him out of his state of self-delusion. On October 24, he wrote to the Canadian-born American financier George McMullen to tell him their agreement could no longer be sustained: "The opposition of the Ontario party will, I think, have the effect of shutting out our American friends from any participation in the road. . . . Public sentiment seems to be decided that the road shall be built by Canadians only."

For Macdonald, the real crisis was now beginning. Lycurgus Edgerton, a Northern Pacific lobbyist with good contacts in Ottawa, reported to Jay Cooke, the banker in the American consortium, that the government was "sorely perplexed to know what to do . . . much trouble is foreboded." On November 28, Macdonald warned Hector-Louis Langevin, who had replaced Cartier as the senior Quebec minister, to be sure to attend the next cabinet meeting, because "there are rocks ahead of the most dangerous character."

Macdonald was referring to pressures building up within the cabinet. On December 6, Joseph Howe advised Macdonald that he was resigning: "I cannot defend that scheme . . . which, I believe, will be a surprise to Parliament and the country, and fraught with consequences deeply injurious to the best interests of the Dominion." Howe was old now, and without any means once his ministerial salary was gone, so his act was one of considerable personal bravery. New Brunswick's Peter Mitchell was also dissatisfied. Throughout this period, as he wrote later, "Macdonald never gave any explanation to his colleagues in Council [cabinet], nor did he attempt to deny or justify any of the charges that were brought against him." By now, Macdonald was performing like a deer caught in the headlights.

In January 1873, Allan agreed to new terms insisted on by the cabinet. He set up a new Canadian Pacific Company, with himself as president and a board of thirteen directors drawn from all six provinces and all properly Canadian. The company's capitalization would be ten million dollars. It was all make-believe. A politically chosen board would have no coherence and no credibility, either with the public or with potential investors in London. Self-delusion now turned into outright fantasy. During an interview with Edgerton, Allan explained how the Canadian Pacific would connect with the lines of the Northern Pacific, meaning that "for the next five or ten years—if not for *all time*—the Canada Pacific must be subservient to and tributary to the interests of the Northern Pacific." It was after this astounding statement that several of Macpherson's associates began to invite Northern Pacific directors to buy their shares at discounted prices. The baffled Northern Pacific president asked why these individuals were doing "just what they accuse Sir Hugh of—selling out to the Americans."

The make-believe continued. Early in January 1873, Macdonald wrote to Cartier in London to report, "Things are going on very quietly here." This feigned cheerfulness helped to sustain the spirits of his terminally ill colleague, but the accurate assessment came from Edgerton: in a report to Jay Cooke, he wrote, "Great events, of a political character, are in the near future in Canada."*

Meanwhile, Macdonald, highly resilient as he was, began to stir into action. He made sure he had the right friend in the right high place, for whenever he might need him.

~

In the summer of 1872, Frederick Temple Blackwood, Lord Dufferin, became the third post-Confederation governor general. Macdonald's first assessment of him was cool: "He is pleasant in manner and has been both by speech and by letter very complimentary to myself. He is, however, rather too gushing for my taste." Macdonald's character review was too glib. Dufferin was indeed an inveterate self-promoter, but in many ways he was a singularly effective governor general. Initially, however, Macdonald was more taken with Lady Dufferin, whom he found "very charming, with nice, unaffected manners." Dufferin would become his admirer; she his friend.

Dufferin, a descendant of the great eighteenth-century playwright Richard Sheridan, brought to the governor general's role an energy and style that transformed the institution. He was shrewd enough to appreciate that the post had lost most of its executive powers and that a major part of British authority would rest henceforth less on power than on the appearance of power—theatrics, social elegance, pomp and ceremony. During their first summer in 1872, the Dufferins went to Quebec City and set about restoring the Citadel. They plunged into local life, and by the time they left the city the whole population lined the streets to

---

* Much of the material in this section has been derived from Pierre Berton's *The National Dream* and from Leonard Irwin's *Pacific Railways and Nationalism in the Canadian-American Northwest, 1845–1873*.

The Dufferins reinvented the role of the governor general, turning it from a post for a diplomat into a platform for a celebrity. In happier days, Lord and Lady Dufferin went curling with Macdonald on the frozen St. Lawrence. During the railway scandal, Dufferin did all he could for Macdonald.

bid them farewell. They then attended all the fall fairs in southern Ontario, sampling the foods and expressing admiration for the farm animals. No governor general had ever reached out to the people in this way, and the Dufferins did so as a couple.* Back in Ottawa, Dufferin inveigled funds from government to add a grand new ballroom to Rideau Hall in which he staged fancy-dress balls and elaborate theatricals.

Perhaps most significant, Dufferin strengthened the country's ties to Britain, but subtly. "Were the curb pressed too tightly," he told the colonial secretary, "Canada might become impatient, the cry for Independence would be raised." He also became enormously important to Macdonald. If anything, he almost fawned

* The Dufferins enjoyed an exceptionally happy marriage. Though naturally shy, Lady Dufferin learned to match her husband's theatrical performances. The king of Greece once remarked admiringly, "No one in the world can enter a room like Lady Dufferin."

over his prime minister. In advance of the 1873 parliamentary session, he declared, "Everybody seems to agree that your management of the House is as neat a specimen of coaching as anyone need wish to witness." He sent the same view back home: "No one in the country [is] capable of administering its affairs to greater advantage."

It didn't take Macdonald long to take Dufferin's measure. Soon, he too laid on the flattery, once even praising a part of Dufferin's speech that was in Greek. When a journalist remonstrated that Macdonald himself knew no Greek, the prime minister agreed, but added, "I do know something about people." As a result, Dufferin was far more partial towards Macdonald than he ought to have been. In the fall of 1873, as the Pacific Scandal reached its climax, Macdonald wrote to a friend: "The Governor General behaved like a brick, and has completely check-mated the Grits." And he could always count on Lady Dufferin. In the summer of 1873, as the odds against his political survival lengthened, Lady Dufferin invited him to become godfather to her new daughter, Victoria May. The child's godmother was Queen Victoria.

SIXTEEN

Decline

[Macdonald has been] hopelessly involved in an infamous and corrupt conspiracy.
The Toronto *Globe*, July 4, 1873

On New Year's Eve of 1872, Macdonald was working in his office on Parliament Hill when George McMullen, the one-time Canadian who had become Allan's principal American partner, arrived unannounced, presented his card and was hurried in for a meeting with the prime minister. They spent two hours discussing the Canadian Pacific project, with McMullen talking at length and often reading from documents he had brought with him detailing his dealings with Sir Hugh Allan.

McMullen was providing Macdonald with answers to some of the questions he had never asked. His revelations were stunning. It was clear that Allan had lied to his American partners, letting them believe they could continue as silent owners of the company long after that possibility was gone. He had also lied repeatedly to Macdonald, concealing his long-standing relationship with the Americans and pretending it hadn't continued for months after he had promised to end it. Allan had even tried to get McMullen to reimburse him for the $350,000 he had given to the Conservatives as election funds. And as if utterly disconnected from reality, he had told the lobbyist Lycurgus Edgerton that the Canadian Pacific would be "subservient and tributary" to the Northern Pacific just one day before he finally informed McMullen that their deal was over. McMullen went on and on. Allan had told him he had secured the support of MPs in return for campaign payments—some of them "very near to you," McMullen said, implying that among them were the two most senior members of cabinet, George-Étienne Cartier and Francis Hincks.

When Macdonald denied that any such bargain had been made, McMullen retorted that Allan must have been an outright swindler. Macdonald conceded nothing; the quarrel, he said, was between McMullen and his associates and Allan, not between them and the government. When McMullen insisted that Macdonald either restore the original agreement between the Canadian Pacific and the Americans or withdraw his commitment to make Allan the president, Macdonald retorted that both demands were impossible. At that point, McMullen turned threatening, talking about the political consequences once the public knew the facts. Macdonald ended the discussion by asking for time to talk to Allan and J.J. Abbott, Allan's lawyer.

Three weeks later, McMullen was back again, accompanied this time by a Chicago banker, Charles Mather Smith. Macdonald expressed his sympathies for the way the Americans had been deceived by Allan, telling them, "If I were in your situation, I would proceed against him." Again, he made no other concession; he would not, he insisted, break his commitment to Allan. In February, Smith wrote a long angry letter to Macdonald pointing out that it had been Allan, not the Americans, who had first proposed the pact: "*We* did not go to him," he said. "The Government alone had the address of our syndicate," so he and his group could only assume that Allan had "direct authority from the cabinet." Smith then ratcheted up the pressure, asking whether Macdonald would have any objection to the syndicate petitioning Parliament for compensation.

Macdonald, naturally, had no end of objections to a public airing of such an abundance of soiled linen. One alternative he discerned was for Allan to negotiate a deal with his one-time American associates, thereby securing their silence. (The value of keeping Allan on his side was no doubt the reason Macdonald consistently refused McMullen's suggestions he remove Allan from the Canadian Pacific presidency.) Macdonald therefore asked Hincks, who was now living in Montreal, to get together with Allan before he left for London to try to secure financial backing for the railway project. A few days later, a letter from Hincks brought the welcome news that the matter had been "quite satisfactorily arranged."

No record remains of those tense negotiations between McMullen and Abbott, but evidence given later to the Royal Commission on the Canadian Pacific Railway suggests that McMullen originally demanded a payment of $200,000, which Abbott argued down to $37,500 in American funds. Abbott paid $20,000 immediately, with the balance written on a cheque that was to be held in a security deposit box at Allan's Merchants' Bank. Also in the box was all the correspondence McMullen had shown Macdonald; once the 1873 parliamentary session had ended, these papers were to be returned to Allan. Effectively, Allan was paying for the chance to destroy all the incriminating documents. Later, rumours circulated, but were never proven, that Macdonald and Allan had each agreed to destroy any revealing memos in their possession.

For Macdonald, this outcome was a considerable coup. Despite the drama and the unrelenting pressure, he had avoided admitting to a single misdeed. Nor had he made any new mistakes, cannily avoiding the temptation to try to bribe McMullen into silence, no doubt because he guessed that McMullen would only ask for additional payments. At the same time, Macdonald had ensured that the government remained completely detached from the negotiations between Allan and McMullen. Against all the odds, there was now a chance that the whole affair might remain a secret. After all, McMullen had to remain silent in order to collect his second cheque.

Two other possibilities did exist: either McMullen might receive a better offer for his papers from someone else, most obviously the Liberals, or other incriminating documents might emerge. Macdonald had surely figured out these possibilities. What he failed to anticipate was that both would become realities.

~

The first session of the Second Parliament of Canada opened on March 6, 1873, amid a day of bright blue skies. The Foot Guards were out in their full colours, and the Ottawa Field Artillery fired off a salute to Governor General Lord Dufferin as he arrived by state carriage to preside at his first opening of Parliament. While the spectacle scarcely matched those Dufferin had been accustomed to in his earlier postings in St. Petersburg, Rome and Paris, he still thought the weather "quite divine" and, after looking over the dignitaries, and their wives and daughters, admitted he was "rather surprised to see what a high bred and good looking company they formed." Dufferin read the Throne Speech, which included the confident declaration that the railway company "has given assurance that this great work will be vigorously prosecuted," and claimed that the favourable state of the money markets in England gave "every hope that satisfactory arrangements will be made for the required capital."

It was all wishful thinking. Word of an impending scandal had begun to make Ottawa's rounds, and the *Globe* showed it possessed some inside knowledge by describing the project as "financially the maddest and politically the most unpatriotic, that could be proposed." No capital could be raised in London, or anywhere, until such suspicions were disposed of.

Three weeks later, Lucius Seth Huntington, a Montreal Liberal MP, gave notice that he intended to move a motion for a parliamentary committee to inquire into matters relating to the Canadian Pacific. For technical reasons, he had to wait until April 2. On that day, the galleries of the House and the corridors of the Parliament Buildings were crowded to overflowing.

The Liberals had selected the right person to make the accusation. Tall, handsome, a sonorous speaker, a one-time junior minister with a fair knowledge of railways, Huntington had an air of gravitas.* His actual speech was surprisingly short—just seven paragraphs—and contained not a scintilla of evidence to support any of his accusations. He claimed that Allan's Canadian Pacific was secretly financed by Americans, that the government knew this was so, that Allan had made enormous election contributions to the Conservative Party, and that he had been offered the railway contract in exchange. Having made these devastating charges, Huntington sat down.

Macdonald remained expressionless throughout, occasionally playing with his pencil. When it was finished, he said not a word, waiting for the Speaker to call a vote. The motion was defeated by thirty-one votes, a larger margin than the government usually commanded.

---

* During the Liberal government that followed, Huntington got involved in a railway scandal in which he, although a cabinet minister, joined a syndicate seeking to buy the Canadian Pacific charter. Other controversies followed, and his political career petered out. His one real accomplishment was to marry a well-off New Yorker and move to her house in that city.

Handsome, gifted with a sonorous voice and married to a rich wife, Lucius Huntington seemed set for a stellar career. He only ever made one mark: his accusations, in the Commons, of massive corruption by Macdonald, set off the Canadian Pacific Scandal.

Public interest had been stirred, but it couldn't be sustained until some actual facts were made public. A week later, Macdonald proposed that the House form a five-member special committee to examine Huntington's charges. He did this, as he told a supporter, because the government's failure to respond had caused "a great uneasiness among our friends" by seeming to suggest it had something to hide.

Here was the first sign that Macdonald, as he seldom allowed to happen to him, was responding to events rather than getting ahead of them, defending rather than attacking, and seeming to be hanging back as if waiting for some event that would itself decide the outcome—almost as if accepting that the effect of this *deus ex machina* could as well be unfavourable to him as favourable. And he was drinking heavily. As Dufferin phrased it delicately to the colonial secretary, "For the last few days he has broken through his usual abstemious habits, and been compelled to resort to more stimulants than suit his peculiar temperament. It is really tragical to see so superior a man subject to such a purely physical infirmity, against which he struggles with desperate courage, until fairly prostrated and broken down."

So began the long death struggle, which always was about Macdonald rather than about the Canadian Pacific. It could have only one of two possible conclusions: either Huntington, after failing to substantiate his accusations, would have to resign his seat;

or Macdonald, having lost the confidence of a majority of the MPs, would have to step down as prime minister and retire ignominiously from public life. Even Allan seemed able at last to comprehend the seriousness of the situation. He wired Macdonald from London to say plaintively that Huntington's accusation was "in all the papers and is very injurious to us. Could you not stop this?"

Most people assumed that the loser would be Huntington. So far, he had failed to produce one bit of evidence. He was also up against formidable opponents: Canada's most skilled politician and its most successful businessman. Further, Macdonald could count on the governor general giving him the benefit of almost every doubt. Dufferin would later write to London that Huntington had "got hold of a mare's nest," and he told Macdonald that his position was "unassailable."

Instead, the Canadian Pacific Scandal would soon completely dominate Canadian public life and become the single political subject talked about. In the meantime, two other events of consequence had taken place: Oliver Mowat, the ablest political opponent Macdonald would ever face, had just returned to the arena, and George-Étienne Cartier, his companion-in-arms since 1855, had left it.

Mowat was little known to the public, having been out of politics for almost a decade. That was about to change. He would go on to become premier of Ontario for twenty-three years, a record never since equalled, and, by perspicacity, determination and the deviousness of his dullness, he laid the foundation for modern Ontario. Macdonald thoroughly detested him, but in their increasingly fierce engagements it was the older man who most often emerged the loser.

Mowat had actually begun his career in Macdonald's office as a junior law clerk. Later, he was recruited by George Brown into the Reform Party. He became a minister in the Great Coalition government that achieved Confederation, but left right after the Quebec Conference to take up the senior judicial post of vice-chancellor of Ontario's Court of Chancery.*

Macdonald had appointed Mowat to the position, quite likely to rid himself of an able political opponent. When the chancellor died, Macdonald did not promote Mowat to the vacancy. If he had, he might have changed the course of Canada's political and legal history. Instead, in 1872, Mowat became Ontario's first Liberal premier. In the years ahead, he would take a string of constitutional cases to Britain's Judicial Committee of the Privy Council and, by winning most of them, turn the highly centralized federation envisaged in the British North America Act into one of the most decentralized in the world. Macdonald never slackened in his nation-building, but even while he added to the country and filled it out, its fundamental character was being altered radically.

For the present, Macdonald and Mowat merely exchanged pleasantries—the political equivalent of boxers touching gloves before the start of a bout. Macdonald's letter of welcome to Mowat on his ascent to the premiership began teasingly: "My feelings . . . are of a composite character . . . with all your political sins, you will impart a respectability to the local govt. which it much wanted." He ended by saying he wished "that the relationship between the Dominion Government & that of Ontario will be pleasant" and saw no reason "why they should not be so." Mowat replied blandly but with a hint of a sharp edge: the success of Confederation, he wrote, depended on "proper relations being maintained between the Dominion and the Local

* Strictly speaking, Ontario was still Canada West at that time.

Governments as such, even when these are not in the hands of the same political party."

Mowat's return to politics as Ontario premier affected Macdonald immediately in one important respect. The day before the March 6 opening of Parliament, the Liberal MPs in Ottawa had at last made the long-delayed decision of choosing a leader. The Liberals had not had an official leader since Confederation, principally because everyone deferred to George Brown, even though he had no seat in the House of Commons. With the Pacific Scandal brewing, the prospect of power focused their minds. As leader, they chose Alexander Mackenzie, who until then had been, like Edward Blake, a member in both Toronto and Ottawa. Simultaneously, the Quebec *rouges*, led by Antoine-Aimé Dorion, at last joined the Liberal Party rather than merely maintaining an informal alliance with it. For the first time since 1867, Macdonald faced a single Liberal Party with a single leader.

Far more consequential to Macdonald at the time was the departure from the stage of George-Étienne Cartier. For almost two decades, Macdonald had called him his "sheet anchor" and his "second-self," the ally without whom Confederation could never have happened and without whose bloc of *bleu* MPs he would not be prime minister.

When Cartier left Canada in September 1872, in the hope of curing his Bright's disease, Macdonald knew that he would never return. Most of the time he was in London, Cartier lived at the Westminster Palace Hotel, later moving to an apartment. His mistress, Luce Cuvillier, crossed the Atlantic to be with him. His estranged wife, Hortense, followed with their two daughters, who took each parent out in turn for walks and carriage rides. His specialist, Dr. George Johnston, prescribed a diet of eggs and milk and a strict regime of "hot-air sweating," in which the patient was covered with flannel blankets while hot air was pumped in underneath, all in the hope of reducing the inflammation in the kidneys.

Cartier and Macdonald wrote to each other constantly. Macdonald reported consistently good news and often remarked that some Canadian just back from London had told him how Cartier's condition had improved, even though the visitor had said nothing of the kind. Cartier's news was equally cheerful and inaccurate. He showed little awareness of what ailed him, and even less that it was incurable. "My illness must have originated in the cold I caught in December last on my way from Quebec to Ottawa," he wrote, and, on another occasion, "I wish so much to be cured so as to be able to return to assist you." By mid-May, Cartier's condition had deteriorated to the point that his letter began, "I am so weak I cannot hold a pen."

The end came quickly. On May 20, 1873, Cartier's daughter Rose telegraphed the news to Macdonald. He opened the envelope in the Commons, read out its contents, stopped and said in a low voice, "I feel myself quite unable to say more at this moment." Back in his seat, he stretched out an arm over Cartier's empty desk and broke down in tears. The other daughter, Josephine, added details of the end: two days before his death, her father had "bade us to read even to minute details the contents of the Canadian newspapers, as if to surmise upon the doings of that Country he beloved, before undertaking his final journey."

The funeral service was in the French Chapel in London's Portman Square. Luce Cuvillier attended, but not Hortense. The body was put into a sealed coffin and placed on board the Allan liner *Prussian*. After a stop at Quebec City, the coffin was transferred to the government boat, *Druid*, which took it up the river to Montreal. The state funeral in the cathedral was preceded by a viewing at the Palais de Justice, where an estimated seventy thousand people passed by the casket. Cartier was buried in the Notre Dame des Neiges cemetery on Mount Royal. The funeral and burial service were hard on Macdonald: Dufferin reported home, "He was in a very bad way . . . indeed quite prostrate."

Macdonald provided his best accounting of his relationship with Cartier long afterwards, at the unveiling of a statue of his friend on Parliament Hill in 1885. He said then of Cartier: "Brave as a lion, he was afraid of nothing. . . . I loved him when he was living; I regretted and wept for him when he died." According to Joseph Pope, during their drive back from the funeral, Macdonald repeated that Cartier was "as bold as a lion," adding, "But for him, confederation could not have carried." The two musketeers were now just one.

Cartier's near-to-last words, according to Josephine, had referred to the "good tidings" from Prince Edward Island, which had at last decided to join Confederation. Again, the decisive factor was a railway, only this time the line had already been built and the consequence was near bankruptcy, of both company and province. The terms of entering Confederation were readily agreed on, with two special provisions: Ottawa would provide an annual subsidy of $45,000 to enable the provincial government to buy up absentee landowners (most of them British) who were retarding the island's agricultural development, and the federal government would commit to maintain "continuous communication . . . winter and summer" with the mainland. The union took place on Dominion Day, 1873. Dufferin attended the ceremonies in Charlottetown and recorded that most islanders were "under the impression that it is the Dominion that has been annexed to Prince Edward Island."*

The five-member special committee Macdonald had proposed to look into Huntington's accusations never got down to work, a victim of his tactic of delaying in the hope that good fortune might burst spontaneously from the inertia. He argued that the committee should begin by questioning the best-informed witnesses, Allan and Abbott. Since both were in England, he suggested that the committee postpone its work until July 2, when they would have returned. The committee's Conservative majority agreed. A new opportunity for delay then presented itself. To get at the real truth, Macdonald suggested that the committee should be able to take evidence under oath. For technical reasons, the Canadian Parliament lacked that authority, so Westminster would have to give its consent. Time passed while British parliamentary experts considered the request. Finally, the answer came that granting a colonial parliament such authority would take a lot of time.

Macdonald now proposed replacing the committee with a Royal Commission, which would have an unquestioned right to compel witnesses to give testimony under oath. Edward Blake spotted what Macdonald was up to and protested forcefully that it would be quite improper for the government to set up a

* The pledge of "continuous communication" with the mainland was not fulfilled in its literal sense until 1997, when an eight-mile bridge was built across the Northumberland Strait. As far back as 1886, though, PEI Senator George Howlan formed a company to build a tunnel to the island, arguing that recent expansions of the London Underground and the Gotthard rail tunnel through the Swiss Alps showed this was possible.

commission to inquire into "matters of charge against itself." More time passed, with the accusations against Macdonald remaining just that—accusations, unsupported by any evidence. Steadily, public interest dwindled.

For Macdonald, this advance was offset by a setback. Allan's mission to London to raise capital for the railway had ended in complete failure, with all of the major financial houses—Glyn's, Baring's, Rothschilds—refusing to have anything to do with the scheme. The reason, as John Rose reported to Macdonald, was the constant press reports of accusations of a vast scandal impending.

Suddenly, the first concrete evidence of what might have happened was made public. Its source was George McMullen, who was at last acting on the threats he had made to Macdonald during their meetings at the start of the year. On July 4, both the Toronto *Globe* and the Montreal *Herald* published an extensive selection of Allan's private correspondence with his secret American backers—seventeen letters in all. Readers could learn about Allan's list of prominent Canadians given free shares, many of them Conservative MPs; about his deal with Cartier and his massive disbursement of election funds to the Conservatives; and about his continuing reassurance to his American partners, long after he had committed to dissolving the relationship, that all would be well for their agreement. The *Globe* claimed that the mass of material showed that Macdonald had been "hopelessly involved in an infamous and corrupt conspiracy."

Conservative newspapers promptly counterattacked, pointing out that the *Globe* and the *Herald* had deliberately failed to print two of Allan's letters, of October 1872, in which he had finally broken off his negotiations with the Americans.

In fact, Macdonald's name appeared only three times in the letters and in no instance was it in connection with any nefarious act. Faced with a specific accusation for the first time since

THE PACIFIC RAILWAY INTRIGUES.

Important Correspondence between Sir Hugh Allan and his American partners.

EXTRAORDINARY DISCLOSURES.

The Charter to be Sold for a Monetary Consideration.

(*By Telegraph from Special Reporters.*)

MONTREAL, July 3.

The following portion of the documentary evidence, showing the corrupt nature of the negotiations between Sir Hugh Allan and the Government in connection with the granting of the Pacific Railway charter, has come into our possession.

(*Telegraph*)

"FATHER POINT, October 8, 1871.

"To C. M. SMITH, of Chicago,

"Metropolitan Hotel, New York.

"Send me by mail, care of Allan, Bros. & Co., Liverpool, the names of the parties engaged with us in the railroad enterprise.

(Signed,) "H. ALLAN."

(*Letter.*)

The Canadian Pacific Scandal began on July 18, 1873, when the Globe *and two other papers printed records stolen from the office of Allan's lawyer, among them Canada's best-known telegram, sent by Macdonald during the 1872 election: "I must have another ten thousand."*

Huntington made his general charges almost four months earlier, Macdonald responded specifically. He insisted that Allan write a long public letter to explain his behaviour. This affidavit, compiled by Abbott, was a masterpiece, interspersing spasms of self-justification amid confessions and admissions. He had contributed election funds, as everyone had the right to do, wrote Allan, but not in exchange for any government commitment other than of the presidency. He had maintained contact with his American backers because of commitments he had made to them, but he had broken away as soon as the government specifically directed him to do so. Most lamely, he argued that his letters had been "written in the confidence of private intercourse in the midst of many matters" and so had been written "with less care and circumspection than might have been bestowed on them had they been intended for publication."

This artfully composed confession made Allan the principal villain in the public's eyes, and for the first time Macdonald allowed himself the luxury of relief: Abbott "has made the old gentleman acknowledge on oath that his letters were untrue," he wrote to Dufferin. To a friend, he wrote triumphantly, "The Huntington matter has ended in a fizzle, as I knew it would." And

In the summer of 1873, Macdonald retreated to a cottage in the resort of Rivière-du-Loup. According to some newspapers, he once stole away to attempt suicide, but in fact he only drank himself into insensibility.

from Dufferin came the sweet sound of support: "Nothing can be more satisfactory than the way in which your own position and that of your colleagues remains unassailed in the midst of all these disreputable proceedings."*

The odds that Macdonald might survive were at least promising now. He felt free to leave Ottawa and holiday in his summer villa overlooking the waters of the Gulf of St. Lawrence near Rivière-du-Loup.

Two weeks later, there came a second eruption in the press—in the *Globe*, the *Herald*, and *L'Événement* in Quebec City. The *Globe*'s headline read, "The Pacific Scandal: Astounding Revelations." Once again, the newspaper reports ran to multiple columns.

* The principal sources for this material are Berton's *The National Dream* and Creighton's *The Old Chieftain*.

McMullen gave a long recounting of his version of events, much of it familiar but with a few new revelations—such as that Hincks, the former finance minister, had asked Allan for fifty thousand dollars in election funds and for a job for his son in the company. Damningly, Asa Foster, a Conservative senator, declared that to his knowledge McMullen's version of events was accurate and that "large sums of money were actually expended for election purposes under the arrangement." Between them, McMullen and Foster created a clear impression of a government prepared to do just about anything to win the election.

The real damage was caused by what appeared farther down in the lengthy newspaper reports. There, for all Canadians to read in amazement and disbelief, was a series of short telegrams and memorandums. One telegram from Cartier to Abbott asked for "a further sum of twenty thousand dollars upon the same conditions as the amount written by me at the foot of my letter to Sir Hugh Allan of the 30th ult." A memorandum from three members of the Conservative central committee confirmed, "Received from Sir Hugh Allan by the hands of J.J. Abbott twenty thousand dollars for General Election purposes." By far the most damaging, because it carried Macdonald's signature, was his August 26, 1872, telegram to Abbott—"I must have another ten thousand"—and Abbott's affirmative reply.

In these the most desperate moments of Macdonald's career, Alexander Campbell, the prime minister's Mr. Fix-It, recognized immediately that the very survival of the government and Macdonald was now at stake. He insisted that Macdonald immediately set up a Royal Commission to investigate the matter, but with "safe" judges. Abbott came up with a list of names and, in addition, dictated a series of editorials in the Montreal *Gazette* making the best possible interpretations of the disclosures. Abbott also tried to figure out how all this material had got into the hands of Liberal editors. He concluded that George Norris, one of his confidential clerks, and Alfred Cooper, a junior clerk, had entered his own office at night and rifled his files. Norris had gone into hiding, but Abbott managed to persuade Cooper to sign an affidavit that the Liberals had paid Norris five thousand dollars to steal the material. Conservative newspapers had great fun pointing out that the virtuous Liberals had abetted a theft.

"It is one of those overwhelming misfortunes that they say every man must meet once in his life," Macdonald wrote to Dufferin after this second round. For weeks now, he had been drinking heavily. On August 3, at Rivière-du-Loup, he broke.

Sometime early that Sunday morning, taking care not to wake Agnes, Macdonald stole quietly out of their house and disappeared. Where he went and what he did over the next two days, nobody knows for sure. The following day, the *Montreal Witness* carried a report that "yesterday afternoon Sir John attempted to commit suicide by jumping from the wharf in the water. He was rescued but now lies . . . in a precarious condition." The *Globe* reprinted this report, adding that he might have suffered some misfortune "accidentally by bathing." The best account of what may have happened was provided months later by Dufferin: "I could get neither an answer to my letter, even to my telegrams," he wrote in a report to London. "No one—not even his wife—knew where he was. He had stolen away, as I subsequently heard, from his seaside villa and was lying *perdu* with a friend in the neighbourhood of Quebec." The least credible account came from Macdonald in a telegram sent to friends and relatives after the suicide story had appeared. "It is an infamous falsehood," he declared. "I was never better in my life."*

* Much of the material in this section is taken from the article "Sir John's Lost Weekend" by Peter Black in *The Beaver*. Later, two Quebec historians wrote that Macdonald most likely spent the time in Lévis in a house rented by his cousin, a Mr. Young, from the poet Louis-Honoré Fréchette.

In practical terms, Macdonald was far too drunk to carry out so demanding a task as killing himself. The likeliest explanation is that he crawled away from his family, like a wounded animal, in search of some place where no one could see his shame as he drank himself into oblivion.

On the third day, Macdonald emerged from hiding. Soon after, he took the train back to Ottawa. A reporter for *Le Canadien* who spotted him at the station in Montreal wrote that he "appeared in excellent health." By then, though, Macdonald must have known that in the dark days ahead there could be but one likely outcome.

This period of some six months, from mid to late 1873, would be the most painful in all Macdonald's political life. He was fighting not just to survive, but for the sake of his honour, his reputation, his place in history. It is somehow fitting that, as nation-builder, he should have accomplished one of the best of all his projects during this most difficult time.

During these months, Macdonald pulled off three nation-building projects: the entry of Prince Edward Island into Confederation as its seventh province; the creation of a new Department of the Interior responsible for western development and the vital land survey; and above all the North-West Mounted Police. With astonishing speed, the Mounted Police became highly regarded by all those they dealt with directly—the Plains Indians, the white settlers and the general public. They changed their name to the Royal Canadian Mounted Police in 1920, and became one of Canada's best-known and most respected institutions (if less so in recent years).*

* The RCMP actually inherited its honorific of "Royal" from its predecessor, the NWMP, which gained the Royal status in 1904.

For decades, to people everywhere, the Mounties were Canada.

Macdonald was the Mounted Police's father and godfather. The original idea was his; he played a major part in its design; he created it; and all his life he supported it unstintingly. Moreover, it was at his insistence that the NWMP was distinctively Canadian. Its purpose, as defined in the act that established it in 1873, was "the preservation of the peace, the prevention of crime." Its objective was not to punish crime, although its members, as magistrates, possessed that authority and exercised it. It was, rather, to prevent crime from happening in the first place. The NWMP didn't so much police the community as become part of it; each year its members would ride horseback over hundreds of miles, getting to know the settlers and the Indians, passing on gossip, weather information, medical advice, delivering and picking up mail or just chatting to the occupants of lonely homesteads.

Macdonald took his time making all this possible, and almost left it too late.* Had he delayed much longer, it's likely that the Liberals, who originally opposed the force on the grounds of cost and later twice tried to abolish the NWMP, would never have set it up. His first description of the force he had in mind was in a letter at the end of 1869 to Captain D.R. Cameron, then accompanying William McDougall on his way to Red River, to whom he wrote "the best Force would be Mounted Riflemen, trained to act as cavalry . . . [and] styled Police." He never altered that basic concept. He was also consistent about its purpose: it was to extinguish the liquor trade, by driving out the American traders

* One of the oddities of Canadian historiography is that this story, well known at the time, was later forgotten. Even Donald Creighton, in his two-volume biography published in the 1950s, makes no mention of Macdonald's role and refers only briefly to the NWMP. The story remained virtually unknown until the publication in 1972 of S.W. Horall's article "Sir John Macdonald and the Mounted Police Force for the Northwest Territories" in the *Canadian Historical Review*.

who were then moving freely across the border, and to keep the peace between the Indians and the steadily increasing numbers of settlers. As he wrote in a letter in 1871, "With emigrants of all Nations flowing into that Country we are in constant danger of an Indian war. . . . This may be prevented only by an early organization of a mounted police."

Not until late in 1872 did Macdonald act. He promised Alexander Morris, the lieutenant-governor of the North-West, that he would introduce enabling legislation the following year. He instructed his deputy minister, Hewitt Bernard, to draft a plan for the force and directed Colonel Robertson-Ross, the head of the militia, to compose a report to be submitted to Parliament.

When the legislation came before the Commons in March 1873 (the same month that Lucius Huntington first spoke out), Macdonald, introducing it as minister of justice, explained that the Mounted Police would be "somewhat similar to the Irish Mounted Constabulary . . . would use the hardy horse of the country, and by being police would be a civil force, each member of which would be a police constable, and therefore a preventive officer." The bill provided for the engagement of three hundred men; all had to be fit, of good character, able to ride, and able to read and write either English or French.

In one respect, Macdonald got it wrong. In the debate, he said the uniform of the force should have "as little gold lace, fuss and feathers as possible." Luckily, Morris, the man on the spot, got it right. He urged that the policemen "be red-coated—as 50 men in red coats are better than 100 in other colours." The change was made, and thereafter everyone in the West knew these men were the Queen's police and not blue-jacketed American cavalry.

The legislation was only enabling. Macdonald still delayed implementing it, rejecting Morris's frantic requests for police to halt the liquor trade that was causing such devastation among the

Just before he went down, Macdonald created the North-West Mounted Police, the first-ever distinctly Canadian institution. Its first uniforms were of scarlet Norfolk jackets and pillbox hats. The bearded officer is F. J. Dickens, son of the famous novelist.

Indians. Then, in August, reports came east of a massacre of several dozen Assiniboine Indians by American traders from Montana. Macdonald approved a start on recruitment, followed by training in Toronto and Kingston, with the force going west the next spring. As his position became more precarious, he changed his mind. On September 24, he wrote to Dufferin, "We find it necessary that the force should be sent up before the close of navigation. . . . If anything went wrong, the blame would lay at our door." Recruitment was undertaken hastily, and a young Irishman, Colonel George Arthur French, who had experience with the Irish Constabulary, was appointed commissioner. On November 1, the force, then of just 150 men, paraded for the first time outside Fort Garry, and the oath of office was administered to officers and men. Four days later, Macdonald was no longer prime minister.

In his absence, the force did him proud. Its first venture, the legendary Great March, right across the prairies from Winnipeg to Fort Whoop-Up, a base for the liquor traders in present-day Alberta, was in fact a near disaster: the contingent lost its way and almost perished for lack of water. Yet the march became an instant epic, gaining the force a reputation for determination and high-mindedness that it retained for decades. In London, the *Times* praised the NWMP as "a corps d'élite." Americans were awed by its laid-back effectiveness; the Fort Benton *Record* coined what would become the Mounted Police's signature phrase, "They always get their man"— its original version being "They fetched their man every time." The highest praise of all came from Blackfoot chief Crowfoot, who explained as his reason for signing a treaty in 1877, "The Mounted Police protected us as the feathers of the bird protect it from the frosts of winter."

The NWMP was never perfect, but it was extraordinary. Because of it, law and order prevailed in Canada's West, while below the border the gun ruled, wielded either by the army or by vigilante squads. Above the border, most of those hauled into the courts by the policemen were whites accused of crimes against Indians; below it, few whites were ever tried, because the all-white juries refused to find them guilty. The Mounted Police did all this with a few hundred men in an area half the size of Europe. Some of this success was circumstance: most of its first recruits came from Ontario and brought with them Upper Canadian deep respect for law and order and, more important, no ingrained hostility to Indians. But still, they did it.

The NWMP didn't just help to build Canada by establishing peace, order and good government in an untamed frontier; rather, it actually helped to build Canada itself. It was in the West that Canada became most distinctive as a nation, developing in a way quite different from the U.S. West, although the two regions were identical and the border between them invisible. In the Canadian West, the prevailing order became community order first, individual interest second. It was the first realization of the "new nationality" that Macdonald's government had once enunciated and then abandoned as impossible. More than a century would have to pass before Canadians came to realize that a "new nationality" could be political rather than ethnic, or one composed of values and attitudes rather than of race. Macdonald himself never had any such goal in mind, but in his pragmatic way he took the first step along that elongated, irregular path.

For the present, however, Macdonald had just one goal in his sights: to survive.

SEVENTEEN

Fall

Your immediate and personal connection with what has occurred, cannot but fatally affect your position as minister.

Governor General Dufferin to Macdonald, October 14, 1873

In the Ontario town of London, on August 28, 1873, Edward Blake's angry oratory rolled down onto the crowd gathered to hear him. "We are a humiliated people," he declared. "It is utterly impossible to urge that those hands are clean, utterly impossible to escape from the conviction that the enormous powers entrusted to the government . . . were used for the purpose of procuring influence and cash from the contractors to whom they agreed to give the contract." From this condemnation he drew the conclusion, "The free voice of the people has been overborne."

Blake was telling the truth. A few days earlier, after returning to Ottawa from Rivière-du-Loup, Macdonald had once again outmanoeuvred the Liberals, winning for himself yet another delay. Earlier, all the parties had agreed that Parliament would reopen on August 13. They now discovered that this reopening was to be postponed to the end of October. The cause of the change was Lord Dufferin's acceptance of a request by Macdonald that he prorogue Parliament immediately after it had assembled so he could announce the establishment of a Royal Commission on the Canadian Pacific Railway. To make that possible—and what particularly angered Blake—the Speaker of the House of Commons had abandoned all pretence of neutrality by refusing to recognize Opposition leader Alexander Mackenzie when he attempted to move a motion of privilege, which always had to be heard before any other business. That lapse gave time for the Usher of the Black Rod, a senior Senate official, to interrupt the Commons proceedings and call all MPs to the Upper Chamber to hear a message from the governor general. Only Conservative MPs followed him down the corridors to the Senate.

For the moment, all the Liberals could do was retreat to a room in the Parliament Buildings to listen to speakers denounce the destruction of "the privileges and independence of Parliament and the rights of the people." A far more effective response was Blake's hastily organized tour of Ontario. He was talking now not like some lofty lawyer but an avenging angel. He had even figured out how to perform like a politician, asking the crowd rhetorically, "What position do we occupy today in relation to the people of the United States?" He then provided his own answer: "We have been accustomed to pride ourselves on the comparative elevation of Canadian morals . . . we can do so no longer." He spoke with the confident authority of a moralist: "The appointment of this Commission is a high contempt of Parliament and . . . the privileges of Parliament are the privileges of the people." As was rare in Canada in those days, Blake was grounding his argument on the foundation of democracy, on the rights of the people, on their sovereignty. Shortly afterwards, a Conservative passed on to Macdonald the disturbing news that the Liberals had printed an astounding thirty thousand copies of Blake's speech to distribute in the right places. Suddenly, the character of the inherently grubby Pacific Scandal changed from being an affair about governmental corruption—scarcely novel—to an affair about democracy, public decency and the relationship between the governing and the governed.

⁓

If the appointment of the Royal Commission wasn't bad enough—it replaced the parliamentary committee all parties had agreed on in the spring—the appointment of the commissioners was even worse. All three were either Conservative supporters or friends of Macdonald. Judge James Gowan was both; in midsummer, he had written to Macdonald to denounce "the evil-speaking slandering,

By the end of the summer of 1873, a sense had taken hold that Macdonald had lost control over the scandal. Grip *magazine caught the mood in this cartoon. For the one and only time, it depicted an out-of-control Macdonald with a bottle peeking out of his pocket.*

vile plotting" to which Macdonald had been subjected, adding, "There is no one capable of taking your place." Another commissioner, Judge Charles Day, had pledged himself to "change the current of public opinion."

Macdonald's last-ditch stand was to appoint a Royal Commission to inquire into the affair. Its three members were Conservatives or friends, or both. They might as well all have been Macdonald himself.

All of this was enough to make Dufferin uneasy for the first time—a condition triggered earlier by a warning note from Colonial Secretary Kimberley seeking an assurance that Dufferin was "fully alive to the necessity of a thorough and immediate investigation into the astonishing charges." Dufferin called Mackenzie in to let him know he had granted prorogation because it was a formal request made by his prime minister, but that he had limited it to ten weeks—less than Macdonald had asked for. And he advised Macdonald that the newspaper disclosures "undoubtedly place your government in a more difficult position." Probably influenced by Lady Dufferin, who adored Macdonald, he soon slipped back to his earlier stance, assuring him that once he was cleared of all accusations, as was certain, "there will set in a glorious reaction in your favour."

Dufferin was no fool. He could sense the tide of opinion shifting, and he asked Macdonald to write a full account of his version of the events. This chronicle contained no new arguments, though Macdonald explained that, in contrast to British practices, where the Carlton and Reform clubs handled such matters for the parties, here in less developed Canada he had been "obliged to get into the [financial] details of the party arrangements." Dufferin took this document with him on his summer holiday to Quebec City and arranged for daily reports of the hearings of the Royal Commission to be hurried to him. He studied them at length and with great care. On his return to Ottawa, he retreated to his private office at Rideau Hall and wrote a long letter to Macdonald. It was dated October 14, just four days before Parliament was due to resume.

"It is with greater pain than ever I did anything in my life, that I now sit down to write to you," Dufferin began. He assured Macdonald that, despite all the accusations made against him, his "personal honour is as stainless as it has ever been." Moreover, no doubt existed that Macdonald had "religiously protected the interests of Canada," against both the American speculators and Sir Hugh Allan. Regardless, continued Dufferin, "It is still an indisputable fact that you and some of your colleagues have been the channels through which extravagant sums of money—derived from a person with whom you were negotiating on the part of the Dominion—were distributed." After that came the verbal equivalent of a judge's gavel descending: "Your immediate and personal connection with what has occurred, cannot but fatally affect your position as minister."

Dufferin had just said he considered Macdonald unfit to continue as prime minister. He did so, he emphasized, with great sadness: "Independent of the personal attachment I feel towards you, I have always had and still have the greatest faith and confidence in your ability, patriotism, integrity and statesmanship." It was to Macdonald that Canada "owes its existence, and your name will be preserved in history as the father and founder of the Dominion." Nevertheless, concluded Dufferin, "no considerations of this kind are sufficient, I fear, to affect the present situation."

One day later, on October 20, Macdonald was summoned to meet with Dufferin at noon at Rideau Hall. Their exchange was entirely amicable but for a mild reproof by Macdonald that

Dufferin had waited so long to send this stinging letter. Dufferin agreed that the evidence exonerated Macdonald of three of four major charges against him—of personal corruption, of selling the railway to the Americans and of entering into an improper pact with Allan. What remained, and what "fatally affect[ed] your position as minister," was that Macdonald had accepted large amounts of money from someone seeking favours from the government and then applied these funds in ways that broke the electoral laws. Speaking to Macdonald as a friend, Dufferin urged him to forestall being ejected from office by losing a vote of confidence, and instead admit publicly that he had made mistakes, dissolve Parliament and put his future into the hands of the people. Dufferin accepted that Macdonald might well lose such an election but argued he would greatly improve his prospects for an eventual recovery.

Macdonald spent most of the following day closeted with his cabinet. He let his colleagues know he was ready to resign. Charles Tupper responded that if Macdonald left, so would he—a deft move by the combative old warrior, because, as the only conceivable alternative leader, he made it far harder for Macdonald to step down. In the middle of these discussions, a message from Rideau Hall summoned Macdonald to meet with Dufferin once again. He had new and, in some sense, encouraging news to impart: a memorandum had just come in from the colonial secretary to say that any decision about the government's future should be taken exclusively by the Canadian Parliament rather than by the governor general. Dufferin therefore advised Macdonald to treat his earlier letter as "in some degree cancelled." Officially, that left him free to go on fighting. But Macdonald can have been in no doubt that, in telling him his tenure as prime minister had been "fatally affected," Dufferin was describing the bitter, unalterable truth.

Parliament opened on October 23 with the customary ceremony and the usual Throne Speech, read by Dufferin and promising a full legislative program. The one newsworthy item was that Allan's Canadian Pacific Company had surrendered its charter because it had not been able to raise the necessary financial backing. Liberal leader Alexander Mackenzie moved for a formal motion of censure. Among Conservative insiders, the guessing was that the government's majority was close to twenty. Early on in the debate, Tupper delivered a four-hour speech, full of sound and fury, which raised the Conservatives' spirits.

The familiar script, though, was no longer being followed. One by one, independent MPs (the largest group being those from Nova Scotia) began to let it be known that their sentiments were with the Opposition. In the corridors, Liberals in particular, but Conservatives also, sought out waverers and whispered words about "possible future considerations."* Estimates of the government's majority began to shrink down to a dozen, even to single figures.

To the surprise of all, and the acute dismay of his own backbenchers, Macdonald remained silent, indeed inactive. Not only did he not lead his troops into battle by delivering a sterling speech, but for long periods he wasn't in the Commons at all. Even when present, he was often too drunk to challenge Opposition speakers with quips and interjections. At times, he gave the appearance of being almost paralyzed, of fearing that some new terrible blow was about to fall on him. Not until November 3, by which time the debate had gone on for a full week, and with his government continually losing support, did Macdonald come alive.

Belatedly, and operating entirely on instinct, he realized at last why no more devastating letters or telegrams had been made

---

* The highest bribe, it was claimed, was for a good government job plus a cash payment of five thousand dollars.

public and why, as made no sense in itself, Blake had not yet risen to give one of his masterful five-hour presentations of the facts, afterwards going on to draw almost unanswerable conclusions from them. The answer was that there were no more incriminating telegrams or documents, so Blake, cannily, to avoid the risk of weakening the Opposition's case, had deliberately not spoken.

At last, Macdonald knew what to do, and he rose to speak. It was too late. Voters had long ago lost interest in the details of the scandal, which were still being churned out in all their contradictions and conflicts by the Royal Commission hearings. All that voters were focused on was the simple fact that something scandalous had happened and that their prime minister was involved in it.

Even though he could not save his government, it wasn't yet inevitable that Macdonald would lose everything. He could still save his image and his honour. As a Scot, he would have known well that a heroic defeat is often remembered more kindly than some spectacular victory. He could still put on a performance that everyone would remember—and that many would recall with a sense of something important having been lost for their country as well as for themselves.

And this is how the event unfolded. Shortly after nine on the night of November 3, word spread quickly from the packed galleries to the crowded corridors in the Parliament Building that "the Old Man is on his feet." A pale, thin, haggard, exhausted and dishevelled old man, his eyes watery, his shoulders slumped, rose to face an exuberant, triumphant Opposition and his own silent supporters, resigned to their fate.

Macdonald began slowly, his voice scarcely audible, his sentences sometimes jumbled, arms waving erratically. Gradually, his shots began to fall nearer to the targets opposite him. He struck out at Lucius Huntington, who had started the whole affair yet favoured a "foreign and alien power"—a reference to Huntington's one-time support for annexation. He charged that Huntington had paid McMullen for his documents. The Montreal MP shouted back, "I challenge the Hon. Gentleman to combat." Macdonald replied coolly, "I hit a sore spot." The next shot targeted David Blain, a lawyer known to have married exceedingly well. He could prove, Macdonald said, that Blain had broken the law by paying someone to vote for him. "Not a cent went out of my pocket," retorted Blain. To which Macdonald responded, "Well, you know, if a man has not a pocket, his wife has." The Opposition sent up cries of "Shame," "Withdraw," "Order."

By now Macdonald was energized, while behind him his supporters were suddenly alert and upright. He set out his basic defence. Allan was the best available man, and no commitment had been made to him except for the presidency. Allan had indeed made election contributions, but all businessmen did. The Americans had been cut out of the project and would never have been allowed to run the company. As for himself, he had never used any of Allan's money.

It was now past 1:30 a.m. More and more, the Liberals were silent and the Conservatives were cheering. In the Speaker's Gallery, Lady Dufferin gazed down in rapt admiration. Macdonald had spoken for more than four hours, at times weakening, but then gaining a new burst of strength. He had arranged for three individuals to provide him with refills of gin in his water glass, so he was assured of constant revivals. Macdonald was no longer speaking about the scandal, but about his future. He moved to his peroration:

> I commit myself, the Government commits itself, to the hands of this House, and far beyond this House, it commits itself to the country at large. We have faithfully done our duty. . . . I have fought the battle of Confederation, the battle of Union, the battle of the Dominion of Canada. I throw myself upon this House; I throw

> myself upon this country; I throw myself upon posterity, and I believe that I know, that not withstanding the many failings in my life, I shall have the voice of this country, and this House rallying around me.
>
> I can see past the decision of this House either for or against me, but . . . there does not exist in Canada a man who has given more of his time, more of his heart, more of his wealth, or more of his intellect and power such as it may be, for the good of this Dominion of Canada.

Macdonald collapsed back into his seat and turned once again into a dishevelled old man. By some strange alchemy, though, he had proved once again more of a leader than anyone else in the House. When she got back to Rideau Hall, Lady Dufferin stayed up until 5 a.m., telling her husband, amid extravagant gestures and excited commentary, about "a very fine speech, full of power."

~

The next morning, the mood among the Conservatives was subdued. The *Globe* began with a brilliant exercise in editorial invective. It admitted that Macdonald's defence "challenges admiration," but continued, "We have heard of men who had the courage of their convictions. . . . He has the unique glory of having the courage of his corruption." In his *Memoirs*, Sir Joseph Pope wrote of an "extreme uneasiness" taking hold among the Conservatives, following with the marvellous (if incomprehensible) remark, "There was a sound of going in the tops of the mulberry trees."

Blake had begun to speak right after Macdonald ended. Despite the emotion and the late hour, he found exactly the right words for the occasion. "I have no feelings of joy and congratulations," he said. Nevertheless, Macdonald had to go, because otherwise, "we may as well at once give up what will have become the farce of representative government." The next day, he continued his speech for close to five hours in all. He indulged in no histrionics, no exaggerated rhetoric, and reduced the whole complex issue to a simple, vivid sentence: "The Government got the money, and Sir Hugh Allan the charter." He continued with a systematic and relentless presentation of the facts. Finally, he concluded, "This House is to a . . . large extent, a purchased and a tainted House." However, "this night or tomorrow night will see the end of twenty years of corruption." He spoke directly to the remaining doubters: "To them I repeat my solemn warning . . . that loyalty to a party or to a man will not be held to justify treason to their country . . . we are here to set up once again the standard of public virtue."

It was soon over. David Laird, the leader of the six brand-new MPs from Prince Edward Island, used his maiden speech to advise the House he would be voting against the government. After him came Donald Smith, now the power in the Hudson's Bay Company and also a Manitoba MP. Desperate Conservatives had arranged a meeting between him and Macdonald, but their encounter went badly from the start. Smith asked that he be repaid for the three thousand dollars of company money he had spent to bribe Métis away from Louis Riel.* Macdonald took offence at this demand, abusing Smith and swearing drunkenly at him. In his speech in the Commons, Smith began by criticizing the Liberals for having abetted the crime of theft and declared that no proof of actual governmental wrongdoing had been established. But, he continued, while there had been "no corruption," there had been "a grave impropriety." Therefore, "for the honour of the country, no government should

---

* At Macdonald's request, Smith presented a bill for $3,367.50, allowing for interest. As one of his final official acts, Macdonald authorized its payment.

exist that has a shadow of suspicion resting on it; and for that reason I cannot give it my support." As he left the Commons after hearing this verdict, Macdonald turned to one of his MPs and said, "I could lick that man Smith quicker than hell could frizzle a feather." Late that night, the exuberant Liberals crammed into the Parliament Building's basement bar singing, "Sir John is dead and gone forever," to the tune of "Oh My Darling, Clementine."

No vote was ever held. The next day the cabinet assembled, and when Macdonald failed to show up they sent emissaries to his house. He was still in bed, but returned with them and told his colleagues, "I suppose I shall have to go to Rideau Hall and hand in your resignations." Soon afterwards, he made his last call on the governor general as prime minister and returned to his home.

Agnes was waiting for him. Though she had listened to his speech of the night before, sitting in a special chair provided for her near to the Speaker, Macdonald had not yet told her what had been going on. He came in and said to her casually, "Well, that's gone along with." "What do you mean?" Agnes asked. "It's a relief to be out of it," he replied. He went upstairs to his bedroom, put on his dressing gown, picked up a book and said not another word. Macdonald never again referred to the defeat, nor, so far as it's possible to know, ever discussed it with anyone.

That same day, Mackenzie met with Dufferin and, somewhat to his surprise, left with an invitation to form a new government. After the Commons' regular opening at 3 p.m., Macdonald rose to announce his resignation and that of his government. He informed the House that the governor general had invited Mackenzie to form a new government. All the Liberals immediately left their seats to cross over to the government side of the chamber, with the Conservatives, more slowly, shifting over to take their place as the Opposition. One Conservative, the British Columbia MP Amor de Cosmos, remained in his seat and was soon engulfed by Liberals. In this way, de Cosmos became the first parliamentarian in Canada—very likely anywhere—to cross the floor without ever leaving his seat.

The election was held in January 1874. The results were a rout; as the editor of the pro-Conservative Ottawa *Citizen* put it, "We have met the enemy, and we are theirs." The Liberals won 138 seats compared to a bare 67 for the Conservatives. Even in Quebec, the Liberals won a majority of the seats.* Only in British Columbia did the Conservatives hold on, winning all 6 seats, not least because Mackenzie had declared publicly that the terms of union with the province were "impossible" and that Macdonald's commitment to bring the transcontinental line across to Vancouver Island could not be fulfilled.

The judgment of the *Globe* on the Pacific Scandal and Macdonald's part in it was predictably harsh. "His *role* as a Canadian politician is played out," it stated. Macdonald possessed exceptional intelligence and judgment, "but these gifts have been poisoned by a cynical view of human nature, which has led him to appeal to the least worthy side of human character." The assessment of Goldwin Smith in *Canadian Monthly* was more nuanced: Macdonald "has kept his own hands clean. If he has sinned, it has been from love of power, not from love of pelf." However, "he has been the centre and organizer of a system, the evil traces of which will be left deep in the character of our people for many a day." The kindest comments were in Dufferin's report to the colonial secretary: "It cut me to the heart that a career so creditable to himself and so serviceable to his

* Besides the Liberal victory, the 1874 contest entered the history books as Canada's first simultaneous election, with almost all ridings voting at the same time.

Country, as that of Macdonald's should have ended in such humiliation." He ended with a most perceptive comment about Macdonald's departure: "I was very much moved by the terror and shame manifested by the people at large, when the possibility first dawned on them of their most trusted statesman having been guilty of such misconduct." Dufferin, there, got right through to the heart of the matter: most Canadians wanted Macdonald to go because of what he had done; a great many also did not really want him to leave. He was the only prime minister most had ever known. And he alone seemed to possess an understanding of what buttons to push and what levers to tug to make this curious, divided, stretched-out country function at all, let alone thrive. Even the scandal that brought him down had been a side effect of his attempt to pull the country together by a transnational railway. He had to be punished, but there was no one now to lead Canadians out of their wilderness. His alternative, Alexander Mackenzie, stirred no one's imagination and provided no inspiration.

Ironically, much of the drama about the Canadian Pacific in 1872 and 1873 was in fact unnecessary. The reason Macdonald was so eager to get the company started was his fear the Northern Pacific Railway would get there first, reducing the Canadian Pacific to a subsidiary and sucking southwards all the commerce from the North-West.

This threat had vanished two months before Macdonald stepped down. Early in September 1873, Jay Cooke found himself unable to market Northern Pacific bonds, and on the eighteenth day of that month his bank declared bankruptcy. All work on the Northern Pacific line stopped. Shortly afterwards, a second American bank closed its doors. A rising financial panic forced the

New York Stock Exchange to shut down for ten days. This credit crisis caused manufacturing plants to lay off workers, construction projects to be stopped, wages to be cut and house prices to collapse. Before long, close to twenty thousand American businesses had closed their doors, and unemployment had reached 14 per cent.

So began what came to be known as the Long Depression, soon spreading to Germany, Austria, Britain, France and Russia, and extending, off and on, until almost the turn of the century. Still, its first casualty was the Northern Pacific. By the time the railway was revived in the mid-1880s, in a much less ambitious form, it was no longer a threat to the Canadian Pacific Railway or to the North-West.*

In the meantime, fortune had once again given Macdonald an encouraging wink: he had been ejected from office at the very moment that the country's economy collapsed into a depression.

*Cooke was bankrupted personally by the collapse of the Northern Pacific, but later regained much of his wealth through a silver mine in Utah.

EIGHTEEN

A Second Act

My fighting days are over.
Macdonald to Charles Tupper, early 1874

Second acts are rare in Canadian politics. Only three prime ministers—Macdonald, Mackenzie King (twice) and Trudeau—have regained office by winning an election after suffering defeat. Of the trio, Macdonald's accomplishment was the most remarkable. He convinced Canadians to change their minds after he had suffered a truly crushing defeat and had been disgraced, personally, in the eyes of most Canadians and of a good many of his own supporters. The tantalizing question is whether Macdonald, once he left office, really wanted to resign as Conservative leader, as he kept offering to do, or whether he aspired from the beginning to regain the post—for the sake of revenge, or of history.

The probability is that from the moment he left office, Macdonald aspired to return to it. Sheer competitiveness would have impelled him to try. As well, the Conservative Party was his creation, one that served both his nation-building plan and his personal need for a second home. A third factor was in play, the same one that influenced Trudeau's behaviour after his election defeat in 1979. Both men thought their careers had been cut short in the midst of unfinished business vital to the nation. For Trudeau, it was the Charter of Rights and Freedoms and patriation of the constitution. For Macdonald, it was the transcontinental spine of steel and the necessary time for Confederation to harden from gristle into bone. Each justification was self-serving, but each man believed deeply in it.

Pragmatic motives applied as well. Beyond the least doubt, Macdonald wanted to regain office in order to regain power. He was convinced that his Liberal successor, Alexander Mackenzie, lacked the stuff to be prime minister. He was also well aware that, without power, he had few other career opportunities: he did go back to being a corporate lawyer, but he was not temperamentally suited to that grind. The best evidence of what Macdonald planned all along to do is the simple fact that he never resigned.

An ideal opportunity to leave relatively gracefully occurred early on. In the 1874 election, Macdonald won his own seat in Kingston by the narrow margin of thirty-seven votes. His opponent initiated a suit for the result to be overturned on the grounds that Macdonald had bribed his voters. Undoubtedly, as was then common, Macdonald had "treated" some electors to small cash handouts and had made overgenerous payments for legitimate electoral services such as printing. The unwritten rule was that party leaders were never subjected to such accusations. The judge called to decide the case, a known Liberal supporter, ruled that the election result was invalid because of breaches of the law, but that Macdonald was not guilty personally because the misdeeds had been committed by his campaign manager, Alexander Campbell. A new election was called for the following month. Macdonald could have left with his head high by claiming he had been driven out by partisan bias. Instead, he contested the by-election—and won by just seventeen votes.

Macdonald did offer to leave—several times. At the caucus meeting the morning after he resigned, he told his MPs and senators he wanted to step down. They roundly rejected his offer. A few days later, at a public dinner at the Russell House hotel for his former ministers, Macdonald returned to the theme: "I cannot last much longer. You will find young men of your party that you will be proud to follow." While certain the party would form the government once more, he said he would "never be a member of any administration again." Later, he told Tupper, "My fighting days are over." Most suggestively, a few weeks after the election debacle, Macdonald wandered into the offices of the pro-Conservative Ottawa *Citizen* and told the staff to "publish an editorial paragraph . . . announcing my resignation of the leadership of the Conservative party." So long as he remained at its head, he explained, the party could never win an election, because it would always be known as the railway "Charter Seller's" party. The editor rushed in and said, "Sir John, my pen will write no such announcement."

Yet if no Conservative dared call for his resignation, some sent out that message silently. In his *Reminiscences*, Sir John Willison, the *Globe*'s editor, recounted how he once observed Macdonald coming down Parliament Hill on a bleak winter day, "dressed in a Red River sash and coat, and the old historic mink-skin cap, tottering down the hill to the eastern gateway alone, others passing him in a wide sweep." What was so telling, and so pathetic, was that no Conservative chose to walk with him. Macdonald's long-time Mr. Fix-It, Alexander Campbell, was more explicit: after the defeat, he told his deputy minister that "had Sir John kept himself straight during the last fortnight, the Ministry would not have been defeated." Campbell continued to serve Macdonald, but he never regained the respect he had once had for him. And there was something pathetic in the way others talked about him: Charles Belford of the Conservative Toronto *Mail* described him as "helpless as a baby."

To many people, it was irrelevant whether Macdonald hung on or resigned; he was finished. In December 1874, Dufferin reported to the colonial secretary, "Sir John Macdonald and his party are entirely routed and nobody expects them to rally during the present Parliament." Speculation he would soon leave kept appearing in the press.

Macdonald fed this speculation by making himself politically invisible. During the 1874 session, he scarcely ever spoke in the House, and often his seat was empty. Tupper took over in effect as the Opposition leader. As Mackenzie wrote to his mentor George Brown, "Sir John is seldom in the House and is gentle as a sucking dove." Some of this quiescence was shame and humiliation, but a substantial part was tactical. In his post-defeat speech at the Russell House, Macdonald told his audience, "You will never find us opposing any measure in the interest of the nation for the sake of opposition." He recognized right away that the new government had to be given a fair chance to show its competence, or otherwise. And his reflexes remained sharp. He avoided divisions in the Commons, because he saw "no advantage in publishing to the world that we numbered only a handful." And to rectify the handicap that there were no political clubs in Canada like Britain's Carlton and Reform, he convinced the party to create a club where Conservatives would eat and drink—and plot. On Dominion Day 1875, he laid the cornerstone for a United Empire Club. Within a year, its membership had climbed to six hundred. By 1879, however, the club had failed and could no longer pay its servants. If Macdonald's goal had not been to make the party less dependent on corporate cash, he had at least attempted to spread the blame for gathering it in.

In the meantime, Alexander Mackenzie and his government were performing not at all badly. One of Mackenzie's first tasks had been to form a cabinet, and he found it difficult: "I was sick, sick, sick before it was done," he said. The Liberals were a loose alliance of anti-Conservatives rather than an organized party. Edward Blake, the party's towering figure, refused to enter the cabinet, then relented under pressure but would accept only the sinecure of president of the council. The two MPs best qualified to be finance minister, Lucius Huntington and Luther Holton, both refused the portfolio, and the best MP from Nova Scotia opted to remain outside the cabinet. This chore done, Mackenzie had to deal with the patronage appointments Macdonald had made just before leaving: Leonard Tilley had become lieutenant-governor of New Brunswick, along with more than one hundred lesser appointments (among them, Charles Tupper's brother). Mackenzie's first instinct was to cancel them all—this "horde of spies . . . who will carry to late Ministers all they can see or hear"—but Dufferin persuaded him not to adopt a "retaliatory policy." Disappointed Liberal supporters who had long been counting on these positions now bombarded Mackenzie with applications. He dealt with them one by one—and in at least one case invented a variety of tests the applicant would have to pass in

Alexander Mackenzie was deeply religious, thoroughly honest and exceptionally hard-working. None of this did him much good—in politics. Almost the day Mackenzie became prime minister, the country plunged into a depression. And while Macdonald was down, he was by no means out.

writing, spelling, composition, algebra and geometry. In another attempt to control the unceasing clamour for favours, Mackenzie arranged to have a staircase built so he could slip out from his office unnoticed. Soon, he was working fourteen-hour days.

Yet things were getting done. The new government enacted sweeping electoral reforms, including introducing the secret ballot and holding all riding elections on the same day. In the summer of 1874, Mackenzie dispatched his strongest possible representative, George Brown, to Washington in an attempt to negotiate a reciprocity agreement, or free-trade pact. To everyone's astonishment, Brown, who was held in high regard in the American capital because of his lifelong opposition to slavery, persuaded Secretary of State Hamilton Fish to agree to a deal by which duties on a wide variety of cross-border products, both primary and manufactured, would be progressively reduced over a number of years. It was a major accomplishment. Although several Conservatives such as Tupper wanted to denounce the treaty as a sellout, Macdonald's response was cautious. His objective, as Dufferin guessed shrewdly, was "to see whether the opponents of the measure were sufficiently strong to make it worth his while to enter into an alliance with them." In the end, Brown's breakthrough came to nothing, because Congress rejected the draft treaty.

In the meantime, Mackenzie had narrowly avoided making a big mistake concerning Macdonald's cherished North-West Mounted Police. In December 1873, alarming reports came in from the North-West about large numbers of American whisky traders crossing the border. Mackenzie's initial response was to propose that a joint Canadian-American expedition be assembled, with the American troops granted authority to cross the border to support the Mounted Police. Canada's national honour was saved when Dufferin pointed out that the request would be "quite incompatible with the dignity of the Dominion." Otherwise, with

THE VACANT CHAIR.
A *RIEL* BOND OF UNION.

question more bedevilled Canadian itics in the mid-1870s than that of amnesty, or of no amnesty, for l: all other acts committed during uprising were forgivable, but not execution of Thomas Scott, most ainly not in Protestant Ontario.

plans to enact temperance legislation and to establish a Supreme Court (a project Macdonald had twice initiated but never completed), Mackenzie's government was off to a creditable start.

In one vital matter, Mackenzie's performance was a good deal more than just creditable. He found a way to settle the long-standing issue of an amnesty for Louis Riel. And he did it by employing the same skills that the Conservatives had perfected: "the fine arts of double-talk, put-it-off, dodge-the-issue, and fool-the-voters."* As magnified the accomplishment even more,

* The quote comes from Jane Graham's exceptional master's thesis, "The Riel Amnesty and the Liberal Party in Central Canada, 1867–1875."

Mackenzie had been a member of the Liberal government in Ontario that had escalated sectarian hostilities by offering a five-thousand-dollar reward for Riel's capture.

The root problem, as Dufferin identified it in an 1874 memorandum to Lord Carnarvon, who had succeeded Lord Kimberley as the colonial secretary, was that "no administration feels itself strong enough to grapple with the question." It was no easier for Mackenzie and the Liberals than for Macdonald and the Conservatives to choose one of the two available ways to settle the affair: either to issue a general pardon that would include Riel, despite his execution of Thomas Scott, or to grant a pardon for all routine misdeeds, but excluding Riel and Ambroise Lépine, who had presided over Scott's trial. The former would cost Ontario's political support, and the latter Quebec's, with either of these choices stirring up sectarian suspicions. Macdonald's solution had been to delay, and to secretly subsidize Riel's exile in the United States while proclaiming his eagerness to bring him to justice. This policy was thoroughly deceitful, and the Liberals discovered that Macdonald, after losing office, had dipped into the secret-service fund to take out $6,600, almost certainly as a further bribe to Riel. Nevertheless, it had served to gain time—the one solution that might heal most of the wounds.

The amnesty issue came to the fore again in the spring of 1874, when Riel, having won the Provencher seat in Manitoba held earlier by Cartier, travelled secretly to Ottawa and, abetted by some French-Canadian MPs, signed the members' register before slipping out of town. Quebec was delighted by Riel's defiance; Ontario, outraged. Mackenzie resorted to a classic Macdonald device—setting up a parliamentary committee, its majority now Liberal, to examine the entire issue, particularly whether the preceding government had made a formal offer of an amnesty. Over six weeks, the committee heard twenty-one witnesses, among them Macdonald, Bishop Alexandre Taché, and Father Noël-Joseph

Ritchot. Macdonald summarized his government's involvement by saying that Cartier and Ritchot had always moved "on different planes" as they discussed the contentious issue—Cartier excluding those involved in Scott's death, and Ritchot including them. After hearing all the witnesses, the committee reached no conclusion but simply published the evidence presented to it.

Mackenzie thus lost the solution he had been hoping for—to be able to declare he had no choice but to grant an amnesty to Riel to fulfill a promise made by his predecessor in office. Dufferin concluded from his study of the committee's report that Macdonald, by his "very guarded" statements to Taché and Ritchot, had made no such promise, while Cartier's comments had been "far more loose and ambiguous than was desirable." Regardless, he reported to London, "No argument will ever persuade the French population that the promises of the Government to Riel and Lépine were not most absolute, explicit and complete."

In October 1874, the situation changed dramatically, making it impossible for Mackenzie to delay any longer. The year before, Lépine had been captured by police after he had sneaked back to his home in Red River. He was tried in Winnipeg for Scott's murder, and to everyone's amazement a jury made up equally of English and French members, several of them Métis, found him guilty. The judge pronounced the sentence of death, despite the jury's recommendation of mercy. In Quebec, opinion was transformed instantly from concern to outrage and bitterness. The provincial legislature passed a unanimous resolution calling for clemency, as did the archbishop and six bishops of Quebec. More than 250 petitions bearing 58,568 names poured into Ottawa from the province.

At this perilous juncture, Mackenzie again resorted to yet one more of Macdonald's well-practised tactics: he asked the Imperial government to express its opinion on the matter. The Colonial

Office agreed, but directed that this judgment be made not in London but in Ottawa, by the governor general. It was an uncommonly clever tactic. Dufferin himself believed that the decision would best be made by the Queen, because in Canada "the Queen's name . . . commands such immediate submission"; nevertheless, he had for a long time been aching to exercise old-style executive authority rather than be confined to the advisory role to which his position had been reduced; more important, he understood fully the politics of this file, warning Carnarvon that the amnesty issue was "severing the Canadian community into its original ethnological divisions." Although he personally thought the Métis leader deserved to be executed for what he repeatedly called "murder," Dufferin described Riel as "a man whom the Government cannot hang"—an exceptionally prescient observation.

Dufferin finally made his decision. On January 21, 1875, the *Royal Gazette* reported that the governor general had reduced Lépine's sentence to one or two years in prison with permanent forfeiture of his political right either to vote or to seek election. Mackenzie followed suit: after first allowing the Ontario election to be safely won by Oliver Mowat's Liberals, he announced a general amnesty for all the Métis except for Riel and Lépine. The penalty for these two men would be banishment for five years and permanent loss of political rights. Riel would never again be able to run for Parliament.

Mackenzie gained little credit for this peacemaking solution in either Ontario or Quebec. In the next election, the Liberals suffered severe losses in Quebec, while in Ontario the *Liberal* (Blake's own newspaper) attacked him for following the governor general's lead rather than leading himself. Macdonald actually came out ahead in public opinion, because the whole exercise reminded everyone of just how artful he could be.

Macdonald now turned his attention from public affairs to private ones. In January 1875, he celebrated his sixtieth birthday, an event that drew attention to the fact that the sand in his hourglass was starting to run out. He enjoyed more leisure time than in previous years and used it to read widely—the novels of Dickens, Trollope and Disraeli, the plays of Sheridan and Shakespeare, Thomas Carlyle's *The Life of Friedrich Schiller*, and a multi-volume tome by the historian Lord Mahon. Every now and then, he would turn to a "yellowback"—the cheap melodramas of the day—using it as a way to turn off his mind (much as a successor, Lester Pearson, would stealthily switch on the TV in his office to watch baseball games).

He had already sorted out his business affairs, although only temporarily as it turned out. In 1874, the biggest client of his law practice, Kingston's Trust and Loan Company, moved its head office to Toronto. In lockstep, Macdonald moved his law practice, now run by James Patton, to the city and opened an office at 25 Toronto Street. Also in that office was the firm's other senior partner, Robert Fleming, and its single junior partner, Hugh John Macdonald.

Hugh John's ambition had been to become a professional soldier, but Macdonald summoned him home after his Red River expedition with Colonel Wolseley and put him to work in his law office. He himself commuted to the business from Ottawa, using a bed in Hugh John's apartment while he was in Toronto. The arrangement didn't work well. Fleming composed a letter of resignation to Macdonald, complaining that Hugh John had not helped "secure business" and had shown "an indifference to the practice of law altogether."

By now in his mid-twenties, Hugh John was feeling cramped by proximity to his famous father. He was determined to be his own man, and early in 1874 he wrote to Macdonald asking him to change his will so as to leave "the bulk of your property to my mother and sister, simply giving me a trifle to show I have not

From the mid-1870s on, probably the most attractive part of Toronto was not the growing but rather dumpy city, but Toronto Island: open, green and a great place to promenade.

been cut off for bad behaviour." As he explained, "If I am ever to be worth my salt, I can make my own living, while they will be dependent on what you leave them."*

By the next year, Hugh John's determination to be independent had escalated into open defiance. He informed Macdonald he had decided to marry Jean King, a widow six years his senior and a practising Catholic. Prompted no doubt by Agnes, who wore her anti-Catholicism on her sleeve, and angered by what he saw as a deliberate act of rebellion, Macdonald engaged in a series of shouting matches with his son. He finally declared that he would refuse to consent to their marriage.

Although Macdonald kept his pledge not to give his blessing to the marriage, he overcame his annoyance sufficiently to attend

---

* The "mother" Hugh John was referring to was his aunt Margaret, who had brought him up since Isabella's death.

the wedding. It would have been better had he stayed away. Goldwin Smith, who hosted Macdonald at his Toronto house, the Grange, recalled his behaviour in his *Reminiscences*: "At the wedding breakfast, he sat perfectly silent. When his health was drunk, he disappointed the company by merely stumbling through two or three disjointed sentences." Only later did Smith discover the reason for Macdonald's distractedness. An American who had apparently done some political service for Macdonald claimed to be owed three thousand dollars and chose that very day to have a writ served on him. Nothing came of this matter, which may well have been an attempt at extortion, but Macdonald managed by his discourteous behaviour to let his son know how small a role he occupied in his life. Before long, Hugh John sent his father a letter to say he planned to leave the family law firm: "I had better go out at the end of this year and start on my own bottom in the beginning of 1876." Macdonald's reply was brutally short: he had taken note of Hugh John's letter, had discussed it with James Patton, and they had agreed "that the end of the year will be a convenient time for you to leave, so that you may consider that as settled." Hugh John moved to Kingston and opened a practice on his own.

If Macdonald's treatment of his son confirmed his capacity to pursue a quarrel with chilling harshness, this period also provided an example of his capacity for uncommon tenderness. Through the winter of 1874–75, the health of Theodora Bernard, Agnes's mother, deteriorated rapidly, and on February 28, while the Macdonalds were in Toronto, she died at their home in Ottawa. Her son, Hewitt, called in the Reverend Thomas Bedford-Jones, the rector of their church, St. Alban's, and they composed two telegrams to be sent two hours apart, the first warning that

Theodora's condition was serious, the second that she had died. The telegraph operator dispatched the second telegram first, and, as Bedford-Jones recalled, "the shock [for Agnes] was awful. . . . For a time we feared she would have permanently lost her reason."

Other than hold his wife's hand, there was nothing Macdonald could do for her. Yet he thought up a way to reach out to his grief-stricken wife. He contacted Bedford-Jones and, in the rector's account, "What passed between us must be sacred. . . . As we parted at a late hour, he held my hand and only said, 'Thank you Doctor.'" The following day, after the funeral service at St. Alban's, Bedford-Jones held a memorial service at the Macdonalds' house on Chapel Street. At an improvised altar in the living room, Agnes knelt beside Hewitt and Hugh John, with Bedford-Jones facing them. To their surprise, he delayed starting the service. Suddenly, Macdonald appeared and knelt beside them, later rising as they got up to receive communion. As Bedford-Jones wrote, "I could scarcely speak the words as I delivered the sacred elements into the open hands of Canada's Premier, himself moved to tears and kneeling upright with his eyes closed." A lifelong Presbyterian, if in no way strongly religious, Macdonald had, the evening before, arranged for Bedford-Jones to receive him into Agnes's own Anglican faith. She was far too intelligent to believe he had really converted to Anglicanism, but she must have been touched deeply by the thoughtfulness of his gesture.

A year later, Macdonald had to attend another funeral, this time of his sister Margaret, who died on April 18, 1876. Macdonald was at her bedside in Kingston, and afterwards wrote to her husband, James Williamson, describing her as "my oldest and sincerest friend [who] has been so through life." Macdonald sorted out the business affairs of both Williamson and his surviving sister, Louisa. Fiercely proud as ever, she once again became the person who rented their joint house, and Williamson became her tenant. During Margaret's illness, Hugh John had kept Macdonald informed about her condition. Father and son now began to grow back together, and Hugh John rejoined the family law firm. When Patton left, they changed the name to Macdonald and Macdonald. At the same time, Macdonald began to accept Jean as a member of the family, and he welcomed her fully in 1877 after she gave birth to his first grandchild. The baby was christened Isabella, after Macdonald's first wife, but the family always called her by her nickname, Daisy.

Through most of 1875, the political dynamics changed little. Mackenzie worked with uncommon diligence and with exemplary honesty, but his efforts always attracted less applause than they merited. In a report home, Dufferin put his finger on the problem: Mackenzie was "honest, industrious, but he has very little talent. He possesses neither 'initiative' nor 'ascendancy.'" In today's language, Dufferin was saying that Mackenzie lacked charisma. George Ross, a Liberal MP and later an Ontario cabinet minister, wrote in his memoir, "Sir John could refuse the request of a deputation with better grace than Mackenzie could grant what was asked." And *Grip* commented that Mackenzie, with his brutally long hours, was behaving "like a clerk; slaving . . . when it would have been better for the party had he been seeing people and wining, dining and poking bartenders in the ribs, jovially, like John A." He also had bad luck: the Long Depression reduced the government's revenues, leaving it little room to manoeuvre. Moreover, he could never escape from the shadow not just of Macdonald but of his own political partner, Edward Blake, who, no matter his temperamental tantrums, was widely accepted as the finest mind in Parliament.

Macdonald's own performance in opposition had not improved. He was often absent from the House, and when he was there he most times remained silent. He was still drinking heavily. Once, at a party at the journalist T.C. Patteson's Toronto house, Macdonald managed to insult Charles Tupper, then tottered upstairs and collapsed on a bed. Lady Macdonald walked out into the garden, sat on an iron bench and was spotted there, shivering in her shawl, at 6 a.m. On another occasion, when he was due to speak at a town on Lake Huron, Macdonald went on a binge during the voyage and fell fast asleep, compelling the ship's captain to protect him by turning his boat around and never entering the harbour.

One of the rare exceptions to his parliamentary passivity came during a debate on the bill to create a Supreme Court. Macdonald had no quarrel with the legislation—it was virtually the same as the bills he had earlier introduced in the Commons but failed to pursue. There was just one change of substance between Macdonald's version and that of Mackenzie's government: the latter proposed that no appeals could be made from the judgments of the new court, thereby eliminating the traditional role in Canadian legal affairs of Britain's Judicial Committee of the Privy Council. Macdonald launched into a rambling speech declaring that, while some might want to loosen, even end, "the colonial connection" to Britain, to him it was "a golden chain, and he . . . was proud to wear its fetters." The bill passed anyway.

That summer, Macdonald and his family spent several weeks at Rivière-du-Loup. Then they packed up and moved to Toronto, first renting a house on Sherbourne Street and later buying a fashionable brick house at 63 St. George Street, near the University of Toronto. By one of life's ironies, a later owner was Premier Mowat.

In the fall, politics resumed. The Conservatives gained a seat in Toronto in a by-election, even as they narrowly lost one in Montreal. Party spirits revived a little, and that November a public dinner was organized in Montreal to help the losing candidate pay off his election expenses. Macdonald was the key speaker, and he chose as his topic Canada's relations with Britain. The real importance of the speech was not what he said but the way he said it. He was funny, animated, clever and scrappy, and he scored several good shots at the government's expense. Once again, Macdonald was thoroughly enjoying the political game. As *Grip* put it, "There's life and spirit in the old man yet."

At this time, though, Canadians were concerned about practical matters. The Long Depression was now into its third year. Many jobs had been lost, plants had closed, house prices had fallen and immigration had dried up. This was the subject Macdonald really had to talk about—especially as the government's response had been to do nothing. An opening for him began to take form in February 1876, when Finance Minister Richard Cartwright brought down a budget based on the principle that it was "no time for experiments": the government's response to the depression was to keep spending down, to hold the deficit to a minimum and to leave the recovery of the economy to the free market. Macdonald recognized instantly that a priceless opportunity had been presented to him—though he had not the least idea yet what he might suggest as an alternative to the government's non-policy.

NINETEEN

Bismarck's Twin

We'll have a country, or we will have none.
Grip magazine

British historians have claimed that the world's first modern election campaign took place in the winter of 1879–80, when Gladstone waged his "Midlothian Campaign," making a whistle-stop tour around southern Scotland, holding large public meetings and delivering a series of speeches on foreign policy. In fact, the Old Country was already behind the times. Macdonald had done it all three years earlier—and a good deal more inventively.

In the summer of 1876, Macdonald initiated a new tactic of "picnic politics," combining food and fun with political speeches. As well, just as Gladstone would soon do, he used these occasions to set out a coherent political platform, in his case a policy of raising tariff rates to protect Canada's manufacturers—to enable them to take root and grow, and thereby create jobs for the country's growing new class of "mechanics," or skilled and semi-skilled urban workers. Integral to Macdonald's protectionist policy was its nation-building potential: a walled-off national market would cause Canadians to

Political picnics, like this one at Napanee, enticed people to come out for the free food, to consume lemonade and beer and enjoy listening to Macdonald joust with hecklers. Once he'd got the crowd on his side, he would work in cracks about the Grits.

buy and sell from each other, and so to get to know and become dependent on each other, thereby moving the country towards becoming a community rather than a "mere geographic expression." To sell this political platform, the first of its kind in Canada, Macdonald minted a couple of slogans. One was "Canada for Canadians," today a banal phrase but then fresh and zesty, because it told Canadians that their country was greater than the sum of its parts. The other slogan was even shorter—Macdonald began to talk of something he called a National Policy.*

Compared with Gladstone's call for a foreign policy based on morality and humanitarianism, rather than Disraeli's "phantoms

* The parentage of this iconic name is uncertain. Charles Tupper claimed it and used it in the Commons as early as 1870, although he was applying it to a higher tariff on Cape Breton coal, which was not a national commodity. Sir John Rose in London may also have suggested the name to Macdonald. The term "National Policy" applied only to tariff policy. In 1913, however, O.D. Skelton, a scholar and senior civil servant, coined the lower-case phrase "national policy" to cover all Macdonald's nation-building programs—the transcontinental railway, the Mounted Police, immigration, western development and tariff protection—giving the impression he had planned them as a coherent whole. But he had not.

of glory," in the Liberal leader's phrase, Macdonald's pledge to raise tariffs to benefit manufacturers was prosaic stuff. Nevertheless, relying entirely on intuition, because no exemplar existed, Macdonald had crafted, together with the political picnics, as populist and professional a campaign as any today. And there was one other similarity between the British and the Canadian campaigns: they both put their leaders back in power.

As a Conservative, Macdonald was by instinct a believer in free trade and the free market. Moreover, in Britain, free trade had gained the status of a secular religion as a result of the efforts of Manchester Liberals such as Richard Cobden and John Bright, who argued that Britain, as the world's industrial leader, would do best by buying raw materials at the cheapest possible price from any source (rather than only from its own Empire) and by selling its manufactured goods to any market. Free trade had indeed improved Britain's economic growth, as it had done for Canada during the eleven-year span (1855–66) of the Reciprocity Treaty with the United States.

Macdonald, though, always put the politically effective ahead of the theoretical. Moreover, he had never been a fanatic about free trade. In an 1864 letter to the warden of Kingston Penitentiary, he had noted that a vineyard in his riding was making "good wine vinegar" and asked that the penitentiary buy some, because "we ought to encourage Canadian production as much as possible." Earlier, in 1859, he told a friend, "I am a protectionist, & warmly interested in this matter, but I cannot speak in the House for lack of knowledge."

After Confederation, Macdonald made determined attempts to master the subject. He got a lot of information from the

Hamilton businessman Isaac Buchanan, who churned out pamphlets calling for a "Patriotic Industrial Policy" and held remarkably progressive attitudes towards industrial workers.* Macdonald convinced a journalist at *Grip* magazine to study the subject and received, in return, some perceptive observations, such as that Britain should "teach her colonies to manufacture for themselves" while itself becoming a "centre of knowledge, of art, of learning."

Macdonald so mastered the complicated topic that in his first major speech on it, in the House in 1876, he put the Liberals on the defensive by pointing out that their hero, John Stuart Mill, had written that protectionism was justified in an underdeveloped nation. In that same speech, Macdonald also quoted from an intriguing Canadian work, *New Principles*, by Scottish-born John Rae, who argued that free trade inhibited development in backward economies like Canada's and that instead governments should intervene to promote new industries and technologies.† By then, Macdonald had become confident enough of his knowledge of the subject to describe economics, then known as "political economy," as "a tentative science, as yet experimental," and to describe free trade, then the all-prevailing economic wisdom, as having been "elevated . . . almost into a religion . . . [and then] into a superstition." His core argument was that for an underdeveloped economy, free trade could only work if it was "reciprocal."

As early as the 1872 election, Macdonald had toyed with the idea of adding tariff protection to the party's cornucopia of promises, and it was then that he first used the phrase "National Policy."

---

* A rarity—a businessman with a capacity for speculative thought—Buchanan argued for reforms to benefit workers which were strikingly close to those being advocated by the American journalist Horace Greeley.

† John Stuart Mill praised Rae's book, published in 1834, whose full title was *Statement of Some New Principles on the Subject of Political Economy*, but his work was generally ignored, principally because he criticized the great Adam Smith.

He wrote to the Toronto financier David Macpherson to say, "Our game is to coquet with the Protectionists": the word "protection" was never to be used, but "we can ring the changes on a National Policy, paying the United States in their own coin [of high tariffs]." He advised T.C. Patteson, editor of the Conservative organ the *Mail*, that "the Paper must go in for a National Policy in Tariff matters": the paper should "advocate a readjustment of the tariff in a way that would assist Canada's manufacturing and industrial interests," but again the word "protection" was to be avoided, so consumers wouldn't fear that the prices of goods would increase (as inevitably they would).

Three factors turned Macdonald into a protectionist. The most urgent was the misery inflicted by the Long Depression, which began in the mid-1870s. To worsen the layoffs, wage cuts and company bankruptcies (the rate doubled between 1873 and 1875), American manufacturers had begun to use Canada as a "slaughter-market" for their surplus goods—some salesmen even followed Canadian ones as they called on customers and offered a discount on any sale that had just been made. Meanwhile, the U.S. Congress continued its highly protectionist policy and rejected the reciprocity deal arranged between Hamilton Fish and George Brown.

Also pushing Macdonald towards protectionism was an unexpected shift in public opinion. Farmers were always strong supporters of free trade. Macdonald, though, never removed his finger from the nation's pulse, and even before the 1872 election he told a supporter he had noticed "the feeling that has grown up in the West [western Ontario] in favour of encouragement of home manufacturers." This shift had occurred because agricultural machines had reduced the need for farm labour, so farmers were sending younger sons into towns and cities to find jobs. A survey done in the mid-1870s by the Grange, an American agricultural organization that had entered Canada, found that one-third of its members supported protection for industries that might employ some of their now surplus sons.

The third factor, far from the least, was that the governing Liberals had just made themselves a sitting target on this issue. Being Liberals, they marched to the free-trade beat of the Manchester Liberals.* Alexander Mackenzie was so passionate about free trade that he described protectionism as "contrary to . . . all just laws, human and divine," although also observing astutely that "some other portion of the community will pay for protecting the particular manufacturers." Richard Cartwright, the Liberal finance minister, believed this creed absolutely. In his budget of February 1876, he took no action to help Canadians cope with the depression, saying that the only solution was for everyone to "atone for past extravagance and folly by the simple recipe of thrift and hard work." Any attempt by the government to intervene, said Cartwright, would be as futile as the effect of "flies on a wheel."

Macdonald recognized a political gaffe the instant it was committed: that fateful "flies on a wheel" phrase would stick to Cartwright for the rest of his career. Macdonald also understood that in the middle of a depression, government intervention, even if it actually accomplished little, would reassure Canadians that they belonged to a community that cared for its members. His reply to Cartwright was unanswerable: "If ever there is a time when it is lawful, or allowable, or wise, or expedient, for a Government to intervene, now is the time."

---

* At the time, the term "liberal," encompassing support for free trade and the free market, had roughly the same meaning as "conservative" does today. Conversely, Macdonald was in many respects far more progressive in his readiness to use public funds to achieve huge projects such as the transcontinental railway. Where Liberals were liberals in today's sense was in their advocacy of election reforms and an expanded franchise.

In the debate that followed Cartwright's budget, Macdonald moved for a motion for "incidental protection" for the country's manufacturers. He got his timing just right. For the first time, in part catalyzed by the hard economic times, nationalism had emerged as a political force in Canada. In October 1874, Edward Blake (who was not in the cabinet at this time) had come close to calling for Canadian independence in a speech he gave in the Ontario hamlet of Aurora. He described Canadians as "four millions of Britons who are not free" and declared that, rather than being just seven provinces, "isolated from each other, [and] full of petty jealousies," Canadians had to find "some common ground on which to unite, some common aspiration to be shared." At the same time, the Canada First nationalists had formed a new National Party. None of this came to anything, and the National Party eventually petered out, especially after Blake decided not to become its leader. But the activity and excitement showed that a generalized interest existed for radical ideas.

From this time on, and through the next century until the advent to power of Brian Mulroney in the 1980s, Liberals would be the free traders and Conservatives the protectionists.

~

As he always did, Macdonald moved cautiously. In a report to London in April 1877, Governor General Dufferin noted that, while many Conservatives had "commit[ted] themselves very unreservedly" to protectionism, "Sir John himself I perceive is remarkably chary of any downright pledges in this direction." His caution was justified. Blocking American imports was one thing, but doing the same to imports from Britain, as high tariffs would do also, quite another; the Liberals might even raise the "loyalty cry" against him.

While manufacturers, naturally, looked kindly on Macdonald's idea, they in fact contributed little to his 1878 campaign. The cause was incompetence: businessmen were poorly organized, and the Dominion Board of Trade could persuade its members to approve only the mildest of protectionist resolutions. Some certainly did help Macdonald: Donald McInnes, the owner of a large textile plant in Cornwall, Ontario, informed him that his employees were "all under my thumb." But the more efficient manufacturers actually opposed protectionism, the president of the farm machinery company Massey saying that the existing tariff was "sufficient protection."

So Macdonald tacked carefully back and forth. When the Liberals charged that he wanted to increase tariff levels by 25 per cent, Macdonald retorted that he had "never proposed an increase, but only a readjustment of the tariff." He managed to give the impression that his National Policy would be all things for all people: "We are in favour of a tariff that will incidentally give protection to our manufacturers," he said in London, adding immediately, "if done, it will give a home market to our farmers. The farmers will be satisfied . . . every man to them is a consumer and that he must have pork and flour, beef and all that the farmers raise."

In 1877, Macdonald again moved a National Policy resolution in the Commons. All the political omens were now in a favourable alignment. The Long Depression showed no signs of ending. In Quebec City, shipbuilding was down by two-thirds, leaving three-quarters of the working population without work, while the Great Western Railway laid off four hundred and offered all who remained the choice of a four-day work week or a one-third wage cut. Everywhere, charities were overstretched.

All these downturns made Macdonald that most potent of all political figures—a man with an idea at a time when new ideas were needed. It was at this moment that he discovered a new way to tell his story to Canadians: open-air picnics.

The picnic rallies were not Macdonald's idea, and the first happened by accident. In the summer of 1876, some Conservatives called on him at his house in Toronto to ask that he speak at a picnic they were holding in the countryside on July 1, Dominion Day. He agreed. When the morning arrived, a special train pulled out from Toronto packed with party notables—Sir John A. and Lady Macdonald, Charles Tupper, William McDougall and others—and chugged off to the village of Uxbridge. There, under tall elms, long cloth-covered tables had been laid out with "substantials" and "delicacies," in Donald Creighton's vivid description—heaping platters of "cold sliced chicken, ornamented tongues, hams in aspic, Milan soufflés, red mounds of strawberries, elaborate moulds of flummery and charlotte russe, tipsy cakes, pound cakes, and cheese cakes, great misted jugs of ice lemonade and raspberry cordial, and clusters of bottles of wine." In the early afternoon, a crowd of several thousand gathered around a temporary platform to listen, awed and delighted, as the Grand Old Man went to work on them. He told jokes. He squashed hecklers. He demonstrated his astounding memory by calling the names, always correctly, of many of those looking up at him. Having primed them, he then delivered his pitch.

"The great question now before the country was as to the best means to relieve it of the existing commercial depression," he said. There was no use looking to Mackenzie, the fanatic free trader, he continued. Rather, there had to be some "incidental protection" for Canadian manufacturers. A few days later the Conservatives won both of two by-elections in Ontario County. As mattered more for the long run, the event at Uxbridge had shown that farmers were no longer frightened by the word "protection." As mattered the most, it was clear that placing Macdonald in the midst of a crowd of voters who had just consumed a lot of free food was like putting the Pied Piper in the midst of a gaggle of frolicking children.

Picnics were hastily organized for Colborne, Guelph, Fergus, St. Catharines, Milton, Woodstock and, on September 12, Belleville, where the crowd numbered an astounding fifteen thousand. Macdonald had found his issue and his voice. "No country is great with only one industry," he said. "Agriculture is our most important, but it cannot be our only staple. All men are not fit to be farmers; there are men with mechanical or manufacturing genius who desire to become operatives or manufacturers of some kind, and we must have means to employ them."

Macdonald was talking about the increasingly urbanized and industrialized Canada that lay ahead, once referring to it directly: "Here and there, all over the land, will be large cities where foundries, factories and workshops will form the centre to which the population has flocked." He was talking about the kind of economy a modern state needed. He was also talking about a Canada in which its people would become interdependent as they had never been before, because "when there is a large body of successful and prosperous manufacturers, the farmer will have a home market for his produce, and the manufacturer a home market for his goods." He was talking like a leader who knew where he wanted to take his country.

In a certain sense, Macdonald's idea for a National Policy was even more ambitious than his commitment to a transcontinental railway. What this conservative Conservative, now in his mid-sixties, was proposing to do was something that had never been attempted before in Canada—nor would be again for another half-century. When it was tried again, it would be once more during hard times—the Great Depression of the 1930s. The innovative idea that Macdonald accepted implicitly with his National Policy was that government should intervene in times of public need. In no way did that make him a progressive, let alone some kind of proto-socialist. Rather, it made him a leader who understood that he was head of a community. He also understood that, in so divided and fragmented a nation, either Canadians accepted they had a responsibility to look out for each other or they would all look outwards, away from the nation. He never articulated this vision. He just did it—because he spotted the need and because he sensed that the path ahead could return him to power.

Intervention by government violated the conventional wisdom of the day. The abiding rule for all governments was simple: the less they did, the better. The prevailing attitude was captured by a *Globe* comment on a proposal made in the Commons in 1881 to regulate the working hours of women and children: "The less the state interferes . . . the better. The employment of women would best be regulated by leaving it to the factory owners," and, anyway, a few hours extra a day would hurt neither "a strong girl nor a lad of sixteen." Governments, especially Conservative ones and particularly Macdonald's, were quite prepared to risk the nation's finances on major infrastructure projects, but social programs were nobody's business except for the churches and individual do-gooders—until the Great Depression.

In Britain, a significant change in the government's sense of responsibility was already taking place, not just by the reform-minded Liberal Gladstone, but also by the Conservative Disraeli, primarily as a response to the radical socio-economic changes under way as a consequence of industrialization and urbanization. Disraeli specifically aimed to create an alliance between the landed gentry and the urban workers. Canada, though, was industrially backward—despite all the railway construction, not one steel rail would be manufactured in the country until the next century. In addition, the great majority of its workers were still self-sufficient farmers. Macdonald was walking a path that no one before him had attempted.

Some parallels did exist, but in far more advanced and larger economies. Despite the free-trade conviction of most economists of the time, several major economies adopted protectionism in the nineteenth century. All of them—Germany, the United States, Japan, France—did exceedingly well.* Indeed, the only nineteenth-century economy to decline, at least comparatively, was freely trading Britain, its share of global manufacturing declining from one-third of the total to one-fifth between the years 1871 and 1901. Like Macdonald, each member of this protectionist group of nations adopted this policy both to bind its national community more closely together and to create jobs for its increasingly better-educated urban workforce.

The nearest parallel to what Macdonald aspired to do was already being done in Germany, by Chancellor Otto von Bismarck. His first step towards building a nation out of the fragmented German statelets had been to resort to the "blood and iron" of military victories over Denmark, Austria-Hungary and France. He then reversed his direction entirely. After the Long Depression in 1873 devastated Germany's economy, he abandoned free trade and protected the country's industries behind high tariff walls. Later, he engaged in a second phase of nation-building from within

---

* Japan's performance was, in context, the most impressive. Long a minimalist society that placed little value on wealth creation, Japan, by the Meiji Restoration of 1867, transformed economic growth into its national religion. While U.S. tariffs were commonly the highest, Japan was easily the most successful in protecting its native industries.

by a series of remarkable and innovative social programs—health insurance, old-age pensions and disability insurance, all of which created a commonality among the German people.

Just how much Macdonald was influenced by such developments is impossible to establish. His adviser, Isaac Buchanan, was unquestionably well informed about what Bismarck was doing, as were a few of the MPs who participated in the National Policy debates in the Commons. Macdonald, though he never shifted his focus from telling Canadians how protectionism would benefit their lives, and did not refer publicly to overseas examples, did in fact keep up with international affairs and could be remarkably astute about distant events. In June 1874, for instance, he wrote to Alexander Galt complaining about right-wing ultramontanism and the "Priest party" in Quebec. He forecast that, as soon as the ultramontane Pope Pius IX died, "there can be little doubt that there is an agreement among the Catholic Powers that the next Pope shall not be ultramontane." And so it happened four years later, with the choice of the liberal Leo XIII as pope.

The comparison with Germany shouldn't be pushed too far. For one thing, Germany's economy was incomparably more advanced than Canada's. For another, Bismarck had a comprehensive program of nation-building from within, including social programs, as Macdonald did not. Still, it is surprising that only one Canadian study has been done of the similarities between these two leaders.*

---

* See Suzanne Zeller's 1976 master's thesis, "The Protective Tariffs of 1879: 'National Policy' in Canada and Germany as a Means of Political and Social Control." An anonymous American writer spotted the connection as early as 1900. That year, a publisher in St. Louis put out a book titled *The World's Best Orations*, which, oddly, put Macdonald up there with Pericles and Jefferson. The book informed readers that Macdonald "attempted to do and did do for the vast country north of the U.S. what Bismarck did in federating and nationalizing Germany."

Macdonald's objective was a good deal harder to attain. He, as a democratic leader, had to sell his program to voters who were primarily anti-free-trade farmers with only one interest in economic policy—for taxes to remain as low as possible. As well, Macdonald had to deal with the angry complaints, inevitable in a regionalized country, that high tariffs would benefit the regions at the centre at the expense of those in the west and east.*

~

Parliament's session of 1877 was as unproductive and as small-minded as any in a long time. The Liberals embarrassed Macdonald by revealing that he had dipped into the secret-service fund, even when he was no longer prime minister, to fulfill an earlier commitment—almost certainly to subsidize Riel in retirement. The Conservatives retaliated by charging the Liberal Speaker, Timothy Anglin, with conflict of interest when a company he owned secured government contracts, and forcing him to resign. As Dufferin put it to Colonial Secretary Carnarvon, "The two parties [have been] bespattering each other with mud in view of the dissolution two years hence."

The following summer, the picnics began again. The Liberals now staged their own, but even if their decorated tongues and cheesecakes were as good as those of Conservative ladies, neither Mackenzie nor Cartwright was a Macdonald. As the *Canadian Magazine* put it, he had again become "a happy soul whom everybody likes." He started out in June in London, and proceeded to Brampton, Orangeville and Markham. Macdonald next tried

* The most detailed study of the phenomenon, by economist Kenneth Norrie, formerly of the University of Alberta, concluded that the National Policy had shifted some manufacturing from the United States to Ontario and Quebec, but scarcely any from the west or east to the centre.

something else new: he became the first leader ever to campaign outside his own province. On July 4, he left Montreal by train for the English-speaking Eastern Townships. At francophone stops such as Saint-Hyacinthe, one of his Quebec ministers would speak for him. Three days later, he was back in Montreal. Some five thousand torch-bearers paraded him through the streets to Dominion Square, where he addressed ten thousand people crammed together and shouting their applause. After a holiday, Macdonald went back to the picnic circuit in eastern Ontario right through to early September. In October, he visited Lindsay and Barrie and continued to Essex County. By the time he got back to Chatham, his voice was failing and his speeches were getting shorter, but never slackening.

On a personal level, Macdonald had made an even more important change—he was steadily drinking less and less. Dufferin reported to Carnarvon, "He certainly can drink wine at dinner without being tempted to exceed, which hitherto he has never been able to do, and during the present [1877] session he has never given way as in former times."

Age was a factor, but credit must be given also to Agnes for her tireless exhortations and prayers. The prime reason was no doubt the humiliation Macdonald had undergone through the Canadian Pacific Scandal. He would still suffer occasional lapses, as during a riotous session in 1878 when Canada's first Temperance Act was passed. Most MPs behaved like bibulous schoolboys—including Macdonald, who had to be carried out of the Chamber to pass the night in the deputy Speaker's office. On the whole, though, Macdonald could give no clearer sign that he was determined to regain the last rung of the "greasy ladder" than to cure himself of his lifelong dependency on alcohol.

Through 1878, only one thing seemed to go right for Mackenzie. That October, he organized a small cabinet shuffle. He brought in a newcomer from Quebec as a junior minister—a country lawyer whose English was imperfect and who was widely regarded as lazy, yet who possessed undeniable charm and effortless eloquence. His name was Wilfrid Laurier.

Earlier, in June, Laurier had given an outstanding speech about religious tolerance at a packed public meeting in Quebec City. He had begun nervously, his voice trembling, but gradually he gained confidence. "I am a liberal," he said. "I am one of those who think that always and everywhere in human things there are abuses to be reformed, new horizons to be opened up, and new forces to be developed." Having defended liberalism, Laurier then criticized it as it existed among his own *rouges*. They had been guilty in the past of arrogance in their eager denunciations of the church. However, Laurier continued, the Programme Catholique strategy of the hardline ultramontanes, of "organiz[ing] all the Catholics into one party, without any other bond than a common religion," could have but one inevitable consequence: it would "organize the Protestant population as a single party and . . . throw open the door to war, a religious war." Instead, he argued, "the right of interference in politics [by clerics] finishes at the spot where it encroaches on the elector's independence." Laurier had brought the fresh voice of a moderate and modern

He was young, inexperienced and thought to be a bit lazy, but Wilfrid Laurier had charm, elegance and eloquence to spare, and adroitly kept a close eye on Macdonald in order to learn his political tricks.

liberal into Quebec's polarized and claustrophobic internal debate.

At the very moment when the old lion was showing that none of his powers had diminished, a sleek young lion had entered the arena. Thereafter, they would circle each other warily, but always with mutual respect. About their relationship there was always a sense of a might-have-been: near to his end, when Macdonald discussed Laurier with his secretary, Joseph Pope, he remarked, "If I were twenty years younger, he'd be my colleague." When Pope suggested this might still happen, Macdonald replied, "Too old, too old."

~

Many people had expected the election in 1877. When that opportunity passed, it had to be in 1878. Mackenzie and the Liberals used the time to get their party onto the best possible election footing, while Macdonald shaped his National Policy into the most alluring possible political shape.

In the 1878 Commons debate on the budget, Macdonald presented a resolution that set out his final version. It called for a National Policy that, by "wise tariff adjustments," would foster agriculture and mining, create jobs at home, restore industry to prosperity, encourage interprovincial trade, end dumping of cut-price products from abroad and even achieve the much-desired reciprocity treaty with the United States. In response, one Liberal MP asked incredulously, "Is that all?" Macdonald replied, "It may be too much for you." He continued, "There are national considerations, Mr. Speaker, that rise far higher than the mere accumulation of wealth, than the mere question of trade advantage; there is prestige, national status, national dominion—and no great nation has ever risen whose policy was free trade." An obvious retort to this would have been that free-trading Britain had gained economic primacy and, simultaneously, the greatest empire since

Rome—except that Britain had adopted free trade *after* it reached the top.

Liberals repeatedly reinforced their free-trade arguments by quoting from the greats—Adam Smith, David Ricardo and John Stuart Mill. Macdonald, who by now really did know his stuff, conceded that free trade accomplished "the liberty of buying in the cheapest market and selling in the dearest." But that ability did not fit Canada's needs. Britain was suffering from the fact that no European country was prepared any longer to compete with her on a level field. Instead, many had turned protectionist, and as a result were now able to compete successfully with Britain. As an example, Macdonald cited the highly protectionist United States: "the people of that country are successfully competing in the English markets, and not only so, but in all the markets to which England has access."

In the case of Canada, continued Macdonald, by relying too much on low tariffs, the country had grown misshapen. "We have no manufacturers here," he declared. "We have no work-people; our work-people have gone off to the United States. These Canadian artisans are adding to the strength, to the power, and to the wealth of a foreign country instead of adding to ours." Free trade had limited Canada to just one industry—agriculture. But "no nation has risen which had only agriculture as its industry. There must be a mixture of industries to bring out the national mind and the national strength and to form a national character."*

By saying all this, Macdonald was functioning like a teacher, talking not to the parliamentarians (their votes already determined) but to the public at large, giving them the information and

---

* Macdonald's arguments echoed those made by Alexander Hamilton in his debates with Thomas Jefferson, Hamilton favouring a more centralized, industrialized America, and Jefferson advocating a democracy based on yeoman farmers.

insights to better understand their own country. Although Canada was only a small country, he said, it had to provide opportunities for its citizens to apply "the skills and genius which God has gifted to them." He was explaining his slogan of "Canada for Canadians." And his message was beginning to be understood. *Grip* magazine, customarily skeptical, came up with an approving ditty:

You this great truth should know,
Countries alone by manufactures grow.
The present's here, the lazy past is done,
We'll have a country, or we will have none.

Two months later, Prime Minister Alexander Mackenzie announced the one bit of information that mattered: the election would be held on September 17, 1878.

TWENTY

The People Change Their Minds

> [A Canadian leader] must have graduated as a horse thief
> or at least have distinguished himself as having chiselled
> a municipality or robbed a Railway Company.
> Alexander Mackenzie to a Liberal MP after the 1878 election

The telegrams arriving in Ottawa early in the evening of September 17, 1878, were encouraging but also worrying. The Conservatives were doing well in Nova Scotia, if less so than Charles Tupper had forecast, but the Liberals were coming on strong in New Brunswick. Then came the astounding news: John A. had gone down in his own seat in Kingston, after thirty-four years. Mrs. Eliza Grimason, a Kingston tavern owner and Macdonald's most devoted supporter, advised Macdonald to tell voters there "to go to the divil."*

Soon afterwards, the news became even more astounding: the Conservatives were decimating the Liberals, not just in Quebec (forty-seven of its sixty-five seats) but even in rural Ontario, where they eventually captured three-quarters of the province's

* Macdonald's surprising defeat in Kingston confirms that "all politics is local." In the preceding years, he'd moved his law office from Kingston to Toronto, less and less often went there and had lost touch with its people.

eighty-eight seats. Combined with a customary sweep of the West, Macdonald's majority would be even larger than Mackenzie's "Scandal" victory of four years earlier. It was larger than the estimate Macdonald had made to Agnes when she asked him in mid-campaign whether she should prepare to move their household back to Ottawa from Toronto. "If we do well," he said, "we shall have a majority of sixty; if badly, thirty." The fact that she had to request this information confirmed how little she now shared his political life.

Better organization was one reason for this success. Macdonald had laid down a firm rule of "no splits," wherein two or more Conservative candidates contested the same riding. "Let us not, like the hunters in the fable, quarrel about the skin before we kill the bear," he quipped. The party had formed a Workingman's Liberal-Conservative Association to capitalize on Macdonald's coquetting with organized labour, and for the moment it had its United Empire Club.

As mattered a great deal, only the Conservatives had anything new to say. As Governor General Dufferin reported to London, Cartwright's dictum that "this is no time for experiments" had left luckless Liberal candidates without "a few sweet morsels to take home to the electorate." Macdonald, in contrast, had been able to talk endlessly about what the National Policy would do. "We will not be trampled upon and ridden over, as we have in the past, by the capitalists of a foreign country," he promised, and, to emphasize the damage already done by the lack of his National Policy, "I have seen the poor men returning from Hay's manufacturery in Toronto, with their heads hanging down in despair, a miserable half-dollar in their pockets."

Best of all, the Conservatives had Macdonald while the Liberals had Mackenzie. The hapless Liberal leader could not believe he had been rejected in favour of the culprit of the Pacific Scandal; as he put it in a letter to one of his MPs, what Canadians seemed to want was a leader who "must have graduated as a horse thief or at least have distinguished himself as having chiselled a municipality or robbed a Railway Company."

The closest equivalent to the 1878 outcome would be, almost exactly a century later, the re-election of Pierre Trudeau. Macdonald and Trudeau both defied a cardinal rule of Canadian elections: a government is always the author of its own defeat. In 1878, as in 1980, Canadians wanted to have back their chastened favourites far more than they wished to heave out the incumbents. On both occasions, Canadians didn't so much re-elect an old leader as recreate him. They parallel those public figures—Frank Sinatra, Judy Garland, Muhammad Ali, as examples—whose careers first soared, then crashed, then reascended. The second time around, they became in a certain sense the property of the public, which had chosen freely to forgive and embrace them again. Thereafter, they became co-dependents with the public: Macdonald, after 1878, went on to win three successive elections, even though two were held in the middle of a depression. Trudeau, while he stepped judiciously aside after a single second term, later re-entered the arena to oppose the Meech Lake Accord, triumphing handily. Essentially, after 1878, Macdonald became a political immortal.*

Macdonald's National Policy of high-tariff protectionism may or may not have been the right idea. It was, though, exactly what he needed to regain office—a strong idea at a time when Canadians were looking for something to haul them out of a depression.

* The implications of Macdonald's quick and easy return to power were recognized at the time; a new Toronto newspaper, the *Telegram*, forecast: "Sir John has a long lease of power, and unless he does some mad thing he will be in office until the close of his career."

Alexander Mackenzie was replaced by Edward Blake, brilliant but cursed with zero emotional intelligence. One formidable rival still remained, but a circumstance both tragic and absurd soon increased even further Macdonald's near immunity from serious political threat. George Brown had left active politics forever after his defeat in 1867, but he remained a major political force through his ownership of the *Globe*, his wealth, his intelligence and his high reputation—renewed by his initial success in negotiating a Reciprocity Treaty with the United States.

On March 25, 1880, a *Globe* employee, George Bennett, who had been discharged by a foreman, came to Brown's office seeking a certificate of service. Brown told him to get it from the foreman. Bennett, who had been drinking, produced a revolver. Brown fearlessly seized hold of him, but the gun went off and wounded his thigh. Bennett was subdued by other workers, and a doctor pronounced the cut superficial. After four days, though, it became inflamed. Brown's condition steadily deteriorated and, on May 9, 1880, he died. Macdonald's response showed him at his competitive worst; he was never able to bring himself to recognize the magnitude of Brown's role in achieving Confederation. The rivalry outlived both men. After Brown's death, his wife, Anne, who detested Canada, moved back to her native Scotland. After Macdonald's death, Lady Macdonald went to Scotland several times on holiday. In the small town of Oban, their carriages sometimes crossed in the streets. Neither ever acknowledged the other, in a mutual salute to their dead spouses.

Macdonald didn't hurry to savour power again. He lingered in Toronto, using the comparative respite to write a raft of letters, among them one in which he gloated to a friend, "I resolved to reverse the verdict of 1874, and have done so to my heart's content." To compensate for the loss of Kingston, he arranged for by-elections in a Manitoba riding and in Victoria, BC—neither of which he had ever visited. He won both and chose the West Coast. He called on Dufferin and received his customary "very gushy" welcome; as Macdonald repeated later to Tupper: "the warmest wish of his heart was gratified by his having the opportunity of charging me with the formation of a Ministry." He was sworn back into office on October 17, 1878.

Macdonald's most important political task was to form a cabinet. Completed a month later, the new ministry contained almost no fresh faces. The old warhorses, Leonard Tilley, Charles Tupper, Alexander Campbell and Hector-Louis Langevin, were all back.* Bad luck was a factor. Thomas White, an accomplished journalist running the Montreal *Gazette*, had just lost his third election in a row, while D'Alton McCarthy, an exceptionally able lawyer, passed up Macdonald's offer because his practice was so lucrative.† Still, it was an uninspired cabinet, even for a prime minister who once joked that his ideal ministry would be composed of "highly respectable parties whom I could send to the penitentiary if I wished." One important newcomer was John Henry Pope, a Quebec farmer, rugged in his looks and plain in his speech, with a first-class mind. The most interesting appointment belonged to Macdonald himself: as minister of the interior he

---

* Tilley had stepped down early as lieutenant-governor of New Brunswick to re-enter politics.

† The law firm that McCarthy founded continues today as McCarthy Tétrault. In his day, McCarthy became famous for his attacks on French Canadians; the firm's website does not mention this point.

would be responsible for western development—another clear indication of where his priorities lay.

He was now sixty-four. "I am in good health, but have not quite regained my strength," he wrote to his sister Louisa. He could still work hard, but his old resilience and stamina had begun to ebb. "I kept up wonderfully well but for the last fortnight of the Sessions had to speak frequently [on] several long Bills," he explained in a letter to Alexander Galt in 1880. "This with no rest at night till morning used me up. . . . I still feel the reaction."

It was around this time that Macdonald became an old man. As Louisa put it to her brother-in-law, James Williamson, in May 1881, "I never saw John looking what I would call old until this time. His hair is getting quite grey." References to liver problems now occur regularly in his letters. In mid-1879, he went down with a bout of cholera, telling Louisa, "The doctor took vigorous steps and has pulled me through, though very weak." Far more alarming was his sudden, unexplained collapse while attending Sunday service in St. Alban's Church in March 1880. His response—more probably Agnes's response—was to take longer holidays at Rivière-du-Loup,* where he had bought an attractive cottage, Les Rochers, looking out on the St. Lawrence. He also slipped away more often to Britain, sometimes on business but also to consult medical specialists. The doctors could find no causes for his ailments except as the legacies of a long, hard life.

While Macdonald's days of excessive drinking were well behind him, he would still occasionally crash. One such occasion was like a flashback to his old, carefree days. Soon after the election, Dufferin returned to England, eventually achieving his long-sought post as viceroy of India. His replacement was the

---

* One other prime minister who holidayed regularly in Rivière-du-Loup was Louis St. Laurent.

Marquess of Lorne and, incomparably more exciting, his wife, Princess Louise—a daughter of the Queen. She was the most intelligent of Victoria's brood, but also the most difficult. Among other reasons for being difficult, she, like her mother, was far more passionate than she appeared, but, unlike her, was married to a homosexual, causing her never to have a child but to indulge in many affairs.* On the train journey to Halifax to greet the ship bringing the Lornes to Canada, Macdonald consumed a great deal of brandy, and he continued to binge while waiting at the elegant residence of the lieutenant-governor. With Their Excellencies about to arrive, a luckless secretary was sent to call Macdonald to duty and, finding him flat on his bed, pleaded with him to get up. Macdonald half-rose, pointed at the hapless man and pronounced, "Vamoose from this ranch."

In the 1878 election, Canadians seized their first chance since sweeping Macdonald out of power to sweep him back in again. The Toronto Telegram *commented shrewdly, "Unless he does some mad thing he will be in office until the close of his career."*

In Ottawa, Macdonald's home was now a large, attractive house called Stadacona Hall in the Sandy Hill district, rented from a lumber baron. There, the small family (still including Agnes's brother, Hewitt Bernard) reassembled. The greatest beneficiary of the new arrangement was Mary, by now close to ten years old. Before, her father had often been away, shuttling

* In this respect Princess Louise did behave herself while in Canada, though in few others. She spent as much of her term in England as she could get away with. Her view of Canadians was once described as "entirely picturesque . . . much the same as she felt for the Cascapedia salmon."

between Ottawa and Toronto and doing the rounds of the picnics. In a letter written in October 1877, she told him achingly, "The house seems so dull and lonely without you, and I miss my evening stories very much." (Mary would have dictated this letter; only later, once typewriters were available, did she learn to write her own letters, doing so with painful slowness but almost never misspelling a word.) Now Macdonald would come home at the end of each day to tell her a story or to recount some outrageous political incident. The Macdonalds organized children's parties for her. In a cruel comment that may not have been intended, Lucianne Desbarats, the wife of the Queen's printer, compared Mary in her diary to "a large rag doll with an oversized head being carried around among gay and active children." E.B. Biggar, in his *Anecdotal Life*, has a poignant description of the young guests preparing to leave one party, at which point Macdonald "quietly persuaded them to stay a little longer. When they resumed the dance, he leaned over to his daughter's chair and said, 'You see Mary, they want a little more of your society, and a little dancing by the way.'"

Mary (in the armchair), with a visiting friend. To Macdonald, she was "Baboo," to whom he read stories and gave funny accounts of his daily doings as soon as he arrived home from the office.

The family member who changed the most as a result of their return to Ottawa was Agnes. Early on in her diary, she had admitted, "My love of Power is strong." Back again in real power, and savouring it because she had not expected to regain it, she yielded more and more to this second love. The image of Lady Macdonald as bossy, bullying and moralistic, ruling social Ottawa with "a rod of iron," takes its form from this time.* It was during this period that she called John Thompson, the minister of justice, a "pervert" because he had abandoned the Presbyterianism of his birth for the Roman Catholicism of his wife. Similarly, she sent Finance Minister George Foster into social exile when he married a divorced woman—a sentence commuted only after Macdonald's death when she lost her power. Yet the lighter "Agnes" character never vanished. Many years later, then a widow living in England, she answered questions in a day book belonging to Mary titled, "*Confessions, Opinions, & Autographs of my Friends.*" To the printed question what country she would like to live in, she answered, "No Man's land"; to whether dress affected character, "Only one's bank account"; to the best sovereign in Europe, "The Gold Sovereign," to the ideal girl of the period, "A glorious creature, in tight skirts," and the ideal man, "Another glorious creature—who smokes."

During her long reign over Ottawa society, Lady Macdonald had only one rival—Princess Louise. These two strong-willed women loathed each other. At the theatre one evening, when Louise rose in the royal box to accept the crowd's applause, she discovered to her fury that Lady Macdonald had risen beside her to share it. Gossip about their rivalry became so widespread that Macdonald had to write a plaintive letter to Lorne, begging him to bring it to an end. A reply from Princess Louise conceded as little as possible: "You must know in how many ways I admire Lady Macdonald and think her a worthy example to every wife."†

---

* The use of the phrase in reference to Lady Macdonald comes from a no less bossy, moralistic and strong woman of the time—Lady Aberdeen, the wife of a future governor general.

† Lorne did as asked, but without enthusiasm, sending back the note "If it is worthwhile to contradict such reports, there is no foundation whatever for the statements made." In 1880, Louise used a sledding accident as an excuse to leave Canada permanently.

That Macdonald ruled again meant that Lady Macdonald again reigned. The younger, more girlish Agnes was increasingly replaced by a sterner, and plumper, consort who ruled Social Ottawa with "a rod of iron."

At the same time, Lady Macdonald fulfilled all her obligations as chatelaine to the last impeccably folded napkin. Thompson, while he detested "that mole-catcher of a wife," as he called her, admired the formal dinners she organized on Macdonald's behalf, and he preserved a menu card that captures the kind of dinner fare she served in the Macdonald house: oysters on the half-shell; consommé; fish or lamb cutlets; and, for dessert, cabinet pudding, charlotte russe, lemon ice or fruit. From Eliza Grimason, who would dearly have loved that responsibility herself, she earned the praise of "looking after him" and the further compliment that "Lady Macdonald keeps her own cow, and hens, and they make their own butter."* Nevertheless, she now looked the part of someone wielding a rod of iron: once statuesque, she had thickened into rotundity; her hair had turned pure white, although she was not yet forty-five years old; and she seldom wore any jewellery other than a small crucifix.

Hugh John, who remained in Toronto, was once again separated from the family. The emotional breach between him and his father over his marriage had healed, however, and Macdonald quickly became besotted with his grandchild, Daisy. Hugh John continued to run the law practice, the bulk of its business coming

* This was several years later, when Mrs. Grimason came to Ottawa to be shown around Parliament by Macdonald and to have tea at Earnscliffe with Lady Macdonald.

in as a tribute to the firm's sleeping partner in the national capital.

To add to Macdonald's contentment, return to power meant an end to financial stringency. He had his prime ministerial salary again, as well as the interest on the trust fund the Toronto financier David Macpherson had organized to help support him, and a share of the law firm's earnings. At the same time, the Macdonalds' expenses had grown; no public funds were provided for all the entertaining they did, and the cost of care for Mary increased as she grew older. Still, it was easier now for Macdonald to take holidays in Britain, where he enjoyed the theatre, scoured London for interesting books and took delight in buying fashionable clothes—especially colourful silk ties and stovepipe hats.

The demands of work could not be postponed. The most exigent for a new prime minister was patronage. Macdonald stalled one claimant for a position in the post office in Stratford by saying, "We find every crevice and cranny in every Department has been filled up by the Grits." He wasn't being evasive; he believed that all governments had a right to appoint their supporters to public positions—and that new governments, his own included, should not turf out their predecessor's choices. He told one disappointed MP that he was "unwilling to remove a civil servant for working for the Government of the day." Intriguingly, Macdonald over time lost much of his zest for the patronage game. In 1882 he wrote to the *Gazette*'s Martin Griffin, "I am bored to death by people applying for judgeships and senateships," and suggested the journalist write an article saying that after making checks in Ottawa he was certain the government would "look with disfavour on any pressure, personal or political, in favour of an individual."

Macdonald's agenda was of course far heavier than it had been in opposition. Two items topped the list: the transcontinental railway and the National Policy. The latter had won him the election, so he moved on it first.

Shortly after he returned to Ottawa, Macdonald received a letter from Goldwin Smith warning that he had stirred up "exaggerated expectations" about what higher tariffs might accomplish. His main point, Smith elaborated, was that he and Macdonald viewed the problem differently: "You regard Canada as part of the British Empire, I as a community of the New World," he said, but in his opinion only "free access to the markets" of the United States could "materially improve its economic prospects."

Macdonald had certainly exaggerated the beneficial effects of high tariffs. The deed had still to be done, and it wasn't easy. The challenge for the government was to come up with a new schedule of tariffs—a task for which there was little expertise within Canada. Fortunately, Macdonald had the right man nearby—Leonard Tilley, now minister of finance. Once a successful druggist, subsequently the premier of New Brunswick, a Father of Confederation and a cabinet minister from 1867 onwards, Tilley possessed qualifications for the job that only the able but erratic Alexander Galt could match. His first cabinet post had been as minister of customs, and in 1873 he had briefly held the finance portfolio. While never popular with the public—he was a teetotaller with a streak of self-righteousness—Tilley was widely respected for his honesty and competence. In his main speech in the budget debate of March 1879, he expressed the core issue in a phrase that passed straight into the Canadian political vocabulary: "The time has arrived when we are to decide whether we will simply be hewers of wood and drawers of water."

Tilley set about his task with dispatch. He recruited a talented staff—a journalist, John MacLean, who had published *Protection and Free Trade*, one of the few Canadian works on the subject, as well as several officials who had worked with him while he was premier of New Brunswick. He also inveigled back a former Nova Scotian, Edward Young, who had headed the U.S. Bureau of Statistics. Together, they worked exceptionally hard for close to four months preceding the budget. Tilley himself laboured so hard he developed serious eye strain and had to rest for several days in darkened rooms.

Tilley's objective was straightforward: "To select for a higher rate of duty those [items] that are manufactured in the country, and to leave those that are not made . . . at a lower rate." Easy to say; difficult to do. Macdonald had not helped matters by his breezy declaration: "We will make every manufacturer, every industry, produce the evidence of what is necessary for the purpose of protecting them in their present struggle into maturity."

The group developed an elaborate classification system going, roughly, from a tariff rate of zero on goods not made in Canada, to 10 per cent on slightly processed goods, to 30 per cent on finished articles. As an example, while the duties on finished textiles went as high as 34 per cent, there were no duties at all on textile machinery, while duties on woollens varied according to differences in weight and in type—Union Tweed, Black Supers or Maramatters, for instance. A major complication was the ferocious lobbying by businessmen. During the pre-budget period, Governor General Lorne reported to London that "everyone who has ever raised a pig or caught a smelt wants protection for his industry."

Finally the task was done. Tilley, who continued as finance minister until 1885, later needed to tinker with only a few of the initial duty rates. In 1890, he wrote proudly to the statistician Young, "It was *well built*. . . . Unlike nearly all the U.S. tariff acts, it did not require subsequent legislation to correct errors or omissions."

Broadly, the changes doubled the average tariff rates, from 15 per cent to 30 per cent. Although high, these tariffs were not as stratospheric as those already in effect across the border; while duties on cotton clothing were 30 per cent in Canada, they went as high as 70 per cent in the United States, and the charge on pig iron was more than three times as high there. Sensibly, all settlers' effects could come in duty free, as could fish, fish oil and seal oil from Newfoundland.

From the start, Macdonald had understood one aspect of the National Policy that was critical to its success: this was that once done, it could not be undone for a long time. The high tariffs would encourage investment in new plants and machinery. If tariffs were then cut sharply, those investments would be devalued and would never be repeated. The effect of the policy, he said, was that "a permanent fixture is certain." In 1882, when calls were raised in the Commons for a reduction of the tariff on sugar beets, Macdonald responded, "We must make the policy a permanent policy." Otherwise, businessmen would cease to invest in Canada.

Macdonald's direct contribution to the implementation of the National Policy was secondary, although he had to reassure the British government that its manufacturers would not be hurt by the new tariffs that would apply to all imports. In a memorandum to the Colonial Office, he managed to argue with a straight face that one of the National Policy's purposes was to "promote trade with Britain"—a "buncombe" argument he fabricated out of concern that lobbying by British firms might persuade the Colonial Office not to approve the program. Pressure was exerted, but the colonial secretary eventually sent the message that London accepted that "the fiscal policy of Canada [is] a matter for decision by the Dominion legislature."

In Britain a year later, Macdonald was accosted by a delegation from the Manchester Chamber of Commerce asking for a reduction in the new duties as they applied to British goods. "The chief difficulty," he explained in an interview with the *Times*, "was that England had nothing to give Canada by way of reciprocity," because it was "the sole exception in adhering in principle and practice to free trade under all circumstances." That Macdonald of all people should have used so dismissive a phrase revealed how strongly he felt about his policy. It also showed a new and more calculating tone in his attitude towards the Mother Country.

As he implemented the National Policy, Macdonald benefited from the most critical element of all: he had enacted it at exactly the right time. By mid-1879 it was clear that the Long Depression was lifting. Everyone's spirits improved, and businessmen and artisans began to look around again for new opportunities.

For several years afterwards, the *Canadian Manufacturer*, the organ of the Canadian Manufacturers' Association, reported ecstatically as new plants were announced: "Score another for the N.P.," it exulted, "More Fruit from the N.P. Treaty," and "The N.P. does it." And it wasn't just cheerleading. From 1878 to 1884, the number of labourers employed in Ontario and Quebec doubled, as did the total value of their wages. Entire new industries appeared—tableware, cutlery and clockmaking. The policy did have one unintended consequence. Many of the new companies were American owned—Singer, Edison, Westinghouse, Gillette, International Harvester—so, while they created jobs, they also competed with Canadian-owned companies and brought no head offices here. Historian Michael Bliss made the most judicious review of the National Policy's achievements in his book *Northern Enterprise*: "Although it neither created nor sustained Canadian manufacturing in any general way, the National Policy moulded both the structure of the Canadian economy and the course of debate about the society's future for many generations." It may not have made Canadians richer, that is, but it made them more Canadian.

The debate on the National Policy ended at the end of April 1879. Not long afterwards, the parliamentary session concluded, freeing Macdonald to make his first trip "home" in the years since he had last held office. After assembling a full agenda of business and pleasure activities, he and Agnes crossed the Atlantic in the middle of the summer.

TWENTY-ONE

A Considerable Man; A Considerable Empire

He believed . . . that the preservation of the union with the mother country was necessary to the making of Canada.
George Monro Grant, about Macdonald

Macdonald's first trip to Britain after an absence of six years started badly. Just as he was about to leave, at the end of June 1879, an attack of cholera delayed his departure for a month. By the time he arrived in London, Parliament's session had ended and almost everyone he wanted to meet had left for country houses to shoot grouse. He managed a long session with the colonial secretary, now Sir Michael Hicks Beach, at which he presented the high tariffs of the National Policy as nothing more than "a somewhat complex re-classification of imports." More persuasively, he argued that Britain should support the transcontinental railway financially because it would enable Britain to trade directly with Japan and China by way of Canada. Hicks Beach was properly diplomatic but urged Macdonald to recognize that Canada's new tariffs had angered many British businessmen, so it would be wiser to postpone his requests for aid from the government.

Macdonald travelled to Guildford to stay at the country house of his old friend Sir John Rose. They had a delicate and difficult conversation. Macdonald let Rose know that he wanted to appoint a diplomatic representative in London—Canada's first. No one could be better qualified than Rose himself, who had carried out similar duties for the previous decade with considerable competence, as well as substantial profit for his private bank.* However, as a British resident with an American wife, Rose would be exposed in such a post to charges of conflict of interest. The choice instead had to be Alexander Tilloch Galt, a former finance minister. Rose reluctantly agreed that Macdonald was right.

Ahead was an incomparably more agreeable engagement. During the 1871 Washington Conference years earlier, Lord de Grey, the head of the British delegation, had let Macdonald know that, as a reward for his services, he should become a member of the Imperial Privy Council—the first colonial to attain such an honour. The Canadian Pacific Scandal had scotched that possibility, but the Canadian public having changed its mind, so could the British government. On the morning of August 14, Macdonald travelled to the Queen's summer home of Osborne House on the Isle of Wight, and that afternoon was sworn in as a member of Her Majesty's Privy Council, elevating his title from "Hon." to "Rt. Hon." By some courtier's blunder, he hadn't been invited to stay for dinner, so he journeyed back to London that same evening.†

Instead, he dined a few days later with his hero, Disraeli, now Lord Beaconsfield, who, on learning of the social gaffe at Osborne, wrote to the governor general, "This vexes me as

---

* Rose's post had been unofficial, and he was always described as someone "enjoying the confidence of the Canadian Government."

† In 1885, the Queen made up for her unintended rudeness by awarding Macdonald the Grand Cross of the Bath. After he received it at a ceremony at Windsor Castle, he both dined with her and spent the night in the castle.

I feel your ministers ought to have been festivaled and banqueted." As a substitute for a royal banquet, Disraeli offered one of his own for just the two of them at his country mansion, Hughenden Manor, in the Chiltern Hills, north of London. Macdonald accepted, and on Monday, September 1, went by rail to High Wycombe, where Disraeli's carriage was waiting.

When Macdonald came to Queen Victoria's house, Osborne, on the Isle of Wight, some hapless courtier had forgotten to invite him to stay on for dinner. The Queen rectified this gaffe a half-dozen years later by extending him an overnight invitation to Windsor Castle, with an excellent dinner included.

"He is gentlemanlike, agreeable and very intelligent; a considerable man," Disraeli wrote afterwards in his diary, adding that he lacked "Yankeeisms except a little sing-song at the end of a sentence." He recorded further that Macdonald, with whom he stayed up well past midnight, had "given me a very bad night and leaving me very exhausted"—meaning that the pair had got into the brandy while exchanging thoughts about the world and, in Joseph Pope's words, "descanted upon the great poets, orators and philosophers of Athens and Rome."*

Disraeli and Macdonald shared a good deal in common—theatricality, wit, tolerance, a keen appreciation of human nature and an amused view of its frailties and follies. And both were Conservatives. Nicholas Flood Davin, who had covered Disraeli as

* Both were partial to brandy, Macdonald enjoying nips of it, while Disraeli often sipped white brandy when giving long public speeches—much as Macdonald once substituted gin for water.

a reporter at Westminster, reckoned, "Sir John is probably the better debater of the two, although not equalling Dizzy in invective or in epigram." Davin judged that, for all Disraeli's sinuous skill, "it may well be doubted if his power of conciliating men and fixing their emotions surpasses that of [Macdonald]." Both were nationalists, no doubt because they were partly outsiders—Disraeli an assimilated Jew, and Macdonald an assimilated Scot. Both were strong believers in the British Empire, Macdonald to avoid becoming American, and Disraeli because he had recently reinvented it, most particularly in India. Disraeli wrote well-regarded novels; Macdonald late in life wished he had been a writer.

There were similarities in their appearance: both had mobile faces with high cheekbones (Disraeli was better at looking sphinx-like), hair that was either crinkly (Macdonald's) or ostentatiously curly (Dizzy's), and both shared a taste for "notice-me" clothes. In 1881, Sir Charles Dilke visited Disraeli on his deathbed, and while he waited later for a train at Euston Station he spotted Macdonald—and believed for a few bewildered moments that Disraeli had somehow made a miraculous recovery.

Yet this dinner was their one and only meeting. The flukes of political timing kept them apart, one or other always being out of power when the other was in. This time, they did overlap, but only until 1880, when Disraeli was defeated by Gladstone. He died the following year.

According to one early Macdonald biographer, there was another missed connection between them. E.B. Biggar claims that, after Disraeli's death, some British Conservatives approached Macdonald to suggest he move to Britain "with a view to succeeding the great English statesman." There may have been a grain of truth to this anecdote. Some leading British Conservatives such as Lord Carnarvon and Sir Stafford Northcote thought highly of

More than once when in London, Macdonald got mistaken for his hero, Disraeli (alone, right). Macdonald spent a night at Disraeli's country house, and the pair stayed up well past midnight talking about "the great poets, orators and philosophers of Athens and Rome."

Macdonald; his heavy drinking days were behind him, and his 1878 recovery from crushing defeat had impressed everybody. In Biggar's version, Macdonald told the British emissaries that "here, he was engaged in the development of a nation; there, he would be struggling to hold together the fabric of an old one." That response sounds like him, and it captures the complex nature of his feelings about Canada's relations with its "home" country.

Macdonald was an unregenerate anglophile: he loved Britain, its history, literature, legal system and political system, and London's bustle and buzz. By comparison, late nineteenth-century Canada—provincial, raw and ridden by religious rivalries—just wasn't very loveable. In Ottawa, he missed his conversations with British public men: "Their tone is so high and their mode of thinking is so correct," he once remarked.

On this side of the Atlantic, though, he was engaged in nation-building. His home was now here; as he once put it, "All my hopes and my remembrances are Canadian; and not only are my principles and prejudices Canadian, but . . . my interests are." His family was here, including those already buried—mother and father, first wife, first-born son and most recently a sister. If the argument advanced in these two volumes is correct—that no Macdonald would have meant no Canada—it is true equally that had there been no Canada, there could have been no Macdonald of renown, instead perhaps just a likeable small-town lawyer who drank too much.

Macdonald's emotional attachment to Britain reinforced, but did not cause, his political conviction that Canada had to remain connected to the world's superpower. He reached that conclusion for reasons of *realpolitik*—Canada's survival. From this conviction he never deviated. He defended the connection on every possible occasion, once calling it "a golden chain" connecting Canada to Britain that he personally was "proud to wear." Most times, his arguments were practical and purposeful. Independence would be "tantamount to annexation." He opposed Edward Blake's contention that Canada should gain the power to negotiate its own treaties. If that happened, he argued, Canada would lose "the prestige of England, the whole diplomatic service of England" and find it hard to get noticed, let alone enforce any treaties it signed. He was well aware that, although all the British soldiers had departed, the Royal Navy remained on both coasts, and that its presence enabled Canada to argue with the United States over its fisheries rights. He knew that Britain's pledge to come to Canada's aid if it was attacked was its only defence, and he once admitted that the Americans, should they ever choose to invade, could "go where they liked, and do what they pleased." He was using Britain's faraway power as a counterweight against the power of a next-door neighbour.

Yet, while he consistently said all the right things about the Mother Country and the British Empire, he actually did remarkably little in return for the benefits of their association. Repeated requests by the Colonial Office for reports on Canada's military capabilities went unanswered. On the subject of an Imperial Federation—the idea of knitting the Empire together more closely by having British and colonial politicians sit in each other's legislatures—he kept official comments to a minimum; in private, he dismissed the notion as unworkable. His National Policy tariffs hit British exports as hard as those of the United States.

At the time, this distinction was little noticed, and most subsequent commentators have slotted Macdonald into the category of a knee-bending colonial. One of the very few people who recognized what he was up to was the principal of Queen's University, George Monro Grant. Macdonald "believed there was room on the continent of America for at least two nations, and he was determined that Canada should be a nation," Grant commented after Macdonald's death. "He believed . . . that the preservation of the union with the mother country was necessary to the making of Canada."

The Mother Country, thus, no matter how much loved by Macdonald personally, was to him a means to an end, an asset to be used to advance Canadian interests—most particularly to gain it time to become a nation. One other observer also figured out his strategy. Sir Charles Dilke once remarked on the curious fact that those in Britain who strongly advocated Imperial Federation and those who dismissed it as a fantasy both supported their case with words from the same source—John A. Macdonald's speeches on the subject.

None of this artfulness lessened Macdonald's love of Britain. Equally, neither did that love ever lessen his readiness to exploit Britain for Canada's benefit.

Macdonald and Disraeli met at exactly the right time. The relationship between the two countries was undergoing a profound change, one that Disraeli had done much to bring about—and one that would alter significantly the nature of the challenges Macdonald faced during the latter part of his second term.

The source of the change was the foreign policy that Disraeli pursued during the years 1874–80. It was an extravagantly expansionist policy. He bought the Suez Canal for Britain in 1875 (from the Khedive of Egypt) and a year later raised Queen Victoria to the rank of Empress of India. Later, at the gathering of all the key statesmen of Europe at the Congress of Berlin, he outfoxed Bismarck and, by undermining the League of the Three Emperors (Germany, Austria-Hungary and Russia), advanced Britain's balance-of-power strategy in Europe.

Partly by intent, partly by circumstance, Disraeli changed Britain itself. He managed the triumph of the pro-Imperial Big Englanders over the Little Englanders and attracted to the Conservative Party many of the newly enfranchised industrial workers, who found in the Empire the glory and excitement lacking in their hard and narrow lives. Because of Disraeli, the Empire, once accumulated in a fit of absence of mind, became a secular religion, a kind of national signature and a source of delight and pride. Potentially powerful arriviste nations such as Germany envied it.

Much of Disraeli's grand foreign policy was his response to an intuitive realization that Britain had entered into an era of economic and military decline, and that from this time on, show—in everything from the colour and precision of its military parades to the impeccably polished decks of its warships—would increasingly have to serve as a substitute for strength. Some observers understood this connection: the bard of empire, Rudyard Kipling, issued a call to "Take up the White Man's burden," but in "Recessional" he penned the melancholy line, "Lo, all our pomp of yesterday / Is one with Nineveh and Tyre!"

Still, the Empire was indubitably splendid. As that chronicler of empire James Morris observed, "There was hardly a moment of the day, hardly a facet of daily living, in which the fact of Empire was not emphasized. From exhortatory editorials to match-box lids, from children's fashions to parlour-games, from music hall lyrics to parish church sermons, the imperial theme was relentlessly drummed."

If the British people were "imperially brain-washed," so were a great many Canadians. They too became New Imperialists. "Imperialism was one form of Canadian nationalism," the historian Carl Berger has written. The nationalist movement of the Canada First intellectuals had by now collapsed, and all talk of "a new nationality" had long since dried up. Just as damaging, the United States no longer performed for Canada's identity the vital role of threatening its existence, or, as effectively, of appearing to. The annexation movement below the border was dead. And so a growing number of Canadians set out to do their bit for national unity by looking abroad, not for a common enemy but for a common friend.

That friend was the British Empire. A cluster of intellectuals, among them George Grant, the teacher and popular historian

George Parkin, the ultra-Tory Colonel George Denison and later the humorist Stephen Leacock and the poet Wilfred Campbell, began to talk up the Empire as the way for Canada to regain energy and spirit. As one of the New Imperialists put it, "How petty our interests, how small most of our public questions, how narrow our sympathies." Canada might not be able to match American energy and dynamism, but the Empire offered glamour, variety, the exotic (really the sexual, as in India) and the prospect of war—a test of manhood dreamed of by many young men in those innocent years before the War to End All Wars.

The Empire also offered a chance at sanctity: rather than trade following the flag, it was now the Bible, as carried by thousands of ardent and athletic missionaries. The New Imperialism was not itself about idealism; the dictum of "the survival of the fittest," derived from Darwin's doctrine of evolution, made it easier to justify the treatment meted out to colonials and indigenous peoples. The assumption became that if these had been truly fit, they would have remained independent—and certainly not have become extinct. Jingoism and racism were as much a part of the New Imperialism as were pith helmets.

Canadians were New Imperialists in a very Canadian way. They weren't imperialistic: no one ever suggested that Canada should acquire colonies. And they were nationalists every bit as much as imperialists. "I am an Imperialist because I do not wish to be a Colonial," Leacock would declare.

Being Canadians, they were eager to make the Empire itself better rather than just bigger. In Grant's view, "In it, the rights of all men are sacred . . . [it] offers most opportunities for all kinds of noblest service to humanity through the serving of fellow-citizens." Even Macdonald was drawn in. In a speech in Montreal in 1875, he said that Britain and its colonies, because they all spoke the same language and lived under the same laws, should operate as "one great nation, as it were, for the purpose of operating as a moral police, and of keeping the peace of the world."

That was Macdonald's one sortie into Imperial altruism. His opinion about the purpose of the Empire was always practical. It was also always vague—and curiously static. It's very likely that the source of both these characteristics was Macdonald's reluctance to be an imperialist himself. His Montreal speech provides the clue. He denounced annexation as a "treasonable proposition" and made his best-known declaration about the transatlantic connection: "A British subject I was born, and a British subject I hope to die." But he said nothing at all about what Canada might contribute to the Empire.

From time to time, Macdonald made some extremely interesting statements about the way the relationship between Canada and its Mother Country might evolve. In that same 1875 speech, he promulgated the idea that "England would be the central power and we the auxiliary nations; that Canada would by degrees have less of dependence and more of alliance than at present." He had said much the same as far back as the Confederation Debate of 1865, when he forecast, "Gradually a different colonial system is being developed, and it will become, year by year, less a case of dependence on our own part . . . and more a case of healthy and cordial alliance." Another decade on, he was still at it: in an 1884 letter to his friend Judge James Robert Gowan, he suggested that colonies such as Canada and Australia should function as "auxiliary kingdoms" by "seeking common cause with England by a quasi-treaty."

These ideas were indeed interesting, and it's even possible to discern in them the outlines of the future Commonwealth. He was certainly savvy enough to recognize early on that the Empire was becoming far more a matter of show than of strength. In that same letter to Gowan, he remarked that the colonies had to "strengthen the shaky old mother." And after learning that the jihad-type uprising in the Sudan had succeeded in capturing the capital, Khartoum, and in killing General Charles Gordon, Macdonald commented to Gowan, "England has I fear culminated, but her children must take care of her." His concerns obviously became known because in 1891 the Imperial magnate Cecil Rhodes wrote to him suggesting they meet to discuss "some tie with our mother country that will prevent separation." Rhodes went on to criticize many of Britain's inhabitants: "They cannot see the future," he complained. "They think they will always be the manufacturing mart of the world." Rhodes's letter, though, reached Ottawa a few days after Macdonald's death.

The most important aspect of Macdonald's musings about some possible new, more equal relationship between the colonies and Britain was that in fact he pursued none of them. Rather, such actions as he took inched Canada away from the Mother Country, even while he was protesting how loyal he and the country were to it. In 1882, when the Colonial Office suggested that Canada send four battalions to Britain so the same number of British battalions could be moved to Egypt, he refused. After the fall of Khartoum, Britain made no request for colonial troops, but Australia and New Zealand sent some anyway. Macdonald commented to Tupper that Canada was not Australia: "The Suez Canal is nothing to us," he wrote. "We do not ask England to quarrel with France or Germany for our sakes. Why should we waste money or men . . . to get Gladstone & Co out of the hole they have plunged themselves into by their imbecility?"

Over the long span, from 1867 to 1891, Macdonald's military policy was consistent and clear. If Britain itself was threatened, Canadian troops would be sent out; but if Britain had started the scrap on some patch of its Empire, the problem was for it to solve. Macdonald spelled out this view when he appeared before an Imperial Defence Commission while he was visiting Britain in

1880. He told the commissioners that, if Britain precipitated some colonial war, the feeling of Canadians would be, "Well, here is a war the mother country has gone into in which we are not interested and about which we have not been consulted." But if Britain itself should be attacked, Canadians, with "their strong affection for the mother country, and their desire to maintain the connection," would immediately offer substantial aid in the form of both men and money.

Macdonald was even more vague about the much-discussed Imperial Federation. In a speech in Toronto in November 1881, he described the scheme as "impossible" and explained why. "We would never agree to send a number of men over to England to sit in Parliament there and vote away our rights and privileges. . . . We will govern our country. We will put on the taxes ourselves." When a founding convention of the Imperial Federation League was held in London in 1884, he directed Charles Tupper, who was then high commissioner, to attend but to say nothing except amiable generalities.

Macdonald got away with so unsentimental a policy because he was genuinely sentimental about his admiration and love for Britain. His feelings about the monarchy were especially strong because the throne was occupied by Queen Victoria. Patently, he enjoyed immensely bending the knee to her. Even here, though, his nationalism showed. In a speech in Toronto in 1875, he referred to her—the first to do so, all but certainly—as "Queen of Canada."* As helped immensely in his daily dealings with the British, high or low, there was "nothing viewy" about Macdonald, as the journalist Nicholas Flood Davin put it, meaning that, unlike some Canadians, he never lectured the British about morality.

* Almost a century had to pass before any British monarch gained that title, it being extended officially to Queen Elizabeth II in 1953, her coronation year.

Being Janus-faced earned him another victory, small but useful, in his "long game" of nudging and tugging Canada towards national maturity. This one involved getting the country onto the international diplomatic stage, even though, as a colony, it had no legal right to be there at all.

One of Macdonald's early acts during his 1879 visit to Britain had been to hand over to Colonial Secretary Hicks Beach a long memorandum titled "Confidential Memorandum on Canada's Representative in London." Its opening sentence defined its purposes: "Canada has ceased to occupy the position of an ordinary possession of the Crown." The country therefore needed someone to represent its national interests at the Imperial centre of London, as no other colony did at the time.

Macdonald had prepared the ground carefully. He informed Governor General Lorne fully on the project and was rewarded with a briefing note from Lorne to London describing him as "perhaps the last statesman who entirely looks to England and who may be believed to be devoted to imperial interests." Much of the credit for Lorne's helpfulness was due to his predecessor, Lord Dufferin, who had sent a perceptive report advising the Colonial Office to yield to Canadian demands for increased autonomy, because the alternative was likely to be "that the cry of Independence would be raised a generation too soon, and Annexation would be the direct and immediate consequence."

Both Hicks Beach and Lord Salisbury, the foreign secretary, had serious reservations about an official Canadian representative. Macdonald resorted to "buncombe" arguments, such as that Canada might be able to benefit the Empire by offering specialized knowledge of what was going on in Washington. When these politicians yielded the field, the bureaucrats took over, arguing at length the proper title for an official Canadian representative. Finally, Macdonald exploded, "We might call him Nuncio or Legate or Letere Gubernatoris if we pleased." Eventually, the title of high commissioner was agreed to—the title used today by all Commonwealth ambassadors in Commonwealth capitals. The bureaucrats won the last round: to Alexander Galt's great disappointment, he was not granted official status as a diplomat.

Galt, able but highly temperamental, did some useful work, principally in attracting immigration. He made major efforts in Ireland, though with little success, because most priests feared that their flock would lose the faith in faraway lands. Galt's great achievement was to convince Lord Rothschild, until then quite hostile to Canada, to sponsor some 1,500 Russian Jews to move to Moosomin in present-day Saskatchewan. Macdonald was ecstatic, telling Galt, "By establishing a Jew colony here, whether ultimately successful or not, a link—a missing link—will be established between Canada and Sidonia" (an ancient Phoenician city). He also negotiated trade pacts with France and Spain, with a Foreign Office official sitting in.

Repeatedly, though, Galt embarrassed Macdonald by interfering in British politics, as by making public speeches calling for Home Rule for Ireland. He also annoyed him by complaining he had insufficient funds to entertain guests.* By 1882, Galt had threatened to resign once too often, and Macdonald accepted his offer. Tupper succeeded him and functioned as high commissioner with previously concealed skill.

---

* Macdonald's guileful response was that Galt should deliberately serve poor food to Canadian guests, who would complain about their treatment when they returned home and so make it easier for the government to increase the entertainment budget.

The New Imperialism remained a political force throughout the remainder of Macdonald's career and on into the First World War. Then, Canadians came to realize they had more in common with American GIs—more open, more egalitarian and above all less class ridden—than with the British Tommies. Many of the effects of the New Imperialism were deeply dysfunctional, because it amounted to the ascendency of Anglo-Saxon Protestantism. It threatened French Canadians and was one of the causes of the bitter sectarian wars of the late 1880s. Its clearest effect was to make English Canadians a great deal more English and so slow the country's progress towards national maturity. This process would take another two-thirds of a century, and, legally, it happened only in 1931, when the Statute of Westminster raised all the dominions to the status of independent nation-states.*

Although Macdonald himself was never a New Imperialist, nor an imperialist of any kind, his love for Britain was absolute. He never accepted a peerage, but he was delighted to receive the highest offer the British establishment could extend to him—membership in the Athenaeum on Pall Mall, London's grandest club, where dukes, ambassadors, bishops and generals turned the pages of the *Times* while sipping Scotch or brandy. Still, as Grant noted, that never stopped him from using Britain as a tool for "the making of Canada."

* Not all British politicians agreed with this concession, one denouncing it as "repellent legalism." His name was Winston Churchill.

TWENTY-TWO

Build It and They Will Come

Catch them, before they invest their profits.
John Henry Pope, minister of agriculture

As railways went, the St. Paul and Pacific Railroad was quite possibly the most woebegone in North America. It had never earned a profit. Designed to run from St. Paul, Minnesota, to the Canadian border, it had never reached anywhere near that far, so didn't connect with the line down from Winnipeg. Its rails were of iron rather than steel, and the company was widely derided as being "two streaks of rust and a right of way." Yet without this little railway to nowhere, there might well never have been a Canadian Pacific Railway to stitch Canada together.

The explanation for this oddity was that although the only attribute the St. Paul and Pacific possessed was a largely unused right of way, such a licence was potentially very valuable, because on both sides of the border above St. Paul, especially on its northern side, there was endless black loam that was widely assumed to be capable of supporting thousands of farms and tens of thousands of settlers. To turn this joke railway into a real one, little more was needed than to use its right of way so the line could stretch all the way up to Winnipeg.

At this time—the late 1870s—there just happened to be a number of entrepreneurs, mostly Canadians, with the smarts to figure this out. One was James Jerome Hill, Canadian-born, though he had spent most of his adult life in the United States doing all kinds of jobs and reading omnivorously. Hill's dream was to own a transcontinental railroad—a goal he would achieve twice over, in two different systems, as a leading partner with the famed banker J.P. Morgan. Another was Donald Smith, now a political power in the North-West as an MP as well as the chief commissioner of the Hudson's Bay Company. He was close to an enterprising HBC officer, Norman Kittson, who operated a steamship service along the Red River. This trio—Hill, Smith and Kittson—figured out that a major part of the ramshackle railway company's bonds was held by some long-suffering Dutch investors. They made a low offer to the Dutch, who rejected it. Smith then turned to his cousin George Stephen for help. Stephen knew so little about the West that he thought Minnesota was "at the North Pole." But he knew a great deal about money.

Stephen would become the irreplaceable man of the Canadian Pacific Railway. Born in Scotland in 1829, the son of a carpenter, he left school at fourteen and after five years in various jobs in Aberdeen emigrated to Canada. He got employment with a dry-goods merchant in Montreal and soon was promoted to be a junior partner. By the late 1860s, he was one of Montreal's leading businessmen, and in 1876 was appointed president of the Bank of Montreal—corporate Canada's top post. Naturally reserved and retiring, he liked to be anonymous. He was obsessive about privacy; he had all his papers burned, avoided talking to the press and banned telephones from his home. He regarded politics with contempt, because it was so public. He didn't even like Canada much, and in 1886, soon after the CPR was completed, he retired to Britain.

George Stephen, first president of the Canadian Pacific Railway, was a brilliant financier with a fine, subtle mind and a talent for hiring executives with unusual abilities. At the same time, he was quick to be hurt by criticism and to lapse into self-pity.

Only in his letters to Macdonald (more than eight hundred of them) did Stephen reveal, unintentionally, some of his inner complexities—his self-doubts, his sense of being misunderstood and treated unfairly, and occasionally even a hint of wishing to be liked. Unquestionably, Stephen was the country's most brilliant financier of the nineteenth century; also, he worked ferociously hard. "It was impressed on me . . . by one of the best mothers who ever lived," he said, "that I must aim at being a thorough master of the work by which I had to get my living . . . to the exclusion of every other thing."

Events moved quickly once Smith introduced Stephen to Hill. In 1878, the Bank of Montreal advanced the group a loan to buy out the Dutch and American investors in the St. Paul and Pacific Railroad. They paid $6.8 million for it and promptly sold most of its land grant for $13 million. They renamed the company the St. Paul, Minneapolis and Manitoba Railroad, then patched and stretched the track so that it reached the Canadian border and connected with the southwards line from Winnipeg. In December 1878, a train—the *Countess of Dufferin*—left the Manitoba capital for the first time. The system was so crude that, for lack of a turntable, the engine had to drive backwards on the return trip. For the first time, however, Canada's North-West was now connected directly to the outside world.

In the late 1870s, it seemed that everything "westophiles" had ever said about the North-West was about to prove true—it was a New Eden, the "garden of the world," Canada's answer to the United States' manifest destiny. The Long Depression lifted, or at least went into remission, and suddenly immigrants came pouring into this vast, unsettled territory—eighteen thousand in 1880, the next year twenty-nine thousand. The 1881 census put Manitoba's population at sixty-six thousand, not counting Aboriginals.

Not all the newcomers were Anglo-Saxons. There were Mennonites fleeing military service in Germany, Icelanders driven out by a volcanic explosion who settled in a place called Gimli ("Paradise"), several thousand Hungarians who grouped together in "Huns Valley," and the "rural Jews" brought out of Russia by Lord Rothschild, initially to Saskatchewan. The English-speaking proportion of Manitoba rose swiftly, from less than half before it joined Confederation to close to 90 per cent—a shift quickened by the departure of many Métis to the Far West, especially to Batoche in present-day Saskatchewan.

Winnipeg now grew rapidly. It was rough and rowdy; in one contemporary judgment, "Winnipeg and Barrie are the two most evil places in Canada."* But it was also go-ahead; by the 1880s, Winnipeg had acquired gas lighting, a telephone system, a street railway, three newspapers and, most remarkable of all, the University of Manitoba. Among those lured westwards by this expansion were two Toronto lawyers, Hugh John Macdonald and Charles Hibbert Tupper, the son of the veteran politician who was

---

* Among Winnipeg's qualifications to be identified as evil was having a saloon for every two hundred residents. The reason for Barrie's inclusion in the list of the infamous remains opaque.

now minister of railways. The senior Tupper, whose patronage practices were legendary, urged Macdonald to steer government business to their sons. Macdonald took offence and told Tupper he would never allow it. For the next two years, these two long-term colleagues never spoke except on formal business. Eventually their hurt feelings healed, with neither harbouring a grudge.

In the meantime, the new owners of the St. Paul, Minneapolis and Manitoba Railroad were making a mint. At this juncture, Macdonald received some of the best advice of his entire career. John Henry Pope, his plain-looking and plain-speaking minister of agriculture, told him about the western railway's owners and advised: "Catch them, before they invest their profits."

During his five years as prime minister, Alexander Mackenzie had been able to advance the transcontinental railway just a few hundred miles. Edward Blake, who always overshadowed him, never stopped denouncing as "insanity" a project that involved, in his term, crossing "a sea of mountains" to serve a market of about twenty thousand (European) people. The principal reason for the slow progress during Mackenzie's term, though, was the contraction of government revenues due to the depression. All he could do was to issue small contracts each year and to shrink the grandiose scheme closer to financial reality—as by cancelling Macdonald's commitment to British Columbia that the line would be extended over to Vancouver Island. Macdonald was back in power now, but he had no clearer idea than Mackenzie how this huge task might actually be done. Moreover, he made things even more difficult by insisting that the line be built entirely in Canada—by running it across the empty, hard-rock expanse above Lake Superior rather than taking the easy and cheap southern route by curling down into the United States at either Sault Ste. Marie or Duluth and returning by way of the St. Paul–Winnipeg line.

Of all Macdonald's cabinet ministers, Charles Tupper was the most exasperating and the most likeable. A medical doctor who kept his bag under his seat in the Commons, large, blousy, loud and ferociously partisan, he provoked everyone he met to describe him in vivid colours. The MP George Ross wrote, "In repose, even, he looked as if he had a blizzard secreted somewhere about his person." Yet Tupper got a lot done: he had manoeuvred Nova Scotia into Confederation and had made it almost impossible for Macdonald to resign after the Canadian Pacific Scandal. Now, he badgered Macdonald into doing what had to be done—to find a syndicate capable of building the CPR.

Charles Tupper was more than a bit of a blowhard, but he was also capable of surprises, such as coming up with the formula that sealed the deal between the government and the CPR. His nickname, "The Ram of Cumberland," was probably unfair, his attentions to the ladies being limited to flirtation.

The Macdonald government's 1880 schedule for railway construction was modest: it involved paying for 125 new miles to be built in British Columbia from Kamloops to the coast. Tupper began to nag his leader: "I want to submit a proposition for building a through line from Nipissing to the Pacific Coast." Macdonald, still harbouring memories of Hugh Allan, warily observed that it would be "a very large order," but he agreed. Tupper plunged ahead and submitted a lengthy memorandum to the cabinet on June 15 asking for authority to negotiate with a group of capitalists "of undoubted means" who he claimed would guarantee not only to construct the line but to operate it as well.

Here, Tupper was being daringly innovative; not only was the line to be built and managed by a private company rather than the government, but in addition this company would be responsible for "the rapid settlement of the public lands." In effect, it would be a national development enterprise, one of Imperial dimensions. Cabinet agreed, and Tupper opened negotiations with Stephen and his partners. Prime among the subjects to be discussed was the scale of the government's assistance in both a cash subsidy and land grants.

At this point, Macdonald decided that he and Tupper should go to England to scout prospects for raising funds for the railway project and to seek out whether any other groups, particularly Canada's largest railway company, the Grand Trunk, might be interested. They sailed from Quebec City on July 10. A day later, the ship stopped at Rimouski to pick up mail. Included in Macdonald's package was a letter from Stephen, convoluted and almost standoffish, but with a hint that he really wanted to be asked to take on the project.

He was, Stephen wrote, rather hesitant to commit himself "to the enormous responsibilities involved in this undertaking." He was sure Macdonald would find others "more or less substantial and with greater courage . . . because they will adopt measures for their own protection" which he would not use. The usual way of building a railway, he continued, was for a company to issue the largest possible number of bonds, so that the real responsibility for the success of the project was transferred to the bondholders, while the company made big profits at the start. He, however, had figured out a better way of getting the job done, by keeping public borrowing to a minimum, financing the project as much as possible from his group's own capital and looking to a respectable return through "the growth of the country and the development of the property"—after the railway was actually in business*. Amid all this roundabout musing he tucked a most alluring argument: because the company would earn its money more from land sales than from ticket sales, it would have a powerful incentive to build the railway as quickly as possible. Stephen closed by saying that although he was "off the notion of the thing now," he might revive his interest if Macdonald and Tupper found that the offers they received in England were not what they expected. The lure worked. In London, Macdonald got no better proposal, so he called Stephen again.

By September, Stephen was writing to Macdonald that both his friends and his enemies had warned him that the railway project would be "the ruin of us all," but he wanted an agreement that would be "*fair* and *creditable* to both the Government and ourselves." But for the details, and for the politics, the deal was done.

One problem appeared. Among the syndicate's directors was Donald Smith, the same man whose vote had ensured Macdonald's defeat in the Commons in 1873. Later, Macdonald and Smith had got into a shouting match in the Commons, with Macdonald calling him "the biggest liar I ever met." The solution agreed on was to omit Smith's name from the published list of CPR directors. That caused new problems. "I have had a terrible bother with Don Smith because his name is not printed," Stephen wrote to John Rose in London, adding, "He has been like a baby over the thing." On the government's side, the problem in fact was not so much Macdonald as it was many of the Conservative MPs. Macdonald's view about

---

* The idea wasn't completely new to Macdonald. Back in 1870, in a debate about the original proposed CPR, he had told MPs one way to finance an intercontinental line was "by means of the lands through which it had to pass." This was why he was so insistent on Ottawa retaining ownership of the Crown lands of the prairies.

political relationships was, as he once told his secretary Joseph Pope, that "a statesman should have no resentments." His Conservative colleagues, however, could never bring themselves to forgive Smith for his disloyalty, and as payback they managed to get Smith's most recent election victory annulled for a technical breach of the law.*

A more fundamental problem now appeared. "Rapid development" of the territory was essential if the CPR was to recoup its costs. To accomplish this end, the company had to have a monopoly over railways in the territory—at least for a time. In a succession of letters to Macdonald, Stephen warned that without a monopoly for the CPR all the money spent on building the line "might as well have been thrown into the Lake." He took a firm position: no monopoly, no contract. Macdonald eventually agreed, but reluctantly, because populist rage against monopolies exploiting their exclusive franchise had become a prime political force all across North America. On October 21, 1880, the contract was signed.

"A stupendous outrage," screamed the *Ottawa Free Press*. "One stands aghast . . . so monstrous are its provisions and so monstrous its omissions," declared the *Montreal Daily Witness*. "A ruinous contract," echoed the *Manitoba Free Press*. These criticisms weren't wrong. The scale of the concessions to the CPR syndicate was without precedent, not only in Canada but even in the far more economically advanced United States, where, during the Gilded Age, the giveaways to railway syndicates and mine operators were truly heroic.

* Smith ran again in the resulting by-election in Manitoba but lost, despite spending a whopping thirty thousand dollars. As one of his aides put it, "The voters have taken your money and voted against you."

The company was to receive a subsidy of $25 million and a grant of 25 million acres of land (in alternative sections of 640 acres each). No duty would be charged on all the construction materials it imported. Its land holdings would be free of taxation for twenty years, and all its structures, such as stations and yards, would be free of tax in perpetuity. The company would be given without charge all the transcontinental line already built—some 710 miles. Most important, the contract included Clause 15, which granted the CPR a twenty-year monopoly over all lines southwards to the border from its own line. The *Ottawa Free Press* calculated that the syndicate was being handed a gift worth $261 million. Stephen denied it, but his mathematics left a lot out.

In exchange, the CPR syndicate agreed to build, to top-class standards, all the uncompleted portions of the line—some 1,900 miles in all, from Ontario to the Pacific coast. At Macdonald's insistence, the line, despite Stephen's strong protests, would be all-Canadian and so would cross the bleak territory above Lake Superior. British Columbia would not get the extension to Vancouver Island it demanded, but it would get a guarantee that the entire project would be completed within ten years—the same time span agreed to when the province entered Confederation (and also, as everyone believed at the time, impossible to meet).

It was horrendously expensive, but it was also magnificently ambitious. As Pierre Berton wrote in *The National Dream*, this contract was designed to be "the instrument by which the nation broke out of the prison of the St. Lawrence lowlands." It would turn Canada into a continental nation, a northern mirror-image of its rival to the south. Goldwin Smith came closest to understanding the magnitude of what was being attempted. "What is truly momentous, and makes this a turning-point in our destiny," he wrote in the *Bystander*, "is the choice which our people are now called upon to make between the continental and the anti-continental system, between the policy of antagonism to our neighbours to the south and that of partnership." It was in this vital respect that the transcontinental railway was the foundation of Macdonald's entire nation-building program. It would make it possible to fully realize his National Policy of tariff protection by creating a national market for Canada's manufacturers. And it would create a true nation, because its citizens would at last be able to come to know each other and to need each other.

The railway was Canada's first *projet national*—the first time, but for Confederation itself, that this fragmented and attenuated nation dared to try to be something grander than the sum of its comparatively small parts. It was a collective aspiration that involved more than merely surviving, or not becoming American by remaining British. This railway would be the first in a series of collective, out-of-the-ordinary undertakings for Canada, including its magnificent participation in the First and Second world wars; its postwar recreation of itself as a welfare state, with universal health care becoming part of the national DNA; Expo 67 and other celebrations of Canada's centennial year; the commitment to peacekeeping; the implementation of national bilingualism and the Charter of Rights and Freedoms; and, today, the policies of multiculturalism and of continuous immigration on a scale, proportionately, far larger than that of any nation on the globe.

Macdonald's project was also that most un-Canadian of events—the taking of a great dare. Out of it would come the country's one major narrative poem, E.J. Pratt's *Towards the Last Spike*, and also the country's most iconic image, of the ceremony (a modest, Canadian affair) that marked the completion of the line. Inevitably, in a nation so divided and thinly stretched, the transcontinental railway project would also produce a great deal of criticism and complaining and carping, both at the time and for decades afterwards. Macdonald could not see into this future; but he could, and did, get the railway built.

~

The next step was to get Parliament's approval. Given Macdonald's majority, the outcome was not in doubt. Far from certain, though, was how long it would take, and how much skepticism about the venture the criticisms of the Opposition would stir up among the citizens. Macdonald underestimated the first challenge and overestimated the scale of the second.

To give the CPR a chance to execute a full construction program for 1881, Macdonald called Parliament into session early, in the middle of December 1880, and immediately tabled the necessary legislation. The debate went on and on and on. To keep it going, Opposition members resorted to reciting everything from "The Charge of the Light Brigade" to "How doth the little busy bee. . . ." From London, Stephen wrote to Macdonald in anguish: "I did not think it possible for political malignity to go so far as it has done in this discussion." After the briefest possible recess for Christmas, the MPs immediately resumed their squabbling. Blake and Tupper exchanged five-hour speeches, neither really saying anything new.

The Opposition did score some points, but overreached itself by promoting the cause of an alternative syndicate that just happened to have a number of well-known Liberals as partners. An illness—perhaps stomach trouble or sheer exhaustion—kept Macdonald away on Parliament's reopening day, and afterwards he let Tupper do all the talking. Then he saw his opportunity. He had to be helped to his feet in the House, and he spoke with long pauses, once saying, "I am not well. But I will be heard." He ridiculed the alternative syndicate as a "farce . . . a political engine." Building a transcontinental railway to connect with the existing

American railways, as planned by the supposed second syndicate, would ruin the policy under which the Dominion of Canada had been created and ruin "our hopes of being a great nation . . . we should become a bundle of sticks as we were before, without a binding cord." In contrast, an all-Canadian line would "give us a great and united, a rich and improving, developing Canada, instead of making us tributary to American bondage, to American tolls, to American freights." Blake wasn't wrong in many of his criticisms about financial improvidence, but he was no match for a national dream.

It still took time. The House often sat until 2 a.m., and once all the way to 8 a.m. The Liberals moved twenty-four amendments. Often weak and pale of face, Macdonald never left the Chamber, and even skipped a fancy-dress ice carnival at Rideau Hall. "I had to betake myself to my bed for a fortnight and am only now beginning to crawl around," he wrote to Alexander Galt, then in London. On January 31, 1881, the bill was given second reading. The final, third reading came on February 1, just before midnight. "At last the CPR is a fixed fact," Macdonald wrote to Galt, again from his bed.

Macdonald was too weary to attend the ceremony at which Governor General Lorne gave royal assent to the bill and it became law. The parliamentary session ended on March 31. A few days later, Macdonald collapsed. "There was no ascertainable cause for it, but suddenly I broke down—pulse at forty-nine, and great pain and disturbance in liver and bowels." For weeks afterwards, he remained fragile and tired.

Some of Macdonald's troubles were actually caused by his physician, Dr. James A. Grant, who continually make alarmist diagnoses such as stomach cancer. When Macdonald finally went to England at the end of May, he came under the more confident care of a Dr. Clark, who told him he saw no evidence of organic disease and prescribed a simple diet and a great deal of rest. Macdonald's condition steadily improved, and by the end of July he was able to go out to dinners and the theatre. Not until mid-September did he book passage home.

Macdonald had set in motion the creation of a new Canada. As for himself, as he told Alexander Campbell, "I have no pleasure nowadays but in work, and so it will be to the end of the chapter."

TWENTY-THREE

The Best of Times

The east-west cousinship, a nation's rise,
Hail of identity, a world expanding,
If not the universe: the feel of it
Was in the air—"Union required the Line."
E.J. Pratt, *Towards the Last Spike*

For Macdonald and a great many Canadians, the early years of the 1880s were the best years of the entire nineteenth century: the economy was booming; new industries were popping up, thanks to the National Policy; the transcontinental railway was being built; immigrants were arriving in droves; public life was free of any deep divisions of religion, race or region. Even nature seemed to be on Canada's side: when the line above Lake Superior reached Sudbury, some workers wandered into the bush to explore. They came across curious yellowish rocks and sent them to be assayed, hoping they might bear gold. They had found the world's largest deposit of nickel and copper. As garnish to all this promise, Canadians thoroughly enjoyed having their seasoned skipper back on the bridge of the ship of state—and he enjoyed being there. Macdonald's one source of discontent was that, with his seventieth birthday coming up fast, he was now experiencing his full share of the aches and ailments of old age.

The most remarkable event during the boom years was Canada's first-ever, American-style, real-estate bubble. It happened when the sixteen thousand citizens of Winnipeg decided that their prairie community was destined to rival Chicago. At the height of the frenzy there were three hundred real-estate dealers in town, and some properties on Main Street topped prices for equivalent properties in the Windy City.

It all ended in a bust. By one estimate, only 5 per cent of the speculators made any money at all, many becoming destitute, together with their victims. But while it lasted—from mid-1881 to mid-1882—the boom served to demonstrate the "animal spirits" of entrepreneurs engaged in a fierce and greedy flight. "Golden Chances! Golden Speculations," ran the headlines in local newspapers. Housing lots were sold up to a ten-mile radius from downtown Winnipeg—enough for a city of half a million. The menus of some hotels featured treats such as quail on toast and oysters on the shell. One real-estate speculator bought so much champagne with his winnings that he filled his bathtub and soaked in it.

Canada's first true real-estate "bubble" took place in Winnipeg in the early 1880s, with some properties selling for as much as they would in Chicago. Then everything went bust.

Once the bubble burst, a mood of retrenchment settled over Winnipeg and Manitoba. The land speculation had extended out to Selkirk, Brandon and other small towns, and even to the open prairie. Many farmers gave up entirely and retreated back east; the immigrants stopped coming. It took the best part of a generation for the province to recover.

Nevertheless, Winnipeg's real-estate boom and bust, echoed in smaller versions in Calgary, Medicine Hat and Moose Jaw, marked the beginnings of the West's sense of itself as a distinctive region, rather than an extension of central Canada. The excesses revealed qualities of dynamism and a can-do spirit different from the more sedate virtues that prevailed in the rest of the country. Regina provided a good illustration. The Irish journalist Nicholas Flood Davin wandered into town, described his trade, and was promptly asked by a group of businessmen to start a newspaper. Davin, a lawyer and poet who had worked on London and Dublin papers, said he would need an impossible five thousand dollars in start-up capital to launch the venture. The full amount was subscribed that evening, and the *Leader* was soon on the stands. As one participant in Winnipeg's boom wrote later, "It was a short life . . . but life with a 'tang' to it." The West's distinctive political creed of populism can be traced back to the sense of outrage when outsiders took advantage of settlers—and before long, protest movements took shape.*

The wildly exaggerated optimism that gripped Winnipeg in the early 1880s derived from one incontrovertible fact: after years of talk and promises and false starts, the railway really was

* Populism—the Grit wing of the Reform Party—first appeared among the farmers of southwestern Ontario. As the Grits moderated into Liberals, populism transplanted itself westwards. There, it later morphed into the United Farmers, Social Credit and the CCF, and in due course reappeared under the historic label of Reform.

coming. It attracted even American farmers, who decided the soil in the free lots available above the border was better than that of the free lots they had picked for themselves below it. Winnipeg was at the dead centre of all of this frenzy. As the single town in the North-West already connected by rail to the outside world, it was about to become a vast supply depot for the gigantic construction project that would stretch out to the Rockies. All the timber, rails and bridge pilings would come through the city, and all the food, provisions and tools for the work teams, including the four thousand bushels of oats needed each day for the contingent of 1,700 horses. For a time, the CPR's head office was situated in Winnipeg, before moving to Montreal. Among those now flourishing in the city was Hugh John Macdonald, who, for two hundred dollars on delivery, had purchased a prefabricated "Chicago House."

For Macdonald, after a decade of effort and criticism and the humiliation of the Canadian Pacific Scandal, vindication was in sight. Predictions of national financial ruin continued, but nothing could alter the cardinal fact that, as poet E.J. Pratt would put it, "Union required the Line." Shortly after the legislation received royal assent, Macdonald told a supporter, "At last the C.P.R. is a fixed fact . . . it now remains for Stephen and Company to show what metal they are made of."

The task was daunting. Within ten years, the company had to build 2,300 miles of "road," or railway track, divided into three sections: 650 miles through the exceptionally difficult country above Lake Superior; 1,250 miles from Winnipeg to Kamloops Lake, mostly across flat, treeless country; and, in British Columbia, 400 miles up and down and through the towering Rocky and Selkirk mountain ranges.

The "road," as rail lines were known, was built everywhere at the same time: these workers laid track in BC's Lower Fraser Valley while others extended lines westwards from Winnipeg and blasted flat the Precambrian Shield above Lake Superior.

Stephen showed his mettle immediately. One day after the law granting the company its charter was enacted, the company posted a million-dollar performance bond with the government and held its first board meeting. Stephen was elected president and a four-member executive committee established, including James Hill, the railway promoter, and the HBC's Donald Smith. Within a fortnight, contracts had been auctioned for half a million railway ties and six thousand telegraph poles. Newly purchased locomotives began hauling huge triple-decker construction cars west of Winnipeg to the End of Track, wherever it was, to be used as dormitories, offices and workshops.

Hill was as decisive as Stephen. He championed the assessment by an Irish-born Canadian botanist and explorer, John Macoun, that almost all the prairies were "of unsurpassed fertility . . . literally the Garden of the whole country." In this, he contradicted earlier explorers such as Henry Youle Hind and John Palliser, who had judged the southern wedge of the prairies to be a desert. Macoun based his analysis on the unusually heavy rainfall he experienced when he crossed this region in 1879 and 1880. From an initial estimate of some 80 million acres of cultivatable prairie land, Macoun raised his estimate to 300 million.

In mid-May the CPR's executive committee decided to follow Macoun's advice and locate the rail line to the south, close to the border. The already-surveyed northerly route, through the rich valley of the North Saskatchewan and on to Edmonton, was abandoned. Towns like North Battleford, long planned as the capital of the Saskatchewan District, were consigned to obscurity, while others suddenly became prominent. Ramshackle Pile of Bones, named after a huge mound of buffalo bones, was now proclaimed the North-West's capital and given the regal title of Regina. The Mounted Police headquarters were shifted there. When Macdonald came through in 1886, making his first and only trip out to the Pacific, he surveyed the scene in Regina and pronounced, "If you had a lit-tle more wood, and a lit-tle more water, and here and there a hill, I think the prospect would be improved."

The CPR's new southern route required that an entirely new route be found through the Rockies in place of the legendary Kicking Horse Pass. Hill engaged another of those extraordinary frontier figures, Major A.B. Rogers. He had earned his military rank in the American Indian Wars and had even graduated from Yale University, but nothing about him—small, thin and capable of inexhaustible profanity—suggested such accomplishment. Determined to become famous, he welcomed the opportunity to find a new pass into the BC interior. By the following summer, he had what he wanted. Rogers Pass, as it came to be called, reduced the CPR's line by seventy miles and brought it so close to the border that the Northern Pacific Railway relinquished all thoughts of thrusting feeder lines northwards. In making this peremptory change in route, though, the CPR had altered the landscape and economy of the prairies without any public discussion and with no explanation of its reasons. Prairie populists took note.

To most westerners and Canadians, all that mattered was that the line was actually being built—and at a pace that outstripped any previous record, in Canada or the world. The credit was due to yet another larger-than-life figure, William Cornelius Van Horne. He had grown up poor in Illinois after his father died suddenly. A tall man with a huge head and wide girth, Van Horne possessed incredible energy. He could go from all-night poker games to long workdays, broken only by vast meals and leisured smokes of his favourite Cuban cigars. "I eat all I can; I drink all I can; I smoke all I can, and I don't give a damn for anything," he proclaimed. Starting out at the age of fourteen in a telegraph office, Van Horne became the youngest railway general manager in the United States before he turned thirty. He could be brutally decisive, firing slackers, incompetent senior executives and union organizers, but he treated good workers well. He was also a fond family man, a keen gardener, a competent artist and a superior collector of paleontology specimens, Old Masters and Japanese porcelain. No one could match his knowledge of railway matters: he could decode entire telegraph messages by listening to the clicks. He

The line that made certain the West would remain Canadian was built by an American, Cornelius Van Horne. Inexhaustibly energetic, Van Horne set world records for the speed with which he constructed the railway. Later, he probably saved the CPR from bankruptcy by rapidly moving the army westwards to put down Riel's 1885 Rebellion.

was lured to the CPR by the offer of the highest general manager's salary of the day and operated on the assumption that "I had only to spend the money while Stephen had to find it."

As soon as he took up his post, on January 2, 1882, Van Horne set a target for himself and the CPR: a record 500 miles of track in that construction season, almost double the amount the year before. Delayed by spring floods, he still managed 420 miles of main track as well as several branch lines and sidings. By the end of the 1883 season, he had extended the line some 960 miles west from Winnipeg, past Calgary to the foothills of the Rockies. The prairie section was completed, though many of the stations (8 miles apart) and divisional points (125 miles apart) had still to be built. Along the main line, two sections remained—the stretch above Lake Superior and, most challenging of all, the track up and over the Rockies and the Selkirks.

For the most part, Macdonald had little more to do than watch with delighted satisfaction. As he wrote to Stephen on September 6, 1882, "All I want is to be able to brag a little next Session as to the progress."

There were occasional bumps. Manitobans, watching the railway being built so fast, soon wanted lines of their own, hoping that competition would bring down the rates. Public pressure forced Premier John Norquay, himself a Conservative, to enact legislation in 1881 to breach the CPR's Clause 15, the "monopoly clause." Macdonald sent Norquay a sharp note: "We shall be compelled to disallow your Acts. We understood that you undertook to discourage and prevent such legislation." In letters to supporters, Macdonald was blunter: "It is a blind stupid policy of these Manitoba people to attempt to injure the C.P.R.," he wrote. There was but one choice: "We shall settle the country [or] the Yankees will supply it and absorb its trade."

A year later, having disallowed yet another Manitoba railway act, Macdonald proclaimed, "Every local interest must be made subordinate to the general policy for the good of all." That same month, he wrote to Stephen, urging him to have his own man in Winnipeg to keep the provincial politicians in check. At this stage, this dispute was only an irritant. Norquay and Macdonald got on well personally, and having his railway bills vetoed by Ottawa saved Norquay the embarrassment of the near-certain bankruptcy of the small companies he was chartering. Still, a distinctive western style was emerging: Manitoba, even though most of its newcomers came from Ontario, was already scrapping with the East.

As the months slipped by, it became clear that something extraordinary was happening: not just that the railway would be completed, but that it would be done faster than anyone had dared imagine. In November 1881, Macdonald went to Toronto to address a provincial party convention being held to warm up the troops for a coming election. For the closing dinner at the Horticultural Gardens, he entered the room to a band's rendition of Handel's "See the Conquering Hero Comes." He had something dramatic to say: the transcontinental railway, he informed the delegates, would not be built in the promised ten years; rather, every foot of it would be done within five years. After the applause had died down, he slipped in a quip: "I now have some chance, if I remain as strong, please God, as I now am, of travelling over it in person before I am just quite an angel."

The confidence, and the cockiness, kept on building. That great Victorian presumption that material progress was possible, even inevitable, was being confirmed. New inventions kept on coming, such as the telephone (by 1882, Ottawa's directory contained some two hundred names) and the typewriter (most were operated by women, known as "typewriters").

The country itself kept growing. In 1880, Britain handed over to Canada its last possessions on the continent—the land and islands from the offshore waters of Greenland west to the 141st meridian and up to the North Pole.* Only Newfoundland remained outside the magical circle. Immigrants now poured in—reaching a nineteenth-century record of 139,000 in 1883. In a deft move, the government offered unmarried females assisted passage to encourage them to become wives for western bachelors. Inevitably, some were not exactly "angels of the house," and the scheme was cancelled despite appeals by western MPs for it to be maintained. Macdonald, to soften the blow, explained solemnly to one MP, "You know, Angus, we must *protect* the Canadian whores."

Canadians even began to find time for some of life's finer things. The Royal Canadian Academy of Art was established in 1880, and the Royal Society of Canada followed two years later. That year, thanks principally to Governor General Lorne, a few works were collected for a future national gallery. The Canadian poet Louis Fréchette won France's prestigious Prix Montyon in 1880, and that same year Charles G.D. Roberts from New Brunswick published his ambitious poem "Orion." Only a few artists could hope to prosper at home, notably the Mohawk poet and performer Pauline Johnson, or Tekahionwake. Most had to go abroad, such as the international opera star Emma Albani, a friend of the Macdonalds. Macdonald was equable about this loss of artistic talent: "The centres of art and civilization, like London and Paris, would certainly attract a great portion of this talent," he said, but "they were Canadians, and would do honour to Canadian genius and Canadian ability."

While culture was nice, commerce was what really mattered. It was blossoming all over. "Money is rolling into the treasury," Lorne wrote to the colonial secretary early in 1882. George

* To avoid stirring up the Americans, the transfer deed deliberately left unspecified whether Canada's new territory included the waters between the Arctic islands.

Stephen described Canada's economic condition in a letter to Macdonald that spring as "prosperous beyond all precedent." The Throne Speech at the start of the 1882 session bragged, "A year of great prosperity . . . farmers have enjoyed a plentiful harvest . . . manufacturing and other industries have been and continue to be developed under favourable auspices."

Macdonald was caught up in the euphoria. He had always been cautious in money matters, keenly aware that Agnes was likely to long outlive him and would have the extra burden of caring for Mary.

By the early 1880s, his prime ministerial salary had been raised to eight thousand dollars, and he began to relax a bit financially. Still, it required all of Agnes's persuasive skills to get him to indulge himself and the family. "I begged Sir John very hard before he would buy it," she said. "I *coaxed hard*" and eventually "had the great satisfaction of knowing that he thoroughly liked and enjoyed the place."

The "place" was Earnscliffe, an imposing three-storey, gabled, limestone house on the city's eastern limits, not far from Rideau Hall, with an exceptional view of the wide Ottawa River and, in the distance, the blue line of the Gatineau Hills. It was built originally in 1857 by John Mackinnon, the son-in-law of Thomas McKay, a railwayman. He passed it on to Thomas Reynolds, who rented it out to the Macdonalds briefly in 1871 and again in 1882 for two months while the house they were renting was undergoing repairs. Macdonald suggested to Reynolds that its name should be Earnscliffe, the prefix "Earn" being an old Scottish name for an eagle.* The deal

* According to Lucianne Desbarats, the Reynolds family had decided to call the cliffside house "Eaglescliffe." When Macdonald heard their choice, he suggested the more euphonious name "Earnscliffe."

was done on January 31, 1883, at a purchase price of $10,400. Predictably, after only a few years had passed, Agnes decided that expansions were needed. Hard coaxing worked again. The most extensive of the changes was the addition of a large new dining room, with the old one turned into an office for Macdonald and an anteroom for a secretary. She had a secret door built in Macdonald's office so he could escape unwanted visitors. The bill for all this work, parts of it extending into 1888, totalled $7,000 dollars, with decorations and furniture to be added. Macdonald told his brother-in-law, Professor James Williamson, "It is the pride of Agnes' heart and she is never weary of showing it off to her friends."

Today the residence of the British high commissioner to Canada, Earnscliffe was the most comfortable, efficient and agreeable house Macdonald ever lived in. It was also the first real home he had ever owned. He built a second-floor retreat for Mary, from which she could look down to watch the dinner guests, and an outdoor belvedere from which she could look out at the river. It was in the attic here that Agnes one day found a box of odd wooden objects, asked Macdonald what they might be, and watched amazed as his eyes filled with tears while he explained they were "John A's"—the toys of his long-dead first-born son. It was here too that Hugh John's daughter, Daisy, came to stay through several summers, and once throughout the winter while she attended the Grey Nuns' school in Ottawa.

At Earnscliffe, Macdonald developed a consistent routine. He got up at about nine and had a cup of tea—no more. He dressed and went down to his office—his "workshop" as he called it—where only his secretary could enter unannounced. He read through the newspapers and then, with his secretary, tackled the daily mound of mail. He answered all the letters himself—by hand until the late 1880s, when he reluctantly agreed to allow a typewriter to be used for routine correspondence. (Macdonald's correspondence contains no evidence he ever made use of that even more intimidating invention, the telephone.) A light eater, Macdonald often combined breakfast with lunch, and even then it consisted of little more than a small portion of fish or game together with toast and butter without salt.

Afterwards, he went by hansom cab to his office on the Hill or to the cabinet room. On some of these drives, he said not a word to the secretary accompanying him, while on others he discussed at length topics such as nature or literature. He usually spent two hours a day on his departmental duties. Afterwards, there were cabinet meetings and, for three months or so each year, long sessions of Parliament. His working days usually ended around 6:30 p.m., giving him time at home to recount the day's events to Mary before he went down to dinner at 7:30. Now that he drank little, Macdonald seldom lingered late in the Parliament Buildings. His dinners usually included a single glass of wine, most often claret. He passed the evenings reading books and magazines or winding down from the day's stresses by playing games of patience. He went early to bed, although he read at length before falling asleep. But for his aches and ailments, Macdonald was in control of his life as never before.

Agnes was a superbly competent chatelaine—the major reason why Macdonald's life ran so smoothly. As important in a different way was his secretary, now Joseph Pope.

During his long career, Macdonald had six personal secretaries in all. Pope served him the longest and was the most able, and a kind of father-son relationship developed between them. Born in Prince Edward Island, he was turned on to politics by witnessing part of the 1864 Charlottetown Conference. His first job, at sixteen, was as a clerk in the office of his grandfather, a provincial cabinet minister. Despite defects—initially, his handwriting was atrocious—he learned fast, and after jobs in banks he went to

Ottawa in 1878 to serve as private secretary to his uncle, a minister in the Macdonald government. After his uncle retired, Pope was taken on as assistant secretary by Frederick White, then serving as both Macdonald's secretary and comptroller of the Mounted Police, or its top civil servant. Within a few months, he had won Macdonald's confidence. That was a key requirement; as Macdonald said, "I do not want anyone about me whom I cannot trust implicitly."

He appointed Pope his secretary, allowing White to concentrate on his police responsibilities. Pope revelled in the job, worked whatever hours were needed, was comprehensively discreet (if excessively cautious), believed as strongly that "forms are things" as did his boss and was even more of an anglophile. One of his important contributions was to persuade Macdonald to buy his holiday house in Rivière-du-Loup. Towards the end of his life, Macdonald entrusted Pope with writing his biography. As he told Agnes, "Joe shall write it; he knows more about me than anyone else." Although the memoir suffers from an excess of admiration, it contains several moments of candour when Macdonald, at the end of a long day, would unburden himself to him. Pope is the source for some of Macdonald's most revealing comments, such as that "a public man should have no resentments," and his partiality to William Pitt's dictum that the "first, second and third rule of a statesman is patience." Nor was Pope afraid to tell a few tales on his hero. One concerned the time when, after Macdonald had delivered a drunken speech, a reporter showed him a draft of his story on it. Macdonald dismissed the draft as incoherent, then delivered a brilliant impromptu speech and gave the reporter invaluable advice: "Young man, never again attempt to report a public speaker when you are drunk."

The trust between prime minister and secretary was so unstinting that Pope was able to maintain a personal friendship with the Liberals' rising star, Wilfrid Laurier, whose wife was related to Pope's wife. In 1887, Macdonald told him, "Laurier will look after you should you need a friend when I am gone." Laurier followed through, ignoring the *Globe*'s demands for heads to roll. He kept Pope in a senior post and eventually appointed him head of the new Department of External Affairs.*

With his own circumstances so satisfactory and those of the country even better, the next obvious step for Macdonald was to ask Canadians what they thought of him.

The 1882 election was the easiest Macdonald ever contested. Peace and prosperity would have been more than enough, but to make his chances ever better, the Liberals had replaced the sad and embittered Alexander Mackenzie with a new leader—Edward Blake. Brilliant but cold and overwhelmingly shy, Blake was the party's worst campaigner until Stéphane Dion early in the twenty-first century, delivering tedious two-hour-long speeches in contrast to Macdonald's snappy, quip-filled conversations with the voters.

As preparation, Macdonald used the 1881 census to "hive the Grits"; that is, to blatantly gerrymander the electoral map, redrawing it into ridings that alternated between those with vast Liberal majorities and those with narrow Conservative pluralities. With only a touch of exaggeration, the *Globe* described this manipulation as "an immortality of infamy by the most unscrupulous of political gamesters." But the ploy didn't work: the Conservatives lost several seats they had counted on winning, while the Liberals held seats they had given up for lost. Macdonald

* In 1910, when the Conservative Robert Borden defeated Laurier, Pope made a second seamless transition and remained in government as a deputy minister.

still won, and handsomely, all but repeating his overwhelming victory of 1878. The real effect was long-term: Macdonald's gerrymandering was so cynical that it led the public to begin demanding a transparent electoral system. Canadians were starting to become democrats.

For the first time, Macdonald began to look like yesterday's man—not just to seem behind the times, but clearly to be behind. Thus, during the 1882 election (and all subsequent ones), Macdonald once again pursued campaign funds with compulsive zeal. He secured support from manufacturers who were prospering under the National Policy, then called them all into the Red Room of the Queen's Hotel in Toronto and announced their donations in front of their colleagues.* And he had almost unlimited access to the coffers of the CPR.

At his age, as was scarcely surprising, he was indeed falling behind the times. By the 1880s, Canada was palpably a Victorian society. The most esteemed qualities were respectability and propriety. In Toronto, unlike liberal-minded Montreal, voters were about to mark their ballots for a ban on the operation of tramcars on Sundays. A national Temperance Act had been drafted. In a great many respects, Macdonald was far more Regency than he was Victorian—he had never apologized for his public drinking bouts, and little in human behaviour ever shocked him. Still, he could be remarkably open to the new, the untried and the innovative. His unstuffiness in such matters derived from the fact that he was able to judge the new, not on the basis of whether it was socially proper, but on whether it worked. This is what he now did.

---

* The Queen's Hotel was the Dominion's finest, but for Montreal's Windsor Hotel. Guests could enjoy such marvels as elevators, central heating by forced hot air and electric bells to summon food and drink.

Early in October 1883, the Kingston *British Whig* ran a most unusual story. A group of people new to the town—an "army of Salvationists"—was holding a meeting to engage in prayers, testimonies and "salvation messages," calling out a lot of "hallelujahs" and singing old songs such as "It Ain't Gonna Rain No More" to new words— "Oh, I Ain't Gonna Sin No More." Even stranger, this service was being led by a woman, a Captain Abigail (Abby) Thompson.

The *Whig*'s most dramatic disclosure came a couple of paragraphs down: "When Abby was reading the Scripture lesson, Sir John Macdonald appeared. He arrived at the hall late and stood for a few minutes at the door, then a Sergt. of the Army invited him forward. As he walked up the aisle people craned their necks and whispered to each other. Captain Abby stopped reading and said, 'Now, don't make a fuss. He's only a gentleman and you all know him.' Abby continued the service, exhort[ing] the people to live so that they would be glad instead of afraid at the second coming of the Saviour."

Most commentators assumed that Macdonald was out to win votes. In fact, among the poor, the unemployed, the alcoholic and the criminal in the hall, few, if any, possessed the property to have the vote. Indeed, even associating with the Salvation Army could lose a politician votes, because most people regarded it as vulgar. The *Whig* speculated that Macdonald was taken by Abby—"strikingly beautiful in her long, tight-fitting Army uniform"—suggesting it was more likely the reporter who was taken by Abby.*

* In fact, Abigail Thompson left Kingston a month later to return to the United States, where she married a fellow Salvation Army officer.

SIR JOHN AND THE SALVATION ARMY.

That a prime minister should take time out—three times—to attend a Salvation Army meeting baffled the press of the day. Reporters assumed he was after votes. In fact, the poor had no votes because they did not own any property. What Macdonald was doing was learning about the effects of the depression on Canada's new class of urban workers.

A better guess would be that Macdonald went to the Salvation Army hall in order to learn. Canada's growing cities and towns were attracting a proletariat of industrial workers, skilled and semi-skilled, who, far more than farmers, were vulnerable during economic downturns. The same was true in Britain, where, in 1878, General William Booth and his wife, Catherine, had established the Salvation Army to reach out to the "submerged ten per cent." (The Booths believed, as was hard to credit then, that women could fill any job in the organization.) Initially, the Booths' concern was for the souls of the victims of industrialization; later, they came to accept that while sin might be a cause of poverty, poverty might also be a cause of sin. This new approach disturbed those who were not poor. As one shrewd observer, Friedrich Engels, said, the Salvation Army "fights capitalism in a religious way . . . which one day may become troublesome to the well-to-do."*

Another shrewd observer was Macdonald. He had been aware for some time of the new forces gaining strength within Canadian society. On October 12, 1880, he had written a remarkable letter to John Rose in London in which he questioned one of the most cherished of his own political assumptions—the sanctity of private property. "Modern opinion seems more and more to incline to the idea that vested rights must yield to the general good," he wrote, adding, "Property has its duties as well as its rights." He visited the Salvation Army citadel in Kingston three times, and, as Pope recorded in his *Memoirs*, "he had always a kind word, and ofttimes something more" in the form of cash for the Salvationists.

Late in 1883, the Long Depression resumed, compelling Macdonald to turn his attention to practical matters. The political and economic stresses that ensued would help generate a second Métis uprising led by Riel and unleash deep sectarian hostilities between Catholics and Protestants, French and English. Still, Macdonald did not forget the Salvationists' message about helping the weak and wounded stand on their feet. In a letter to George Stephen in 1890, he wrote, "I always thought the Salvation Army would be productive of great good and was laughed at somewhat for Countenancing the movement at Kingston. Their mode is contrary to the taste of the educated classes, but it gets at the multitude."

Having allowed his imagination to take him where it might, Macdonald now had to get on with his job.

---

* Later, when General Booth came to Ottawa he dined with Macdonald at Earnscliffe.

TWENTY-FOUR

A Dream Baulked

The judicial lawmakers, not John A. Macdonald . . . are the real authors of Canadian constitutional law.

John T. Saywell, *The Lawmakers*

As the mid-1880s approached, Macdonald must have been supremely confident that his nation-building objective was within his grasp. All British North America, from the Atlantic to the Pacific and north to the Pole, had been added to the new nation—excepting only Newfoundland. Canada was now as large as the United States. The transcontinental railway was well under way and, fortunately, the National Policy had produced many of the new manufacturing companies and jobs Macdonald had promised so blithely. The North-West Mounted Police had forged good relations with most of the native people of the prairies, assuring incoming settlers of a peaceable environment. And Canadians had just re-elected him handily, extending his term in office to 1887.

In one vital respect, though, Macdonald's nation-building project had already begun to falter and would soon decline. He would be astonishingly slow to realize what was happening, almost certainly because the cause was an institution peopled by individuals he admired unreservedly—the British legal system and some of its most distinguished judges.

From the early 1880s on, the members of Britain's Judicial Committee of the Privy Council (JCPC) would reinterpret the Canadian constitution (the British North America Act) in a way that would change its balance radically. Macdonald himself had composed most of the original text, and it had been signed by all the Fathers of Confederation and by the British government and parliament of the day. Now, these judges, who were three thousand miles away in London and knew nothing about Canada nor ever visited there, began to execute the single most intrusive act of colonialism in Canada's entire post-Confederation history. They dismissed as irrelevant to their considerations any argument based on Canadian history, politics, customs or conditions. It was almost as if they were tinkering with a theoretical model of their own imagining. Yet they executed these changes with scarcely a word of complaint from Macdonald or from any Canadian politician, lawyer, scholar, journalist or public figure.

The JCPC's decisions during Macdonald's last decade in office, and later rulings based upon precedents set during this period, would constitute unconstrained judicial activism: that is, judges making the law rather than just interpreting it. Their activism caused the highly centralized federation envisaged by the BNA Act to be turned into one of the most decentralized such systems in the world. Among the measures of this condition are that more barriers to trade exist among the provinces in Canada than in any other federal nation, and that in contrast to the nearest equivalent, the contemporary system in the U.S., itself originally highly decentralized, Ottawa accounts for only about one-third of spending by all governments, compared to Washington's two-thirds share, and is excluded from any say about education or the management of health care.*

Given that Canada is an attenuated nation divided by two official languages and distinct geographical regions, it would be reasonable to assume that so fragmented a system of governance could not possibly work. Yet it does, and by most international comparisons it works well. While the JCPC judges knew nothing about the country, their remote, abstract decisions may well have been in Canada's best interests.

Certainly, it's difficult to make the case that a more centralized federation would have fared better. The one clearly negative consequence was how long it took Canada to mature as a nation. Formal independence was achieved only in 1931 (by the Statute of Westminster),† Canadian citizenship in 1947, freedom from the arbitration of the JCPC in 1949, a national flag in 1965 and a patriated and fully Canadianized constitution in 1982. Despite the British constitutional theoretician A.V. Dicey's declaration that "federalism is . . . legalism," or endless legal arguments over who is responsible for what, perhaps Canada works largely because of Canadians themselves, their ingrained pragmatism, aptitude for compromise and readiness to listen to contrary views. If so, it's possible that had the JCPC not intervened, Canadians would have figured out how to make the more centralized constitution that Macdonald and the Fathers of Confederation intended work as effectively for them.

The JCPC judges don't merit all the blame. Canada's constitution was thin. Unlike the U.S. constitution, it entirely lacked poetry; its only definition of purpose was that it was "similar in

---

* The only federations which may be more decentralized than Canada's are those of Switzerland and Belgium.

† Canada achieved effective independence as an "autonomous community" five years earlier, by the Balfour Declaration of 1926.

principle" to Britain's constitution.* The BNA Act even lacked the quality of connectedness of its nearest equivalent, the Australian constitution, which declares in the preamble, " . . . the people of New South Wales, Victoria, South Australia, Queensland and Tasmania, relying on the blessing of Almighty God, have agreed to unite in one indissoluble federal commonwealth." Only in 1982, when their constitution was changed radically by adding to it the Charter of Rights and Freedoms, and was itself at last brought home, did Canadians possess a constitution that truly belonged to them—if, inevitably, not all of them, Quebecers most particularly.

For a full decade after Confederation in 1867, scarcely any harsh words were exchanged about the constitution's meaning. The provincial governments were preoccupied with figuring out what they were, and because all the experienced politicians and civil servants were in Ottawa, looked to the capital for advice about the law. Edward Blake did attempt to stir up controversy when Macdonald offered "better terms" first to Nova Scotia and later to others, but he attracted little support in his own Liberal Party and none at all from the general public.

Yet Macdonald was careful not to overplay his hand. In 1868, he circulated to the premiers a memorandum describing how he intended to exercise the awesome power of being able to disallow provincial legislation—a hangover from Britain's earlier right to disallow errant colonial legislation. To provincial applause, Macdonald pledged to exercise this right "with great caution and

---

* The "Peace, Order and Good Government" phrase, while now accepted as the constitution's essence, was originally merely standard wording inserted at that time into the constitutions of a great many British colonies.

only in cases where the law and the general interests of the Dominion imperatively demand it." During his first six years in power, Macdonald disallowed only five provincial acts, compared to eighteen by Alexander Mackenzie's Liberal government over a similar span. In the case of the New Brunswick law abolishing Catholic separate schools, Macdonald refused calls to intervene, telling a Reverend Quinn in 1873, "the Constitution would not be worth the paper it is written on unless the rights of the Provincial Legislatures were supported." The cure would have to be political action by local Catholics; the effect of any attempt by Ottawa to intervene would be that "all hope for the Catholic minority was gone."

Several of Macdonald's early steps towards centralization would have greatly benefited the country. As one, Canada might have had fewer and cheaper lawyers. In 1871, Macdonald asked the lieutenant-governor for the North-West to allow members of the bar in all the other provinces to practise in Manitoba. Nothing was done. One of his successful acts of centralization has been of unquestioned value. Although immigration was constitutionally a joint responsibility, Macdonald persuaded the provinces to let Ottawa make the decisions: as he told his Quebec friend Brown Chamberlin, the editor of the Montreal *Gazette*, "The Local Governments would do nothing, and the French were not *very* anxious on the subject."* Even in his nation-building projects, he remained within the constitutional limits. The BNA Act made policing a provincial responsibility; Macdonald therefore limited the mandate of his Mounted Police to the North-West Territory, excluding Manitoba despite calls for the force by its lieutenant-governor. When one leading citizen pleaded for federal action to

* Most provinces have now negotiated joint agreements with Ottawa, Quebec being the first to have done so.

improve the schools, Macdonald replied that "we at Ottawa had no right of interference or supervision of any kind," even though he believed in "a comprehensive system of education for the youth of the Dominion, based on broad principles and not on local prejudices."

Macdonald's interest was in nation-building, not in building up the national government by new social and economic legislation. Only with his protectionist National Policy of 1879 did he engage in legislation that might compete with provincial aspirations. At this time, Ontario alone had any such ambitions; in Quebec, social programs were the concern of the church—as one historian has observed, "the church was the state."

Arguments about Canada's constitution began with Macdonald's return to power in 1878. The initiator was Ontario's Oliver Mowat.

Macdonald had always known that disagreements between the two levels of government were inevitable. In an 1868 letter to Chamberlin, he agreed that "a conflict may, ere long, arise between the Dominion and the States Rights people." He continued confidently, "The powers of the General Government are so much greater than those of the United States in its relations with the local Governments, that the central power must win." Macdonald even wondered if the provinces might end up as enlarged municipalities, telling one correspondent that they merited no more attention "than the ruling party in the corporation of Quebec [City] or Montreal."

Macdonald didn't think of himself as a centralist; rather, he said he followed "the happy medium." In another 1868 letter, he said that unlike Chamberlin, "an ardent Dominion man," he felt he was "taking the middle and correct course" in relation to "the provincial magnates." He nevertheless had no doubt about the "proper place" for the provinces: they should be subordinate to the federal government rather than sovereign within their own jurisdiction. Macdonald came by this view naturally; singular sovereignty was integral to the British tradition. Sir William Blackstone, the great eighteenth-century legal scholar, had laid down the precept that sovereignty had to be "a supreme, irresistible, absolute, uncontrolled authority."

Macdonald's view of the role of the federal government was clear: "*We* represent the interests of all the Provinces of Canada," he told Justice Minister Alexander Campbell. His most explicit public description of his vision was his declaration in Parliament in 1882: "Sir, we are not half a dozen provinces. We are one great Dominion." Laurier's counter-vision, expressed three years later, was "we have not a single community in this country. We have seven different communities."

Besides British history and legal theory, Canada's own constitution confirmed Macdonald's presumption. The clear objective of the Fathers of Confederation had been to create a centralized federation in order to avoid a northern version of the Civil War, precipitated, in their view, by the highly decentralized system in the United States. It was no coincidence that the BNA Act repeatedly used the word "union" rather than "federation." At the same time, as a practical politician, Macdonald accepted that any attempt to create a British-style unitary state in Canada was impossible: in his words, Quebec's concerns about its cultural particularities would have been "enough to secure the repudiation of Confederation by the people of Lower Canada."

The powers of the central government, as set out in the BNA Act, were so extensive that, other than to have granted it the right to abolish the provinces (as happened in New Zealand), it wasn't easy to imagine what else might have been ceded to the centre. Ottawa had the power to disallow or reserve (set aside) provincial legislation that, in its judgment, infringed federal jurisdiction. It could raise revenues by any form of taxation, and spend them in areas of provincial jurisdiction (if by practice rather than specific legal sanction). In a conscious reversal of the U.S. system, all powers not specifically assigned to the provinces resided with the federal government. It possessed the comprehensive override clause of "Peace, Order and Good Government." It could designate any public undertaking as being "for the general Advantage of Canada." The economy was to function as a single market. Unlike the original arrangement in the United States, the federal government had exclusive authority over banking and currency. As Macdonald saw it, the central government possessed "all the great subjects of legislation . . . all the powers that are incidental to sovereignty." The only broad power granted to the provinces was the secondary one of control over "Property and Civil Rights."

This lopsided division of powers was the work of the Fathers of Confederation. George Brown had declared that the provinces "should not be expensive and should not take up political matters." At the Quebec City Conference, Mowat himself had proposed the clause that gave Ottawa the right to disallow provincial legislation, and he insisted that the Criminal Code be standardized, because "it would weld us into a nation."

The Fathers may not have really known what they were doing. During the debates in the pre-Confederation legislature, an independent member, Christopher Dunkin, observed that as time passed, "all talk of your new nationality will sound but strangely"; in its place, "some older nationality will then be found to hold the first place in most people's hearts." Dunkin had foreseen the future: the "older" loyalties were to Britain or to historic entities such as Upper Canada or Nova Scotia. Confederation itself added little to any sense of pan-Canadianism. As Goldwin Smith commented in 1878, "Sectionalism still reigns in everything, from the composition of the Cabinet down to that of a Wimbledon Rifle team." Then and for many decades to come, Canada's condition was comparable to Italy's; as that country's nineteenth-century nationalist leader Count Cavour commented on the achievement of union, "We have made Italy, now we must make Italians."

Not until the First World War, as a result of the sacrifices paid by its soldiers, would Canada begin to see itself as a society greater than the sum of its parts. In earlier years, little sense of nationhood existed, other than that provided by the stature that first Macdonald and after him Laurier achieved, and, as essential to national survival, that strange, stubborn refusal by Canadians to become Americans.

Macdonald understood this mood. He worried that the new nation had "no associations, political or historical, connected with it." Just a few trace elements of such feelings existed. After Confederation, ships' captains took to flying a Canadian version of the Red Ensign, with the national coat of arms in its fly, even though no official approval existed. The great national holiday was not Dominion Day, July 1, but Queen Victoria's birthday, May 24. Macdonald, skeptical of emotion and sentimentality, did little to develop such associations and institutions. He failed to appreciate the disintegrative effects of the Long Depression, when harsh conditions turned people's attention towards the immediate and the local. And he failed to appreciate the effectiveness of the emerging provincial champion—Oliver Mowat.

Mowat's most evident political quality was his blandness—confirmation that, from Ontario's beginning, bland worked: for a quarter-century, from 1872 to 1896, Mowat never lost an election, an all-time record. Modern Ontario dates from him, because in these years he steered through the transition from a mostly rural and small-town society to a mostly industrial and urban province. Above all, he made Ontario well governed—an attribute then unique among the provinces.

Physically, Mowat resembled a clerk—he was "desky," in the taunt of the Conservative *Mail*. Eloquence was foreign to him. His best-remembered utterance is the ill-considered line, his slogan in his first, 1857 election: "Vote for the Queen and Mowat, not for the Pope and Morrison [his opponent]," causing him ever after to be vulnerable to the accusation of being anti-Catholic. He called himself "a Christian statesman" and drank not a drop. He also ran Canada's most efficient and extensive patronage machine. Mowat's principal political gift was inexhaustible guile, "a genius for reconciling duty and opportunity," according to *Globe* editor John Willison. His determination was as inexhaustible: "He was a Mameluk when roused," commented one senior minister.

Oliver Mowat, stubby and cross-eyed, was Ontario's longest-serving premier and Macdonald's most effective opponent. In a great put-down Macdonald once said what he most admired about Mowat was "his hand-writing." Macdonald underestimated him, probably because Mowat had once been an apprentice in his law office.

Macdonald's great mistake was to underestimate Mowat, his former clerk in his law office in Kingston. In debates, Macdonald could dance rings around him: on one occasion, when asked what he most admired about Mowat, he replied, "His hand-writing." But somehow he missed the rigour and determination of Mowat's campaign for provincial rights. Partly, Mowat was motivated by self-interest: by bashing Ottawa, he made it easier for Ontario voters to forgive his failings. But there was also an important principle at stake. The Liberals had long demanded provincial autonomy, principally for two reasons: the first democratic, to get government as near to the people as possible; the second populist, to get French Canada off the back of Ontario's English-Canadian Protestants. Instead, after Confederation, George-Étienne Cartier's *bleus* seemed to exercise as much influence as ever, if now from the vantage-point of Ottawa.

Once Mowat became premier in 1872, the exchange of letters between him and Macdonald was chilly, if polite. During the year that remained before the Canadian Pacific Scandal, they engaged in just one tussle. In 1873, two bills came before the Ontario legislature to permit the Orange lodges to incorporate. Catholics protested, and the provincial cabinet split over the issue. The bills passed eventually, and with Mowat's approval, but he cannily convinced the lieutenant-governor to reserve the acts, so the responsibility for offending either the Orangemen or the Irish Catholics was transferred to Ottawa. Macdonald, describing himself as "too old a bird to be caught with such chaff," lobbed the ball right back to Mowat. In the end, Mowat withdrew the bills, which pleased the Catholics but did not really offend the Orangemen, because he soon brought down general legislation allowing everyone to gain incorporation. Mowat had proved he was master at Queen's Park, while Macdonald had confirmed that, in Ottawa, there was no one to match him.

One letter defined the real debate that would take place between these giants after Macdonald's return in 1878. In a note to Mowat of January 7, 1873, about a dispute over whether Queen's

Counsels could be appointed by provinces, Macdonald commented that "each Province is a quasi-Sovereignty." This statement directly contradicted the claim Mowat had made on his first day in office—that the provinces were fully sovereign within their own jurisdiction. For the next six years, peace prevailed while the Liberals held power in Ottawa; as soon as Macdonald was back, everything changed.

During the intervening five years, Mowat provided a fair amount of good government in the form of social and economic reforms. His most considerable accomplishment, though, was to prepare himself for constitutional battle with Macdonald. His preparations were tactically impeccable. Before attempting to decentralize power away from Ottawa, Mowat first centralized power within the province itself, so enabling him to speak on behalf of a united Ontario.

The Long Depression hit a number of Ontario municipalities hard. Mowat responded by setting up a Municipal Loan Board to extend relief to those seriously threatened. A side-consequence was to make the municipalities dependent on Queen's Park and, no less agreeably, to expand Mowat's opportunities to exercise patronage. Mowat went on to repeat this pattern in the fields of education, liquor licensing and agriculture. Ever more power got transferred to Queen's Park, together with the numbers of Ontarians ready to say, "Ready, aye, ready," when Mowat asked.

Macdonald spotted the threat immediately, describing Mowat as "that little tyrant who had attempted to control public opinion by getting hold of every little office." By 1883, he was complaining that "the whole system of the Liberal Administration in the Province of Ontario has been centralized. They have taken the right of deciding everything connected with taverns and with the licensed victuallers; they have taken the clerkships of courts and the appointments of bailiffs."

Mowat's patronage machine may well have been the most efficient ever assembled in Canada. It was comprehensive: Willison wrote in the *Globe*, "For over a generation, not a Conservative was appointed to the public service in Ontario." And it was intensive: unlike Macdonald, Mowat insisted that appointees do their public duties properly, even as he maintained a close eye on what they were doing for the party. As well, he kept his own hands at a respectable distance from it all, as the real work was done by party secretary W.T.R. Preston, who came to be known as "Hug the Machine." Mowat himself made no apology, declaring that "the right of patronage" belonged to "the party in power."

While he was premier, Mowat always spoke only about Ontario—he never gave a speech on general dominion issues nor showed any interest in events beyond Ontario's borders. The one brief exception was a conference of dissident provinces held in 1887 at the call of Quebec premier Honoré Mercier. Mowat attended and steered through resolutions calling for more money from Ottawa and more power over provincial jurisdiction. Nothing happened to any of these demands, and Mowat never again spoke about provincial rights in general.

Although he has entered the history books as "the father of provincial rights," Mowat was really only the father of Ontario's rights. Indeed, the more autonomy Mowat gained for Ontario, the harder it would be for Macdonald to redistribute to other provinces any of the revenues sent to Ottawa by prosperous Ontario. As one of his senior ministers, Christopher Fraser, put it, Ontario would not be "the milk cow for the whole concern."

Mowat's real role was as the father of what historian H.V. Nelles has called "Empire Ontario." The long-term effect of this accomplishment, though, would be the exact opposite of Mowat's intent: once confident of their province's autonomy, Ontarians became enthusiastic advocates of a coast-to-coast national identity.

In the summer of 1878, Ontario took a long step towards becoming Empire Ontario. On August 3, an inquiry set up years earlier by Alexander Mackenzie to resolve a long-running argument over the location of Ontario's western boundary abruptly announced its decision. The boundary line, the commissioners ruled, should be drawn well west of the Lakehead (today, Thunder Bay), adding 110,000 square miles to the province. This decision was made after only three days of hearings and with no explanation given to justify it.

Ontario's western boundary had been an issue ever since the North-West entered into Confederation. The first inquiry, initiated by Macdonald in 1872, fell apart in internal wrangling. The second, by Mackenzie, did nothing until Mowat realized that Macdonald might well win the 1878 election. Mackenzie revived the commission, which came down resoundingly on Ontario's side. When Macdonald gained office two months later, he dismissed its findings. He argued that the interests of Manitoba should be taken into account, its attraction to Macdonald being that its government was Conservative. Two provinces now claimed control of the same territory. Both appointed magistrates in the principal community, Rat Portage (today, Kenora), and sent out policemen, who at one point began arresting each other. After more wrangling, Macdonald and Mowat agreed to refer the issue for a binding decision by Canada's highest legal body, the Judicial Committee of the Privy Council.

Macdonald had helped to make it possible for the JCPC to exercise this authority. Canada's court of last resort did not have to have been a handful of British judges sitting in a small room in London. An alternative existed, the Supreme Court of Canada, but in the coming contest for judicial supremacy, it would lose out to the JCPC—and an intervention by Macdonald that hobbled

This Grip *cartoon shows Ontario Premier Oliver Mowat asking for "more" in the manner of Oliver Twist and, by a decision of the British judges, getting it in the form of a major increase in Ontario's size.*

its chances of succeeding. He in fact strongly supported the creation of a Supreme Court. Twice during his first term, he had introduced the necessary legislation but set it aside for other priorities. After the Liberals gained power, Télesphore Fournier, the new minister of justice, introduced similar legislation. Macdonald applauded the initiative, and approval seemed certain.

At this point a minor historical figure changed history's course: a backbench Liberal MP, Aemilius Irving, moved an amendment that the Supreme Court should become the sole arbiter of Canadian law, including constitutional cases.* If this Clause 47 had been accepted, the role the JCPC performed all over the Empire would have ended in Canada. Macdonald's feelings about Britain

* Irving was following up a suggestion by Justice Minister Fournier in his opening speech when he'd said he would "very well like to see a clause introduced declaring that this right of appeal to the Privy Council no longer existed."

retaining its oversight over Canadian law were mixed. He once told W.R. Meredith, the Conservative leader in Ontario, that "Canada is so separated by position from England that it may be considered another country and its legislation therefore . . . a matter of indifference to the Mother Country." Yet he also informed Judge James Robert Gowan that Canada's laws "should in principle be the same as in England . . . [giving] the inestimable advantage of having English decisions as authority in our Courts."

During the Commons debate, Macdonald, at times sounding as though he had imbibed too liberally, declared passionately that Irving's Clause 47 threatened the "golden chain" linking Canada to Britain. Eliminating it could "excite in England" a conviction that Canada was gripped by "an impatience . . . of even the semblance of Imperial authority." The bill still passed.

Alerted by Macdonald's intervention, the Colonial Office sent worried inquiries across the Atlantic. By another accident of history, Edward Blake, a strong nationalist, had just returned to Mackenzie's cabinet as minister of justice. He strongly favoured Clause 47, and by exerting his considerable legal skills persuaded the Colonial Office that Canada did indeed have the right to limit, even to abolish, appeals to the JCPC. At this point Lord Cairns, Britain's Lord Chancellor, joined the dispute. Highly regarded as a legal scholar, he concluded that Macdonald had been right and that passing Clause 47 would be "equivalent to a complete severance in its strongest tie between our Colonies and the Mother Country." There was now a real risk that London might disallow the legislation, provoking a first-class transatlantic political row.*

---

* One of Cairns's arguments was that only the JCPC itself could decide whether Canada had the right to end appeals to it. He was correct, technically: in 1949, it was accepted that the JCPC could only be abolished if it first consented to its own extinction.

The problem was resolved by an exercise in high-level Imperial chicanery. By now, the Mackenzie government had already begun setting up the Supreme Court; to back down would be a severe humiliation. Hastily, Blake was invited to present his case to Cairns in London. The two engaged in high-stepping legal arguments and arrived at a solution: Canada would complete the establishment of a Supreme Court, but both parties agreed to treat Clause 47 as inoperative, enabling the JCPC to continue as if nothing had happened. Blake regretted backing down, saying in a Commons debate, "The true spirit of our Constitution, can be made manifest only to the men of the soil. I deny it can be well expounded by men whose lives have passed, not merely in another, but in an opposite sphere of practice." Canadian judges, he astutely remarked, "such as they are, *they are our own*." Blake was more than half a century ahead of his time. In the meantime, Macdonald would learn that the "golden chain" he so favoured could also choke.

~

For four years, the Supreme Court had the field largely to itself, with constitutional cases going first to it. During this span, all but one of its six constitutional decisions favoured federal jurisdiction over provincial—a striking consensus given that all its judges had been appointed by Mackenzie's Liberal government.

As a harbinger of the future, Mowat appeared before the Supreme Court in one case, declaring, "I claim for the Provinces the largest power they can be given," and adding, "It is the spirit under which Confederation was agreed to." He lost that case. In another, Macdonald's first appointee to the court, Justice John Gwynne, described the provinces as "subordinate bodies . . . having jurisdiction *exclusive* though not 'Sovereign.'" Historian John Saywell reckoned that "in time, the Supreme Court, in spite of its shortcomings, would have shaped the federal constitution. . . . But there was no time." By 1879, the JCPC was ready and eager to decide what Canadians should do.

The change was quick and dramatic. Appellants, particularly Mowat, took to submitting their cases directly to the JCPC, bypassing the Supreme Court. Before long, the British court was overruling one in two of the Supreme Court decisions. Inexorably, the Supreme Court's stature and credibility went into decline, where they would remain for two-thirds of a century.

The JCPC met the cardinal requirements for institutional credibility in Britain: it was ancient, and it was eccentric. It could be traced back to the fifteenth century or further. Its members sat around a circular table rather than an elevated long one, and it wasn't truly a court that issued judgments but a committee that gave advice to the monarch— so its members wore neither gowns nor wigs. (Always, one chair around the table was left empty so the king or queen could attend; none ever did.) In substance, however, it was one of Britain's highest courts, hearing cases from 150 colonies as well as the Admiralty and the Church of England.*

The JCPC had decided defects for the role it was about to perform for Canada. No member knew anything about Canada or about federalism—Britain itself providing no guidance, since it was a unitary state and had no written constitution. It relied unduly on advice from Judah P. Benjamin, the former attorney general for the Confederate States of America, who had fled to London after the Civil War, and who, inevitably, was a strong

* The JCPC is still in business today, hearing cases from such places as Bermuda and the Falkland Islands.

advocate of states' rights. The two members who moved it furthest along the decentralist path—lords Watson and Haldane—were both Scots, and favoured keeping their nation as far apart as possible from English entanglements. Lastly, Imperial Federation was much in vogue at the time, and judges like Watson and Haldane, in anticipation of the day when the Empire could no longer be held together by force of arms, may well have been using Canada as a test case for Imperial devolution.

The JCPC's leading initial authority on Canadian affairs was William Watson. A conservative Conservative, he had had an undistinguished early career and was the second choice when appointed to the JCPC in 1880. Ennobled as Lord Watson, he was the decisive force in determining Canadian cases until his death in 1899. As his successor, Haldane, wrote of his role, "In a series of masterly judgments, [Watson] expounded and established the real constitution of Canada." In other words, he engaged in judicial activism. Haldane described him as "a statesman as well as a jurist, [who] fill[ed] in the gaps which Parliament has deliberately left in the skeleton constitution and laws." About his own later interventions, most particularly those which contracted the meaning of the "Peace, Order and Good Government" clause to near nullity, thereby reducing Ottawa to near impotence during the Great Depression, Haldane explained without apology that the JCPC was "giving administrative assistance."

Compared to the Supreme Court, the JCPC possessed considerable advantages. It published no dissenting opinions, so giving itself an aura of infallibility, and it wrote off Canadian history and political practice as "of great historical value but not otherwise pertinent." In effect, its judges interpreted the BNA Act as an ordinary statute, freeing themselves from the constitution's context and dealing only with the words used in it, and how they chose to interpret them.

Citizen's Insurance Co. v. Parsons, in 1881, was the JCPC's first major Canadian constitutional case. It confirmed the Supreme Court's earlier dismissal of an Ontario claim that "the provincial parliament has the exclusive right to create within the province, rights of property." While the judgment favoured Macdonald's constitutional position, Justice Gwynne warned him that the arguments presented in the case could be "the thin edge of the wedge to bring about provincial sovereignty[,] which I believe Mr. Mowat is endeavouring to do." Macdonald ignored Gwynne's warning. It is possible that Mowat's ultimate constitutional ambitions went further than sovereignty within Ontario's own borders. At one JCPC hearing, Mowat's counsel informed the judges, "The provinces are virtually separate countries. . . . Each is a separate state." Although Mowat never made this claim, Haldane would later describe the provinces as "independent kingdoms over which the Dominion has little control."

For a brief span, it seemed that Macdonald might have been right to be so confident. In 1882, *Russell v. the Queen* came before the JCPC. Charles Russell of Fredericton, New Brunswick, had been fined in magistrate's court for selling intoxicating liquors without a provincial licence, despite his argument he was justified because the federal Canada Temperance Act regulated the liquor trade right across the country. Russell fought back through all the courts. The JCPC's ruling could not have pleased Macdonald more; it rejected the claim that the Temperance Act breached provincial jurisdiction and anchored this finding in Ottawa's "Peace, Order and Good Government clause." Macdonald gleefully told Campbell, "My opinions are strongly supported. . . . This decision will be a great protection to the Central Authority."

One year later, the case of *Hodge v. the Queen* changed everything. Archibald Hodge, a Toronto innkeeper who had a licence under the federal Temperance Act, had appealed a provincial fine that he incurred when he allowed his patrons to play billiards past Ontario's Saturday closing hour of 7 p.m. After hearing the arguments, the JCPC ruled, on December 15, 1885, that provincial powers under Section 92 of the act were in no way diminished by the federal powers in Section 91. Rather, the provincial legislature was "supreme and has the same authority as the Imperial Parliament or the Parliament of the Dominion would have under like circumstances." The provinces were not subordinate to Ottawa, and within their prescribed area of jurisdiction were in fact supreme.

This decision would lead historian W.L. Morton to conclude, "On Mr. Hodge's billiard table, then, the Macdonaldian concept for Confederation was baulked."

Afterwards came the deluge. The single most definitive confirmation of the new order, in *Liquidators of the Maritime Bank of Canada v. Receiver-General of New Brunswick*, was made public in 1892, one year after Macdonald's death (although the case had passed through the lower courts for years earlier). The JCPC's judgment, written by Watson, held: "The object of the B.N.A. Act was neither to weld the provinces into one, nor to subordinate the provincial governments to a central one"; rather, the provinces' powers were "exclusive and supreme." The provinces were sovereign—and not just within their jurisdiction as enumerated in Section 91, but over an ever-expanding list as the judges progressively diminished the reach of the federal "Peace, Order and Good Government" override clause and expanded the provinces' "Property and Civil Rights" equivalent.

Macdonald never complained publicly about this rewriting of the constitution by means of radically reinterpreting it. He did once burst out in exasperation, "Mowat has all the luck." The truth was, though, that Mowat made most of his luck himself.

Macdonald never quite seemed to understand what was going on. He sent able lawyers across to London to represent the federal side, Alexander Campbell and D'Alton McCarthy among them. Mostly, though, he remained detached. In a letter to Gowan while in London in 1884, Macdonald mused, "I agree with much that you say about the Judicial Committee of the P.C.—but we must put up with it—I don't move in the legal region at all here." He reacted politically, worrying about the next election rather than about the next case due to be heard by the JCPC. Most simply, Macdonald, in his reverence for the law and for Britain, could not bring himself to say out loud that some of the best judges in Britain might have been grievously wrong for a cluster of reasons, the most decisive being that they knew nothing about Canada, nor were in the least bothered by this shortcoming.

One major attempt has been made since then to claim that the JCPC judges did care. In an influential 1971 article, the distinguished constitutional scholar Alan Cairns argued, "It is impossible to believe that a few elderly men in London . . . caused the development of Canada in a federalist direction that the country would not otherwise have taken." Instead, the JCPC's rulings were "not in isolation of deeply rooted, popularly supported trends in Canada."

This proposition is unpersuasive. The single instance Cairns cited of the JCPC being in accord with "popularly supported trends" was the hero's welcome given Mowat when he returned from Britain in 1884 after winning a favourable ruling on Ontario's western boundary. That same year, though, Macdonald received as rapturous a welcome in Toronto for the anniversary of his fortieth year in politics. Overlooked is the one objective measure of popular sentiment that does exist: the 1883 election in Ontario, when Mowat made his constitutional quarrel with Macdonald the centrepiece of his campaign. Never before or afterwards did Mowat have a harder time, and his majority was reduced from twenty-five to nine. This result doesn't mean that Ontarians preferred Macdonald's more centralist policy; it simply means that, then as now, Ontarians had little interest in constitutional quarrels.

Canada's constitution was indeed given "a new form" (Haldane's phase) by "a few elderly men in London," as Saywell wrote in his seminal but neglected work, *The Lawmakers: Judicial Power and the Shaping of Canadian Federalism*. They inflicted on Macdonald his one clear nation-building defeat. Yet he still implemented almost all his nation-building agenda. It has to be added that things haven't turned out at all badly in the decentralized nation that the JCPC judges concocted in place of Macdonald's vision for it; also, that even though nothing could have been further from the British judges' intentions or interests, Canada's decentralization ("provincialisation" would really be a more accurate term) is one of the political characteristics that clearly differentiates the Canadian political system from America's.

TWENTY-FIVE

The Worst of Times

The Americans may say with truth that if they do not annex Canada, they are annexing Canadians.
Goldwin Smith

The Long Depression resumed around the end of 1883. This time, it wasn't precipitated by some financial panic or corporate scandal but just seemed to happen. International prices for commodities such as grain and lumber began to fall, touching off a domino effect in real estate, and in quick succession banks tightened credit, manufacturers cut back, unemployment increased and wages dropped. From Canada's perspective, there was one fundamental difference between this downturn and the first phase of the Long Depression from 1873 to 1878. It affected Canada much more deeply than the United States until 1893, when a financial panic precipitated an all-out crash below the border.

In many respects, the United States still boomed. The Gilded Age was in full flower, powered by mass immigration, the settlement of the West, an outburst of technological creativity and the acquisitive energies of tycoons such as John D. Rockefeller, Cornelius Vanderbilt, Andrew W. Mellon and Andrew Carnegie.

In between a series of small recessions, the country expanded, and by the end of the century its manufacturing output exceeded that of Britain, Germany and France.

Never has the contrast between Canada and the United States been wider. In historian J.M.S. Careless's phrase, the span from the mid-1880s to the turn of the century was Canada's "age of failure." Its effects were felt more acutely than those of all the earlier downturns because the growing class of urban industrial workers were so vulnerable—unlike farmers, unable to grow their own food, and few owning their own houses. Although the depression's scope was global, its psychological and political impact on Canadian society went especially deep, and it came to induce a sense of national failure. Because Americans were faring so much better, Canadians began to question the national assumption that their way—the British way—was superior. They came to doubt their society and themselves more than they ever had before, or ever would again, even during the Great Depression of the 1930s, when, while many despaired for their personal future, few doubted their country's ability to exist.

Although not a "failed state," Canada towards the last decade of the nineteenth century came perilously close to failing its people in material terms, and failing to fulfill the dreams once held for it by visionaries such as D'Arcy McGee and Charles Mair. Goldwin Smith spoke for the opposite view of the country's prospects when he said that Canadian nationality was "a lost cause" and "the ultimate union of Canada with the United States appears now to be morally certain."

There was a particular reason for Canada's gloom. At a time when most measures of economic progress were imprecise, the one exception was population counts. Censuses were widely believed to be scrupulously accurate, and these showed that through the last two decades of the nineteenth century Canada's population had changed little, edging up from just over 4 million to just over 5 million. Given the enormous increase in its physical size and the high rate of immigration earlier in the century, this was deeply disappointing. But for the fecundity of Quebec wives and their obedience to their curés, the population might even have contracted. Every year, more people left the country than entered it. Canada's net immigration numbers were lower comparatively than those not only of the United States, but also of its "new nation" rivals—Australia, New Zealand, Argentina and Brazil. During Macdonald's last decade, 1880 to 1890, net out-migration would reach 207,000, an all-time record. By the century's end, more than one million Canadians were living in the United States, close to one for every five at home; many more Canadians had probably moved south but were living there invisibly.

This situation applied most depressingly in the North-West, where the greatest influx of immigrants had been anticipated. By the end of the century, the population there was around a hundred thousand European Canadians—little different from Prince Edward Island. The long-dreamed-of transcontinental railway was being built, but few people were arriving to use it.

No immediate cure existed for this failure. Immigrants to North America overwhelmingly headed to the American West, attracted by the milder climate and higher level of development, and they would keep going there until 1892, when the frontier was officially declared closed. There were some immigration success stories here. The Icelanders did well as farmers, and their numbers increased to seven thousand. Mennonites also did exceptionally well, in about the same numbers. Jews driven out of Russia by pogroms, and later from Poland and Austria, fled to Western Europe, with some continuing on to Canada; they were traders rather than farmers, so most soon left the prairies for Winnipeg and other towns. Lastly, a number of French Canadians who had

For years after the buffalo were gone, some people on the prairies made a living by gathering their bones and dung. For lack of wood, dwellings were made of sod. The hardness of pioneer life is confirmed by the fact that this is described as "better" than what went before.

moved to the United States were attracted back by the promise of state-supported separate schools in the West.

Attempts to attract large-scale emigration from Ireland failed, however, despite these separate schools. Irish nationalists now saw Canada's attempts to entice its people as "forcing the Irish into Exile, at the instance of the [British] Govt., or the Landlord," as Macdonald put it in one letter. Nothing would change until the first decade of the twentieth century, when a combination of rising grain prices and the closure of the American West sent immigrants pouring into the prairies. Soon, Laurier would be able to predict that the twentieth century might belong to Canada.*

Macdonald missed this moment of national reaffirmation. From the mid-1880s until his death in 1891, his principal nation-building

---

* Laurier made his famous prediction in a speech to the Canadian Club of Ottawa in 1904.

task would be to keep the nation going—and together—until things turned around.

~

Macdonald was renowned for his resilience and capacity for optimism under the bleakest of circumstances—qualities that sustained him through the disappointments of his personal life. He also had some priceless assets. His guile and wiliness had been refined by years of experience. And he had a hold on the affections of Canadians that few other leaders would ever approach.

Yet time ticked inexorably by. When Macdonald celebrated his seventieth birthday in 1885, at a party at the Windsor Hotel in Montreal, he quoted from Shakespeare's *As You Like It*: "My age is as a lusty winter / Frosty but kindly." Aches and ailments had become part of his daily condition, with an occasional warning of something more drastic ahead. "I am breaking down. I can't conceal it from myself, perhaps not even from my friends," he told a civil servant after the end of the 1883 session. Macdonald still viewed life with too much sardonic amusement to ever become a grumpy old man, but he was beginning to get out of date: in 1883, he referred to the North-West as "a Crown Colony," as though it still belonged to Britain. He complained to Charles Tupper about his own cabinet: "We are too old." His administrative practices became slapdash. After 1883, he "developed the habit of putting some of the most perplexing files aside, to be looked at later. These, in turn, got buried by other files," Janet Sowby writes in her master's thesis. He was entering his "Old Tomorrow" era.*

* This nickname is often credited to Indian leaders such as Big Bear or Poundmaker or Crowfoot, but no supportive evidence exists. Macdonald took it in good heart: asked what title he would take if the current rumour he was to be offered a peerage was correct, he answered, "Lord Tomorrow."

Macdonald was now trapped in the office he had held for so long. Stepping down had become almost impossible: he had no successor, and too many of his supporters depended on him. More and more, the people around him told him what they guessed he wanted to hear rather than what they genuinely believed.

As the depression continued, sectarianism raised its ugly head. Desperate people needed scapegoats to explain their economic misery. In Ontario, annoyance grew that its hinterland colony, the North-West, had been stolen from it by Macdonald's creation of the province of Manitoba. In the West, the view took hold that French Canadians were running the country, because Macdonald depended, permanently, on the bloc of *bleu* MPs. And soon Quebec would join the ranks of disaffected provinces. There was more to come: a rebellion in the North-West; a serious risk of Canada's first Indian war; a second outbreak of separatism in Nova Scotia; the rise of a "nativist" movement hostile to all immigrants, especially those from China; a contraction in the government's revenues just when the Canadian Pacific Railway needed to be rescued from bankruptcy; and a large number of prairie Aboriginals who needed to be saved from starvation.

It's been said that Macdonald called Canada "a hard country to govern." The only evidence he ever did say this is an unsubstantiated claim by *Saturday Night* magazine editor Hector Charlesworth in his memoirs of 1927. In fact, the initiator of the phrase was Laurier, who wrote in a 1906 letter to the *Globe*'s John Willison, "This is a difficult country to govern." True beyond doubt is that Canada had never been harder to govern than it was during Macdonald's last decade. Most of the time he was on the defensive, hanging on, much as was the country. He made some bad mistakes. But he never made the one mistake that would have mattered: he never gave up.

There is, though, a clear and unfamiliar note of defeatism in a letter he wrote on November 3, 1884, to Judge James Robert Gowan from London, where he had gone as much as anything to get away from it all. "I did run away as you supposed, from dyspepsia and worry—having at the same time enough public work to do to keep me from rusting on this Side," he confessed. However, he had seen his physician, who told him he was "wonderfully Sound" and that he could not discover the door "through which my Soul will some day escape for realms unknown." Eventually, Macdonald recovered his customary good spirits, returned home and went to work.

Among the effects of the return of the Long Depression was the first appearance of prairie populism on the national stage.* Western alienation dates from this time, as does the West's sense of itself as a distinct region rather than a hinterland extension of the old Canada. Western populism would have manifested itself eventually anyway, because it suited the temper and topography of the area: when space is almost limitless, individuals all shrink to the same size. Hard times, though, quickened its appearance on the national stage.

The movement began in Brandon. On October 19, 1883, a settler named Charles Stewart, who had graduated from Cambridge University, wrote to the local *Sun* calling for a protest meeting "to obtain for ourselves that independence which is the birth right of every British subject." Out of this came the Manitoba and North-West Farmers' Union, which held its inaugural convention in Winnipeg on December 19 that same year. The gathering agreed

* It can be argued that its first expression was Riel's uprising of 1869–70, though that was really an expression of Métis, rather than prairie, populism.

to a Declaration of Rights calling for an end to Ottawa's disallowance of local railways, removal of high National Policy tariffs on agricultural equipment, and the transfer to the province of control over Crown lands. The declaration was sent to Macdonald in Ottawa; he paid not the least attention.

A second convention, in Winnipeg in March 1884, approved an "anti-immigration" resolution urging that potential immigrants to Manitoba be asked not to come until Ottawa had settled the West's grievances. This excess, worsened by excited talk about separation, cost the movement its credibility. A new organization, a Protective Union, took over and launched an innovative program to buy up members' wheat, ship it in bulk to Ontario and use the profits to buy binder twine in large quantities for its members. An Ontario manufacturer won the contract, though, provoking protests against "Eastern domination."*

The real causes of the difficulties in the West were far beyond anyone's reach. A worldwide surge in wheat production (in the United States, South America and Australia as well as Canada) pushed down prices, from $1.21 a bushel in 1880 to as low as 81 cents by 1888. The new agricultural machinery—such as Massey-Harris self-binders and steam-locomotive threshers—improved productivity, but, because bought with bank loans, made farmers more vulnerable to price declines and crop failures. Populism fed on the basic truth that the prairie pioneers had it extraordinarily hard: time and again, the frost came early, and droughts and locusts ravaged the land. The necessary techniques for dry-land farming would not be developed for years. In the meantime, one song popular on the prairies went, "This country's a regular fraud, O, / And I want to go home to Mamma."

---

* Charles Stewart, the original protester, became an ardent separatist, prompting Protective Union moderates to "secede" Stewart from the hall—into a snowbank.

Right from the start, western populists identified the people they held responsible for their troubles: "For the discontent which is keeping out immigration, for the hideous robbery to which people are daily subjected by the extortionate railway rates," said the *Manitoba Free Press*, "Sir John Macdonald and his ministers alone are to blame." In fact, after the turn of the century, as soon as grain prices rose and immigrants came, the West roared off on a three-decade-long boom. But this earlier experience gave westerners a target to unite against. As Frank Oliver, editor of the *Edmonton Bulletin*, put it, "The idea that the North-West is to eastern Canada as India is to Great Britain is one that will, if not abandoned, lead to the rupture of confederation." Within Confederation there was now a lusty, brawling newcomer.

This western discontent was expressed most loudly in the north of present-day Saskatchewan. There, the CPR had abruptly switched its line far southwards, making Regina the territorial capital rather than North Battleford. The region went doubly into a depression. A Settlers' Union was formed in Prince Albert, the largest town, and outraged resolutions were passed and sent to Ottawa. There, they vanished. The settlers became even more enraged. The same anger arose among a particular group of westerners living nearby in an area known as the South Branch of the Saskatchewan River. Its principal community was known as Batoche.

~

The Métis had been moving there, mostly from Red River, since the early 1870s, hoping to find buffalo farther west and a place in the North-West that was not English and Protestant. A settlement practice of the Métis—derived from Québécois settlements along the St. Lawrence River—was that their lots were long and narrow, fronting directly onto the river, rather than the square homestead properties standard everywhere else.

Batoche was in no way a fancy community, but neither was it impoverished. Most of its houses were flat-roofed log cabins, with buffalo hides stretched across the open door and windows. The first issue of the *Saskatchewan Herald* described it as "large and very flourishing." The home of its most successful trader, with its "six roomy bedrooms sumptuously furnished with marble-topped dressers," was regarded as the finest house west of Winnipeg. Another trader had installed a billiard table and, for his wife, a hand-operated washing machine. He was known as Gabriel Dumont, a legendary buffalo hunter who now operated a ferry across the Saskatchewan River at Batoche.

Still, it was an unsettled community. Its people were French and Catholic, and Métis. Many were illiterate and spoke little English. Despite disadvantages, indeed because of them, they possessed a sense of collective rights. This condition, together with their traditional preference for their elongated lots, complicated the task of settling their land claims. Early in 1884, a solution seemed imminent when a lands inspector, William Pearce, visited and suggested that square lots already surveyed be subdivided to create rectangular ones. For reasons now unclear, the Métis were not satisfied—and officials took no follow-up action. Historians Bob Beal and Rod Macleod suggest that the "Metis and their priests misunderstood the government's land regulation and that compromises might have been worked out." They continue that "the government had seemed to ignore the Metis," who in turn assumed "it was up to the government to make rules that . . . coincided with their demands."

The root problem was quite different—and likely impossible to resolve. The Métis' main economic activity, the buffalo hunt, ended with the vanishing of the once-huge herds. Simultaneously, their subsidiary economic activity as freighters and teamsters on the riverboats and in convoys of Red River carts was being displaced by steamships and the railway. This change of life mattered incomparably more than difficulties over settling land claims, but the land-claim issue became the emotional focus for all the Métis anxieties. Pleas and petitions went out to Ottawa, but there disappeared.

In March 1884, some twenty-five South Branch Métis gathered to discuss what should be done. The most decisive was Gabriel Dumont. He told the others they should take matters into their own hands and "force the government to give us justice." A decision was reached to bring in an expert to argue their case with Ottawa.

The expert they selected was someone they knew well: Louis Riel, now a teacher living on St. Peter's Mission in the backcountry of Montana. A delegation of four, headed by Dumont, made the six-hundred-mile horseback journey to visit him. Riel listened to their story and their request that he go back north with them, and he said he would give his answer the following day. When dawn broke, he agreed he would return. Now forty, he was plumper than he had been and had grown an impressive reddish-brown moustache. He even had a hardiness about him, probably because for the first time in his life he had gone out with the Métis on buffalo hunts. He had also married a Métisse named Marguerite and was the father of two young children.

Two aspects of this encounter would have lasting importance. Although three of the four visitors were French Métis, one was an English Métis. But there was no representative from the largest of all the prairie groups, the Aboriginals, nor any representative of the white settlers. The other distinction resided in Riel himself. In explaining to the quartet why he needed a day to consider their proposal, he had used a curious formula. The delegation had

The Riel who came back in 1884 to help the Métis achieve their land claims looked like the Riel of old, strong and bulky with piercing eyes. But he now had a family to care for—his wife, Marguerite, his son, Jean-Louis, and his daughter, Marie-Angélique. The more radical difference was that he was now fulfilling a "divine mission"; among the Métis of Batoche he could find a congregation that believed in it, too.

arrived on June 4, he said, so God had sent him a message by dispatching "four of you who have arrived on the fourth and you wish to leave with a fifth." He concluded: "I cannot answer today. You must wait until the fifth." The Riel who returned with them was no longer the man they had once known in Red River. This Riel now received messages directly from God.

For the time being, however, all that mattered was that Riel was coming home.

TWENTY-SIX

God's Messenger

The bankers invite me to their table.
Louis Riel

The news of Louis Riel's return in the summer of 1884 caused no great concern. His five years of exile had expired in 1880, so he had every right to come back. He had turned up in Winnipeg the year before, spoken freely with journalists and called on Bishop Taché—but they no longer trusted each other, so it was a chilly encounter. The newspaper reports on his visit were positive: the *Winnipeg Daily Sun* observed that "his eyes danced and glistened in a manner that riveted attention." There were some worrying signs. While Riel was still in Montana, one U.S. federal agent had advised his superior, "He can wield the Half Breeds at will, and also probably the Cree." And while in Winnipeg, Riel sent a kind of warning signal to a friend: "No one wanted me in the influential circles," he wrote. "I am forgotten as if I were dead." Clearly, Riel hungered as much as ever for attention and fame.

Otherwise, everything went equably. Before leaving Montana, Riel told the Sun River *Sun* he wouldn't be gone long, and he informed the quartet of Métis accompanying him, "My intention is to come back in the fall." His own Métis met him at South Bend's southernmost point in fifty Red River carts and gave him a rapturous reception. On July 8, he made his first public speech in Canada since 1870, at the house of a cousin, Charles Nolin. On this occasion, he sounded so much the peacemaker that *Le Manitoba* reported on some Métis' disappointment at his lack of belligerence. He also had a meeting with Father Alexis André, a confident and forceful Oblate serving as a parish priest and much admired by the Métis because he was physically strong and hardy. André had been worried by Riel's proven ability to stir up the Métis, but he was now reassured. He wrote to Lieutenant-Governor Edgar Dewdney, "I do not entertain the least suspicion about Riel causing any trouble. He acts quietly and he speaks wisely."

A fortnight later, Riel confirmed André's assessment by charming an audience of white businessmen and settlers at a public meeting in Prince Albert. The priest reported to Dewdney that the meeting had been packed and the reaction enthusiastic, with only one person shouting at Riel—"and he was put out quickly." Most encouragingly, Riel had said that all their objectives could be achieved, provided they "acted orderly and peaceably."

The Prince Albert meeting had been arranged by another of those larger-than-life frontier characters. William Jackson had spent three years at the University of Toronto before he had to drop out after his storekeeper father ran out of money. Small, intense and excitable, he joined the family in Prince Albert, where his brother ran a pharmacy. A born agitator, Jackson started a newspaper, the *Voice of the People*, in which he forecast "a fierce and prolonged struggle with the numerous monopolies which are fastening their talons upon the vitals of this infant country." Jackson sought out Riel; they talked all night and became instant friends and intellectual soulmates. Jackson had found his hero, and Riel was delighted to have a well-educated white on his side. He made Jackson his secretary, and they both settled in Batoche. All through that summer, Riel, with Jackson tagging along, met with French and English Métis to hear their grievances. Jackson added the views of Prince Albert businessmen—or at least his version of them. Out of all of this mix was to come a petition to be sent to Ottawa.

Back in Ottawa, Macdonald at this time held all the western portfolios himself: he was minister of the interior and also responsible for both Indian Affairs and the North-West Mounted Police. In addition, all the key decisions about the transcontinental project were made in the prime minister's office. In every respect, Macdonald was *the* minister for everything in the West. Although he passed the Interior portfolio in 1882 to an old friend, Senator David Macpherson, it was to a man with little energy or insight, and nothing changed. Macpherson, despite Riel's return, took off for his annual health cure in Europe in the summer of 1884, pronouncing that everything was peaceable in the West.

The officials Macdonald put in charge provide another reason why all important western decisions ended up on his own desk. His departmental deputy minister was Lawrence Vankoughnet, an old family friend, who was competent enough, but in a narrow, bureaucratic way. His overriding interest was to keep costs down. Out west, the top official was Edgar Dewdney, again Macdonald's personal friend, who held the double title of lieutenant-governor and commissioner of Indian affairs for the North-West. Although comparatively progressive, he possessed an unseemly addiction to using his inside knowledge in land deals. Dewdney was also utterly awed by Macdonald, telling him what he thought Macdonald wanted to hear rather than providing objective advice. Dewdney told his wife after his first meeting with Macdonald that he was "a strong and singularly gifted man . . . [who] filled the population's admiration." Knowing how heavy Macdonald's workload was, he did all he could to keep his recitations of problems to a minimum. Dewdney's intentions were good, but they served Macdonald ill.

Edgar Dewdney, the senior Indian Affairs official in the North-West Territory, was comparatively moderate. His defects were an inordinate enthusiasm for making money and a worshipful awe of Macdonald, from whom he repeatedly withheld unpleasant news.

Throughout the West, Macdonald's power wasn't so much ministerial as proconsular. Everything passed through his hands—immigration, land grants, Indian policy, railway policy and the police. He also had the CPR at his beck and call. Often called the government's "sleeping partner," it was described better as "the Conservative Party on wheels."

The problem wasn't that Macdonald had the powers of a dictator but that he was an erratically engaged dictator. When Opposition critic David Mills complained that Macdonald was letting his department "take care of itself," the prime minister admitted he often had to "rely on memory and the improvisation of the moment" to deal with questions about western affairs. Age was a factor, along with his assorted ailments, but the combination of his having to deal with Riel's activities and the financial problems of the CPR at the same time amounted to the political equivalent of a two-front war.

As a further handicap, Macdonald knew far less about the West than he thought he did. He did have experience in western affairs, going back to Riel's first uprising of 1869–70, the creation of Manitoba and the formation of the Mounted Police. But he had never been there. For once, his knowledge was abstract. He had no appreciation of the zeitgeist of the West, the immensity of its distances and the effect they had on the people. He did not realize that settlers there thought they were building the nation from scratch, not just filling it up, or that the life of the Plains Indians was so different from that of the Indians he was familiar with in the East. Macdonald knew the prose of the West, but not its poetry.*

He was decidedly confident, even cocky, about Riel's return to Batoche. On August 5, he reported to Lord Lansdowne, who had replaced Lord Lorne as governor general, "There is, I think, nothing to be feared from Riel." The Métis leader had spoken of "some claims he had against the government. I presume these refer to his land claims which he forfeited on conviction and banishment. I think we shall deal liberally with him and make him a good subject again." Macdonald wrote this letter from his cottage in Rivière-du-Loup, where he had gone for his summer holiday. By most of the signs and portents, it was a well-timed break.

Some alarmist messages had begun to come in. A Mounted Police sergeant advised his superiors that, while the South Branch Métis seemed outwardly calm, "they advocate very different measures in their councils," with one Métis leader urging that they should "take up arms and commence killing every white man they can find." The Indians had also started to stir. In June 1884, two of the

* Still, it has to be said that, of Canada's first seven prime ministers, Macdonald would be the only one to travel west before 1911, when Laurier went there during an election campaign. Macdonald's one visit was in 1886, however, when all the critical decisions were behind him.

most powerful Cree chiefs, Big Bear and Poundmaker, got together on Poundmaker's reserve to stage a Thirst Dance and to discuss ways to get the government to fulfill the terms of their treaties. Over that summer, Big Bear also met privately with Riel. In fact, no pact or alliance was achieved at this encounter, and it was clear that the Indian chiefs were extremely wary of getting too close to Riel.* Most reassuring, Father André had passed on to Dewdney a sound reason to remain untroubled. "A Man will not bring his wife and children along with him if he intended to raise a rebellion," he wrote, and the fact that Riel had brought his family to Saskatchewan provided "the best proof he has no bad intentions."

More worrying indicators did exist, although it would have taken a traitor to uncover them. There was a highly revealing letter Riel had written to his brother, Joseph: "Not long ago I was a humble schoolmaster on the distant banks of the Missouri and here I am today in the ranks of the most popular public men in Saskatchewan. . . . The bankers invite me to their table." This was the tone of someone thoroughly enjoying power and unlikely to return soon to Montana. As always with Riel, his ego, once inflated, kept on expanding. Early in August he gave a public speech criticizing the clergy for not supporting the Métis' political objectives. This episode precipitated a furious row between him and Father André in which Riel accused the priest of being a supporter of the government. André retorted that Riel had become a "true fanatic" and should stop rambling on about his "heretical and revolutionary ideas."

Macdonald's lack of awareness of the profound psychological change in Riel since their last contest contributed to his twice

* The gloomiest and most perceptive observer was the poet and ex–Canada Firster Charles Mair. Now living in Prince Albert, he scented trouble and moved his wife and family to Windsor, Ontario.

missing opportunities that might have altered the course of events. The first, in mid-August, was a visit that his Quebec lieutenant, Public Works Minister Hector-Louis Langevin, announced he would make to Batoche during a tour of the North-West. In high anticipation, Riel organized a gala dinner and wrote out notes for a speech. But once Langevin reached Regina by train, he decided not to make the 350-mile trip northwards by cart. He didn't even send a telegram to Riel, implicitly letting him know that Ottawa failed to take him seriously.

The second missed chance occurred when Dewdney, on Macdonald's instruction, commissioned a local judge, Charles Rouleau, to investigate what was going on in the area. Rouleau reported that, although the Métis in South Branch were quiet, their anger was rising, so a settlement of their land claims should be made "under the shortest delay possible." He also warned that unless the government provided food and clothing to the Indians, "there will be great misery and starvation among them during this winter." When Macdonald received this information, his only response was to increase the Mounted Police force by one hundred men. As he explained, "I don't apprehend myself any rising, but with these warnings it would be criminal negligence not to take any precautions."

At just this time, Macdonald's attention was focused elsewhere: the CPR was in real trouble.

Not long after the CPR began work on its ambitious task, it encountered a perplexing problem: it was building its line too fast and as a consequence was rapidly running out of cash. William Van Horne had created this problem by the exceptional efficiency with which he had organized the construction crews and driven them through the work seasons of 1882 and 1883. Ottawa's bureaucracy magnified the problem by falling far behind in making the payments due to the company as it finished each section. At the same time, the resumption of the Long Depression made investors and banks far more cautious about extending credit.

When George Stephen had promised Macdonald "no financial fireworks," he had failed to allow for Van Horne's efficiency and the difficulty of getting British banks interested in any project that included the word "Canada." In London, he now told Macdonald, a P.T. Barnum circus with an elephant named Jumbo "was a matter of ten times more interest." As early as the summer of 1883, Stephen had to warn Macdonald that even the costs of the easy prairie section had turned out to be "enormously in excess of our estimate."

To make matters worse, the CPR and the Grand Trunk Railway could find no compromise to the intense rivalry between them over their competing lines in central Canada. In the succeeding propaganda war, the Grand Trunk almost always came out ahead, not least because it was backed by several British banks. In November, the *Wall Street Daily News* described CPR stock as "a dead skin" and predicted that buyers would "lose every cent." At risk now was the CPR itself and, by extension, Macdonald's government, which had made the nation's financial reputation hostage to the corporation's fortunes. On December 1, 1883, Macdonald wired Charles Tupper, now Canada's high commissioner in London: "Pacific in trouble. You should be here." Tupper cabled back: "Sailing on Thursday."

As a first response to the crisis, Stephen persuaded Macdonald to grant the CPR a government guarantee of three percentage points of the 5 per cent dividend the company was committed to paying. The shares still fell. Tupper, once in Ottawa, signed a letter guaranteeing repayment of an outstanding cash advance made earlier to the company. This guarantee enabled Stephen to obtain a loan from the Bank of Montreal. But it was still not enough.

In January 1884, Stephen asked for a government loan of \$22.5 million, almost as large as its original subsidy. That was far too much for Macdonald. At a meeting at Earnscliffe, he heard out the CPR executives, then told them, "You might as well ask for the planet Jupiter. I would not give you the millions you ask, and if I did the Cabinet would not agree."

Before returning to Montreal in the evening, the group went by hansom cab to report their failure to the acting minister of railways, the bluff, straight-talking John Henry Pope. He heard them out while downing a Scotch and smoking a cigar, called a carriage and disappeared. An hour and a half later, at around 2 a.m., he was back: "Well boys, he'll do it." What he had done, Pope explained, was to go to Earnscliffe, rouse Macdonald from his bed and tell him, "The day the Canadian Pacific busts, the Conservative Party busts the day after."

Over fierce objections by the Opposition, Tupper got the Commons to agree to legislation to authorize a \$22.5 million government loan to the CPR. In exchange, the company pledged to finish the job in 1886—a scarcely believable date. In return for their support for the government's new loan, Macdonald's *bleus* exacted a promise of a multi-million-dollar payment to Quebec to bail out a money-losing line along the north shore of the St. Lawrence. Maritime MPs resorted to the same tactic and exacted a commitment that the CPR would build a new "short" line to Halifax.

This virtual blackmail produced one offsetting gain. Donald Smith had played a key part in the CPR's recovery, keeping it going by pledging his personal assets, as had Stephen. But because of his old quarrel with Macdonald dating back to his negative vote during the Canadian Pacific Scandal, Smith's role as a member of the CPR's executive committee had been kept secret. Smith was now able to appear in the gallery of the Commons on the same day the relief measure went through. The peacemaker was his cousin George Stephen, who brought Macdonald and Smith together over a bottle of Scotch. In his monumentally self-centred way, Smith later summed up their meeting: "I know—without his saying it—that [Macdonald] is today a much happier man."

The settlement brought the CPR relief—for about eight months. By then, the CPR's financial situation was back to where it had been at the beginning of the year. It was during this time that Riel made the journey from Montana to South Branch.

From this point on, Macdonald was fighting both against Riel and for the CPR. The strain showed. "I would leave the Government tomorrow," he told Tupper in midsummer, except that if he did "George Stephen would throw up the sponge." And he confided to Stephen, "It is only because I want to be *in* on the completion of the CPR that I remain where I am. . . . I may say I groan for rest."

By late 1884, the CPR was eking out its dwindling cash reserves by paying its workers ever more slowly. "I feel like a man walking on the edge of a precipice," Stephen told Macdonald. Near the year's end, Stephen and Smith staved off creditors for one month by pledging their personal credit to raise an £80,000 loan for the company. Stephen celebrated by sending Smith Canada's second-best-known telegram: "Stand fast, Craigellachie." As Scots, both men were familiar with the great rock of Craigellachie, where the clans used to rally to bellow out defiance at their enemies.

Gestures, no matter how splendid, could not change reality. In January 1885, rumours that the company was close to financial collapse appeared in the press. CPR stock immediately tumbled to an all-time low. Grave doubts now existed whether the company could fulfill its next dividend payment, due in April. Allowing the dividend to "pass" would be an admission of imminent bankruptcy.

Yet Macdonald still refused to make any commitment—refused even to discuss the crisis. Stephen turned frantic and accusatory: "It is as clear as noonday, Sir John," he wrote in mid-January, "that unless you yourself say what should be done, nothing but disaster will result." Macdonald knew that perfectly well, but he could see no path to take him safely ahead. Three of his ministers were adamantly opposed, one to the point of threatening to resign if the company was bailed out again. Finance Minister Leonard Tilley was certain many Conservative MPs would refuse to vote for another loan. On January 26, Macdonald wrote in despair to Tupper, "We dare not ask for another loan. How it will end, I do not know." Tupper responded, "If you let the C.P.R. go down, you will sacrifice both the country and the party."

By now it had become habitual for Macdonald to live up to his nickname, "Old Tomorrow," doing nothing in the hope that some near-miraculous turn of luck would do the job for him. This time, though, he seemed to be waiting aimlessly, as if mesmerized. As the days slipped past, he kept silent, and Stephen grew more frantic. Then, by a mysterious alchemy, two unrelated lines of development began to converge onto a single track: Macdonald and the CPR on one path, and Riel and the Métis on the other.

Through the summer of 1884, Riel, with William Jackson's assistance, had canvassed the opinions of all the potentially interested groups—the French and English Métis, the settlers, the Prince Albert businessmen and, in this instance very superficially, the Indian bands in the region. In mid-September, a draft document was completed and circulated for comment and approval. All that remained was to send the final text to Ottawa.

During this period, Riel neither said nor did anything threatening or aggressive, other than to engage in occasional rows with Father André over religion and politics. Some of the excitement and tension generated by his arrival began to ebb away. Yet a radical change was under way, one with far-reaching implications. A Riel quite unlike the man who had come to northern Saskatchewan only a few months earlier was beginning to emerge.

The old Riel had been invited as an expert to help the Métis settle their grievances over land claims. The new Riel would be a prophet called upon by God to bring about an entirely new political and social order in the North-West, and an entirely new religious order within the Roman Catholic Church.

Back in February 1875, Prime Minister Alexander Mackenzie had announced that Riel would receive an amnesty for his role in the Red River Resistance provided he stayed in exile for five years. The absence of a pardon meant that Riel's career as a leader of the Métis was over, as well as any political career he might aspire to as an MP in Ottawa. Instead, he would become a nobody. Riel expressed his feelings in poetry, as he often did now: "Those of homeland dispossessed / Though with many friendships blessed / May receive the gift of tenderness / And yet feel a profound sadness."*

For Riel, exile was a hard and a humiliating experience. He was anonymous and dependent on the charity of friends. He never had a job, except as a teacher in a Métis hamlet during his last year in Montana. Much of the time he was lonely, cut off from his family and friends in Manitoba. One of the priests who looked after Riel during his time in the United States remarked that he had "the appearance of a man overwhelmed by boredom."

---

* This moving poem is quoted in Maggie Siggins's biography *Riel: A Life of Revolution*.

Then he found a sustaining creed and an ennobling cause. While slipping back and forth across the border during the early years of his exile, Riel had several times met in Montreal with Bishop Ignace Bourget, the leader of the conservative ultramontanes. After a visit on July 14, 1875, Bourget wrote him a note of encouragement, assuring him he would receive, sooner than he expected, "the reward for all those mental and moral sacrifices" he had made. "God, who has always led you and assisted you . . . has given you a mission which you must fulfill in all respects," Bourget concluded.

For Bourget, the words were probably no more than an encouraging pleasantry. To Riel, his spiritual mentor had sent him a direct message from God. All his life, Riel kept this letter on his person, its pages ever more crumpled and worn. It was the proof, he wrote later in his diary, that "God [had] anointed him with his divine gifts and fruits of his Spirit, as prophet of the New World."

The reward of conviction was ecstasy. On December 8, while attending high mass in a church in Washington, Riel experienced the first of a series of visions, this one enveloping him with "a joy which took such possession of me." In other epiphanies, he wrote that "the spirit of God comes upon him . . . transports him to the fourth heaven and instructs him about the nations of the earth." Before long, Riel recorded in his diary, "people began to treat me like a madman." While staying with a priest, he constantly cried and shouted, and even behaved the same way in church.

In January 1876, arrangements were made for him to visit the St. Jean de Dieu asylum in a Montreal suburb. The doctor there was impressed by Riel's intelligence, though not at all sure whether his patient was having hallucinations or acting out a part. He agreed to admit Riel under the cover name of Louis R. David—the surname Riel had given himself in deference to the great Jewish king. The treatment at the asylum was harsh—a visiting British alienist described it as "a chamber of horrors." Every time Riel challenged one of the "cures," he was punished by being strapped into a straitjacket. On one occasion, it took three men to bring him under control. Later, he was moved to a second asylum, near Quebec City, where he tore off his clothes and sometimes described himself as "Prophet, Infallible Pontiff, and Priest-King." Gradually, he became calmer, and the asylum chaplain reported to Bishop Taché that "he is beginning to forget his role as prophet." He concluded: "He isn't Pope any longer." Eventually, Riel seemed to recognize he had suffered delusions, saying he now laughed "at the proud hallucinations" of his mind. The doctor pronounced him cured, "more or less," and he was discharged in January 1878.

Riel's experiences in the two asylums persuaded him not to talk openly any more about his religious convictions. As he wrote later from Montana, "Alone amongst people who don't want to hear my ideas, I have to be silent and keep to myself the grandeur of my hope in God." As later events made apparent, however, none of this changed any of Riel's religious convictions. He was certain he had been assigned a "divine mission" to save both the Métis and the Catholic Church. In his vision, the two merged into one. The Métis were God's new chosen people, descended from the ancient Israelites. They would bring about the third kingdom of God, Métis Catholicism, following on from the kingdom of the Jews and then that of Roman Catholicism. Before that could happen, the Vatican had to leave corrupt Rome for Montreal, with Bishop Bourget becoming pontiff. Later, the papacy would move to its real home, in Manitoba. Riel knew this chronology because he was the "Prophet of the New World."

The most extensive study of Riel's religious ideas is Thomas Flanagan's highly original work *Louis "David" Riel: Prophet of the New World*. Flanagan paid Riel the compliment, which many commentators have avoided, of taking seriously that part of his life that meant the most to him. "Faced with the annihilation of his people's way of life," he wrote, "Louis Riel tried to create a new identity, a new life, and a new future. His insanity—if it may be called that—was a message of hope."

"Hope" was indeed what Riel brought to the Métis of the North-West, no matter how briefly. At that time, the condition of the Métis was in no way as painful as that of the Plains Indians: no Métis experienced starvation, and none were subject to the orders of Indian agents and farm instructors. Yet the Métis faced the same threat of "annihilation" as did the Indians. They too were in the process of being dispossessed by the new socio-economic order spreading across the West through the railway and the settlers.

In a certain sense, the Métis were more vulnerable. They were suspended between their dual heritages—Indian and European. They might call themselves a "New Nation," but no such status was recognized in Canada or the United States, or anywhere. The Indians, in contrast, possessed the special confidence of knowing they were the heirs to centuries of ancestors—a unique attribute that was recognized in treaties and reserves. However the new order might unfold, it was impossible to see any place in it for the Métis except as individuals—as people, but not as a people.

Riel possessed the intelligence to understand this situation, and from his time in the United States he had acquired considerable knowledge about the kind of future his people faced. The one remedy he could offer was the "hope" of a distinctive national church—the kind of covenant given by God to a chosen people. To outsiders, Riel's religious notions were fantastical, absurd, insane, but many Métis grasped his core intentions. A distinctive religion for the Métis would make them a distinctive people, in the same way that Judaism, for which he had immense respect, defined the Jews.

Perhaps it was all insane. But if insane, it was politically and operationally rational. Riel knew that the new socio-economic order was unstoppable and that the specific reason he had come north, to settle the Métis land claims, could at best make only a marginal difference to the condition of his people. Perhaps the source of Riel's insanity was really that he knew too much.

Besides a national Métis church, Riel wanted to create a new form of government that could preserve the Métis as a distinctive people—as a "New Nation," in their own phrase. He had first expressed this notion during the 1869–70 resistance at Red River, when he insisted that the Métis had the right to negotiate their terms of entry into Confederation. To Riel, the North-West belonged to the Métis and the Indians. Without their consent, Canada's possession of that area was illegal, no differently, from his perspective, than its original attempt to take over the North-West Territory in 1869 had been. Specifically, Riel came up with the idea that the Métis were entitled to a one-seventh share of the North-West Territory; within this space, they would be able to create an autonomous state with its own distinctive government.

Riel always played down these notions, because any suggestion of separation would have lost him the support of the white settlers he was courting. Included in the surviving papers of his secretary William Jackson, however, is a page with the notations "Petition Brit. Govt. to appoint Commit.[ee] & transfer Govt. to [Métis] Council. In case of refusal, declare Independence." This memo suggests strongly that Riel considered outright independence an option. Moreover, Riel would have known that his own Métis agreed with him. When the four Métis delegates invited Riel to come north with them in June 1884, they brought along a document which declared that Canada had "taken possession of the North-West Territories without the consent of the natives [Métis]," who possessed "an exclusive right to those lands, along with the Indians."

In his other book on the topic, *Riel and the Rebellion: 1885 Reconsidered*, Tom Flanagan provides the defining comment on this issue: "The concrete [land claims'] grievances of the Metis had become merely a means to these ends." While important, the Métis' land claims were not an existential issue, as they've often been portrayed. They had legitimate grievances with bureaucratic incompetence and with political indifference, the Toronto *Mail* later commenting shrewdly, "Had they [the Métis] had votes like white men . . . without doubt the wheels of office would have revolved for them." But, no differently from any settler, each Métis in the North-West could claim 160 acres under the Homestead Act and could later double the size of his lot, making it significantly more than the 240 acres they were seeking, as had been granted in Manitoba. And while they lacked "patents," or titles to their lots, squatters did have rights in the territories, and everywhere else. What Riel sought instead for his Métis was collective survival. A national church was one way to attain it. A "reserve," in the form of a one-seventh share of the entire territory, was another. There was, though, never any realistic chance that Riel could achieve either goal, or that he could frighten Macdonald into granting what he wanted by staging an uprising. If Riel's actions before he started the uprising, and even more after it had begun, were often strange and outright self-destructive, the reason may have been that he was too intelligent not to know how improbable was victory, politically as much as militarily.

Here may lie an answer to one of the great puzzles of the 1885 Rebellion.* Given the huge disparity in the forces, the rebellion was bound to be crushed. Gabriel Dumont recognized this from the

---

* The 1885 uprising is properly called a rebellion, unlike the uprising in 1869–70, because there was no question but that Canada was the legal owner of the North-West.

beginning. Yet he stood by Riel, not just to the final defeat but beyond it, attempting to rescue his leader from jail. Dumont's deference to Riel, an attitude sometimes held toward the well-educated by the illiterate, had to be a factor in his loyalty. A larger cause was, as Dumont later put it: "I had confidence in his faith and his prayers and that God would listen to him." To succeed, Riel needed a miracle. Since he was on a "divine mission," he must have counted on one. None came, though, and a great many died uselessly.In the judgment of most contemporary commentators, though, it is Riel who has emerged the moral winner. In one of his poems, some tantalizing lines suggest he sensed this might be the outcome of his confrontation with Macdonald: "And on you history will lay the blame. / I pine away in exile but remain / In spite of you my nation's true leader."

That one man had to lose and the other win was not the real tragedy in the confrontation between Macdonald and Riel. It was, rather, that the goals of each man were fundamentally the same. Macdonald's was to create a nation; Riel's was to save a nation. But there was not sufficient room in the country to accommodate both of their legitimate goals.

TWENTY-SEVEN

The One White Than Whom There Is No Higher

Two generations ago, historians wrote of European saints and Indian savages. In the last generation, too many scholars had been writing about Indian saints and European savages. The opportunity for our generation is to go beyond the calculus of saints and savages altogether.

David Hackett Fischer, *Champlain's Dream*

A case can be made that the single most important aspect of the North-West Rebellion in northern Saskatchewan was what *didn't* happen: the Indians did not join forces with Riel. A small number of Indians did rise up, though surprisingly few. Of these, all but a handful did so not as allies of Riel but for their own purposes and in their own way. If, instead, there had been a general uprising among the 25,000 or so Plains Indians as well as of the Métis, the consequences would have been a prolonged war, the loss of a great many lives, extensive destruction and a severe cost to the country. To suppress such an insurgency, Canada would almost certainly have been forced to appeal to London for military aid, and quite possibly to Washington as well.

Macdonald was well aware of the danger. In letters he wrote in the months between Riel's return in the summer of 1884 and the start of the spring rebellion, he refers often to the "risks of an Indian war." The possibility that the few hundred Métis of South

Branch would take up arms was to him little more than an annoyance. Once the crisis broke, though, he acted swiftly and decisively to reduce to the minimum any possibility of a widespread Indian uprising.

Yet the role the Indians played, or did not play, in this pivotal episode in Canadian history has received comparatively little attention. The only full descriptions are in *Prairie Fire*, by historians Bob Beal and Rod Macleod, and in *Loyal till Death*, by historians Bill Waiser and Blair Stonechild (himself an Aboriginal).* In effect, Riel has taken up all the oxygen in the room. What follows is an account, deliberately excluding the actions of Riel and the Métis, of the role of the Plains Indians before, during and after the North-West Rebellion of 1885.

~

The decisive event in the history of the Plains Indians during the last quarter of the nineteenth century was the vanishing of the buffalo almost to the point of extinction. This happened with terrifying and bewildering speed, over little more than a decade, a blink of an eye in the record of any people, from roughly the mid-1870s to the mid-1880s. In terms of biological catastrophes throughout the North and South American continents, no equivalent exists but for the collapse of the northern cod stocks of Newfoundland, which in the late 1980s and early 1990s dropped to just 1 per cent of their once vast scale.

Until this disaster occurred, the Plains Indians had enjoyed one of the highest standards of living of any Aboriginal people on

---

* In terms of effect on public opinion, the most influential work on the rebellion is the excellent graphic biography *Louis Riel*, by Chester Brown. In it, only one Indian appears—a minor character, and on only one page.

the continent—and higher than that of Scottish Highlanders or Irish peasants. The buffalo were the foundation for their way of life, these once near-limitless herds providing the Indians with a seemingly inexhaustible source of high-quality fresh meat and from which came long-lasting pemmican, as well as warm winter robes and teepees made from hides, water bottles from the animals' bladders and a host of bone artifacts ranging from needles to snowshoes. At the very same time that the buffalo were reduced to extinction by over-hunting, European Canadians began to move rapidly across the flat and treeless prairies in a way that hadn't been possible in the more challenging terrain of the eastern U.S. and Canada; right after them came railways, liquor supplies, towns, and weapons the Indians could never match. Virtually overnight, an entirely new, technology-based socio-economic order enveloped the Indians' way of life, threatening to send it the way of the buffalo.

Ottawa's response to the loss of the buffalo was to pressure Indians to take up farming on their reserves as the only way they could sustain themselves. The scale of the challenge the Indians faced was not understood then, nor is it easy to comprehend even in hindsight. In essence, the Plains Indians underwent a cultural catastrophe that encompassed every aspect of their lives—not just the material and political, but the social, the economic, the spiritual, the cultural, the psychological; each of these was either shattered or reduced to the redundant, the retrograde or, in the eyes of many outsiders, the comic. It is not easy to identify any people anywhere who have had to cope with so complete and swift an extinction of their way of life other than those defeated in war, occupied and reduced to slavery. Perhaps the best intellectual analysis of this transformational trauma is that by the American philosopher Jonathan Lear in his book *Radical Hope*. There, he explores the dimensions of a comment made by Chief Plenty Coups of the Crow Nation that, after the buffalo disappeared, "Nothing happened."

Chief Plenty Coups was saying that once the buffalo were gone, his people became like the living dead.* To compound the challenge, the Plains Indians were nomads, following the game as it moved. Everywhere, nomads, whether the Aboriginals of North America, the Aborigines of Australia, the Bedouin of North Africa or the Roma of Europe, have always been exceptionally resistant to modernization or to being remade into bourgeoisie.

For all of the country's Aboriginals, but most acutely for the Indians of the Plains, this is the great tragedy of Canadian history; and it is one that is not yet ended. Macdonald happened to be in office at the time when the disasters touched off by the disappearance of the buffalo were set in motion. It therefore became his responsibility to find palliatives that might, with great difficulty and only over considerable time, enable Aboriginal people to regain their centuries-old confidence and pride—to become again, as they had been for time immemorial, a free people, self-sufficient and at one with their environment.

Macdonald made many mistakes and paid far too little attention to his ministerial duties, principally because he was applying most of his time and energy to the railway—to *his* project, rather than to one inflicted on him. Yet, while clearly he could have done better, Macdonald was unquestionably the best available man for a task that, at its core, was near to impossible. So his involvement with the Indians—as with Riel and the Métis—became his tragedy.

---

* The nearest Canadian equivalent to Lear's book, *Radical Hope: Ethics in the Face of Cultural Devastation*, published in 2006, is the work of the Alberta writer Rudy Wiebe, most particularly his novel *The Temptations of Big Bear*, which Wiebe has described as "an imaginative report on our land."

Macdonald's attitudes towards Indians, and his policy prescriptions for them, derived from two sources. His formal Indian policy was essentially British Indian policy. While pre-eminently practical—to gain military allies, first against the French and then against the Americans—it was also remarkably enlightened. One major cause of the revolt by the Thirteen Colonies in 1763 was that the British redcoats prevented American colonists from stealing Indian lands. British Indian policy had two key facets: to protect Aboriginal people from destructive contact with settlers, and to civilize them, or to bring them up to the level of the newcomers in the way they lived and in their religious beliefs. Although idealistic, these two objectives directly contradicted each other, creating a tension left unchanged by later Canadian legislation such as the Gradual Civilization Act of 1857 (enacted by Macdonald) and the Indian Act of 1876 (enacted by the Mackenzie government).

The other source for Macdonald's Indian policy came from direct contact with the people themselves. Far more than any other public figure of the time, he knew Indians personally. As a young lawyer he had defended several in criminal cases and had sung in a local Mohawk choir. As was then most unusual, his early friends included mixed-bloods such as the Reverend Peter Jones (Kahkewaquonaby) and John Cuthbertson. He maintained this attitude all his life, sending his granddaughter, Daisy, to a school in Ottawa run by a Métisse, Abby Maria Harmon. As prime minister, he became a close friend of Canada's most successful Indian of the time, Peter Martin (Oronhyatekha), a medical doctor and founder of the Independent Order of Foresters who named his son John Alexander after him.*

---

* Despite the uniqueness of Macdonald's personal dealings with Indians and their far-reaching consequences, only one study has been done on the topic, Donald Smith's "John A. Macdonald and Aboriginal Canada," in *Historic Kingston*.

Macdonald knew more about Indian policy and the Indians themselves than any of his predecessors, or any of his successors until Jean Chrétien and Paul Martin a century later. He was superintendent general of Indian Affairs (its minister) for almost a decade, from 1879 to 1887; for much of that time he was also minister of the interior. Throughout his entire second term, he was responsible for the Mounted Police. In May 1881, Macdonald wrote to Edgar Dewdney, his top official in the West: "Indian matters and the land granting system form so great a portion of the general policy of the Government that I think it necessary for the First Minister, whoever he may be, to have that in his own hands."

On one occasion, Macdonald developed a policy initiative that, had it lasted, might have made a measurable difference to the evolution of relations between Canada's Aboriginals and its European population. His proposal was built on the premise that the two peoples had to trust each other. This small epiphany is a rare shaft of light in a long and bleak chronicle.

In February 1885, a month before the rebellion broke out, Macdonald put a Franchise Bill before Parliament. As one reform of the electoral system, he suggested a way both to "protect" Indians and to "civilize" them. Indians, he declared, should be granted the right to become enfranchised—to gain the vote and so become full citizens—but without, as in the past, having to give up in exchange any of their special rights as Aboriginals, either those gained by treaty or by the Indian Act. Opposition criticism was ferocious, one Liberal MP saying it would "bring a scalping party to the polls." Another called it Macdonald's "crowning act of rascality," claiming he was doing it only to win Indian votes. Macdonald's motives may not have been pure, but any votes he gained would have been more than cancelled by those of outraged western settlers. Despite a conspicuous absence of enthusiasm among Conservative MPs, Macdonald piloted the measure through successfully. In his major speech in May 1885, he advanced a deft argument. The runaway slaves who had come to Canada by the Underground Railway, he said, "although unaccustomed to freedom," got the vote as soon as they came to Canada—and no one had objected to that. The Indians, in contrast, "who had formerly owned the whole of this country, were prevented from sitting in the House and from voting for men to represent their interests there."

Macdonald didn't just enact the measure but continued to promote it. In August 1886, he wrote to an Indian leader, Peter Edmund Jones (the son of the famous Peter Jones), that his objective had been "to place [Indians] on a footing of equality with the white brethren." He assured Jones that the Franchise Act would not "affect or injure the rights secured by treaty or by the laws relating to the Red Men of the Dominion," and concluded, "I hope to see some day the Indian race represented by one of themselves on the floor of the House of Commons."

In fact, this measure lasted only to 1898, when it was scrapped by the Laurier government. One Liberal MP told the House then that it had been "an insult to the free white people of this country to place them on a level with pagan and barbarian Indians." It was not restored until 1960, by John Diefenbaker—by then too late to penetrate the walls of mistrust between Aboriginals and European Canadians.

This imaginative initiative has all but vanished from the Canadian historical record. It extended a kind of citizenship-plus to Indians, giving them a higher status than that enjoyed by European Canadians—if only to a small number, because like all others who possessed the vote, they had to own a minimum amount of property. Many chiefs opposed enfranchisement as a threat to their authority. Yet it is seldom mentioned, or it is described as applying only to the peaceable Indians in the East. The exact opposite was the case. After introducing the measure in the Commons in March

1885, by which time the rebellion had already begun, Macdonald was asked by the Opposition critic, David Mills, whether it would "include Indians in Manitoba and British Columbia." Macdonald answered, "Yes." Mills then asked, "Poundmaker and Big Bear?" referring to the chiefs of the most belligerent of the Indian bands. Again, Macdonald answered, "Yes." It was then that Mills made his "scalping party" comment. Only later did public outrage at a slaughter of whites by Indians cause Macdonald to yield to political necessity and limit the measure to eastern Indians.*

A number of Macdonald's more general comments about Aboriginal people at the time possessed this same uncommon understanding, especially in contrast to the prevailing opinions of his day. They too are all but absent from the historical record, despite being preserved in plain sight in the pages of Hansard. Macdonald's attitude to Aboriginal people can be compared to the views about French Canadians he expressed back in 1854—that if they were treated "as a nation," they would respond "as a free people usually do, generously."†

Debates of substance about Indian affairs were rare in the House of Commons, because almost no Aboriginals had the vote. The government's attempts to convince the Plains Indians to change from hunters to farmers, however, roused considerable interest and criticism among MPs, especially the program that provided agricultural implements, farm instructors and some supplies of basic foods to

* The one reasonably extended account is in Olive Dickason's *Canada's First Nations*, in which she writes admiringly, "It speaks volumes for Macdonald's political expertise that he was able to get the bill passed."

† The full text of Macdonald's expression of opinion about relations with French Canadians is contained in volume one of this biography, pages 128–29.

help Indians on reserves make the transition to farming. Complaints about costs were incessant. Opposition critic Mills said that Macdonald's food policy was "tending to make the Indians a dependent population instead of civilizing them and making them more self-reliant," while Edward Blake, the party leader, warned, "We are training the Indians to look to us for aid . . . [and] teaching them to rely on us for everything."

In 1880, a new Department of Indian Affairs was established, with Macdonald as its minister. He spoke twice that session, once on April 23 on the department's spending estimates, and again on May 5. He made three cardinal points: that Indians possessed certain inalienable rights; that they were not whites, and in a fundamental sense never would be; and that successful change would take many decades. About the key issue of special rights for Indians, he was explicit. In theory, he said, it could be argued that it would be better if the Indians were assimilated and "disappear[ed] from the continent," so "the Indian question would cease to exist."* But, he continued, "We must remember that they are the original owners of the soil, of which they have been dispossessed by the covetousness or ambition of our ancestors. Perhaps if Columbus had not discovered this continent—had left them alone—they would have worked out a tolerable civilization of their own." The only certainty was that "the Indians have been the great sufferers by the discovery of America and the transfer to it of a large white population."

Macdonald doubted that assimilation would ever succeed. He agreed that a small number of Indians had made a successful transition to white society, but "the exception proves the rule." Specifically, he rejected the U.S. policy of encouraging assimilation

* It's worth noting that Macdonald used the phrase "Indian question" rather than "Indian problem," as was common then and for decades afterwards.

by allowing Indians to own outright a personal share of reservation land rather than all of it being owned collectively. The consequence would be, he said, that "the Indian gets his deed and by some injurious or unfortunate process sells or leases his land and becomes a vagrant without property." Instead, said Macdonald, he accepted the general rule "that you cannot make an Indian a white man." The source for this belief, he said, was an Indian chief, who had told him, "We are the wild animals; you cannot make an ox out of a deer"—or, as Macdonald rephrased it, "You cannot make an agriculturalist out of an Indian."*

In a later intervention in the Commons in 1885, Macdonald provided his estimate of how long it would take for Indians to reach the stage when they would be able to blend in with whites while still remaining Indian. "There is only one way, patience, patience, patience," he said. "In the course of ages—it is a slow process—they will be absorbed in the country. You must treat them, and our children and our grand-children and our great grand-children, must treat them in the same way, until, in the course of ages, they are absorbed in the general population." At the time this commentary is being written, one direct great-great-grandson of Macdonald, now in his nineties, survives. His great-great-grandfather had it just about right.

Unfortunately, Macdonald's understanding of Aboriginal people was not translated into effective action. An opportunity did exist, but only briefly. The buffalo disappeared far faster than anyone

---

* Here, Macdonald was quoting almost word for word a comment made to him forty years earlier by an Anglican clergymen, who had in turn heard it from the chief of an Indian reserve where he was serving.

had anticipated, and the difficulty of teaching warriors and hunters to settle for being farmers proved to be formidable. Farm instructors often turned out to be failed farmers themselves, and the Indians, accustomed to "country food" they had shot or trapped themselves, found processed food such as bacon almost inedible. It was excruciatingly difficult for Aboriginals, for centuries warriors and hunters, to abandon all that to become sedentary farmers scraping at the soil. The government, like all administrations in its day, had no notion that it should subsidize the indigent and unemployed. Macdonald shared fully the prevailing fear of creating a permanently dependent underclass. So he vacillated, temporized and clung to the hope that things would somehow sort themselves out.

They didn't. As early as 1879, an Oblate missionary to the Blackfoot reported that many on his reserve had been reduced to "eat[ing] the flesh of poisoned wolves" and that some parents were sleeping in the open in below-zero temperatures to escape the constant crying of their children, for whom they could do nothing. An 1882 study by a Mounted Police officer described one Cree band as "literally in a starving condition and destitute." One winter, a large gathering of Indians near the Mounted Police outpost at Fort Walsh survived only because the policemen shared their own rations with them. The next year, the department closed Fort Walsh. After Lawrence Vankoughnet, Macdonald's departmental deputy minister, toured the desperate region in 1882, he imposed a series of spending cuts, including laying off many of the farm instructors.

Macdonald knew what was going on. Edgar Dewdney sent him an accurate description of some 1,300 Indians near Calgary being "in a very destitute condition and many on the verge of starvation." Thomas White, the able editor of the Montreal *Gazette*, whom Macdonald would soon appoint minister of the interior, advised him that many Indians now believed that "the treaties are

Despite the tensions, misunderstandings and failures, the North-West Mounted Police retained the trust of a great many of the Plains Indians, but after the uprising, this relationship was never the same again.

made simply as a means of getting possession of the country." Thereafter, the Indians of the Plains endured what became known as the Great Famine. Three Cree chiefs, all known as moderates, sent Macdonald a despairing appeal: "If we must die by violence, let it be done quickly," they wrote.

But Macdonald continued along his ambivalent path. Although his department's unofficial operating slogan was "work or starve," he admitted the obvious truth that "we cannot in conscience let them starve." One year, he claimed that the transition to farming was succeeding; the next year, he admitted the progress had been illusory. He proclaimed that his officials were "doing all they can, by refusing food until the Indians are on the verge of starvation, to reduce the expense." But he also told MPs, "It is better to feed them than to fight them." Western opinion pressed down on him, and the *Saskatchewan Herald* complained that the Indians were being "encouraged to believe that the Government would do everything for them."

The suffering was real and widespread. The number of Plains Indians declined—from about 32,000 in 1880 to some 20,000 five years later, according to Blair Stonechild, though this annual death rate of nearly 10 per cent seems high. The principal cause of Indian deaths was European diseases such as smallpox, scarlet fever and whooping cough. The shortage of warm winter clothing due to the lack of buffalo robes was also a factor, as was the effect of "multiple insanitation," in the phrase of one missionary, caused by the exchange of well-aired teepees for closed huts on the reserve. And without doubt some young Indian males simply lost the will to live in a world where no opportunities existed to prove their manhood. All things considered, as Beal and Macleod point out in *Prairie Fire*, "The policy the North-West Indians so detested was not so much a policy of John A. Macdonald's government as it was a policy of the Canadian people."

Public opinion indeed played a major part in the government's behaviour. Quite unlike Canadians today, nineteenth-century Canadians felt no guilt about their country's treatment of Indians. Rather, they felt great pride in Canada's policy and practice; and they were quite right to do so.

At this time, Canadian Indian policy was far superior, in effectiveness and sensitivity, to American Indian policy. As the Halifax *Chronicle* put it, the policy and treatment here were "humane and successful," while in the United States the approach was of "war and extermination." The *Globe* similarly described American policy as "a dark record of broken pledges, undisguised oppression and triumphant cruelty." A great many Americans thought exactly the same way. A report to the House Committee on Indian Affairs concluded admiringly that Canadians would be "known in history as having striven to do justice to the aborigines," and a study for the U.S. Board of Indian Commissioners described Canada's system as "immeasurably superior to our own."

Most important, Indians agreed. Their name for the border was the Medicine Line, meaning that above it there was healing. Except for the Loyalists, all the major moves of population north into Canada were by Indians, beginning with the Six Nations and followed by groups such as the Potawatomis, Chippewas and Ottawas. The most recent arrival was Sitting Bull, who, after his victory over General Custer at Little Bighorn in 1876, led his warriors across the border because they would be safe there, protected by the law and the North-West Mounted Police.

Today, by contrast, it's quite possible that American Indians are in the better state. Contemporary cross-border comparisons are curiously difficult to find, but a 1988 study by the Lakehead Centre for Northern Studies in Thunder Bay found that the health and education levels of Canadian Indians were "considerably lower" than of their American counterparts, as were the numbers of them in the labour force. In other words, in Canada many more Indians, proportionately, were imprisoned in the dependency trap.*

The results of any nineteenth-century cross-border comparison would have been quite different. The defining difference was that Canadians did not kill Indians; in the course of the nineteenth century, some forty thousand American Indians were killed, principally by the U.S. Army of the West; above the Medicine Line, the only deaths were the small number killed during the North-West Rebellion. The difference can largely be attributed to the Mounted Police, who arrested many more whites than Indians—the exact

* Among specifics, the Lakehead Centre found that only 26 per cent of Indians here were high school graduates, compared to 55 per cent in the United States, and that the infant mortality rate was almost twice as high (19 per cent to 10 per cent).

opposite of the situation below the border. Not until 1879 was an Indian here arrested for the murder of a white. The police suppressed the liquor trade, which had devastated Aboriginal people below the border.

At the level of official policy in the United States, the "removal" of Indians from land ceded to them as reservations under treaties went on continually. In Canada, in contrast, Macdonald told an inquirer as early as 1867 that Indian reserves "cannot be dispossessed nor can the property be alienated from them without their consent." He responded the same way in the middle of the North-West Rebellion, informing a correspondent that although "Indian reservations will prove to a certain extent obstructive of settlement . . . this cannot be helped." It was his duty, he said, "to protect the Indians and sustain them in their rights."

Personal attitudes really expressed the difference on each side of the Medicine Line. In Canada, few would have said, as did General Philip Sheridan, the commander of the U.S. Army of the West, "The only good Indian is a dead Indian."* In the United States, no Indian said, as did Chief Crowfoot of the Blackfoot, that he had decided to take treaty in 1877 because "The Police have protected us as the feathers of the bird protect it from the frosts of winter." Some differences were less agreeable. In the United States a strong pro-Indian lobby existed, severely criticizing governments for the "removal" of Indians from land they possessed in law and for the widespread corruption in the Department of the Interior. In Canada, debate of any kind, let alone criticism, was rare. As a result, once Canadians were in a mood to give up the high ground, they did so quickly—and silently.

---

* General Sheridan's actual original comment was "The only good Indians I ever saw were dead."

At this traumatic time in their history, the Indians of the Plains possessed one priceless asset other than their own extraordinary stoicism and capacity for endurance. They had three exceptional leaders—the Cree chiefs Big Bear (Mistahimaskwa) and Poundmaker (Pihtokahanapiwiyin or Pitikwahanapiwiyin) and the Blackfoot chief Crowfoot (Isapo-Muxika). To step sideways into counterfactual history, or might-have-beens, it's impossible not to wonder what might have happened had these three ever been able to talk directly to Macdonald about what was going on, and whether, as a result, the historical record just might have been greatly changed.

Of the trio, two, Poundmaker and Big Bear, can usefully be described here, with the portrait of Crowfoot reserved for later. In the view of the Toronto *Mail*, Poundmaker resembled one of James Fenimore Cooper's "noble-looking" heroes with "black and piercing eyes." A white friend, a schoolteacher, remarked that "his bearing was so eminently dignified and his speech so well adapted to the occasion as to impress every hearer." Poundmaker's particular qualities, besides his record as a warrior, were those of eloquence and intelligence. He made his first appearance in history during the negotiation of a treaty with most of the Cree leaders at Fort Carlton in 1876, discomfiting the Canadian team by bursting out, "This is our land. It isn't a piece of pemmican to be cut up and given in little pieces back to us." Most of the Cree leaders agreed to sign the treaty after securing a pledge that a medicine chest would be stationed on each reserve and a written promise of food rations should "any pestilence or general famine occur"; Poundmaker likewise signed, but refused to settle on any reserve for three years, because, as he said, he could not see how he would be able "to clothe my people and feed them as long as the sun shines and the waters flow." An encounter with Governor General

During this time in their history, by far the hardest ever, the Indians of the Plains had one priceless asset: three exceptional chiefs (clockwise, from top left), the Cree leaders Poundmaker and Big Bear, and Crowfoot of the Blackfoot. The odds against them were still too long to be overcome.

Lorne, who was touring the West, changed his mind. During their long talks, Lorne was amazed to discover that rather than telling him about war-making and hunting, Poundmaker held him captivated by his commentaries on politics and on spiritual matters. In turn, Poundmaker came to recognize, as he told his people, "the whites will fill the country. . . . It is useless to dream that we can frighten them, that time is passed." He now chose a reserve, in northern Saskatchewan, and made a serious attempt at farming; it did well briefly but then failed. Thereafter, he and his band endured the Great Famine.

Big Bear was like Poundmaker in some ways, in others quite different. He most certainly was not noble-looking, but rather was short, wrinkled and plain ugly. Neither, although a superb horseman, did Big Bear have a record as a warrior. He was, though, unusually intelligent, and in particular possessed of exceptional cunning. Dewdney's impression of him was of "a very independent character, self-reliant and appears to know how to make his living without begging from government." A white friend described him as gifted, with "a keen intellect, a fine sense of humour, quick perception and splendid powers of expression, and great strength of purpose." One of Big Bear's most highly respected skills was his ability to read dreams. His own most powerful dream concerned his going out to hunt buffalo and spotting a coyote that was laughing at him. Looking more closely, he realized that the coyote was laughing not at him but at a prairie lily from which was spouting a fountain of blood that soon covered the earth around. The vision Big Bear was recounting was of what lay ahead for the Cree.

To avoid that fate for his people, Big Bear came up with an idea that conceivably might have changed the course of history: that his people should "not fight the Queen with guns. We should fight her with her own laws."

In March 1884, the *Saskatchewan Herald* carried an intriguing story. It was that Big Bear had "conversed with many of the chief officers of Indian Affairs, but had found that none seems to be 'the head'—there is always one higher. To settle who this higher power is has now become the one object of his life. . . . If there is a head to the Department, he is bound to find him, for he will deal with no one else." That summer, Big Bear convened a grand council of the Cree, and after long discussions about the government's failure to provide rations and farm implements, he told the chiefs, "What I see is this: I speak for my band as a Chief speaks for his People, but the White agent I speak to isn't like that. There is always someone higher behind him whom I never see. I say: who wastes a bullet on a tail when he knows at another end the bear's teeth are waiting?" Instead, said Big Bear, "It is time to talk to that one White than whom there is no higher."

Macdonald, of course, was the person "than whom there is no higher." Yet no meeting between him and these three Aboriginal leaders of quite uncommon ability was ever held. Even had it been, it is most unlikely anything would have been accomplished. Macdonald was old and tired, and his gaze was fixed firmly on the railway. Nor is there any certainty the chiefs would have risen to the occasion, Indian decision-making being convoluted and protracted. All that can be stated with certainty is that Crowfoot, the one member of the trio who maintained close relations with Macdonald, ended his life deeply disillusioned at how little he had been able to do for his people. Nevertheless, had the highest representatives of both these two founding peoples ever talked to each other, the chiefs might have learned something—and so might Macdonald.

As the 1880s wore on, evidence accumulated that large numbers of Plains Indians were indeed suffering severe hunger, and at times outright starvation. The department's principal response continued to be denial. "The Government is doing much to assist [the Indian]," Dewdney reported to Ottawa, adding, hopefully, "After a sharp trial, during which they will doubtless be not a little suffering, let us hope that the crisis will be overcome."

Macdonald remained as erratic as ever. In 1884, he tried to have it both ways, telling MPs, "The Indian will always grumble, they will never be satisfied . . . if there is an error, it is in exceedingly large supply being furnished to the Indians." He was now in full Old Tomorrow mode. His interest was directed principally at what Riel was up to. By September 1884, he had become concerned enough to tell the comptroller of the Mounted Police, "It would appear that the situation is getting serious . . . with these warnings it would be criminal negligence not to take every precaution."

In fact, trouble had already begun—but among the Indians. One Indian agent was horsewhipped by a Cree for refusing to distribute rations, and another was stabbed. On Poundmaker's reserve, a standoff between militant braves and policemen came to the brink of a general riot. By February 1885, Hayter Reed, the most hardline senior officer in the department, was warning Macdonald that the Indians were "beginning to look up to [Riel] as the one who will be the means of curing all their ills and of obtaining all their demands." A Métis-Indian uprising was now a real possibility.

TWENTY-EIGHT

A Defiant, Doomed Gesture

You must have known that in taking up arms we should be beaten.

Gabriel Dumont to Riel after the Battle of Batoche

Not until December 19, 1884, did Louis Riel at last dispatch to Ottawa his petition about the South Branch Métis land grievances. Of all the documents associated with the rebellion, this one is the most puzzling. Nowhere does it contain Riel's own name or signature. The only author identified is Riel's assistant, William Jackson, who in a covering letter described himself as "Secretary, General Committee."

The Métis land grievances, the issue that had brought Riel northwards, were addressed in just two single-sentence paragraphs in the petition. Everything else either was of interest only to white settlers or concerned general political issues relating to the North-West. The only points raised on behalf of the Métis were: "That the Half-breeds of the Territory have not received 240 acres of land each, as did the Manitoba Half-breeds"; and "That the Half-breeds who are in possession of tracts of land have not received patents [titles] therefore."

That was it, although one other paragraph called for more food supplies to be provided to the Indians. After six months in the making, the document was extraordinarily skimpy: it advanced no new arguments about Métis land claims. Most astonishingly, it made no mention of the issue that most agitated the Métis—confirmation of their traditional Quebec-style lots, long and narrow and extending to the riverbanks.

It is fair to question just how much of the petition Riel actually wrote himself. The text sounds rather like Jackson, a political and naïve radical: it declares that "settlers are exposed to coercion at elections" and that the territory needed free trade, representation in the federal Parliament and a railway to Hudson Bay. Further, Jackson commented provocatively in his covering letter that consideration had been given to sending the petition to "the Privy Council of England . . . rather than the federal authorities," as though Britain could tell Canada what to do within its borders. All in all, the document was more a grandiloquent political manifesto than a petition seeking redress of land grievances.

The consequence in Ottawa was confusion. When he was asked later in the Commons whether he had received Riel's petition, Macdonald answered, "The Bill of Rights had never been officially or in any way promulgated so far as we know, and transmitted to the government."* This response was not evasion but a genuine misunderstanding—by this time, Riel and Jackson were known to be working on a Bill of Rights, though it was never completed. Mostly, the petition conveyed the impression that Riel, under Jackson's influence, was trying to forge some kind of alliance with the settlers.

---

* To increase the confusion, the document sent to Ottawa carried the title "Petition of Rights."

Initially, Macdonald responded relatively speedily. He acknowledged the petition immediately, a formality Jackson misinterpreted as evidence that a satisfactory answer would follow. Macdonald put the key question before the cabinet—whether the territory's land policy should be changed to allow the South Branch Métis to make land claims similar to those granted in Manitoba. In that province, many Métis had sold their scrip to speculators at sums far below its value. Macdonald told Governor General Lord Lansdowne in disgust: "The scrip is sold to the sharks and spent in whiskey." Despite his own misgivings, however, he secured cabinet agreement for a settlement similar to the terms in Manitoba.

But Macdonald bungled the delivery of this message. On January 28, 1885, the news was sent from Ottawa to Lieutenant-Governor Edgar Dewdney that the government would set up a Half-Breed Commission "with a view of settling equitably the claims of half-breeds." This commission did eventually do some useful work, but the announcement was written in near-incomprehensible bureaucratese. When he was asked in the Commons what action he was taking, Macdonald was needlessly provocative, explaining to MPs that he had agreed to the commission "with the greatest reluctance," but "at the last moment I yielded and I said [to the cabinet]: 'Well, for God's sake, let them have the scrip; they will either drink it or waste it or sell it, but let us have peace.'" To compound his apparent indifference, Macdonald did not get around to selecting the members of the commission until mid-March.

Most damaging of all, no notice of the announcement was sent to Riel. Instead, it went to Dewdney, who forwarded it to a local politician, who passed it on to Charles Nolin, a moderate Métis, who at last, on February 8, handed over a copy to Riel.

Understandably, Riel interpreted this roundabout route as an attempt to circumvent him. After reading the document, he said angrily to the Métis, "In 40 days, Ottawa will have my answer"—a span of time that matched the period of Christ's withdrawal into the desert.

This accounting of the events differs substantially from the traditional victim/oppressor version, which holds that Riel's petition was treated with contemptuous indifference by Ottawa, inciting him to a rebellion he might not otherwise have initiated. The principal source for this alternative analysis is Thomas Flanagan's *Riel and the Rebellion: 1885 Reconsidered.* There, Flanagan wrote, "The North-West Rebellion was as much a religious movement as a political uprising." He argued that "the Metis' grievances were at least partly of their own making" and that the government "was on the verge of resolving them when the Rebellion broke out." He also questioned whether Riel was motivated by "disinterested idealism" or by self-interest in securing a settlement of his personal finances as part of an overall settlement with the government.*

Both the traditional and the revisionist versions contain elements of the truth. It's difficult to disagree with Flanagan on his key point that by this time Riel's religious convictions took precedence over everything else, including the Métis' land claims. He was right also to note that Macdonald was, belatedly, taking action to address these claims. But his conclusion that Riel was prompted as much by his personal financial interests (although these certainly existed) is highly improbable. Riel may have misled the Métis, but he would not have cheated them.

Riel was most certainly still obsessed with the future of his people. But his focus had shifted. He was primarily concerned

---

* This revisionist analysis provoked claims that Flanagan was a racist—and even demands for his dismissal from the University of Calgary.

now with their religious future—the realization of the "divine mission" assigned to him by God via Bishop Bourget. Riel also saw the Métis' future not so much in terms of additional land for individuals as in some kind of reserve in the North-West. One comment in Jackson's covering letter is particularly revealing: he called on Ottawa to negotiate the North-West's "entry into Confederation." Riel believed that the survival of the Métis as a people could be achieved only by their securing a sort of self-governing reserve, one comparable to, but with greater autonomy than, the reserves of the Indians. In contemporary parlance, he seems to have had in mind some form of a distinct society, even of sovereignty-association, terms and concepts that of course did not then exist.

In Ottawa, the prevailing view, expressed repeatedly by Macdonald, was that the Métis could identify themselves either as whites or as Indians, but they could not claim the privileges of both groups. Nor was it easy to imagine how a reserve for the Métis could actually work; Father Albert Lacombe, the much-loved missionary to the Blackfoot, attempted to create one later in Alberta, but it attracted few Métis and was soon closed. The painful truth was that with the buffalo gone, the Métis could not avoid coming to terms with the new socio-economic and technological order—with, for instance, the railway and steamships already taking away many of their traditional jobs as teamsters and boatmen. Lastly, the notion of a Métis-settler alliance of some kind was quite unrealistic. While enraged that the CPR's decision to shift its line to the south had severely damaged the economy of northern Saskatchewan, the settlers would never have marched with the Métis in rebellion against their own government. Riel must have known he was seeking the impossible. Yet he possessed still one indomitable sustaining force—the depth and intensity of his religious convictions.

A critical difference between Riel's 1869 to 1870 resistance and his rebellion of 1885 was that the priests were no longer with him. Father Alexis André, well-liked by the Métis, regarded Riel's religious views, such as that the Vatican should leave Rome for Canada, as those of an outright heretic.

Once in South Branch, Riel became a changed man. Earlier, in the asylums in Quebec and during his time in Montana, he had stopped talking about his "divine mission" because people laughed at him. In South Branch, no Métis laughed, though some surely did so in private openly. He had, now, a congregation that believed in him. As early as September 1884, the local bishop, Vital Grandin, was warning that Riel had become to the Métis "a saint; I would say rather a kind of God." The local missionaries were deeply shocked. Their disbelief only reinforced Riel's certitude. "I had terrible struggles with him, and I aroused his anger so much he lost all control of himself," Father André later recalled, adding, "He became in those moments truly a maniac, twisting himself into contortions in a rage." André tried to warn Riel that his way "could only end in war, that it would bring down on them all sorts of evils and cover the country with ruin and blood." To Riel, certain he was doing what God wanted him to do, a solution to the apparent impossibility did exist. Should it be necessary, God would work a miracle for him.

Macdonald never gave any indication he took seriously the reports reaching him about Riel's all-consuming religiosity; his likeliest response would have been to dismiss them as evidence of another incomprehensible squabble among Catholics. The reports he did take seriously were those claiming Riel was asking to be bribed so he could quit and go home.

The source for these reports was Father André, who quarrelled constantly with Riel about religion and told the "veritable fanatic" that his views about the Catholic Church and the Pope moving from Rome to the North-West were heresies. When André got the Métis leader talking about subjects other than religion, he noticed that Riel kept referring to his personal financial claims, saying he was worried about his family's needs (his wife was pregnant with their third child). Among Riel's claims were the original 240 acres awarded in 1870 to all the Métis in Manitoba, as well as some other land claims he believed he was entitled to as compensation for expenses he'd incurred while helping to bring Manitoba and the North-West Territories into Confederation.

At a meeting on December 23, André asked Riel outright whether, if the government met his terms, Riel might in exchange return to Montana. Afterwards, André wrote to Dewdney urging him to let Macdonald know that "$3,000 to $5,000 would cart the whole family across the border." A local politician present at the meeting corroborated this discussion, claiming that Riel had said that if the government would "pay him a certain amount in settlement of these claims he would arrange to make his illiterate and unreasoning followers well satisfied with almost any settlement of their claims for land." The tone of these reports indicates that André and his companion were telling Macdonald not so much what they had heard but what they had wanted to hear. In fact, Riel had never concealed from the Métis his personal financial claims, and none of them ever accused him of false motives.

Macdonald himself thought otherwise. He told the Commons, "I believe he came in for the purpose of attempting to extract money from the public purse." He added dismissively, "Of course that could not be entertained for a moment." Ever since Riel had slipped back into Canada after being sent money to stay in the

United States, Macdonald had become personally hostile to him, his attitude gradually hardening into outright contempt.

After it was all over, George Denison, the old Canada Firster turned passionate imperialist, wrote in exasperation, "The whole dispute was mainly about some red tape regulations as to surveying some forty or fifty thousand acres of land on which people were already settled . . . [this] in a wilderness of tens of millions of acres." A finagling of the regulations, thus, could have saved the country a great deal of blood and treasure. This escape-hatch was never resorted to, however, for two reasons: Riel had succumbed to religious zealotry, and Macdonald had forgotten his ruling maxim: "A public man should have no resentments."

The most distinctive attribute about the rebellion was that its outcome was inevitable from the start. Riel's strategy, to use that term loosely, was to repeat exactly what he had done in 1869–70: proclaim a provisional government, seize hostages for bargaining purposes and avoid causing casualties so the government could negotiate with him. He realized, although never admitting it, that the execution of Thomas Scott had been a terrible mistake. The circumstances in 1885, however, were utterly different. This time, no priests or American annexationists were on his side, and the English Métis, though supportive, had no intention of taking up arms. This time, insurgents would no longer be resisting outside interference but rebelling against a legitimate government. Most critically, a railway over which troops could be rushed to the West was now close to completion.

Riel did have one asset he had lacked before. Beside him now was Gabriel Dumont—a man who inspired admiration, even love, from almost all who met him. At forty-eight, he was stocky, bull-shouldered, handsome, with long hair like an Indian. He was open, generous and fearless. As a hunter, he had few equals—he was a superb shot, an outstanding horseman and, rare on the prairies, an exceptional swimmer. Sam Steele, the celebrated Mounted Police officer, said Dumont knew the prairies "as a housewife knows her kitchen"; he could always find the buffalo and "always brought them down."

Dumont's admiration for Riel was absolute, and he was himself a passionate Métis nationalist. He believed fervently in Riel's religious beliefs, saying, "God would listen to his prayers." (Riel also impressed him by being able to beat him at billiards, Dumont's greatest passion after gambling.) The Métis looked up to him as a warrior-prince, and the Indians held him in awe. His personal appeal even attracted some Indians, though still very few, to the Métis side. Riel, though, all but threw away this priceless asset. Dumont wanted to wage a guerrilla war, harassing the army as it approached, especially at night. But Riel was convinced that if no casualties occurred, the government would negotiate with him. "Mine was the better plan," Dumont said, after it was all over. Unquestionably, he was right.

In every respect but one, Riel's position in 1885 was incomparably weaker than it had been in Red River. The advantage: Gabriel Dumont, a natural guerrilla fighter. But Riel never made use of this asset until it was too late.

Above all, Riel still possessed his direct connection to God. Despite Father André's protestations, he became increasingly explicit about his beliefs. He was "a prophet of the New World"; a sacred king; a descendent of Saint Louis, the king of France, who would defeat the forces of evil in the world. His piety became ever more embracing. At one all-night wedding, while the guests danced and enjoyed their refreshments, Riel spent the night upstairs on his knees praying. He developed a special diet consisting of milk, vegetables and cooked blood. His personal vanity became ever more pronounced: in his diary, he described himself as "unusually wise and farsighted," with an intelligence "far above any other."

On February 24, a community meeting was held at the church in Batoche to discuss the government's announcement of the land claims commission. Riel told the gathering he had done all he could by sending in the petition and would now return to the United States. The entire congregation roared back, "No, No." After promising to stay, Riel asked, "And the consequences?" Back came the unanimous response: "We will suffer the consequences." At a meeting on March 5, Dumont and ten others signed an oath to "save our country from a wicked government by taking up arms." Then the whole audience joined in prayer. By mid-March, Riel had welded together Métis nationalism and his religious vision into an indissoluble whole.

The actual rebellion began on March 18, exactly forty days after Riel first read the government announcement. He sent armed Métis to a store in Batoche to seize arms and ammunition, and later imprisoned hostages. He proclaimed that he had decided to divide the North-West into seven parts, one for the Métis, the others for nations such as the Irish, Germans and Italians. When a priest rebuked him, Riel silenced him, declaring, "Rome has fallen." He created a provisional government, calling it "Exovedate"—a Latinized word of his own invention, meaning "from out of the flock." The Exovedate's first act was to proclaim Riel "a prophet in the service of Jesus Christ." Later, it renamed the days of the week—Monday, for instance, became Christ Aurore. Throughout the rebellion, the Exovedate concerned itself almost entirely with religious matters rather than the prosecution of the insurgency. The outcome of the rebellion depended now, not on Riel and Dumont, or Macdonald and General Frederick Middleton, a British officer and commander of Canada's militia, but on God.

It has been said that the best-planned war strategy never lasts longer than the first encounter with the enemy. Riel's plan to take up arms but not inflict any casualties lasted less than a week. Soon after the rebellion began, a report reached Batoche that a force of five hundred Mounted Policemen was marching on the community to arrest Riel. In fact, no such scheme existed; rather, fifty policemen and an equal number of local militia, commanded by Superintendent Leif Crozier, had moved from Fort Carlton, an old Hudson's Bay Company post, to be nearer to the South Branch district. In response, Riel and Dumont set out with several hundred Métis for Fort Carlton. The two groups met at the hamlet of Duck Lake. There, misunderstandings occurred, tempers flared and a few shots were fired. By the time it was over, twelve members of Crozier's force were dead and five Métis. Crozier retreated with his wounded, first to Fort Carlton and then to Battleford. Fearing a follow-up attack from the Métis, the police and townspeople barricaded themselves into the local barracks.

The Métis had scored a considerable victory, but Riel's strategy had been undone by the spilling of blood. So he temporized. Dumont wanted to pursue Crozier and ambush him, then go on to Fort Carlton and seize its stores. Riel insisted that they turn around and return to Batoche—and there the Métis stayed for almost the full duration of the rebellion. Riel was now conducting a contradiction in terms—a rebellion that sat on its hands. Worse, he had failed to take account of the changed military dynamic created by the nearly completed railway. Most self-defeating of all, he was gravely underestimating Macdonald.

The rebellion had not surprised Macdonald. He had government informers in South Branch, and Superintendent Crozier had sent a warning five days before Riel's call to arms: "Half-breed rebellion likely to break out any moment. . . . If Half-breeds rise, Indians will join them."

Macdonald was now performing at his best. On March 23, even before the bad news from Duck Lake came in, he wired Edgar Dewdney in cipher: "General Middleton proceeds to Red River tonight. Orders sent to Winnipeg militia to be ready to move." Macdonald followed with a second telegram, which he transmitted openly: "The land claims of the half-breeds are to be adjusted without delay. A Commission is to proceed to the spot immediately." A few days later, he telegraphed Father Albert Lacombe, urging him to call on Chief Crowfoot to make certain the Blackfoot would remain loyal. Lacombe made the visit, and the militarily formidable Blackfoot remained quiet. One reason for their passivity was that, the previous summer, Dewdney had arranged for Crowfoot and other Blackfoot Confederacy chiefs to go by train to Winnipeg, where they saw for the first time the size and technological abundance of the coming new order. As additional countermeasures, extra rations were suddenly made available to the Blackfoot and to several Cree bands—a step that could have been taken much earlier.

In fact, prompted by some instinctive sense of the scale of the challenge coming down on him, Macdonald had snapped out of

Canadian Pacific Railway Co
24 collect
WESTERN DIVISION.
The following message received at C *Time* 8.45P *M.*
By Telegraph from Blackfoot Crossing
Date 30th 1885
To Sir John Macdonald
Ottawa
I have seen Crowfoot & all the Blackfeet all quiet promised me to be loyal no matter how the things may turn Elsewhere
Father Lacombe

Once the rebellion actually began, Macdonald acted swiftly and decisively. One of his best moves was to get Father Lacombe, a much-loved missionary, to convince Chief Crowfoot to remain neutral. Lacombe soon wired back that the militarily formidable Blackfoot would "be loyal."

his Old Tomorrow mode even earlier. In February, he had introduced into the Commons a Franchise Bill that he would call "the greatest triumph of my life." It was no such thing, but it had the useful objective of making the federal government, rather than the provinces, responsible for the administration of federal elections. As an added benefit, a great swatch of provincial patronage, such as the appointment of returning officers, would now be the property of the federal government—in other words, of Macdonald. Embedded in the bill were two imaginative initiatives: the first, already described, extended to Indians the right to be able to vote without losing any of their other rights; the second, an idea then unique in the world, proposed to extend the vote to women.

That same month, Macdonald had to deal with the possibility of having to send troops abroad. When the dramatic news reached Canada that Sudanese followers of the Mahdi had stormed Khartoum and killed General Charles Gordon after a year-long siege, it unleashed across Canada a tidal wave of feeling for the Empire. To add to the pressure, Australia and New Zealand voluntarily announced that they would send troops to support the British. But Macdonald sent no troops. "England is not at war," he explained to Charles Tupper, the Canadian high commissioner in London, "but is merely helping the Khedive [of Egypt] to put down an insurrection[,] and now that Gordon is gone the motive of aiding in the rescue of our own countrymen is gone with him."

One more challenge Macdonald had to confront came from British Columbia. For several years, the BC government and its MPs in Ottawa had been demanding action to halt the influx of workers from China. Macdonald stalled, arguing that in the absence of a large local population the CPR line could only be completed by outside workers in that province. He kept disallowing acts passed by the BC government to ban the employment of Chinese workers. In mid-1884, he set up a Royal Commission to study the subject and requested a report by the spring of 1885.

Lastly, Macdonald had had to find time and energy to worry about the CPR as its cash reserves dwindled, the price of its stock fell and bankers turned away from its requests for loans. On March 18, the same day that Riel issued his call to arms, George Stephen asked the government for yet one more loan—for five million dollars. The cabinet said no, simply because Parliament would never grant it. So Macdonald waited for a more propitious moment to come along.

Unfortunately for Riel, he challenged Macdonald just at the time when the Old Chief was in a mood to act like a leader who knew where he wanted to go.

~

Riel's return to Batoche after his victory at Duck Lake changed the insurrection into two parallel but quite separate rebellions. The Métis remained in their homes, and a small number of Indians went on the warpath. For years, Riel had tried to achieve a full-scale alliance with the Indians. While still in Montana, he had on several occasions approached Canadian Indians hunting for buffalo below the border and suggested that the two groups should combine to drive the white man from the North-West. He spoke at length to the Cree chief Big Bear, who was interested but suspected Riel might not act in good faith. Riel next turned his attention to Crowfoot, the Blackfoot chief.

Crowfoot was the ideal chief for a warlike tribe. He had fought in nineteen wars, and on one occasion, armed only with a spear, had killed a grizzly bear. He was tall, lithe, confident, dignified, hot-tempered, intensely proud and so manly that he had ten wives.* As early as 1876, he had taken treaty because he saw no sense in fighting the white invaders. In 1879, Crowfoot led a Blackfoot hunting party south of the border in search of buffalo. Riel sought him out, and they held long talks. As Crowfoot later related, "He wanted me to join with the Sioux [Chief Sitting Bull] and the Crees and the half-breeds . . . to have a general uprising and capture the North-West and hold it for the Indian race and the Metis." In the end, Crowfoot refused to cooperate in Riel's plan. Once he arrived in Canada in the summer of 1884, Riel repeated his attempt to achieve a pan-Aboriginal alliance, but again without any success.

The Métis victory at Duck Lake transformed the situation. Young braves welcomed this chance to prove their mettle in war. Their enthusiasm was magnified by widespread anger on the reserves about shortages of government-supplied food and the general conviction that treaty promises had been broken. Father Lacombe warned Dewdney, "One who knows the Indian character could very easily perceive they were not pleased when told of victories of the whites; on the contrary they were sorry and disappointed."

The feared Indian War never happened, though. By one estimate, only 4 per cent of Indians in the North-West took up arms, and almost all of them went their own way. The Indians were

---

* This account is based on Hugh Dempsey's excellent biography, *Crowfoot, Chief of the Blackfeet*.

simply never persuaded that their interests were the same as those of the Métis. Not even the admired Gabriel Dumont could overcome this perception. As a further constraint, Canadian Indians were well aware of what had happened to their kin in Indian wars below the border. Far from least, they had signed peace treaties with the Queen and her Canadian government representatives, and they took the words in these documents seriously.

Only two substantial groups of Indians did take up arms—Cree belonging to the bands led by Poundmaker and Big Bear. Here resided one of the great tragedies of the rebellion. Both chiefs had deliberately kept their bands away from the new order overtaking the West by refusing to go into a reserve for as long as they could. At the same time, though, neither had any doubt about the irresistible power of the new order. Poundmaker had told his people, "It is useless to dream that we can frighten them," while Big Bear, with his typical cunning, told them, "We should not fight the Queen with guns. We should fight her with her own laws."

But by their prolonged resistance to retreating into reserves, which made them ineligible to receive food rations (issued only to bands attempting to become farmers), Big Bear and Poundmaker had weakened their own leadership. The condition of their bands was pitiable, and many members had slipped away. Those who still followed them tended to be the most militant of the braves. Once the rebellion started, these hardliners formed warrior societies, which by tradition had the exclusive right to make decisions about peace or war, Big Bear's own son Imasees being a member. Poundmaker and Big Bear still retained great respect, but their authority had shrunk.

The news of the Métis victory at Duck Lake catalyzed the warrior societies of these bands into action. Both voted for war. Led by Wandering Spirit, the angriest of all the braves, Big Bear's warriors set off for a tiny hamlet called Frog Lake, where Thomas

Quinn, a particularly hard Indian agent, lived. Big Bear, fearing violence, took off on a hunt, hoping he could satisfy his people with a huge feast. Back in Frog Lake, Wandering Spirit got into a shouting match with Quinn when the agent refused his request for rations. The argument became ever more heated, until Wandering Spirit raised his rifle and killed Quinn with a single shot. Despite Big Bear's hasty return and his cries of "No, no, no," a general massacre followed in which all but one of Frog Lake's ten adult males were slaughtered, including two priests. "It was as if they were trying to lash out against years of deprivation, abuse and wounded pride," writes Blair Stonechild of this terrible outburst.*

Poundmaker faced a comparable challenge, though one without any imminent risk of a rampage. After the Métis victory at Duck Lake, he led a group of Indians from several Cree reserves, together with some Assiniboine and Stoney braves, to Battleford, where the townspeople and a few police had barricaded themselves inside a makeshift fort. Their goal was to secure some food for their people. They did get the supplies, but as tensions mounted some of the braves looted and burned houses that had been abandoned by the townspeople. The Indians then pulled back and established a camp outside the town at Cut Knife Hill. When they received a message from Riel to "destroy Fort Battle[ford], seize the stores and munitions and bring the forces and animals here," they took no action.

Meanwhile, Big Bear's band lingered at Frog Lake, then eventually moved west to seize the supplies at Fort Pitt. The fort protected a small police detachment led by Inspector Francis

---

* Later accounts have blamed the massacre on some of the Indians having drunk patent medicines they found in the hamlet that contained alcohol. However, the single survivor, William Cameron (protected by some because well regarded), wrote in his later book, *Blood Red the Sun*, that he took the two boxes of Perry Davis' Painkiller and hid them in a chimney.

Dickens, a son of the famous novelist Charles Dickens. This time, Big Bear intervened successfully to prevent violence. He convinced the policemen to abandon the fort on the promise they would not be hurt. Dickens and his crew of police scuttled off downriver in a scow, leaving behind civilians who were taken hostage but not harmed in any way.

The decisive event remained the massacre at Frog Lake. It had the same effect on Canadian public opinion as the murder of a Quebec cabinet minister by FLQ terrorists a century later. From it came rage and fear and patriotism. The consequence was Canada's first-ever genuinely national army.

General Middleton, a decorated veteran of British colonial wars, faced two problems as the army's commander. One was that Macdonald kept telling him what to do; for instance, informing him, "The first thing to be done is to localize the insurrection so as to prevent the flame from spreading westwards." The other was that the Canadian militia were poorly trained and lacked any experience of war. In response, he ignored Macdonald's messages and put his troops through rigorous training.

Some militia troops did exist in the West—the 90th Rifles, based in Winnipeg, included Lieutenant Hugh John Macdonald among its members. Middleton hurried west, got the Winnipeg militia moved to Qu'Appelle (in present-day southern Saskatchewan) and immediately set to training these raw recruits. But moving an entire army to the West was quite another matter.

William Van Horne, the uncommonly efficient, hard-driving general manager of the CPR, now proved to be exactly the right man in the right place. During the Civil War, he had moved many Union soldiers over the railways. After a talk with John Henry

Pope, the acting minister of railways, he put a proposition to the government: the CPR would move the entire army to the West on the condition that Van Horne had complete and exclusive charge. "Has anyone got a better plan?" Macdonald asked the cabinet. Van Horne soon came up with a detailed proposal—an excellent one for the army and the government, and every bit as much for the CPR.

About the railway itself, Macdonald had been close to despair. "Our difficulties are immense . . . we have blackmailing all round," he wrote to Charles Tupper in London, referring to the demands of Quebec and Maritime MPs for regional payoffs for their votes to bail out the CPR. "How will it end, God knows." Out of nowhere, Van Horne had given him the solution: the railway would transport the army to the West, and in return a grateful nation would save the CPR.

Given the go-ahead, Van Horne declared he could transport to Qu'Appelle, the rail point nearest to Batoche, an army of some 3,300 men from Quebec, Ontario and the Maritimes. The first troops would be delivered to their destination within ten days. It seemed impossible. In the railway line above Lake Superior, there were still four gaps totalling eighty-six miles. Somehow, the men, horses, artillery pieces and supplies would have to be dragged over the bare rock and muskeg amid temperatures that could fall to −4 °F (−20 °C).

Militia members had already been ordered to assemble, and thousands gathered in drill halls in Montreal, Toronto, Ottawa, Quebec City and Halifax, and in all the towns of the Loyalist Strand out to Kingston. After a few days, they were put on parade and given inspirational speeches by their commanders and blessings by their clergymen. A unit from the University of Toronto sang songs in Latin as they marched through huge crowds to the railway station. In Toronto and elsewhere in English Canada, the bands played such tunes as "The British Grenadiers"; in Montreal, they played "La Marseillaise." Untrained volunteers smuggled themselves aboard the trains.

Van Horne exceeded his target and got the men there in just nine days. In the rough tract above Lake Superior, he had hot meals waiting for them wherever they stopped, and at every gap in the line the troops were bundled into waiting dogsleds. Many suffered frostbite or snow blindness, but only one man died.

The first troops reached Qu'Appelle on March 28. Middleton's strategy was simple and sensible: once he had assembled a large enough army and had drilled them, he would march off directly to the heart of the rebellion. By April 6, only three weeks after the rebellion had begun, he started out for Batoche, 230 miles to the north, with four hundred foot soldiers as well as cavalry and artillery. A week later, with his army reinforced by newcomers, he was only 100 miles from Batoche. Riel wrote in his diary, "I have seen the giant; he is coming; he is hideous. It is Goliath."

In fact, the first engagement between the soldiers and the insurgents involved neither Middleton nor the Métis. It was between some soldiers and Poundmaker's Indians—and the soldiers lost as badly as their compatriots had at Duck Lake, with Poundmaker's intervention alone preventing an utter rout. An ambitious officer, Colonel William Otter, had been sent by Middleton to hurry a force to Battleford, where civilians and policemen were threatened by the Indians encamped on Cut Knife Hill. Otter relieved the town, but without any authority set off next to attack the Indian camp. He found it easily and began shelling the teepees. The Indians quickly realized the shells did little real damage, so they crept out through the bushes and encircled Otter's force. Before long, two dozen soldiers were dead or badly wounded, and Otter beat a retreat. The Indians wanted to pursue them, but Poundmaker stopped them by holding up the sacred pipe-stem, the Oskichi, and saying, "They have come here to fight us and we have fought them; now let them go."*

Excited by their success, but knowing that Middleton's army was nearing Batoche, the braves were uncertain what to do. Métis messengers sent by Gabriel Dumont urged them to join in the decisive battle. Poundmaker bowed to the wishes of the warrior society and put his mark on a letter saying he would come. His band did move, but with conspicuous slowness.

For more than six weeks, Riel and his Métis had been engaged in a rebellion in which the insurgents remained motionless, except for scouts sent south by Dumont to keep watch on Middleton's progress. The only topic of discussion was religion. Riel himself never carried a gun, only a large crucifix, while the rebel flag included a large picture of Our Lady of Lourdes. Aware that the enemy was coming nearer, Riel wrote in his diary, "I pray you to keep away the sons of evil. Stagger them when the fight takes place so . . . they will know the Almighty is prepared to inflict retribution upon them."

At last, on April 23, Riel allowed Dumont to take the fight to the enemy. Dumont set off with about 130 Métis for Fish Creek, South Branch's most southerly point, to ambush Middleton's forces. He arrived too late for a night attack, Riel having slowed the march by insisting on saying a full rosary at each halt, and early the next morning exchanged shots with army scouts. Outnumbered three to one, Dumont was soon in serious trouble and at risk of being surrounded. The Métis sharpshooters held the soldiers back, however, and Middleton failed to press his advantage. In Batoche,

* Otter announced a victory by claiming he had forestalled an Indian attack on Battleford. (None was planned.) Later, he did well in South Africa, winning a considerable victory at Paardeberg, was promoted to general, and in 1907 became the first Canadian to command Canada's militia. Macdonald, as one of his letters shows, never believed Otter had won at Cut Knife Hill.

where Riel had returned, he prayed with his arms outstretched in the form of a cross. His prayers were answered in the sense that Middleton squandered a victory that was his for the taking.*

Three days later, his contingent now increased to 900 and equipped with a Gatling gun, a forerunner of the machine gun, Middleton arrived in Batoche to face some 250 to 300 Métis and about 30 Indians. Even here, only about one in two adult male Métis had turned out to fight for Riel.

The fighting began on May 9 and extended over three days. The Métis, entrenched in dugouts, suffered few casualties. Dumont confused his foes by constantly moving his troops, making his forces seem much larger than they actually were, while his troops demoralized the soldiers by the accuracy of their fire. In contrast, the army's cannon did little damage and mostly hit buildings, while the wildly firing Gatling gun sent a hail of bullets over the rebels' heads. The Métis were running out of ammunition, though, and at night they crept over the battlefield to pick up bullets dropped by the soldiers. Eventually they had nothing but nails and pebbles to fire at them.

Skill and bravery could only do so much. On the fourth day, Middleton planned a careful, probing attack. Frustrated militiamen simply got up and charged the enemy. The Métis ranks broke, and perhaps as many as fifty men were killed. The soldiers, now roaring in triumph, broke into Batoche and freed the prisoners. Afterwards, they looted the Métis' houses and burned them. It was the single Canadian victory of the entire campaign.

In a wood above the town, Dumont and Riel found each other. Riel asked, "What are we going to do? We are beaten." Dumont

---

* In the Fish Creek encounter, Hugh John Macdonald came as close as he ever would to actual combat. He wanted to lead a charge against the Métis, but his superior overruled him. If he had, the skilled Métis would have sliced down his troops.

responded, "You must have known that in taking up arms we should be beaten." Three times over the next four days, Dumont slipped back into Batoche, to steal blankets, dried meat and a horse. Each day, he searched for Riel, but, as he said later, "The good Lord did not wish me to see poor Riel again. I wanted to advise him not to surrender." Eventually, carrying six buckwheat cakes as supplies, Dumont set off for the border. He made it safely.

Riel never gave any thought to trying to escape. In the last desperate moments, he told one Métis, "I'm the one they want, and when my enemies have me they'll be over-joyed; but my people will be at peace and they will get justice." On May 15, two army scouts walking in the woods came upon a weary, shoeless Métis. Asked who he was, he answered, "Louis Riel."

Once Riel was escorted back to the army camp, he was brought to General Middleton. The two men talked for the rest of the day on a variety of subjects, principally about the Catholic Church. Riel said the church was thoroughly corrupt and that "religion should be based on morality and humanity and charity." Middleton said later, "He was a man of rather acute intellect. He seemed quite able to hold his own on any argument or topic we happened to touch on." Captain George Young, the officer who guarded Riel during the nine-day journey from Batoche to Regina, thought likewise: "I found that I had a mind against my own, and fully equal to it; better educated and much more clever than I was myself." To neither man was Riel in any way insane.

TWENTY-NINE

Wickedly, Maliciously and Traitorously

If you hang him, you make a patriot of him. If you send him to prison, he is only an insane man.
Annie Thompson, wife of John Thompson,
Macdonald's minister of justice

The most famous trial in Canadian history began with the usual legal jousting. Riel's lawyers argued that a capital case should not be presided over by a stipendiary magistrate but by a full judge, and should not be decided by a jury of only six men but by the usual twelve. The magistrate, Judge Hugh Richardson, ruled that the present arrangements had been provided for under the North-West Territories statutes and confirmed by the Appeal Court of Manitoba in a recent murder trial. The court clerk then read out the charges, six in all, accusing Riel of high treason because he, "most wickedly, maliciously and traitorously, did levy and make war against our said Lady, the Queen."* He

* These archaisms were the wording of the ancient Statute of Treasons of 1352, under which Riel was charged. Though routinely used in Britain, the statute became part of Canadian law only in 1868 and was not extended to the North-West Territories until 1873. Macdonald himself had doubts about it, telling his justice minister, "I hope we shall not be obliged to have recourse to the Statute. . . . The proceedings are complicated."

asked Riel how he intended to plead. The prisoner replied, "I have the honour to answer the court that I am not guilty." The proceedings were then adjourned for a week to give the defence time to bring in several priests and "alienists" (doctors specializing in mental health) as witnesses.

This two-week trial in Regina has become the most intensively studied in Canadian legal history. Every aspect has been examined minutely, and every possible misstep and legal error scrutinized. In recent years, the conclusions have usually been severely critical of the role played by the government and by Macdonald. One historian, Lewis Thomas, has described the proceeding as "judicial murder."*

At the time, few people thought this way. Wilfrid Laurier, soon to become Liberal leader, declared, "I never saw any fair ground of attack against the tribunal." Riel's own defence team never made unfairness part of their appeal, while his principal lawyer, Charles Fitzpatrick, said, "It is impossible to pretend that Riel was unfairly tried." This team was exceptionally strong: its members included future chief justices of the Supreme Court and of Quebec's Superior Court.† They accepted tacitly the validity of the charge of treason and argued Riel's innocence on the grounds of insanity. In Quebec, fierce complaints would be made about Riel's actual execution, most famously and most eloquently by Laurier; the trial itself, though, and the verdict and even the

* Readers looking for a balanced analysis should turn to Desmond Morton's introduction to the trial transcript, *The Queen v Louis Riel.*

† One weakness of Riel's team, organized for him by Quebec friends, was that all were prominent Liberals. Riel was astute enough to recognize this problem, and he wrote to Macdonald suggesting that, if found innocent, he would add his political support to the Conservative Party. The prosecution team, assembled by Justice Minister Alexander Campbell, was every bit as strong, and in courtroom terms a good deal more effective.

sentence, inspired relatively little criticism, although a major reason for this attitude was the widespread presumption by French Canadians that Macdonald would respond to the jury's call for clemency.

Beyond question, several aspects of the trial were seriously flawed. Richardson's charge to the jury was grossly unbalanced and in several instances plain wrong. It was indefensible that all the jurors were English-speaking; Riel spoke English well but not with complete ease.* A better ethnic balance, though, might not have produced a different outcome. A decade earlier, in Winnipeg, a twelve-member French-English jury that included several Métis had handed down a guilty verdict on Ambroise Lépine, the president of Riel's court which had sentenced Thomas Scott to death. Even though all six jury members at Regina were English and Protestant, they deliberated carefully; the jury foreman appears to have argued for a verdict of innocence (according to one newspaper, he "cried like a baby" while delivering the verdict); and the jury unanimously urged clemency.†

Riel did everything he could to defeat the defence team's argument that he should not be found guilty of treason because he was insane. During his pre-trial meetings with his lawyers, he specifically instructed them to base their arguments on the merit of his actions—that these were a legitimate response to the "wrongs" done to the Métis—and not on the state of his mental health. Once he realized they were ignoring his instructions, he attempted to question hostile witnesses himself. His senior lawyer intervened, telling Riel he was "obstructing the proper management

---

* Of the thirty-two original potential jurors, only one was a French Canadian, and he was unable to take part because of an accident.

† In an attempt at fairness, all six were chosen from the southern Saskatchewan area, where no one had suffered from the rebellion, and one was bilingual.

of the case" and warning that if he persisted, "it will be perfectly useless for us to endeavour to continue any further." Judge Richardson advised Riel he would have to be silent or conduct his own defence. Riel responded eloquently: "My counsel comes from Quebec, from a far province. . . . They cannot follow the thread of the questions. They lose more than three-quarters of the opportunities." Richardson intervened to help Riel, saying Riel could give his lawyers the questions he wanted asked; as well, the leader of the prosecution team said the Crown would have no objection to Riel examining witnesses, provided his own counsel agreed. After a recess, Riel's lead lawyer put an end to the discussion: "The law says that when a man appears by counsel, that counsel must act for him during the whole trial." Riel continued to argue, but eventually accepted he had no choice but to depend on his lawyers.

In this defeat, Riel surrendered not one iota of his dignity. He told the court, "Here I have to defend myself against the accusation of high treason, or I have to consent to the animal life of an

The bearded Riel delivered his final speech to the jury seated opposite him during his trial in Regina. A terrible paradox of the trial was that Riel's speech, while at times eccentric on religious matters, demonstrated that he could function as well as any sane person, undermining his lawyer's attempt to save him from execution by proving him insane.

asylum. I don't care much about animal life, if I am not allowed to carry with it the moral existence of an intellectual being." He would prefer to be executed, Riel was saying, than to suffer a sub-human existence in an asylum and have his life's work trivialized as the mouthings of a madman. This statement was not just extraordinarily brave but the rational conclusion of someone who, if eccentric, had made a logical choice between the only two alternatives available to him. Indeed, one jury member said later that Riel's two major speeches during the trial made him seem "as sane as anyone else who addressed us in the court-room." Nor did Riel ever stop trying to demonstrate his sanity: in his closing speech, he quipped adroitly that he had been "contending with an insane and irresponsible government."

Another difficulty the defence team faced was that Riel had initiated a rebellion that had led to a large number of deaths, including unarmed civilians—about one hundred in all, though no exact count exists. It had also caused the destruction of a great deal of property and the terrorizing of settlers, especially women and children. Ample proof existed of a readiness to commit violence, such as the letter Riel had sent to Mounted Police Superintendent Leif Crozier threatening "a war of extermination." Further, the government, even if "insane and irresponsible," was unquestionably a legitimate government and the representative of the "said Lady, the Queen," against whom Riel had taken up arms. He had committed treason and so, unless insane, was legally guilty.

Extenuating circumstances certainly existed. The Métis had been treated badly and their grievances either ignored or never seriously addressed until too late. These were the issues, including the question of political reforms throughout the North-West, that Riel had hoped would be debated during the trial. Even if valid, though, they did not alter the nature of the rebellion. Only clear evidence of his insanity could do that. And Riel, throughout the trial, did all he could to prove he was sane.

Riel's lawyers may have done him harm by their strategy. The McNaughten rules, the binding legal guide of the time, required conclusive proof that "at the time of committing the act the accused was labouring under such a defect of reason, from disease of the mind, as not to know the nature and quality of the act he was doing." The defence thus had to prove not so much insanity in general, but that at the particular time he acted Riel had lost the ability to distinguish right from wrong. The alternative—a persuasive argument about extenuating circumstances—would not have secured a verdict of innocence but it would have generated material to strengthen an appeal for mercy, a tactic used successfully by one lawyer in another of the rebellion trials.*

The central question has never been whether Riel's trial could have been better conducted. By the rough and ready frontier standards of the time, it was acceptably fair. Richardson later gave many Métis defendants light sentences, so he bore no obvious bias. Blame for the rebellion had been fixed exclusively on Riel during the trial, and there was no discussion of the government's failure to take action that could have made the insurrection unnecessary. In these circumstances, the core question becomes why Macdonald, once the trial had ended so satisfactorily for him, did not follow his customary course of compromise by looking for a way to avoid making Riel a martyr—as he had done after the

---

* An example of what might have been done for Riel was provided by the lawyer Henry Clarke, who told his jury, "The achievements of the suffering people rising in their might and crushing their tyrants are the brightest pages with which history is gilded." This splendid hyperbole earned an acquittal, although it helped materially that the evidence of actual treasonable acts by Clarke's client was weak.

1869–70 uprising, when he made secret payments to Riel to get him out of the country.

The conditions in Regina, however, were incomparably more demanding. The trial was closely watched, and suspicions were rife that Macdonald might arrange for Riel to escape. *The Week* even ran a satiric account of a successful jail escape by Riel, with Macdonald's connivance. Riel was in fact surrounded by so many soldiers and policemen that an escape would have been virtually impossible. Whenever he was let out to exercise, he was shackled to a ball and chain.

A way out for Macdonald did exist. After the trial, and after two appeals against the verdict and sentence had failed, Macdonald set up a hasty three-member medical commission to examine Riel's mental health. His motive was to provide political cover to allow French-Canadian ministers to claim that every possible step to save Riel had been taken. Macdonald could have moved a further half-step forwards. He could have deliberately chosen experts likely to say that the accused had become insane since the beginning of the trial, thereby making him ineligible to be executed. Instead, he leaned towards alienists likely to judge Riel sane and so qualified to be hanged. Two of the doctors reported that they found Riel to be fully sane. The third, Dr. F.X. Valade, described him as being at different times sane and insane—as when he suffered "hallucinations on political and religious subjects"—but his opinion was rewritten in the version made public by the government to make it accord with the other two conclusions. Macdonald made no attempt whatever to avoid Riel's execution. In fact, he seems to have regarded it as his duty to see it through.

The most common analysis of what happened is that Macdonald allowed Riel to hang to appease Ontario, preferring it rather than Quebec because Ontario sent more MPs to Ottawa, and because the West would have voted with Ontario.

In fact, it's an open question whether Macdonald would have lost Ontario had he instead appeased Quebec by dispatching Riel to an asylum. Through the trial itself, the appeals, and the inquiry by the three doctors, Ontario, in contrast to Quebec, had remained quiescent. This response came easily to Ontarians, because in Riel's conviction and the dismissal of his appeals they had been getting all they wanted. Initially, many in Ontario had doubted that Macdonald would even allow Riel to go to trial, for fear of breaking up his *Bleu* bloc. His own son, Hugh John, implied as much when he told his wife, "Had our fellows taken [Riel] he would have been brought home in a coffin and all the troubles about his trial would have been avoided." Suspicions among the English and Protestants began to form only as the fall progressed

WHAT WILL HE DO WITH HIM?

After Riel's defeat at Batoche and his surrender, the decision about what to do with him rested with Macdonald. Canadians clearly told him what to do—depending entirely on whether they spoke in English or French.

and the execution was delayed while Riel's lawyers launched appeals to the Manitoba Court of Appeal and the Judicial Committee of the Privy Council in London.

Moreover, the picture often drawn of Ontarians, incited to a frenzy by Popish-hating Orangemen waiting impatiently for Riel's arrival at the gibbet, is greatly exaggerated. For a long time, Ontario's response was remarkably relaxed. Long afterwards, the government made public all the petitions and appeals sent to it about Riel. Among them were just 3 petitions calling for Riel to be hanged—one from Ontario and the other two from Saskatchewan. By contrast, 149 anti-hanging petitions were sent in from Quebec. The Quebec petitions contained more than 12,000 signatures, in contrast to just 127 from English Canada. In all, the Orange lodges passed only a half-dozen resolutions on the subject, the one from Kingston calling for Riel to have "a full and fair hearing." The Ontario press was similarly judicious. The *London Advertiser* commented after Riel's capture, "We must all hope that Riel will get the punishment he so richly deserves, but it must be done in a legal way . . . a fair trial." As time passed, Ontarians became progressively more agitated. What stirred them up was less what might or might not be done to Riel than what Quebecers were doing.

For quite a while, Quebecers had also been strikingly quiescent—more so than during the Red River affair. Francophone Quebecers had formed part of General Middleton's expeditionary force. On their return, *La Revue Canadienne* praised "nos braves volontaires." After Batoche, *La Presse* hailed the victory and called for legal action to be taken against "les insurgés."

Anxiety rose in Quebec as the trial date loomed. A group of nationalist intellectuals agreed to pay for Riel's legal team, but, unlike in 1869–70, the French clergy were deeply hostile to Riel because of his outrageous heresies about the Catholic faith. In the summer of 1885, French missionaries in the North-West circulated a joint letter condemning Riel's double disloyalty to the church and the law. As it happened, very few Quebecers had emigrated there, although many were emigrating to eastern Ontario and the United States, so the North-West was really a distant country that meant little to the province. Initially, Quebecers agreed that Riel should be punished to maintain the law and peace. *Le Pionnier de Sherbrooke* described him as "a dangerous lunatic who cannot be treated with the full rigour of the law, but who must be put into a situation in which he cannot do any more harm or start up with his wild escapades."

What changed Quebec's attitude was the news that Riel, once found guilty, had instantly been sentenced to death. Quebec's political elite had failed to prepare the public for the consequences of legal logic. This unreality persisted. On the same November day that Riel was hanged, *La Minerve*, the newspaper run by Macdonald's Quebec lieutenant, Hector-Louis Langevin, carried an editorial predicting he would not be touched. Most Quebecers took it for granted that to hold the religious views Riel did meant that he was *fou* (mad), as their priests kept saying, thereby making actual implementation of the death penalty unthinkable.

Random incidents can transform events, just as a lost horseshoe nail can change the outcome of a battle. Soon after Riel's trial ended, William Jackson, his secretary, came into the same Regina courtroom charged with the lesser count of treason-felony. After just a half-day of hearings, the jury, without bothering to retire, acquitted him on the grounds that he was transparently insane. He was consigned to an asylum in Winnipeg for life. Soon after, he walked out and strolled all the way to the border, without anyone bothering to chase after him.

Objectively, the two cases were quite different. Jackson had never advocated rebellion nor been present at any battle. Everyone regarded him as insane—his own family, the Métis (who kept him under house arrest during the rebellion), the Crown and defence counsel, and the soldiers who brought him to Regina and who witnessed his wild behaviour. But the Quebec press had its own interpretation. *L'Électeur* pointed out that the reason he was treated differently from Riel was "because Jackson is English while Riel is a French-Canadian," and the overwhelming majority of francophone Quebecers agreed. As the editorial continued, "It is his nationality they want to punish through him; it is his nationality that we want to defend." From this moment on, the fateful phrase "La lutte des races," began to appear in Quebec's newspapers. Riel became not a madman but a martyr, together with the Jesuit martyrs and those who had died defending New France on the Plains of Abraham.

A case can be made that Quebec's contemporary collective consciousness dates from this time. This consciousness was always there, created by Quebecers' sense of rootedness to the soil and of belonging to a new nation composed not of transplanted Frenchmen but of French-speaking Canadiens. After the Conquest, the British had accepted the distinctiveness of Quebec's law, religion and language. But they were gone now, and power in the country was exercised by English Canadians, who, by Confederation, were out to build their own new nation.

Within this changed political and demographic equation, Macdonald had long performed a critical role. He personified the best that Quebecers could expect from the rest of the country. He had treated Quebecers "as a nation"—with respect, with a share of power in Ottawa and with a great deal of patronage. Even if essentially just a political bargain, Macdonald's pact with Quebec had been one of trust. Now he was breaking it—he was about to send a Frenchman to the gallows for the sake of Ontario votes. If Macdonald could do that, what would all succeeding English Canadians do once he was gone?

Far more than any identification with Riel, it was this existential anxiety that Macdonald failed to understand. Once Riel was executed, *La Minerve* declared, "The hopes of an entire nation have been dashed." Just before it happened, Adolphe Chapleau, the ablest of Macdonald's francophone ministers, wrote, "An electric current is running through Quebec, the force of which is not known even to those using it." The signal Macdonald missed was that, once Quebecers came to question whether they really could count on him, and by extension on his likely successors, they were bound to question whether they could count for survival on anybody but themselves.

This agitation in Quebec provoked a counter-agitation in Ontario. Its newspapers now wrote that Quebecers wanted Riel to escape justice, not because he was insane, but because he was French. Partisan politics escalated this anger into outrage. As the Toronto *Globe* editor John Willison wrote later, the Liberals, whom he knew so well in his role as a key adviser to the party, all along assumed that Macdonald would never dare to "defy Quebec." When Macdonald did just that by allowing Riel's execution to proceed, continued Willison, the Liberals went into "deep dismay," because he had destroyed their election strategy. They had planned to wait until Macdonald reduced Riel's sentence and then charge that this clemency was "irrefutable evidence" of "French domination" over the rest of the country.

If Macdonald had placated Quebec by sending Riel to an asylum, it is far from certain that Ontario would have turned on him. His own MPs would have followed him, and his box of political tricks was far from empty. He did, after all, win the next election in 1887 and then again in 1891, even though he campaigned against the free trade with the United States that so many Ontarians wanted as an antidote to their economic miseries. Moreover, by no means were all Ontarians paranoid about the supposed appeasement of the French. Even the *Globe* ran editorials pointing out that "the Metis have a case." Moreover, a number of public figures in Ontario were arguing openly that appeasing Quebec was more important to the country than punishing Riel.

Among these voices of sanity was, astonishingly, William McDougall, the former cabinet minister whose thick-headedness had provoked the disaster at Red River. In an article in the *World*, he sent a prescient warning to Macdonald: "Canada cannot afford to have her future content disturbed by any portion of her population believing that Riel died as a martyr." The most sensible analysis came from Annie Thompson, the wife of Justice Minister John Thompson. She wrote to her husband: "If you hang him, you make a patriot of him. If you send him to prison, he is only an insane man."* The most significant intervention came from an unidentified individual who, in an encounter with Macdonald, spoke truth to power. Macdonald purportedly responded, "He shall hang though every dog in Quebec bark in his favour."

Often quoted, this comment is perhaps the most damaging to his reputation Macdonald ever made. Yet on every occasion it has been quoted, including by several professional historians, it has been misused and cited without the context in which it was made—if it was made at all. The evidence that Macdonald did make the comment is in itself too skimpy for it to be taken seriously. It derives from a single passage in a slim memoir about Macdonald published long afterwards, in 1909, by the popular historian George Parkin. In it, Parkin wrote, "When a life-long friend, unconnected with either party, urged on him the need for mercy in order to conciliate Quebec, the old man turned on him

---

* It is impossible to know whether Thompson passed on Annie's comment to Macdonald, but Thompson was in no way awed by the Grand Old Man and was not afraid to disagree with him in cabinet.

with toss of head and stamp of foot, all the lion in him aroused, 'He shall hang,' he said fiercely, 'though every dog in Quebec bark in his favour.'"*

Even if Parkin's source, unidentified and unsubstantiated, had it more or less right, Macdonald's comment was made to an old friend in a moment of anger during a private meeting. No record exists of what may have been said, the time and place of the meeting (if any) are unknown, and, because private, the discussion had no political or any other effect at the time. Yet this historical minutia has repeatedly been portrayed as a deliberate public insult by Macdonald to French Canadians.

All this said, something may have been going on. Historian Desmond Morton has suggested that Macdonald's visitor may have been George Monro Grant, the principal of Queen's University. He may very well have been right. Grant certainly knew Macdonald well enough to get an appointment with him, and he possessed the moral authority to challenge him. That September, he made a speech in Halifax in which he declared he believed that "the enlightened sense of the 19th century was opposed to death sentences for political offences." Here, Grant got to the heart of the issue: treason is a political crime, not a criminal one. In any meeting with Macdonald, Grant would have repeated this argument—that the political cost of Quebec's alienation did not justify executing Riel. Macdonald may have lashed out intemperately not because Grant disagreed with him, but because his argument was persuasive. By the time Grant made his case, however, it was too late for Macdonald to change his mind. Any last-minute reduction in Riel's sentence would have confirmed to English and Protestant Ontarians that

---

* The comment has been used frequently since it was quoted by the distinguished historian George Stanley in his groundbreaking 1935 work, *The Birth of Western Canada*, a reprint of his doctoral thesis.

they had been right all along—their country was run by French-Canadian Catholics.

These possibilities can only be speculation. During the six months from Riel's surrender to his death on November 16, Macdonald wrote few letters on the subject. None suggests he ever had any doubt that Riel should be executed for treason. A kind of mirror image of Macdonald's likely thinking can be found in letters sent to him during this period by his old friend Judge James Robert Gowan. In September, Gowan wrote that it would be "a fatal blunder to interfere with the due course of law in this case." On November 18, two days after the execution, he concluded, "It would have been an act of political insanity to yield, simply because the man was of French blood." If these opinions do mirror Macdonald's, it is clear he had objective reasons for allowing the sentence to proceed. Whether his reasons were right or wrong in themselves is quite another matter.

Insofar as the national interest was concerned, Macdonald was never persuaded that the agitation in Quebec—the "Francesa furioso" as he called it—would be more than temporary.* After all, his three francophone ministers had stood by him, and Quebec's clergy, always influential, had condemned Riel in the strongest possible terms. Indeed, the Riel affair was one of the very few occasions when Quebecers ignored the opinions of their priests.

Macdonald was well aware of the scale of anger and anxiety in Quebec. His appointment of the medical commission to determine the state of Riel's mental health and his legal fitness to be executed showed his uneasiness—if only that of a politician. Still, the government's manipulation of the ambiguous assessment by

---

* At the beginning of the process, Macdonald had been more concerned about Ontario opinion. In a June 4 letter to Gowan, he referred to "people grumbling at his not being hanged off hand." He thought that Quebec opinion would be determined by the clergy's general hostility to Riel.

Dr. Valade confirms Thomas Flanagan's critical summation that, in this instance, Macdonald stands to be accused "not of delays or misjudgments, but of bad faith."

One straightforward explanation for Macdonald's behaviour does exist: that he genuinely believed Riel had committed treason, and that, for so serious an offence to society, the law properly required the ultimate penalty. The fact that nineteenth-century Canadians attached such deep importance to the virtue of loyalty would only have amplified Macdonald's conviction—particularly as he realized he was one of the few forces holding the country together. His reading of the law was straightforward: Riel had raised a rebellion, an act for which there were no extenuating circumstances.* This interpretation was not new to Macdonald. As a young lawyer, he had defended, unsuccessfully, Americans who had come into Canada to raise a rebellion; during the Fenian raids in 1866, he had described treason in a letter to Governor General Lord Monck as "the highest crime known to the law, involving the severest penalties." Macdonald's conclusion was essentially the same as that of Riel's lawyers: he was legally guilty and his only chance to escape would have been to be proven insane. Peter Waite, one of the ablest historians to study the issue, put it this way: "Although it is sometimes averred that Riel was sacrificed to Ontario opinion, that is the truth inside out. Riel was a victim of the law."† Beyond argument, Macdonald revered the law; during

* At that time, just one justification for treason existed. It was described best in the sixteenth-century epigram of Sir John Harington: "Treason doth never prosper: what's the reason? Why, if it prosper, none dare call it treason."

† In fact, the law can always be bent to political reality. In the United States, none of the Confederate leaders was prosecuted after the Civil War. While many of the first batch of Patriote rebels of 1837 were executed or transported to penal colonies, later ones had their charges of treason annulled and were allowed back from exile, four becoming pre-Confederation premiers—among them George-Étienne Cartier.

the same Fenian raids, he rejected calls for individuals to be arrested on mere suspicion of being Fenians, because, "This is a country of law and order, and we cannot go beyond the law." Macdonald may well have been wrong—politically he certainly was—but he acted as he did, not for political gain, but because he thought he was doing what the law required.

The end was quick and ugly, but not pathetic. Riel's dignity and courage raised it far above the tawdry. On November 15, Father André, who had been Riel's confessor throughout his term in jail, brought him the news he would mount the gibbet the next day. Riel wrote two letters, the first to his mother: "And when your last day will come, may God be so pleased with you that your pious spirit will leave the earth on the wings of the love of the angels." He then wrote to his wife, Marguerite: "Take courage, I bless you." His last meal, at his request, was three eggs and a glass of milk. He spent most of the time with Father André, praying, saying the rosary and receiving his last communion. The fact that, in Catholic doctrine, the host cannot be given to someone who is insane reveals the feelings of both men about Riel's state of mind. As his last words, Riel wrote, "I die Catholic and in the only true faith."

At 8.15 on a cold, clear morning, Riel, accompanied by several priests, walked slowly to the scaffold, where a crowd of officials, soldiers and policemen were waiting. At the base of the structure, he knelt in prayer, surrounded by the priests. He mounted the stairs to the platform without help, Father André stumbling behind him. The hangman put a hood over Riel's head and the noose around his neck. Father André, now crying uncontrollably, led him in the Lord's Prayer: "Our Father who art in heaven,

I have devoted my life to my country. If it is necessary for the happiness of my country that I Should now Soon cease to live, I leave it to the Providence of my God.

Louis Riel.

His execution imminent, Riel wrote this statement. Throughout his ordeal, he retained his dignity and calm demeanour, causing the foreman of the jury to burst into tears as he read out the guilty verdict, and Father André to do the same as he walked with Riel up the stairs to the scaffold.

hallowed be thy name. Thy kingdom come, thy will be done . . ." At that instant, the trap door sprang open.

Edgar Dewdney informed Macdonald by telegram that the deed had been done. Macdonald replied it was "satisfactory." It was the worst mistake of his entire career.

THIRTY

Knocking Off the Queen's Bonnet

Pity the children of my tribe. Pity the old and helpless of my people.

Big Bear to the court after he received his sentence

In the moments before the noose was placed around his neck, Riel had prayed. A few days later—at the foot of a scaffold in Battleford rather than in Regina—eight other native people used their last moments to chant out death songs. All were Indians, the only native people to pay the ultimate penalty for rising up in rebellion.

The last days of these men were radically different from the last days of Riel. None understood a word of the language—English—in which their trials were conducted; none of them was represented by counsel; no jury was empanelled to pronounce a verdict and perhaps add a request for mercy; and their executions, unlike Riel's, were public, even though such spectacles had long been banned by law.* Above all, while Riel's trial and execution

---

* Following Britain's abolition of public executions in 1868, the same reform was enacted in Canada one year later. The last was staged on December 7, 1869, when Nicholas Melady was hanged in Goderich, Ontario, for the murder of a rich farmer.

went on to become Canada's best-known judicial process, the trials and executions of the Indians are little known today and their names have long ago slipped into oblivion. They were Wandering Spirit, Round the Sky, Bad Arrow, Miserable Man, Itka, Man without Blood, Iron Body and Little Bear.

In all, eighty-one Indians were brought into the courtrooms in Battleford and Regina, almost twice as many as the forty-six Métis who came to trial. Of these Métis defendants, many were acquitted or given nominal one-year sentences. Few Indians got off so lightly. Both of the white men charged with taking part in the rebellion, one being William Jackson, were acquitted—a white-native disparity some commentators have made much of, although the evidence against the two men was scanty. One real difference among the three ethnic groups did exist: the whites and the Métis were treated as Canadians, while the Indians were treated as Indians.

Some attempts at fairness were made. The first to be tried, Chief One Arrow—whose case followed Riel's in the same courtroom—was represented by an able Winnipeg lawyer, Beverley Robertson, hired by the Crown to defend him. Yet the process—its rules, rituals, terminology and the language used—was incomprehensible to the accused and to all his kin. Translations in Cree were provided, but their quality was poor. When the indictment of treason-felony was read out, the interpreter so mangled his version that One Arrow thought he was being accused of "knocking off the Queen's bonnet and stabbing her in the behind," and he protested that the interpreter had to be drunk. Robertson did his best for his client, but admitted, "I cannot acquire his confidence. I don't know Indians enough." One Arrow was found guilty and given a three-year sentence. Missing from the sentencing process, as in all the Indian trials, were the testimonials by priests and local settlers which had been provided for the Métis; Father André, for instance, advised the court during the trial of one Métis that, except for a few leaders, "not one of the other half-breeds had the least idea or suspicion that there was any probability or danger of rebellion."

After the trials were over, all Indians were subjected to new restrictions on their movements and behaviour, including many who belonged to tribes and bands judged to have been "loyal." The real change, though, was in attitude—and it affected all Aboriginal people after the rebellion. For close to a century, to be an Indian was to be invisible, so far as the government and the majority of Canadians were concerned.

Except in the cases of the two white men, Macdonald took no recorded interest in any of the trials after Riel's. The idea for the public hanging of the eight Indians came from Hayter Reed, the hardliner in the Department of Indian Affairs, who urged that "the punishment be public as I am desirous of having Indians witness it . . . [as] would cause them to meditate for many a day." Macdonald had to have assented to this plan. Earlier, he had directed Justice Minister Alexander Campbell to get the government lawyers to lay charges against as many white settlers as possible. His motive here was to apprehend those whom he suspected, correctly, had encouraged Riel to act aggressively in order to pressure Ottawa to deal with their own political complaints. But the lawyers could not find enough evidence to charge more than the two white men.

The most dramatic Indian trial was that of Wandering Spirit and four others charged with the slaughter at Frog Lake of unarmed civilians, including two priests.* At the same time, three other

* The most detailed accounts of the trials of the Indians are in Bob Beal and Rod Macleod's *Prairie Fire* and Bill Waiser and Blair Stonechild's *Loyal till Death*, and in Myrna Kostash's *The Frog Lake Reader*, published in 2009.

Indians were tried, and convicted, for the separate killings of two white settlers and a policeman. As well, three more were tried for the killing of an Indian woman who had turned into a witch, a *wehitkow*, but were acquitted for lack of evidence. Most of the defendants readily pleaded guilty, most particularly Wandering Spirit, the principal instigator of the Frog Lake massacre, who had become deeply ashamed of what he had done and made an unsuccessful attempt at suicide.

The choice of the presiding judge, though, was glaringly inappropriate, particularly in the absence of a jury. Judge Charles Rouleau lived in Battleford, and during its siege his house had been burned down, destroying his valuable collection of legal volumes. Rouleau made no attempt to conceal his bias, telling Dewdney as soon as the rebellion was over, "It is high time . . . Indians should be taught a severe lesson." Once Rouleau had declared the guilty verdicts, no legal appeals were made on behalf of the eight Indians, nor, in contrast to Riel, were appeals for clemency advanced by influential individuals and institutions across the country.

By deliberate intent, the eight convicted men were sent to their deaths in front of a huge crowd of their kin brought in from all the neighbouring reserves, including boys from the Battleford Industrial School. After their execution, the largest ever in Canadian history, all were buried in a common grave and their names promptly forgotten.*

---

* Forgetfulness set in immediately. Unlike the throng of multinational journalists who watched Riel take his last walk, only two local reporters came out to see the eight Indians meet their ends, and one was there simply to secure a stipend for signing the death warrants.

By far and away the most important Indian trials were those of the Cree chiefs Poundmaker and Big Bear, both charged with treason-felony. These proceedings were better balanced in the sense that juries were empanelled in both cases and Rouleau was replaced by Judge Hugh Richardson, who had presided over Riel's trial. Each trial lasted only two days, though, and nothing could alter the strangeness of the process and the legal terminology for the chiefs. Beverley Robertson, once again hired by the government to defend the accused, did all he could for the chiefs, particularly as he became convinced that anti-native racism was playing a major part in their treatment. In his final plea for Poundmaker, he asked the jurymen to remember "that this poor man is an Indian, that although he is defended here he is very imperfectly defended . . . if I had a white man to defend . . . it would be a very different thing." The jury's verdict was guilty, almost certainly because of the letter to Riel, promising to join the Métis leader at Batoche, which the warrior society had persuaded Poundmaker to put his mark to.

Asked if he had anything to say before being sentenced, Poundmaker made a brief plea, its few words providing the only insight available into what he thought about the charges against him. "There is nothing of it true," he said. "I did everything to stop bloodshed. If I had not done so, there would have been plenty of blood spilled this summer." When Richardson sentenced him to three years in the Stony Mountain Penitentiary in Winnipeg, Poundmaker shouted back, "I would prefer to hang than to be in that place." For an Indian accustomed to going as he willed across the prairies, with the wind in his face and the earth beneath his moccasined feet, incarceration inside stone walls was like being entombed alive.

Big Bear's experience in the courtroom followed the same pattern. After Riel's defeat at Batoche, he had avoided arrest for another two months, fighting off pursuing troops in a drawn battle at Frenchman's Butte, the insurgency's last engagement. After his band dissolved, he moved undetected through the forests, accompanied only by his fourteen-year-old son, Horse Child, until hunger and exhaustion forced him to surrender to a surprised police detachment.

The trial, starting on September 11, was one of the last rebellion trials. On Big Bear's behalf, Robertson, again acting as defence counsel, argued that he had lost control of his band to the war party before the rebellion began and that, once hostilities broke out, he had done all he could to prevent any violence. The jury's verdict was guilty, but with a recommendation for mercy. In a long speech to the court, Big Bear protested his innocence: "You think I encouraged my people to take part in the trouble. I did not. I advised against it." And he made one plea: "Pity the children of my tribe. Pity the old and helpless of my people . . . send out and pardon and give them help." Richardson's sentence was the same as for Poundmaker—a three-year term in Stony Mountain Penitentiary.

The last rebellion in Canadian history was over, but only in the literal sense. Among French Canadians, its consequences—emotional, symbolic, political—were far from ended, even though they were briefer than is often assumed. Macdonald did suffer a loss of seats in Quebec in the next election, in 1887, but he still won a majority there, and in his final election, in 1891, he won more votes in the province, if fewer seats, than the Liberals. The real change in Quebec did not happen until the 1896 election, by which time French Canadians' interest in the West had withered away and their political choices were determined by new factors, particularly the fact that one of their own, Wilfrid Laurier, had established himself as a credible national leader.

The consequences for Canada's Aboriginal people were of a quite different order of magnitude. Indians would be affected radically for decades, and in some respects they still feel the effects of those long-ago events. Before the North-West Rebellion, Canadians had seen them as "our Indians," in an expression of national pride, because the relationship between the two groups was so much superior to its American equivalent. Afterwards, Aboriginal people came to be regarded as just "the Indians" or, worse, as "the Indian problem"—a complication, an irritant, a disappointment.

The consequences for the Métis were negative also, but in a more complicated way. Many of their land grievances were settled by the Half-Breed Commission, though, as Macdonald expected, much of the scrip was quickly sold to speculators. The rise in racist attitudes towards Aboriginal people damaged the Métis in particular, however, because, unlike Indians on their reserves, many lived within the white communities and were exposed to direct discrimination and exclusion. The underlying problem of the Métis remained: the arrival of a new socio-economic order, which would completely dominate the West once hundreds of thousands of immigrants flooded in after the turn of the century. Thereafter, few opportunities existed for people without education or agricultural skills. The Métis' real enemy was modernity.

After the rebellion, the greatest effect of Riel's execution was in Quebec. Macdonald's initial response to the news of the death sentence was grossly optimistic. As he wrote in a long letter to Governor General Lansdowne, "There is, it is true, some sympathy in the Province of Quebec, with Riel. This is principally worked up by the *Rouge* Party for political purposes." He went on to refer to the Patriotes' rising of 1837, commenting, "The attempt now being made to revive that feeling in his favour will not extend far, and will be evanescent." What Macdonald overlooked was that Riel, whatever his failings and his religious beliefs, was French.

The news of Riel's execution hit Quebecers like a slap in the face. One week after his death, a crowd of some fifty thousand gathered in Montreal's Champs de Mars to listen to the speeches of thirty-seven notables while flags flew at half-mast and effigies of Macdonald burned. The speakers compared Riel to Joan of Arc and Quebec's own Jesuit martyrs. Two in particular would be remembered long afterwards. The first was the rising federal Liberal star, Laurier, who told the crowd, "If I had been on the banks of the Saskatchewan, I too would have shouldered my musket to fight against the neglect of government and the greed of speculators."

The second notable speaker was Honoré Mercier, Jesuit educated, a lawyer, a first-rate organizer and an attractive speaker. He had opposed Confederation, and although at forty-five he had already been in provincial politics for a decade and a half, he had never enjoyed power, because the Conservatives still held on to it so firmly. Deeply religious and a fierce nationalist, Mercier now dominated the evening by his oratory. "Riel our brother is dead, victim of his devotion to the cause of the Métis," he thundered, "victim of fanaticism and treason—of the fanaticism of Sir John and some of his friends, of the treason of three of our people who sold their brother to keep their portfolios." Picking up a theme first enunciated by *La Presse*—that Riel's death had turned everyone in Quebec who had once been Conservative or Liberal into "Patriots or Traitors"—Mercier

By becoming premier in 1887, principally because of Quebecers' fury at Riel's execution, Honoré Mercier changed Canada's character as the first nationalist to exercise power in Quebec since Confederation.

called for the creation of a new party, the Parti National, "to unite to punish the guilty" (Macdonald's francophone ministers) and to protect "our national interests." Quebecers, he was saying, could from now on count only on themselves.

The passion unleashed by the rally could not be sustained. By spring, it seemed that Quebec's "blaze of straw," as Macdonald unwisely called it, was indeed burning out. The Catholic bishops, particularly Bishop Alexandre Taché in the West, were warning their people not to embrace an apostate such as Riel. And Laurier edged back from extremism, reminding Quebecers in a speech in the House of Commons that the creation of Mercier's all-French party would "cause the majority to organize as a political party, and the result must be disastrous to themselves."

At this point, it was the Ontario newspapers that revived the cause. "Must it be said that the rights and liberties of the English people in this English colony depend upon a foreign press?" declared the *Orange Sentinel*, going on to warn, "The day is near when an appeal to arms will be heard in all parts of Canada." Toronto's *Evening News* was even more provocative: "Ontario pays about three-fifths of Canada's taxes. . . . Quebec, since the time of Intendant Bigot, has been extravagant, corrupt and venal. Quebec now gets the pie. Ontario gets the mush, and pays the piper." The more respectable *Mail* was as harsh: the French were "seeking to suspend the operations of the law when a representative of their race is in its toils"; rather than submit, "Ontario would smash Confederation into its original fragments." In case its meaning was unclear, the newspaper wrote later that, should Quebecers push too hard, "the Conquest will have to be fought over again."

These sentiments handed Mercier all the ammunition he needed. In the provincial election campaign of early 1886, he made almost one hundred speeches. The result itself was a stalemate, but Mercier soon outmanoeuvred the floundering Conservative government. On January 1, 1887, he was sworn in as Quebec's first-ever non-Conservative premier.

Anger against the execution of Riel was by no means the only cause of this political transformation. Quebec's out-migration was continuing in large numbers, and additional social anxieties were unleashed by the drift of surplus farmers to cities and towns, above all Montreal. The continuing Long Depression magnified the pessimism. Yet Riel's role was critical. His execution confirmed to French Canadians the cardinal character of Canada as refashioned by Confederation—that within it the French would always be the minority and the English not merely the majority, but an ever more dominant one. This realization would have taken hold eventually, but Quebec's failure to win a commutation for Riel marks the dividing line between Canada's past—the alliance first of Robert Baldwin and Louis-Hippolyte LaFontaine in the 1840s, then of Macdonald and Cartier from the 1850s to the early 1870s—and its future, with Quebec ever more self-contained and detached from the rest of the country.

Some of the consequences of the rebellion were more positive. White settlers benefited marginally when, after the rebellion, Macdonald granted the North-West four seats in the House of Commons. Real political change, however, did not begin until 1905, when Alberta and Saskatchewan were granted provincial status—though, as continued to be the case for Manitoba, without gaining ownership of their own resources as was the case in all other provinces.

The single clear winner was the Canadian Pacific Railway. William Van Horne, soon to be promoted to president of the CPR, had read the political entrails correctly. The speed and efficiency with which he had moved the army out to the prairies earned the company the nation's gratitude—and particularly Macdonald's. Indeed, Van Horne had also played a role in creating Canada's first post-Confederation sense of national consciousness, even though it lasted only briefly. Out on the prairies, the soldiers from Ontario, Quebec, the Maritimes and the West itself discovered they were all engaged in a common cause—one carried out exclusively by Canadians rather than by British redcoats (but for General Middleton). This mood didn't last long, and in the West it was soon succeeded by almost continual criticisms of the CPR for everything from high rates to poor service. For its part, the railway paid little attention to public relations: as soon as the rebellion was over, it submitted a bill for transporting the troops calculated to the last penny: $852,331.32.

The decisive change for the CPR was that all thought of allowing it to go bankrupt vanished overnight. As well, as Van Horne noted, "There is no more talk about the construction of the Lake Superior line having been a useless expenditure of money, nor about the road having been built too quickly." Macdonald, reverting to his Old Tomorrow mode, took his time to settle this account. His dilatoriness reduced George Stephen to despairing frustration: "It is impossible for me to carry on the struggle," he wrote, and, later, "It is very hard having to fight both enemies and friends." At one point, Macdonald got so annoyed by Stephen's incessant demands that he reminded him that only his own "personal influence with our supporters and a plain indication of my resignation" had stiffened his MPs to the point of resisting the widespread demands for the government to take over possession of the line. The CPR's woes were real, though. Van Horne wired Stephen, "Have no means paying wages, pay car can't be sent out, and unless we get immediate relief we must stop." In the Rockies, workers downed their tools, and Mounted Police had to be brought in to prevent riots.

Macdonald made his move on May 1, 1885, an odd time to choose, because the battle at Batoche had yet to be won. A CPR bond payment was due, and without a government loan there would be a default, and then, as Stephen wrote to Macdonald, it would be "goodbye to the CPR." At a hastily called cabinet meeting, Macdonald told his ministers that the government had to intervene. So it did: John Henry Pope, the acting railway minister, delivered the good news to CPR executives assembled in a nearby room. They waited for Pope to leave and then, in Van Horne's recollection, "We tossed up chairs to the ceiling; we trampled on desks. I believe we danced on the tables." Not long afterwards, Stephen cabled in code from London, "Railway now out of danger"—the CPR's bonds had soared.

Macdonald's greatest single achievement as a nation-builder, aside from Confederation itself, was realized on November 7, 1885. The plan had been for the last spike of the CPR's line to be driven

On November 7, 1885, in the middle of the Rockies, at a station called Craigellachie, the line from the West met the line from the East. Donald Smith bent the first last spike with a clumsy hammer blow. He hit true at the second last spike. The ceremony was modest, casual and thoroughly Canadian.

in at Craigellachie by Governor General Lansdowne, but bad weather forced him to return to Ottawa. Without him and the special silver spike he had taken back with him, the ceremony was plain and brief—stereotypically Canadian, in contrast to the rambunctious and lavish American equivalents. No speeches were made and except for railway executives no dignitaries were present. Donald Smith, Macdonald's old opponent, botched his first hammer blow, bending the iron spike. As a professional photographer from Winnipeg clicked the shutter of his camera a second time, Smith's next try hit fair and square. In dead silence, but for the gushing of a small mountain stream, Smith hammered home the spike. At last cheers broke out, amplified by the whistles of waiting locomotives. Called on to say something, Van Horne mumbled, "All I can say is that the work has been done well in every way." There were more cheers and handshakes, and a rush for souvenir chips from the last wooden tie. Smith pocketed the twisted spike. For the first time, a conductor uttered the iconic cry, "All aboard the Pacific." Later, the workers restaged the ceremony, adding to the history books a photograph of themselves.

When this news reached Macdonald, he commented triumphantly, "We have been made one people by the road." Just one week later, Riel made his last walk to the centre of the prison yard in Regina—and irrevocably divided the nation. Macdonald was talking about a Canada that no longer existed.

The most powerful memory of the rebellion was, and will always remain, the hanging of Louis Riel. Its most important event, though, was something that did not happen: there was no Indian war. Only a few Indians took up arms, and they did so on their own terms—not to join Riel but to protest the treatment they

THE GREAT NORTH WESTERN TELEGRAPH COMPANY OF CANADA.

OPERATING THE LINES OF THE MONTREAL, DOMINION AND MANITOBA TELEGRAPH COMPANIES.

This Company transmits and delivers messages only on conditions limiting its liability, which have been assented to by the sender of the following message.

Errors can be guarded against only by repeating a message back to the sending station for comparison, and the Company will not hold itself liable for errors or delays in transmission or delivery of unrepeated messages, beyond the amount of tolls paid thereon, nor in any case where the claim is not presented in writing within sixty days after sending the message.

This is an unrepeated message, and is delivered by request of the sender, under the conditions named above.

H. P. DWIGHT, General Manager. ERASTUS WIMAN, President.

Money orders by telegraph between principal telegraph offices in Canada and the United States.

TELEGRAM.

Use this space for Continuation of Lengthy Addresses, or INSTRUCTIONS TO MESSENGER.

To Rt Hon Sir J.A. Macdonald KCB

No. 3 Check 27 Pd

Rec'd No. 2 From A Sent CD Rec'd by mc Time 3p

Ottawa, 188

From Craigellachie Eagle pass BC 7

Thanks to your far seeing policy and unwavering support the Canadian Pacific Railway is completed the last rail was laid this (Saturday) morning at 9:22

W.C. VanHorne

A telegram from Van Horne brough the news to Macdonald that what Lady Macdonald called "the darlin dream of his heart" had been realize

had received from government and, for some long-tamed young braves, to show their warrior spirit.

Macdonald was inordinately lucky in this outcome. Nevertheless, this general restraint indicates that the Indians of the Plains still retained some measure of respect for the government, and above all for the Mounted Police. Neither then nor later did Canada experience any of the bloody conflicts that occurred so often south of the Medicine Line. As well, while Macdonald bore a full share of responsibility for the mistakes and insensitivities of his officials, he himself retained a degree of regard among the Aboriginal people, at least for having tried to understand what they were going through during this time of cultural catastrophe; afterwards, his largely amicable relations with Indians in the East remained unchanged.

Yet, in return for having escaped the ultimate disaster of an Indian war, Macdonald failed to maintain his side of the implicit pact of trust he had established with the Aboriginal people. According to Hayter Reed, twenty-eight of the tribes and bands in the region had been "disloyal." All were penalized: their food rations were cut even further, and they were forced to turn in their rifles and, in some instances, their horses. Gradually, this strict, closely scrutinized regime based on mistrust was extended to all the Indians of the Plains.* Even Crowfoot of the Blackfoot, who had been honoured, brought to Ottawa to meet the governor general and provided with money for himself and extra rations for his tribe, died in 1890 a deeply disappointed man, wholly uncertain whether his policy of accommodation had been the right one for his people. Macdonald reserved his harshest comment about the events in Saskatchewan until after it was all safely over: "The execution of Riel and of the Indians will, I hope, have a good effect on the Metis and convince the Indians that the white man governs."

After the rebellion, all Indians ceased to be treated as independent people who had signed treaties with the government and were reduced progressively to mere wards of the state. For the better part of a century, the old ideals of protecting and civilizing Canada's Indians were replaced by the practicalities of administration and control.

Macdonald played little part in the implementation of this new order. Several times, he in fact suggested that the regulations should be less restrictive. When Hayter Reed proposed a strict application of the pass system to control the movement from their reserves not just of the "disloyal" tribes, but of all Indians on the prairies, Macdonald pointed out that the pass system violated the

---

* In the most blatant example of the restrictiveness of the new regime, when some tribes did succeed as farmers, settlers' complaints that their work was being subsidized led to a rule that Aboriginals should be limited to "peasant farming" on small, unmechanized plots, so that their output could not compete in the marketplace.

treaty terms and insisted that, if the Indians protested, the new rules should not be enforced. He also made changes in a plan to disarm the Indians, telling Dewdney, "The only way of effecting this is by way of peaceable exchange . . . Fowling Pieces instead of Winchester Rifles, [us] paying the difference." But he wrote "approved" on his deputy minister's memorandum calling for a comprehensive "management of Indians," and he went along with the banning of the Sun Dance (or Thirst Dance). At the same time, Macdonald continued to reject any demand for American-style "removals" of Indians from their reserve lands, and to the end of his life he insisted that the treaties must not be violated.*

Conservative and cautious would best describe Macdonald's response. His principal concern was to ensure that no further violence broke out, so potential immigrants would not be discouraged and the railway not damaged. In his attitude, a more profound change took place. His dominant mood became one of sheer weariness with "the Indian problem." In all probability, at some level Macdonald felt let down by the Indians, perhaps even betrayed. Or perhaps he had come to accept that any real change would take so long to effect that there was little he could do in the time left to him.

His loss of interest was easy to track. In 1886, an extended debate on Indian policy took place in the Commons as a result of a motion moved by Liberal MP Malcolm Cameron, who had strongly criticized the government's actions before and during the rebellion. Macdonald, once so ready to talk about Aboriginal affairs, said nothing at all in rebuttal, relying instead on a self-serving account of the events published by the Department of Indian Affairs. Within a year, he had given up the portfolio, although it

---

* Explicit violations of treaties really date from the early years of the twentieth century, when Clifford Sifton, Laurier's minister of the interior, wanted to increase the amount of land available to the mass of immigrants then pouring into the prairies.

must be added that his total of ten years as minister has never been equalled since. On his one trip west, late in 1886, he made no effort to meet Indian leaders other than Crowfoot.

During the 1886 Commons debate, Cameron, who was something of an authority on the subject, made one telling point: "We are not in a position to point to our Indians as proudly as we did before." He was right, both about the circumstances and about the attitudes of Canadians. Not all felt that way. After Poundmaker's conviction and sentencing, *The Week* protested that his sentence was "disproportionate to any offence of which he has been shown to be guilty." Presbyterian minister James Pitblado, a former militia chaplain, delivered a fiery sermon in Winnipeg, telling his parishioners that the Indians' "national life has been paralyzed by our presence. . . . They have been corrupted by our vices. They have been pauperized by our charities."

The prevailing mood was expressed more accurately by the *Saskatchewan Herald*: "Good and loyal Indians are a thing of the past." And official attitudes so changed that the 1889 report of the Department of Indian Affairs expressed regret that Indians "should be so lacking in intelligence" as to resist becoming farmers. If no Canadian ever said in public, "The only good Indian is a dead Indian," a good many thought that way. One important person came close to saying it openly. David Mills, one-time Liberal minister of the interior, lectured Macdonald in the Commons on the fact that "the doctrine of the survival of the fittest is a necessary law of human existence," and that by providing food to Indians because they refused to farm, "we frustrate the operation of that law."

Mills was here paraphrasing Charles Darwin, who, in *The Origin of Species*, observed that "vaccination has preserved thousands, who from a weak constitution would formerly have succumbed"—with consequences "highly injurious to the race of man." Darwin was no Social Darwinist. He nevertheless used the phrase "survival of the fittest," which had been coined by the philosopher Herbert Spencer, and came close to endorsing it, writing later in *The Descent of Man* that "at some future period . . . the civilized races of man will almost certainly exterminate, and replace, the savage races throughout the world." Although few Canadians at the time bothered to engage in theoretical speculation, social Darwinism had become part of their intellectual conversation.

What was happening then to Indians seemed to confirm the view that they were not fit to survive. In 1886, there were some 128,000 Indians in Canada; by 1900, the count was down to 98,000, despite considerable advances in medicine. Not until the 1920s would the Aboriginal population begin to increase again—a phenomenon not really appreciated until the 1960s.

In fact, death would constitute the last involvement by the Indians of the Plains in the rebellion of 1885. Poundmaker's declaration that he would prefer to be hanged than be immured in a penitentiary was confirmed by events. Cut off from the land and his country food, and sustained only by permission to retain his waist-length hair (a concession by the government to his adopted father, Crowfoot), he declined rapidly. To avoid the embarrassment of his dying in jail, Poundmaker was released after less than a year. He made the long journey on foot to the Blackfoot reserve to see Crowfoot and died there of tuberculosis on July 4, 1886.

Big Bear's story was the same. Old and sick, he too was let out early, on July 27, 1887. On the outside, he was utterly alone, without either a tribe or a family—a condition for an Indian akin to a death sentence. Eventually, a daughter came to look after him until he died, on January 17, 1888. The third chief to be imprisoned, One Arrow, likewise died within weeks of being released early. The story of the Plains Indians in the 1880s was over.

It wasn't over for Riel, though. Time would have to pass before it happened, but he would be reborn—to the point that, today, he is in a sense still alive.

Once Quebecers' gaze had turned inward, Riel was soon largely forgotten. In the rest of the country, his disappearance was complete. *The Chronicles of Canada*, a popular multi-volume work published early in the twentieth century, didn't even mention his name. No historian bothered with him until George Stanley wrote his epic work of 1936, *The Birth of Western Canada: A History of the Riel Rebellions*, but it sold few copies in Canada. Riel survived only in western folklore; John Diefenbaker loved to recount how as a young boy he had met Gabriel Dumont, one of his heroes.

As would have nettled Macdonald, it was an American who stirred Canadians to take Riel seriously again. In 1952, a curious historical novel, *Strange Empire*, by a leftist writer, Joseph Kinsey Howard, was published. In his telling, Riel championed the cause of downtrodden Aboriginals against capitalists and the political establishment. Inaccurate in historical details, the book was right on target emotionally. A belated realization that a moving and powerful story, and one distinctively Canadian, had been overlooked precipitated an outpouring of accounts about Riel—fiction and non-fiction, operas and stage plays, radio and television plays, and poems and docudramas.

Riel has gone on to become the most discussed person in all Canadian history, with Trudeau the only rival and Macdonald lagging several laps in the rear. Riel alone has had every single known word he ever uttered or wrote transcribed, translated, annotated and published. Books about him such as Maggie Siggins's *Riel: A Life of Revolution* and Chester Brown's "comic-strip biography" *Louis Riel* have been bestsellers. Works that take a more critical stance about those long-ago events are rare now, limited really to Thomas Flanagan's *Riel and the Rebellion: 1885 Reconsidered.** In the twenty-first century, the flood has slackened, though in 2004 the opera *Riel*, first performed in 1967, was restaged in Montreal, and in 2008 the Dominion Institute organized a three-part repeat of Riel's trial for CBC Television, which attracted an audience of half a million and a poll result of 87 per cent for acquittal.

This record confirms the protean quality of Riel's appeal. If it ebbs somewhere, as has happened in Quebec, it flows strongly elsewhere, as among westerners, who now view Riel as the founder of Manitoba, with public statues in Winnipeg and Regina. At one time, progressives looked askance at Riel as a right-wing religious fanatic; today, the left sees him as a champion of the poor and oppressed and of Aboriginal people. Indians themselves, though, identify little with Riel, as shown by Bill Waiser and Blair Stonechild's *Loyal till Death*, and some Métis have come to question his dominance over their narrative and find themselves emotionally closer to Gabriel Dumont. Overall, hero worship of Riel is now centred in English Canada.

Here resides an intriguing paradox. One factor behind the appeal of Louis Riel is that in most ways he was European—from his fine education to the French language in which he wrote. The fact that he was only one-eighth Métis is irrelevant: he felt himself to be Métis and was accepted as that. The reason he can be seen today as a champion of Aboriginal peoples, though, is

* Flanagan's other related work, *Louis "David" Riel: Prophet of the New World*, is a highly original but not inherently critical study of Riel's religiosity.

precisely because his European attributes make him easy to understand. In contrast, the fully native quality of Big Bear, Poundmaker and Crowfoot makes them unsatisfactory as interlocutors for European Canadians.

The core reason for Riel's enduring relevance is that he was a martyr. Otherwise, he would just be known as a local eccentric with difficult religious views. Macdonald made him a martyr by sending him to a gibbet rather than to an asylum. Had the asylum been Riel's fate, against all his own wishes, he might today be as little known as Wandering Spirit and the seven other Indians who shared his fate.

As the first Canadian commentator to appreciate Riel's importance, George Stanley deserves the last word. Late in his life, he returned to his first scholarly topic of the 1930s and admitted he had often wondered what would have happened if Macdonald and Riel had ever met. "Of one thing only I am certain," wrote Stanley, " . . . the impossibility of understanding the history of Canada during the last one hundred years without a thorough study of the personalities, thoughts and actions of these men." Riel haunts us still, as does Macdonald too, with his knowing, sardonic smile.

Those old struggles are not yet over. In February 2011, the Supreme Court of Canada announced it would hear an appeal by the Manitoba Metis Federation against decisions by the Manitoba courts rejecting its claim for compensation for the way the lands promised to the Métis and their children by the Manitoba Act in 1870 were distributed by the governments of Macdonald and Mackenzie.

In one aspect, though, closure has been achieved. In 1967, the year of Canada's centennial, a party of Cree from northern Saskatchewan travelled to the Blackfoot reserve in what by then was Alberta. There, they were given the remains of Poundmaker, who had been buried on Crowfoot's reserve. The Cree took the relics back to Saskatchewan, and on Cut Knife Hill, overlooking Poundmaker's old reserve, reburied them in the centre of a circle of inward-leaning teepee poles set in concrete. There Poundmaker lies, his remains in contact with the earth, as would be those of a deer, or of an Indian of old.

THIRTY-ONE

You'll Never Die

The darling dream of his heart . . .
Lady Macdonald

As soon as the rebellion and its immediate aftermath were over, Macdonald took off for England—to do some business and to see his doctors, but mostly for rest and recuperation. His trip began on a humiliating note. As usual, the Macdonalds went by train from Ottawa to Montreal, but rather than board the *Polynesian* there, they continued straight on by train to Rimouski, where Macdonald alone embarked hurriedly on the steamer. He had been warned that, so soon after Riel's execution, he would be at risk if he lingered in Montreal. Lady Macdonald and Mary left him here and went off on a railway tour of the Maritimes. Macdonald stayed in England by himself for five weeks, over Christmas and his birthday, returning to Canada only in mid-January 1886.

He had a grand time over there. He turned down entreaties by both CPR president George Stephen and his old friend Sir John Rose to stay at their houses and instead settled into his favourite hotel, Batt's. He went out almost every night, often to the theatre or the prestigious Athenaeum Club, and once to the pantomime *Aladdin*. He was also regularly invited to dine at the very best houses.

At some point during this holiday, it seems that the suggestion was made to him, in the usual discreet, deniable way, that he might play a role in the June 1887 celebrations commemorating Queen Victoria's fiftieth anniversary of her accession to the throne. As the Empire's senior colonial statesman, would he, perhaps, consider accepting an elevation to the peerage? In fact, Macdonald never rose above the rank of knight. But Lady Macdonald confirmed that something was afoot by her comment to Macdonald's sister, Louisa: "You may be sure that he will never take a peerage! It would make us both look ridiculous." The real problem, Macdonald knew, was that being Lord Something or Other would distance him from voters.

In 1888, speculation bubbled up that Macdonald might be made Britain's ambassador to Washington after a mini-scandal compelled the hasty retirement of the incumbent, Sir Lionel Sackville-West.* Although this appointment was never likely, there may well have been some talk about it at Westminster. What is interesting is the confirmation this provides of how well regarded Macdonald was in Britain—and, despite his admiration for the Mother Country, also of his determination not to move there to live, as so many other successful Canadians had done.

In Britain, Macdonald's health recovered with near-miraculous speed. Reporters waiting for him in Montreal advised their readers he was "as ruddy as a red apple."

Lady Macdonald was also having a grand time. She and Mary

---

* Lionel Sackville-West's real claim to fame was that his daughter, Victoria, was the mother of Vita Sackville-West, the novelist, poet and lover of Virginia Woolf, and a good many others.

travelled all over the Maritimes. Once back in Ottawa, she set off again, this time without Mary, on a far more ambitious trip. Late in December 1885, she took a CPR train, a special one consisting of a private car and a second car housing a butler and maid, out to the West, first to Winnipeg to spend time with Hugh John and his new wife, Gertrude (Vankoughnet), whom he had married following the sudden death of Jean. Afterwards, she crossed the flatlands—"prairies undulating in soft swelling," as she recorded—to the foothills of the Rockies, where the train reversed and raced back to Ottawa so she could greet her husband on his return. The newspapers had got it right about Macdonald: "He was so tired and worried when he went away that it quite enspirits me to see him so cheery," she wrote in her diary.

The trip also brought out her second, more youthful and ebullient side. She wrote excitedly of the "brilliantly fine and clear" prairie skies and contrasted the West to the capital: "Ottawa seems so dull & tame & stupid & *old* after that wonderful new western world with its breadth and clear air & and wonderfully exhilarating atmosphere that always seems to lure me out. [I] feel a new person." The original Agnes, far more physical, at times downright girlish, was emerging, someone quite unlike the stern guardian of morality she had become.

While Macdonald went to Britain after the drama of 1885, Lady Macdonald went to the West. She fell wholly in love with it, and often returned to the West, staying at the CPR's log mansion at Banff Hot Springs.

For two decades now, she had been Macdonald's hostess, chatelaine, nurse and assistant, sitting in the galleries of the House of Commons and taking notes of the debates when he was away or ill. She had hosted dinners twice a week for his MPs, and coped with the lot that life had handed her, of "constantly nursing the sick and housekeeping in Ottawa for a large household & looking after all sorts of things daily," as she wrote to Louisa, herself by now in deep decline and housebound in Kingston.

Much about the relationship between John A. and Agnes can never be more than speculation, principally because no letters between them have survived. Soon after their marriage, she had fallen hopelessly in love, and was always immensely proud of him. His prolonged drunkenness would have deeply pained her, but the gesture he had made in becoming an Anglican to help ease her grief after her mother's death must have touched her to her core. They had experienced many triumphs and setbacks together and were bonded by their fierce, protective love for Mary. Many of the pursuits Macdonald took on in later life to earn extra money, such as accepting in 1887 the strictly nominal but salaried post of president of the Manufacturers Life Insurance Company (today, Manulife Financial), had but one purpose: to build up a nest egg to protect Agnes and Mary after he was gone.*

When they took their separate holidays in the winter of 1885–86, there was no rupture between them. In all probability, though, they were preparing for the solitariness that, with Macdonald now in his seventies, couldn't be far off. At the same time, she was just entering her fifties, in full middle-aged vigour. From this point on, Agnes would often either plunge off on her own or allow him to do the same, though she continued to accompany him on election

* Right after Macdonald's death, Lady Macdonald was elevated by the Queen to the rank of baroness. Macdonald would have given his consent to this honour earlier, most likely at the time he turned down a peerage for himself.

campaigns. As she wrote to Louisa on one occasion, "I hope Sir John will go to England. Perhaps I may go too, but I don't greatly care about it." Essentially, she preferred the Canadian landscape to the grandest of cities, her favourite being the new resort of Banff Hot Springs, where the CPR built a wooden mansion for tourists, following Van Horne's instructions to "capitalize the scenery." Macdonald distanced himself from her in more subtle ways: often in the years ahead, he buried himself in government work to an extent far beyond what was really needed.

The best-known trip of their lives they made together, to the far west coast. Agnes badgered him into going to fulfill a pledge she had made to Louisa that she would "never rest till he too goes." They set out from Ottawa on July 10, 1886, a few days after the first transcontinental train had left Montreal for the BC terminus of Port Moody. They went in a special train, comfortably settled in the "Jamaica" private car. Agnes described their quarters later in a lively article for Britain's *Murray's Magazine*: it was crammed with sofas and plump armchairs, and an abundance of books and games, "all somewhat resembling the cabin of a fine ship."* There's a proud affection in her comment that Macdonald, looking out from the stateroom, was seeing "the realization of the darling dream of his heart—a railway from ocean to ocean, the development of many million acres of magnificent country, and the birth of a new nation."

Winnipeg surprised everybody in their group. Agnes called it "a prodigy among cities." Joseph Pope, Macdonald's trusted secretary, noted in his diary, "It is excellently paved from end to end

* Actually, the greatest luxury was the new type of fine mesh screen that Van Horne had put up on the windows to keep out mosquitoes and soot.

with wooden blocks . . . and furnished with all the appeals of modern civilization, including a first-rate line of street cars." When they reached Regina, Agnes raved at the sight of the Mounted Police, "in their bright red coats as they . . . rode compactly together, and wheeled into a low enclosure of the Police fort." At a reception held for him there, Macdonald was asked by a Belgian bishop why one of the guests was wearing a skirt rather than pants. Noticing a kilted Highlander standing nearby, Macdonald told the puzzled cleric that his extraordinary outfit was but a local custom: "In some places people take off their hats as a mark of honour to distinguished guests; here, they take off their trousers."

In present-day southern Alberta, the Macdonalds met with Crowfoot, the illustrious Blackfoot chief, who was wearing rags, in mourning for his recently deceased adopted son, Poundmaker. Although Crowfoot pledged undying loyalty to the Canadian government, he also pointed out that sparks from the engines roaring across his reserve often caused fires. Macdonald answered that the railway mostly brought good, and then proceeded to lecture the

In 1886, the Macdonalds travelled the CPR's special VIP car "Jamai all the way from Ottawa to the Pac terminus at Port Moody, then cross to Victoria. Through the Rockies, Lady Macdonald sat on the cowcatcher at the train's front. Macdonald did the same, but brief

Indians on their need to "dig and plant and sow like white men." His sermon was received in silence.

The Rockies were next on their itinerary. At Laggan, a stop early in the mountains (today, Lake Louise), Agnes got out to inspect the new powerful engine that had come to pull them up the steep inclines. As she later recorded, "from the instant my eyes rested on the broad, shining surface of the buffer-beam and cowcatcher" on the exposed front of the engine, she made up her mind to sit there for the remaining six hundred miles. She asked "the Chief" for permission, and when he called her proposition "rather ridiculous," she deliberately misunderstood his response and did what she wanted to do. As the train hurtled along, it passed through a pack of pigs, and one got hooked up in the engine's apparatus. Suddenly, there was "a squeal, a flash of something near," which just missed her. She was extremely lucky to avoid direct impact. Still, she remained immobile on her perch, "a soft felt hat well over the eyes, and a linen carriage cover tucked round me from waist to foot." She was well aware of the risk she was taking, "but the wild spell of the mountains is strong upon me, and I sit watching the stars gleam out over the mountains." To general consternation, she managed to persuade Macdonald to join her—briefly—but he chose not to spend too long outside on the cowcatcher.

The train at last made it to the CPR's western terminus at Port Moody. There, Macdonald made a short speech from the rear platform of the railway car, saying nothing memorable. In his *Memoirs*, Pope tried to fill the gap: "I could not help feeling as I stood by that old man standing on the shores of the Pacific, with his grey hair blowing over his forehead, what an exultant moment it must have been for him." The Port Moody *Gazette* reported that "Sir John looks as gay as a lark." He also proved that age hadn't dimmed one of his most valuable political assets—his near-photographic memory for faces and names. When a man came up to say they had once met before, Macdonald replied instantly, and correctly, that it had been at a picnic in Ontario in 1856 and that the day had been rainy. The group spent little time in the new town of Vancouver, which had burned to the ground a couple of months earlier. Instead, they sailed across to Victoria, where they stayed for three weeks. Macdonald found the town slow-paced, if not sleepy. After that, they boarded the train again for the long journey back to Ottawa.

Agnes, having succeeded in having one article published, went on to sell others to *Murray's Magazine*. In one of her best, "Men and Measures in Canada," she recounted watching the House of Commons in action on an especially hot summer day: "I counted four pages asleep round the steps of a chair in which the Speaker had gone to bed. Five members in one row lay back sleeping peacefully; in the next, one was making a sketch with ink on a reclining sleeper's bald and shiny crown, while another dropped ice-water into his neighbour's left ear."* No wonder she preferred Banff!

As soon as the parliamentary session of 1887 had ended, Agnes took off for a two-week fishing holiday on New Brunswick's Restigouche River. She slept on the floor of a crude cabin, ate beans from a tin plate, kept out the mosquitoes by tying her veil tightly with a rubber band, and after listening carefully to the advice of seasoned fishermen, landed a twenty-five-pound salmon

* This article was anonymous, not to protect Agnes's identity, but in accordance with *Murray's* practice for all political articles.

after an hour-long struggle. She had found, she wrote, the answer to the ultimate question: "Is life worth living?"

By this time, the Macdonalds had settled into a routine that fulfilled both their needs, whether apart or together. Their Ottawa home, Earnscliffe, was a most agreeable place, especially after the renovations were completed in January 1889. Mary was now in her late teens. Physically, nothing had changed. Much-touted and expensive treatments, such as "the Swedish massage," and a trip to New York to see a specialist, accomplished little. She was unable to stand, got around in a wheelchair and was painfully slow in her speech. Yet she seemed content. As Hugh John remarked to Professor Williamson, "She is a gentle amiable girl, and no one who sees much of her can help being fond of her."

In 1888, Macdonald yielded to Lady Macdonald's urging and commissioned major renovations to the Earnscliffe house he'd bought five years earlier. Besides a new dining room and a veranda from which Mary could look out on the Ottawa River, he now had a capacious office with a secret door so he could escape unwanted visitors.

Macdonald's contribution surely counted the most towards her happiness. "Where's my Baboo?" he would call as soon as he returned home each day. He wrapped her in his arms, told her the day's gossip and read her stories. And his absences left a huge hole in her life. During his long stay in Britain at the end of 1885, she wrote him (dictated, that is) a poignant letter: "I suppose you will soon be thinking of coming home. I hope so for I miss you very much, but of course as it is going to do you good I must not grumble. . . . [Have] you seen Her Majesty the Queen? Do you remember what you told me last year about kissing her hand? . . . What are you going to do on Christmas day? I will miss you very much. I suppose you will be out in time for your birthday and then wont we hug and kiss each other. Were you very sick crossing? . . . I must say good-bye, hoping that if you do not sail soon after this letter, you will let me have one in return." Mary ended, "Many kisses for your dear old self." In a later letter, when she was in Banff with her mother, Mary ended: "Are you very lonely without us, do you miss our evening talk?" By contrast, Lady Macdonald's approach, if every bit as loving, was more demanding: as she told her sister-in-law, Louisa, "I have tried to teach Mary what my mother tried to teach me, that she must do, or have done, what was best for her & and for others, & not grumble."

For those times, the care and love with which the Macdonalds surrounded Mary were exceptional. And their attentions never slackened. In the spring of 1889, the famous Canadian-born opera singer Emma Albani came to Ottawa to perform at a concert. Because Mary could not attend, the Macdonalds arranged for Albani to come to Earnscliffe a few days later for Mary's birthday party, where she performed for her and her guests.

In one respect, the Macdonalds' care may have been misjudged. Hugh John spotted it and told Williamson that, after a long stay at Earnscliffe in 1888, he had become "perfectly convinced that

[Mary's] mind was developing and that she was becoming more of a woman and less of a child." Her apparent childishness, he wrote, "is, I think, accounted for by the fact that both my father and mother treat her as a child." Hugh John was right; much later, when both her parents had passed on, Mary would reveal a long-hidden maturity.

By now, Hugh John was doing well in Winnipeg as a lawyer. His role as a militia officer during the rebellion had boosted his confidence: "I was pleased and rather surprised to find I was quite cool under fire and perfectly able to handle my men," he wrote proudly to his father. Soon, he was confident enough to argue with his father over politics, taking a far harder stand on the issue of bilingualism in the West than did Macdonald.

The strongest bond between father and son was Daisy, Hugh John's daughter Daisy often spent part or all of her summers with the Macdonalds, both at Earnscliffe and at their cottage in Rivière-du-Loup. Mary showed no resentment of this new female competition. As Patricia Phenix writes perceptively in *Private Demons*, Mary was "lacking in ego." One of Mary's few recorded comments about Daisy was that she took "great pride in her lessons." If Macdonald didn't quite dote on Daisy, he certainly delighted in her. She had a way with him, ending her letters, "Your little puss." And he had a way with young girls, knowing exactly how to treat them with mock seriousness and, even better, how to make them laugh.

Relations between father and son greatly improved when Hugh John remarried, this time to a family friend, Gertrude Vankoughnet. Their son was named John Alexander.

Early in 1891, the last year of his life, Macdonald received a letter from a girl he had never met. Lottie Prentiss, aged eleven and living in Chelsea on the Quebec side of the Ottawa River, had written to him after learning that Macdonald's birthday fell on the same day as her own. She wished him well and then worked in the subject that really interested her—that a boy she liked had been "real mean" to her, because he had not bothered to answer a letter she had sent him. Macdonald replied immediately, on January 6:

> My dear Little Friend,
>
> I am glad to get your letter, and to know that next Sunday you and I will be of the same age. I hope and believe, however, that you will see many more birthdays than I shall, and I trust that every birthday may find you strong in health, and prosperous, and happy.
>
> I think it was mean of that young fellow not to answer your letter. You see, I have been longer in the world than he, and know more than he does of what is due young ladies.
>
> I send you a dollar note, with which pray buy some small keepsake to remember me by.
>
> Believe me. Yours sincerely,
>
> John A. Macdonald

No wonder, in *Globe* editor John Willison's comment, so many women, and girls, "worshipped" him.

That was Macdonald at his best. His late-life dealings with old relatives nearing their end sometimes revealed him at less than his best. This emotional awkwardness showed itself most clearly in his relationship with his remaining sister, Louisa. She had always been his favourite, stubborn and difficult as she was, but also exceptionally courageous, and he had always gone out of his way to accommodate her eccentricities. After the death in 1876 of Macdonald's other sister, Margaret, the two remaining members of that household, Louisa and the widower James Williamson, moved into the centre of Kingston, where they rented rooms in a boarding house. They didn't get on. Louisa complained that Williamson left books lying all over the house, and before long that he had begun to fall apart, drinking and "dining out," and, most startlingly, going "off to the club with a lot of girls." Macdonald tried to smooth things over by sending money, but he kept finding reasons not to fulfill his promise to Williamson to attend various Queen's University functions. In an attempt to repair the damage, Macdonald wrote to Louisa, "I fear the Professor is breaking up & shall advise him to retire and devote himself to literary pursuits." Paradoxically, this implied threat worked, causing Williamson to apply himself harder to hold on to his university post.

By this time, though, Macdonald was finding reasons to avoid coming to Kingston to visit not just the errant Williamson, but the increasingly lonely and sick Louisa. "I am chained by the leg here just now," he wrote, "and cannot leave town for the moment as the negotiations with Washington are going on [over the fisheries] and I am receiving cipher messages hourly which require immediate answer." He did spring into action by letter when her doctor issued Louisa a stern warning. Macdonald told her in no uncertain terms, "Complete rest, he says, is your best medicine, and you won't take it. He objects especially to your going up & down those stairs . . . my dear Louisa, you really must take better care of yourself or you and I will quarrel." Finally, at the end of 1887, he did go down by train, aboard the "Jamaica," for a one-day visit. Louisa's spirits were much improved as a result: Williamson reported that she was "the better in health for your visit, and goes up this evening to take tea at Mrs. John's."

Louisa's improvement was only temporary. A year later, word was sent to the family that her end was near. Macdonald rushed to Kingston, to find her considerably improved. He returned to Earnscliffe, and was there when a telegram arrived announcing her death. At Louisa's funeral, at St. Andrew's Church in Kingston, Macdonald wept, making no attempt to halt the tears. She was later interred in Cataraqui Cemetery, in the family plot.

All of Macdonald's original family was gone now, except for Maria, Isabella's sister. She had married one of the Macpherson clan and still lived in Kingston, but they had never been close.* As for Williamson, Hugh John best described to the professor the consequences of Louisa's death: "[You] and she had lived together for so long I don't think either of you realized how much you were to each other." Thereafter, the letters between Williamson and Macdonald dwindled away to brief notes, usually about money, and they met for the last time when Macdonald was in Kingston for his final election, in 1891.

~

The death, impending or actual, of family members and old friends was an inevitable fact of Macdonald's last years, with the same inevitability applying to himself. Macdonald, though, found a way to make the subject a part of his political character. In 1884, on the occasion of the fortieth anniversary of his entry into politics, a monster celebratory rally was staged in Toronto. When

---

* A second, more remote relative also existed. Another of Isabella's sisters, Ann, had moved to New Zealand. In 1888, she wrote to Macdonald to urge him to retire to "honest private life."

Macdonald remarked on how few were left of those who had "entered [politics] full of hope, life and the earnestness of youth," all of them now, "like myself, feeble old men," cries of "No, no, no," burst out from all over the hall. Then someone called out, "You'll never die, John A."

One of the most memorable of all Canadian political slogans had been born. At once defiant and melancholy, it encapsulated what it was that his government and the Conservative Party now stood for—Macdonald himself, a Grand Old Man, unflagging and alluring, if flawed, battling on unbowed on behalf of his country even in the face of his own impending death. For the rest of his career, Macdonald would be lifted up, as if on the shoulders of ordinary Canadians, by that iconic war cry, "You'll never die, John A."

Only two of Canada's prime ministers have died in office. The other, Sir John Thompson, was comparatively young, and his death from a heart attack was unexpected. Macdonald took a long time to die, and he was often in poor health. For several years, therefore, Canadians watched their leader slowly dying while still he fought for their national survival.

Although Macdonald often told those close to him he would soon have to step down—as in his 1885 letter to Lord Carnarvon, when he wrote that, "With the CPR completed and the Franchise Bill passed, I can sing my *nunc dimittis* and retire"—he probably never meant it, except to keep his supporters in order. Equally, only some temporary frustration caused him to tell the CPR's George Stephen in 1888 that he had "lost all interest in public service." The reality was that he immensely enjoyed his job and was exceptionally good at it, and that there was no one to take his place. As well, the adrenalin rush of politics filled up some of the void in his private life. "When a man like myself has once entered on the track, he cannot go back," he said. "Having assumed certain duties, he cannot, in justice to himself, in justice to his constituents, or in justice to his own principles, recede. He cannot retire."

Macdonald had become convinced that without him Canada—his creation and in a sense his child—might not survive. He never lost his mistrust of Americans, and in later years, amid the disaffections unleashed by the never-ending Long Depression, it is probable that he came to question just how much his own Canadians could be trusted not to sell out to the attractive alternative next door. Beyond any doubt, he was certain that Confederation still needed time to jell, and that no one else possessed the skill, determination, guile and deviousness it took to ensure that Canadians got the time they needed to achieve that transformation. In the end, it was this goal for Canada, and not the CPR, that was his real "darling dream."

And so it happened. Uniquely among Canadian leaders, Macdonald stayed on the bridge to his end, giving up only after he had got the country through as considerable a challenge to its existence as any it has faced. He of course did die, but only when his going made no difference.

THIRTY-TWO

The Wheels of His Mind

An impression of enormous reserves of latent force . . .
British diplomat Lord Frederick Hamilton on Macdonald

Early in 1885, in a conversation with his long-time associate Alexander Campbell, Macdonald remarked, "We must let in new blood to the system." That was an understatement. All his most important ministers—Leonard Tilley, Charles Tupper, Hector-Louis Langevin and Campbell himself—had been around from the beginning; others, such as John Henry Pope and David Macpherson, were in poor health. The government itself had expressed no new ideas in the decade since Macdonald concocted his high-tariff National Policy. Campbell had told Macdonald bluntly not long before how poorly his government was performing: "The constant giving way to truculent demands and our delays and the irritation and mischief they produce are in everybody's mouth."

Macdonald's age and indifferent health were major causes of this decline: he was now measuring his pace and shortening his stride in every way possible, including ever-longer afternoon naps. He even turned down an invitation from Governor General Lord

Lansdowne to go fishing: "I have been too-long engaged in Catching, or trying to Catch, 'loose fish' to enter into a competition with Salmo Salar," he explained. His legendary optimism was clouded now by occasional displays of bleak pessimism, as in his querulous comment to George Stephen about western attempts to build local lines to compete with the CPR: "Don't be disgusted at the ingratitude of the Manitobans. I have been long enough in public life to know how little of that commodity [gratitude] there exists in this world."

As so often, Macdonald's trigger for action was political necessity. The last election had been held in 1882, and the next one could not be delayed beyond 1887. The omens were not good: both of the large provinces were now held by the opposition—by Oliver Mowat in Ontario and Honoré Mercier in Quebec. In Nova Scotia a separatist movement was stirring, and in Manitoba, Conservative premier John Norquay was fast losing his hold on power. Macdonald had no choice but to recruit new talent.

His interests went a good deal further than partisan politics. From the mid-1880s on, Macdonald began for the first time to think beyond nation-building itself to the kind of nation he ought to be trying to build. He did so even though a series of events beyond his control was now radically altering the national agenda: deep sectarian divisions threatened to tear the country apart; soon afterwards, the Liberals would suddenly embrace cross-border free trade, even consider an outright economic union. To Macdonald, these measures challenged Canada's very existence. So he once again readied himself for a fight. He might be an old volcano, but he was by no means extinct. Getting a better cabinet was just his first step.

Back then, cabinet-making was a good deal more difficult than it is today. The number of portfolios was fixed, first at thirteen, then at fourteen—unlike today, when all kinds of new posts are invented to create cabinet spots for promising newcomers or to satisfy overlooked regions and interest groups. Nor was it acceptable then for portfolio responsibilities to be chopped and changed to fit the available talent.

Macdonald began the task soon after he returned from his sojourn in Britain, in January 1886. He once even went so far as to consider committing the ultimate Canadian political heresy: as he told a colleague, "I think we must choose men for their qualifications rather than for their locality." He didn't take that risk, and in payment for past loyalties during the Riel crisis, he left untouched the cabinet's most glaring weakness—his francophone ministers, Adolphe-Philippe Caron, Joseph-Adolphe Chapleau and Hector-Louis Langevin. All three now lacked lustre back home. He did, though, recruit four promising newcomers.

Among the quartet was Thomas White, a capable journalist and long his protégé, whom Macdonald slotted into the beleaguered Interior Ministry. George Foster was another; Macdonald had overheard him giving an eloquent lecture on temperance while visiting Kingston, and shortly afterwards, this New Brunswicker found himself in the cabinet, eventually becoming finance minister. It was as a lover, though, that Foster made his most considerable mark in the history books. A bachelor in his mid-forties, he suddenly married Adeline Davies, a divorcee—and it was this couple that Lady Macdonald exiled from Ottawa society. The third was Charles Hibbert Tupper, the son of the old warhorse Charles Tupper. He began badly, when he importuned the prime minister to find a job for a constituent and received the testy reply, "Skin your own skunks." Before long, however, Macdonald was praising the son to his father, saying, "His only fault—if it be a fault—is that he would like to carry all his reforms in a day—but I was young once myself, altho' it was a long time ago."

Macdonald's most important recruit was John Thompson—a later prime minister. As a lawyer, Thompson had been appointed to the Nova Scotia Supreme Court and was greatly admired for his judgments. Once in Ottawa, he would accomplish, twice over, the near impossible. He bested the formidable Edward Blake, winning decisively their first encounter in a debate in 1886 on the government's handling of affairs in the North-West. As well, he was not intimidated by Macdonald, arguing uninhibitedly with him at cabinet meetings, with neither taking their disagreements personally.

Thompson had flaws. Intelligent and respected for his integrity, he had none of Macdonald's understanding of human nature. He had another, more serious political defect: raised a Presbyterian, he converted to the Catholic faith of his wife, Annie. That

To improve his cabinet, Macdonald belatedly recruited some newcomers. John Thompson, the new justice minister, was the star, able enough to best Edward Blake in debate. Annie Thompson had good political instincts, warning her husband that, if executed, Riel would become "a martyr."

prompted Lady Macdonald to call him openly "a pervert." Macdonald considered naming Thompson his successor but feared that Ontario would never accept him.*

Macdonald snared Thompson with great deftness. Charles Tupper's latest return to London as high commissioner had created an opening in the cabinet for a Nova Scotian. Macdonald persuaded Alexander Campbell, his minister of justice, to move over to the Post Office, a demotion that Campbell never forgave. That response inspired Macdonald to one of his great insights about human nature: when Joseph Pope observed that Campbell owed Macdonald for many past favours, he replied, "That is just why he hates me. There are some people in the world who resent nothing so much as a sense of obligation."

Thompson rejected the first offer, but Macdonald's careful reading of his letter prompted him to quote Byron's *Don Juan* to a colleague: "A little while she strove, and much repented, / And whispering 'I will ne'er consent'—consented." Macdonald guessed right. Annie Thompson made up her husband's mind for him by asking whether he really wanted to spend the rest of his life among the "sere old crows" on the bench. After a by-election was opened up by a promise to the incumbent Liberal of a spot on the bench, Thompson was sworn in as minister of justice.

To the public and everyone else in the government, only Macdonald ever mattered. Canada's system of presidential prime ministers, often assumed to be a modern invention, can be traced back to him. Certainly he believed that his powers were near presidential. In an 1890 letter to John Schultz, Riel's one-time opponent in Red River, who was now considered so respectable as

---

* After Macdonald's death, Thompson made it to the top post in 1892, but he died suddenly two years later during a trip to Britain. Had he survived, Canadian political history might have been radically different.

to be appointed lieutenant-governor of Manitoba, Macdonald laid down the law: "*The Premier is in fact the ministry*, and should there be any difference of opinion between him and any member of the cabinet, his advice must prevail with you."*

On several occasions during his long political career, Macdonald had shown genuine, but often little-recognized, originality in his understanding of the nation's character. For example, his original call for the Mounted Police to be composed of a "co-mingling" of Europeans and Aboriginals, and his fine distinction about how to treat the Mother Country—that Canada owed Britain support if it was under direct threat, but not when it got itself into difficulties by some colonial venture. What was different after the mid-1880s was that Macdonald was now consciously searching for ideas about what to do.

Macdonald possessed the capacity for this creativity because, although often pragmatic and opportunistic, he was also capable of being subtle and protean. One of the most perceptive comments ever made about him was by Archibald McLelan, an otherwise unremarkable cabinet minister from Nova Scotia, who in a letter to Macdonald in 1889 said that a phrase his father sometimes applied to those he admired also applied to Macdonald: "There are wheels in that man's mind that haven't been yet moved." Lord Frederick Hamilton, a senior British diplomat who met Macdonald several times while in Ottawa, reached the same conclusion: "He conveyed an impression of enormous reserves of latent force behind his genial manner," he wrote in his diary. While Macdonald most times

* Probably because it had been his pre-Confederation title, Macdonald often referred to himself as "premier" rather than his official title of prime minister.

hid his intellect so as not to distance himself from voters, the capaciousness of his mind shone through in the breadth of his reading and the quickness of his wit. He once told Joseph Pope that had he been able to have a university education, he would probably have "entered the path of literature and acquired distinction therein." Perhaps so; perhaps not. What is certain is that, late in his life, he put into motion some of the unused wheels in his mind.

He had already extended the franchise to Indians without their having to lose any of their rights—an idea that became a permanent part of Canadian law only three-quarters of a century later. The interest he had taken in the Salvation Army reflected his readiness to try to figure out how to connect to the poor and the dispossessed. His most imaginative idea, already referred to briefly, was not merely progressive but revolutionary—how best to extend the vote to women. For reasons difficult to comprehend, this story has disappeared entirely from the country's history books. It's time to get it back into the national chronicle.

When Macdonald introduced the Franchise Bill in the Commons in January 1885, it set off a filibuster that went on for months, with Opposition MPs reading out passages from books such as *Robinson Crusoe* to keep the obstruction going. Their skepticism was merited. Ostensibly a nation-building measure to make the federal government rather than the provinces responsible for the administration of national elections, the bill's real purpose was to transfer to the Conservative Party a large slice of patronage—such as the jobs for returning officers. Tucked into the body of the bill was a clause that was even more contentious than that of extending the vote to Indians: it provided for extending the vote to women.

Ever since, this initiative has been quite unknown or dismissed.* A 2007 pamphlet, *A History of the Vote in Canada*, by the chief electoral officer, described it as "a sacrificial lamb" concocted by Macdonald to get his hands on all the election patronage. That analysis makes no sense; in the 1880s, the notion of votes for women was so outlandish that Macdonald would not have gained any bargaining advantage from it. In Canada, few women espoused it; in Lady Macdonald's opinion, "Those silly women . . . do more harm than good, as women generally do when they put their dainty fingers into the political pie."† Nor could the initiative win Macdonald any votes: while some women might be grateful, far more men would be outraged. Opposition MPs argued that it "would make women coarser" and that "the majority of Canadian women are more proud to be known as good mothers than as good voters."

An alternative explanation exists for why Macdonald took up the cause of votes for women, and at a time when scarcely a man espoused it but for John Stuart Mill: he actually believed what he was saying, even though politically its principal effect would be to cause many to look on him as an aging eccentric. This analysis doesn't exclude political considerations, which always were near the top of his priorities. According to Pope, Macdonald believed that "women, as a whole, were conservative." Beyond any question, they strongly favoured him. As *Globe* editor John Willison saw it, because "women know men better than they know themselves,

* A rare exception, really the only one, is the 2009 master's thesis by Colin Grittner, "A Statesmanlike Measure with a Partisan Tail." His title comes from the shrewd headline description of the Franchise Act in the Montreal *Daily Star*, of May 16, 1885.

† A group of women in Toronto figured out how to get their fingers into the pie: they formed a book club, but as soon as they closed the door they switched to discussing the suffrage, confident that no man would ever enter a room filled with women talking about novels.

and better than men ever suspect, there was among women a passionate devotion to Sir John Macdonald such as no other leader in Canada has ever inspired."

The case that he meant what he said rests upon what he actually said. During the debate, on April 27, Macdonald commented that he had long hoped "that Canada should have the honour of first placing woman in the position that she is certain, after centuries of oppression, to obtain . . . of completely establishing her equality as a human being and as a member of society with man." By this phrase, he was telling MPs not only that women deserved the vote but, as was truly revolutionary, that they deserved equal treatment in every aspect of public life. He went on to tell them, "It is merely a matter of time." Indeed, a half-century before the famed Persons Case of 1929 that established legal equality between the genders (in respect of appointments to the Senate), Macdonald, in the proposed enabling clause he wrote himself, declared that "Persons means men . . . and women who are unmarried or widows."

Macdonald's limitation of the vote to widows and spinsters—on the grounds that married women's votes would be decided for them by their husbands—makes his proposal seem a minimal concession when viewed from today's perspective. But it was carefully calculated, deriving from his governing maxim, "Never refuse a step in advance." In fact, this limitation already existed in law in Ontario, although only in municiple elections.* More usefully, it reassured MPs they would not have to cope with demanding wives who held different political opinions from their own.

---

* These radical ideas weren't new to Macdonald. Earlier, in February, 1884, in a kind of warning of what he intended to ask MPs to accept, he'd used a Commons debate on Indian affairs to tell them, "By slow degrees, the idea of placing woman on an equality with man has grown in the civilized world," adding that he didn't know whether this was true also among Indians.

In the event, nothing happened. Macdonald's own *bleu* Quebecers were adamantly opposed, and it was reckoned that only four Conservatives were ready to vote for him. After a one-day debate, Macdonald withdrew the measure. He didn't forget the idea, though. In 1890, he circulated a memorandum among his ministers, asking in which provinces women were able to vote in municipal elections, how many actually voted and whether they could be members of school boards and of institutions such as the Guardians of the Poor. Clearly, he was working up to giving a speech on the subject.

Ultimately, it's unprovable whether Macdonald meant what he said about votes for women. It is puzzling that, having introduced the measure and spoken eloquently in favour of it, he then withdrew it quickly, the likely explanation being that he never wasted time on causes certain to be lost. The cardinal fact is that he made the attempt, even though it offered him no conceivable political benefit—indeed, the exact opposite. He was both right and far ahead of his time in attempting to extend the vote, initially, to some women, and in his judgment that its advent was "a mere matter of time." Two facts are unquestionable: he was the first national leader in the world to attempt to grant women the vote, and because of him Canada's Parliament was the first in the world to debate the issue.* Perhaps the reason why this extraordinary initiative has vanished from the country's history books is shame that Canada had the chance to be a global social pioneer but let it slip by. Instead, the suffrage equality crown was won by New Zealand in 1893, with Canada delaying until 1918.

---

* The debate in Ottawa was limited and uninformed by the standards of the public discussions of "the women question" going on in the United States and Britain during the 1880s.

Macdonald's most interesting train of speculative thought can be dated back to a letter he wrote to Sir John Rose in London on October 12, 1880. He noted then that "there is now and always has been a prejudice in the minds of the people of Canada against corporations holding large properties." There was, he continued, "a general feeling that these companies lie on their oars and . . . allow their lands to be increased in value by the combined action of the Government and the settlers." Change had to happen; "Property has its duties as well as its rights," and "vested rights must yield to the general good." He finished by saying, "I might write an essay on this subject." Sadly, he never got around to it.

Nevertheless, Macdonald sensed the way the future was beginning to take shape. From the mid-1880s on, radical social and economic change was becoming visible in Canada. A rural society at the edge of a wilderness was beginning its transition to an urbanized, industrial society. In no way was the change as dramatic as that under way in countries such as the United States, Britain, Germany, France and Japan. Still, industries were getting larger, especially in Montreal, Toronto and Hamilton, and some were already large, such as Massey, the agricultural implements manufacturer. The National Policy helped, while the CPR created a national market for the first time. Companies employed an ever-growing new class of workers, of artisans and "mechanics," who, unlike the yeoman farmers Macdonald had always known, possessed technical expertise and espoused collective goals.

This new class of urban, industrial workers effected far-reaching social and economic change. Between 1870 and 1890, Canada's urban population increased from 18 per cent of the national total to 35 per cent. Alarming new creeds such as communism and socialism were starting to be discussed. Religious leaders began to think not only of the heaven that awaited everyone, but of the hellish conditions many urban dwellers lived in on earth. Their concern would develop into the social gospel, a major national political force throughout much of the twentieth century. As the General Conference of Methodists put it, all Christians had "a duty . . . to make all proper efforts to secure the most satisfactory economic conditions through appropriate legislation."

Unions also began to revive. In 1883, the first meeting of the Trades and Labour Congress was held. The most powerful union for a time was the American-based Knights of Labor, which combined evangelical Christianity and unionism, generating working-class pride and solidarity across regions and religions. Despite this inclusiveness, the Knights strongly criticized the influx of Chinese workers.

There was strong opposition to these new ideas and ideals. Goldwin Smith argued that "injustice is human . . . it is idle, for any practical purpose, to assail it as an injustice." The view of the *Nation* was that poorhouses (on the British model) "are a step towards creating a pauper population with all its attendant misery, disease, and crime . . . all sexes, ages, and vices mixed together like a rank, unwholesome, world." The predominant view remained that the unemployed were not "honest" but idle, and that helping them only injured them by making them dependent on the state.

Macdonald's response, late in 1886, was to set up the Royal Commission on the Relations of Labour and Capital. In one respect it was unique, not only at the time, but in all Canadian history. With seven of its fifteen members drawn from labour, it was Canada's most worker-oriented national inquiry ever. Its high-minded objectives were to improve the "material, social, intellectual and moral prosperity" of workers, but its actual accomplishments were sparse. Only one of its recommendations was ever implemented—to create a new national holiday, Labour Day. Yet it laid a foundation for the future. Its core conclusion was that "to offer a very large percentage of workers the smallest amount of wages appears to be the one fixed and dominant idea [of employers]." And it made the shrewd point that "there is no bond of sympathy existing between the capitalist of the large mill and his employees, such as prevailed when smaller works were the rule." It also made a number of shocking findings: that child employees, girls as well as boys, were regularly beaten in cigar factories in Montreal; that eleven-and-a-half-hour days were common in cotton mills; that rest periods were rare in most factories and that employees commonly ate while continuing with their work.

The report, published in 1889, totalled 734 pages—a length Macdonald no doubt found intimidating. Still, he was able to edge matters forward a few short steps. The next year, the right of unions to strike was strengthened, and an amendment to the Criminal Code protected female employees from seduction by their bosses. But Macdonald's general inattention to the report is revealed in the plaintive letter he received from one commission member: "You are too busy a man, Sir John, to be able to read the report. Will you not, in justice to us, ask some trustworthy friend to read it?" Still, Canada's slow long march towards becoming a welfare state began with this inquiry into capital and labour that was biased, deliberately, towards labour.

Perhaps the most remarkable example of Macdonald's readiness to allow his imagination to take flight is contained in a letter to his old friend Judge James Robert Gowan in January 1886. Gowan had taken a hard line on Quebec's turn towards nationalism in response to Riel's execution. Macdonald replied soothingly that there might be much in what he said about Quebec matters, but then took off in a quite different direction. "Looking at them [Quebecers] from a patriotic rather than a party point of view, is it not to be regretted that the French should [not] be more equally divided between the two existing parties?" Before the Riel affair, he wrote, "they went nearly all *one* way and altho' it was *my* way—it was not particularly wholesome . . . their unanimity had to be paid for."

In an uncanny prefiguration of how Canada's political future would unfold, Macdonald was saying that it would be far better for the country if Quebecers supported both parties rather than supporting one overwhelmingly. He had no idea how complete the tilt away from the Conservatives would be nor how long it would last, but he sensed that national harmony depended on both races being represented in the two national parties.

If in some ways Macdonald saw the future more clearly than most people did, in others he remained behind the times. An unexpected effect of his Franchise Act of 1885 was that it handed no electoral advantage to the Conservatives. Voters, it seemed, wanted elections to be for them, and not just for the parties. Canadians were becoming converts to democracy and were less ready to assume that the version that existed below the border was mere mobocracy.

Heresies began to be uttered out loud. In 1883, the Toronto *News* explained that democracy was "nothing but a government of the people, by the people, for the people." By 1890, the Victoria *Times* had declared, "Democracy is upon us. We cannot get rid of it if we could. We must, therefore, make the best of it." Macdonald's opinion remained that democracy in the form of universal franchise was unsound in itself, because it gave electoral power to those with no stake in the system—to those who owned no property. Equally damning, it was the way Americans did things. In 1890, he wrote to Colonial Secretary Lord Knutsford, urging that "the monarchical idea should be fostered in the colonies, accompanied by some gradation of the classes." He added the explanation that Canadian annexationists used advances in democracy to argue that "our national sympathies are with the Americans."

On other matters, Macdonald embraced the wrong side of history. He continued to chase election funds in the wrong places as avidly as he ever did—from companies doing business with the government. The evidence comes from a letter written to him by George Stephen, the former president of the Canadian Pacific Railway, on July 29, 1890, which was uncovered by historian Michael Bliss while he was researching his 1974 book, *A Living Profit*. Although the letter is extraordinary, it has been almost entirely ignored. Stephen complains to Macdonald that the government is ignoring him and that "in almost every transaction we have had with the Govt. arising out of this contract, we have been taken advantage of and duped and deceived in the most cruel manner." He is particularly annoyed that Joseph Hickson, the general manager of the rival Grand Trunk Railway, has been promised a "subsidy for the Toronto and Ottawa line" even "without doing anything"—without having sent money to the Conservative Party.

Then comes the almost unbelievable paragraph: "On the other hand, you know that I have personally & otherwise thro [Railway Minister] Pope, *alone* spent over one million dollars since 1882." According to Stephen, the CPR poured more than $1 million—in today's currency at least $30 million—into the Conservative coffers over an eight-year span. Moreover, this largesse was provided by Stephen alone (as he emphasized), strongly implying that the full tally was even higher.

This largesse was staggering, not only in itself, but even more in the context that the electorate in the late nineteenth century was only around 400,000 and campaign expenses were simple and small. It's possible Stephen exaggerated in a bout of self-pity, but no reply from Macdonald exists, and this enormous figure was never mentioned again in any other correspondence. Whatever the exact amount, it is obvious that the CPR functioned like a cornucopia cascading cash into the Conservative coffers.

Back in 1882, after he secured the charter for the transcontinental railway, Stephen wrote to Macdonald, "The Canadian Pacific Railway is in reality in partnership with the government." This partnership was not just about getting the railway built but about making certain that Macdonald's administration remained the government forever. Clearly, Macdonald had learned nothing from the disaster of his first attempt, a quarter-century earlier, to create a company able to build the railway. He was very lucky that Stephen's letter from 1890 never surfaced in his own time. What would have happened then is unknowable, but Macdonald certainly would not have apologized for what he had done. He believed that the national interest justified a mutually beneficial government-business partnership. As he once said, "The Conservative party in England does not repudiate the actions of the brewers and distillers and the Association of Licensed Victuallers in electing candidates in their interest, and we do not repudiate or reject the influence of the railway interests." On another key issue, Macdonald wasn't behind the times but just plain wrong: on how best to contain the arrival of ever-larger numbers of Chinese workers into Canada's west coast.

~

By the standards of the day, Macdonald was liberal on most matters of race. All his political life he sought harmony between the French and the English. His views about the proper treatment of Indians—"the original owners of the soil" in his repeated phrase—were far more liberal than most. He also took it for granted that blacks in Canada had the same rights as anyone else, telling one correspondent, "There should be no reason why the red man . . . should not have the same privileges as the British subjects either White or Black." In 1882, when blacks were attacked by a crowd of whites and fought back, he came down strongly on their side, telling his justice minister, "The Judge was I think wrong in excluding evidence as to the Cries of the Whites . . . such as for instance Hang the Niggers . . . and [the blacks] might naturally think it necessary to cut their way through." He actively sought Jews as immigrants, and praised his representative in London, Alexander Tilloch Galt, for persuading the Rothschilds to sponsor Jews fleeing from pogroms in Russia to come to Canada: "You have made a great strike by taking up the Old Clo' cry and going in for a Jew immigration into the North-West."

All of this derived from Macdonald's conviction that no distinction should be made among Canadians except where racial distinctions existed in the law itself, as in the case of Aboriginal peoples or of francophones in terms of their education and religion and language. Neither did he accept that any distinction should be made, again in terms of the law, between those who had long lived in the country, such as descendants of United Empire Loyalists, and newcomers, such as Hungarians, Icelanders, Moravians, Mennonites, Jews and blacks.

His attitude towards outsiders was decidedly different, though. He made a sharp distinction between those he believed could assimilate, such as Jews, and those he believed could not—blacks (other than those already here) and Chinese. When a senior Jamaican politician visited him in Ottawa to ask about the island's possible entry into Confederation, Macdonald wrote to Francis Hincks on September 18, 1884, "Commercial union would be valuable, but I dread the political union which a union opens to us—The Negro question, defence, &, &." He treated as warily a similar expression of interest in union by Barbados.

In the 1880s, the newcomers who were stirring national debate were the Chinese workers in British Columbia. Some had come up from California in the mid-1870s, but the real influx took place in the mid-1880s, especially once construction of the CPR created a demand for large numbers of unskilled labourers along the line through the Rockies, where, unlike on the prairies, there was no local population to fill the available jobs. In all, some seventeen thousand Chinese worked on the railway. The great majority were temporary workers from Guangdong province who had left their families at home and come to the "Golden Mountain" to earn enough money to buy land when they returned, in the hope of escaping their hereditary status as indentured peasants.

The first demand for the number of Chinese to be reduced or the influx stopped entirely was made in the Commons as early as 1878 by the former BC premier Amor de Cosmos. Year after year, comparable resolutions were moved and defeated. Only when the CPR construction teams entered the Rockies did the issue become urgent. After the company had itself arranged for additional workers to be brought in from China, Macdonald's position became "Either you can have this [Chinese] labour, or you can't have the CPR." He disallowed a succession of bills passed by the BC legislature to restrict immigration. And he rejected calls from trade unions across the country, including from a mass rally in Hamilton by the Knights of Labor, for the importation of labour to end. The accusations at the heart of the clamour: that the Chinese reduced the general level of wages, and that they competed for jobs sought by Canadians in coal mines and by Indians in berry picking and fish cleaning in British Columbia.*

The Chinese paid a high price for their striking success as railway workers. About four thousand of them died, many from malnutrition because of the unfamiliar Canadian food they were offered. They also endured injuries and died as a result of these, because few medical facilities were provided for them. Macdonald refused to halt the immigration of Chinese temporary workers, despite demands he do so, because he feared that without this supply of labour the railway's construction would stretch out for years, multiplying the risk of bankruptcy for the CPR.

All along, though, Macdonald had a second concern he felt strongly about. In 1882, he told the Commons, "I share very much the feeling of the people of the United States and the Australian colonies against a Mongolian or Chinese population in our country as permanent settlers. . . . I believe it is an alien race in every sense, that would not and could not be expected to assimilate." Two years later, he elaborated on this view: "They are not of our people, they are not of our race; they do not kindly mix with us." The following year, he was even more blunt: "It is not considered advantageous to the country that the Chinese should come and settle. . . . It may be right or wrong, but the prejudice is universal."

While commonplace at the time, these opinions were not universal. Even in British Columbia, where the prejudice was most explicit, the Victoria *Colonist* noted that the Chinese were "the most orderly and the most sober" in the town. Queen's University principal George Monro Grant declared that "discrimination based on race, colour, creed or sex" was "contrary to the spirit of Christianity."

---

* Chinese workers typically received wages at half the level of those received by whites doing similar work. As a result, Chinese domestic servants were in high demand in Victoria.

Still, there was massive, open prejudice and anti-Chinese rioting in British Columbia. Even in Toronto, where few if any Chinese workers came, the *News* compared them to "a yellow-skinned, almond-eyed, long-haired, swarm of grasshoppers." Even Grant's moderation derived from his concern to maintain trade ties to China.

Until the rail line was finished, Macdonald temporized, resorting in 1884 to the device of setting up a Royal Commission to study the issue. Co-chaired by Joseph-Adolphe Chapleau, one of his own ministers, and by John Gray, a well-regarded BC judge, its findings were strikingly moderate. The Chinese were "not an inferior race," but were first-rate workers. Even though their presence in large numbers in a province with only thirty thousand European settlers had provoked "irritation, discontent and resentment," equilibrium could be restored by "moderate restrictions" rather than by a U.S.-style outright ban on all Chinese immigration. It is highly probable that the commission was saying what Macdonald wanted it to say.

In the mid-1880s, Macdonald enacted Canada's first-ever explicitly discriminatory legislation in the form of a head tax on Chinese workers. As the Grip *cartoon shows, though, most Canadians wanted far harsher action.*

Published in May 1885, the commission's report was denounced by the BC press as "absurd" and "a farce." At a mass rally in Victoria, protestors carried banners reading, "No Yellow Slave Shall Eat Our Children's Bread." Macdonald at last acted. He decreed that Chinese immigrants—more accurately, temporary workers, except for very small numbers—would not be excluded, but there would be legislation to "Restrict and Regulate" their entry. Future arrivals would pay a head tax of fifty dollars, and there would be a limit on the number allowed on any incoming ship. The new law sharply reduced the inflow of Chinese workers, from 4,000 in 1885 to just 214 in 1886, with the total continuing to decrease until 1890, when it rose to 1,000. The later Laurier government increased the head tax to a prohibitive five hundred dollars, and in 1923 Canada followed the United States with a complete exclusion of immigrants from China.

Most Canadians wanted far harsher measures. Their demands do not alter the fact that Macdonald implemented Canada's first explicitly discriminatory, race-based regulation—and that he did it twice over: at the same time as he imposed the race-based head tax he amended the original definition of "Person" in the Franchise Act to exclude those of "Mongolian or Chinese race," so withdrawing the vote from them. Here, he was discriminating against immigrants already in Canada rather than acting against temporary workers. He did so for the sake of votes in British Columbia, but also because he genuinely believed that Chinese would never be more than "sojourners" in Canada. It has taken most of a century to prove Macdonald wrong.

By the end of the 1880s, Macdonald was less than a fortnight short of his seventy-fifth birthday, and his burst of intellectual energy had run its course. Piled up on his desk were files about sectarian hatreds, separatism in Nova Scotia, nationalism in Quebec, alienation in the West, the never-ending depression and the beginnings of talk about the need not merely for cross-border free trade, but for an outright economic union with the U.S. To Macdonald, this last proposal could end only in political union. For the remaining years of his life, he applied all his available energy to trying to stamp out the political fires that now stretched across Canada, or that came at it from the south.

THIRTY-THREE

The Second Bell

We thought we saw an open path
On which rare joys await.
O foolish we, that thus had hoped!
Such lines no land shall have;
This poor old Canada now sinks,
Back into her old time grave.

"Troubadour," writing to Sir John A. Macdonald

In the summer of 1886, Macdonald began his picnic parade across Ontario once again, now accompanied by his new star, John Thompson. The justice minister was impressed by Macdonald's skill and energy; he told his wife, Annie, how Macdonald would "shake hands with everyone & kiss all the girls." He was not so keen on the picnics, which were "nothing but a lot of people walking about a field and some nasty provisions spoiling on a long table in the sun." Still, things having gone better than expected, Macdonald dissolved Parliament and set the election date for February 22, 1887. A few days later, Honoré Mercier became premier of Quebec, at the head of a government of nationalists and Liberals, and joined actively in the campaign.

Macdonald still won handily. His majority dropped from sixty-eight to thirty-seven, but that was ample. Inevitably, he lost ground in Quebec, but even there just stayed ahead, thirty-three to thirty-two. Canadians still liked and trusted him—and certainly preferred him to the aloof Edward Blake. By June, Blake had resigned; Macdonald regretted his going, because, as he said, "We could not have a weaker opponent." Blake's self-chosen successor was still a long way from being a national figure, yet he clearly possessed natural political talent. He was Wilfrid Laurier, who had learned a lot about leadership by observing Macdonald carefully. For the first time, Macdonald faced an opponent of real mettle*.

The 1887 election victory would turn out to be the last bit of good news Macdonald heard for the next four years.

His difficulties had begun to multiply a few months earlier when, near the end of the 1886 session of Nova Scotia's legislature, the new premier, William S. Fielding, put a most unusual motion before the mentors: the best interests of all of the Maritime provinces, he claimed, would be advanced by "withdrawing from the Canadian Federation and uniting under one Government." Once again, Nova Scotians appeared to want out.

What the province really wanted was, again, "better terms"—in other words, more money. Fielding, a former newspaperman in his mid-thirties, was pursuing his goal with considerable skill. His appeal to local patriotism gave his Liberals an unbeatable issue in the election, winning him twenty-nine of the thirty-eight seats. And his call for separation was risk free, because there was no way the other Maritime provinces would ever join Nova Scotia as junior partners in a regional union, in or out of Confederation.

* At the time Laurier became leader, most Liberals and political observers regarded him as only a stopgap because he was so inexperienced. Among the few to detect his potential when he was young and callow was Macdonald.

Macdonald had already rejected Fielding's request, and to strengthen his hand had called Charles Tupper back from London. The presence of the "Cumberland Warhorse," together with local anxieties that separation (or repeal, as it was called) might actually happen, earned Macdonald fourteen of Nova Scotia's twenty-one federal seats in the election. Soon after, Fielding cancelled his motion. As the Halifax *Morning Herald* put it, "The legislature of Nova Scotia consigned the repeal jackass to the silent tomb."

Nevertheless, Fielding and his Liberals were still the provincial government.* And a conviction of unfairness had taken hold among the population, one that would last for almost a century. Paradoxically, there was no justification for this view at this time. The Maritimes had done well from Macdonald's protectionist National Policy: of the twenty-three cotton mills across the country, eight were down east, as were both of the nation's steel mills and six of its twelve rolling mills. What had changed was that the golden age of the sailing ship was over: between 1864 and 1887, Nova Scotia's annual output of wooden ships shrank from 73,000 tons to 14,000. And about this, no one could do anything.

The real cause of the letdown was psychological. As an 1886 editorial in the Halifax *Morning Chronicle* put it, "The Upper Canadian comes here to sell, but he buys nothing but his hotel fare. . . . [He] generally conveys the impression that in his own estimation he is a very superior being." The journalist concluded that "fusion" of Upper Canada and the Maritimes was "absolutely impossible."

---

* Fielding would have a most successful career. He was premier for a decade, then joined Laurier's government as minister of finance and held the post for a record fifteen years. In 1919, he ran for the Liberal leadership, losing to Mackenzie King by just thirty-eight votes.

There was truth in this argument. Although Canada had acquired some of the physical attributes of a nation-state, such as a transnational railway, scarcely any national feeling existed. Goldwin Smith understood why: "To make a nation there must be a common life, common sentiments, common aims and common hopes," and he could see "none" of these qualities in Canada. Some commonalities did exist. The nation had filled itself out, not only from sea to sea, but, by the addition of Britain's Arctic territories, also now encompassing everything between the forty-ninth parallel and the Pole. It had a national capital with Parliament as its centrepiece, and the distinctive North-West Mounted Police. There was also the Conservative Party—perhaps the most "national" government Canada has ever had, certainly so over so long a span, with strong support in every region from east to west and among both French and English. And there was Macdonald himself—the founding father turned guardian of a troubled infant. But that was about it.

The principal attribute Canadians had in common was that they were anti-American, and that most people were immensely proud of being British. They had little sense of being Canadian, though. A Nova Scotia MP, A.G. Jones, summed it up in a single phrase: "I am a Canadian by an Act of Parliament." It was a fact, thus, but not a feeling.

Because the times were bad, Canadians from the mid-1880s on turned increasingly inwards. Local concerns took precedence over the national structures Macdonald had built. Pan-Canadianism, in the form of bilingualism in Manitoba, would soon be challenged directly, Orangemen labelling the province "a second Quebec." The same fate awaited the protectionist National Policy; the new industries it had created were now taken for granted while being blamed for increasing consumers' costs. The transcontinental railway was criticized almost as soon as built, as westerners pushed their politicians to charter independent railway companies to take their grain to southern markets. Most radical of all, calls were now being made for free trade (reciprocity) with the United States, even for an outright economic union despite its political risks. Simultaneously, there were rising demands for "provincial rights," not only in Ontario where they began but across the country.

The anonymous poet Troubadour was exaggerating when he wrote to Macdonald that "poor old Canada now sinks, back into her old time grave." Still, in contrast to the United States, Canada was clearly becoming a state that was failing its people. Nothing magnified the mood of defeatism more than the constant exodus of its people—a loss of population comparable only to Ireland's during the Great Famine.*

An article by Goldwin Smith captured the circumstances Macdonald had to contend with at this time, even if published a few years earlier. On April 10, 1884, Smith had written, "The task of his political life has been to hold together a set of elements, national, religious, sectional and personal as motley as the component patches of any 'crazy quilt,' and actuated each of them by paramount regard for their own interests. . . . It is more than doubtful that anyone could have done better. . . . Let it be written on his tomb, that he held out for the country against the blackmailers until the second bell had rung." Macdonald would respond to the threat posed by free trade and economic union in his last election, in 1891. His immediate task was to deal with the deep internal divisions arising out of language rights and provincial rights. About the scale of the challenge, he had no doubts: "The present is a grave crisis in the political history of Canada," he wrote a friend in mid-1887.

---

* About one million Canadians left during the last decades of the nineteenth century. Ireland's loss during the Great Famine was a million and a half, but from an original population of eight million, close to double that of Canada. Ireland, though, also lost a million people by outright starvation.

Since gaining the Quebec premiership at the start of 1887, Honoré Mercier had performed exceptionally well. He had immediately ordered reviews of the government's finances and administrative machinery, then had followed up with measures to establish industrial schools for workers and to modernize the road system. He also undertook one daring initiative: he announced he would host a conference of the premiers to consider "their financial and other relations."

Macdonald's response was consistently negative. When Mercier wrote to ask for a "confidential interview on the subject," Macdonald offered only an "official" meeting. When Mercier declined this, Macdonald refused to attend the conference. To further minimize the gathering's importance, he persuaded the Conservative premiers of British Columbia and Prince Edward Island to send their regrets. This enabled him to dismiss the conclave as "a Grit caucus," even though one Conservative premier, Manitoba's John Norquay, took part. As weakened the gathering further, the federal Liberals, uneasy about their long-standing opposition to "better terms," stayed silent about the whole affair.

By outward appearances, the conference went well. Five premiers got together for a week in October 1887 and, with Oliver Mowat in the chair, approved all but one of twenty-four resolutions, ranging from demands that Ottawa cease disallowing provincial legislation, to Senate reform, to better financial terms. These accomplishments were illusory. Macdonald ignored the recommendations on the grounds he had played no part in concocting them. Soon after, they all vanished into the archives. Nevertheless, the event was important. For the first time, provincial premiers had been able to get together to discuss their grievances. Having done it once, they could do it again.

Further, a coherent intellectual argument had been advanced that the provinces were in effect co-governors of the country together with the federal government. Its source was a series of essays titled "Letters upon the Interpretation of the Federal Constitution," written by T.J.J. Loranger, a leading Quebec Liberal lawyer, and published in Quebec City's *Morning Chronicle* in 1884. Loranger advanced the argument that Confederation had been a "compact," or treaty, among the provinces, rather than the creation of a new national government with the provinces as its subsidiaries. The provinces were the components of Confederation, he argued, and they had created the federal government to deal with certain common interests.

In itself, that notion is hard to credit; no one involved in the Confederation negotiations ever expressed any such intent, the British government included. Ontario and Quebec hadn't existed before Confederation; even if they had, neither they nor the

In 1887, Quebec Premier Honoré Mercier, backed by Ontario's Oliver Mowat, convened the first-ever gathering of provincial premiers. Mowat sits in the centre with Mercier to his left and Nova Scotia's W.S. Fielding to his right; farther right is Manitoba's John Norquaym and on the extreme left is the tallest of them all, New Brunswick's Andrew Blair. They agreed that Ottawa should give them more money and more autonomy. Macdonald paid not the least attention.

newcomers, Nova Scotia and New Brunswick, because just colonies, possessed the authority to sign a treaty with anyone. This was why Confederation had come into existence by an act of the British Parliament. Nevertheless, Loranger's essays imparted credibility to an idea now taking hold—that Canada had to be a highly decentralized confederation, a development already under way as a result of the constitutional decisions of the Judicial Committee of the Privy Council in London. Macdonald's view of Canada was rapidly becoming out of date.

Macdonald began to adjust himself to the new order. For some time now, his most bitter intergovernmental battles had been not with Ontario but with Manitoba. Macdonald had disallowed far more legislation emanating from that small province than from any other—this was why Norquay broke party ranks to attend Mercier's conference.

Distinctive because he was a Métis, and of imposing size (six foot four and three hundred pounds), Norquay was the right man in the right place when he became Manitoba's premier in 1879.* As a moderate, he did as well as anyone could have done in minimizing conflicts between all the disparate groups—Métis and whites, French and English, old and new settlers. His connection with Macdonald enabled him repeatedly to secure "better terms," including increases in Manitoba's original size.

Yet the ground was shifting under Norquay's feet too. The ever-increasing English majority—90 per cent by the end of the 1880s—made language tensions inevitable. Far fewer immigrants

* Norquay took great pride in his ancestry, wearing both a suit and moccasins in the legislature.

arrived than had been hoped for; the techniques of dry-land farming took a long time to master; and the Long Depression had sharply reduced the selling price of grain. Together, these factors catalyzed a new political force—an amalgam of regional alienation and populism. The *Manitoba Free Press* caught its temper in an editorial on August 24, 1887: "For the hideous robbery to which the people are subjected by the extortionate railway rates, for the misfortunes of the farmers, and for the blight from which the prospects of this great and glorious portion of God's country are suffering so terribly, Sir John Macdonald and his ministers are alone to blame."

In fact, the principal reason life on the prairies was difficult then was because the flatlands, far from markets and with a severe climate, were a hard place to make a living. Yet there was more than paranoia to the conspiracy theory. The question whether national interests or local interests should have precedence has gone on to become the essence of Canada's never-ending tug of war between the federal and provincial governments. In its first clear expression, in Manitoba in the late 1880s, the issue was easy to grasp—whether the CPR should exercise monopoly power throughout the West, or whether local interests should be accommodated by allowing competing local lines to be built, thereby benefiting prairie farmers but at the cost of draining traffic away from the national company and central Canada. As to how these could be resolved, Charles Tupper put it bluntly: "Are the interests of Manitoba and the North-West to be sacrificed to the interests of Canada? I say, if it is necessary, yes."

As soon as the CPR line across the prairies was finished, agitation began for local lines to be built. Time and again, Macdonald disallowed legislation for the competing lines—four in one year alone. The public pressure on him was relentless. The *Edmonton Bulletin* came up with a splendid bit of invective: "The sun rises in

Halifax, shines all day straight over Montreal and Ottawa, and sets in Toronto."

Eventually, Norquay chartered a line southwards from Winnipeg, even though it would run between two CPR lines. Macdonald successfully pressured the lieutenant-governor of Manitoba to set aside the legislation. Norquay, just back from the premiers' meeting, responded by staging a sod-turning ceremony. Macdonald then stalled the start of construction by passing word to American and Canadian bankers that Ottawa didn't want the project to proceed. On a trip to New York to raise money for his line, Norquay seems to have had a breakdown, precipitated by rumours that he had been involved in financial irregularities. By the end of 1887, he was out of office.

In the short term, Macdonald appeared to have won. Yet he accepted that he could not forever deny public opinion. When Norquay's successor, the Liberal Thomas Greenway, came to Ottawa for negotiations, Macdonald advised him he would not disallow any new railway legislation. It all ended badly: the resulting local line was bought up by the U.S. Northern Pacific Railway and its rates quickly rose to match those of the CPR. Anyway, CPR president George Stephen had by now concluded that the monopoly wasn't worth the trouble it caused, because the company could buy up many of the new lines cheaply while getting paid handsomely by Ottawa for agreeing to cancel Clause 15, which had granted the monopoly to the CPR.

For the first time, however, provincial rights had won, and this had been achieved not because of decisions made by distant British judges, but because of the force of local public opinion. The West had made its first contribution to the national debate.

The West's second national intervention would be a good deal less constructive. The target of populist anger now became the iniquity of the East, most particularly Macdonald, in imposing a requirement for bilingualism on the West, even though its population was overwhelmingly English-speaking and becoming ever more so.

~

Although all the predictable epithets of sectarian extremism—"Rome-worshipping Papists" and "Orange fanatics"—would be hurled across the Ottawa River in the late 1880s, the force dividing the country was not religion but rather race (or, in today's terminology, ethnicity). Religion certainly mattered: French Canadians were overwhelmingly Catholic and of the right-wing ultramontane persuasion, while English Canadians were overwhelmingly Protestant, the exceptions of course being Irish Catholics. The sectarian war that now broke out, however, was far less about religious matters such as separate schools than about language.

The person who understood this distinction most clearly was D'Alton McCarthy, the man who did the most to magnify the divisions between the two sides. Although a member of the elite, and an exceptional orator, he possessed an uncommon understanding of popular opinion, which he maintained by always remaining an active farmer. He was flawed, though, by a fascination with extremism: in the shrewd assessment of historian J.R. Miller, he "perhaps preferred preaching to the exercise of power." As a result, his once highly promising political career would peter out.* McCarthy emigrated from Ireland as a child with his father

* A major source for the material in this chapter is Miller's book *Equal Rights: The Jesuits' Estates Act Controversy* as well as his articles on the subject in the *Canadian Historical Review* and the *Journal of Canadian Studies*.

and later did exceptionally well as a corporate lawyer.* An indulgent father and a celebrated host, he yet could also, as one newspaper put it, be "as cold-blooded as an executioner." While his comments about French Canadians were often brutal, he was never a member of the Orange Order, and at his father's funeral refused to allow Orangemen to pay their respects unless they removed their regalia.

McCarthy began his lonely path with a speech in Barrie during the 1887 election, in which he declared, provocatively but presciently, "It is not religion which is at the bottom of this matter but race feeling. . . . Do they mix with us, assimilate with us, intermarry with us? Do they read our literature or learn our laws?" To McCarthy, it was the Frenchness of French Canadians, not their Catholicism, which constituted what he called "the great danger to Confederation." As he saw it, so long as Canada remained both French and English, it could never become a true nation-state in the manner of Britain or the United States or France. McCarthy never challenged the constitutional protections for the French language in Quebec, but he did all he could to suppress the use of French outside the province. The protests he stirred up would lead to the abolition of bilingualism in Manitoba and the North-West, and later in Ontario. McCarthy thus played a critical part in creating a Canada that would no longer be Macdonald's Canada—still less Pierre Trudeau's Canada.

The sectarian war began as a confrontation over that quintessentially Canadian religious dispute—the treatment of Jesuits. One of the reforms Honoré Mercier initiated as premier concerned a long-standing dispute over what were known as the Jesuits' Estates. The disputed lands had once been owned by the

* McCarthy was so able a lawyer that he would be offered the prime portfolio of minister of justice by both Macdonald and, much later, Laurier.

Jesuits but had reverted to the Crown when the order was dissolved by the Pope in 1773. When the Jesuits were later reprieved, in 1814, they returned to the province. The distribution of these lands among claimants ranging from Laval University to the Jesuits themselves became an issue of financial consequence and great political moment.

Mercier's solution, announced in 1889, was eminently sensible. Laval and the Jesuits would both get shares, as would other Catholic institutions and Quebec's Protestants. As a demagogue, however, Mercier understood the value of having an enemy of the right kind. His act was just one page long, but preceding it was a fifteen-page preamble that included all his correspondence on the matter with the Vatican, including the statement that "the Holy Father reserves to himself the right of settling the question." In the Quebec legislature, this bill, so deferential to the Pope, delighted the ultramontanes and passed easily. The Ontario press, though, took note that the Pope, a foreign potentate, had been asked to decide a strictly domestic Canadian affair. The *Orange Sentinel* demanded that Macdonald's government "apply the veto power" to Mercier's bill and promised that such action would receive "the hearty endorsement and commendation of all who love their country."

The scene was set for a confrontation between Ontario and Quebec, with Macdonald as the certain loser. Without Ontario's Orange vote, he could never win a majority in the province. Yet if he disallowed Mercier's law, his *bleu* supporters would rebel and he would lose Quebec. That fall, Mercier came to Ottawa to see Macdonald, and during a walk together he asked Macdonald whether he intended to disallow his Jesuits' Estates legislation. In Joseph Pope's recollection, "Suddenly the old man unbent, his eyes brightened, his features grew mobile as he half looked back over his shoulder, and said in a stage whisper, 'Do you take me for a damn fool?'" No doubt Mercier was deeply disappointed—to have provincial legislation vetoed by the same man who had executed Riel would have been the ultimate political gift. In mid-January 1889, Macdonald leaked word that the government had decided that "the subject-matter of the Act is one of provincial concern only." There was to be no disallowance.

Ontario newspapers, including mainstream ones such as the *Globe*, now denounced the government for failing to veto Mercier's legislation, on such grounds as that the Jesuits were "a disloyal society." By March, mass meetings in Toronto had led to the creation of an Equal Rights Association dedicated to suppressing the rights of French Canadians. Anger at Quebec extended far beyond the hardline Orange Order. In the magazine *Grip*, the satirist Bengough, so often a progressive, as on votes for women and fair treatment for Aboriginals, wrote that "the French element" would prevent the development of the Canadian nation, because they were out to "transform this Dominion into a mediaeval Province of Popedom."

Grip *caught the mood of sectarian hatred and fear and suspicion with its cartoon of Macdonald clinging to a Quebec cleric while the errant Conservative, D'Alton McCarthy, advances on him at the head of a throng of honest, respectable Ontario Protestants.*

Macdonald responded with irritation modulated by anxiety. He told his friend Judge James Robert Gowan, "The demon of religious animosity which I had hoped had been buried in the grave of George Brown has been revived"; the consequence might be "dragon's teeth [which] I fear may grow into armed men." He warned Charles Tupper that although "the unwholesome agitation" was confined to Ontario and Quebec, "the drum ecclesiastic is now being beaten so loudly that the sound may reach the other provinces." By early 1890, Macdonald had to admit there was "fanaticism both in the East and the West." This transformation was McCarthy's doing.

Although his relations with McCarthy had become severely strained, Macdonald did all he could to avoid an outright break. Early in 1889, a Conservative MP allied to McCarthy moved a resolution in the Commons calling on the government to disallow Mercier's Jesuits' Estates Act. The measure was defeated overwhelmingly, with only thirteen dissident Conservatives voting for it. Macdonald later dubbed them "the Devil's dozen." He didn't speak during the debate, but allowed Justice Minister John Thompson to respond with a brilliant and crushing analysis of McCarthy's long and sometimes eloquent speech. Afterwards, Macdonald worried that Thompson had done too well and perhaps incensed the humiliated McCarthy. He recalled the advice Elizabeth I gave to Walter Raleigh: "Anger makes men witty, but it keeps them poor." Instead, the tactic Macdonald settled on was to avoid criticizing the many Conservatives who supported the Equal Rights Association on the grounds that, if admonished, they would find it hard to later change their minds.

In early April, Macdonald wrote a long letter to McCarthy which has been lost, but McCarthy's reply to it, of April 17, conveys the state of their relationship. "Our views are so wide apart," he wrote, "that I do not see how they can be reconciled." To McCarthy, the fundamental national question was "not whether we are to be annexed or to remain a part of the British Empire, but whether this country is to be English or French." To Macdonald, the answer was that Canada had to be both.

McCarthy made his public break with Macdonald on July 12, 1889—the "Glorious Twelfth" to all Orangemen. Provoked by a fiery speech delivered by Mercier on Saint-Jean-Baptiste Day,

Quebec's June 24 holiday, McCarthy gave a talk in the Ontario hamlet of Stayner in which he referred to the French as a "bastard nationality" that threatened Confederation. He called for the abolition of French-language schools in Ontario and urged that bilingualism be ended in the North-West. If the "ballot box" did not provide a solution for this generation, he proclaimed, "bayonets will supply it in the next."

McCarthy now embarked on a tour of the West, where he gave speeches in Portage la Prairie and in Calgary. Neither was especially inflammatory, dealing principally with the need for a strong central government, yet both had a galvanic effect on the race issue. The reason was that, at Portage, he was followed by Manitoba's attorney general, Joseph Martin, who not only dismissed French as "a foreign language" but declared that the government would abolish separate schools and cease printing government documents in French. This speech was so popular—among its supporters was the prominent Winnipeg lawyer Hugh John Macdonald—that Premier Greenway, even though a moderate, was soon obliged to confirm his attorney general's pronouncements. The next year, the government introduced legislation to end public funding of separate schools and of publishing the official Gazette in French. The "fanaticism" Macdonald had feared was out of control.

So far, Macdonald had said as little as possible, conserving his strength for a critical moment. But he could no longer linger on the sidelines. In January 1890, McCarthy moved a private member's bill in the Commons to cancel the guarantees in the North-West Territories Act for the use of French in the legislature and in the courts. His reasoning was that "in the interests of national unity in the Dominion, there should be community of language among the people of Canada." Historian Peter Waite has described what followed as "one of the great debates in the history of the Canadian

Parliament . . . [about] what Canada was and what it should be." The finest single speech came from Wilfrid Laurier, who argued for calm, reason and respect.* McCarthy's effort was also one of his best, moderate in its language yet woundingly divisive in its consequences. Macdonald's speech, while not one of his best, was one of his most memorable, because it turned out to be his final appeal for harmony between the races. And what he said would become the source of one of the greatest tributes ever paid to him.

Macdonald spoke twice, always in conciliatory terms, trying to edge those on the extremes back towards the centre. On February 17, right after Laurier, he began by saying that any attempt to "oppress the [French] language or to render it inferior would be impossible if it were tried and it would be foolish and wicked if it were possible." It had often been said, he continued, "that this is a conquered country." Even if true, this meant nothing: "Whether it was conquered or conceded, we have a constitution now under which all British subjects are in a position of absolute equality, having equal rights of every kind—of language, of religion, of property and of person." The truth was, he continued, "there is no paramount race in this country: we are all British subjects, and those who are not English are none the less British subjects on that account." As for the bill's objective of changing the language rules in the North-West, "whether the people occupy a Territory or occupy a Province, if they want to use the French language they should be allowed to use it, and if they want to use the English language they should be allowed to use it, and it should be left to themselves."

Three days later, Macdonald intervened again. By this time

* One far-sighted observation by Laurier was that English "is today, and must be for several generations, perhaps several centuries, the commanding language of the world."

Thompson had put forward a compromise proposal based on the recognition that the North-West Legislative Assembly did have the right to decide in which languages or language its own proceedings should be published. All other protections for French, though, should continue. In making his argument that this compromise should be accepted, Macdonald asked MPs to compare themselves to the Canadian parliamentarians who had come before them. He recalled that back in 1793, soon after the Province of Upper Canada had been created, its legislature had met for the first time in Newark (today, Niagara-on-the-Lake). The members of this infant legislature, all of them "Englishmen," had discussed the fact that, in the new province's extreme southwest, there were some small settlements of "Frenchmen" in present-day Essex County.

That old pioneering legislature had then passed an order that Macdonald now read out: "That such acts as have been already passed, or may hereafter pass the Legislature of this Province, be translated into the French language for the benefit of the inhabitants of the western district of this Province and other French settlers who may come to reside." At this point, Macdonald put a question to his audience: "Are we, one hundred years later, going to be less liberal to our French-Canadian fellow-subjects than were the few Englishmen, United Empire Loyalists, who settled Ontario?" When the vote was taken, McCarthy's bill was defeated overwhelmingly.

None of this agitation had any immediate effect, but in 1892 the North-West Legislative Assembly would abolish the official use of French throughout the region. In Manitoba, provincial legislation was enacted to limit the public funding of separate schools and was appealed all the way up to the Judicial Committee of the Privy Council in London, but upheld by that body. The issue would be settled in 1896 by a compromise negotiated between

Laurier and Premier Greenway that limited instruction in French to schools where a sufficient number of students required it. Later, a similar restriction was implemented in Ontario. As Laurier had to explain to his own Quebecers, "There was no other solution for this question . . . [because of] the necessity for the people of Quebec to maintain inviolate the principle of local autonomy." Implicitly, Laurier was accepting that Canada was no longer Macdonald's Canada but McCarthy's—and so in the form in which it would remain until the Official Languages Act of 1969.

Macdonald had said his last words about the relationship between the two founding European races. The final word about the goal of harmony between them, which he had tried for so long to maintain, had yet to be said, however. By the 1920s, it had become the practice for a Quebec MP to sponsor each year a private member's bill to give French-Canadian civil servants a bonus for the translation work they did for unilingual colleagues. None of these bills ever passed, but they did keep alive the idea of bilingualism.

In 1927 bilingualism's greatest champion of the time joined the debate. He was Henri Bourassa, the founder of *Le Devoir.* Bourassa intervened to say that, rather than try to justify the motion by quoting the complaints of French Canadians, he would instead cite the words of "the one man who best understood and to a large extent best applied the spirit of confederation." That person was Sir John A. Macdonald. Bourassa then recounted the history lesson Macdonald had given the parliamentarians of his day about the generosity shown by their ancestors. The bill still went nowhere. But a third of a century after Macdonald's death, these two uncommon Canadians reached out and shook each other's hand.

THIRTY-FOUR

Loyalty versus the Dollar

O Canada, sweet Canada,
John Bull is much too old
For such a winsome lass as you.
Leave him to fuss and scold,
Tell him a "Neighbour" you will be,
He loves you not so much as we.
Fair maiden, stand not thus perplexed,
Come, sweetheart, come and be annexed.

Brother Jonathan's "Love Song"*

Toronto had never before experienced an event like the meeting at the Academy of Music on February 17, 1891. King Street was entirely blocked by a crowd of fifteen thousand ecstatic fans. Inside the hall, more than four thousand people filled every inch of space, from the windowsills to the edges of the stage. Some had got in by breaking a basement window, while others had clambered up a twelve-foot ladder brought by an enterprising boy who first

* By the 1860s, Uncle Sam had become the cartoonists' personification of the United States. In Canada, however, earlier versions, most particularly Brother Jonathan, continued to be used for several years.

charged a nickel, then a dime, and eventually a quarter.* Macdonald was driven to the front door, but the crush was so great he couldn't leave his carriage. A flying wedge of policemen and the burliest of his supporters finally got him to the stage. The moment Macdonald appeared, a roar burst out that, in the words of *Empire* reporter Alice Freeman, "broke in great waves over the house, falling and rising again and again, spontaneous, irrepressible, magnetic."† It was as though Canadians had gathered to say hail to their chief, but also farewell.

By the way they greeted Macdonald, Canadians were also saluting their country. Canada in 1891 was weary, depressed and self-doubting, more so than ever before or since. Macdonald, pale with fatigue, began his last campaign by telling them, "A British subject I was born—a British subject I will die." He would be a Canadian and not an American to the end of his days; and so should they. That war cry sums up Macdonald's story, and a good deal of Canada's.

The 1891 election campaign had really begun almost four years earlier, with a speech given in October 1887 in the Ontario town of Ingersoll by Richard Cartwright, the Opposition financial critic and now Ontario's senior federal Liberal. The speech was his response to a call by the party's new leader, Laurier, for policy ideas that might reverse the party's endless succession of defeats. Cartwright talked about a policy he had long favoured—commercial union, or a

* Among those who had to pay to use the ladder was Charles Tupper, who almost fell off.

† Alice Freeman was her real name; as did many female writers then, she used a pen name, hers being Faith Fenton.

customs union with the United States. The party embraced his idea, and in March 1888 he moved a motion in the Commons calling for negotiations to secure what he now called unrestricted reciprocity. Both schemes would achieve cross-border free trade, with commercial union standardizing tariff schedules and other items between the two countries.

The change in nomenclature was astute politically: the years of the Reciprocity Treaty, 1854–66, had been a boom period for Canadians, and the new policy was less vulnerable politically than commercial union, which effectively amounted to complete economic union. In fact, the wide gap in the economic size and strength of the two countries made it likely—not inevitable, but highly likely—that both reciprocity and commercial union would evolve first into economic union and, not long afterwards, into outright political union. The Philadelphia *Record* understood this progression: "No scheme in which Canada would have an equal voice . . . could be entertained," it declared. Canadians would be voiceless on all important matters of economics and finance unless they gained representation in the places that counted—the White House and Congress. The only way to achieve such a voice would be by political union, or annexation. The Regina *Leader* nicely summed up the consequences: "The eagle and the beaver would repose together, but the beaver would be inside the eagle."

Cartwright understood the risks of the policy he was advancing, but he also knew that the Liberals had to stand for something new and attractive. As he said later, "We had to adopt this project or go to pieces." Embedded in this political calculation was one serious defect: while unrestricted reciprocity gave the Liberals a policy to offer the voters, it also gave Macdonald a target. Criticizing free trade itself wasn't that difficult: many Canadian manufacturers long protected by the National Policy would go under; duty-free access for American goods would discriminate against the Mother Country; and because tariffs were the principal source of government revenues, the loss caused by cross-border free trade would have to be made up by increases in other taxes. At the same time, though, free trade was also easy to sell: many goods would become cheaper, and in politically critical Ontario farmers would enjoy expanded markets for their products.

Just by being bold, the Liberals had revived their prospects. People were in a mood for something new and ambitious. Other novel ideas were being discussed freely at this time: Imperial Federation to transform the British Empire into a kind of global confederation; Canadian independence, with the country casting aside its colonial status; and even outright political union with the United States. When the *Globe* asked readers to express their opinions, one in three of those who responded said they supported annexation. In 1887, a Commercial Union League was formed, with Goldwin Smith as its president, followed a year later by an Imperial Federation League, with D'Alton McCarthy as president. Even the Conservative Montreal *Gazette* no longer felt constrained by the old verities: "It is not improbable," it declared, "that the people will, sooner than many now imagine, be called on to determine whether the Confederation is to be preserved or allowed to lapse into its original fragments, preparatory to absorption into the United States."

As always, Goldwin Smith had the most to say. He had concluded long before that Canadian nationality was "a lost cause" and that Canada's natural market was "the market of the continent." Now he was drawing large audiences for his speeches about the attractions of commercial union. Active also was Edward "Ned" Farrer, the editor of the *Mail*, and from mid-1890 on, the chief editorial writer for the *Globe*. A shadowy, intriguing figure, educated by the Jesuits and once destined for the priesthood, Farrer advanced a "two bites" doctrine, in which the first bite would be commercial union with the United States and the second, political union.

Influential also were a couple of Canadian-born businessmen who had done well in the United States—Erastus Wiman, the developer of Staten Island, and S.J. Ritchie, who had extensive holdings in railways and mines on both sides of the border. They provided funds for the commercial union cause as well as political contacts in Washington. Both Wiman and Goldwin Smith had a romantic expectation that Canada could help end the division in the Anglo-Saxon world between the United States and Great Britain. In a variant of social Darwinism, Wiman believed that "the world moves as the Anglo-Saxon civilization progresses."

As it happened, a number of American politicians had been listening to this talk going on in Canada. These men, many in Ohio but with allies from Illinois to Maine, were interested principally in the idea that an economic deal might serve as a stepping stone to annexation. They knew not to mention political union in public, although sometimes they forgot. Ohio congressman Benjamin Butterworth advised the Canadian Club of New York in a speech in 1888 that "Canadians are satisfied with their form of government. There is no desire on this side to change it." Shortly afterwards, in a speech in Congress, he contradicted himself by urging President Grover Cleveland to seek "the assimilation & unity of the people of the Dominion of Canada and the United States under one Government."

Cleveland, a Democrat, was defeated in the fall 1888 election and succeeded by the Republican Benjamin Harrison. Neither man said much publicly about any policy towards Canada, though at one point Cleveland, in an effort to force Canada to stop fining American fishing ships operating illegally in its waters, threatened to end the long-standing passage through the United States of Canadian goods in bond. Harrison appeared to call for Canada's annexation in one of his election speeches, but later claimed his words had been quoted out of context.

The secretaries of state in each regime were far more active. On behalf of Cleveland, Thomas Bayard showed a refreshing readiness, as he told Charles Tupper, to accept that "the Confederation of Canada and the construction of the CPR have brought us face to face with a nation and we may as well discuss policy questions from that point of view." Bayard and Tupper reached an agreement on current fisheries disputes, in which the United States claimed, correctly, that Canada was seizing its boats, and Canada responded, also correctly, that these boats were breaking the regulations. The deal, however, was rejected by the Senate.

Harrison's secretary of state, James G. Blaine, who had served an earlier term in this post, was of Irish descent and had no love for Britain. As a resident of Maine, he also had little love for Canada because of the incessant fisheries confrontations. Of greatest significance, he was an ardent annexationist. "Canada is like an apple on a tree just beyond our reach," he said. "Let it alone, and in due time it will fall into our hands." He was willing to give that tree a little shake, once saying he was "teetotally opposed to giving the Canadians the sentimental satisfaction of waving the British Flag . . . and enjoying the actual cash remuneration of American markets." He told President Harrison that Canada "will find she has a hard row to hoe and will ultimately, I believe, seek admission to the Union."

As a counterbalance to such ambitions, few ordinary Americans were interested in the effort required to add northern territories to their already huge country. Blaine therefore moved carefully and deftly; chatter in public about a political union died away while those seeking it considered how to advance the cause by offering Canada some form of free-trade deal.

Although the Liberals had backed away from their original support for commercial union to the safer territory of unrestricted reciprocity, few Canada-watchers below the border regarded the free-trade option as credible because approval by the protectionist-minded Senate was highly improbable. Instead, the majority of those Americans interested in relations with Canada favoured commercial union precisely because it might well end up in a political union and so win approval in Congress. At some point, some senior Liberals seem to have connected the dots and realized that, if they sent discreet messages southwards that the party was ready to engage in a serious debate with American leaders about a possible eventual political union, Washington in return might be amenable to the free-trade pact that the Liberal platform called for.

Just what happened next is an intriguing unknowable of Canadian history. The case that some kind of chicanery was put in motion rests upon a remarkable letter written to Laurier on January 14, 1891, by John Willison, the *Globe* editor. In it, he posed the existential question "Do you think these men at Washington are favouring Reciprocity because they want to build up a great British or a great rival power on this continent?" The only possible honest answer was that, all but certainly, these Americans hoped to use the lure of a trade deal to attract Canada into a process of which the likeliest end would be political union. Some influential Liberals thus appear to have hoped to pull off the election-winning plum of gaining free trade by implying to influential Americans that full union might actually be possible, even while in no way intending to give up the country. It amounted to a kind of devil's pact.

No evidence exists that Laurier himself was in any way party to this plan or knew about it. But it is impossible not to suspect that some senior Liberals, desperate not to lose yet another election, attempted to outsmart annexation-minded American politicians. Given Canada's national fragility, such a venture was somewhat like engaging in high-fives with a gorilla.

Nothing, of course, was ever admitted publicly. In a speech to New York's Board of Trade, Cartwright reminded his audience, "We have our history, our traditions, our aspirations, just as you have." Immediately afterwards, though, he made an unannounced trip to Washington. The pro-annexationist Farrer also slipped south, and secured a private interview with Blaine with suspicious ease. The Detroit *Tribune*, a newspaper close to Blaine, came out with a revealing editorial declaring that "the plans of our secretary of state affecting our relations with Canada comprise vastly more than appears on the surface." It went on to urge the administration to "examine the question of commercial union with Canada and afterwards of its actual annexation."*

The highly suggestive question that Willison put to Laurier at the election's start became public only many years later, and so was unknown to Macdonald. He did, however, learn of Cartwright's and Farrer's secret trips to Washington. During the election campaign he would hurl the accusation of "veiled treason" against his opponents. He had used this tactic many times before, but this time he may actually have been right, at least up to a point.

~

Macdonald meanwhile was developing his own policy. It came in two parts, which, not unusually for him, contradicted each other. One was his decade-old high-tariff National Policy: "Our manufacturers are too young and weak yet," he told Tupper. "Ten years hence they might agree they would gain by the opening of the

* Much of this material is based on *Secret Craft*, an excellent 1992 biography of Farrer by the retired journalist Carman Cumming.

market of 60 millions to them on even terms, by opening our market of 5½ millions—but they would be crushed out just now." The United States thus still needed to be kept at a safe difference. His second policy was designed to pull it closer, by showing Canadians that the Conservatives could also bring them free trade. Macdonald announced that he was prepared to negotiate with Washington a revival of the old 1854–66 Reciprocity Treaty on "natural products," such as fish, lumber, grain and other foods. Although his plan was more modest than the Liberals' unrestricted reciprocity, it kept him from looking like a hidebound protectionist. As Macdonald said to a friend, "We must countermine when they begin to mine." What he didn't say was that his trade notion had not the least chance of getting through the U.S. Senate.

Politically, though, Macdonald had positioned himself in a sweet spot. The National Policy could still win votes in cities and towns. As for free trade, he was now able to tell Ontario farmers that he, no less so than the Liberals, wanted lower tariffs on the products that interested them. As a bonus, he had been right all along to dismiss from its beginning—as "a dead duck"—the commercial union originally favoured by the Liberals: it never gained any support outside some business circles. Luck also broke his way: a leading British politician, Joseph Chamberlain, soon to become colonial secretary, came over and warned the Toronto Board of Trade

A lean Macdonald faces down a plump American capitalist to capture the essence of the 1891 election: at stake was a choice between his National Policy of protective tariffs and the Liberals' promise of cross-border free trade. To many, including the ex–Liberal leader Edward Blake, the real choice was between independence and annexation.

that unrestricted free trade could "pave the way for the surrender of . . . political independence."

Two events then unhinged Macdonald's strategy. With the Republicans back in power, one of their rising stars, William McKinley, a congressman who later became president, introduced into Congress a radical new tariff regime and won approval for it. His changes were massive: tariff rates were to be almost doubled, to an average of 48 per cent, the highest in American history. Suddenly, all the major exports of Canadian farmers—cereals, eggs, farm animals—were at risk. In this new environment, the Liberals' policy of unrestricted reciprocity came to be seen not merely as desirable but as essential to Canada's survival. With McKinley's tariffs due to come into effect just a few months away, the Liberals talked about nothing but their commitment to cross-border free trade.

Macdonald's other setback also originated outside the country—in Newfoundland. In the summer of 1890, an island cabinet minister, Robert Bond, travelled to Washington to meet with Secretary Blaine; astoundingly, after only a few months they had agreed on a comprehensive deal to open Newfoundland's fishery to American boats in exchange for duty-free entry for the island's marine products into U.S. markets. Macdonald was outraged, principally because the Colonial Office had failed to advise him of the talks, in which the British ambassador had participated, but also because he had been outfooted by a tiny colony. An embarrassed London hastily made approval of any Newfoundland-U.S. deal contingent on a parallel negotiating success by Canada. The affair eventually petered out, chiefly because, under congressional pressure, Blaine progressively whittled down his original offer to Bond.

To compensate for its clumsiness, Britain sent its ambassador back to see Blaine and secured an agreement, given with great reluctance, for what the secretary of state called "a full but private conference" with Canadian representatives on all outstanding cross-border issues, including a limited "natural products" free-trade pact of the kind Macdonald was advocating.

Talks behind closed doors didn't really fit Macdonald's political needs, though. So he cheated on Blaine. On January 14, 1891, the *Empire*, a leading Conservative Toronto newspaper, came out with a major story that, in response to a specific request by the American government, negotiations were about to start in Washington on a possible free-trade pact with Canada. The affair was now public, to Macdonald's great political benefit. Except that Blaine now cheated on him in return. He got a Republican congressman to circulate word to the newspapers that not only were "no negotiations whatever" planned with Canada, but that "no such reciprocity with the Dominion confined to natural products will be entertained by this Government."

"We have burned our boats and must now fight for our lives," Macdonald responded, in full combat mode. He set the time for the start of the campaign at the earliest possible date, February 3, 1891. Thereafter, he fought the election of his life.

~

But for Pierre Trudeau's first "Trudeaumania" campaign of 1968, the 1891 election is probably the best known in all Canadian history. From it came one of the most potent of all Canadian election slogans: "The Old Flag, the Old Policy, the Old Leader." It also produced that brilliant poster with the triple "Old" slogan along its foot and, above, a drawing of Macdonald being borne along in the burly arms of a farmer and a factory worker.* And it

* The actual author of the slogan, the first ever used in a Canadian political campaign, was Louis P. Kribs, editor of the *Empire*.

inspired Macdonald's war cry: "A British subject I was born—a British subject I will die."

His appeal here wasn't for loyalty to Britain, although that mattered, but for loyalty to the founding idea of Canada itself. At the time, little distinction existed between the two: everyone in Canada was a "British subject," with the term "Canadian citizen" still far in the future.* Nevertheless, the electoral artifacts Macdonald chose to use in this campaign suggested a subtle shifting of his perception of these loyalties. The flag used in the famous poster, although described as the "Old Flag," was not in fact the Union Jack, but rather the Red Ensign, a banner that was steadily gaining ground as the unofficial national flag. As well, he made a subtle change in his "British subject" invocation. Macdonald had used the phrase twice before in the Commons; this time, though, he made a critical alteration to its wording. Earlier, he had always ended the chant, "a British subject I hope to die." This time, his last words were "a British subject I will die."

Knowing that his end was near, and knowing also that most Canadians knew it, Macdonald by these devices was challenging voters to stay with him, their founding father, in the last appeal he would ever make to them to remain Canadians rather than become Americans. A letter-writer to *The Week* said it all in one short sentence: "Wait a little, friends, and let the old gentleman serve out his time as a veteran servant of the state, and then do what you like." So they did what he wanted.

---

* Legally, no Canadian citizens existed until the enactment in January 1947 of the Canadian Citizenship Act.

For his last election, Macdonald unfurled Canada's first, and possibly most effective, campaign poster. Intriguingly, the slogan is wrong. It isn't the "Old Flag," or Union Jack, that Macdonald is holding up, but the Red Ensign, which was fast gaining ground as the national flag.

The election wasn't won easily. Amid the bleak economic times, the Liberals' advocacy of unrestricted reciprocity exerted a powerful appeal. In Toronto, one food bank was ladling out seventy gallons of soup a day. Macdonald's reserves of energy were fading fast, yet he continued to wage one of his most energetic campaigns ever. Quite literally, he kept going until he could no longer stand.

On February 3, right after the campaign's start, Macdonald moved to Toronto, where he set up his headquarters. He fired off letters in all directions urging loyalty and action. "I really think this Election is the crisis of Canada's fate. . . . This is the last time of asking—it is the fifth Act of the drama and I want the curtain to fall on me with all my friends around me," went one. Another read, "You manufacturers must rouse yourselves & fight as you have never fought before. . . . Our defeat means every Canadian industry crushed by American tariffs and American rings." His most important appeal went to the CPR's head office. Van Horne reported back, "Our canvass is very nearly complete and the CPR vote will be practically unanimous—not one in one hundred even doubtful." He cabled Tupper in London, yet again asking him to join the campaign; Tupper, as always, immediately recrossed the Atlantic. He recruited candidates, briefed pro-Conservative reporters and personally chose the towns and cities he would visit.

Before appearing at his first public rally on February 17, Macdonald's principal concern was to compose a manifesto that he circulated widely and used throughout the campaign as his key election speech. He wrote out the entire text and then edited a typed version, though all his changes were minor, as in changing "CPR" to "Canadian Pacific Railway." Its closing paragraphs constituted Macdonald's political will and testament:

> The question which you will shortly be called upon to determine resolves itself into this: shall we endanger our possession of this great heritage bequeathed to us by our fathers, and submit ourselves to direct taxation for the privilege of having our tariff fixed at Washington with the prospect of ultimately becoming a portion of the American Union?
>
> I commend these issues to your determination and to the judgment of the whole people of Canada, with an unclouded confidence that you will proclaim to the world your resolve to show yourselves not unworthy of the proud distinction you enjoy of being numbered among the most dutiful and loyal subjects of the Queen.
>
> As for myself, my course is clear. A British subject I was born—a British subject I will die. With my utmost effort, with

> my latest breath, I oppose the veiled treason which attempts by sordid means and mercenary profit to lure our people from their allegiance. During my long public service of nearly half a century, I have been true to my country and its best interests, and I appeal with equal confidence to the men who have trusted me in the past, and to the young hope of the future, with whom rests its destinies for the future, to give me their united and strenuous aid in this, my last effort, for the unity of the Empire and the preservation of our commercial and political freedom.

A few days later, he was driven by carriage to the Academy of Music.

After well over an hour of waiting through the preliminary presentations, Macdonald at last rose to speak. He began by criticizing himself. He was, he told the crowd, "the aged leader, and perhaps the weak and inefficient leader." Predictably, loud shouts of "No, no, no," burst out. Having tugged the audience to his side, Macdonald pointed the way for it to go: "I believe that this election, which is the great crisis on which so much depends, will show the Americans that we prize our country as much as they do, that we would fight for our existence as they would."

Right afterwards, he had some important information to make public. "I now take the opportunity of making the charge," he said, drawing a document from his pocket as his captivated audience watched. The accusation he now made had as its source a pamphlet on the issues of free trade and political union which had been commissioned by an American customer from Ned Farrer—a person Macdonald described as "the ambassador between the *Globe* or Sir Richard Cartwright and Washington."* What Farrer's pamphlet did, explained Macdonald, was to give this American advice on how best to pressure Canada into a political union. Macdonald had great sport with the report's conclusion—that no attempt at annexation could succeed before "Sir John's disappearance from the stage." He pointed out gleefully that since he had now reached the age of seventy-six, the conspirators should not have long to wait.

In fact, despite the drama Macdonald invested in it, his accusation of a backstage conspiracy didn't add up to much. He produced no evidence to connect the document to the Liberal Party; further, any advice given to an American on how to annex Canada, if a shabby act, was certainly not "treason," veiled or otherwise. Earlier Macdonald had shown the document to Governor General Lord Stanley, who advised him it was too slight to use.

A few days later, though, Macdonald was able to make a second revelation. This time, he made public the secret visits to Washington by Cartwright and Farrer. He revealed also that Farrer had told people in Washington that their best way forward was by taking "two bites"—free trade first, and later political union.

Everything else about the affair was murky, and hindsight has made it no clearer. Macdonald, though, had succeeded in his principal objective: he had pushed the Liberals back onto the defensive. Thereafter, they kept insisting on how loyal they were, even persuading Premier Mowat to come out with his own version of Macdonald's "British subject" declaration. He said the same thing as Macdonald, but without the passion or poetry: "I am glad that I was born a British subject: a British subject I have lived for

* Macdonald obtained the pamphlet from a supporter in the print shop that had produced it.

three-score years, and something more—I hope to live and die a British subject."

Another of Mowat's contributions to the party was more helpful. By now, Edward Blake, the former leader, had concluded that free trade would indeed lead to political union by way of an intermediate stage of economic union. Mowat persuaded Blake to keep his opinion to himself until the election was over. But Cartwright, who repeatedly said the wrong thing at the wrong time, put the Liberals back onto the defensive with a speech in Almonte, a town near Ottawa, in which he openly discussed political union, even though not sanctioning it himself.

As the tide turned, Macdonald paddled ever harder. From Toronto he went the next day to Hamilton, where he and Tupper each held two-hour meetings at different locations before switching over to the other's rally. Macdonald went on to Strathroy, London, Stratford, St. Mary's, Guelph, Acton and Brampton, day after winter day, and sometimes twice a day, keeping up the "double rally" practice as long as he could, but eventually limiting his engagements to one a day. One feature of this tour was unique. He was accompanied not by Lady Macdonald, but by his secretary, Joseph Pope. The reason had to be that his secretary, unlike his wife, could not order Macdonald to cut back his schedule to save his health.

For most of Sunday February 22, Macdonald rested in Toronto, but that evening he took the overnight train for Kingston, arriving early Monday morning. Right away, he left his private car, the "Jamaica," for the British American Hotel to meet local supporters, and that evening, despite a raging storm, spoke to a huge crowd at Martin's Opera House. The weather in his home town was now bitterly cold, and, as Pope would write, "To this sudden change of temperature I attribute the chill, from the effects of which he never fully recovered."

The next morning Macdonald and Pope set off by train for Napanee. There, he was driven to his engagement in the town hall in an open carriage. He gave his speech, leaning heavily on a walking stick, but ended utterly exhausted. Despite Pope's pleas, the local organizers insisted he go to a second planned rally, again in an open carriage. Eventually, Macdonald made it back to his train. Pope picked up some telegrams, took them into Macdonald's compartment and found him lying across the bed, "his face of ashen grey." The next morning, Pope sent out the message that the tour was halted, with all outstanding engagements cancelled. For a week, frequently in pain, Macdonald remained in Kingston; there, Senator Michael Sullivan, a physician, diagnosed his condition as "commencing bronchitis, loss of voice, congested soft palate and pharynx, pain on inspiration of left lung, and irregular pulse."

Only on March 4, the day before polling, was he able to travel back to Ottawa. At Earnscliffe, Lady Macdonald put him immediately to bed. The next evening, Macdonald followed the early returns as they came in by a special wire, but at ten o'clock, with barely half the constituencies reported, slipped away to his bedroom. Not until the next morning did he know he had won.

Before most elections, Macdonald overestimated his prospects. This time, he was too pessimistic. "I was surprised and aggrieved to find the hold unrestricted reciprocity had got of our farmers," he wrote to George Stephen after the election. The results, which he attributed mostly to the "defection" of Ontario farmers, "have left us with a diminished majority and an uncertain future."

In fact, although the government's majority had been slimmed to twenty-seven, its share of the total vote had actually increased from the 1887 election. Macdonald did lose seats in rural Ontario, but in the ever-growing urban centres he lost only one seat, in London. Overall in Ontario, he won more votes than the Liberals, and only a few unlucky electoral breaks left him four seats behind. In the Maritimes and the West, he gained seats, despite the strong support for free trade in both regions. This outcome prompted Cartwright to yet another indiscretion: he dismissed the results from the five eastern and western provinces as those of Confederation's "shreds and patches." In Quebec, where the trade issue was of small consequence, Macdonald did lose some ground, but far less—a net drop of just five seats—than most had expected, given that the Liberals were now led by Laurier and that Premier Mercier again campaigned actively. Even there, Macdonald won the popular vote handily, confirming that Riel was by now a political irrelevancy in the province.

One of the election results gave Macdonald particular pleasure. Among the freshman MPs was Hugh John Macdonald, who disliked politics and told his father he hoped he would lose, but instead won by a comfortable five hundred votes. Some political skills had been handed down across the generations. A year earlier, Hugh John had warned his father, "There is practically no Conservative Party in Canada at the present time," only a "John A. party." He forecast that "a process of rapid disintegration will set in when anyone else attempts to take command." When Hugh John first took his seat in Parliament, at its opening on April 29, 1891, he was brought into the chamber by his father. Their once-strained relationship had become close.

As in all elections, statistics about vote percentages and seats won and lost matter little; only the overall result counts. Macdonald had won perhaps his most important post-Confederation victory. Confronted by the most difficult national circumstances Canadians would ever have to face, they had voted to go on being Canadians. Macdonald's skill and deviousness had played a major part in determining the result, but the essence of what had happened was unmistakable. Compelled to make a choice between loyalty and economic advantage, Canadians had decided, freely, that they wanted their nation to be theirs.

Once it was over, Canadians were told by one of their most highly regarded public figures that they had made the correct choice. Right after the election, Edward Blake dispatched a letter to his West Durham constituents. He wrote that what he called "absolute free trade" should be implemented only as "a well-understood precursor of political union." He was saying that Macdonald had been right.

The Liberal Party soon reached the same conclusion. Within a year, the party cancelled its policy of unrestricted reciprocity in favour of a commitment to something called "Fairer Trade." Had Macdonald still been around, he would have noted approvingly that this new policy meant anything, and nothing.

Without Macdonald ever knowing it, he received yet another tribute for defeating free trade—this time from the best-informed individual on the continent. When Secretary of State Blaine briefed President Harrison about some Canadian approaches during the winter of 1891–92 for a possible reopening of talks about ongoing cross-border problems, he advised him to reject the proposition, because "Canada can offer us nothing we cannot duplicate." Afterwards, Harrison wrote to Blaine, setting out his views should the topic of cross-border reciprocity ever be revived: "I have never seen," he stated, "how we could arrange a basis of reciprocity with Canada short of a complete customs union by which they would adopt our tariff and everything should be free between the two countries. This would be an absolute commercial union and it is probably not practicable unless it is accompanied by political union." Harrison was also saying that Macdonald had been right.

Macdonald had made his last contribution to his country.

THIRTY-FIVE

A Last Bow from the Stage

He believed that there was room on the continent of America for at least two nations, and he was determined that Canada should be a nation.

George Monro Grant, writing about Macdonald

Macdonald faded away quietly, much as old soldiers are said to do. His exceptional constitution still allowed him one last burst of energy, or at least a show of it. The election over, he stayed at Earnscliffe through the rest of March and well into April, much of the time resting in bed but also receiving many more visitors than Lady Macdonald would have wished, and churning out letters on such urgent government matters as whether the baggage-master at Hampton merited an increase in pay to $1.50 a day. In Macdonald's opinion, he did not.

The approach of spring and the opening of the first session of the new Parliament brought Macdonald into the open with a small lift to his step, even though he wearied quickly. For the opening occasion in the House he knew so well, he wore his signature outfit of a frock coat, soft grey trousers, a stovepipe hat and a large and floppy red necktie. Proudly, he and Hugh John signed their names one after the other in the register. During the Throne

Speech debate, Macdonald spoke briefly but deftly, teasing Laurier over his electoral disappointment: "J'y suis, j'y reste. We are going to stay here and it will take more than the power of the Hon. Gentleman with all the phalanx behind him, to disturb us or to shove us from our pedestal." One reporter wrote of him, "His eye was clear, his step elastic." Hugh John advised Professor Williamson in Kingston that his father was "now very much better."

In fact, he had made his last bow on the stage. On May 12, Macdonald went to his parliamentary office to discuss with Governor General Stanley the possibility of an Anglo-American confrontation in the Bering Strait because of a Canada-U.S. dispute over seal-hunting rights. While explaining the matter, he found he could no longer speak properly. He asked Joseph Pope to bring in John Thompson. Once Thompson arrived, Macdonald, looking highly embarrassed and utterly weary, asked him to brief the governor general. At that point, Stanley noticed that Macdonald's mouth was drawn and twisted. As soon as Stanley had left, Macdonald turned to Pope, a note of fear sounding clearly through his thickened voice, and told him, "I am afraid of paralysis. Both my parents died of it and I seem to feel it creeping over me." Macdonald's fear was not that the next stroke might fell him, but that it would not. As he explained to one of his doctors, "I hope to God I don't hang on like Mackenzie," the former Liberal leader, who still lingered in the House, forever shaking and almost never speaking. Because this stroke was a mild one, Macdonald managed to conceal from Agnes what had happened.

That evening, all the symptoms of his stroke eased, and his speech returned to near normal. His doctor urged him to take a complete rest away from Ottawa. Macdonald refused to leave while Parliament was in session; he did agree to rest as much as possible, but insisted he had to be present at cabinet meetings and debates in Parliament. Back in the chamber again, his spirits revived and he sat listening to the debates, sometimes cheering on a Conservative MP or discomfiting a Liberal with some quip.

Friday May 22 was a soft, warm day, and Macdonald spent it on the Hill. In Thompson's words to Annie, he was "very well and bright again." Early in the evening, Macdonald went down to the basement for a shave by the parliamentary barber, Napoleon Audette. While there, he studied a framed engraving of the Legislature members of 1855, a decade after he had first entered politics. He called out their names—Morin, Augers, Caron, Mackay, Dunkin, Short, Meredith, LaFontaine, Drummond—and told Audette, "All gone, all gone." Back in the chamber, Mackenzie Bowell, one of his ministers, teased Macdonald into agreeing that it was time for two oldsters like them to be "at home in bed." Macdonald responded, "I will go. Good-night." These were the last words he ever spoke in the House of Commons.

For several days, he continued to maintain much of his regular schedule, insisting, over Agnes's protests, that they have their usual Saturday dinner for Conservative MPs and staying up until the guests had left. That night, Macdonald woke up at 2:30 a.m. to discover Agnes bending over him. She had come into his bedroom in response to his incoherent shouts, and he admitted to her he had lost all feeling in his left leg. The next morning, Macdonald managed to talk to Thompson about government business in slow, painfully prolonged whispers. His leg had recovered.

Word of his illness began to circulate beyond his inner circle, and his doctors issued regular bulletins on his condition. On Thursday May 28, they reported he had experienced "a return of his attack of physical and nervous prostration" for which they had prescribed "entire freedom from public duties."

One day later, Macdonald suffered a third stroke. It left all his right side paralyzed and all but ended his ability to speak, although he still could reply to carefully enunciated questions from visitors—Agnes, Hugh John, Pope or one of the doctors—by squeezing their hands. Lord Stanley later described to the Queen the unflagging care Lady Macdonald provided her dying husband: "She never left his side, always thinking he would be able to say some last words to her, but they never came and it was only by the pressure of his hand that she knew that he knew she was at his side."

By now, word of the seriousness of Macdonald's condition had spread out across the entire country. All the barges on the Ottawa River silenced their whistles as they passed Earnscliffe, and horse-drawn carriages along Sussex Drive no longer used their bells. Outside the house, reporters stood on guard day and night, and a special telegraph wire was set up to flash the news outwards. The doctors continued their bulletins, although not making public the diagnosis of one senior specialist, James Grant: "Hemorrhage on the brain. Condition hopeless."

On June 1, the weather turned hot. The heavy curtains in his bedroom were pulled tight shut. Sometimes, Macdonald would swallow a glass of milk or beef tea in small sips, and even take a little champagne. Everyone spoke in whispers. His grandson, Jack, Hugh John's son, insisted on seeing him and prattled away at his bedside, unable to understand why his grandfather never answered his questions. Macdonald's own Mary was then brought into the bedroom and managed by some intuitive skill to convince Jack to remain quiet. Their very presence, though, seemed to revive him.

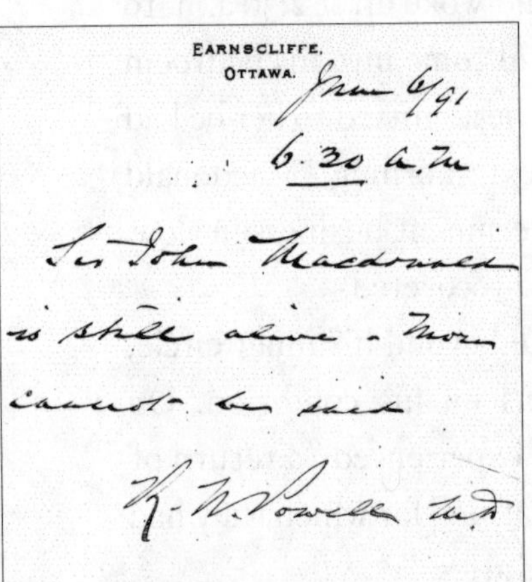
EARNSCLIFFE,
OTTAWA. June 6/91
6.30 a.m.

Sir John Macdonald
is still alive – More
cannot be said

R. W. Powell M.D.

At 6:30 a.m. on June 6, 1891, the doctors issued a bulletin that Macdonald was "still alive." Their next bulletin, at 10 a.m., reported his death, and the news flashed by telegram across the country.

Meanwhile, government ministers were frantically exchanging gossip and opinions about who might succeed him. Would it be Mackenzie Bowell,

J.J. Abbott, Charles Tupper or Hector-Louis Langevin, the most senior cabinet member but one mired in a scandal? Or should it be John Thompson, by far the ablest man, but politically flawed because he had converted to Catholicism? Clearly, Macdonald either hadn't made up his mind who should succeed him, or could no longer tell his ministers what he wanted done.

The doctors' bulletins described a patient fighting to the end. On Thursday June 4, they reported: "Sir John A. Macdonald passed a fairly comfortable night. . . . His cerebral symptoms are slightly improved." The next day, the tone was sombre: "We find Sir John Macdonald altogether in a somewhat alarming state. . . . In our opinion, his powers of life are steadily waning."

Shortly after 10 a.m. on Saturday June 6, 1891, Joseph Pope emerged from the door at Earnscliffe with a message for the crowd of reporters waiting in the grounds outside. "Gentlemen," he said, "Sir John Macdonald is dead." He then pinned the doctors' last bulletin onto the gate.

All the churches in Ottawa began to toll their bells. As the news spread out by telegraph and telephone, through towns and hamlets connected by railway lines, along the coasts by calls shouted from one fishing boat to another, and out in the countryside by solitary riders passing farmers in the fields, church bells everywhere began to toll—from Cape Breton to Vancouver Island, all the way across the impossible magnitude of the country Macdonald had created.

As always, Laurier was the most eloquent. In the Commons two days later, he said, "The place of Sir John Macdonald in this country was so large and so absorbing that it is almost impossible to conceive that the political life of this country, the fate of this country, can continue without him . . . as if indeed one of the institutions of the land had given way." Before him, Langevin had tried to speak but could only say, "My heart is full of tears; I cannot proceed." Although a coincidence, it was appropriate that both of the official eulogies for Macdonald should have been given by French Canadians.

Afterwards, others said what Langevin had tried to say. Thompson told the Montreal *Daily Star*, "He was the founder and father of the country. . . . There is not one of us who had not lost our heart to him." Goldwin Smith wrote, "He combined lifelong experience with consummate tact. . . . He had singular attractiveness of manner with a playful wit. He had great social versatility. . . . He was a thorough man of the world, with nothing about him narrow or fanatical." No one better captured John A. Macdonald's essence than did his constant critic J.W. Bengough, at *Grip* magazine: "He was no harsh, self-righteous Pharisee."

Not everyone thought this way. Sir Daniel Wilson, president of the University of Toronto, declared that Macdonald had been a "clever, most unprincipled party leader [who] developed a system of political corruption that has demoralized the country. Its evils will long survive him."* Years later, Richard Cartwright, by then Laurier's minister of trade and industry, declared that no statue of Macdonald should go up on Parliament Hill unless its inscription included "Canadian Pacific Scandal."

The response of ordinary Canadians was utterly different. *The Week* admitted that its erudite commentaries had completely missed the most important part of Macdonald's political life: "It is now seen that the dying Premier had a hold not only upon the

---

* Wilson had an exceptionally low opinion of all politicians and had quarrelled with Macdonald over his having been made, in 1888, only a knight bachelor, a lower honour than that granted to politicians.

popular intellect and imagination but upon the popular heart, to a degree which few, probably, had believed or imagined. . . . There must have been in the man, as distinct from the politician, depths of genuine feeling and sympathy, of the existence of which many a week ago would have been incredulous." John Willison, in his *Reminiscences*, said it more directly: "It was no common man who so touched a nation's heart."

On the Monday, the day of Langevin's and Laurier's eulogies, the Commons chamber was draped in black, similarly Macdonald's seat, with a spray of white flowers on his desk. He lay in state in the Senate chamber for two and a half days, with the public allowed to come in only for the last day. During that time, more than twenty thousand people—as many as Ottawa's total population—walked past his coffin. After the funeral service at St. Alban's Church, his body was taken to the railway station to make its last journey to Kingston. The route took him past all the familiar towns and hamlets—Stittsville, Carleton Place, Perth, Sharbot Lake, Harrowsmith—with crowds gathered everywhere along the line, all the men bare-headed. At Kingston, he lay in state in the City Hall, his open casket guarded by military cadets. There, some ten thousand walked past the casket—double the town's population.

He was buried in Cataraqui Cemetery near to the graves of his mother and father, his sisters and his infant son, John Alexander. Above his grave, the inscription on the simple Latin cross read, "Sir John A. Macdonald, 1815–1891. May he rest in Peace." The cemetery is close enough to the Toronto–Montreal main line for the whistles of the trains to be heard as they thunder along, some heading westwards by the all-Canadian route, around Lake Superior, across the prairies and over the Rockies, to the end of the line at the edge of the Pacific. One detail of all this ceremony might have caused Macdonald to raise an eyebrow: his casket, of rolled steel painted the colour of rosewood, had been imported from the United States.

After his open casket had lain in state in the Parliament Buildings for two and a half days, a special train carried Macdonald to Kingston past bare-headed throngs standing along the track. After a ceremony, a huge procession accompanied the casket to Cataraqui Cemetery, where he was buried beside his family, beneath a plain stone cross inscribed, "Sir John A. Macdonald, 1815-1891. May he rest in Peace."

Epilogue

The last person to have known Macdonald personally, his granddaughter Daisy, by then Mrs. Isabella Gainsford, died in Winnipeg in 1959. Her son, Hugh Gainsford, Macdonald's great-grandson and his last surviving direct descendant, is still living at the time this narrative is being written. The last person who had known him politically, William Jackson, Riel's secretary, died in New York in 1951. Those who knew Macdonald and who lived on after him can be grouped into family members, politicians and others.

Agnes Macdonald Soon after Macdonald's death, Lady Macdonald was raised to the peerage as Baroness Macdonald of Earnscliffe. Although always worried about her finances, she was well taken care of. Macdonald's estate, including a life-insurance policy, amounted to $100,000, and her own trust fund's value was now $80,000. Yet, as she put it, "joy" had "gone out of" her life.

For a time, Agnes travelled constantly, almost frantically, to Banff, to New Jersey (to be close to her ailing brother, Hewitt Bernard), and to their old summer cottage at Rivière-du-Loup. It was at Banff that Lady Aberdeen, the wife of the incoming governor general, encountered her and made the cruel entry in her diary about Lady Macdonald's "unconcealed grief at her loss of power." She did in fact try to hang on to it, attempting immediately after Macdonald's death, if unavailingly, to convince the governor general to pick Charles Tupper as the new prime minister.

Alone now at the age of fifty-four, Agnes's abiding rule was to do what she guessed Macdonald would have wanted. After her trip to New Jersey, she never again crossed the border, telling Professor Williamson, "I know Sir John would not approve of our spending so much time in the States." In 1892, at the start of a new parliamentary session, she told Joseph Pope that she found herself "going in spirit to the old place . . . and seeing again the tall figure with its decorations and well known face standing so erect & earnest at his post. I used to watch him—master of them all—with pride and triumph." In 1901, she poured out her feelings to a friend, saying she was "longing for just one moment as it was before he was struck down. But I would not call him back to this troublesome world. I know so well he's well and at rest, but he is always near us, and my mind through all the world's din is dwelling all the time on him." When she and George Brown's widow, Anne, encountered each other in the narrow streets of the Scottish town of Oban, neither acknowledged the other.

She escaped from Ottawa and her memories by moving to Britain, making her first trip in 1893, and soon after settling there. As a baroness, she was invited to the Queen's garden party and to the wedding of a future king (George V), and took her seat in the House of Lords. The British winters, however, always drove her to Italy. In all these travels, she was accompanied by Mary.

There may have been, briefly, someone else. In 1897, Agnes wrote to Joseph Pope, "I am in truth only a very sad old woman—with a past, alas!, wholly unforgotten and unforgettable." The cause of this outburst was a newspaper report that she was about to remarry. In a follow-up letter to Pope, Agnes sounded somewhat defensive, saying, "I have always had a fair share of my own way & like to please myself as to *who* I see much of & when but apart from that there is really no *shadow of reason* for such a silly, unknown rumour." And living alone changed some of her views on life. In 1885, she'd been scornful of Macdonald's attempt to extend the vote to women. In 1910, answering the printed questions in Mary's day book, her answer to whether she believed in women's suffrage was "With all my heart."

She returned to Canada only once, in 1896, and decided to sell Earnscliffe, although the actual sale and three-day auction of the furniture and household effects did not take place until 1900. Her last decades were uneventful but marred by a break in relations between her and Pope, she feeling, with justification, that he had mismanaged her trust fund. Agnes died in 1920, at the age of eighty-four, in the south-coast town of Eastbourne, where she was buried.

Mary Macdonald When told her father had died, Mary, by then twenty-two but mentally still a child, said in her slow, deliberate way, "I must try and be a comfort to mother now, instead of a burden to her."

Unable to feed herself or even to turn over in bed, Mary could not help but be a burden. She was a light burden, however, because she had inherited much of her father's charm and sunny disposition. There is just a trace of rueful envy in a comment Agnes once made to Pope: "Everyone pets & humours her as usual & she is quite the little Queen I hear."

In London a different Mary began to emerge. She discovered the South Kensington Museum (now the Victoria and Albert) and, with her Canadian companion, Kay Peacock, in attendance, began to go there regularly. She also went to the Royal Aquarium, and to Hyde Park to watch the passing parade of people, horses and carriages. Most remarkably, Mary began to go to the theatre.

Agnes sometimes accompanied her to comic operas and plays such as *Iolanthe* and *The Great Millionaire*, but she had her doubts about them, saying, "Everything is beautiful at the plays—but the *morals*."

A turning point in Mary's development came when she astonished her mother by telling her, "I shall never grow any older, Mother, I shall always be more or less a child." Agnes recognized this self-awareness as an "awakening intelligence." Thereafter, Mary no longer lived as she had, in a large nursery, but in the world—or as much of it as she could manage.

At this critical moment, the right person entered her life. In 1906, Agnes engaged Sarah Coward, the daughter of a Yorkshire farmer, as a maid-companion for Mary. With infinite patience, Coward began to teach Mary how to enunciate her words and how to read. Later, she taught her how to use a typewriter (a 1922 Corona), using just three fingers. She was very slow, but almost never made a typing mistake. Later, she learned some Italian and some French.

Lady Macdonald and Mary in mourning clothes. In their different ways, each mourned him for the rest of their lives.

It was evident now that Mary was likely to outlive her mother. Agnes found the solution in Sarah Coward—"clever, entirely trustworthy, judicious, deeply religious"—and she made a contract with her to look after Mary for the rest of her life. After Agnes's death, Mary and Coward bought a house in the southern seaside town of Hove. Each day, Sarah took Mary out in her wheelchair for a stroll along the promenade; each evening, a full dinner was served to them, with silverware and fine china on the table, the linen napkins folded into the shape of water lilies. One of Mary's particular pleasures was listening to the news over the wireless.

Mary lived until 1933, by then a remarkable sixty-four years old. Coward, to whom Mary left two thousand pounds a year in her will, lived on until 1944. The last line on the cross above Mary's grave is "Blessed are the pure in heart."*

Hewitt Bernard and *James Williamson* Macdonald's surviving relatives by marriage both died a few years after him, Agnes' brother, Hewitt, in 1893, and James Williamson, the widower of Macdonald's sister Margaret, in 1895.

Hugh John Macdonald Macdonald's son Hugh John always disliked politics. He slipped away to Winnipeg in 1893, but was persuaded to return to Ottawa in 1896 by Charles Tupper, by then prime minister. Hugh John stayed for four years, and later served a brief term as Manitoba's premier (his one legislative accomplishment being to enact a Temperance Act). In 1911, he was appointed police magistrate of Winnipeg. At last, Hugh John had found his true vocation. As a politician, he had been well to the right of his father, and during the Winnipeg General Strike of 1919 he called for the deportation of all Eastern Europeans and German Jews as "Bolsheviki." On the bench, though, he was a progressive and sometimes delivered exceptionally imaginative judgments. On one occasion, he discharged a young prostitute because she had been married that morning; on another, he sent a vagrant to jail to save him from freezing to death on the streets.

* Most of the material on Mary's later life is taken from two remarkable articles in *Historic Kingston* by Margaret Cohoe, who reassembled the story of Sarah Coward's care for Mary by locating two of her nieces, Edith and Margaret Coward, who as little girls had gone often to her house.

He also gave homeless offenders temporary shelter in his own house and searched for jobs for them.

By the time of his death in 1929, at the age of seventy-nine, Hugh John Macdonald had become one of Winnipeg's most beloved characters.* All the flags in the city were lowered to half-mast, and the police wore black arm bands. His house in Winnipeg, Dalnavert, is now a national historic site; built in 1895, it included such state-of-the-art features as central heating, walk-in closets and electricity.

Isabella "Daisy" Gainsford (née Macdonald) A favourite of her grandfather (she once declared she would rather be in hell with John A. than in heaven without him), Daisy had a hard life in many ways. Her mother died when she was four. Her half-brother, Jack, who was always in poor health, died at the age of twenty.

Daisy was a fun-loving extrovert, excelling at fencing, pistol shooting and dancing. In 1915, at the age of thirty-eight, she married George Gainsford, a British engineer. They had two children, Hugh and Lionel, but the younger boy developed spinal meningitis and died young.

Gainsford was always a heavy drinker, and Hugh remembers his mother crying late into the evenings until his father reeled home. In the early 1930s, Gainsford slipped away one day and was never heard from again. Although always short of money, Daisy remained an active member of Winnipeg's social scene. She died in 1959.

Hugh Gainsford At the time this book is being written, Hugh is ninety-three years old. His life was transformed by his father's

---

* In 1927 a skin infection caused Macdonald to have one of his legs amputated. When the disease reappeared, he refused a second amputation.

flight. He had just passed the examination to enter the University of Manitoba, but now had to look after his mother and took a job with the Manitoba Liquor Control Commission. He remained there all his working life, except when a soldier during the Second World War. He and his wife had no children of their own, but they adopted a boy and a girl.

Today, Hugh Gainsford lives in a retirement home in Brandon. Among his few relics of his ancestor are John A.'s gold signet ring and a buffalo horn.

Sir John Thompson The ablest of all Macdonald's ministers, Thompson, had he lived longer, might well have changed Canada's political history. He succeeded as prime minister the ineffectual J.J. Abbott (his one memorable statement being "I hate politics"), and immediately won a string of by-elections. His political successes included settling the Bering Strait dispute with the United States, revising the Criminal Code and settling the separate-schools issue in the North-West Territories.

Thompson worked impossibly hard, never exercised, and consumed inordinate amounts of food. Though only five foot seven, he pushed his weight to 225 pounds. On a trip to Britain in December 1894, he was felled by a massive heart attack during a lunch given by the Queen at Windsor Castle.

Charles Tupper For four years after Macdonald's death, Tupper remained in London as high commissioner. The sudden death of Prime Minister Thompson created a crisis within the Conservative government. Mackenzie Bowell succeeded Thompson briefly but was toppled by a ministerial coup. On the eve of the 1896 election, Tupper was brought back to Ottawa and appointed prime minister in a desperate effort to avoid an utter rout. The old warhorse turned out to have a remarkable amount of wind left in him. On election night, Tupper actually won the most votes, but fell behind in the seat count because Quebecers voted overwhelmingly for their own—Wilfrid Laurier. Tupper stayed on as leader until the next election in 1900, but resigned after he once again lost to Laurier.

Tupper's last years were decidedly agreeable. He lived most of the time with his daughter Emma at Bexleyheath, wintering with her in Italy and even in his eighties taking lessons in Italian. He died in 1915, the last survivor of the Confederation Fathers. His son Charles Hibbert Tupper was the last survivor of all of Macdonald's ministers, dying in 1927 in Vancouver.

Opposition leaders During his long political career, Macdonald faced several leaders of the Opposition. Antoine-Aimé Dorion, leader of the pre-Confederation *rouges* and a strong opponent of Confederation, died just two weeks before Macdonald himself. Alexander Mackenzie, the cause of his single election defeat, died, after a long decline, only a year later. Edward Blake, his most formidable intellectual opponent, left Canada in 1892 to become an Irish nationalist MP at Westminster. He made no great mark there and never achieved his heartfelt wish to be appointed to the Judicial Committee of the Privy Council. He retired to Toronto and died there in 1912. His house still stands on Jarvis Street.

Wilfrid Laurier As prime minister, Laurier possessed in abundance the most valuable of all political gifts—luck. Soon after his 1896 victory, the Long Depression ended, grain prices rose, and with the American West at last filled up, immigrants soon poured into the Canadian prairies. By his eloquence, elegance and charm, Laurier stirred up a spirit of optimism and confidence among Canadians, he forecasting that the approaching twentieth century would belong to them. In many ways, he presided over the realization of the

Canada that Macdonald dreamed of achieving. Lady Macdonald recognized this, telling Joseph Pope, "Laurier has taken in the strangest way, not only the policy but also the personality of Sir John."

Joseph Pope Of all Macdonald's secretaries, Pope was the one who served him best and knew him best, going on to be his official biographer, publishing three books in all. Pope also connected Macdonald to Laurier, with whom, with Macdonald's full approval, he maintained a close friendship. When the Conservatives were defeated in 1896, Pope moved easily into the new administration and eventually headed the new Department of External Affairs. After Laurier lost the 1911 election, Pope effected a second seamless transition to the government of the Conservative Robert Borden. As the years passed, he fell behind the times, particularly because he remained an unquestioning anglophile and imperialist. Nevertheless, he remained a deputy minister to his death in 1926.

Eliza Grimason Among all the women captivated by Macdonald, Grimason was his most ardent supporter. "There's not a man like him in the livin' earth," she said. When he was near death, she too fell seriously ill. They met for the last time when he came to Kingston during the 1891 election, spotted her in the crowd, and called on her to come up and stand beside him on the stage, as she did. An astute businesswoman, Grimason accumulated considerable wealth and became one of Kingston's leading citizens. She bought a plot next to Macdonald's in Cataraqui Cemetery. When she died in 1916 at the age of ninety-five, she was buried there, as close as possible to the man she adored.

Louis Riel Just as his death was a tragedy, so were the deaths of his family. His wife, Marguerite, succumbed to tuberculosis six months after Riel mounted the scaffold. Shortly before his execution, she gave birth to a son who died within hours. Their children, Marie-Angélique, a pretty brunette, and Jean-Louis, exceptionally handsome, were brought up by their grandmother; both died young, she at the age of fourteen, he at twenty-six. Neither had children, so Riel left no direct descendants.

Gabriel Dumont After his last meeting with Riel, Dumont crossed the border without difficulty. He made plans for an attempt to rescue his leader, but had to abandon them. He moved freely in the United States, joining Buffalo Bill's Wild West Show, where, along with Annie Oakley, he dazzled audiences with his marksmanship. His undimmed detestation of the way the Métis had been treated earned him an invitation by Quebec nationalists to make a speaking tour of the province, but he quickly lost support by making ferocious attacks on the clergy for having failed to support Riel. After wanderings back and forth, Dumont returned to the North-West, built himself a small cabin and lived by hunting and fishing. He died in 1906.

William Jackson Another ardent supporter of Riel, Jackson enjoyed an even longer and stranger life—perhaps the most heroic of the losers in 1885. After walking away from the Winnipeg asylum to the border, Jackson settled in Chicago, became a union organizer, ran the Anarchist Defense Fund and became a champion of Métis rights—for which he changed his name to Honoré Jaxon. Union officials arranged a speaking tour for him, but he lost his audiences by speaking for six hours in impassioned but incomprehensible detail. He did marry, but his absorption with left-wing politics left the pair perennially penniless. He ended his life as a janitor in New York, dying in 1951 at the age of ninety-three.

Perhaps the best summary of Macdonald's political life was written some years after his death by Queen's University principal George Monro Grant. The only extant version is contained in George Parkin's slim 1908 biography of Macdonald, but without any description of why or when and where Grant wrote it. Grant's assessment was:

> He believed that there was room on the continent of America for at least two nations, and he was determined that Canada should be a nation. He believed in the superiority of the British constitution to any other for free men, and that the preservation of the union with the mother country was necessary to the making of Canada. He had faith in the French race, and believed that a good understanding between French and English people was essential to the national welfare.

To that analysis, Grant added an exceptionally perceptive description of why Macdonald was able to accomplish so much of what he set out to achieve: "The people followed him, not only as a leader but as an actual embodiment of these fundamental ideas."

Whether viewed within the context of his own times or in hindsight, Grant's summation needs little addition. Macdonald's lifelong mission was to ensure that a second "new nation" besides the United States could exist in North America. That is what he set out to do, and it is what he did.

A near century and a half later, Macdonald's old Canada of 1867—of farmers, loggers and fishermen, of churches overflowing with Protestant and Catholic believers, of small towns and clearings in the forests—has slipped to the country's margins. Most Canadians now live in ever-expanding cities, and the country's demography increasingly resembles a miniature of the world. Canadians no longer look southwards in fear and envy, but rather with an un-Canadian cockiness— at least for the time being. In this new Canada, the handwritten letters Macdonald poured out in such profusion have been replaced by tweets.

Returning today, while Macdonald would feel strange, he would in no way feel a stranger. Despite all the changes caused by economic, cultural and population growth, as well as by the physical transformations effected by new structures and new technologies, he would be able to identify the foundations he laid down. He would note that while relations between French and English matter less today than they did in his time, they remain critical—not only in themselves, but as a model for achieving accommodations among the nation's multiplicity of peoples. He would note with approval that the legal and political systems borrowed from Britain, though substantially Canadianized over the years, have in fact served the country pretty well; he would draw satisfaction from the fact that the Scottish-style banking and financial system implemented by his government has served the country exceedingly well. With some surprise and disappointment, he would realize that the degree of understanding between Aboriginals and other Canadians (the term "European Canadians" being obsolete now) has scarcely advanced from his time, if at all. He would take pleasure from the fact that the protectionist impulse he conjured into existence by his National Policy, reflecting his appreciation of the country's innate fragility, remains stubbornly persistent among Canadians, if not among economists. Though he could hardly anticipate the importance Canadians now give to the notion of "Peace, Order and Good Government," there's not a word in that defining phrase he would wish to alter.

Had there been no Macdonald, there almost certainly would be today no Canada.

In a great many ways, what Canadians have become began with him. He, a nation-maker, made us.

John A

Acknowledgments

Among the many who helped make this book possible, four deserve my undying gratitude: my wife, Carol Bishop-Gwyn; my publisher at Random House Canada, Anne Collins; my historical consultant at the Library of Parliament in Ottawa, George Ekins; and my editor, Rosemary Shipton.

Carol contributed directly to the book by amassing an array of exceptional photographs and cartoons and then playing a key part in the choice of those actually used. Simultaneously, even though fully engaged in her own project of a biography of Celia Franca, the founder of the National Ballet of Canada (also due to be published in 2011), Carol took on an unconscionable share of the domestic chores and kept up my spirits during the seven years it has taken to do the research, structure the story, and write the text for both volumes, then rewrite it again, and again. Thank you, my love.

Anne Collins, together with Louise Dennys, the executive publisher of the Knopf Random Canada Publishing Group, made the original decision to publish this biography. They thereby took a considerable gamble because, as is said incessantly, Canadians have little interest in history. To my later suggestion that two volumes would be needed to properly cover John A. Macdonald's life, Anne, contravening the publishing maxim that second volumes are frequently one too many, interrupted to say, "Yes, of course"—so we went off for a most agreeable lunch. Thereafter, her consistent contributions were to care passionately about the project and to insist on excellence in every respect—writing, editing, production.

George Ekins is a little-known national treasure. His knowledge of Canadian history is wide, deep and exact. For the sake of his private passion and nothing else, he gave me the priceless gift of his exceptional capabilities as a researcher. Some of the best "raisins to add to the rice pudding"—a prescription for making writing readable coined by my late wife, Sandra—are in fact George's doing, such as his tracing the origin of Macdonald's description of Victoria, BC, as a place where "the day is always in the afternoon" back to Tennyson's poem *The Lotos-Eaters*. He also scanned the text for errors, not just once, as did several others, but all over again with the final draft.

Rosemary Shipton is, I'm convinced, the best editor of nonfiction in the country. History is her specialty, but her skills and sensitivity have been applied to elaborate books on art and porcelain as well. She edited volume one, and contributed hugely to it. Her contribution to this volume has been even more extensive. Besides having to edit the text more substantively, not least because I was flagging by then, she also had to prune the manuscript to a length bearable to readers and to Random House. We came to know each other so well and with such mutual respect that we functioned like partners in a joint enterprise.

My purpose in writing this biography was to try to make Canadian history alive and relevant again—a goal that I believe deeply is attainable because, despite all the demographic and technological changes that have taken place during the century and a half since Macdonald set out to make a nation, a vital part of the way we are today is still unchanged from the way Canadians were then. If I have made any progress towards this goal by this book, I know it could not have happened but for Carol, Anne, George and Rosemary.

Others have made major contributions too. A number of individuals, most of them professional historians, gave generously of their time and expertise by reading early drafts to identify factual errors and, at times, to challenge my analysis and conclusions. This group included Michael Bliss, Bob Beal, Gerald Friesen, Roger Hall, Peter H. Russell, Joseph Martin, Donald B. Smith and, in the cold outside academe, George Anderson, an authority on federalism. As goes without saying, none bear any responsibility for the mistakes that remain.

Invaluable help was provided by two men from Macdonald's "home town" of Kingston. The journalist Arthur Mills is both an indefatigable researcher and an instigator of interest in all Canadian prime ministers and American presidents. If Macdonald's bicentenary in 2015 is celebrated in some of the style deserved for a "Nation-Maker," the person the country should thank is Arthur. Also tireless in the assistance he extended to me was Brian Osborne, a geographer turned history enthusiast.

The quality of the book itself and the undeviating attention to detail in its production are the work of my meticulous copy editor, Alexander Schultz, and several Random House staffers, particularly Deirdre Molina and Caleb Snider, and also by Jane McWhinney. My agents, first John Pearce, now Hilary McMahon, have done all they could to assist. Lastly, I am grateful to my brother-in-law Gordon Fulton for the author photograph on the back of the jacket.

Bibliography

A NOTE ON SOURCES

While at Library and Archives Canada (LAC), surrounded by brown cardboard boxes, or scanning works in the stacks at the University of Toronto's amazing Robarts Library—the fact that researchers can access the actual stacks makes it certain they will stumble upon relevant material they never knew existed—I never doubted I was following a trail thoroughly marked long before my exploration of the terrain. The pathfinder was of course Donald Creighton, as he quested for material for his two magisterial volumes of biography on Macdonald—*The Young Politician* and *The Old Chieftain*—published in the 1950s. His research was voluminous, assiduous, and highly imaginative the greater part of it entirely original—he thus making public for the first time Lady Macdonald's diary. His accomplishment was unprecedented in Canadian historiography. If I have stretched the trail further and changed its direction here and there, it is because I was standing on Creighton's shoulders. I have benefited also from subsequent original research by many academic historians. My task, although its duration—seven years—was far longer than I'd ever anticipated, was immensely satisfying, and at several eureka moments it elevated into ecstasy. But I always knew I was following the footprints of others.

In order to pare down the length of this volume, the usual detailed Source Notes have been placed on the Random House website, www.randomhouse.ca, as well as on my own website, www.richardjgwyn.ca. The full Notes identifying the origins of the specific contents of the text will appear as well in the soft-cover edition, particularly because its readers are more likely to be students.

Here, two forms of bibliographic material are presented: first, a description of the primary sources for material on Macdonald and his principal associates and opponents; afterwards, a detailed bibliography of the secondary sources used during the research.

PRIMARY SOURCES

The treasure trove of Macdonaldiana in its primary form is at Library and Archives Canada (LAC) in Ottawa; it comprises some six hundred "volumes," each encased in a large rectangular cardboard box. Thanks to the diligence of Macdonald's secretary, Sir Joseph Pope, a great many of his original letters have survived (almost all handwritten; some typewritten during his last years). There are two sizeable gaps: scarcely any letters remain from his period in opposition, 1873 to late 1878, no doubt because he lacked a secretary; and no letters between him and Lady Macdonald have survived, undoubtedly because she chose to destroy them at some time during her long widowhood. Conversely, the richest period for primary material is the three months when Macdonald was at the Washington Conference of 1871, writing often to cabinet ministers and friends back in Ottawa because he could no longer talk directly to them in some parliamentary nook or over a dinner at Earnscliffe.

The base of the LAC collection was provided by Pope. As Macdonald's literary executor, he sorted out the mass of material, culled out items concerned with minor matters, and donated the remainder—some 714 "bundles" of letters—to the then Public Archives. Pope insisted he had not discarded anything that "could not stand the light of day"; on the evidence, he was telling the truth. Over the years, considerable material has been added, the most recent being a dozen letters written by Macdonald during the 1870s to Alexander Morris, a cabinet minister and important figure in the west, and bought by a Canadian at an auction in London.

LAC's Macdonald Collection, or Fonds, all of it classified as MG26-A, comprises some 100,000 letters, by him and to him, as well as a great deal of supplementary material, from tax receipts to his various wills. Its contents include files on subjects ranging from "Alaska Boundary" all the way to "Wrecking on the Great Lakes." Among the files containing letters from Macdonald's correspondents, the most comprehensive are those of George Stephen, Alexander Campbell, Alexander T. Galt and Charles Tupper, and also, because of Macdonald's long tenure as minister of Indian Affairs, those of his two senior officials, Edgar Dewdney and Lawrence Vankoughnet. Separate volumes deal with family members, although these are best read in J.K. Johnson's excellent *Affectionately Yours.*

The most accessible part of the collection can be found in volumes 571 to 576c. These are transcripts of Macdonald's letters that were copied soon after he wrote them by means of a letterpress. In the 1950s, all of these were microfilmed and distributed to libraries. Because the technology was poor, all are now virtually unreadable. However, a project by LAC to publish all of Macdonald's letters properly transcribed and annotated, even though long since abandoned for lack of funds, has resulted in a great many of the fast-fading, original letters being transcribed; all are easy to read. (The last published volume only goes to 1861, but a third, unpublished, volume, covering the period up to Confederation, is available as Volume 589.)

No new history-changing dark secrets or fresh scandals are revealed by any of Macdonald's letters. But quite a few add considerably to the historical record, sometimes clarifying it, at other times making it more ambiguous. As an example, the often-made claim that Macdonald blundered impulsively into the west in 1869 is at the very least overstated: rather, it's clear that he knew he knew little about it and so set out to "grope along." Many add considerably to our understanding of his personality, often showing his character as more complex, more contradictory and more human. Above all, because Macdonald so clearly enjoyed putting pen to paper, his personal letters provide aspirant biographers with what they most crave—a simulacrum of their subject's actual voice.

A cluster of other primary sources exists. One useful advance is that the Library of Parliament has completed its project of creating, out of newspaper accounts of the time, virtual Hansards for the post-Confederation years before 1878, when the official record of Parliamentary debates began. As is exceptionally useful, a considerable number of documents and official papers are now available in published books. Among these (see Secondary Sources for details) are Michael Bliss's *Canadian History in Documents, 1763–1966*, H.D. Forbes's *Canadian Political Thought*, J.L. Granatstein's *First Drafts: Eyewitness Accounts from Canada's Past*, J.H. Reid's A *Source-book of Canadian History*, R.C. Brown's *Canadian Historical Documents*, J.H. Bumsted's *Documentary Problems in Canadian History*, David De Brou's *Documenting Canada* and John Saywell's *Original Documents.* Add to this the Champlain Society's *Dufferin-Carnarvon Correspondence*. Douglas Francis's *Destinies* contains useful web addresses for those seeking, as an example, *British Columbia*, *Terms of Union.* Daily copies of the *Globe*, back to 1844, are available online through the Toronto Public Library. *Canada's Founding Debates*, edited by Janet Ajzenstat, extends to the post-Confederation debates in British Columbia, Manitoba, Newfoundland and Prince Edward Island.

Other primary material relevant to Macdonald resides in the archival records of individuals who knew him well as friend or foe. Those at LAC include the records of George Brown (MG24-B40), George-Étienne Cartier (MG27-D4), Brown Chamberlin (MG24-B19), (Alexander T. Galt (MG27-ID4), James Gowan (MG27-1E17), Francis Hincks (MG24-B68), Joseph Howe (MGB-29), Hector-Louis Langevin (MG27-D), Wilfrid Laurier (MG-26-G), Alexander Mackenzie (MG-26-B), Alexander Morris (MG21-A), John Thompson (MG26-D) and Charles Tupper (MG26-F), while John Rose is in volumes 258–9. Equivalent records at the Archives of Ontario include those of Edgar Blake (vols. 136–273) and Alexander Campbell (vols. 469–87), as well as the papers of T.C. Patteson.

SECONDARY SOURCES

This bibliography is extensive for several reasons: Macdonald held office or was on his way back into it for a full quarter of a century; he engaged in an unusual number of major events, several involving the country's very survival; and, as the country's first prime minister, he set precedents that in several instances long outlasted him—his protectionist National Policy largely surviving until the cross-border free trade pact of 1988, his North West Mounted Police today the RCMP. The list of secondary sources is also inclusive; besides describing Macdonald as a person and political leader, I have tried to bring alive the Canada of years past to provide today's readers the social and political framework of Macdonald's actions, and the context within which to judge his successes and failures.

The standard way of presenting secondary sources—books, articles, theses—is to list them in alphabetic order by author. As a guide to researchers, and to help them find materials of interest without "searching for needles in a haystack," the list that follows has been broken down into subject headings and sub-headings: for instance, SOCIETY AND DAILY LIFE: *Women.* To the extent possible, although a certain arbitrariness has been unavoidable, these categories correspond to Macdonald's principal spheres of activity over the years. Within each section, the listing of the materials remains alphabetical.

MACDONALD AND HIS FAMILY: *The 1891 Election*

ABORIGINAL PEOPLES
ATLANTIC PROVINCES
BIOGRAPHIES AND MEMOIRS
CONSTITUTION AND THE JUDICIARY
DEFENCE
THE ECONOMY AND BUSINESS

FEDERAL-PROVINCIAL RELATIONS: *Ontario*, *Manitoba*, *British Columbia*
HISTORICAL STUDIES AND DOCUMENTS
IMMIGRATION CHINESE WORKERS
IMPERIALISM AND THE EMPIRE
LABOUR AND UNIONS
MÉTIS AND THE BUFFALO
NATIONAL POLICY AND TRADE
NATIONALISM
POLICE: NORTH-WEST MOUNTED
POLITICS, PARLIAMENT AND THE FRANCHISE
QUEBEC
RAILWAYS
RELIGION
RIEL, LOUIS: 1869–70
RIEL, LOUIS: 1884–85: *Louis Riel*, *Postscript*
SOCIETY AND DAILY LIFE: *Women*
U.S.-CANADIAN RELATIONS; U.S.-BRITISH RELATIONS
THE WEST AND THE NORTHWEST

(Abbreviations: CHA—Canadian Historical Association; *CHR—Canadian Historical Review*; *CJEPS—Canadian Journal of Economic & Political Science*; *CJPS—Canadian Journal of Political Science*; *JCS—Journal of Canadian Studies*; *JPS—Journal of Political Studies*; *QQ—Queen's Quarterly*)

The single most valuable secondary source for this work, and certainly the one resorted to most often, was the Canadian Dictionary of Biography, available online at www.biographi.ca.

MACDONALD AND HIS FAMILY

Biggar, E.B. *Anecdotal Life of Sir John Macdonald*. Montreal: Lovell, 1891.

Black, Peter. "Sir John A.'s Lost Weekend" *Beaver* Oct/Nov (2007).

Bliss, Michael. *Right Honorable Men: The Descent of Canadian Politics from Macdonald to Chrétien*. Toronto: HarperPerennial Canada, 2004.

Burt, A.L. "Peter Mitchell on John A. Macdonald" *CHR* 42, no. 3 (1961).

Cohoe, Margaret. "John A.'s Daughter and the Faithful [Sarah] Coward" *Historic Kingston* 37 (1993).

———. "John A. Macdonald—The Family Man" *Historic Kingston* 33 (1989).

———. "Mary, Margaret, Theodora, Macdonald, 1969–1933" *Historic Kingston* 45 (1997).

Collins, Joseph Edmund. *Life and Times of the Rt. Hon. Sir John A. Macdonald, Premier of the Dominion of Canada*. London: Rose, 1883.

Commonwealth Relations Office, London. *Earnscliffe, Home of Canada's First Prime Minister, and Since 1930 Residence of High Commissioners for the United Kingdom in Canada*. London: 1955.

Creighton, Donald Grant. *John A. Macdonald*. Vol. 1, *The Young Politician*, and vol. 2, *The Old Chieftain*. Toronto: Macmillan, 1952 and 1955.

———. *John A. Macdonald, Confederation and the West*. Winnipeg: Manitoba Historical Society, 1967.

Eggleston, Stephen David. "Emergence of National Parties and the Development of Party Cohesion in Early Post-Confederation Canada: 1867–1896." Ph.D. thesis, Queen's University, 1992.

Ewart, John S. *Sir John A. Macdonald and the Canadian Flag*. Toronto: 1908.

Gibson, Jane, and Karyn Patterson. "A Recollection [of Macdonald]" *Historic Kingston* 34 (1986).

Giffin, Ronald. "Sir John Macdonald and the Canadian Pacific Railway." B.A. (Hons.), Acadia University, 1963.

Grenville, John. "In Memoriam: Kingston Mourns Sir John A. Macdonald" *Historic Kingston* 40 (1992).

Guest, Henry James. "The Old Man's Son Sir Hugh John Macdonald." Papers read before the Historical and Scientific Society of Manitoba, Series 3, no. 29, 1973.

———. "Reluctant Politician: A Biography of Sir Hugh John Macdonald." Master's thesis, University of Manitoba, 1973.

Guillet, Edwin Clarence. *You'll Never Die, John A!* Toronto: Macmillan, 1967.

Gwyn, Sandra. *The Private Capital: Ambition and Love in the Age of Macdonald and Laurier*. Toronto: McClelland & Stewart, 1984.

Heick, Welf Henry. "Mackenzie and Macdonald: Federal Politics and Politicians in Canada, 1873–1878." Ph.D. thesis, Duke University, 1965.

Johnson, J.K. *Affectionately Yours: The Letters of Sir John A. Macdonald and His Family*. Toronto: Macmillan, 1969.

Johnson, Keith J. "Sir John A. Macdonald, 1815–1891, A Tribute" *Historic Kingston* 23 (1975).

Lewis, J.P. "'The Lion and the Lamb Ministry': John A. Macdonald and the Politics of the First Canadian Federal Cabinet." Master's thesis, University of Guelph, 2005.

Lockhart, A.D. "The Contribution of Macdonald Conservatism to National Unity, 1854–78" *CHA Report*, 1939.

Lower, Arthur. "Sir John A. Macdonald in Caricature" *CHA Report*, 1940.

MacDermot, Terence. "The Political Ideas of John A. Macdonald" *CHR* 14 (1933).

Maclean, William F. "The Canadian Themistocles" *Canadian Magazine* 4 (1895).

Macpherson, J. Pennington. *Life of the Right Hon. Sir John A. Macdonald.* Saint John, N.B.: Earle Publishing House, 1891.

Martin, Ged. *Favorite Son: John A. Macdonald and the Voters of Kingston, 1841–1891*. Kingston: Kingston Historical Society, 2010.

McNaught, Kenneth. "Sir John A. Macdonald and the Idea of Canada" *Historic Kingston* 39 (1991).

Morton, W.L. "The Formation of the First Federal Cabinet" *CHR* 36, no. 2 (1955).

Moyles, Gordon. *"Happy Jack" Macdonald on the Salvation Army*. Salvation Army, Kingston Advisory Board (May 2008).

Muller, Steven. "The Canadian Prime Ministers, 1867–1948: An Essay on Democratic Leadership." Ph.D. thesis, University of Ann Arbor, Michigan, 1958.

Newman, Lena. *The John A. Macdonald Album*. Toronto: Tundra, 1974.

Parkin, George Ross. *Sir John A. Macdonald*. London and Edinburgh: T.C. & E.C. Jack, 1909.

Phenix, Patricia. *Private Demons: The Tragic Personal Life of John A. Macdonald*. Toronto: McClelland & Stewart, 2006.

Pope, Joseph. *Correspondence of Sir John A. Macdonald*. Toronto: Doubleday, Page, 1921.

———. *The Day of Sir John Macdonald: A Chronicle of the First Prime Minister of the Dominion*. Toronto: Brook, 1915.

———. *Memoirs of the Right Honourable Sir John Alexander Macdonald, G.C.B., First Prime Minister of the Dominion of Canada*. Ottawa: J. Durie and Son, 1894 (repr. Toronto: Musson, 1930).

———. *Sir John A. Macdonald Vindicated: A Review of the Right Honourable Sir Richard Cartwright's Memoirs*. Toronto: The Publishers' Association of Canada, 1912.

Pope, Maurice A., *Public Servant: The Memoirs of Sir Joseph Pope*. Toronto: Oxford University Press, 1960.

Preece, Rod. "The Political Wisdom of Sir John A. Macdonald" *CJPS* 17, no. 3 (1984).

Preston, Richard Arthur. "Sir John A. Macdonald and the United States" *Historic Kingston* 37 (1989).

Reynolds, Louise. *Agnes: The Biography of Lady Macdonald*. [Toronto: Samuel Stevens, 1979]; Montreal and Kingston: McGill-Queen's University Press, 1990.

Roy, James. "John A. Macdonald: Barrister and Solicitor" *Canadian Bar Review* 26 (1948).

Smith, Cynthia M., and Jack McLeod, eds. *Sir John A.: An Anecdotal Life of Sir John A. Macdonald.* Toronto: Oxford University Press, 1989.

Sowby, Joyce Katharine. "Macdonald the Administrator: Department of the Interior and Indian Affairs, 1878–1887." Master's thesis, Queen's University, 1984.

Stanley, George F.G. "The Man Who Made Canada, 1865–1867." Address to Conference of Public Relations Society of America, Montreal, 1964.

Stewart, Alice. "The Imperial Policy of Sir John A. Macdonald, Canada's First Prime Minister." Ph.D. thesis, Radcliffe College, Harvard University, 1946.

Stewart, Gordon. "John A. Macdonald's Greatest Triumph" *CHR* 63, no. 1 (1982).

Swainson, Donald. *Sir John A. Macdonald: The Man and the Politician.* 2nd ed. Kingston: Quarry Press, 1989.

Tassé, Joseph. *Lord Beaconsfield and Sir John A. Macdonald: A Political and Personal Parallel.* Montreal, 1891.

Thomas, Earle. "Sir John A. Macdonald in Opposition, 1873–1878." Master's thesis, Queen's University, 1951.

Thomas, Walter K. "Canadian Political Oratory in the Nineteenth Century" *Dalhousie Review* 39 (1959/60).

Travill, A.A. "Sir John A. Macdonald and His Doctors" *Historic Kingston* 29 (1981).

Waite, Peter B. "Chartered Libertine? A Case against Sir John Macdonald and Some Answers" *Manitoba Historical Society* Series 3, no. 32 (1975/76).

———. Introduction to Donald Grant Creighton, *John A. Macdonald: The Young Politician: The Old Chieftain.* Toronto: University of Toronto Press, 1998.

———. *Macdonald: His Life and World.* Toronto: McGraw-Hill Ryerson, 1975.

———. "The Political Ideas of John A. Macdonald." In *The Political Ideas of the Prime Ministers of Canada*, edited by Marcel Hamelin. Ottawa: Les Éditions de l'université d'Ottawa, 1969.

———. "Sir John A. Macdonald: The Man" *Dalhousie Review* 47 (1967).

Wilson, Keith. *Hugh John Macdonald.* Winnipeg: Peguis Publishers, 1980.

The 1891 Election

Beck, Murray. *Pendulum of Power: Canada's Federal Elections.* Scarborough, Ont.: Prentice-Hall, 1968.

Creighton, Donald Grant. *John A. Macdonald.* Vol. 2, *The Old Chieftain* (chapter 15). Toronto: Macmillan, 1955.

Cumming, Carmen. *The Secret Craft: The Journalism of Edward Farrer.* Toronto: University of Toronto Press, 1992.

Grant, Ian. "Erastus Wiman: A Continentalist Replies to Canadian Imperialism" *CHR* 53, no. 1 (1972).

Lewis, Margaret Mae. "Canadian-American Reciprocity, 1854–1935." Master's thesis, University of Colorado, 1942.

Master, D.C. "Reciprocity, 1846–1911." Ottawa: CHA Booklet, no. 12, 1961.

MacKirdy, K.A. "The Loyalty Issue in the 1891 Federal Election Campaign" *Ontario History* 55 (1963).

Smith, Goldwin. "Loyalty." Speech given at Young Men's Liberal Club, Toronto, Feb. 2, 1891. In *Canadian History since Confederation*, edited by Bruce Hodgins and Robert Page. Georgetown, Ont.: Irwin-Dorsey, 1972.

Vevier, Charles. "American Continentalism: An Idea of Expansion, 1845–1910" *American Historical Review* 65, no. 1 (1960).

Waite, Peter B. *Canada, 1874–1896, Arduous Destiny.* Toronto: McClelland & Stewart, 1971.

Warner, Donald, *The Idea of Continental Union: Agitation for the Annexation of Canada to the United States, 1849–1893.* Lexington: University of Kentucky Press, 1960.

ABORIGINAL PEOPLES

Ahenakew, Edward. *Voices of the Plains Cree.* Regina: Canadian Plains Research Center, 1995.

Barron, F. Laurie. "The Indian Pass System in the Canadian West, 1882–1935" *Prairie Forum* 13, no. 1 (1988).

———, and James B. Waldram. *1885 and After: Native Society in Transition.* Regina: Canadian Plains Research Center, University of Regina, 1986.

Bartlett, Richard. "Citizens Minus: Indians and the Right to Vote" *Saskatchewan Law Review* 44 (1980).

Bingaman, Sandra Estlin. "The Trials of Poundmaker and Big Bear" *Saskatchewan History* 28 (1975).

Brown, Jennifer. *Reading Beyond Words: Context for Native History.* Peterborough, Ont. Broadview Press, 1996.

Buckley, Helen. *From Wooden Ploughs to Welfare.* Montreal and Kingston: McGill-Queen's University Press, 1992.

Bumsted, J.M. "Thomas Scott and the Daughter of Time" *Prairie Forum* 23, no. 3 (1998).

Campbell, Robert A. "Making Sober Citizens: The Legacy of Indigenous Alcohol Regulation in Canada, 1777–1985" *JCS* 42, no. 4 (2008).

Carter, Sarah. *Aboriginal People and Colonizers of Western Canada to 1900.* Toronto: University of Toronto Press, 1999.

———. "Demonstrating Success: The File Hills Farm Colony" *Prairie Forum* 16, no. 3 (1991).

———. *Lost Harvest: Prairie Indian Reserve Farmers and Government Policy.* Montreal and Kingston: McGill-Queen's University Press, 1990.

Chamberlin, J.E. *The Harrowing of Eden: White Attitudes toward Native Americans.* New York: Seabury Press, 1978.

Dempsey, Hugh. *Big Bear: The End of Freedom.* Vancouver: Douglas & McIntyre Books, 1984.

———. *Crowfoot, Chief of the Blackfoot.* Edmonton: Hurtig, 1976.

Dickason, Olive. *Canada's First Nations: A History of Founding Peoples from Earliest Times.* Toronto: McClelland & Stewart, 1992.

Dyck, Noel. "An Opportunity Lost: The Initiative of the Reserve Agricultural Programme in the Prairie West." In *1885 and After: Native Society in Transition*, edited by Laurie Barron. Regina: Canadian Plains Research Center, University of Regina, 1986.

Flanagan, Thomas. "Aboriginal Title." In *An Introduction to Canadian History*, edited by A.I. Silver and Carl Berger. Toronto: Canadian Scholars' Press, 1991.

Francis, Dani. *The Imaginary Indian: The Image of the Indian in Canadian Culture.* Vancouver: Arsenal Pulp Press, 1992.

Frideres, James. *Aboriginal People in Canada*. Toronto: Prentice Hall/Pearson Education, 2008.

Friesen, Gerald. "Prairie Indians, 1840-1900: The End of Autonomy." In *The Challenge of Modernity: A Reader in Post-Confederation Canada*, edited by Ian McKay. Toronto: McGraw-Hill Ryerson, 1992.

Friesen, John W. *Rediscovering the First Nations of Canada*. Calgary: Detselig Enterprises, 1997.

Getty, Ian, and Antoine S. Lussier, eds. *As Long as the Sun Shines and Water Flows: A Reader in Canadian Native Studies*. Vancouver: UBC Press, 1983.

Helin, Calvin. *Dances with Dependency: Indigenous Success through Self-Reliance.* Vancouver: Orca Spirit Publishing, 2006.

Horsman, Reginald. *Expansion and American Indian Policy.* East Lansing: Michigan State University Press, 1967.

Larmour, Jean, B.D. "Edgar Dewdney, Commissioner of Indian Affairs and Lieutenant-Governor of the Northwest Territories." Master's thesis, University of Saskatchewan, 1969.

———. "Edgar Dewdney and the Aftermath of the Rebellion," *Saskatchewan History* (1970).

Lear, Jonathan. *Radical Hope: Ethics in the Face of Cultural Devastation.* Cambridge, Mass.: Harvard University Press, 2006.

Leighton, Douglas. "The Development of Federal Indian Policy in Canada." Ph.D. thesis, University of Western Ontario, 1975.

———. "A Victorian Civil Servant at Work: Lawrence Vankoughnet and the Canadian Indian Department, 1874–1893." In *As Long as the Sun Shines and Water Flows*, edited by Ian Getty and Antoine Lussier. Vancouver: UBC Press, 1983.

Lutz, John Sutton. *Makuk: A New History of Aboriginal-White Relations*. Vancouver: UBC Press, 2008.

Lux, Maureen K. *Medicine that Walks: Disease, Medicine and Canadian Plains Native People, 1880–1940*. Toronto: University of Toronto Press, 2001.

MacLeod, R.C. *Swords and Ploughshares: War and Agriculture in Western Canada*. Edmonton: University of Alberta Press, 1993.

McCoy, Ted. "Legal Ideology in the Aftermath of the Rebellion: The Convicted First Nations Participants, 1885" *Social History* 42, no. 2 (2009).

Miller, J.R. "Canada and the Aboriginal People, 1867–1927." Ottawa: CHA Booklet, 1997.

———. *Compact, Contract, Covenant: Aboriginal Treaty-Making in Canada*. Toronto: University of Toronto Press, 2001.

———. *Reflections on Native-Newcomer Relations*. Toronto: University of Toronto Press, 2004.

———. *Skyscrapers Hide the Heavens: A History of Indian-White Relations in Canada*. Toronto: University of Toronto Press, 1989.

———. *Sweet Promises: A Reader on Indian-White Relations.* Toronto: University of Toronto Press, 1991.

Montgomery, Malcolm. "The Six Nations Indians and the Macdonald Franchise" *Ontario History* 57 (1965).

Morrison, R. Bruce, and Roderick C. Wilson. *Native Peoples: The Canadian Experience.* Toronto: McClelland & Stewart, 1974.

Nichols, Roger L. *Indians in the United States and Canada: A Comparative History.* Lincoln and London: University of Nebraska Press, 1998.

Owram, Douglas. "White Savagery: Some Canadian Reaction to American Indian Policy, 1867–1885." Master's thesis, Queen's University, 1971.

Pennanen, Gary. "Sitting Bull: Indian without a Country" *CHR* 51, no. 2 (1970).

Samek, Hana. *The Blackfoot Confederacy: A Comparative Study of Canadian and U.S. Indian Policy.* Albuquerque: University of New Mexico Press, 1987.

———. "Evaluating Canadian Indian Policy: A Case for Comparative Historical Perspective" *American Review of Canadian Studies* 16 (1986).

Smith, Donald. "Aboriginal Rights in 1885." In *Swords and Ploughshares: War and Agriculture in Western Canada*, edited by R.C. MacLeod. Edmonton: University of Alberta Press, 1993.

———. "John A. Macdonald and Aboriginal Canada" *Historic Kingston* 50 (2002).

Spry, Irene. "The Tragedy of the Loss of the Commons in Western Canada." In *As Long as the Sun Shines and Water Flows*, edited by Ian Getty and Antoine Lussier. Vancouver: UBC Press, 1983.

Stanley, George. "The Indian Background of Canadian History." Ottawa: CHA Bulletin, 1952.

Stonechild, Blair, and Bill Waiser. *Loyal Till Death: Indians and the North-West Rebellion*. Calgary: Fifth House, 1997.

Surtees, Robert J. *The Original People*. Toronto: Holt, Rinehart and Winston, 1971.

Taylor, Colin F., ed. *The People of the Buffalo: The Plains Indians of North America*. Wyk auf Foehr, Germany: Tatanka Press, 2003.

Taylor, J.L. "Canada's North-West Indian Policy in the 1870s." In *Sweet Promises: A Reader on Indian-White Relations*, edited by J. Miller. Toronto: University of Toronto Press, 1991.

Taylor, Leonard. "The Development of an Indian Policy for the Canadian North-West." Ph.D. thesis, Queen's University, 1976.

Titley, Brian. *The Frontier World of Edgar Dewdney*. Vancouver: UBC Press, 1999.

Tobias, John L. "Canada's Subjugation of the Plains Cree, 1879–1885" *CHR* 64, no. 4 (1983).

———. "Protection, Civilization, Assimilation: An Outline History of Canada's Indian Policy." In *As Long as the Sun Shines and Water Flows*, edited by Ian Getty and Antoine Lussier. Vancouver: UBC Press, 1983.

Weller, Geoffrey R., and Joyce M. Kramer. "North American Native Health: A Comparison between Canada and the United States." Paper presented to Midwestern Association for Canadian Studies, Detroit, October 1988.

ATLANTIC PROVINCES

Beck, J. Murray. *Joseph Howe*. Vol. 2, *The Briton Becomes Canadian, 1848–1873*. Montreal and Kingston: McGill-Queen's University Press, 1983.

———. "Joseph Howe: Opportunist or Empire-builder?" *CHR* 41, no. 3 (1960).

Buckner, Phillip. "CHR Dialogue: The Maritimes and Confederation: A Reassessment" *CHR* 71, no. 1 (1990).

Francis, R. Douglas. "An Unwilling Newfoundland and a Reluctant Prince Edward Island." In R. Douglas Francis, Richard Jones and Donald B. Smith, *Destinies: Canadian History since Confederation*, vol. 2. Toronto: Holt, Rinehart and Winston of Canada, 1988.

Harvey, D.C. "Confederation in Prince Edward Island" *CHR* 14, no. 2 (1933).

Hiller, James, and Peter Neary, eds. *Newfoundland in the Nineteenth and Twentieth Centuries: Essays in Interpretation*. Toronto: University of Toronto Press, 1980.

Howell, Colin. "W.S. Fielding and the Repeal Elections of 1886 and 1887 in Nova Scotia" *Acadiensis* 11, no. 2 (1979).

McMillan, Charles. *Eminent Islanders: Prince Edward Island, From Colony to Cradle of Confederation*. Bloomington, Indiana: AuthorHouse, 2008.

Pryke, Kenneth. G. *Nova Scotia and Confederation, 1864–74*. Toronto: University of Toronto Press, 1979.

———. *The Atlantic Provinces and the Problems of Confederation*. St. Johns: Breakwater, 1979.

Rawlyk, G.A. "Nova Scotia Regional Protest, 1867–1967" *QQ* 75 (1968).

Stanley, G.F.G. "Sir Stephen Hill's Observations on the Election of 1869 in Newfoundland" *CHR* 29, no. 3 (1948).

Warner, Donald. "The Post-Confederation Annexation Movement in Nova Scotia" *CHR* 28, no. 2 (1947).

BIOGRAPHIES AND MEMOIRS

Abbott, Elizabeth L. *The Reluctant P.M.: Notes on the Life of Sir John Abbott, Canada's Third Prime Minister.* Montreal: Elizabeth L. Abbott, 1997.

Batt, Elisabeth. *Monck, Governor General, 1861–1868.* Toronto: McClelland & Stewart, 1976.

Beck, J. Murray. *Joseph Howe.* Vol. 2, *The Briton Becomes Canadian, 1848–1873.* Montreal and Kingston: McGill-Queen's University Press, 1983.

Careless, J.M.S. *Brown of the Globe.* Vol. 1, *The Voice of Upper Canada, 1815–1859*, and vol. 2, *Statesman of Confederation, 1860–1880.* Toronto: Macmillan, 1959, 1963.

Cartwright, Sir Richard. *Reminiscences.* Toronto: William Briggs, 1912.

Collard, Edgar Andrew. *Canadian Yesterdays.* Toronto: Longmans, Green, 1955.

Cumming, Carman. *Secret Craft: The Journalism of Edward Farrer.* Toronto: University of Toronto Press, 1992.

Dent, John Charles. *The Last Forty Years.* Vol. 2, *The Union of 1841 to Confederation.* Toronto: George Virtue, 1981.

Desbarats, Lilian Scott. *Recollections.* Ottawa: Leclerc, 1957.

De Kiewiet, C.W., and F.H. Underhill, eds. *Dufferin-Carnarvon Correspondence, 1874–1878.* Toronto: The Champlain Society, 1955.

Evans, Margaret A. *Sir Oliver Mowat.* Toronto: University of Toronto Press, 1992.

Fraser, Barbara. "The Political Career of Sir Hector Louis Langevin" *CHR* 42, no. 2 (1961).

French, Doris. *Ishbel and the Empire: A Biography of Lady Aberdeen.* Toronto and Oxford: Dundurn Press, 1988.

Grant, A.R.C., and Caroline Combe, eds. *Lord Roseberry's North American Journal 1873.* London: Sidgwick & Jackson, 1967.

Hodgins, Bruce. *The Political Career of John Sandfield Macdonald to the Fall of His Administration in March, 1864*. Durham, North Carolina: Duke University Press, 1967.

Koester, Charles. *Mr. Davin MP: A Biography of Nicholas Davin*. Saskatoon: Western Producer Prairie Books, 1980.

Land, Andrew. *Life, Letters and Diaries of Sir Stafford Northcote, First Earl of Iddesleigh*. Edinburgh and London: William Blackwood & Sons, 1891.

Morton W.L., ed. *Monck Letters and Journals, 1863–1868*. Toronto: McClelland & Stewart, 1970.

Murray, Jock. *Sir Charles Tupper: Fighting Doctor to Father of Confederation*. Markham, Ont.: Fitzhenry & Whiteside, 1999.

Phelan, Josephine. *The Ardent Exile: The Life and Times of Thomas D'Arcy McGee*. Toronto: Macmillan, 1951.

Pope, Joseph. *Public Servant: The Memoirs of Sir Joseph Pope*. Toronto: Oxford University Press, 1960.

Ross, Sir George W. *Getting into Parliament and After*. Toronto: William Briggs, 1913.

Schull, Joseph. *Edward Blake: The Man of the Other Way, vol. 2, 1833–1881*. Toronto: Macmillan, 1975.

———. *Laurier: The First Canadian*. Toronto: Macmillan, 1965.

Skelton, Oscar D. *The Life and Times of Sir Alexander Tilloch Galt*. Toronto: Oxford University Press, 1920.

Slattery, T.P. *The Assassination of D'Arcy McGee*. Toronto: Doubleday Canada, 1968.

Smith, Donald B. *Honoré Jaxon: Prairie Visionary*. Regina: Coteau Books, 2007.

Smith, Goldwin. *Reminiscences*. Arnold Haultain, ed. New York: Macmillan, 1910.

———. *A Selection from Goldwin Smith's Correspondence, 1846–1910*. Arnold Haultain, ed. New York: Duffield & Co. 1913.

Smith, W.I. *The Cumberland War-horse: Sir Charles Tupper*. Unpublished manuscript at LAC, 2000.

Swainson, Donald. "Alexander Campbell: General Manager of the Conservative Party" *Historic Kingston* 17 (1969).

Sweeny, Alistair. *George-Étienne Cartier: A Biography*. Toronto: McClelland & Stewart, 1976.

Thompson, Samuel. *Reminiscences of a Canadian Pioneer, 1833–1883*. Toronto: McClelland & Stewart, 1968.

Thomson, Dale C. *Alexander Mackenzie: Clear Grit*. Toronto: Macmillan, 1960.

Waite, Peter B. *The Man from Halifax: Sir John Thompson, Prime Minister*. Toronto: University of Toronto Press, 1985.

Wallace, Elisabeth. *Goldwin Smith: Victorian Liberal*. Toronto: University of Toronto Press, 1957.

Warkentin, Germaine. "'D'Arcy McGee and the Critical Act': A Nineteenth-Century Oration" *JCS* 17, no. 2 (1982).

Willison, Sir John. *Reminiscences, Political and Personal*. Toronto: McClelland & Stewart, 1919.

Young, Brian. "The Defeat of George-Étienne Cartier in Montreal East in 1872" *CHR* 51, no. 4 (1981).

———. *George-Étienne Cartier: Montreal Bourgeois*. Montreal and Kingston: McGill-Queen's University Press, 1981.

CONSTITUTION AND THE JUDICIARY

Barrett, Maxwell. *The Law Lords: An Account of the Workings of Britain's Highest Judicial Body and the Men Who Preside Over It*. Basingstoke: Macmillan, 2001.

Black, Edwin R. *Divided Loyalties: Canadian Concepts of Federalism*. Montreal: McGill-Queen's University Press, 1975.

Cairns, Alan C. *Constitution, Government, and Society in Canada*. Toronto: McClelland & Stewart, 1988.

Dickinson, H.T., and Michael Lynch. *The Challenge to Westminster: Sovereignty, Devolution and Independence*. East Linton, Scotland: Tuckwell Press, 2000.

DiGiacomo, Gordon. "Support for a Centralist Vision of Labour Policy in Early Canada" *JCS* 38, no. 3 (2004).

Farr, D.M.L., J.S. Moir and S.R. Mealing. *Two Democracies*. Toronto: Ryerson Press, 1963.

Forsey, Eugene. "The British North America Act and Biculturalism" *QQ* 71, no. 2 (1964).

Gibson, Dale. "The Development of Federal Legal-Judicial Institutions in Canada" *Manitoba Law Journal* 23, Canadian Legal History Project, 1992 (1996).

Howell, P.A. *The Judicial Committee of the Privy Council, 1833–1876*. Cambridge: Cambridge University Press, 1979.

Koerner, Wolfgang. "Foundations of Canadian Federalism." Parliamentary Research Branch, Background Paper, Dec. 1988.

Krikorian, Jacqueline. "British Imperial Politics and Judicial Independence" *CJPS* 33 (2000).

La Forest, G.V. "Disallowance and Reservation of Provincial Legislation." Ottawa: Department of Justice, 1955.

Laskin, Bora. "'Peace, Order and Good Government' Re-examined" *Canadian Bar Review* 25 (1947).

MacKinnon, Frank. "The Establishment of the Supreme Court of Canada" *CHR* 17, no. 3 (1946).

McConnell, W.H. *Commentary on the British North America Act*. Toronto: Macmillan, 1977.

Morton, W.L. "Confederation, 1870–1896: The End of the Macdonaldian Constitution and the Return to Duality" *JCS* 1, no. 2 (1966).

———. "The Conservative Principle in Confederation" *QQ* 71, no. 4 (1965).

Paquin, Stephane. "The Myth of the Compact Theory of Confederation" www.canadahistory.com/sections/papers/paquin.htm

Paterson, Alan. *The Law Lords*. Toronto: University of Toronto Press, 1982.

Pierson, Coen G. *Canada and the Privy Council*. London: Stevens & Sons, 1960.

Pue, Wesley W., and Barry Wright, eds. *Canadian Perspectives on Law & Society: Issues in Legal History*. Ottawa: Carleton University Press, 1983.

Risk, Richard. "The Privy Council and Its Scholars: Canadian Constitutional Law." Canadian Legal History Project Working Paper Series. University of Manitoba, Faculty of Law, 1992.

Roach, Kent. *The Supreme Court on Trial: Judicial Activism or Democratic Dialogue*. Toronto: Irwin Law, 2001.

Rogers, Norman McLeod. "The Genesis of Provincial Rights" *CHR* 14, no. 1 (1933).

Romney, Paul. *Getting It Wrong: How Canadians Forgot Their Past and Imperilled Confederation.* Toronto: University of Toronto Press, 1999.

———. "Provincial Equality, Special Status and the Compact Theory of Canadian Confederation" *CJPS* 32 (1999).

Russell, Peter H. *Constitutional Odyssey: Can Canadians Become a Sovereign People?* Toronto: University of Toronto Press, 2004.

———. *The Judiciary in Canada: The Third Branch of Government*. Toronto: McGraw-Hill Ryerson, 1987.

Saywell, John T. *The Lawmakers: Judicial Power and the Shaping of Canadian Federalism*. Toronto: University of Toronto Press, 2002.

Scott, Frank. "The Consequences of the Privy Council Decisions" *Canadian Bar Review* 15 (1935).

Simeon, Richard, and Ian Robinson. *State, Society, and the Development of Canadian Federalism*. Toronto: University of Toronto Press, 1990.

Smiley, Donald V., ed. *The Rowell-Sirois Report*, Book 1 (abridgement). Toronto: McClelland & Stewart, 1968.

Smith, Jennifer. "The Origins of Judicial Review in Canada" *JCS* 16, no. 1 (1983).

Snell, James G., and Frederick Vaughan. *The Supreme Court of Canada: History of the Institution*. Toronto: University of Toronto Press, 1985.

Stanley, George. *A Short History of the Canadian Constitution*. Toronto: Ryerson Press, 1969.

Stevenson, Garth. *Unfulfilled Union: Canadian Federalism and National Unity.* Toronto: Gage, 1983.

Vaughan, Frederick. *The Canadian Federalist Experiment: From Defiant Monarchy to Reluctant Republic*. Montreal and Kingston: McGill-Queen's University Press, 2003.

———. "Critics of the Judicial Committee of the Privy Council: The New Orthodoxy and an Alternative Explanation" *CJPS* 19 (1986).

Vipond, Robert C. "Confederation and the Federal Principle." In *An Introduction to Canadian History*, edited by A.I. Silver and Carl Berger. Toronto: Canadian Scholars' Press, 1991.

———. "Constitutional Rights and the Legacy of the Province Rights Movement in Canada" *CJPS* 18 (1985).

———. "Federalism and the Problem of Sovereignty: Constitutional Politics and the Rise of the Provincial Rights Movement in Canada." Ph.D. thesis, Harvard University, 1983.

———. *Liberty and Community: Canadian Federalism and the Failure of the Constitution*. Albany: State University of New York Press, 1991.

DEFENCE

Hitsman, J. MacKay. *Safeguarding Canada, 1973–1871*. Toronto: University of Toronto Press, 1968.

Preston, Richard A. *Canadian Defence Policy and the Development of the Canadian Nation, 1867–1917*. Ottawa: CHA Booklet 25, 1970.

———. *The Defence of the Undefended Border: Planning for War in North America, 1867–1939*. Montreal: McGill-Queen's University Press, 1977.

Senior, Hereward. *The Last Invasion of Canada: The Fenian Raids, 1866–1870*. Toronto: Dundurn Press, 1991.

Stacey, C.P. "Britain's Withdrawal from North America, 1864–1871" *CHR* 36, no. 3 (1955).

———. "British Military Policy in the Era of Confederation" CHA *Annual Report*, 1934.

———. *Canada and the Age of Conflict: A History of Canadian External Policies. Vol. 1, 1867–1921*. Toronto: University of Toronto Press, 1961.

———. *Canada and the British Army*. Toronto: University of Toronto Press, 1963.

Stanley, George. *Toil and Trouble: Military Expeditions to Red River.* Toronto: Dundurn Press, 1989.

Stewart, Alice. "Sir John A. Macdonald and the Imperial Defence Commission of 1879" *CHR* 26, no. 4 (1954).

THE ECONOMY AND BUSINESS

Bliss, Michael. "Canadianizing American Business: The Roots of the Branch Plant." In *An Introduction to Canadian History*, edited by A.I. Silver and Carl Berger. Toronto: Canadian Scholars' Press, 1991.

———. *A Living Profit: Studies in the Social History of Canadian Business.* Toronto: McClelland & Stewart, 1974.

———. *Northern Enterprise: Five Centuries of Canadian Business.* Toronto: McClelland & Stewart, 1987.

Cross, Michael S. *Canada's Age of Industry, 1849–1896*. Toronto: McClelland & Stewart, 1982.

Easterbrook, W.T. and M.H. Watkins. *Approaches to Canadian Economic History*. Toronto: McClelland & Stewart, 1967.

Firestone, O.J. *Canada's Economic Development, 1867–1953*. London: Bowes and Bowes, 1958.

Goodwin, Craufurd D.W. *Canadian Economic Thought: The Political Economy of a Developing Nation, 1814–1914*. Durham, North Carolina: Duke University Press, 1961.

Longley, R.S. "Sir Francis Hincks, Finance Minister of Canada, 1869–1873" CHA *Annual Report*, 1939.

Macmillan, David S. *Canadian Business History, Selected Studies, 1497–1971*. Toronto: McClelland & Stewart, 1972.

McCalla, Douglas. *Perspectives on Canadian Economic History*. Toronto: Copp Clark Pitman, 1987.

Naylor, R.T. *The History of Canadian Business. Vol. 1, 1867–1914*. Toronto: James Lorimer, 1975.

Norrie, Kenneth, and Douglas Owram. *A History of the Canadian Economy*. Toronto: Harcourt Brace Jovanovich, 1991.

Porter, Glenn, and Robert Cuff. *Enterprise and National Development: Essays in Canadian Business and Economic History*. Toronto: Hakkert, 1973.

Rae, John. *New Principles of Political Economy*. London: Macmillan, 1905.

FEDERAL-PROVINCIAL RELATIONS

Cook, Ramsay. *Provincial Autonomy, Minority Rights and the Compact Theory, 1867–1921*. Studies of the Royal Commission on Bilingualism and Biculturalism. Ottawa: The Queen's Printer, 1969.

La Forest, G.V. *Disallowance and Reservation of Provincial Legislation*. Ottawa, Department of Justice, 1955.

Rogers, Norman McLeod. "The Genesis of Provincial Rights" *CHR* 14, no. 1 (1933).

Romney, Paul. "Provincial Equality, Special Status and the Compact Theory of Canadian Confederation" *CJPS* 32, no. 1 (1999).

Rowell-Sirois Report. *An Abridgement of Book One of the Rowell-Sirois Report on Dominion-Provincial Relations*. Toronto: McClelland & Stewart, 1963.

Stevenson, Garth. *Ex Uno Plures: Federal-Provincial Relations in Canada, 1867–1896*. Montreal and Kingston: McGill-Queen's University Press, 1993.

Vipond, Robert. "Constitutional Politics and the Legacy of the Provincial Rights Movement in Canada" *CJPS* 18, no. 2 (1985).

Ontario

Armstrong, Christopher. "The Mowat Heritage in Federal-Provincial Relations." In *Oliver Mowat's Ontario*, edited by Donald Swainson. Toronto: Macmillan, 1972.

———. *The Politics of Federalism: Ontario's Relations with the Federal Government, 1867–1942*. Government of Ontario, Historical Studies Series. Toronto: University of Toronto Press, 1981.

Morrison, J.C. "Oliver Mowat and the Development of Provincial Rights in Ontario: A Study in Federal-Provincial Relations, 1867–1896." In *Three History Theses*. Toronto: Ontario Department of Public Records and Archives, 1961.

Ontario Historical Society. *Profiles of a Province: Studies in the History of Ontario*. Toronto: Ontario Historical Society, 1967.

Romney, Paul. "From the Rule of Law to Responsible Government: Ontario Political Culture" *CHA Historical Papers* (1980).

Swainson, Donald, ed. *Oliver Mowat's Ontario*, Toronto: Macmillan, 1972.

Zaslow, Morris. "The Ontario Boundary Dispute." In *Profiles of a Province*. Toronto: Ontario Historical Society, 1967.

Manitoba

Begg, Alexander. *The Creation of Manitoba; or, A History of the Red River Troubles*. Yarmouth, N.S.: A.H. Hovey, 1871.

Ens, Gerhard. *Homeland to Hinterland: The Changing Worlds of Red River Metis in the Nineteenth Century*. Toronto: University of Toronto Press, 1996.

Friesen, Gerald. *River Road: Essays on Manitoba and Prairie History*. Winnipeg: University of Manitoba Press, 1996.

McCutcheon, Brian R. "The Birth of Agrarianism in the Prairie West" *Prairie Forum* 1, no. 2 (1976).

Morton, W.L. *The Birth of a Province*. Vol. 1. Manitoba Record Society Publications, 1965.

———. *Manitoba, A History*. Toronto: University of Toronto Press, 1967.

British Columbia

Angus, Henry Forbes. *British Columbia and the United States: The North Pacific Slope, from Fur Trade to Aviation.* Toronto: Ryerson Press, 1891.

Barman, Jean. *The West beyond the West: A History of British Columbia.* Toronto: University of Toronto Press, 1991.

Helmcken, John Sebastian. *The Reminiscences of Doctor John Sebastian Helmcken.* Edited by Dorothy Blakey Smith. Vancouver: UBC Press, 1975.

Hind, Henry Youle. *A Sketch of an Overland Route to British Columbia.* Toronto: W.C. Chewett & Co, 1862.

Roy, Patricia. *A History of British Columbia.* Toronto: Copp Clark Pitman, 1989.

Sage, Walter N. "British Columbia Becomes Canadian, 1871–1901" *QQ* 52, no. 2 (1945).

Shelton, George W. *British Columbia and Confederation.* Victoria: Morriss Printing Co., 1967.

HISTORICAL STUDIES AND DOCUMENTS

Berger, Carl. *Approaches to Canadian History.* Toronto: University of Toronto Press, 1967.

Bliss, Michael. *Canadian History in Documents, 1763–1966.* Toronto: Ryerson Press, 1968.

Bothwell, Robert. *The Penguin History of Canada.* Toronto: Penguin Group, 2006.

Brown, R.C., and M.E. Prang. *Canadian Historical Documents. Vol. 3, Confederation to 1949.* Scarborough, Ont.: Prentice-Hall of Canada, 1966.

Bumstead, J.M. *Documentary Problems in Canadian History. Vol. 2, Post-Confederation.* Georgetown, Ont.: Irwin-Dorsey, 1969.

———. *Interpreting Canada's Past. Vol. 2, After Confederation.* Toronto: Oxford University Press, 1986.

———. *The Peoples of Canada: A Post-Confederation History*. Toronto: Oxford University Press, 1992.

Careless, J.M.S. and Craig Brown, eds. *The Canadians, 1867–1967*, Part 1. Toronto: Macmillan, 1980.

Cook, Ramsay, John Ricker and John Saywell. *Canada: A Modern Study.* Toronto: Clarke, Irwin & Co., 1977.

De Brou, David, and Bill Waiser. *Documenting Canada: A History of Modern Canada in Documents.* Saskatoon: Fifth House Publishers, 1992.

Finlay, J.L., and D.M. Sprague. *The Structure of Canadian History*. Scarborough, Ont.: Prentice-Hall Canada, 1997.

Francis, R. Douglas, Richard Jones and Donald B. Smith. *Destinies: Canadian History Since Confederation*, 6th Ed. Scarborough, Ont.: Nelson Education, 2008.

Gaffield, Chad. *Constructing Modern Canada: Readings in Post-Confederation History*. Toronto: Copp Clark Longman, 1994.

Granatstein, J.L. *First Drafts: Eyewitness Accounts from Canada's Past*, Toronto: Thomas Allen, 2000.

Hodge, Bruce, and Robert Page, eds. *Canadian History since Confederation: Essays and Interpretations*. Georgetown, Ont.: Irwin-Dorsey, 1979.

Horn, Michael, and Ronald Saborin, eds. *Studies in Canadian Social History*. Toronto: McClelland & Stewart, 1974.

Lower, Arthur R.M. *Colony to Nation: A History of Canada*. Toronto: Longmans, Green, 1946.

McInnis, Edgar. *Canada: A Political and Social History*. Toronto: Holt, Rinehart and Winston of Canada, 1982.

McKay, Ian, ed. *The Challenge of Modernity: A Reader on Post-Confederation Canada*. Toronto: McGraw-Hill Ryerson, 1992.

Moir, John S. *Character and Circumstances: Essays in Honour of Donald G. Creighton*. Toronto: Macmillan, 1970.

Morton, W.L. *The Critical Years: The Union of British North America, 1857–1873*. Toronto: McClelland & Stewart, 1964.

Reid, J.H. Stewart, Kenneth McNaught and Harry S. Crowe. *A Source-book of Canadian History: Selected Documents and Personal Papers.* Toronto: Longmans, Green, 1964.

Saywell, John, and John C. Ricker, eds. *Nation-Making: Original Documents on the Founding of the Canadian Nation and the Settlement of the West, 1867–85.* Don Mills, Ont.: Burns and MacEachern, 1967.

Silver, A.I., and Carl Berger, eds. *An Introduction to Canadian History.* Toronto: Canadian Scholars' Press, 1991.

Sprague, D.N. *Post-Confederation Canada: The Structure of Canadian History since Confederation.* Scarborough, Ont.: Prentice-Hall, 1990.

Waite, Peter B. *Arduous Destiny: Canada, 1874–1896.* Toronto: McClelland & Stewart, 1971.

IMMIGRATION AND CHINESE WORKERS

Barman, Jean. "The West Beyond the West: The Demography of Settlement in British Columbia" *JCS* 25, no. 3 (1990).

Chiel, Arthur. *The Jews in Manitoba: A Social History.* Toronto: University of Toronto Press, 1961.

Con, Harry. *From China to Canada: A History of the Chinese Communities in Canada.* Toronto: McClelland & Stewart, 1982.

Goutor, David. "Constructing the 'Great Menace': Canadian Labour's Opposition to Asian Immigration, 1880–1914" *CHR* 88, no. 4 (2007).

Holland, Kenneth. "A History of Chinese Immigration in the United States and Canada" *American Review of Canadian Studies* 37, no. 2 (2007).

Li, Peter. *Chinese in Canada.* Toronto: OUP, 1988.

MacDonald, Norman. *Canada: Immigration and Colonization, 1841–1903.* Aberdeen: Aberdeen University Press, 1966.

Munro, John A. "British Columbia and the 'Chinese Evil': Canada's First Anti-Asiatic Immigration Law" *JCS* 6, no. 4 (1971).

Roy, Patricia. "A Choice Between Evils: The Chinese and the Construction of the Canadian Pacific Railway in British Columbia." In *The CPR West*, edited by Hugh Dempsey. Vancouver: Douglas & McIntyre, 1984.

———. *A White Man's Province: British Columbia Politicians and Chinese and Japanese Immigrants, 1858–1914*. Vancouver: UBC Press, 1989.

Sack, Benjamin. *History of the Jews in Canada*. Montreal: Harvest House, 1965.

Tulchinsky, Gerald, ed. *Immigration in Canada: Historical Perspectives*. Toronto: Copp Clark Longman, 1994.

Ward, W. Peter. *White Canada Forever: Popular Attitudes and Public Policies towards Orientals in British Columbia*. Montreal and Kingston: McGill-Queen's University Press, 2002.

Winks, Robin W. *The Blacks in Canada: A History*. Montreal and Kingston: McGill-Queen's University Press, 1977.

Woodsworth, Charles. *Canada and the Orient*. Toronto: Macmillan, 1941.

IMPERIALISM AND THE EMPIRE

Berger, Carl. *Studies in the Ideas of Canadian Imperialism, 1867–1914*. Toronto: University of Toronto Press, 1970.

Bodelson, C.A. *Studies in Mid-Victorian Imperialism*. New York: Howard Fertig, 1968.

Bourne, Kenneth. *Britain and the Balance of Power in North America, 1815–1908*. Toronto: Longmans, 1967.

Buckner, Phillip ed. *Canada and the British Empire*. Oxford: Oxford University Press, 2008.

———, and R. Douglas Francis. *Canada and the British World: Culture, Migration and Identity*. Vancouver: UBC Press, 2006.

Bumsted, Michael. "From the Red to the Nile: William Nassau Kennedy and the Manitoba Contingent of Voyageurs in the Gordon Relief Expedition, 1884–1885" *Manitoba History* 42, Manitoba Historical Society, 2001/2002.

Coates, Colin M. *Imperial Canada, 1867–1917*. University of Edinburgh, Canadian Studies Conference, May 1995.

Davison, Helen Louise. "Sir John A. Macdonald and the Imperial Relations in the Period 1878–1891." Master's thesis, University of Ottawa, 1957.

Dyck, Harvey, and Peter Krosby, eds. *Empire and Nation.* Toronto: University of Toronto Press, 1969.

Farr, David M.L. *The Colonial Office and Canada, 1867–1887.* Toronto: University of Toronto Press, 1955.

———. "Sir John Rose and Imperial Relations: An Episode in Gladstone's Administration" *CHR* 33, no. 1 (1952).

Glazebrook, G.P. de T. *A History of Canadian External Relations.* Toronto, New York: Oxford University Press, 1950.

Horan, James Francis. "Patterns of Canadian Foreign Policy: A Study in the Shaping of Canadian External Relations from Confederation to Suez." Ph.D. thesis, University of Connecticut, 1958.

Hodgins, Thomas. *British and American Diplomacy Affecting Canada, 1782–1899.* Toronto: Rowell and Hutchinson, 1900.

Hyam, Ronald. *Britain's Imperial Century, 1815–1914: A Study of Empire and Expansion.* London: B.T. Batsford, 1976.

———, and Ged Martin. *Reappraisals in British Imperial History.* London: Macmillan, 1975.

Jenkins, Brian. *Fenians and Anglo-American Relations during Reconstruction.* Ithaca: Cornell University Press, 1969.

MacLaren, Roy. *Commissions High: Canada in London, 1870–1971.* Montreal and Kingston: McGill-Queen's University Press, 2000.

Martin, Ged. "Queen Victoria and Canada" *American Review of Canadian Studies* 13 (1983).

Moore, Steve, and Debi Wells. *Imperialism and the National Question in Canada.* Toronto: Moore, 1975.

Morris, James. *Heaven's Command: An Imperial Progress.* New York: Harcourt Brace Jovanovich,1980; London: Faber and Faber (1973) 2003.

Moyles, R.G., and Doug Owram. *Imperial Dreams and Colonial Realities: British Views of Canada, 1880–1914.* Toronto: University of Toronto Press, 1988.

Parsons, Timothy. *The British Imperial Century, 1815–1914.* Lanham, Maryland: Rowman and Littlefield, 1999.

Porter, Bernard. *The Absent-Minded Imperialists: Empire, Society and Culture in Britain*. Oxford: Oxford University Press, 2004.

Smith, Goldwin, "Loyalty." In *Canadian History since Confederation*, edited by Bruce Hodgins and Robert Page. Georgetown, Ont.: Irwin-Dorsey, 1972.

Stacey, C.P. *Canada and the Age of Conflict: A History of Canadian External Policies*. Toronto: University of Toronto Press, 1984.

———. "Canada and the Nile Expedition of 1884–85" *CHR* 33, no. 4 (1952).

———. "John A. Macdonald on Raising Troops in Canada for Imperial Service, 1885" *CHR* 38, no. 1 (1957).

Stewart, Alice. "Sir John A. Macdonald and the Imperial Defence Commission of 1879" *CHR* 35, no. 2 (1954).

———. "The Imperial Policy of Sir John A. Macdonald, Canada's First Prime Minister." Ph.D thesis, Radcliffe College, Harvard University, 1946.

Thornton, A.P. *The Imperial Idea and Its Enemies: A Study in British Power*. London: Macmillan; New York: St. Martin's Press, 1959.

Troop, William H. "Canada and the Empire: A Study of Canadian Attitudes to the Empire and Imperial Relations since 1867." Ph.D. thesis, University of Toronto, 1933.

Winks, Robin W. *The Age of Imperialism*. New Jersey: Prentice-Hall, 1969.

LABOUR AND UNIONS

Allen, Richard. "The Social Gospel and the Reform Tradition in Canada, 1890–1928" *CHR* 49, no. 4 (1968).

Bercuson, David, ed. *Canadian Labour History: Selected Readings*. Toronto: Copp Clark Pitman, 1987.

Bullen, John. "Hidden Workers: Child Labour." In *The Challenge of Modernity: A Reader in Post-Confederation Canada*, edited by Ian McKay. Toronto: McGraw-Hill Ryerson, 1992.

Cross, Michael S., ed. *The Workingman in the Nineteenth Century*. Toronto: University of Toronto Press, 1974.

Gagan, David, and Rosemary Gagan. "Working-class Standards of Living in Late Victorian Urban Ontario" *Journal of the Canadian Historical Association* 1, no. 1 (1970).

Kealey, Greg, ed. *Canada Investigates Industrialism*. Toronto: University of Toronto Press, 1973.

———. *Essays in Canadian Working Class History*. Toronto: McClelland & Stewart, 1976.

———, and Bryan Palmer. *Dreaming of What Might Be: The Knights of Labour in Ontario, 1880–1900*. Toronto: New Hogtown Press, 1987.

Langdon, Steven. *The Emergence of the Canadian Working Class Movement, 1845–1875*. Toronto: New Hogtown Press, 1975.

Marks, Lynne. "The Knights of Labour and the Salvation Army: Religion and Working-Class Culture in Ontario, 1882–1890." In *Constructing Modern Canada*, edited by Chad Gaffield. Toronto: Copp Clark Longman, 1994.

Ostry, Bernard. "Conservatives, Liberals, and Labour in the 1870s" *CHR* 41, no. 2 (1960).

Palmer, Bryan, ed. *The Character of Class Struggle: Essays in Canadian Working-Class History, 1850–1985*. Toronto: McClelland & Stewart, 1976.

Scott, Jack. *Sweat and Struggle: Working Class Struggles in Canada. Vol.8, 1789–1899*. Vancouver: New Star Books, 1974.

Watt, F.W. "The National Policy, the Workingman, and Proletarian Ideas in Victorian Canada" *CHR* 40, no. 1 (1959).

Zerker, Sally. "George Brown and the Printers' Union" *JCS* 10, no. 1 (1975).

MÉTIS AND THE BUFFALO

Arthur, George. "The North American Plains Bison: A Brief History" *Prairie Forum* 9, no. 2 (1984).

Bumsted. J.M. *Thomas Scott's Body, and Other Essays on Early Manitoba History*. Winnipeg: University of Manitoba Press, 2000.

Ens, Gerhard J. "The Border, the Buffalo, and the Manitoba Metis." In *The Borderlands of the American and Canadian West*, edited by Sterling Evans. Lincoln: University of Nebraska Press, 2006.

———. "Dispossession or Adaptation? Migration and Persistence of the Red River Metis, 1835–1890." CHA Historical Papers, 1988.

———. *Homeland to Hinterland: The Changing Worlds of the Red River Metis in the Nineteenth Century.* Toronto: University of Toronto Press, 1996.

Foster, John. "The Metis: The People and the Term." In A.S. Lussier, ed., *Louis Riel and the Metis.* Winnipeg: Pemmican Publications, 1991.

Geist, Valerius. *Buffalo Nation: History and Legend of the North American Bison.* Saskatoon: Fifth House Publishers, 1996.

Horanday, William T. *The Extermination of the American Bison, 1854–1937.* Washington, D.C.: Smithsonian Institution Press, 2002.

Lussier, Antoine. *The Other Natives: The/Les Métis.* Winnipeg: Manitoba Métis Federation Press, 1978.

MacLeod, Margaret A. "A Note on the Red River Hunt by John Norquay" *CHR* 38, no. 2 (1957).

McLean, Donald G. *Home from the Hill: A History of the Métis in Western Canada.* Regina: Gabriel Dumont Institute of Native Studies, 1987.

Miller, J.R. "From Riel to the Metis" *CHR* 69, no. 1 (1988).

Morton, W.L. "The New Nation." In *A Social History of the Manitoba Métis*, edited by Emile Pelletier. Winnipeg: Manitoba Métis Federation Press, 1977.

Pannekoek, Frank. "The Historiography of the Red River Settlement, 1830–1868" *Prairie Forum* 6, no. 1 (1981).

Payment, Diane P. *The Free People—Les Gens Libres: A History of the Métis Community of Batoche, Saskatchewan.* Calgary: University of Calgary Press, 2009.

Pelletier, Emile, ed. *A Social History of the Manitoba Métis.* Winnipeg: Manitoba Métis Federation Press, 1977.

Purich, Donald. *The Métis.* Toronto: James Lorimer, 1988.

Roe, Frank Gilbert. *The North American Buffalo: A Critical Study of the Species in its Wild State.* Toronto: University of Toronto Press, 1951.

Sealey, Bruce, and Antoine Lussier. *The Métis, Canada's Forgotten People.* Winnipeg: Manitoba Métis Federation Press, 1975.

Sprague, D.N. *Canada and the Métis, 1869–1885.* Waterloo: Wilfrid Laurier University Press, 1988.

Sprenger, H.S. "The Métis Nation: Buffalo Hunting vs. Agriculture at Red River Settlement, 1810–1870." In *A Social History of the Manitoba Métis*, edited by Emile Pelletier. Winnipeg: Manitoba Métis Federation Press, 1977.

Stanley, George. "The Metis and the Conflict of Cultures in Western Canada" *CHR* 27, no. 4 (1947).

NATIONAL POLICY AND TRADE

Berns, Rima. *The Real Story Behind Free Trade (A History of the Canadian Tariff).* Baltimore: Johns Hopkins School of Advanced International Studies, 1988.

Bliss, Michael. "Canadianizing American Business: The Roots of the Branch Plant." In *Introduction to Canadian History*, edited by A.I. Silver and Carl Berger. Toronto: Canadian Scholars' Press, 1991.

Brown, Robert Craig. *Canada's National Policy: A Study in Canadian-American Relations, 1883–1900.* Princeton: Princeton University Press, 1964.

———. "The Nationalism of the National Policy." In *Nationalism in Canada*, edited by Peter Russell. Toronto: University of Toronto Press, 1966.

Crankshaw, Edward. *Bismark.* London: Macmillan, 1981.

Craven, Paul, and Tom Traves. "The Class Politics of the National Policy" *JCS* 14, no. 3 (1979).

Dales, John, ed. "Canada's National Policies." In *The Protective Tariff in Canada's Development*, edited by John Dales. Toronto: University of Toronto Press, 1966.

———. "'National Policy' Myths, Past and Present" *JCS* 14, no. 3 (1979).

Forster, Benjamin. "The Coming of the National Policy: Business, Government and the Tariffs, 1876–1879" *JCS* 3, no. 3 (1979).

———. "Tariffs and Politics: The Genesis of the National Policy." Ph.D. thesis, University of Toronto, 1981.

Forster, Jakob, J.B. *A Conjunction of Interests: Business, Politics and Tariffs, 1825–1879*. Toronto: University of Toronto Press, 1986.

Fowke, V.C. "The National Policy—Old and New" *CHR* 18, no. 3 (1952).

Goodwin, Craufurd. *Canadian Economic Thought: The Political Economy of a Developing Nation, 1814–1914*. Durham: Duke University Press, 1961.

Norrie, Kenneth H. "The National Policy and the Prairie Region: A Reappraisal of the National Policy Tariffs and Their Effect on the Developing Wheat Economy." Ph.D. thesis, University of Ann Arbor, Michigan, 1971.

———. "The National Policy and the Rate of Prairie Settlement: A Review" *JCS* 14, no. 3 (1979).

Smiley, Donald V. "Canada and the Quest for a National Policy" *CJPS* 8, no. 1 (1975).

Williams, Glen. "The National Policy Tariffs: Industrial Underdevelopment Through Import Substitution" *CJPS* 12, no. 2 (1979).

Zeller, Suzanne. "The Protective Tariffs of 1879: 'National Policy' in Canada and Germany as a Means of Political and Social Control." Master's thesis, University of Windsor, 1976.

NATIONALISM

Berger, Carl. *The Sense of Power: Studies in the Ideas of Canadian Imperialism, 1867–1914*. Toronto: University of Toronto Press, 1970.

———. "The True North Strong and Free." In *Nationalism in Canada*, edited by Peter Russell. Toronto: University of Toronto Press, 1966.

Cole, Douglas L. "Canada's 'Nationalistic' Imperialists" *JCS* 5, no. 3 (1950).

Cook, Ramsay. *The Maple Leaf Forever: Essays on Nationalism and Politics in Canada*. Toronto: Macmillan, 1974.

Cupido, Robert. "Appropriating the Past: Pageants, Politics and the Diamond Jubilee of Confederation" *Journal of the CHA*, 9 (1998).

Farrell, D.R. "The Canada First Movement and Canadian Political Thought" *JCS* 4, no. 4 (1969).

Friesen, Gerald. *Citizens and Nation: An Essay on History, Communication, and Canada*. Toronto: University of Toronto Press, 2000.

Gagan, David. "The Relevance of 'Canada First'" *JCS* 5 (November 1970).

Henley, Kevin. "The International Roots of Economic Nationalist Ideology in Canada, 1846–1885" *JCS* 24, no. 4 (1989/90).

Martin, Chester. *Foundations of Canadian Nationhood,1882–1958*. Toronto: University of Toronto Press, 1955.

———. "The United States and Canadian Nationality" *CHR* 18, no. 1 (1937).

Russell, Peter H. ed. *Nationalism in Canada*. Toronto: University of Toronto Press, 1966.

Rutherford, Paul. "The New Nationality, 1864–1897." Ph.D. thesis, University of Toronto, 1973.

Scott, Frank. "Political Nationalism and Confederation" *CJEPS* 22 (1945).

Shrive, Norman. *Charles Mair: Literary Nationalist*. Toronto: University of Toronto Press, 1965.

Smith, Allan. *Canada—An American Nation? Essays on Continentalism, Identity and the Canadian Frame of Mind*. Montreal and Kingston: McGill-Queen's University Press, 1994.

Stacey, C.P. "Fenianism and the Rise of National Feeling in Canada at the Time of Confederation" *CHR* 12, no. 3 (1931).

Stewart, Wallace. "The Growth of Canadian National Feeling" *CHR* 1, no. 2 (1920).

University League for Social Reform. *Nationalism in Canada*. Toronto: McGraw-Hill, 1966.

Wise, S.F. and Robert Craig Brown. *Canada Views the United States: Nineteenth-Century Political Attitudes*. Seattle: University of Washington Press, 1967.

POLICE: NORTH-WEST MOUNTED

Atkin, Ronald. *Maintain the Right: The Early History of the North-West Mounted Police, 1873–1900*. Toronto: Macmillan, 1973.

Baker, William M., ed. *The Mounted Police and Prairie Society*. Regina: Canadian Plains Research Center, University of Regina, 1998.

Beahan, William, and Stan Horrall. *Red Coats on the Prairies: The North-West Mounted Police, 1886–1900*. Regina: Centax Books, 1998.

Dempsey, Hugh A., ed. *Men in Scarlet*. Calgary: McClelland & Stewart West, 1974.

Denny, Cecil E. *The Law Marches West.*Toronto: J.M. Dent, 1972.

Evans, Sterling. *The Borderlands of the American and Canadian West*. Lincoln, Nebraska: University of Nebraska Press, 2006.

Horrall, W.F. "Sir John A. Macdonald and the Mounted Police Force for the Northwest Territories" *CHR* 53, no. 2 (1972).

Jennings, John. "The North West Mounted Police and Indian Policy after the 1885 Rebellion." In *1885 and After: Native Society in Transition*, edited by Laurie Barron and James Waldram. Regina: Canadian Plains Research Center, University of Regina, 1986.

MacBeth, R.G. *Policing the Plains*. London: Hodder and Stoughton, 1923.

Macleod, R.C. *Canadianizing the West: The North-West Mounted Police as Agents of the National Policy, 1873–1905*. In *The Prairie West: Historical Readings*, edited by Francis Douglas. Edmonton: Pica Pica Press, 2001.

———. "The Mounted Police and Politics." In *Men in Scarlet*, edited by Hugh Dempsey. Calgary: McClelland & Stewart West, 1974.

———. *The NWMP and Law Enforcement, 1873–1905*. Toronto: University of Toronto Press, 1976.

Morton, Desmond. "Cavalry or Police: Keeping the Peace on Two Adjacent Frontiers, 1870–1900" *JCS* 12, no. 1 (1977).

Sharp, Paul F. *Whoop-Up Country: The Canadian-American West, 1865–1885*. Minneapolis: University of Minnesota Press, 1955.

Walden, Keith. *The Great March of the Mounted Police in Popular Literature*. CHA Historical Papers, 1980.

Wilson, Garrett. "The North-West Mounted Police." In *Frontier Farewell: The 1870s and the End of the Old West*, edited by Garrett Wilson. Regina: Canadian Plains Research Center, University of Regina, 2007.

POLITICS, PARLIAMENT AND THE FRANCHISE

Beaven, Brian. "Partisanship, Patronage and the Press in Ontario, 1880–1894: Myths and Realities" *CHR* 44, no. 3 (1983).

Beck, Murray J. *Pendulum of Power: Canada's Federal Elections*. Scarborough, Ont.: Prentice-Hall of Canada, 1968.

Bell, David. *The Roots of Disunity: A Look at Canadian Political Culture*. Toronto: McClelland & Stewart, 1979.

Bond, C.C.J. "The Canadian Government Comes to Ottawa, 1865–1866" *Ontario History* 55, no. 1 (1963).

Burke, Sister Teresa Avila. "Mackenzie and His Cabinet, 1873–1878" *CHR* 41, no. 2 (1960).

Careless, J.M.S. *Brown of the Globe*. Vol. 2, *Statesman of Confederation*. Toronto: Macmillan, 1963.

Carty, R. Kenneth. *National Politics and Community in Canada*. Vancouver: UBC Press, 1986.

Dawson, MacGregor. "The Canadian Civil Service, 1867–1880" *CHR* 7, no. 1 (1926).

———. "The Gerrymander of 1882" *CJEPS* (May 1935).

Forbes, H.D. *Canadian Political Thought*. Toronto: Oxford University Press, 1985.

Forster, Ben. "A Conservative Heart: The United Empire Club, 1874–1882" *Ontario History* 78, no. 2 (1986).

Gibbons, Kenneth M. *Political Corruption in Canada: Cases, Causes and Cures*. Toronto: McClelland & Stewart, 1976.

Graham, J.E. "The Riel Amnesty and the Liberal Party in Central Canada, 1869–1875." Master's thesis, Queen's University, 1967.

Greer, Allan. "Historical Roots of Canadian Democracy" *JCS* 34, no. 1 (1999).

Grittner, Colin. "'A Statesmanlike Measure with a Partisan Tail': The Development of the Nineteenth-Century Dominion Electoral Franchise." Master's thesis, Carleton University, 2009.

Heick, W.H. "Mackenzie and Macdonald: Federal Politics and Politicians in Canada, 1873–78." Ph.D. thesis, Duke University, 1965.

Kerr, D.G.G. "The 1867 Elections in Ontario: The Rules of the Game" *CHR* 51, no. 4 (1970).

Lewis, J.P. "'The Lion and the Lamb Ministry': John A. Macdonald and the Politics of the First Canadian Federal Cabinet." Master's thesis, University of Guelph, 2001.

Livermore, J.D. "The Personal Agonies of Edward Blake" *CHR* 56, no. 1 (1975).

Morton, Desmond. "Reflecting on Gomery: Political Scandals and the Canadian Memory" *Policy Options*, June 2005.

Morton, W.L. "The Extension of the Franchise in Canada: A Study in Democratic Nationalism" *CHA Report* 22 (1943).

Neatby, Blair. *Laurier and Liberal Quebec: A Study in Political Management.* Toronto: McClelland & Stewart, 1973.

Noel, S.J.R. "Dividing the Spoils: The Old and New Rules of Patronage in Canadian Politics" *JCS* 7, no. 2 (1987).

———. *Patrons, Clients, Brokers: Ontario Society and Politics, 1979–1896.* Toronto: University of Toronto Press, 1990.

Office of the Chief Electoral Officer of Canada. *A History of the Vote in Canada.* 2nd ed. Ottawa: 2007.

Schull, Joseph. *Edward Blake: The Man of the Other Way, 1833–1881.* Toronto: Macmillan, 1978.

———. *Laurier: The First Canadian.* Toronto: Macmillan, 1965.

Simpson, Jeffrey. *Spoils of Power: The Politics of Patronage.* Toronto: Collins, 1988.

Smith, David E. "Patronage in Britain and Canada: An Historical Perspective" *JCS* 22, no. 2 (1987).

Stairs, William J. "Political Corruption and Public Opinion: The Evolution of Political Ethics in Canada, 1840–1896." Ph.D. thesis, Université Laval, 1991.

Stewart, Gordon. "John A. Macdonald's Greatest Triumph" *CHR* 63, no. 1 (1982).

———. *The Origins of Canadian Politics: A Comparative Approach*. Vancouver: UBC Press, 1986.

———. "Political Patronage under Macdonald and Laurier" *American Review of Canadian Studies* 10, no. 2 (1980).

Tausky, Thomas E. "In Search of a Canadian Liberal: The Case of Sara Jeannette Duncan" *Ontario History* 83, no. 2 (1991).

Thomson, Dale C. *Alexander Mackenzie: Clear Grit*. Toronto: Macmillan, 1960.

Underhill, Frank H. *Canadian Political Parties*. Ottawa: CHA Booklet, 1957.

———. "The Development of National Political Parties in Canada" *CHR* 16, no. 4 (1935).

———. "Laurier and Blake, 1882–1891" *CHR* 24, no. 2 (1939).

———. *Political Ideas of the Upper Canada Reformers, 1867–78*. Ottawa: CHA Booklet, 1942.

Ward, Norman. *The Canadian House of Commons Representation*. Toronto: University of Toronto Press, 1950.

———. "The Formative Years of the House of Commons, 1867–1891" *CJEPS* 18, no. 4 (1952).

Wiseman, Norman."The Gerrymander of 1882" *CJEPS* 1 (1935).

———. *In Search of Canadian Political Culture*. Vancouver: UBC Press, 2007.

———. "The Origins of Canadian Politics and John A. Macdonald." In *Politics Is Local: National Politics at the Grassroots*, edited by Kenneth Carty and Munroe Eagles. Toronto: Oxford University Press, 2006.

QUEBEC

Cook, Ramsay. *Canada and the French-Canadian Question*. Toronto: Macmillan, 1966.

———. *Watching Quebec: Selected Essays*. Montreal and Kingston: McGill-Queen's University Press, 2005.

Dickinson, John A. *A Short History of Quebec:* Montreal and Kingston: McGill-Queen's University Press, 2008.

Fraser, Barbara. "The Political Career of Sir Hector Louis Langevin" *CHR* (June 1961).

Hall, D.J. "'The Spirit of Confederation': Ralph Heintzman, Professor Creighton, and the bicultural compact theory" *JCS* 9, no. 4 (1974).

Heintzman, Ralph. "The Political Culture of Quebec, 1840–1960" *CJPS* 16, no. 1 (1983).

———. "The Spirit of Confederation: Professor Creighton, Biculturalism, and the Use of History" *CHR* 52, no. 1 (1971).

Linteau, Paul-André, René Durocher and Jean-Claude Robert. *Quebec, A History, 1867–1929*. Toronto: James Lorimer, 1983.

Monet, Jacques. *French-Canadian Nationalism and the Challenge of Ultramontanism*. CHA Historical Papers, 1966.

Neatby, Blair. *Laurier and a Liberal Quebec: A Study in Political Management*. Toronto: McClelland & Stewart, 1975.

Neatby, Blair, and John Saywell. "Chapleau and the Conservative Party in Quebec" *CHR* 37, no. 1 (1956).

Seigfried, André. *The Race Question in Canada*, edited by Frank Underhill. Ottawa: Carleton University Press, 1966.

Silver, A.I. "Quebec and the French-speaking Minorities, 1864–1912." Ph.D. thesis, University of Toronto 1973.

———. *The French-Canadian Idea of Confederation, 1864–1900*. Toronto: University of Toronto Press, 1982.

———. "Some Quebec Attitudes in an Age of Imperialism and Ideological Conflict" *CHR* 57, no. 4 (1976).

Trofimenkoff, Susan Mann. *The Dream of Nation: A Social and Intellectual History of Quebec*. Toronto: Gage, 1983.

Wade, Mason. *The French-Canadians, Vol. 1: 1760–1911*. Toronto: Macmillan, 1968.

Young, Brian. "Federalism in Quebec: The First Years after Confederation." In *Federalism in Canada and Australia*, edited by Bruce Hodgins, Don Wright and W.H. Heick. Waterloo: Wilfrid Laurier University Press, 1978.

———. *George-Etienne Cartier: Montreal Bourgeois*. Montreal: *MQUP*, 1981.

RAILWAYS

Berton, Pierre. *The Last Spike, 1881–1885*. Toronto: McClelland & Stewart, 1971.

———. *The National Dream: The Great Railway, 1871–1881*. Toronto: McClelland & Stewart, 1970.

Bliss, Michael. *Northern Enterprise: Five Centuries of Canadian Business*. Toronto: McClelland & Stewart, 1987.

Dempsey, Hugh. *The CPR West: The Iron Road and the Making of a Nation*. Vancouver: Douglas & McIntyre, 1984.

Gilbert, Heather. *Awakening Continent: The Life of Lord Mount Stephen Vol. 1: 1829–91*. Aberdeen: Aberdeen University Press, 1965.

Irwin, Leonard B. "Pacific Railways and Nationalism in the Canadian-American Northwest, 1845–1873." Ph.D. thesis, University of Pennsylvania, 1939.

Lamb, W. Kaye. *History of the Canadian Pacific Railway*. New York: Macmillan, 1977.

Lavallee, Omer. *Van Horne's Road: The Building of the Canadian Pacific Railway*. Saskatoon: Fifth House Publishers, 2007.

MacDougall, Lorne. "The Character of the Entrepreneur: The Case of George Stephen." In *Canadian Business History*, edited by David Macmillan. Toronto: McClelland & Stewart, 1972.

Newman, Peter C. *Company of Adventurers: How the Hudson's Bay Empire Determined the Destiny of a Continent*. Toronto: Penguin Canada, 1985.

den Otter, A.A. "Nationalism and the Canadian Pacific Scandal" *CHR* 69, no. 3 (1988).

RELIGION

Clark, Lovell. *The Manitoba School Question: Majority Rule or Minority Rights.* Toronto: Copp Clark, 1968.

Dalton, Roy C. *The Jesuits' Estates Question, 1760–1888.* Toronto: University of Toronto Press, 1968.

Forbes, H.D., ed. "The Programme Catholique: Pastoral Letter of the Bishops of the Ecclesiastical Province of Quebec." In *Canadian Political Thought*, edited by H.D. Forbes. Toronto: Oxford University Press, 1985.

Miller, J.R. "Anti-Catholic Thought in Victorian Canada" *CHR* 6, no. 4 (1985).

———. *Equal Rights: The Jesuits' Estates Act Controversy.* Montreal and Kingston: McGill-Queen's University Press, 1979.

———. "The Jesuits' Estates Act Crisis: An Incident in a Conspiracy of Several Years' Standing" *JCS*, 9, no. 2 (1974).

Moir, John S. *The Church in the British Era, from the British Conquest to Confederation.* Toronto: McGraw-Hill Ryerson, 1972.

Perin, Robert. "Nationalism and the Church in French-Canada, 1840–1880." *Bulletin of Canadian Studies* 1, no. 2 (1977).

Senior, Hereward. "D'Alton McCarthy, Equal Rights, and the Origins of the Manitoba School Question" *CHR* 54, no. 4 (1973).

———. "Orangeism in Ontario Politics, 1872–1896." In *Oliver Mowat's Ontario*, edited by Donald Swainson. Toronto: Macmillan, 1972.

———. *Orangeism: The Canadian Phase.* Toronto: McGraw-Hill Ryerson, 1972.

RIEL, LOUIS, 1869–70

Begg, Alexander. *The Creation of Manitoba; or, A History of the Red River Troubles.* Toronto: A.H. Hovey, 1871.

———. *Reporting the Resistance.* Winnipeg: University of Manitoba Press, 2003.

Bowsfield, Hartwell. *Louis Riel: Selected Readings.* Toronto: Copp Clark Pitman, 1988.

———. *The United States and Red River Settlement*, Manitoba Historical Society Transactions 3, no. 23 (1967).

Bumsted, J.M. *Louis Riel v. Canada: The Making of a Rebel*. Winnipeg: Great Plains Publications, 2001.

———. *The Red River Rebellion*. Winnipeg: Watson and Dwyer, 1996.

———. *Thomas Scott's Body and Other Essays on Early Manitoba History*. Winnipeg: University of Manitoba Press, 2000.

Ens, Gerhard J. "Dispossession or Adaptation? Migration and Persistence of the Red River Metis, 1835-1900." CHA Historical Papers, 1988.

———. *Homeland to Hinterland*. Toronto: University of Toronto Press, 1996.

Flanagan, Thomas. "The Half-Breed Land Grants." In *Louis Riel Selected Readings*, edited by Hartwell Bowsfield. Toronto: Copp Clark Pitman, 1988.

Gluek, Alvin C. *Minnesota and the Manifest Destiny of the Canadian Northwest: A Study in Canadian-American Relations*. Toronto: University of Toronto Press, 1968.

———. "The Riel Rebellion and Canadian-American Relations" *CHR* 36, no. 3 (1955).

Hafter, Ruth. "The Riel Rebellion and Manifest Destiny" *Dalhousie Review* 45, no. 4 (1965/66).

Huel, Raymond J.A. *Archbishop A.-A. Taché of St. Boniface: The "Good Fight" and the Illusive Vision*. Edmonton: University of Alberta Press, 2003.

Lamb, R.E. *"Thunder in the North": Conflict over the Riel Risings, 1870–1885*. New York: Pageant Press, 1957.

Lussier, A.S., ed. *Riel and the Métis*. Winnipeg: Pemmican Publications, 1991.

Mailhot, Philippe. "'Ritchot's Resistance': Abbé Noel Joseph Ritchot and the Creation and Transformation of Manitoba." Ph.D. dissertation, University of Manitoba, 1986.

Melnyk, George. *Riel to Reform: A History of Protest in Western Canada*. Saskatoon: Fifth House Publishers, 1992.

Morton, W.L., ed. *Alexander Begg's Red River Journal and Other Papers Relative to the Red River Resistance of 1869–70*. Toronto: The Champlain Society, 1956.

Owram, Doug. "'Conspiracy and Treason': The Red River Resistance from an Expansionist Perspective." In *The Prairie West: Historical Readings*, edited by Douglas Francis and Howard Palmer. Edmonton: Pica Pica Press, 2001.

Patterson-Smith, James. "The Riel Rebellion of 1869: New Light on British Liberals and the Use of Force on the Canadian Frontier" *JCS* 30, no. 2 (1995).

Silver, A.I. "French-Canada and the Prairie Frontier, 1870–1890" *CHR* 50, no. 1 (1969).

Stanley, George. *Louis Riel*. Toronto: Ryerson, 1963.

———. "The Half-Breed 'Rising' of 1875." In *The Other Natives: The-Les Métis*, edited by Antoine Lussier. Winnipeg: Manitoba Métis Federation Press, 1978.

———. *Toil and Trouble: Military Expeditions to Red River*. Canadian War Museum Publication No. 25, 1989.

RIEL, LOUIS, 1884–85

Adams, Howard, "Causes of the 1885 Struggle." In *Riel to Reform: A History of Protest in Western Canada*, edited by George Melnyk. Saskatoon: Fifth House Publishers, 1992.

Association of Métis and Non-Status Indians of Saskatchewan. *Louis Riel: Justice Must Be Done*. Winnipeg: Manitoba Métis Federation Press, 1979.

Barron, Laurie, and James Waldram, eds. *1885 and After: Native Society in Transition*. Regina: Canadian Plains Research Center, University of Regina, 1986.

Beal, Bob. "Attacking the State: The Levying War Charge in Canadian Treason Law." Master's thesis, University of Alberta, 1994.

———, and Rod Macleod. *Prairie Fire: The 1885 North-West Rebellion*. Edmonton: Hurtig; Markham: Penguin Canada, 1984.

Bingaman, Sandra. "The Trials of the 'White Rebels,' 1885" *Saskatchewan History* 25, no. 2 (1973).

Bowsfield, Hartwell, ed. *Louis Riel: Rebel of the Western Frontier or Victim of Politics and Prejudice?* Toronto: Copp Clark, 1969.

Boyden, Joseph. *Louis Riel and Gabriel Dumont*. Toronto: Penguin Canada, 2010.

Brown, Chester. *Louis Riel: A Comic-strip Biography*. Montreal: Drawn and Quarterly Press, 2006.

Brown, D.H. "The Meaning of Treason in 1885" *Saskatchewan History* 28, no. 1 (1975).

Cameron, William B. *Blood Red the Sun*. Calgary: Kenway, 1950.

Chambers, Brian. "Louis Riel: A Critical Examination of the Psychiatric Evidence." Master's thesis, University of Calgary, 1976.

Clarke, C. "A Critical Study of the Case of Louis Riel" *QQ* 12, no 1 (1905).

Davin, Nicholas Flood. "Interview with [Louis Riel], November, 1885." In *Louis Riel, Rebel of the Western Frontier or Victim of Politics and Prejudice?* edited by Hartwell Bowsfield. Toronto: Copp Clark, 1969.

Ens, Gerhard J. "Prologue to the Red River Resistance: Pre-liminal Politics and the Triumph of Riel" *CHA Review* 5, no. 1 (1994).

Flanagan, Thomas. "Aboriginal Title." In *Introduction to Canadian History*, edited by A.I. Silver and Carl Berger. Toronto: Canadian Scholars' Press, 1991.

———. "Comment on Ken Hatt the North West Rebellion Scrip Commissions, 1885-1889." In *1885 and After: Native Society in Transition*, edited by Laurie Barron and James Waldram. Regina: Canadian Plains Research Center, University of Regina, 1986.

———. *Louis "David" Riel: "Prophet of the New World"*. Toronto: University of Toronto Press, 1979.

———. "Metis Land Claims at St. Laurent: Old Arguments and New Evidence" *Prairie Forum* 12, no. 3 (1987).

———. *Riel and the Rebellion: 1885 Reconsidered*. Saskatoon: Western Producer Books, 1983.

———."The Riel 'Lunacy Commission': The Report of Dr. Valade" *Revue de l'Université d'Ottawa* 46, no. 1 (1976).

Graham, Jane. "The Riel Amnesty." Master's thesis, Queen's University, 1967.

Huel, Raymond J.A. "'A Parting of the Ways': Louis Schmidt's Account of Louis Riel and the Metis Rebellion." In *As Long as the Sun Shines and Water Flows*, edited by Ian Getty and Antoine Lussier. Vancouver: UBC Press, 1983.

Kostach, Myrna. *The Frog Lake Reader*. Edmonton: NeWest Press, 2009.

Lamb, R.E. "Friction between Ontario and Quebec Caused by the Rising of Louis Riel." Master's thesis, University of Ottawa, 1953.

Littmann, S.K. "A Pathography of Louis Riel" *Canadian Psychiatric Journal* 23, no. 4 (1978).

McNaught, Kenneth. "Political Trials and the Canadian Political Tradition" *University of Toronto Law Journal* 24, no. 1 (1974).

Morton, Desmond. *The Last War Drum: The North West Campaign of 1885*. Toronto: Hakkert, 1972.

———, ed. *The Queen v Louis Riel*. Toronto: University of Toronto Press, 1984.

Mumford, Jeremy R. "Why Was Louis Riel, a United States Citizen, Hanged, as a Canadian Traitor in 1885?" *CHR* 88, no. 2 (2007).

Payment, Diana. "Batoche after 1885: A Society in Transition." In *1885 and After: Native Society in Transition*, edited by Laurie Barron and James Waldram. Regina: Canadian Plains Research Center, University of Regina, 1986.

Silver, A.I. "The Impact on Eastern Canada on Events in Saskatchewan in 1885." In *1885 and After: Native Society in Transition*, edited by Laurie Barron and James Waldram. Regina: Canadian Plains Research Center, University of Regina, 1986.

Smith, Donald B. *Honoré Jaxon: Prairie Visionary*. Regina: Coteau Books, 2007.

Stanley, George. *The Birth of Western Canada: A History of the Riel Rebellion*. Toronto: University of Toronto Press, 1970.

———. *Louis Riel: Patriot or Rebel*. Ottawa: CHA Booklet, 1979.

Sprague, D.N. *Canada and the Metis, 1869–1885*. Waterloo: Wilfrid Laurier University Press, 1988.

———. "The Manitoba Land Question, 1870–1882" *JCS* 15, no. 3 (1980).

Thomas, Lewis H. "A Judicial Murder—The Trial of Louis Riel." In *The Settlement of the West*, edited by Howard Palmer. Calgary: University of Calgary and Comprint Publishing, 1977.

Wiebe, Rudy. *Big Bear*. Toronto: Penguin Books, 2008.

———. *The Temptations of Big Bear.* Toronto: Vintage Canada, 1973.

Woodcock, George. *Gabriel Dumont, The Metis Chief and his Lost World.* Edmonton: Hurtig Publishers, 1975.

———. "The Little Republic of St. Laurent." In *Canadian History since Confederation*, edited by Bruce Hodgins and Robert Page. Georgetown, Ont.: Irwin-Dorsey, 1972.

Louis Riel, Postscript

Braz, Albert R. "The False Traitor: Louis Riel in Canadian Literature." Ph.D. thesis, University of Toronto, 1999.

Hathorn, Ramon, and Patrick Holland, eds. *Images of Louis Riel in Canadian Culture*. Lewiston: Edwin Meller Press, 1992.

Mattes, Catharine. "Whose Hero? Images of Louis Riel in Contemporary Culture and Metis Nationhood." Master's thesis, Concordia University, 1998.

Owram, Doug. "The Myth of Louis Riel" *CHR* 63, no. 3 (1982).

Reid, Jennifer. *Louis Riel and the Creation of Modern Canada: Mythic Discourse and the Postcolonial State*. Albuquerque: University of New Mexico Press, 2008.

Stanley, George. "The Last Word on Louis Riel—the Man of Several Faces." In *1885 and After: Native Society in Transition*, edited by Laurie Barron and James Waldram. Regina: Canadian Plains Research Center, University of Regina, 1986.

Swainson, Donald. "Rieliana and the Structure of Canadian History" *Journal of Popular Culture* 14, no. 3 (1980).

SOCIETY AND DAILY LIFE

Bliss, Michael. "'Pure Books on Avoided Subjects': Pre-Freudian Sexual Ideas in Canada." CHA Historical Papers, 1970.

Bradbury, Bettina. "Family Strategies in the Face of Death, Illness and Poverty, Montreal, 1860–1885." In *An Introduction to Canadian History*, edited by A.I. Silver and Carl Berger. Toronto: Canadian Scholars' Press, 1991.

Burr, Christina. "Gender, Sexuality, and Nationalism, in J.W. Bengough's Verses and Political Cartoons" *CHR* 83, no. 4 (2002).

Careless, J.M.S. *Frontier and Metropolis: Regions, Cities and Identities in Canada before 1914*. Toronto: University of Toronto Press, 1989.

———. *The Regenerators: Social Criticism in Late Victorian English Canada*. Toronto: University of Toronto Press, 1985.

Creighton, Luella. *The Elegant Canadians*. Toronto: McClelland & Stewart, 1967.

Cumming, Carmen. *"Sketches from a Young Country": The Images of Grip Magazine*. Toronto: University of Toronto Press, 1997.

Finlay, John L. *Canada in the North Atlantic Triangle: Two Centuries of Social Change*. Toronto: Oxford University Press, 1975.

Gaffield, Chad. *Constructing Modern Canada: Readings in Post-Confederation History*. Toronto: Copp Clark Longman, 1994.

Gardiner, John. *The Victorians: An Age in Retrospect*. London and New York: Hambledon and London, 2002.

Gwyn, Sandra. *The Private Capital: Ambition and Love in the Age of Macdonald and Laurier*. Toronto: McClelland & Stewart, 1989.

Horn, Michel, and Ronald Sabourin. *Studies in Canadian Social History*. Toronto: McClelland & Stewart, 1974.

Loo, Tina. *Historical Perspectives on Law and Society in Canada*. Toronto: Copp Clark Longman, 1994.

Lower, Arthur R.M. *Canadians in the Making: A Social History of Canada*. Toronto: Longmans Green and Co., 1958.

McInnis, Edgar. *Canada: A Political and Social History*. Toronto: Clarke, Irwin, 1959.

McKillop, A.B. *A Disciplined Intelligence: Critical Inquiry and Canadian Thought in the Victorian Era*. Montreal and Kingston: McGill-Queen's University Press, 1979.

Morton, W.L., ed. *The Shield of Achilles: Aspects of Canada in the Victorian Age*. Toronto: McClelland & Stewart, 1968.

Roome, P. "The Darwin Debate in Canada, 1860–1889." In *Science, Technology and Culture in Historical Perspective*. Calgary: University of Calgary Studies in History, No. 1 (1976).

Rutherford, Paul. *A Victorian Authority: The Daily Press in Late Nineteenth-Century Canada*. Toronto: University of Toronto Press, 1982.

Smith, Allan. "The Myth of the Self-made Man in English Canada, 1850–1914" *CHR* 59, no. 2 (1978).

Strange, Carolyn. *Making Good: Law and Moral Regulation in Canada, 1867–1939*. Toronto: University of Toronto Press, 1997.

Torrance, Judy M. *Public Violence in Canada, 1867–1982*. Montreal and Kingston: McGill-Queen's University Press, 1986.

Wallace, Elisabeth. "The Origin of the Social Welfare State in Canada, 1867–1900" *CJEPS* 16, no. 3 (1950).

———. "A Study of the Changing Conception of the State as Revealed in Canadian Social Legislation, 1867–1943." Ph.D. thesis, Columbia University, 1950.

Vance, Jonathan. *A History of Canadian Culture*. Don Mills: Oxford University Press, 2009.

Waite, P.B. *Macdonald: His Life and World*. Toronto: McGraw-Hill Ryerson, 1975.

Wilson, A.N. *The Victorians*. London: Hutchinson, 2007.

Women

Abrahamson, Una. *God Bless Our Home: Domestic Life in Nineteenth-Century Canada*. Toronto: Burns & MacEachern, 1966.

Cook, Ramsay, ed. *The Proper Sphere: A Woman's Place in Canadian Society*. Toronto: Oxford University Press, 1976.

L'Espérance, Jeanne. *The Widening Sphere: Women in Canada, 1870–1940*. Ottawa: [Public Archives, National Library of Canada] LAC, 1982.

Mitchison, Wendy. "The WCTU: 'For God, Home and Native Land': A Study of Nineteenth-Century Feminism." In *Readings in Canadian Social History*, 5 vols., edited by Michael Cross. Toronto: McClelland & Stewart, 1984.

Prentice, Alison. *Canadian Women: A History*. Toronto: Harcourt, Brace, Jovanovich, 1985.

Thompson, Joanne Emily. "The Influence of Dr. Emily Howard Stowe on the Woman Suffrage Movement in Canada" *Ontario History* 54, no. 4 (1962).

U.S.-CANADIAN RELATIONS; U.S.-BRITISH RELATIONS

Baker, William M. "The Anti-American Ingredient in Canadian History" *Dalhousie Review* 53, no. 1 (1973).

Brebner, John B. *North Atlantic Triangle: The Interplay of Canada, the United States, and Britain*. New Haven: Yale University Press, 1945.

Callahan, James M. *American Foreign Policy in Canadian Relations*. New York: Macmillan, 1937.

Campbell, Charles S. *From Revolution to Rapprochement: The United States and Great Britain, 1793–1900*. New York: Wiley, 1974.

Chester, M. "The United States and Canadian Nationality" *CHR* 18, no. 1 (1937).

Cook, Adrian. *The Alabama Claims: American Politics and Anglo-American Relations, 1865–1872*. Ithaca: Cornell University Press, 1975.

Doyle, James. *North of America: Images of Canada in the Literature of the United States, 1775–1900*. Toronto: ECW Press, 1983.

Finlay, John. *Canada in the North Atlantic Triangle: Two Centuries of Social Change*. Toronto: OUP, 1975.

Fridley, Russell W. "When Minnesota Coveted Canada" *Minnesota History* 41, no. 2 (1968).

Gardner, Lloyd. *Creation of the American Empire: U.S. Diplomatic History*. Chicago: Rand McNally, 1973.

Gluek, Alvin C. *Minnesota and the Manifest Destiny of the Canadian Northwest: A Study in Canadian-American Relations.* Toronto: University of Toronto Press, 1965.

Granatstein, J.L. *Yankee Go Home? Canadians and Anti-Americanism.* Toronto: HarperCollins, 1996.

Hansen, Marcus L. *The Mingling of the Canadian and American Peoples.* New Haven: Yale University Press, 1940.

Hollander, Paul, ed. *Understanding Anti-Americanism: Its Origins and Impact at Home and Abroad.* Chicago: Ivan R. Dee, 2004.

Jenkins, Brian. *Fenians and Anglo-American Relations during Reconstruction.* Ithaca: Cornell University Press, 1969.

LaFeber, Walter. *The New Empire: An Interpretation of American Expansionism, 1860–1898.* Ithaca: Cornell University Press, 1963.

Lecker, Robert, ed. *Borderlands: Essays in Canadian-American Relations.* Toronto: ECW Press, 1991.

Lewis, Margaret Mae. *Canadian-American Reciprocity, 1854–1935.* Master's thesis, University of Colorado, 1942.

Lumsden, Ian. *Close the 49th Parallel: The Americanization of Canada.* Toronto: University of Toronto Press, 1970.

Martin, Lawrence. *The Presidents and the Prime Ministers, 1867–1982.* Toronto: Doubleday Canada, 1982.

Merk, Frederick. *Manifest Destiny and Mission in American History.* New York: Alfred Knopf, 1963.

Moffett, Samuel E. *The Americanization of Canada* [1907]. Toronto: University of Toronto Press, 1972.

Monro, Alexander. *The United States and the Dominion of Canada: Their Future.* Saint John, N.B.: Barnes & Co., 1879.

Munro, William B. *American Influences on Canadian Government.* Toronto: Macmillan, 1929.

Nevins, Allan. *Hamilton Fish: The Inner History of the Grant Administration.* New York: Dodd, Mead and Co., 1936.

Paolino, Ernest N. *The Foundations of the American Empire: William Henry*

Seward and U.S. Foreign Policy. Ithaca: Cornell University Press, 1973.

Plesur, Milton. *America's Outward Thrust: Approaches to Foreign Affairs, 1865–1890*. DeKalb: Northern Illinois University Press, 1971.

Sams, Russell F. "The Congressional Attitude Towards Canada during the 1860s." Master's thesis, Queen's University, 1947.

Shippee, Lester B. *Canadian-American Relations, 1849–1874*. New Haven: Yale University Press, 1939.

Smith, Allan. *Canada—An American Nation? Essays on Continentalism, Identity and the Canadian Frame of Mind*. Montreal: McGill-Queen's University Press, 1994.

Smith, Goldwin A. *The Treaty of Washington, 1871: A Study in Imperial History*. Ithaca: Cornell University Press, 1941.

Smith, Jean. *Grant*. New York: Simon & Schuster, 2001.

Snell, James G. "'The Eagle and the Butterfly': Some American Attitudes towards British North America, 1864–1867." Ph.D. thesis, Queen's University, 1970.

Stewart, Gordon. *The American Response to Canada since 1776*. East Lansing: Michigan State University Press, 1992.

Stouffer, Allen P. "Canadian-American Relations, 1861–1871." Ph.D. thesis, Claremont Graduate School, 1971.

Stuart, Reginald C. *United States Expansionism and British North America, 1775–1871*. Chapel Hill: University of North Carolina Press, 1988.

Tansill, Charles C. *Canadian-American Relations, 1875–1911*. New Haven: Yale University Press, 1943.

Tyler, Alice F. *The Foreign Policy of James G. Blaine*. Minneapolis: University of Minnesota Press, 1927.

Warner, Donald F. *The Idea of Continental Union: Agitation for the Annexation of Canada to the United States, 1849–1893*. Lexington: Mississippi Valley Historical Association and the University of Kentucky Press, 1960.

Weinberg, Albert K. *Manifest Destiny: A Study of Nationalist Expansionism in American History*. Baltimore: Johns Hopkins Press, 1958.

Wise, S.F., and Robert Craig Brown. *Canada Views the United States:*

Nineteenth-Century Political Attitudes. Seattle: University of Washington Press, 1967.

THE WEST AND THE NORTH-WEST

Allen, Richard, ed. *Man and Nature on the Prairies*. Regina: Canadian Plains Research Center, University of Regina, 1976.

Bercuson, David, ed. *Western Perspectives*. Western Canadian Studies Conference. Toronto: Holt, Rinehart and Winston of Canada, 1974.

Berger, Carl, and Ramsay Cook, eds. *The West and the Nation: Essays in Honour of W.L. Morton*. Toronto: McClelland & Stewart, 1976.

Francis, R. Douglas, and Howard Palmer, eds. *The Prairie West: Historical Readings*. Edmonton: Pica Pica Press, 2001.

Friesen, Gerald. *The Canadian Prairies: A History*. Toronto: University of Toronto Press, 1984.

———. "Studies in the Development of Western Canadian Regional Consciousness." Ph.D. thesis, University of Toronto, 1974.

MacEwan, Grant. *Grant MacEwan's West: Sketches from the Past*. Saskatoon: Western Producer Prairie Books, 1990.

Martin, Chester. "'Dominion Lands' Policy." In *Canadian Frontiers of Settlement*, edited by A.S. Morton and C. Martin. Toronto: Macmillan, 1938.

Melnyk, George, ed. *Riel to Reform: A History of Protest in Western Canada*. Saskatoon: Fifth House Publishers, 1992.

Merk, Frederick. *History of the Westward Movement*. New York: Alfred A. Knopf, 1978.

Morton, Arthur S. "History of Prairie Settlement." In *Canadian Frontiers of Settlement*, edited by A.S. Morton and C. Martin. Toronto: Macmillan, 1938.

Morton, W.L. *The West and Confederation*. Ottawa: CHA Booklet, 1958.

Newman, Peter C. *Company of Adventurers: How the Hudson's Bay Empire Determined the Destiny of a Continent*. Toronto: Penguin Canada, 1985.

den Otter, A.A. *Civilizing the West: The Galts and the Development of Western Canada*. Edmonton: University of Alberta Press, 1982.

Owram, Douglas. "Disillusionment: Regional Discontent in the1880s." In *From Riel to Reform: A History of Protest in Western Canada*, edited by George Melnyk. Saskatoon: Fifth House Publishers, 1992.

———. "The Great North West: The Canadian Expansionist Movement and the Image of the West in the Nineteenth Century." Ph.D. thesis, University of Toronto, 1976.

———. *Promise of Eden: The Canadian Expansionist Movement and the Idea of the West, 1856–1900*. Toronto: University of Toronto Press, 1980.

Palmer, Howard, ed. *The Settlement of the West*. Calgary: University of Calgary Press, 1977.

Paxon, Frederic L. *History of the American Frontier, 1763–1893*. Boston, New York: Houghton Mifflin, 1924.

Swainson, Donald, ed. *Historical Essay on the Prairie Provinces*. Toronto: McClelland & Stewart, 1970.

Wilson, Garrett. *Frontier Farewell: The 1870s and the End of the Old West*. Regina: University of Regina, Canadian Plains Research Center, 2007.

Zaslow, Morris. *The Opening of the Canadian North, 1870–1914*. Toronto: McClelland & Stewart, 1971.

Picture Credits

Art Collection, BMO Financial Group

George Stephen (p. 329)

Glenbow Museum

Louis Riel—drawing, 1870 NA-1406-69 (p. 103)

Fort Gary, Manitoba NA-354-13 (p. 125)

Thomas Scott NA-576-1 (p. 127)

Father Noël-Joseph Ritchot NA-1406-215 (p. 135)

Main St., Winnipeg, 1880–1881 NA-1255-2 (p. 342)

Louis Riel NA-504-3 (p. 394)

Gabriel Dumont NA-1063-1 (p. 442)

Father Lacombe rebellion telegram NA-1713-8 (p. 446)

Grip cartoon—"What will he do with him?" NA-3012-4 (p. 464)

Riel's written statement NA-720-2 (p. 474)

The Globe

Doctor's bulletin in paper (p. 142)

The Printers' Strike (p. 196)

The Pacific Railway Intrigues (p. 234)

Library and Archives Canada

John A. Macdonald political caricature E008072619 (p. ii)

John A. Macdonald C006956 (p. 8)

McCord Museum of Canadian History

Sir Francis Hicks MP 1991126 (p. 81)

Donald Smith I66959 (p. 115)

Sir Hugh Allan, 1871 I-635411 (p. 181)

Ravenscrag, Montreal, QC 4867 (p. 187)

Royal BC Museum, BC Archives

The Beginning of better times E-07919 (p. 386)

Index

A page number in italic indicates a photograph or other illustration. The lowercase letter "n" following a page number indicates a footnote.